GOD'S WORD

DAILY REFLECTIONS 2022

ST PAULS

Editor: Michael Goonan SSP, Fr Joshy Joseph SSP

Associate Editor: Julie Whiteford

Contributors:

January	Robert Nixon OSB	July	Michelle Vass
February	Debra Vermeer	August	Michael Goonan SSP
March	Brian Grenier CFC	September	Grace Roclawska CSFN
April	Carmel Jones RSJ	October	Joby Mathew SSP
May	Fiona Basile	November	Flora Ricupero PBVM
June	Ruben C. Areño SSP	December	Fr John Dunn (NZ)

GOD'S WORD 2022

ISBN: 978-1-910365-88-5

Cover design Domenika Fairy

Internal layout by St Pauls/Better Yourself Books, India

Illustrations by Dorothy Woodward RSJ

Cover painting: The Return of the Prodigal Son (1773) by Pompeo Batoni. Other artwork: Madonna and Child by Giovanni Battista Salvi (Il Sassoferrato, 1609-1685); detail of the face of Jesus by Heinrich Hoffman (1889). All artwork in the Public Domain, sourced through Wikimedia Commons.

ST PAULS by Westminster Cathedral
Morpeth Terrace, Victoria
London, SW1P 1EP
Ph: +44 (0) 207 828 5582
www.stpauls.org.uk

ST PAULS Publishing
Moyglare Road, Maynooth
Co. Kildare, Ireland
Ph: +353 (1) 628 5933
www.stpauls.ie

Printed by Melita Press, Malta.

ST PAULS PUBLICATIONS is an activity of the priests and brothers of the Society of St Paul who place at the centre of their lives the mission of evangelisation through the modern means of communication.

MESSAGE

Dear friends,

The Word of God changes lives. Even today, as a Christian of many years, I am again and again delighted to discover new depths and meanings to God's Word, now being encouraged by it, now consoled, now edified. Let me urge you to set aside a portion of each day to sit quietly and read **God's Word 2022**. St Ambrose said: "We speak to God when we pray; we listen to Him when we read the Scriptures." The treasure of the Scriptures brings us closer to God, and the simple format of God's Word 2022 makes it accessible and engaging to all. It helps us to listen to Him. There's even space in these pages to jot down your own thoughts and prayers. My prayer for you is that you will dedicate more of this coming year to the Word of God. Let this guide help you do exactly that.

May God bless you in 2022!

+Leo Cushley
Archbishop of St Andrews & Edinburgh

01
JAN SAT

MARY, MOTHER OF GOD, Solemnity

(Octave of Christmas)

White

Numbers 6:22-27

The Lord spoke to Moses and said, 'Say this to Aaron and his sons: "This is how you are to bless the sons of Israel. You shall say to them: May the Lord bless you and keep you. May the Lord let his face shine on you and be gracious to you. May the Lord uncover his face and bring you peace."

This is how they are to call down my name on the sons of Israel, and I will bless them.'

Psalm 66:2-3, 5, 6, 8. R. v. 2

O God, be gracious and bless us.

Galatians 4:4-7

When the appointed time came, God sent his Son, born of a woman, born a subject of the Law, to redeem the subjects of the Law and to enable us to be adopted as sons. The proof that you are sons is that God has sent the Spirit of his Son into our hearts: the Spirit that cries, 'Abba, Father', and it is this that makes you a son, you are not a slave anymore; and if God has made you son, then he has made you heir.

Luke 2:16-21

The shepherds hurried away to Bethlehem and found Mary and Joseph, and the baby lying in the manger. When they saw the child they repeated what they had been told about him, and everyone who heard it was astonished at what the shepherds had to say. As for Mary, she treasured all these things and pondered them in her heart. And the shepherds went back glorifying and praising God for all they had heard and seen; it was exactly as they had been told.

When the eighth day came and the child was to be circumcised, they gave him the name Jesus, the name the angel had given him before his conception.

Reflection

It is fitting that the new year commences with the solemnity of Mary, the great Mother of God, the virgin Queen of Heaven, and the immaculate paradigm of all virtue and sanctity. Through Mary's motherhood a new and glorious epoch dawned. Of all mortals, Mary alone was holy enough to bear in her womb and in her arms the supreme and only God. She nursed him, comforted him, wiped away his infant tears, and kissed away his pain. She taught him how to pray and how to believe. She taught him how to be brave, how to be kind and good, and how to love. And she will surely do the same for us, if we but let her, if we but call upon the name of this most sweet and gentle of maidens: *Holy Mary, Mother of God, pray for us sinners, now and at the hour of our death. Amen.*

02
JAN SUN

SECOND SUNDAY OF CHRISTMAS
– England, Wales & Ireland

EPIPHANY OF THE LORD, Solemnity
– Scotland
see Thursday, 6th January
White

Ecclesiassticus 24:1-2.8-12

Wisdom speaks her own praises, in the midst of her people she glories in herself. She opens her mouth in the assembly of the Most High, she glories in herself in the presence of the Mighty One; "Then the creator of all things instructed me, and he who created me fixed a place for my tent. He said, 'Pitch your tent in Jacob, make Israel your inheritance.' From eternity, in the beginning, he created me, and for eternity I shall remain. I ministered before him in the holy tabernacle, and thus was I established on Zion. In the beloved city he has given me rest, and in Jerusalem I wield my authority. I have taken root in a privileged people in the Lord's property, in his inheritance."

Psalm 147

The Word was made flesh, and lived among us.

Ephesians 1:3-6.15-18

Blessed be God the Father of our Lord Jesus Christ, who has blessed us with all the spiritual blessings of heaven in Christ. Before the world was made, he chose us, chose us in Christ, to be holy and spotless, and to live through love in his presence, determining that we should become his adopted sons, through Jesus Christ, for his own kind purposes, to make us praise the glory of his grace, his free gift to us in the Beloved.

That will explain why I, having once heard about your faith in the Lord Jesus, and the love that you show towards all the saints, have never failed to remember you in my prayers and to thank God for you. May the God of our Lord Jesus Christ, the Father of glory, give you a spirit of wisdom and perception of what is revealed, to bring you to full knowledge of him. May he enlighten the eyes of your mind so that you can see what hope his call holds for you, what rich glories he has promised the saints will inherit.

John 1:1-18

In the beginning was the Word:
the Word was with God
and the Word was God.
He was with God in the beginning.
Through him all things came to be,
not one thing had its being but through him.
All that came to be had life in him
and that life was the light of men,
a light that shines in the dark,
a light that darkness could not overpower.
A man came, sent by God.

His name was John.
He came as a witness,
as a witness to speak for the light,
so that everyone might believe through him.
He was not the Light,
only a witness to speak for the light.
The Word was the true light
that enlightens all men;
and he was coming into the world.
He was in the world
that had its being through him,
and the world did not know him.
He came to his own domain
and his own people did not accept him.
But to all who did accept him
he gave power to become children of God,
to all who believe in the name of him
who was born not out of human stock
or urge ofthe flesh
or will of man
but of God himself.
The Word was made flesh,
he lived among us,
and we saw his glory,
the glory that is his as the only Son of the Father,
full of grace and truth.
John appears as his witness. He proclaims:
"This is the one of whom I said:
He who comes after me
ranks before me
because he existed before me."
Indeed, from his fullness we have, all of us, received –
yes, grace in return for grace,
since though the Law was given through Moses,
grace and truth have come through Jesus Christ.
No one has ever seen God;
it is the only Son, who is nearest to the Father's heart,
who has made him known.

Reflection

"The Word became flesh and lived among us. The light shone in the darkness, and the darkness did not overcome it." In John's Gospel, Jesus reveals to us who God is, and says that he is the true light of the world. And this light is here among us. In Jesus, darkness cannot exist, and truths are revealed. Let us continue to share with all the grace and the light of Christ.

03
JAN MON

MONDAY AFTER EPIPHANY – Scotland
see Appendix A-1

Monday before Epiphany, The Most Holy Name of Jesus
(Optional, White) or **Saint Munchin**, Bishop

1 John 2:29-3:6

You know that God is righteous – then you must recognise that everyone whose life is righteous has been begotten by him. Think of the love that the Father has lavished on us, by letting us be called God's children; and that is what we are. Because the world refused to acknowledge him, therefore it does not acknowledge us. My dear people, we are already the children of God but what we are to be in the future has not yet been revealed; all we know is, that when it is revealed we shall be like him because we shall see him as he really is. Surely everyone who entertains this hope must purify himself, must try to be as pure as Christ. Anyone who sins at all breaks the law, because to sin is to break the law. Now you know that he appeared in order to abolish sin, and that in him there is no sin; anyone who lives in God does not sin, and anyone who sins has never seen him or known him.

Psalm 97:1,3-6

All the ends of the earth have seen the salvation of our God.

John 1:29-34

The next day, seeing Jesus coming towards him, John said, 'Look, there is the lamb of God that takes away the sin of the world. This is the one I spoke of when I said: A man is coming after me who ranks before me because he existed before me. I did not know him myself, and yet it was to reveal him to Israel that I came baptising with water.' John also declared, 'I saw the Spirit coming down on him from heaven like a dove and resting on him. I did not know him myself, but he who sent me to baptise with water had said to me, "The man on whom you see the Spirit come down and rest is the one who is going to baptise with the Holy Spirit." Yes, I have seen and I am the witness that he is the Chosen One of God.'

Reflection

John uses so many titles for Jesus because Jesus is a mystery that cannot be captured in this or that title! He means different things to different people. All those who go to him with their expectations encounter him uniquely. However, even after all the titles possible are used for Jesus, he still remains above all titles. We require openness and receptivity because God keeps revealing Himself in ways we can never imagine. Any kind of limitation that we may impose on this revelation, any restriction that we set on it may result in precluding the freshness with which Jesus always comes to us. To insist only on one or another name for Jesus is to miss the fullness of his grace, his peace, his love; indeed, it is to miss the fullness of life

04
JAN TUE

TUESDAY AFTER EPIPHANY – Scotland
see Appendix A-2

1 John 3:7-10

My children, do not let anyone lead you astray: to live a holy life is to be holy just as he is holy; to lead a sinful life is to belong to the devil, since the devil was a sinner from the beginning. It was to undo all that the devil has done that the Son of God appeared. No one who has been begotten by God sins; because God's seed remains inside him, he cannot sin when he has been begotten by God. In this way we distinguish the children of God from the children of the devil: anybody not living a holy life and not loving his brother is no child of God's.

Psalm 97:1,7-9. R. v. 3

All the ends of the earth have seen the salvation of our God.

John 1:35-42

As John stood with two of his disciples, Jesus passed, and John stared hard at him and said, 'Look, there is the lamb of God.' Hearing this, the two disciples followed Jesus. Jesus turned round, saw them following and said, 'What do you want?' They answered, 'Rabbi,' – which means Teacher – 'where do you live?' 'Come and see' he replied; so they went and saw where he lived, and stayed with him the rest of that day. It was about the tenth hour.

One of these two who became followers of Jesus after hearing what John had said was Andrew, the brother of Simon Peter. Early next morning, Andrew met his brother and said to him, 'We have found the Messiah' – which means the Christ – and he took Simon to Jesus. Jesus looked hard at him and said, 'You are Simon son of John; you are to be called Cephas' – meaning Rock.

Reflection

John the Baptist points Jesus out to his disciples as the one who will save people by giving his life as a ransom for all. The disciples start following Jesus not fully knowing what this will entail. This, however, is the turning point in their lives. John signifies this by stating that "It was the tenth hour", the hour when one had to decide for or against. The disciples decide for Jesus. They become mediators or witnesses of God's Word. This time, however, God's Word is not simply verbal. It is manifest in the most perfect of ways, in Jesus.

05
JAN WED

WEDNESDAY AFTER EPIPHANY – Scotland
see Appendix A-3

Wednesday before Epiphany | White
(Optional, White)

1 John 3:11-21

This is the message as you heard it from the beginning: that we are to love one another; not to be like Cain, who belonged to the Evil One and cut his brother's throat; cut his brother's throat simply for this reason, that his own life was evil and his brother lived a good life. You must not be surprised, brothers, when the world hates you; we have passed out of death and into life, and of this we can be sure because we love our brothers. If you refuse to love, you must remain dead; to hate your brother is to be a murderer, and murderers, as you know, do not have eternal life in them. This has taught us love – that he gave up his life for us; and we, too, ought to give up our lives for our brothers. If a man who was rich enough in this world's goods saw that one of his brothers was in need, but closed his heart to him, how could the love of God be living in him? My children, our love is not to be just words or mere talk, but something real and active; only by this can we be certain that we are children of the truth and be able to quieten our conscience in his presence, whatever accusations it may raise against us, because God is greater than our conscience and he knows everything. My dear people, if we cannot be condemned by our own conscience, we need not be afraid in God's presence.

Psalm 99

Cry out with joy to the Lord, all the earth.

John 1:43-51

After Jesus had decided to leave for Galilee, he met Philip and said, 'Follow me.' Philip came from the same town, Bethsaida, as Andrew and Peter. Philip found Nathanael and said to him, 'We have found the one Moses wrote about in the Law, the one about whom the prophets wrote: he is Jesus son of Joseph, from Nazareth.' 'From Nazareth?' said Nathanael 'Can anything good come from that place?' 'Come and see' replied Philip. When Jesus saw Nathanael coming he said of him, 'There is an Israelite who deserves the name, incapable of deceit.' 'How do you know me?' said Nathanael. 'Before Philip came to call you,' said Jesus 'I saw you under the fig tree.' Nathanael answered, 'Rabbi, you are the Son of God, you are the King of Israel.' Jesus replied, 'You believe that just because I said: I saw you under the fig tree. You will see greater things than that.'

And then he added 'I tell you most solemnly, you will see heaven laid open and, above the Son of Man, the angels of God ascending and descending.'

Reflection

"Can anything good come out of Nazareth?" Nathanael wondered, and he asked the question because of the fact that Galilee, in which Nazareth was located, was believed to be a place of ill repute, from which no prophet had ever come (John 7:52). So it is no likely place for the Messiah to come. To be a Galilean or a Nazarene would only invite contempt. This mode of judging is not uncommon. Such judgements are made not by examining evidence, but by prejudice. Without examining the case in question many persons allow their minds to be filled with prejudice against others or their religion, and then pronounce judgements without examination. Philip found that the best answer would be to "Come and see". There was no need to reason with Nathanael or find out cases to the contrary, but the best way would be to go and examine for himself by meeting Jesus and staying with him. Personal knowledge and experience are the only ways to remove prejudice from our minds.

06

JAN THU

THE EPIPHANY OF THE LORD, Solemnity

THURSDAY AFTER EPIPHANY – Scotland
see Appendix A-4

Psalter Week 2

White

Isaiah 60:1-6

Arise, shine out Jerusalem, for your light has come, the glory of the Lord is rising on you, though night still covers the earth and darkness the peoples.

Above you the Lord now rises and above you his glory appears. The nations come to your light and kings to your dawning brightness.

Lift up your eyes and look round: all are assembling and coming towards you, your sons from far away and daughters being tenderly carried.

At this sight you will grow radiant, your heart throbbing and full; since the riches of the sea will flow to you; the wealth of the nations come to you; camels in throngs will cover you, and dromedaries of Midian and Ephah; everyone in Sheba will come, bringing gold and incense and singing the praise of the Lord.

Psalm 71:1-2, 7-8, 10-13. R. v. 11

All nations shall fall prostrate before you, O Lord.

Ephesians 3:2-3, 5-6

You have probably heard how I have been entrusted by God with the grace he meant for you, and that it was by a revelation that I was given the knowledge of the mystery. This mystery that has now been revealed through the Spirit to his holy apostles and prophets was unknown to any men in past generations; it means that pagans now share the same inheritance, that they are parts of the same body, and that the same promise has been made to them, in Christ Jesus, through the gospel.

Matthew 2:1-12

After Jesus had been born at Bethlehem in Judaea during the reign of King Herod, some wise men came to Jerusalem from the east. 'Where is the infant king of the Jews?' they asked. 'We saw his star as it rose and have come to do him homage.' When King Herod heard this he was perturbed, and so was the whole of Jerusalem. He called together all the chief priests and the scribes of the people, and enquired of them where the Christ was to be born. 'At Bethlehem in Judaea,' they told him 'for this is what the prophet wrote: And you, Bethlehem, in the land of Judah, you are by no means least among the leaders of Judah, for out of you will come a leader who will shepherd my people Israel.'

Then Herod summoned the wise men to see him privately. He asked them the exact date on which the star had appeared, and sent them on to Bethlehem. 'Go and find out all about the child', he said 'and when you have found him, let me know, so that I too may go and do him homage.' Having listened to what the king had to say, they set out. And there in front of them was the star they had seen rising; it went forward and halted over the place where the child was. The sight of the star filled them with delight, and going into the house they saw the child with his mother Mary, and falling to their knees they did him homage. Then, opening their treasures, they offered him gifts of gold and frankincense and myrrh. But they were warned in a dream not to go back to Herod, and returned to their own country by a different way.

Reflection

The visit of the Magi or three kings to the infant Jesus is a beautiful and touching event, recorded in Matthew's Gospel only. Each of the gifts offered is an eloquent symbol of Christ's future destiny. The splendour of gold represents kingship and sovereignty. Frankincense, delicate and richly aromatic, expresses the mystery of his divinity. The bitterness of myrrh, an analgesic sap extracted from a small, thorny tree, foretells the pain and suffering which lay ahead. Let each of us, like the Magi, seek out and follow the star which will lead us to our Saviour. No matter how oppressive the blackness may be which envelops us, no matter how empty and barren may seem the sky which looms above us, the small star – Hope – shall not fail to shine through, if we seek it with open eyes. May we follow its golden radiance, even if it be but the faintest glimmer; for it will surely lead us to that tranquil resting place where our God abides.

07
JAN FRI

FRIDAY AFTER EPIPHANY
– Scotland
see Appendix A-5

Friday after Epiphany | White
or **St Raymond of Penyafort,** *priest* (Optional, White)

1 John 3:22-4:6
Whatever we ask God, we shall receive, because we keep his commandments and live the kind of life that he wants. His commandments are these: that we believe in the name of his Son Jesus Christ and that we love one another as he told us to. Whoever keeps his commandments lives in God and God lives in him. We know that he lives in us by the Spirit that he has given us. It is not every spirit, my dear people, that you can trust; test them, to see if they come from God, there are many false prophets, now, in the world. You can tell the spirits that come from God by this: every spirit which acknowledges that Jesus the Christ has come in the flesh is from God; but any spirit which will not say this of Jesus is not from God, but is the spirit of Antichrist, whose coming you were warned about. Well, now he is here, in the world. Children, you have already overcome these false prophets, because you are from God and you have in you one who is greater than anyone in this world; as for them, they are of the world, and so they speak the language of the world and the world listens to them. But we are children of God, and those who know God listen to us; those who are not of God refuse to listen to us. This is how we can tell the spirit of truth from the spirit of falsehood.

Psalm 2:7-8,10-11
I will give you the nations for your heritage.

Matthew 4:12-17,23-25
Hearing that John had been arrested, Jesus went back to Galilee, and leaving Nazareth he went and settled in Capernaum, a lakeside town on the borders of Zebulun and Naphtali. In this way the prophecy of Isaiah was to be fulfilled: 'Land of Zebulun! Land of Naphtali! Way of the sea on the far side of Jordan, Galilee of the nations! The people that lived in darkness has seen a great light; on those who dwell in the land and shadow of death a light has dawned.' From that moment Jesus began his preaching with the message, 'Repent, for the kingdom of heaven is close at hand.' He went round the whole of Galilee teaching in their synagogues, proclaiming the Good News of the kingdom and curing all kinds of diseases and sickness among the people. His fame spread throughout Syria, and those who were suffering from diseases and painful complaints of one kind or another, the possessed, epileptics, the paralysed, were all brought to him, and he cured them. Large crowds followed him, coming from Galilee, the Decapolis, Jerusalem, Judaea and Transjordania.

Reflection
We are given one more opportunity to celebrate the gift of Jesus to us today in the liturgy as the light of the world. He also calls us to be his disciples and shares his light with us. He makes us light as well so that we can shine and put an end to the darkness in our corner of the world and in the lives of those around us. He noted once: "you are the light of the world... let your light shine." Christ's light in us shines brightly when we seek to do his will and work with him to spread God's kingdom of love, justice and peace. So, let your light shine. Lord, dispel the darkness of our daily struggles and pain! Amen

Saturday after Epiphany
White

08
JAN SAT

SATURDAY AFTER EPIPHANY
– Scotland
see Appendix A-6

1 John 4:7-10
My dear people, let us love one another since love comes from God and everyone who loves is begotten by God and knows God. Anyone who fails to love can never have known God, because God is love. God's love for us was revealed when God sent into the world his only Son so that we could have life through him; this is the love I mean: not our love for God, but God's love for us when he sent his Son to be the sacrifice that takes our sins away.

Psalm 71:1-4,7-8
All nations shall fall prostrate before you, O Lord.

Mark 6:34-44
As Jesus stepped ashore he saw a large crowd; and he took pity on them because they were like sheep without a shepherd, and he set himself to teach them at some length. By now it was getting very late, and his disciples came up to him and said, 'This is a lonely place and it is getting very late. So send them away, and they can go to the farms and villages round about, to buy themselves something to eat.' He replied, 'Give them something to eat yourselves.' They answered, 'Are we to go and spend two hundred denarii on bread for them to eat?' 'How many loaves have you?' he asked. 'Go and see.' And when they had found out they said, 'Five, and two fish.' Then he ordered them to get all the people together in groups on the green grass, and they sat down on the ground in squares of hundreds and fifties. Then he took the five loaves and the two fish, raised his eyes to heaven and said the blessing; then he broke the loaves and handed them to his disciples to distribute among the people. He also shared out the two fish among them all. They all ate as much as they wanted. They collected twelve basketfuls of scraps of bread and pieces of fish. Those who had eaten the loaves numbered five thousand men.

Reflection
Christian discipleship is a 24x7 mission. We cannot take a break from being good and doing good! All the same, we need a time-out to recuperate and rejuvenate ourselves so that we can continue the good work. Jesus knew his disciples who returned from their mission trip needed rest and so invited them to do so. However, their rest seemed to have been interrupted by the crowd that was eager to hear them! Jesus breaks the schedule and "sets out to teach them at some length." His reaction to the people who disrupted his well-earned break was to feel sorry for them and to help them. How willing am I to break my schedules for the sake of the mission to those who are less privileged than I am?

09
JAN SUN

THE BAPTISM OF THE LORD, Feast
Psalter Week 1
White

Isaiah 40:1-5, 9-11
'Console my people, console them' says your God. 'Speak to the heart of Jerusalem and call to her that her time of service is ended, that her sin is atoned for, that she has received from the hand of the Lord double punishment for her crimes.' A voice cries, 'Prepare in the wilderness a way for the Lord. Make a straight highway for our God across the desert. Let every valley be filled in, every mountain and hill be laid low, let every cliff become a plain, and the ridges a valley; then the glory of the Lord shall be revealed and all mankind shall see it; for the mouth of the Lord has spoken.' Go up on a high mountain, joyful messenger to Zion. Shout with a loud voice, joyful messenger to Jerusalem. Shout without fear, say to the towns of Judah, 'Here is your God.' Here is the Lord coming with power, his arm subduing all things to him. The prize of his victory is with him, his trophies all go before him. He is like a shepherd feeding his flock, gathering lambs in his arms, holding them against his breast and leading to their rest the mother ewes.

Psalm 103:1-2, 3-4, 24-25, 27-30. R. v. 1
Bless the Lord, my soul! Lord God, how great you are.

Titus 2:11-14; 3:4-7
God's grace has been revealed, and it has made salvation possible for the whole human race and taught us that what we have to do is to give up everything that does not lead to God, and all our worldly ambitions; we must be self-restrained and live good and religious lives here in this present world, while we are waiting in hope for the blessing which will come with the Appearing of the glory of our great God and saviour Christ Jesus. He sacrificed himself for us in order to set us free from all wickedness and to purify a people so that it could be his very own and would have no ambition except to do good. When the kindness and love of God our saviour for mankind were revealed, it was not because he was concerned with any righteous actions we might have done ourselves; it was for no reason except his own compassion that he saved us, by means of the cleansing water of rebirth and by renewing us with the Holy Spirit which he has so generously poured over us through Jesus Christ our saviour. He did this so that we should be justified by his grace, to become heirs looking forward to inheriting eternal life.

Luke 3:15-16, 21-22
A feeling of expectancy had grown among the people, who were beginning to think that John might be the Christ, so John declared before them all, 'I baptise you with water, but someone is coming, someone who is more powerful

than I am and I am not fit to undo the strap of his sandals; he will baptise you with the Holy Spirit and fire.' Now when all the people had been baptised and while Jesus after his own baptism was at prayer, heaven opened and the Holy Spirit descended on him in bodily shape, like a dove. And a voice came from heaven, 'You are my Son, the Beloved; my favour rests on you.'

Reflection

Although Jesus, as the sinless Son of God, had no need for re-birth through baptism, he chose, in his humility, to accept the washing by John in the waves of the Jordan. In doing so, he imparted sacramental power to the waters of baptism, whereby our own being is restored to its original blessedness and purity. When Christ emerged from the water, the Spirit descends upon him as a dove, while the voice of the Father proclaims, 'You are my Son, my Beloved; my favour rests upon you.' This descent of the Spirit and proclamation of love and favour from the Father is a reality for each baptised person. It is a reality which is renewed constantly, or rather has a potency which is indelible and eternal. If we still our minds from distractions, worries, aspirations and fears, and look upwards to the heavens, we shall see the Holy Spirit hovering above us, as the white dove of hope and faith. And if we listen intently, we shall not fail to hear our God proclaim with infinite love and joy to each of us personally, 'You are my beloved child, and my favour rests upon you.'

1 Samuel 1:1-8

There was a man of Ramathaim, a Zuphite from the highlands of Ephraim whose name was Elkanah son of Jeroham, son of Elihu, son of Tohu, son of Zuph, an Ephraimite. He had two wives, one called Hannah, the other Peninnah; Peninnah had children but Hannah had none. Every year this man used to go up from his town to worship and to sacrifice to the Lord of hosts in Shiloh. The two sons of Eli, Hophni and Phinehas, were there as priests of the Lord. One day Elkanah offered sacrifice. He used to give portions to Peninnah and to all her sons and daughters; to Hannah, however, he would give only one portion, although he loved her more, since the Lord had made her barren. Her rival would taunt her to annoy her, because the Lord had made her barren. And this went on year after year; every time they went up to the temple of the Lord she used to taunt her. And so Hannah wept and would not eat. Then Elkanah her husband said to her, 'Hannah, why are you crying and why are you not eating? Why so sad? Am I not more to you than ten sons?'

Psalm 115:12-19. R. v. 17

A thanksgiving sacrifice I make to you, O Lord.

Mark 1:14-20

After John had been arrested, Jesus went into Galilee. There he proclaimed the Good News from God. 'The time has come' he said 'and the kingdom of God is close at hand. Repent, and believe the Good News.' As he was walking along by the Sea of Galilee he saw Simon and his brother Andrew casting a net in the lake – for they were fishermen. And Jesus said to them, 'Follow me and I will make you into fishers of men.' And at once they left their nets and followed him. Going on a little further, he saw James son of Zebedee and his brother John; they too were in their boat, mending their nets. He called them at once and, leaving their father Zebedee in the boat with the men he employed, they went after him.

Reflection

Jesus calls his first disciples and apostles, Simon and Andrew, to leave behind their business as fishermen, their nets, boats, and way of life, and to follow him. Each of us may ask ourselves: What am I being called to leave behind to follow Christ more faithfully? There are, perhaps, parts of our lives which are holding us back and limiting our freedom. These might be vices, prejudices, fears, bitterness, addictions, unhelpful relationships, or simply bad habits. Each of us – even the most devout – carries within us something which would be better left behind. Let us examine ourselves carefully today, and find at least one thing (big or small) which we are called to renounce or surrender. And, with God's help, let us strive to do that, so that we may draw closer to the perfect freedom of radical detachment.

11 JAN TUE

1st Week in Ordinary Time
Green

1 Samuel 1:9-20

After they had eaten in the hall, Hannah rose and took her stand before the Lord, while Eli the priest was sitting on his seat by the doorpost of the temple of the Lord. In the bitterness of her soul she prayed to the Lord with many tears and made a vow, saying, 'Lord of hosts! If you will take notice of the distress of your servant, and bear me in mind and not forget your servant and give her a man-child, I will give him to the Lord for the whole of his life and no razor shall ever touch his head.' While she prayed before the Lord which she did for some time, Eli was watching her mouth, for she was speaking under her breath; her lips were moving but her voice could not be heard. He therefore supposed that she was drunk and said to her, 'How long are you going to be in this drunken state? Rid yourself of your wine.' 'No, my lord,' Hannah replied 'I am a woman in great trouble; I have taken neither wine nor strong drink – I was pouring out my soul before the Lord. Do not take your maidservant for a worthless woman; all this time I have been speaking from the depth of my grief and my resentment.' Then Eli answered her: 'Go in peace,' he said 'and may the God of Israel grant what you have asked of him.' And she said, 'May your maidservant find favour in your sight'; and with that the woman went away; she returned to the hall and ate and was dejected no longer.They rose early in the morning and worshipped before the Lord and then set out and returned to their home in Ramah. Elkanah had intercourse with Hannah his wife and the Lord was mindful of her. She conceived and gave birth to a son, and called him Samuel 'since' she said 'I asked the Lord for him.'

1 Samuel 2:1, 4-8. R. cf. v. 1

My heart exults in the Lord.

Mark 1:21-28

Jesus and his disciples went as far as Capernaum, and as soon as the sabbath came he went to the synagogue and began to teach. And his teaching made a deep impression on them because, unlike the scribes, he taught them with authority. In their synagogue just then there was a man possessed by an unclean spirit, and it shouted, 'What do you want with us, Jesus of Nazareth? Have you come to destroy us? I know who you are: the Holy One of God.' But Jesus said sharply, 'Be quiet! Come out of him!' And the unclean spirit threw the man into convulsions and with a loud cry went out of him. The people were so astonished that they started asking each other what it all meant. 'Here is a teaching that is new' they said 'and with authority behind it: he gives orders even to unclean spirits and they obey him.' And his reputation rapidly spread everywhere, through all the surrounding Galilean countryside.

Reflection

The early hearers of Jesus were struck at once by a certain confidence and power which he conveyed, by the fact that, 'unlike the scribes, he taught them with authority.' Christ was, at this time, a relatively young and unknown man who had no official status or position. What, then, was the source of his mysterious authority which so greatly impressed his hearers? Presumably it was not personal charisma nor rhetorical skill alone. Rather, his authority came from perfect purity of heart, simplicity and honesty. He was not motivated by self-interest or political agendas. Jesus simply spoke the truth and, more importantly, spoke the truth with love. When we are called upon to explain or defend the teachings of our faith, let us always endeavour to do the same.

12
JAN WED

1st Week in Ordinary Time
Green

1 Samuel 3:1-10, 19-20

The boy Samuel was ministering to the Lord in the presence of Eli; it was rare for the Lord to speak in those days; visions were uncommon. One day, it happened that Eli was lying down in his room. His eyes were beginning to grow dim; he could no longer see. The lamp of God had not yet gone out, and Samuel was lying in the sanctuary of the Lord where the ark of God was, when the Lord called, 'Samuel! Samuel!' He answered, 'Here I am.' Then he ran to Eli and said, 'Here I am, since you called me.' Eli said, 'I did not call. Go back and lie down.' So he went and lay down. Once again the Lord called, 'Samuel! Samuel!' Samuel got up and went to Eli and said, 'Here I am, since you called me.' He replied, 'I did not call you, my son; go back and lie down.' Samuel had as yet no knowledge of the Lord and the word of the Lord had not yet been revealed to him. Once again the Lord called, the third time. He got up and went to Eli and said, 'Here I am, since you called me.' Eli then understood that it was the Lord who was calling the boy, and he said to Samuel, 'Go and lie down, and if someone calls say, "Speak, Lord, your servant is listening."' So Samuel went and lay down in his place. The Lord then came and stood by, calling as he had done before, 'Samuel! Samuel!' Samuel answered, 'Speak, Lord, your servant is listening.' Samuel grew up and the Lord was with him and let no word of his fall to the ground. All Israel from Dan to Beersheba came to know that Samuel was accredited as a prophet of the Lord.

Psalm 39:2, 5, 7-10. R. vv. 8, 9

Here am I, Lord! I come to do your will.

Mark 1:29-39

On leaving the synagogue, Jesus went with James and John straight to the house of Simon and Andrew. Now Simon's mother-in-law had gone to bed with fever, and they told him about her straightaway. He went to her, took her by the hand and helped her up. And the fever left her and she began to wait on them. That evening, after sunset, they brought to him all who were sick and those who were possessed by devils. The whole town came crowding round the door, and he cured many who were suffering from diseases of one kind or another; he also cast out many devils, but he would not allow them to speak, because they knew who he was. In the morning, long before dawn, he got up and left the house, and went off to a lonely place and prayed there. Simon and his companions set out in search of him, and when they found him they said, 'Everybody is looking for you.' He answered, 'Let us go elsewhere, to the neighbouring country towns, so that I can preach there too, because that is why I came.' And he went all through Galilee, preaching in their synagogues and casting out devils.

Reflection

In today's Gospel, we are told that Jesus rose before dawn and went off to a lonely place to pray. This practice is related numerous times in the Gospels and was evidently an important part of the spiritual life of Christ. In our modern world, with its habitual business, true solitude is a rare thing. But a few minutes spent each day in silent reflection can be a wonderful source of strength and energy. Our moments of solitude are precious treasures beyond any price. For it is when we are most truly alone that we are most truly in the presence of God.

13
JAN THU

1st Week in Ordinary Time | Green
or **St Hilary,** *bishop, doctor* (Optional, White)

Saint Kentigern (Mungo), Bishop, Feast – Scotland, see Appendix A-7

1 Samuel 4:1-11

It happened at that time that the Philistines mustered to fight Israel and Israel went out to meet them in battle, encamping near Ebenezer while the Philistines were encamped at Aphek. The Philistines drew up their battle line against Israel, the battle was hotly engaged, and Israel was defeated by the Philistines and about four thousand of their army were killed on the field. The troops returned to the camp and the elders of Israel said, 'Why has the Lord allowed us to be defeated today by the Philistines? Let us fetch the ark of our God from Shiloh so that it may come among us and rescue us from the power of our enemies.' So the troops sent to Shiloh and brought away the ark of the Lord of hosts, he who is seated on the cherubs; the two sons of Eli, Hophni and Phinehas, came with the ark. When the ark of the Lord arrived in the camp, all Israel gave a great shout so that the earth resounded. When the Philistines heard the noise of the shouting, they said, 'What can this great shouting in the Hebrew camp mean?' And they realised that the ark of the Lord had come into the camp. At this the Philistines were afraid; and they said, 'God has come to the camp.' 'Alas!' they cried 'This has never happened before. Alas! Who will save us from the power of this mighty God? It was he who struck down Egypt with every kind of plague! But take courage and be men, Philistines, or you will become slaves to the Hebrews as they have been slaves to you. Be men and fight.' So the Philistines joined battle and Israel was defeated, each man fleeing to his tent. The slaughter was great indeed, and there fell of the Israelites thirty thousand foot soldiers. The ark of God was captured too, and the two sons of Eli died, Hophni and Phinehas.

Psalm 43:10-11, 14-15, 24-25. R. v. 27

Redeem us, O Lord, because of your love.

Mark 1:40-45

A leper came to Jesus and pleaded on his knees: 'If you want to' he said 'you can cure me.' Feeling sorry for him, Jesus stretched out his hand and touched him. 'Of course I want to!' he said. 'Be cured!' And the leprosy left him at once and he was cured. Jesus immediately sent him away and sternly ordered him, 'Mind you say nothing to anyone, but go and show yourself to the priest, and make the offering for your healing prescribed by Moses as evidence of your recovery.' The man went away, but then started talking about it freely and telling the story everywhere, so that Jesus could no longer go openly into any town, but had to stay outside in places where nobody lived. Even so, people from all around would come to him.

Reflection

In our first reading today, we witness the Philistines and the Hebrews meeting in battle. The Hebrews possess the ark of the Lord, and for this reason the Philistines are initially overtaken with fear. But they are urged to take courage and be strong. Somewhat unexpectedly, they end up defeating the Hebrews. The advice to 'be strong' is one which is very useful as we face the many challenges and adversities of life. But the strength to which we are called is not the hard and unfeeling strength of iron or of stone, but rather the flexible resilience of the young palm branch. Such a branch, though green and easily pliable, is extremely difficult to break. Let us prepare ourselves for the battle of life, not with the weapons of hardness and rigidity, but rather those of flexibility, patience and gentleness.

14
JAN FRI

1 Samuel 8:4-7, 10-22

All the elders of Israel gathered together and came to Samuel at Ramah. 'Look,' they said to him 'you are old, and your sons do not follow your ways. So give us a king to rule over us, like the other nations.' It displeased Samuel that they should say, 'Let us have a king to rule us,' so he prayed to the Lord. But the Lord said to Samuel, 'Obey the voice of the people in all that they say to you, for it is not you they have rejected; they have rejected me from ruling over them.' … *(Please see the Appendix B-1)*

Psalm 88:16-19. R. cf. v. 2

I will sing for ever of your love, O Lord.

Mark 2:1-12

When Jesus returned to Capernaum, word went round that he was back; and so many people collected that there was no room left, even in front of the door. He was preaching the word to them when some people came bringing him a paralytic carried by four men, but as the crowd made it impossible to get the man to him, they stripped the roof over the place where Jesus was; and when they had made an opening, they lowered the stretcher on which the paralytic lay. Seeing their faith, Jesus said to the paralytic, 'My child, your sins are forgiven.' Now some scribes were sitting there, and they thought to themselves, 'How can this man talk like that? He is blaspheming. Who can forgive sins but God?' Jesus, inwardly aware that this was what they were thinking, said to them, 'Why do you have these thoughts in your hearts? Which of these is easier: to say to the paralytic, "Your sins are forgiven" or to say, "Get up, pick up your stretcher and walk?" But to prove to you that the Son of Man has authority on earth to forgive sins,' – he said to the paralytic – 'I order you: get up, pick up your stretcher, and go off home.' And the man got up, picked up his stretcher at once and walked out in front of everyone, so that they were all astounded and praised God saying, 'We have never seen anything like this.'

Reflection

Jesus performs two miracles or wondrous actions in today's Gospel. He heals a man of physical paralysis and also forgives his sins. In a way, the physical healing is a symbol for the forgiveness of sins. Often sins can tend to paralyse our hearts and souls. We can feel held back and immobilised because of mistakes we have made in the past. Yet Jesus is able to restore our liberty, to free us from the burdens which restrain us. In big ways or small ways, we are all in need of the forgiveness of the Lord. We all suffer some form of spiritual paralysis or impairment which is holding us back from our full potential. This full potential is, of course, nothing less than the perfect freedom of the children of God, and the perfect joy and peace that comes from knowing we are dearly loved by our heavenly Father.

15 JAN SAT

1st Week in Ordinary Time
Green

1 Samuel 9:1-4, 17-19; 10:1

Among the men of Benjamin there was a man named Kish son of Abiel, son of Zeror, son of Becorath, son of Aphiah; a Benjaminite and a man of rank. He had a son named Saul, a handsome man in the prime of life. Of all the Israelites there was no one more handsome than he; he stood head and shoulders taller than the rest of the people. Now some of the she-donkeys of Saul's father Kish had strayed, so Kish said to Saul, 'My son, take one of the servants with you and be off; go and look for the she-donkeys.' They passed through the highlands of Ephraim and passed through the land of Shalishah, but did not find them; they passed through the land of Shaalim, they were not there; they passed through the land of Benjamin, but did not find them. When Samuel saw Saul, the Lord told him, 'That is the man of whom I told you; he shall rule my people.' Saul accosted Samuel in the gateway and said, 'Tell me, please, where the seer's house is?' Samuel replied to Saul, 'I am the seer. Go up ahead of me to the high place. You are to eat with me today. In the morning I shall take leave of you and tell you all that is in your heart.' Samuel took a phial of oil and poured it on Saul's head; then he kissed him, saying, 'Has not the Lord anointed you prince over his people Israel? You are the man who must rule the Lord's people, and who must save them from the power of the enemies surrounding them.'

Psalm 20:2-7. R. v. 2

O Lord, your strength gives joy to the king.

Mark 2:13-17

Jesus went out to the shore of the lake; and all the people came to him, and he taught them. As he was walking on he saw Levi the son of Alphaeus, sitting by the customs house, and he said to him, 'Follow me.' And he got up and followed him. When Jesus was at dinner in his house, a number of tax collectors and sinners were also sitting at the table with Jesus and his disciples; for there were many of them among his followers. When the scribes of the Pharisee party saw him eating with sinners and tax collectors, they said to his disciples, 'Why does he eat with tax collectors and sinners?' When Jesus heard this he said to them, 'It is not the healthy who need the doctor, but the sick. I did not come to call the virtuous, but sinners.'

Reflection

When Jesus encounters criticism from the Pharisees for choosing to associate with tax collectors and sinners, his response is that he has come not to call the virtuous, but sinners to repentance. Of course, this does not mean that Christ wishes to exclude the 'virtuous', or people who are judged as good by the standards of society. Indeed, many Pharisees, scribes and priests came to be his closest followers. Rather, Jesus' words teach us that, in order to receive his gracious gift of salvation, we need firstly to recognise our need for mercy and to acknowledge our need for healing. Each of us, even the strongest, carries a multitude of weaknesses, wounds and worries, some of which may be visible to the world, but most of which probably are not. Let us reveal them openly and honestly to our God, the wise and loving physician who alone can bring us perfect wholeness and peace.

16
JAN SUN

SECOND SUNDAY IN ORDINARY TIME

Psalter Week 2

Green

Isaiah 62:1-5

About Zion I will not be silent, about Jerusalem I will not grow weary, until her integrity shines out like the dawn and her salvation flames like a torch. The nations then will see your integrity, all the kings your glory, and you will be called by a new name, one which the mouth of the Lord will confer. You are to be a crown of splendour in the hand of the Lord, a princely diadem in the hand of your God; no longer are you to be named 'Forsaken', nor your land 'Abandoned', but you shall be called 'My Delight' and your land 'The Wedded' for the Lord takes delight in you and your land will have its wedding. Like a young man marrying a virgin, so will the one who built you wed you, and as the bridegroom rejoices in his bride, so will your God rejoice in you.

Psalm 95:1-3, 7-10 R. v. 3

Proclaim the wonders of the Lord among all the peoples.

1 Corinthians 12:4-11

There is a variety of gifts but always the same Spirit; there are all sorts of service to be done, but always to the same Lord; working in all sorts of different ways in different people, it is the same God who is working in all of them. The particular way in which the Spirit is given to each person is for a good purpose. One may have the gift of preaching with wisdom given him by the Spirit; another may have the gift of preaching instruction given him by the same Spirit; and another the gift of faith given by the same Spirit; another again the gift of healing, through this one Spirit; one, the power of miracles; another, prophecy; another the gift of recognising spirits; another the gift of tongues and another the ability to interpret them. All these are the work of one and the same Spirit, who distributes different gifts to different people just as he chooses.

John 2:1-11

There was a wedding at Cana in Galilee. The mother of Jesus was there, and Jesus and his disciples had also been invited. When they ran out of wine, since the wine provided for the wedding was all finished, the mother of Jesus said to him, 'They have no wine.' Jesus said, 'Woman, why turn to me? My hour has not come yet.' His mother said to the servants, 'Do whatever he tells you.' There were six stone water jars standing there, meant for the ablutions that are customary among the Jews; each could hold twenty or thirty gallons. Jesus said to the servants, 'Fill the jars with water,' and they filled them to the brim. 'Draw some out now' he told them 'and take it to the steward.' They did this; the steward tasted the water, and it had turned into wine. Having no idea where it came from – only the servants who had drawn the water knew – the steward called the bridegroom and said, 'People generally serve the best wine first, and keep the cheaper sort till the guests have had plenty to drink; but you have kept the best wine till now.' This was the first of the signs given by Jesus: it was given at Cana in Galilee. He let his glory be seen, and his disciples believed in him.

Reflection

It may strike us a slightly curious that the first miracle performed by Jesus in John's Gospel is not a cure or exorcism of some kind, but rather it is the conversion of water into wine – fine wine and in a generous quantity. Wine is an almost universal symbol of celebration and joy, and reveals much of Christ's vision of human life. He came, after all, that we may have life and have it more abundantly. Christian life is thus a gift and an expression of God's gracious love, not merely a duty or a trial. It is good to ask ourselves from time to time, 'Am I enjoying life? Am I taking the time to do things that make me happy?' Such a question is born not of mere selfishness, but rather reflects true gratitude for God's gifts. Moreover, we have very little chance of being kind, patient and generous with others unless we are firstly kind, patient and generous with ourselves – that is to say, unless we take the time to drink the wine (real or metaphoric) of the good things of creation.

17
JAN MON

2nd Week in Ordinary Time
St Anthony, *abbot,* **Memorial** | White

1 Samuel 15:16-23

Samuel said to Saul, 'Stop! Let me tell you what the Lord said to me last night.' Saul said, 'Tell me.' Samuel continued, 'Small as you may be in your own eyes, are you not head of the tribes of Israel? The Lord has anointed you king over Israel. The Lord sent you on a mission and said to you, "Go, put these sinners, the Amalekites, under the ban and make war on them until they are exterminated." Why then did you not obey the voice of the Lord? Why did you fall on the booty and do what is displeasing to the Lord?' Saul replied to Samuel, 'But I did obey the voice of the Lord. I went on the mission which the Lord gave me; I brought back Agag king of the Amalekites; I put the Amalekites under the ban. From the booty the people took the best sheep and oxen of what was under the ban to sacrifice them to the Lord your God in Gilgal.' But Samuel replied: 'Is the pleasure of the Lord in holocausts and sacrifices or in obedience to the voice of the Lord? Yes, obedience is better than sacrifice, submissiveness better than the fat of rams. Rebellion is a sin of sorcery, presumption a crime of teraphim. 'Since you have rejected the word of the Lord, he has rejected you as king.'

Psalm 49:8-9, 16-17, 21, 23. R. v. 23

I will show God's salvation to the upright.

Mark 2:18-22

One day when John's disciples and the Pharisees were fasting, some people came and said to Jesus, 'Why is it that John's disciples and the disciples of the Pharisees fast, but your disciples do not?' Jesus replied, 'Surely the bridegroom's attendants would never think of fasting while the bridegroom is still with them? As long as they have the bridegroom with them, they could not think of fasting. But the time will come for the bridegroom to be taken away from them, and then, on that day, they will fast. No one sews a piece of unshrunken cloth on an old cloak; if he does, the patch pulls away from it, the new from the old, and the tear gets worse. And nobody puts new wine into old wineskins; if he does, the wine will burst the skins, and the wine is lost and the skins too. No! New wine, fresh skins!'

Reflection

St Anthony of Egypt, whose feast is celebrated today, is sometimes referred to as the 'Father of monasticism'. Anthony's influence and personality gave a huge impetus to the monastic movement in Egypt. The story of his life was immensely popular in Western Europe, and influenced St Benedict, St Francis and innumerable other religious founders. The charism of St Anthony was to seek God in silence and solitude. Not only did he encounter God, but also was confronted with a multitude of temptations and challenges, and thus came to a very profound self-knowledge. Indeed, there is no true knowledge of God without knowledge of self, and no true knowledge of self without knowledge of God. Let us journey with St Anthony into the silence of our hearts and into the unexplored deserts of our souls, and meet there the unknown God who transcends all our words and surpasses all our thoughts.

18 JAN TUE

2nd Week in Ordinary Time
Green

1 Samuel 16:1-13

The Lord said to Samuel, 'How long will you go on mourning over Saul when I have rejected him as king of Israel? Fill your horn with oil and go. I am sending you to Jesse of Bethlehem, for I have chosen myself a king among his sons.' Samuel replied, 'How can I go? When Saul hears of it he will kill me.' Then the Lord said, 'Take a heifer with you and say, "I have come to sacrifice to the Lord." Invite Jesse to the sacrifice, and then I myself will tell you what you must do; you must anoint to me the one I point out to you.'

Samuel did what the Lord ordered and went to Bethlehem. The elders of the town came trembling to meet him and asked, 'Seer, have you come with good intentions towards us?' 'Yes,' he replied 'I have come to sacrifice to the Lord. Purify yourselves and come with me to the sacrifice.' He purified Jesse and his sons and invited them to the sacrifice. … *(Please see the Appendix B-1)*

Psalm 88:20-22, 27-28. R. v. 21

I have found David, my servant.

Mark 2:23-28

One sabbath day Jesus happened to be taking a walk through the cornfields, and his disciples began to pick ears of corn as they went along. And the Pharisees said to him, 'Look, why are they doing something on the sabbath day that is forbidden?' And he replied, 'Have you never read what David did in his time of need when he and his followers were hungry – how he went into the house of God when Abiathar was high priest, and ate the loaves of offering which only the priests are allowed to eat, and how he also gave some to the men with him?'

And he said to them, 'The sabbath was made for man, not man for the sabbath; so the Son of Man is master even of the sabbath.'

Reflection

Our reading from the book of Samuel tells the story of David being selected as future king of Israel. Now, David is the youngest of many brothers. Yet it is not any of his brethren – who are older, taller, stronger and more experienced – whom is chosen, but the one who is apparently the least. And David, who is a mere shepherd boy, goes on to become an invincible warrior, the greatest of kings and an inspired prophet. It is a striking instance of the Gospel maxim, 'The first shall be last'. God often works in unexpected ways, and God's graces flow through channels we may not expect. Are there people whom we have overlooked, dismissed, or even 'written off'? Are there areas in our lives or even our own personalities that we habitually ignore or neglect? Let us open our eyes and our hearts to these, and perhaps find therein new potentialities and unexpected graces.

1 Samuel 17:32-33, 37, 40-51

David said to Saul, 'Let no one lose heart on his account; your servant will go and fight this Philistine.' But Saul answered David, 'You cannot go and fight the Philistine; you are only a boy and he has been a warrior from his youth.' 'The Lord who rescued me from the claws of lion and bear,' David said, 'will rescue me from the power of this Philistine.' Then Saul said to David, 'Go, and the Lord be with you!'

He took his staff in his hand, picked five smooth stones from the river bed, put them in his shepherd's bag, in his pouch, and with his sling in his hand he went to meet the Philistine. The Philistine, his shield-bearer in front of him, came nearer and nearer to David; and the Philistine looked at David, and what he saw filled him with scorn, because David was only a youth, a boy of fresh complexion and pleasant bearing. The Philistine said to him, 'Am I a dog for you to come against me with sticks?' And the Philistine cursed David by his gods. ...

(Please see the Appendix B-1)

Psalm 143:1-2, 9-10. R. v. 1

Blessed be the Lord, my rock.

Mark 3:1-6

Jesus went into a synagogue, and there was a man there who had a withered hand. And they were watching him to see if he would cure him on the sabbath day, hoping for something to use against him. He said to the man with the withered hand, 'Stand up out in the middle!' Then he said to them, 'Is it against the law on the sabbath day to do good or to do evil; to save life, or to kill?' But they said nothing. Then, grieved to find them so obstinate, he looked angrily round at them, and said to the man, 'Stretch out your hand.' He stretched it out and his hand was better. The Pharisees went out and at once began to plot with the Herodians against him, discussing how to destroy him.

Reflection

The narrative of David and Goliath possesses a powerful and ever-relevant resonance. The message is very simple: sometimes the smaller and apparently weaker person may defeat a bigger and stronger adversary. Even if our hearts are entirely set upon peace, it is virtually impossible to avoid encountering adversity or enmity of one kind or another. In each conflict, we should ask ourselves, am I the David or the Goliath in this battle? This question can never be answered with absolute certainty or real objectivity. It is always tempting to imagine that we are the 'underdog' fighting against some oppressive and bloated Goliath. But other people – our adversaries – may equally see us as the Goliath, and themselves as David, the 'underdog'. Can we imagine a world in which David and Goliath sat down and discussed their differences in a civil way? Perhaps this is what our world needs most today.

20 JAN THU

2nd Week in Ordinary Time
or **St Fabian,** *pope, martyr* | or **St Sebastian,** *martyr* (Opt., Red)

1 Samuel 18:6-9; 19:1-7

On their way back, as David was returning after killing the Philistine, the women came out to meet King Saul from all the towns of Israel, singing and dancing to the sound of tambourine and lyre and cries of joy; and as they danced the women sang: 'Saul has killed his thousands, and David his tens of thousands.'

Saul was very angry; the incident was not to his liking. 'They have given David the tens of thousands,' he said 'but me only the thousands; he has all but the kingship now.' And Saul turned a jealous eye on David from that day forward.

Saul told Jonathan his son and all his servants of his intention to kill David. Now Jonathan, Saul's son, held David in great affection; and so Jonathan warned David; 'My father Saul is looking for a way to kill you,' he said 'so be on your guard tomorrow morning; hide away in some secret place. Then I will go and keep my father company in the fields where you are hiding, and will talk to my father about you; I will find out what the situation is and let you know.'

So Jonathan spoke well of David to Saul his father; he said, 'Let not the king sin against his servant David, for he has not sinned against you, and what he has done has been greatly to your advantage. He took his life in his hands when he killed the Philistine, and the Lord brought about a great victory for all Israel. You saw it yourself and rejoiced; why then sin against innocent blood in killing David without cause?' Saul was impressed by Jonathan's words and took an oath, 'As the Lord lives, I will not kill him.' Jonathan called David and told him all these things. Then Jonathan brought him to Saul, and David attended on him as before.

Psalm 55:2-3, 9-14. R. v. 5 ***In God I trust: I shall not fear.***

Mark 3:7-12

Jesus withdrew with his disciples to the lakeside, and great crowds from Galilee followed him. From Judaea, Jerusalem, Idumaea, Transjordania and the region of Tyre and Sidon, great numbers who had heard of all he was doing came to him. And he asked his disciples to have a boat ready for him because of the crowd, to keep him from being crushed. For he had cured so many that all who were afflicted in any way were crowding forward to touch him. And the unclean spirits, whenever they saw him, would fall down before him and shout, 'You are the Son of God!' But he warned them strongly not to make him known.

Reflection

Today's Gospel tells of Jesus and his disciples seeking to flee the crowds, and having to get on to a boat to avoid being crushed by the sheer multitude of people. Often in life, it is possible to feel that we are about to be crushed or obliterated – either by the weight of too many responsibilities, too much work, too many demanding human relationships, or excessively high expectations which we or others have placed upon us. We can very easily 'spread ourselves too thin.' Perhaps, like Christ and the disciples, we also need somewhere to which we can flee, to escape the crush of life. It is good to remind ourselves that God does not actually need our service or busyness. All God asks is that we love him. Let us take some moments to be unproductive, to do nothing but be still in the presence of our God.

21
JAN FRI

2nd Week in Ordinary Time
St Agnes, *virgin, martyr,* **Memorial** | Red

1 Samuel 24:3-21

Saul took three thousand men chosen from the whole of Israel and went in search of David and his men east of the Rocks of the Wild Goats. He came to the sheep-folds along the route where there was a cave, and went in to cover his feet. Now David and his men were sitting in the recesses of the cave; David's men said to him, 'Today is the day of which the Lord said to you, "I will deliver your enemy into your power, do what you like with him."' David stood up and, unobserved, cut off the border of Saul's cloak. Afterwards David reproached himself for having cut off the border of Saul's cloak. He said to his men, 'The Lord preserve me from doing such a thing to my lord and raising my hand against him, for he is the anointed of the Lord.' David gave his men strict instructions, forbidding them to attack Saul.

Saul then left the cave and went on his way. After this, David too left the cave and called after Saul, 'My lord king!' Saul looked behind him and David bowed to the ground and did homage. Then David said to Saul, 'Why do you listen to the men who say to you, "David means to harm you"? … *(Please see the Appendix B-2)*

Psalm 56:2-4, 6, 11. R. v. 2

Have mercy on me, God, have mercy.

Mark 3:13-19

Jesus went up into the hills and summoned those he wanted. So they came to him and he appointed twelve; they were to be his companions and to be sent out to preach, with power to cast out devils. And so he appointed the Twelve: Simon to whom he gave the name Peter, James the son of Zebedee and John the brother of James, to whom he gave the name Boanerges or 'Sons of Thunder'; then Andrew, Philip, Bartholomew, Matthew, Thomas, James the son of Alphaeus, Thaddaeus, Simon the Zealot and Judas Iscariot, the man who was to betray him.

Reflection

In today's Gospel, Jesus sends his apostles forth to proclaim the message of salvation. God never ceases to provide witnesses to this saving message, who announce the Gospel in a multitude of ways. One of the most powerful ways is in the lives and deaths of the martyrs. St Agnes, whom we honour today, suffered martyrdom as a mere child, of twelve or thirteen. She held firm to her innocence and purity in the face of violent threats, and so was cruelly executed. We modern Christians are unlikely to suffer physical violence because of our faith, but we still may be misunderstood, excluded, mocked or face discrimination. Following the noble example of Agnes, let us be faithful to the God who gave his very life for our sake. In doing so, we may also be bearing witness to the Gospel of love in ways we cannot possibly know or imagine.

22
JAN SAT

2nd Week in Ordinary Time
or **St Vincent,** *deacon, martyr* (Optional, Red)

2 Samuel 1:1-4, 11-12, 17, 19, 23-27

David returned from his rout of the Amalekites and spent two days in Ziklag. On the third day a man came from the camp where Saul had been, his garments torn and earth on his head. When he came to David, he fell to the ground and did homage. 'Where do you come from?' David asked him. 'I have escaped from the Israelite camp,' he said. David said to him, 'What happened? Tell me.' He replied, 'The people have fled from the battlefield and many of them have fallen. Saul and his son Jonathan are dead too.'

Then David took hold of his garments and tore them, and all the men did the same. They mourned and wept and fasted until the evening for Saul and his son Jonathan, for the people of the Lord and for the house of Israel, because they had fallen by the sword.

Then David made this lament over Saul and his son Jonathan: 'Alas, the glory of Israel has been slain on your heights! How did the heroes fall? Saul and Jonathan, loved and lovely, neither in life, nor in death, were divided. Swifter than eagles were they, stronger were they than lions. O daughters of Israel, weep for Saul who clothed you in scarlet and fine linen, who set brooches of gold on your garments. How did the heroes fall in the thick of the battle? O Jonathan, in your death I am stricken, I am desolate for you, Jonathan my brother. Very dear to me you were, your love to me more wonderful than the love of a woman. How did the heroes fall and the battle armour fail?'

Psalm 79:2-3, 5-7. R. v. 4

Let your face shine on us, O Lord, and we shall be saved.

Mark 3:20-21

Jesus went home, and such a crowd collected that they could not even have a meal. When his relatives heard of this, they set out to take charge of him, convinced he was out of his mind.

Reflection

The incident of Jesus' family members coming to collect him, believing him to be out of his mind, must have been a painful experience for our Lord on a human level. He certainly loved his mother and family members and had no wish to see them upset. But troubles and divisions within families are virtually an inevitable part of our human condition, and it was into this human condition, with all its complexities and pain, that God truly entered through the Incarnation of the Son. This God came to share fully and experientially the pains and troubles of humanity, including those which lie hidden deep within our hearts. Let us spare a thought and prayer today for families, especially those who experience pain, trauma and misunderstandings of various kinds. Let us also remember those who suffer from mental and psychological afflictions, and all those who care for them and love them.

23
JAN SUN

THIRD SUNDAY IN ORDINARY TIME

Sunday of the Word of God

Psalter Week 3

Green

Nehemiah 8:2-6, 8-10

Ezra the priest brought the Law before the assembly, consisting of men, women, and children old enough to understand. This was the first day of the seventh month. On the square before the Water Gate, in the presence of the men and women, and children old enough to understand, he read from the book from early morning till noon; all the people listened attentively to the Book of the Law. Ezra the scribe stood on a wooden dais erected for the purpose. In full view of all the people – since he stood higher than all the people – Ezra opened the book; and when he opened it all the people stood up. Then Ezra blessed the Lord, the great God, and all the people raised their hands and answered, 'Amen! Amen!'; then they bowed down and, face to the ground, prostrated themselves before the Lord. And Ezra read from the Law of God, translating and giving the sense, so that the people understood what was read. Then Nehemiah – His Excellency – and Ezra, priest and scribe (and the Levites who were instructing the people) said to all the people, 'This day is sacred to the Lord your God. Do not be mournful, do not weep.' For the people were all in tears as they listened to the words of the Law. He then said, 'Go, eat the fat, drink the sweet wine, and send a portion to the man who has nothing prepared ready. For this day is sacred to our Lord. Do not be sad: the joy of the Lord is your stronghold.'

Psalm 18:8-10, 15 R. John 6:63

Your words are spirit, Lord, and they are life.

1 Corinthians 12:12-30 *(Shorter form 12:12-14, 27)*

Just as a human body, though it is made up of many parts, is a single unit because all these parts, though many, make one body, so it is with Christ. In the one Spirit we were all baptised, Jews as well as Greeks, slaves as well as citizens, and one Spirit was given to us all to drink. Nor is the body to be identified with any one of its many parts. If the foot were to say, 'I am not a hand and so I do not belong to the body', would that mean that it stopped being part of the body? If the ear were to say, 'I am not an eye, and so I do not belong to the body,' would that mean that it is not a part of the body? If your whole body was just one eye, how would you hear anything? If it was just one ear, how would you smell anything? Instead of that, God put all the separate parts into the body on purpose. If all the parts were the same, how could it be a body? As it is, the parts are many but the body is one. The eye cannot say to the hand, 'I do not need you,' nor can the head say to the feet, 'I do not need you.' What is more, it is precisely the parts of the body that seem to be the weakest which are the indispensable ones; and it is the least honourable parts of the body that we clothe with the greatest care. So our more improper parts get decorated in a way that our more proper parts do not need. God has arranged the body so that more dignity is given to the parts which are without it, and so that there may not be disagreements inside the body, but that each part may be equally concerned for all the others. If one part is hurt, all parts are hurt with it. If one part is given special honour, all parts enjoy it. Now you together are Christ's body; but each of you is a different part of it. In the Church, God has given the first place to apostles, the second to prophets, the third to teachers; after them, miracles, and after them the gift of healing; helpers, good leaders, those with many languages. Are all of them apostles, or all of them prophets, or all of them teachers? Do they all have the gift of miracles, or all have the gift of healing? Do all speak strange languages, and all interpret them?

Luke 1:1-4; 4:14-21

Seeing that many others have undertaken to draw up accounts of the events that have taken place among us, exactly as these were handed down to us by those who from the outset were eye-witnesses and ministers of the word, I in my turn, after carefully going over the whole story from the beginning, have decided to write an ordered account for you, Theophilus, so that your Excellency may learn how well founded the teaching is that you have received. Jesus, with the power of the Spirit in him, returned to Galilee; and his reputation spread throughout the countryside. He taught in their synagogues and everyone praised him. He came to Nazara, where he had been brought up, and went into the synagogue on the sabbath day as he usually did. He stood up to read, and they handed him the scroll of the prophet Isaiah. Unrolling the scroll he found the place where it is written: The spirit of the Lord has been given to me, for he has anointed me. He has sent me to bring the good news to the poor, to proclaim liberty to captives and to the blind new sight, to set the downtrodden free, to proclaim the Lord's year of favour. He then rolled up the scroll, gave it back to the assistant and sat down. And all eyes in the synagogue were fixed on him. Then he began to speak to them, 'This text is being fulfilled today even as you listen.'

Reflection

When Jesus returned to his hometown of Nazareth, while many people were delighted with his gracious words, there were others who were reluctant to accept him as anything extraordinary. 'Surely, this is Joseph's son!' they exclaim. Frequently we overlook the uniqueness of persons with whom we are familiar, and can come to take them for granted. People and things which we see or experience often soon cease to impress us, and our appreciation can grow cold or disappear altogether. In this context, it is good to remind ourselves of the incalculable worth of other individuals – not merely their merits or usefulness to us, but their uniqueness, value and dignity in the sight of God. In many cultures, 'over-familiarity' with another person is considered a sign of discourtesy and disrespect. There is perhaps a hidden wisdom in such traditions. Let us never presume to know others completely; let us never presume to define or limit them. For each of them truly bears the image of the unknown God – ineffable, infinite and transcendent.

24
JAN MON

3rd Week in Ordinary Time
St Francis de Sales, *bishop, doctor,* **Memorial** | White

2 Samuel 5:1-7, 10

All the tribes of Israel came to David at Hebron. 'Look' they said 'we are your own flesh and blood. In days past when Saul was our king, it was you who led Israel in all their exploits, and the Lord said to you, "You are the man who shall be shepherd of my people Israel, you shall be the leader of Israel."' So all the elders of Israel came to the king at Hebron, and King David made a pact with them at Hebron in the presence of the Lord, and they anointed David king of Israel. David was thirty years old when he became king, and he reigned for forty years. He reigned in Hebron over Judah for seven years and six months; then he reigned in Jerusalem over all Israel and Judah for thirty-three years. David and his men marched on Jerusalem against the Jebusites living there. These said to David, 'You will not get in here. The blind and the lame will hold you off.' (That is to say: David will never get in here.) But David captured the fortress of Zion, that is, the Citadel of David. He grew greater and greater, and the Lord, the God of hosts, was with him.

Psalm 88:20-22, 25-26. R. v. 25

My truth and my love shall be with him.

Mark 3:22-30

The scribes who had come down from Jerusalem were saying: 'Beelzebul is in him' and, 'It is through the prince of devils that he casts devils out.' So Jesus called them to him and spoke to them in parables, 'How can Satan cast out Satan? If a kingdom is divided against itself, that kingdom cannot last. And if a household is divided against itself, that household can never stand. Now if Satan has rebelled against himself and is divided, he cannot stand either – it is the end of him. But no one can make his way into a strong man's house and burgle his property unless he has tied up the strong man first. Only then can he burgle his house. 'I tell you solemnly, all men's sins will be forgiven, and all their blasphemies; but let anyone blaspheme against the Holy Spirit and he will never have forgiveness: he is guilty of an eternal sin.' This was because they were saying, 'An unclean spirit is in him.'

Reflection

When Jesus is accused of deriving his power to cast out devils from Beelzebub, the prince of devils, we witness a very grievous act of calumny. The radiantly sinless Son of God is accused of being in partnership with the forces of darkness. Arguably, this reflects the very human reality that whenever an individual does something which makes them stand out from the crowd – as Jesus certainly did – their actions are likely to be treated with a degree of suspicion and hostility. It is good for us to examine our own attitudes towards others who are different from ourselves. Christian charity demands that we interpret the actions of others with as much kindness and generosity as we possibly can. May the Holy Spirit, and the example of Jesus, help us always to do that.

The Conversion of St Paul, Apostle

Feast | White

25
JAN TUE

Acts 22:3-16 *(Alternate Reading: Acts 9:1-22)*

Paul said to the people, 'I am a Jew and was born at Tarsus in Cilicia. I was brought up here in this city. I studied under Gamaliel and was taught the exact observance of the Law of our ancestors. In fact, I was as full of duty towards God as you are today. I even persecuted this Way to the death, and sent women as well as men to prison in chains as the high priest and the whole council of elders can testify, since they even sent me with letters to their brothers in Damascus. When I set off it was with the intention of bringing prisoners back from there to Jerusalem for punishment. 'I was on that journey and nearly at Damascus when about midday a bright light from heaven suddenly shone round me. I fell to the ground and heard a voice saying, "Saul, Saul, why are you persecuting me?" I answered: who are you, Lord? and he said to me, "I am Jesus the Nazarene, and you are persecuting me." The people with me saw the light but did not hear his voice as he spoke to me. I said: What am I to do, Lord? The Lord answered, "Stand up and go into Damascus, and there you will be told what you have been appointed to do." The light had been so dazzling that I was blind and my companions had to take me by the hand; and so I came to Damascus. 'Someone called Ananias, a devout follower of the Law and highly thought of by all the Jews living there, came to see me; he stood beside me and said, "Brother Saul, receive your sight." Instantly my sight came back and I was able to see him. Then he said, "The God of our ancestors has chosen you to know his will, to see that Just One and hear his own voice speaking, because you are to be his witness before all mankind, testifying to what you have seen and heard. And now why delay? It is time you were baptised and had your sins washed away while invoking his name."'

Psalm 116:1-2. R. Mark 16:15

Go out to the whole world; proclaim the Good News.

Mark 16:15-18

Jesus showed himself to the Eleven and said to them, 'Go out to the whole world; proclaim the Good News to all creation. He who believes and is baptised will be saved; he who does not believe will be condemned. These are the signs that will be associated with believers: in my name they will cast out devils; they will have the gift of tongues; they will pick up snakes in their hands, and be unharmed should they drink deadly poison; they will lay their hands on the sick, who will recover.'

Reflection

The conversion of St Paul is one of the most dramatic of the post-resurrection appearances of Christ. Paul, intent upon persecuting the emerging Church, beholds a vision of blinding light and hears a voice from heaven. While many people are able to recount some personal 'Damascus moment' of sudden enlightenment, for most Christians the daily practice of the faith, year in and year out, is more a process of patient perseverance than wondrous revelations. Yet, if we look with open eyes, we shall not fail to perceive manifestations of God's glory and love. Perhaps this may be seen when someone extends to us an unexpected act of consideration or kindness, or equally when a situation calls upon us to act as a conduit of God's mercy and love. True conversion, even for St Paul, is never an instantaneous event, but a life-long process – an ever-deepening penetration into the splendid light of God's love.

26
JAN WED

3rd Week in Ordinary Time | Green
or **Sts Timothy and Titus,** *bishops* (Optional, White)

2 Timothy 1:1-8
(Please see the Appendix B-2)

Psalm 95:1-3,7-8,10
Proclaim the wonders of the Lord among all the peoples.

Mark 4:1-20
Jesus began to teach by the lakeside, but such a huge crowd gathered round him that he got into a boat on the lake and sat there. The people were all along the shore, at the water's edge. He taught them many things in parables, and in the course of his teaching he said to them, 'Listen! Imagine a sower going out to sow. Now it happened that, as he sowed, some of the seed fell on the edge of the path, and the birds came and ate it up. Some seed fell on rocky ground where it found little soil and sprang up straightaway, because there was no depth of earth; and when the sun came up it was scorched and, not having any roots, it withered away. Some seed fell into thorns, and the thorns grew up and choked it, and it produced no crop. And some seeds fell into rich soil and, growing tall and strong, produced crop; and yielded thirty, sixty, even a hundredfold.' And he said, 'Listen, anyone who has ears to hear!'

When he was alone, the Twelve, together with the others who formed his company, asked what the parables meant. He told them, 'The secret of the kingdom of God is given to you, but to those who are outside everything comes in parables, so that they may see and see again, but not perceive; may hear and hear again, but not understand; otherwise they might be converted and be forgiven.'

He said to them, 'Do you not understand this parable? Then how will you understand any of the parables? What the sower is sowing is the word. Those on the edge of the path where the word is sown are people who have no sooner heard it than Satan comes and carries away the word that was sown in them. Similarly, those who receive the seed on patches of rock are people who, when first they hear the word, welcome it at once with joy. But they have no root in them, they do not last; should some trial come, or some persecution on account of the word, they fall away at once. Then there are others who receive the seed in thorns. These have heard the word, but the worries of this world, the lure of riches and all the other passions come in to choke the word, and so it produces nothing. And there are those who have received the seed in rich soil: they hear the word and accept it and yield a harvest, thirty and sixty and a hundredfold.'

Reflection
When we pay attention to Jesus' word, we will gain a deeper understanding of Him. The more we know about Jesus, the better we will be able to witness Him and bear fruits in abundance. Today's liturgy honours two great men, Timothy and Titus, who heeded Christ's teachings and bore testimony to him throughout their lives. We, too, have been commissioned to preach the gospel and bear witness to Christ.

27
JAN THU

2 Samuel 7:18-19, 24-29

After Nathan had spoken to David, the King went in and, seated before the Lord, said:

'Who am I, Lord, and what is my House, that you have led me as far as this? Yet in your sight, Lord, this is still not far enough, and you make your promises extend to the House of your servant for a far-distant future. You have constituted your people Israel to be your own people for ever; and you, Lord, have become their God. Now, Lord, always keep the promise you have made your servant and his House, and do as you have said. Your name will be exalted for ever and men will say, "The Lord of hosts is God over Israel." The House of your servant David will be made secure in your presence, since you yourself, Lord of hosts, God of Israel, have made this revelation to your servant, "I will build you a House"; hence your servant has ventured to offer this prayer to you. Yes, Lord, you are God indeed, your words are true and you have made this fair promise to your servant. Be pleased, then, to bless the House of your servant, that it may continue for ever in your presence; for you, Lord, have spoken; and with your blessing the House of your servant will be for ever blessed.'

Psalm 131:1-5, 11-14. R. Luke 1:32

The Lord God will give him the throne of his father David.

Mark 4:21-25

Jesus said to the crowd: 'Would you bring in a lamp to put it under a tub or under the bed? Surely you will put it on the lamp-stand? For there is nothing hidden but it must be disclosed, nothing kept secret except to be brought to light. If anyone has ears to hear, let him listen to this.' He also said to them, 'Take notice of what you are hearing. The amount you measure out is the amount you will be given – and more besides; for the man who has will be given more; from the man who has not, even what he has will be taken away.'

Reflection

When Christ says that 'there is nothing hidden that shall not be disclosed, and nothing kept secret except to be brought to light', he offers a wonderful gem of practical wisdom. Of course, all our actions and thoughts are always fully visible to God. The keen awareness of this is perhaps our most useful guide in drawing us to choose those actions which are most consistent with God's love, mercy and justice. It is helpful to ask ourselves at times, 'Would I want what I am saying now freely repeated to other people?', 'Would I be happy for this email to be made public?', or 'If there was someone here who could read my mind, would I have anything to be ashamed of?' True simplicity of soul arises from harmony of interior and exterior, and from congruity of thought, speech and action. With God's help, let us earnestly aspire to such simplicity.

28
JAN FRI

2 Samuel 11:1-10, 13-17

At the turn of the year, the time when kings go campaigning, David sent Joab and with him his own guards and the whole of Israel. They massacred the Ammonites and laid siege to Rabbah. David however remained in Jerusalem.

It happened towards evening when David had risen from his couch and was strolling on the palace roof, that he saw from the roof a woman bathing; the woman was very beautiful. David made inquiries about this woman and was told, 'Why, that is Bathsheba, Eliam's daughter, the wife of Uriah the Hittite.' …
(Please see the Appendix B-3)

Psalm 50:3-7, 10-11. R. cf. v. 3

Have mercy on us, Lord, for we have sinned.

Mark 4:26-34

Jesus said to the crowd: 'This is what the kingdom of God is like. A man throws seed on the land. Night and day, while he sleeps, when he is awake, the seed is sprouting and growing; how, he does not know. Of its own accord the land produces first the shoot, then the ear, then the full grain in the ear. And when the crop is ready, he loses no time: he starts to reap because the harvest has come.'

He also said, 'What can we say the kingdom of God is like? What parable can we find for it? It is like a mustard seed which at the time of its sowing in the soil is the smallest of all the seeds on earth; yet once it is sown it grows into the biggest shrub of them all and puts out big branches so that the birds of the air can shelter in its shade.'

Using many parables like these, he spoke the word to them, so far as they were capable of understanding it. He would not speak to them except in parables, but he explained everything to his disciples when they were alone.

Reflection

The comparison of the kingdom of God with a mustard seed is a dearly beloved icon of the possibility of great things springing from small and apparently insignificant beginnings. Often a little act of consideration, a kind word or a smile can make all the difference between a 'good day' or a 'bad day' for someone. Since the kingdom of God means, amongst other things, a world in which peace, joy and love prevail, we can each make a contribution to the realisation of this wonderful kingdom. It is interesting to reflect on why Jesus chose a mustard seed, rather than another tree species. Mustard is a spice which, while apparently insubstantial in itself as a foodstuff, imparts a zest, energy and vibrancy to other foods. And just so should our Christian faith animate all aspects of our lives with something of the spice of God's eternal glory.

29
JAN SAT

3rd Week in Ordinary Time
Green

2 Samuel 12:1-7, 10-17

The Lord sent Nathan the prophet to David. He came to him and said: 'In the same town were two men, one rich, the other poor. The rich man had flocks and herds in great abundance; the poor man had nothing but a ewe lamb, one only, a small one he had bought. This he fed, and it grew up with him and his children, eating his bread, drinking from his cup, sleeping on his breast; it was like a daughter to him. When there came a traveller to stay, the rich man refused to take one of his own flock or herd to provide for the wayfarer who had come to him. Instead he took the poor man's lamb and prepared it for his guest.'

David's anger flared up against the man. 'As the Lord lives,' he said to Nathan 'the man who did this deserves to die! He must make fourfold restitution for the lamb, for doing such a thing and showing no compassion.' ...
(Please see the Appendix B-3)

Psalm 50:12-17. R. v. 12

A pure heart create for me, O God.

Mark 4:35-41

With the coming of evening, Jesus said to his disciples, 'Let us cross over to the other side.' And leaving the crowd behind they took him, just as he was, in the boat; and there were other boats with him. Then it began to blow a gale and the waves were breaking into the boat so that it was almost swamped. But he was in the stern, his head on the cushion, asleep. They woke him and said to him, 'Master, do you not care? We are going down!' And he woke up and rebuked the wind and said to the sea, 'Quiet now! Be calm!' And the wind dropped, and all was calm again. Then he said to them, 'Why are you so frightened? How is it that you have no faith?' They were filled with awe and said to one another, 'Who can this be? Even the wind and the sea obey him.'

Reflection

In the Gospel today, Jesus stills the fury of a raging tempest, causing the sea to become calm. Christ has the unique ability to restore tranquillity, even in the midst of the most violent turbulence. Apart from the tempestuous conditions which often surround us in life, we can also experience storms within our own hearts: conflicting emotions, frustrated impulses, unfulfilled desires and pains and wounds which remain hidden in the depths of our being. Of course, there are many useful and helpful formulas for attaining inner peace, such as 'Accept what you cannot change', or 'It's all in God's hands', or 'Everything passes'. Yet none of these have any real efficacy, except through divine grace. It is Jesus alone who has power to bring true peace to the human heart. This peace is not merely stoic resignation, but a golden ray of light which both promises and leads us forth into eternal joy.

30
JAN SUN

FOURTH SUNDAY IN ORDINARY TIME

Psalter Week 4

Green

Jeremiah 1:4-5, 17-19

In the days of Josiah, the word of the Lord was addressed to me, saying,

'Before I formed you in the womb I knew you; before you came to birth I consecrated you; I have appointed you as prophet to the nations. So now brace yourself for action. Stand up and tell them all I command you. Do not be dismayed at their presence, or in their presence I will make you dismayed. I, for my part, today will make you into a fortified city, a pillar of iron, and a wall of bronze to confront all this land: the kings of Judah, its princes, its priests and the country people. They will fight against you but shall not overcome you, for I am with you to deliver you – it is the Lord who speaks.

Psalm 70:1-6, 15, 17. R. v. 15

My lips will tell of your help.

1 Corinthians 12:31–13:13 *(Shorter form 13:4-13)*

Be ambitious for the higher gifts. And I am going to show you a way that is better than any of them.

If I have all the eloquence of men or of angels, but speak without love, I am simply a gong booming or a cymbal clashing. If I have the gift of prophecy, understanding all the mysteries there are, and knowing everything, and if I have faith in all its fullness, to move mountains, but without love, then I am nothing at all. If I give away all that I possess, piece by piece, and if I even let them take my body to burn it, but am without love, it will do me no good whatever.

Love is always patient and kind: it is never jealous; love is never boastful or conceited; it is never rude or selfish; it does not take offence, and is not resentful. Love takes no pleasure in other people's sins but delights in the truth; it is always ready to excuse, to trust, to hope, and to endure whatever comes.

Love does not come to an end. But if there are gifts of prophecy, the time will come when they must fail; or the gift of languages, it will not continue for ever; and knowledge – for this, too, the time will come when it must fail. For our knowledge is imperfect and our prophesying is imperfect; but once perfection comes, all imperfect things will disappear. When I was a child, I used to talk like a child and think like a child, and argue like a child, but now I am a man, all childish ways are put behind me. Now we are seeing a dim reflection in a mirror; but then we shall be seeing face to face. The knowledge that I have now is imperfect; but then I shall know as fully as I am known.

In short, there are three things that last: faith, hope and love; and the greatest of these is love.

Luke 4:21-30

Jesus began to speak in the synagogue, 'This text is being fulfilled today even as you listen.' And he won the approval of all, and they were astonished by the gracious words that came from his lips. They said, 'This is Joseph's son, surely?' But he replied, 'No doubt you will quote me the saying, "Physician, heal yourself" and tell me, "We have heard all that happened in Capernaum, do the same here in your own countryside."' And he went on, 'I tell you solemnly, no prophet is ever accepted in his own country. 'There were many widows in Israel, I can assure you, in Elijah's day, when heaven remained shut for three years and six months and a great famine raged throughout the land, but Elijah was not sent to any one of these: he was sent to a widow at Zarephath, a Sidonian town. And in the prophet Elisha's time there were many lepers in Israel, but none of these was cured, except the Syrian, Naaman.' When they heard this everyone in the synagogue was enraged. They sprang to their feet and hustled him out of the town; and they took him up to the brow of the hill their town was built on, intending to throw him down the cliff, but he slipped through the crowd and walked away.

Reflection

In today's beautiful passage from the first letter to the Corinthians, Paul speaks of the wonders of love – the love which is always patient and kind, which is always ready to forgive, which delights in the truth, and which does not come to an end. As such, love, in its purified form, reflects the character of the divinity, the essence of God himself. Each of us has experienced and participated in love in some way or another. It is a universal and even constitutive part of our human condition. But human love is often marred by possessiveness, inconstancy, lust or insecurity, and is therefore but an imperfect image of heavenly love. Yet it remains always an authentic and genuine (if, at times, somewhat tarnished) reflection of God's love and a manifestation of the divine essence which is itself love. Let us not be afraid to love, ardently and passionately, all that is noble, beautiful and true. For in whomever and whatever we love, it is God himself who is ultimately both the lover and the beloved.

31
JAN MON

4th Week in Ordinary Time
St John Bosco, *priest,* **Memorial** | White

2 Samuel 15:13-14, 30; 16:5-13
(Please see the Appendix B-3)

Psalm 3:2-8. R. v. 8
Arise, Lord; save me, my God.

Mark 5:1-20
Jesus and his disciples reached the country of the Gerasenes on the other side of the lake, and no sooner had he left the boat than a man with an unclean spirit came out from the tombs towards him. The man lived in the tombs and no one could secure him any more, even with a chain; because he had often been secured with fetters and chains but had snapped the chains and broken the fetters, and no one had the strength to control him. All night and all day, among the tombs and in the mountains, he would howl and gash himself with stones. Catching sight of Jesus from a distance, he ran up and fell at his feet and shouted at the top of his voice, 'What do you want with me, Jesus, son of the Most High God? Swear by God you will not torture me!' – For Jesus had been saying to him, 'Come out of the man, unclean spirit.' 'What is your name?' Jesus asked. 'My name is legion,' he answered 'for there are many of us.' And he begged him earnestly not to send them out of the district. Now there was there on the mountainside a great herd of pigs feeding, and the unclean spirits begged him, 'Send us to the pigs, let us go into them.' So he gave them leave. With that, the unclean spirits came out and went into the pigs, and the herd of about two thousand pigs charged down the cliff into the lake, and there they were drowned. The swineherds ran off and told their story in the town and in the country round about; and the people came to see what had really happened. They came to Jesus and saw the demoniac sitting there, clothed and in his full senses – the very man who had had the legion in him before – and they were afraid. And those who had witnessed it reported what had happened to the demoniac and what had become of the pigs. Then they began to implore Jesus to leave the neighbourhood. As he was getting into the boat, the man who had been possessed begged to be allowed to stay with him. Jesus would not let him but said to him, 'Go home to your people and tell them all that the Lord in his mercy has done for you.' So the man went off and proceeded to spread throughout the Decapolis all that Jesus had done for him. And everyone was amazed.

Reflection
In today's first reading, King David is cursed by a man of the family of the former monarch, Saul. This man denounces David for his violence and his treacherous usurpation (as he sees it) of his kinsman. When one of David's officers volunteers to kill the man, David orders him not to do so. He recognises that, from this man's perspective at least, he has indeed acted reprehensibly. Many things, events and people in life look completely different when seen from different perspectives. Before judging others as being in the wrong, we should always endeavour to understand the issue from their point of view. This means not simply 'placing ourselves in their situation', but also seeing that they are not who we are, and we are not who they are. God alone sees human actions with perfect understanding and infinite mercy – and, for this reason, God alone can judge.

4th Week in Ordinary Time
Green

01
FEB TUE

SAINT BRIGID, ABBESS, SECONDARY PATRON OF IRELAND

see Appendix A-8

2 Samuel 18:9-10, 14, 24-25, 30–19:3
(Please see the Appendix B-4)

Psalm 85:1-6. R. v. 1 ***Turn your ear, Lord, and give answer.***

Mark 5:21-43
When Jesus had crossed in the boat to the other side, a large crowd gathered round him and he stayed by the lakeside. Then one of the synagogue officials came up, Jairus by name, and seeing him, fell at his feet and pleaded with him earnestly, saying, 'My little daughter is desperately sick. Do come and lay your hands on her to make her better and save her life.' Jesus went with him and a large crowd followed him; they were pressing all round him. Now there was a woman who had suffered from a haemorrhage for twelve years; after long and painful treatment under various doctors, she had spent all she had without being any the better for it, in fact, she was getting worse. She had heard about Jesus, and she came up behind him through the crowd and touched his cloak. 'If I can touch even his clothes,' she had told herself 'I shall be well again.' And the source of the bleeding dried up instantly, and she felt in herself that she was cured of her complaint. Immediately aware that power had gone out from him Jesus turned round in the crowd and said, 'Who touched my clothes?' His disciples said to him, 'You see how the crowd is pressing round you and yet you say, "Who touched me?"' But he continued to look all round to see who had done it. Then the woman came forward, frightened and trembling because she knew what had happened to her, and she fell at his feet and told him the whole truth. 'My daughter,' he said 'your faith has restored you to health; go in peace and be free from your complaint.' While he was still speaking some people arrived from the house of the synagogue official to say, 'Your daughter is dead: why put the Master to any further trouble?' But Jesus had overheard this remark of theirs and he said to the official, 'Do not be afraid; only have faith.' And he allowed no one to go with him except Peter and James and John the brother of James. So they came to the official's house and Jesus noticed all the commotion, with people weeping and wailing unrestrainedly. He went in and said to them, 'Why all this commotion and crying? The child is not dead, but asleep.' But they laughed at him. So he turned them all out and, taking with him the child's father and mother and his own companions, he went into the place where the child lay. And taking the child by the hand he said to her, 'Talitha, kum!' which means, 'Little girl, I tell you to get up.' The little girl got up at once and began to walk about, for she was twelve years old. At this they were overcome with astonishment, and he ordered them strictly not to let anyone know about it, and told them to give her something to eat.

Reflection: 'Do not be afraid; only have faith.' The Gospel for today sees Jesus up-end some of the Jewish people's rules about what is required of them to live a good life, in favour of the one thing necessary: faith. Both the bleeding woman and the young girl who has died would be considered 'unclean' under Jewish law (Leviticus 15:25, Numbers 19:11). But rather than Jesus becoming unclean by touching them, the exact opposite happens. They become healed by Jesus' touch because of their faith. As Christians we are called not only to have faith in Jesus' healing power, whether that be spiritual, physical, emotional, but also to do as Jesus does. We are invited to step beyond our comfort zone, to reach out to the outcasts and the spiritually dead in our world today and bring Jesus' love and healing touch to them.

02
FEB WED

THE PRESENTATION OF THE LORD, Feast

White

Malachi 3:1-4

The Lord God says this: Look, I am going to send my messenger to prepare a way before me. And the Lord you are seeking will suddenly enter his Temple; and the angel of the covenant whom you are longing for, yes, he is coming, says the Lord of hosts. Who will be able to resist the day of his coming? Who will remain standing when he appears? For he is like the refiner's fire and the fullers' alkali. He will take his seat as refiner and purifier; he will purify the sons of Levi and refine them like gold and silver, and then they will make the offering to the Lord as it should be made. The offering of Judah and Jerusalem will then be welcomed by the Lord as in former days, as in the years of old.

Psalm 23:7-10. R. v. 10

Who is the king of glory? He, the Lord, he is the king of glory.

Hebrews 2:14-18

Since all the children share the same blood and flesh, Jesus too shared equally in it, so that by his death he could take away all the power of the devil, who had power over death, and set free all those who had been held in slavery all their lives by the fear of death. For it was not the angels that he took to himself; he took to himself descent from Abraham. It was essential that he should in this way become completely like his brothers so that he could be a compassionate and trustworthy high priest of God's religion, able to atone for human sins. That is, because he has himself been through temptation he is able to help others who are tempted.

Luke 2:22-40 *(Shorter form: 2:22-32)*

When the day came for them to be purified as laid down by the Law of Moses, the parents of Jesus took him up to Jerusalem to present him to the Lord – observing what stands written in the Law of the Lord: Every first-born male must be consecrated to the Lord – and also to offer in sacrifice, in accordance with what is said in the Law of the Lord, a pair of turtledoves or two young pigeons. Now in Jerusalem there was a man named Simeon. He was an upright and devout man; he looked forward to Israel's comforting and the Holy Spirit rested on him. It had been revealed to him by the Holy Spirit that he would not see death until he had set eyes on the Christ of the Lord. Prompted by the Spirit he came to the Temple; and when the parents brought in the child Jesus to do for him what the law required, he took him into his arms and blessed God, and he said: 'Now, Master, you can let your servant go in peace, just as you promised; because my eyes have seen the salvation which you have prepared for all the nations to see, a light to enlighten the pagans and the glory of your people Israel.'

As the child's father and mother stood there wondering at the things that were being said about him, Simeon blessed them and said to Mary his mother, 'You see this child: he is destined for the fall and for the rising of many in Israel, destined to be a sign that is rejected – and a sword will pierce your own soul too – so that the secret thoughts of many may be laid bare.'

There was a prophetess also, Anna the daughter of Phanuel, of the tribe of Asher. She was well on in years. Her days of girlhood over, she had been married for seven years before becoming a widow. She was now eighty-four years old and never left the Temple, serving God night and day with fasting and prayer. She came by just at that moment and began to praise God; and she spoke of the child to all who looked forward to the deliverance of Jerusalem.

When they had done everything the Law of the Lord required, they went back to Galilee, to their own town of Nazareth. Meanwhile the child grew to maturity, and he was filled with wisdom; and God's favour was with him.

Reflection

The Presentation of Jesus in the temple marks an important occasion in the story of salvation history, and therefore, an important occasion for all of us. The Church helps us to grasp the significance of this scene by giving us the prophecy from the Prophet Malachi as our first reading: 'And the Lord you are seeking will suddenly enter his temple.' So now we can see. This isn't just any baby being brought to the temple in his mother's arms as was the Jewish requirement. This baby is the Messiah, entering his temple for the very first time. He is the Lord that the ageing Simeon had been seeking. And, through the power of the Holy Spirit, both Simeon and Anna, conditioned by lives of prayer, recognise him when they gaze at him. We too, through the Holy Spirit are invited to gaze on the face of Jesus and know him. Like Mary, we are warned that life in Christ won't be easy, but it is where our salvation lies.

03
FEB THU

4th Week in Ordinary Time | Green or **St Blaise,** *bishop, martyr* | or **St Ansgar,** *bishop* (Optional, Red/White)

1 Kings 2:1-4, 10-12

As David's life drew to its close he laid this charge on his son Solomon, 'I am going the way of all the earth. Be strong and show yourself a man. Observe the injunctions of the Lord your God, following his ways and keeping his laws, his commandments, his customs and his decrees, as it stands written in the Law of Moses, that so you may be successful in all you do and undertake, so that the Lord may fulfil the promise he made me, "If your sons are careful how they behave, and walk loyally before me with all their heart and soul, you shall never lack for a man on the throne of Israel."'

So David slept with his ancestors and was buried in the Citadel of David. David's reign over Israel lasted forty years: he reigned in Hebron for seven years, and in Jerusalem for thirty-three.

Solomon was seated upon the throne of David, and his sovereignty was securely established.

1 Chronicles 29:10-12. R. v. 12

You, Lord, are the ruler of all.

Mark 6:7-13

Jesus made a tour of the villages, teaching. Then he summoned the Twelve and began to send them out in pairs giving them authority over the unclean spirits. And he instructed them to take nothing for the journey except a staff – no bread, no haversack, no coppers for their purses. They were to wear sandals – but, he added, 'Do not take a spare tunic.' And he said to them, 'If you enter a house anywhere, stay there until you leave the district. And if any place does not welcome you and people refuse to listen to you, as you walk away shake off the dust from under your feet as a sign to them.' So they set off to preach repentance; and they cast out many devils, and anointed many sick people with oil and cured them.

Reflection

'Take nothing for the journey.' Wait. Not even a little carry-on sized bag crammed with the essentials for a trip – a book, some toiletries, a change of clothes or two? No, in today's Gospel reading, Jesus is sending the apostles out on mission. He doesn't want them to be focused on what they're carrying, what's weighing them down. He wants them to be free and agile when they share the Good News. He also wants them to be dependent on others, not self-sufficient, because it's in our vulnerability that we truly encounter Christ in others. The reading also shows us something of what Jesus wants his Church to be. He sent the apostles out to heal people, cure their diseases, cast out demons and proclaim the kingdom of God. Every baptised Christian is sent out on mission, to reach out to the suffering and offer the healing love of Jesus Christ to the people we meet.

4th Week in Ordinary Time
Green

04
FEB FRI

Sirach 47:2-11
(Please see the Appendix B-4)

Psalm 17:31, 47, 50-51. R. cf. v. 47
Praised be the God who saves me.

Mark 6:14-29
King Herod had heard about Jesus, since by now his name was well-known. Some were saying, 'John the Baptist has risen from the dead, and that is why miraculous powers are at work in him.' Others said, 'He is Elijah'; others again, 'He is a prophet, like the prophets we used to have.' But when Herod heard this he said, 'It is John whose head I cut off; he has risen from the dead.'

Now it was this same Herod who had sent to have John arrested, and had him chained up in prison because of Herodias, his brother Philip's wife whom he had married. For John had told Herod, 'It is against the law for you to have your brother's wife.' As for Herodias, she was furious with him and wanted to kill him; but she was not able to, because Herod was afraid of John, knowing him to be a good and holy man, and gave him his protection. When he had heard him speak he was greatly perplexed, and yet he liked to listen to him.

An opportunity came on Herod's birthday when he gave a banquet for the nobles of his court, for his army officers and for the leading figures in Galilee. When the daughter of this same Herodias came in and danced, she delighted Herod and his guests; so the king said to the girl, 'Ask me anything you like and I will give it to you.' And he swore her an oath, 'I will give you anything you ask, even half my kingdom.' She went out and said to her mother, 'What shall I ask for?' She replied, 'The head of John the Baptist.' The girl hurried straight back to the king and made her request. 'I want you to give me John the Baptist's head, here and now, on a dish.' The king was deeply distressed but, thinking of the oaths he had sworn and of his guests, he was reluctant to break his word to her. So the king at once sent one of the bodyguard with orders to bring John's head. The man went off and beheaded him in prison; then he brought the head on a dish and gave it to the girl, and the girl gave it to her mother. When John's disciples heard about this, they came and took his body and laid it in a tomb.

Reflection: When King Herod hears of the arrival of Jesus, of his compelling preaching and his attraction of big crowds, he immediately thinks it is John the Baptist come back from the dead to cause him trouble. Why? Because Herod had famously beheaded John and has lived with the guilt of that action ever since. You see, Herod had not wanted to kill John. In fact, we read that he liked listening to John's preaching, even though it perplexed him. He sensed something good in John and was attracted to it. But the disordered way Herod was living his life, having married his brother's wife, and his love of power, saw him commit a crime which continues to haunt him. When we order our lives around anything else but God, disorder begins to rule in our hearts and then in our actions and we begin to trade a life of peace for a life of disharmony, guilt and fear.

05
FEB SAT

4th Week in Ordinary Time
St Agatha, *virgin, martyr,* **Memorial** | Red

1 Kings 3:4-13

King Solomon went to Gibeon to sacrifice there, since that was the greatest of the high places – he offered a thousand holocausts on that altar. At Gibeon the Lord appeared in a dream to Solomon during the night. God said, 'Ask what you would like me to give you.' Solomon replied, 'You showed great kindness to your servant David, my father, when he lived his life before you in faithfulness and justice and integrity of heart; you have continued this great kindness to him by allowing a son of his to sit on his throne today. Now, Lord my God, you have made your servant king in succession to David my father. But I am a very young man, unskilled in leadership. Your servant finds himself in the midst of this people of yours that you have chosen, a people so many its number cannot be counted or reckoned. Give your servant a heart to understand how to discern between good and evil, for who could govern this people of yours that is so great?' It pleased the Lord that Solomon should have asked for this. 'Since you have asked for this' the Lord said 'and not asked for long life for yourself or riches or the lives of your enemies, but have asked for a discerning judgement for yourself, here and now I do what you ask. I give you a heart wise and shrewd as none before you has had and none will have after you. What you have not asked I shall give you too: such riches and glory as no other king ever had.'

Psalm 118:9-14. R. v. 12

Lord, teach me your statutes.

Mark 6:30-34

The apostles rejoined Jesus and told him all they had done and taught. Then he said to them, 'You must come away to some lonely place all by yourselves and rest for a while'; for there were so many coming and going that the apostles had no time even to eat. So they went off in a boat to a lonely place where they could be by themselves. But people saw them going, and many could guess where; and from every town they all hurried to the place on foot and reached it before them. So as he stepped ashore he saw a large crowd; and he took pity on them because they were like sheep without a shepherd, and he set himself to teach them at some length.

Reflection

'Come away to a lonely place … and rest for a while.' Whenever I read this passage, I'm reminded of an exhausted mother of young children, who ducks away to a quiet spot in the house (often the bathroom) just to rest for a few moments and regain her strength. But we all know how the story ends. She isn't in there for two minutes before little hands start tapping at the door and seeking her presence. It was like that for Jesus and the apostles. As the message of Jesus spread, more and more people sought him out to be in his presence and hear him speak. This passage shows us that Jesus clearly understood the need to rest and re-charge. And it also shows his extraordinary compassion for people, a compassion which moved his heart to put aside his own tiredness just for now and be a loving shepherd to his flock.

06
FEB SUN

FIFTH SUNDAY IN ORDINARY TIME

Psalter Week 1

Green

Isaiah 6:1-8

In the year of King Uzziah's death I saw the Lord seated on a high throne; his train filled the sanctuary; above him stood seraphs, each one with six wings. And they cried out one to another in this way, 'Holy, holy, holy is the Lord of hosts. His glory fills the whole earth.' The foundations of the threshold shook with the voice of the one who cried out, and the Temple was filled with smoke. I said: 'What a wretched state I am in! I am lost, for I am a man of unclean lips and I live among a people of unclean lips, and my eyes have looked at the King, the Lord of hosts.'

Then one of the seraphs flew to me, holding in his hand a live coal which he had taken from the altar with a pair of tongs. With this he touched my mouth and said: 'See now, this has touched your lips, your sin is taken away, your iniquity is purged.'

Then I heard the voice of the Lord saying: 'Whom shall I send? Who will be our messenger?' I answered, 'Here I am, send me.'

Psalm 137:1-5, 7-8. R. v. 1

Before the angels I will bless you, O Lord.

1 Corinthians 15:1-11 *(Shorter form 15:3-8, 11)*

Brothers, I want to remind you of the gospel I preached to you, the gospel that you received and in which you are firmly established; because the gospel will save you only if you keep believing exactly what I preached to you – believing anything else will not lead to anything.

Well then, in the first place, I taught you what I had been taught myself, namely that Christ died for our sins, in accordance with the scriptures; that he was buried; and that he was raised to life on the third day, in accordance with the scriptures; that he appeared first to Cephas and secondly to the Twelve. Next he appeared to more than five hundred of the brothers at the same time, most of whom are still alive, though some have died; then he appeared to James, and then to all the apostles; and last of all he appeared to me too; it was as though I was born when no one expected it.

I am the least of the apostles; in fact, since I persecuted the Church of God, I hardly deserve the name apostle; but by God's grace that is what I am, and the grace that he gave me has not been fruitless. On the contrary, I, or rather the grace of God that is with me, have worked harder than any of the others; but what matters is that I preach what they preach, and this is what you all believed.

Luke 5:1-11

Jesus was standing one day by the Lake of Gennesaret, with the crowd pressing round him listening to the word of God, when he caught sight of two boats close to the bank. The fishermen had gone out of them and were washing their nets. He got into one of the boats – it was Simon's – and asked him to put out a little from the shore. Then he sat down and taught the crowds from the boat. When he had finished speaking he said to Simon, 'Put out into deep water and pay out your nets for a catch.' 'Master,' Simon replied, 'we worked hard all night long and caught nothing, but if you say so, I will pay out the nets.' And when they had done this they netted such a huge number of fish that their nets began to tear, so they signalled to their companions in the other boats to come and help them; when these came, they filled the two boats to sinking point.

When Simon Peter saw this he fell at the knees of Jesus saying, 'Leave me, Lord; I am a sinful man.' For he and all his companions were completely overcome by the catch they had made; so also were James and John, sons of Zebedee, who were Simon's partners. But Jesus said to Simon, 'Do not be afraid; from now on it is men you will catch.' Then, bringing their boats back to land, they left everything and followed him.

Reflection

'Do not be afraid; from now on it is men you will catch.' When Jesus shows us the abundance he has in store for us, when we get a glimpse of the utter goodness of God, it is natural for us to respond by saying we are not worthy. We are sinners. This was the case with Simon Peter when the Lord asked him to go out into the deep and put out his nets for a catch. A fisherman all his life, Peter told Jesus that he'd worked hard all night, but caught nothing, so what is likely to change now? But in obedience, he does was Jesus asks and catches so many fish that his nets break. Jesus meets Peter's lack with overflowing abundance and Peter is overcome by his sinfulness and unworthiness. But what we learn here is that God's goodness doesn't depend on our worthiness. We can't earn his abundance. It just is. And having strengthened Peter by giving him this glimpse of how God provides, Jesus urges him to banish his fears and step out in faith to share the message of God's goodness with others.

1 Kings 8:1-7, 9-13

Solomon called the elders of Israel together in Jerusalem to bring the ark of the covenant of the Lord up from the Citadel of David, which is Zion. All the men of Israel assembled round King Solomon in the month of Ethanim, at the time of the feast (that is the seventh month), and the priests took up the ark and the Tent of Meeting with all the sacred vessels that were in it. In the presence of the ark, King Solomon and all Israel sacrificed sheep and oxen, countless, innumerable. The priests brought the ark of the covenant of the Lord to its place, in the Debir of the Temple that is, in the Holy of Holies, under the cherubs' wings. For there where the ark was placed the cherubs spread out their wings and sheltered the ark and its shafts. There was nothing in the ark except the two stone tablets Moses had placed in it at Horeb, the tablets of the covenant which the Lord had made with the Israelites when they came out of the land of Egypt; they are still there today.

Now when the priests came out of the sanctuary, the cloud filled the Temple of the Lord, and because of the cloud the priests could no longer perform their duties: the glory of the Lord filled the Lord's Temple.

Then Solomon said: 'The Lord has chosen to dwell in the thick cloud. Yes, I have built you a dwelling, a place for you to live in for ever.'

Psalm 131:6-10. R. v. 8

Go up, Lord, to the place of your rest!

Mark 6:53-56

Having made the crossing, Jesus and his disciples came to land at Gennesaret and tied up. No sooner had they stepped out of the boat than people recognised him, and started hurrying all through the countryside and brought the sick on stretchers to wherever they heard he was. And wherever he went, to village, or town, or farm, they laid down the sick in the open spaces, begging him to let them touch even the fringe of his cloak. And all those who touched him were cured.

Reflection

There's a lot happening in this short Gospel reading from Mark! Jesus and his disciples cross to the other side of the lake, land and tie their boat up. No sooner have they stepped out of the boat than Jesus is recognised by the people who start hurrying through the countryside to see him and to bring him the sick on stretchers for healing. This continues wherever Jesus goes – 'to village, town, or farm'. Mark seems intent on showing us that Jesus never tired of going out to meet the people where they were at and bringing his healing love to them. And the people *recognised* him. Do I recognise Jesus when I see him? Do I recognise him in the Eucharist? Do I recognise Christ in others? Do I move with haste and urgency to meet him? Do I present in prayer my 'stretcher' of needs for his healing? *Dear Lord, let me recognise you in the quiet of the Church and the busyness of the street. Let me rush to you in faith and rest in your healing love. Amen.*

5th Week in Ordinary Time | Green
or **St Jerome Emiliani** (Optional, White)
or **St Josephine Bakhita,** *virgin* (Optional, White)

1 Kings 8:22-23, 27-30
(Please see the Appendix B-5)

Psalm 83:3-5, 10-11. R. v. 2
How lovely is your dwelling-place, Lord, God of hosts.

Mark 7:1-13
The Pharisees and some of the scribes who had come from Jerusalem gathered round Jesus, and they noticed that some of his disciples were eating with unclean hands, that is without washing them. For the Pharisees, and the Jews in general, follow the tradition of the elders and never eat without washing their arms as far as the elbow; and on returning from the market place they never eat without first sprinkling themselves. There are also many other observances which have been handed down to them concerning the washing of cups and pots and bronze dishes. So these Pharisees and scribes asked him, 'Why do your disciples not respect the tradition of the elders but eat their food with unclean hands?' He answered, 'It was of you hypocrites that Isaiah so rightly prophesied in this passage of scripture: This people honours me only with lip-service, while their hearts are far from me. The worship they offer me is worthless, the doctrines they teach are only human regulations.

'You put aside the commandment of God to cling to human traditions.' And he said to them, 'How ingeniously you get round the commandment of God in order to preserve your own tradition! For Moses said: Do your duty to your father and your mother, and, Anyone who curses father or mother must be put to death. But you say, "If a man says to his father or mother: Anything I have that I might have used to help you is Corban (that is, dedicated to God), then he is forbidden from that moment to do anything for his father or mother." In this way you make God's word null and void for the sake of your tradition which you have handed down. And you do many other things like this.'

Reflection
Jesus doesn't mince his words in today's Gospel passage, labelling the Pharisees as hypocrites because of the way they clung to their long list of laws, which often prevented them from doing what really matters – loving God and neighbour. It stings to be called a hypocrite. But it's a good wake-up call for me to examine whether I sometimes fit the hypocrite bill. Do I profess a faith which I don't put into action, happy to sit back and just observe the rules instead? Today we celebrate St Josephine Bakhita, an African woman who was kept as a slave for many years until she converted to Christianity and was eventually freed with the help of Christian supporters. She too suffered in a system where people kept slaves because 'that's the way things had always been done'. But she reached true freedom when she and others challenged that way of doing things, driven by the law of love for God and neighbour.

1 Kings 10:1-10

The fame of Solomon having reached the queen of Sheba, she came to test him with difficult questions. She brought immense riches to Jerusalem with her, camels laden with spices, great quantities of gold, and precious stones. On coming to Solomon, she opened her mind freely to him; and Solomon had an answer for all her questions, not one of them was too obscure for the king to expound. When the queen of Sheba saw all the wisdom of Solomon, the palace he had built, the food of his table, the accommodation for his officials, the organisation of his staff and the way they were dressed, his cup-bearers, and the holocausts he offered in the Temple of the Lord, it left her breathless, and she said to the king, 'What I heard in my own country about you and your wisdom was true, then! Until I came and saw it with my own eyes I could not believe what they told me, but clearly they told me less than half: for wisdom and prosperity you surpass the report I heard. How happy your wives are! How happy are these servants of yours who wait on you always and hear your wisdom! Blessed be the Lord your God who has granted you his favour, setting you on the throne of Israel! Because of the Lord's everlasting love for Israel, he has made you king to deal out law and justice.' And she presented the king with a hundred and twenty talents of gold and great quantities of spices and precious stones; no such wealth of spices ever came again as those given to King Solomon by the queen of Sheba.

Psalm 36:5-6, 30-31, 39-40. R. v. 30 ***The just man's mouth utters wisdom.***

Mark 7:14-23

Jesus called the people to him and said, 'Listen to me, all of you, and understand. Nothing that goes into a man from outside can make him unclean; it is the things that come out of a man that make him unclean. If anyone has ears to hear, let him listen to this.'When he had gone back into the house, away from the crowd, his disciples questioned him about the parable. He said to them, 'Do you not understand either? Can you not see that whatever goes into a man from outside cannot make him unclean, because it does not go into his heart but through his stomach and passes out into the sewer?' (Thus he pronounced all foods clean.) And he went on, 'It is what comes out of a man that makes him unclean. For it is from within, from men's hearts, that evil intentions emerge; fornication, theft, murder, adultery, avarice, malice, deceit, indecency, envy, slander, pride, folly. All these evil things come from within and make a man unclean.'

Reflection

Once again, in today's Gospel passage we see Jesus emphasising that what makes us pure and clean in God's eyes is not the keeping of the many Jewish laws – in this case, the laws about clean and unclean food – but rather, our internal disposition. It's the state of our heart that matters. We've all seen people who keep all the rules of society on the surface and seem to live exemplary lives, but are later exposed for poor behaviour. The husband who seems like such a great family man, but is having an affair. The businesswoman who we admire as a success story, but has been quietly siphoning off a portion of the company's takings on the side. And of course, tragically, the betrayal of some clergy and religious who were scrupulous about keeping to the rubrics in Mass, but were committing criminal abuse on young and vulnerable people. Jesus isn't interested in us 'keeping up appearances'. He wants us to focus on keeping our hearts pure and nourished by him, and from there, goodness will flow.

10 FEB THU

5th Week in Ordinary Time
St Scholastica, *virgin,* **Memorial** | White

1 Kings 11:4-13

When Solomon grew old his wives swayed his heart to other gods; and his heart was not wholly with the Lord his God as his father David's had been. Solomon became a follower of Astarte, the goddess of the Sidonians, and of Milcom, the Ammonite abomination. He did what was displeasing to the Lord, and was not a wholehearted follower of the Lord, as his father David had been. Then it was that Solomon built a high place for Chemosh the god of Moab on the mountain to the east of Jerusalem, and to Milcom the god of the Ammonites. He did the same for all his foreign wives, who offered incense and sacrifice to their gods. The Lord was angry with Solomon because his heart had turned from the Lord the God of Israel who had twice appeared to him and who had then forbidden him to follow other gods; but he did not carry out the Lord's order. The Lord therefore said to Solomon, 'Since you behave like this and do not keep my covenant or the laws I laid down for you, I will most surely tear the kingdom away from you and give it to one of your servants. For your father David's sake, however, I will not do this during your lifetime, but will tear it out of your son's hands. Even so, I will not tear the whole kingdom from him. For the sake of my servant David, and for the sake of Jerusalem which I have chosen, I will leave your son one tribe.'

Psalm 105:3-4, 35-37, 40. R. v. 4

O Lord, remember me out of the love you have for your people.

Mark 7:24-30

Jesus left Gennesaret and set out for the territory of Tyre. There he went into a house and did not want anyone to know he was there, but he could not pass unrecognised. A woman whose little daughter had an unclean spirit heard about him straightaway and came and fell at his feet. Now the woman was a pagan, by birth a Syrophoenician, and she begged him to cast the devil out of her daughter. And he said to her, 'The children should be fed first, because it is not fair to take the children's food and throw it to the house-dogs.' But she spoke up: 'Ah yes, sir,' she replied 'but the house-dogs under the table can eat the children's scraps.' And he said to her, 'For saying this, you may go home happy: the devil has gone out of your daughter.' So she went off to her home and found the child lying on the bed and the devil gone.

Reflection

This is one of those Gospel readings which contain a 'hard' saying of Jesus, which can be jarring for us to hear. Is Jesus really calling this woman a dog, or is something else going on? Firstly, we see that Jesus has left the Jewish areas where he was being mobbed with crowds and headed to Tyre, a Gentile region, no doubt seeking a rest. But this woman heard he was there and went to Him, begging him to cure her daughter. Jesus responds with an allegory, harsh to our ears, but instantly understandable to the Gentile woman – there is an order to things. First Jesus was sent to the people of Israel and then to those outside. The woman gets it. She responds with humility, confident that even the crumbs from Jesus will be enough. Jesus delights in her response, in her perseverance and faith, and he heals her daughter. The passage shows us that Jesus came to bring his healing love to all who have faith. And it gives us a model for persevering in prayer and reaching out to Jesus with our needs.

11
FEB FRI

5th Week in Ordinary Time | Green
or **Our Lady of Lourdes,** (Optional, White)

1 Kings 11:29-32; 12:19

One day when Jeroboam had gone out of Jerusalem, the prophet Ahijah of Shiloh accosted him on the road. Ahijah was wearing a new cloak; the two of them were in the open country by themselves. Ahijah took the new cloak he was wearing and tore it into twelve strips, saying to Jeroboam, 'Take ten strips for yourself, for thus the Lord God speaks, the God of Israel, "I am going to tear the kingdom from Solomon's hand and give ten tribes to you. He shall keep one tribe for the sake of my servant David and for the sake of Jerusalem, the city I have chosen out of all the tribes of Israel."' And Israel has been separated from the House of David until the present day.

Psalm 80:10-15. R. vv. 11, 9

I am the Lord your God: listen to my warning.

Mark 7:31-37

Returning from the district of Tyre, Jesus went by way of Sidon towards the Sea of Galilee, right through the Decapolis region. And they brought him a deaf man who had an impediment in his speech; and they asked him to lay his hand on him. He took him aside in private, away from the crowd, put his fingers into the man's ears and touched his tongue with spittle. Then looking up to heaven he sighed; and he said to him, 'Ephphatha,' that is, 'Be opened.' And his ears were opened, and the ligament of his tongue was loosened and he spoke clearly. And Jesus ordered them to tell no one about it, but the more he insisted, the more widely they published it. Their admiration was unbounded. 'He has done all things well,' they said 'he makes the deaf hear and the dumb speak.'

Reflection

Fittingly, on this feast day of Our Lady of Lourdes, the Gospel is once again all about healing. A man who is deaf and has a speech impediment is brought to Jesus. Jesus touches him, looks up to heaven in prayer and says: 'Be opened'. Nobody was more marginalised in Jesus' time than those who lived with disability. Here, we see his compassion and concern for those with disability and his desire to be with them, to reach out to them and to love them. But at another level, I too am like this man. Too often I am deaf to the Word of God and I fail to speak of God's goodness in my life and in the world. I too need to 'Be opened' so that the healing love of Jesus can flow through me and outward to others. *Our Lady of Lourdes, who appeared to the young St Bernadette, pray for us that we may be opened to the love of our Lord Jesus and become channels of his healing presence in the world. Amen.*

5th Week in Ordinary Time
Green

12
FEB SAT

1 Kings 12:26-32; 13:33-34

Jeroboam thought to himself, 'As things are, the kingdom will revert to the House of David. If this people continues to go up to the Temple of the Lord in Jerusalem to offer sacrifices, the people's heart will turn back again to their lord, Rehoboam king of Judah, and they will put me to death.' So the king thought this over and then made two golden calves; he said to the people 'You have been going up to Jerusalem long enough. Here are your gods, Israel; these brought you up out of the land of Egypt!' He set up one in Bethel and the people went in procession all the way to Dan in front of the other. He set up the temple of the high places and appointed priests from ordinary families, who were not of the sons of Levi. Jeroboam also instituted a feast in the eighth month, on the fifteenth of the month, like the feast that was kept in Judah, and he went up to the altar. That was how he behaved in Bethel, sacrificing to the calves he had made; and at Bethel he put the priests of the high places he had established.

Jeroboam did not give up his wicked ways after this incident, but went on appointing priests for the high places from the common people. He consecrated as priests of the high places any who wished to be. Such conduct made the House of Jeroboam a sinful House, and caused its ruin and extinction from the face of the earth.

Psalm 105:6-7, 19-22. R. v. 4

O Lord, remember me out of the love you have for your people.

Mark 8:1-10

A great crowd had gathered, and they had nothing to eat. So Jesus called his disciples to him and said to them, 'I feel sorry for all these people; they have been with me for three days now and have nothing to eat. If I send them off home hungry they will collapse on the way; some have come a great distance.' His disciples replied, 'Where could anyone get bread to feed these people in a deserted place like this?' He asked them, 'How many loaves have you?' 'Seven,' they said. Then he instructed the crowd to sit down on the ground, and he took the seven loaves, and after giving thanks he broke them and handed them to his disciples to distribute; and they distributed them among the crowd. They had a few small fish as well, and over these he said a blessing and ordered them to be distributed also. They ate as much as they wanted, and they collected seven basketfuls of the scraps left over. Now there had been about four thousand people. He sent them away and immediately, getting into the boat with his disciples, went to the region of Dalmanutha.

Reflection

The story of Jesus feeding the crowd with loaves and fishes is one of the most familiar passages in the Gospels and one of the richest. What stands out for you? Is it the compassion Jesus felt for the people who had travelled a great distance to see him and were hungry? For surely that is all of us at some point in our life. Or is it the unmistakable eucharistic overtones – that Jesus took bread, gave thanks, broke it and distributed it? Perhaps it is the portrait of the absolute overflowing abundance of God. That I can bring what little I have to Jesus and he will bless it and multiply it and there will be enough not only for me but surplus to share with others too. I don't have to have everything sorted out. I don't have to have the answers or solutions to every problem in my life. All I need to do is bring what I do have to Jesus and let him bless it and grow it in ways I could never imagine.

13
FEB SUN

SIXTH SUNDAY IN ORDINARY TIME

Psalter Week 2

Green

Jeremiah 17:5-8

The Lord says this:

'A curse on the man who puts his trust in man,
who relies on things of flesh,
whose heart turns from the Lord.
He is like dry scrub in the wastelands:
if good comes, he has no eyes for it,
he settles in the parched places of the wilderness,
a salt land, uninhabited.

'A blessing on the man who puts his trust in the Lord,
with the Lord for his hope.
He is like a tree by the waterside
that thrusts its roots to the stream:
when the heat comes it feels no alarm,
its foliage stays green;
it has no worries in a year of drought,
and never ceases to bear fruit.'

Psalm 1:1-4. R. Psalm 39:5

Happy the man who has placed his trust in the Lord.

1 Corinthians 15:12, 16-20

If Christ raised from the dead is what has been preached, how can some of you be saying that there is no resurrection of the dead? For if the dead are not raised, Christ has not been raised, and if Christ has not been raised, you are still in your sins. And what is more serious, all who have died in Christ have perished. If our hope in Christ has been for this life only, we are the most unfortunate of all people. But Christ has in fact been raised from the dead, the first-fruits of all who have fallen asleep.

Luke 6:17, 20-26

Jesus came down with the Twelve and stopped at a piece of level ground where there was a large gathering of his disciples with a great crowd of people from all parts of Judaea and from Jerusalem and from the coastal region of Tyre and Sidon who had come to hear him and to be cured of their diseases.

Then fixing his eyes on his disciples he said:

'How happy are you who are poor; yours is the kingdom of God.

Happy you who are hungry now: you shall be satisfied.

Happy you who weep now: you shall laugh.

'Happy are you when people hate you, drive you out, abuse you, denounce your name as criminal, on account of the Son of Man. Rejoice when that day comes and dance for joy, for then your reward will be great in heaven. This was the way their ancestors treated the prophets.

'But alas for you who are rich: you are having your consolation now.

Alas for you who have your fill now: you shall go hungry.
Alas for you who laugh now: you shall mourn and weep.
'Alas for you when the world speaks well of you! This was the way their ancestors treated the false prophets.'

Reflection

Luke's account of Jesus' great sermon containing his teaching on the Beatitudes is a shorter version than in Matthew's Gospel, but is very similar in its content and message. It seems counter-intuitive. How can we be happy if we are poor, hungry, weeping, if people hate us, drive us out, abuse us, denounce our name as criminal on account of the Son of Man? But Luke's Gospel is all about highlighting how Jesus up-ended the expected conventions. In this most famous of sermons, Jesus is showing us the way to be truly, deeply happy in this broken world, and that is to align ourselves to the kingdom of God. We do this by avoiding an overattachment to pleasure and fleeting happiness, such as the pleasures found in money, possessions, food and good times. It is when we come, little and poor, to Jesus, hungering for his merciful love, that we are blessed, both now and in the next life.

14
FEB MON

Sts Cyril, *monk* **and Methodius,** *bishop,*
Patrons of Europe, Feast | White

Acts 13:46-49

Paul and Barnabas spoke out boldly. 'We had to proclaim the word of God to you first, but since you have rejected it, since you do not think yourselves worthy of eternal life, we must turn to the pagans. For this is what the Lord commanded us to do when he said:

I have made you a light for the nations,
so that my salvation may reach the ends of the earth.'

It made the pagans very happy to hear this and they thanked the Lord for his message; all who were destined for eternal life became believers. Thus the word of the Lord spread through the whole countryside.

Psalm 116

Go out to the whole world and proclaim the Good News.

Luke 10:1-9

The Lord appointed seventy-two others and sent them out ahead of him, in pairs, to all the towns and places he himself was to visit. He said to them, 'The harvest is rich but the labourers are few, so ask the Lord of the harvest to send labourers to his harvest. Start off now, but remember, I am sending you out like lambs among wolves. Carry no purse, no haversack, no sandals. Salute no one on the road. Whatever house you go into, let your first words be, "Peace to this house!" And if a man of peace lives there, your peace will go and rest on him; if not, it will come back to you. Stay in the same house, taking what food and drink they have to offer, for the labourer deserves his wages; do not move from house to house. Whenever you go into a town where they make you welcome, eat what is set before you. Cure those in it who are sick, and say, "The kingdom of God is very near to you."'

Reflection

The job is going to be difficult and dangerous, the Lord warns the newly recruited messengers as they are sent out. Lambs in the midst of wolves are certainly not safe and secure. The messengers are instructed not to expect any safety or security nor to count on any resources. But the Lord's command, "Go, I am sending you…" has an extraordinary power in it. Relying on that power alone the disciples embarked on their mission. The Lord sustained them with his presence and power. As disciples of Jesus today we too must be challenged by the same command of the Lord, "Go, I am sending you…."

15
FEB TUE

6th Week in Ordinary Time
Green

James 1:12-18

Happy the man who stands firm when trials come. He has proved himself, and will win the prize of life, the crown that the Lord has promised to those who love him.

Never, when you have been tempted, say, 'God sent the temptation'; God cannot be tempted to do anything wrong, and he does not tempt anybody. Everyone who is tempted is attracted and seduced by his own wrong desire. Then the desire conceives and gives birth to sin, and when sin is fully grown, it too has a child, and the child is death.

Make no mistake about this, my dear brothers: it is all that is good, everything that is perfect, which is given us from above; it comes down from the Father of all light; with him there is no such thing as alteration, no shadow of a change. By his own choice he made us his children by the message of the truth so that we should be a sort of first-fruits of all that he had created.

Psalm 93:12-15, 18-19. R. v. 12

Happy the man whom you teach, O Lord.

Mark 8:14-21

The disciples had forgotten to take any food and they had only one loaf with them in the boat. Then Jesus gave them this warning, 'Keep your eyes open; be on your guard against the yeast of the Pharisees and the yeast of Herod.' And they said to one another, 'It is because we have no bread.' And Jesus knew it, and he said to them, 'Why are you talking about having no bread? Do you not yet understand? Have you no perception? Are your minds closed? Have you eyes that do not see, ears that do not hear? Or do you not remember? When I broke the five loaves among the five thousand, how many baskets full of scraps did you collect?' They answered, 'Twelve.' 'And when I broke the seven loaves for the four thousand, how many baskets full of scraps did you collect?' And they answered, 'Seven'. Then he said to them, 'Are you still without perception?'

Reflection

Once again we find the disciples in a situation where they are worried about not having enough food. But they do have Jesus with them in their boat, so why should they be anxious? In fact, it seems that they have either forgotten, or they never fully grasped, the meaning of Jesus' miraculous action in multiplying the loaves and fishes for the crowd. We're lucky when we read these Gospel accounts because we know how the story ends. We know that these eucharistic occasions are pointing forward to the Last Supper, the crucifixion and the resurrection. The disciples are still trying to work it all out. And yet, even though I know the ending, when Jesus fires off his nine questions to the disciples, he could be asking them of me too. Do I still not understand who Jesus is? Do I have no perception? Is my mind closed? Have I forgotten all that Jesus has done so far in my life? Jesus himself is the bread of life. If he's in my boat, I need not fear.

James 1:19-27

Remember this, my dear brothers: be quick to listen but slow to speak and slow to rouse your temper; God's righteousness is never served by man's anger; so do away with all the impurities and bad habits that are still left in you – accept and submit to the word which has been planted in you and can save your souls. But you must do what the word tells you, and not just listen to it and deceive yourselves. To listen to the word and not obey is like looking at your own features in a mirror and then, after a quick look, going off and immediately forgetting what you looked like. But the man who looks steadily at the perfect law of freedom and makes that his habit – not listening and then forgetting, but actively putting it into practice – will be happy in all that he does.

Nobody must imagine that he is religious while he still goes on deceiving himself and not keeping control over his tongue; anyone who does this has the wrong idea of religion. Pure, unspoilt religion, in the eyes of God our Father is this: coming to the help of orphans and widows when they need it, and keeping oneself uncontaminated by the world.

Psalm 14:2-5. R. v. 1

The just will live in the presence of the Lord.

Mark 8:22-26

Jesus and his disciples came to Bethsaida, and some people brought to him a blind man whom they begged him to touch. He took the blind man by the hand and led him outside the village. Then putting spittle on his eyes and laying his hands on him, he asked, 'Can you see anything?' The man, who was beginning to see, replied, 'I can see people; they look like trees to me, but they are walking about.' Then he laid his hands on the man's eyes again and he saw clearly; he was cured, and he could see everything plainly and distinctly. And Jesus sent him home, saying, 'Do not even go into the village.'

Reflection

In many of the previous stories of healing, Jesus acted because of the faith of the person seeking healing. In today's account, it is actually the friends of the blind man who bring him to Jesus. They seem to be the ones who have faith that Jesus can heal their friend. We don't know if he came willingly and shared their faith or if they dragged him along. But we do know that through his encounter with Jesus, he was healed. Not immediately, mind you. Rather, it was a gradual process. This is a metaphor for our faith life. When we come to Jesus and encounter him, we begin to see. At the beginning of our faith journey we may see only dimly the great treasures of the kingdom of God. But if we stay with Jesus, our faith-sight will grow clearer and clearer. Do I ever lead my friends to Jesus? Do I ask Jesus to help me see more clearly – not seeking to see the whole picture all at once, but rather, 'one step enough for me' (St John Henry Newman)?

6th Week in Ordinary Time | Green or **Seven Holy Founders of the Servite Order** (Optional, White)

17 FEB THU

James 2:1-9

My brothers, do not try to combine faith in Jesus Christ, our glorified Lord, with the making of distinctions between classes of people. Now suppose a man comes into your synagogue, beautifully dressed and with a gold ring on, and at the same time a poor man comes in, in shabby clothes, and you take notice of the well-dressed man, and say, 'Come this way to the best seats'; then you tell the poor man, 'Stand over there' or 'You can sit on the floor by my foot-rest.' Can't you see that you have used two different standards in your mind, and turned yourselves into judges, and corrupt judges at that? Listen, my dear brothers: it was those who are poor according to the world that God chose, to be rich in faith and to be the heirs to the kingdom which he promised to those who love him. In spite of this, you have no respect for anybody who is poor. Isn't it always the rich who are against you? Isn't it always their doing when you are dragged before the court? Aren't they the ones who insult the honourable name to which you have been dedicated? Well, the right thing to do is to keep the supreme law of scripture: you must love your neighbour as yourself; but as soon as you make distinctions between classes of people, you are committing sin, and under condemnation for breaking the Law.

Psalm 33:2-7. R. v. 7

This poor man called; the Lord heard him.

Mark 8:27-33

Jesus and his disciples left for the villages round Caesarea Philippi. On the way he put this question to his disciples, 'Who do people say I am?' And they told him, 'John the Baptist,' they said 'others Elijah; others again, one of the prophets.' 'But you,' he asked 'who do you say I am?' Peter spoke up and said to him, 'You are the Christ.' And he gave them strict orders not to tell anyone about him. And he began to teach them that the Son of Man was destined to suffer grievously, to be rejected by the elders and the chief priests and the scribes, and to be put to death, and after three days to rise again; and he said all this quite openly. Then, taking him aside, Peter started to remonstrate with him. But, turning and seeing his disciples, he rebuked Peter and said to him, 'Get behind me, Satan! Because the way you think is not God's way but man's.'

Reflection

'But you … who do you say I am?' Is there any more penetrating question in the whole of the Gospels? Jesus was saying to his disciples, 'You've seen the miracles, you've heard the teaching, you've spent time in my company – now, who do you say I am?' Peter was quick with his faith-filled reply, 'You are the Christ'. But then, having affirmed that Jesus is the Messiah they have been waiting for, Peter can't handle the reality of what that means. As Jesus explains that he is destined to suffer, die and be raised again after three days, Peter tries to intervene, to end this talk of suffering, to put Jesus back in a safe 'box' according to Peter's own limited understanding. Don't I try to do this to Jesus too? I confess with my lips and my heart that he is My Lord and My God, but I still try to fence him in and shape him according to my own understanding, rather than letting God be God.

18

FEB FRI

6th Week in Ordinary Time

Green

James 2:14-24, 26

Take the case, my brothers, of someone who has never done a single good act but claims that he has faith. Will that faith save him? If one of the brothers or one of the sisters is in need of clothes and has not enough food to live on, and one of you says to them, 'I wish you well; keep yourself warm and eat plenty,' without giving them these bare necessities of life, then what good is that? Faith is like that: if good works do not go with it, it is quite dead.

This is the way to talk to people of that kind: 'You say you have faith and I have good deeds; I will prove to you that I have faith by showing you my good deeds – now you prove to me that you have faith without any good deeds to show. You believe in the one God – that is creditable enough, but the demons have the same belief, and they tremble with fear. ... *(Please see the Appendix B-5)*

Psalm 111:1-6. R. cf. v. 1

Happy the man who takes delight in the commands of the Lord.

Mark 8:34–9:1

Jesus called the people and his disciples to him and said, 'If anyone wants to be a follower of mine, let him renounce himself and take up his cross and follow me. For anyone who wants to save his life will lose it; but anyone who loses his life for my sake, and for the sake of the gospel, will save it. What gain, then, is it for a man to win the whole world and ruin his life? And indeed what can man offer in exchange for his life? For if anyone in this adulterous and sinful generation is ashamed of me and of my words, the Son of Man will also be ashamed of him when he comes in the glory of his Father with the holy angels.'

And he said to them, 'I tell you solemnly, there are some standing here who will not taste death before they see the kingdom of God come with power.'

Reflection

Having foreshadowed his own suffering, death and resurrection, Jesus now outlines the conditions for being one of his followers. It involves self-denial, a willingness to accept suffering and hardship and a commitment to follow Jesus, wherever he takes us in our life and beyond. It's not hard to see why Mark emphasised the need for us to 'take up our cross'. He was writing at a time shortly after the Roman emperor Nero let loose with a terrible Christian persecution. Many Christians were dying for their belief. Mark was also addressing a Jewish community which was torn on the question of whether the Messiah could possibly have been killed on a cross, as criminals were. Tragically, today, more people than ever are being persecuted around the world for their Christian belief. And all of us will encounter some kind of suffering and hardship. Our hope lies in taking up our cross, uniting it with the suffering, death and resurrection of Jesus and following him. Because when we follow him, we are assured of going where he is and it is this promise which anchors our Christian life in joy.

6th Week in Ordinary Time
Green

19
FEB SAT

James 3:1-10

Only a few of you, my brothers, should be teachers, bearing in mind that those of us who teach can expect a stricter judgement. After all, every one of us does something wrong, over and over again; the only man who could reach perfection would be someone who never said anything wrong – he would be able to control every part of himself. Once we put a bit into the horse's mouth, to make it do what we want, we have the whole animal under our control. Or think of ships: no matter how big they are, even if a gale is driving them, the man at the helm can steer them anywhere he likes by controlling a tiny rudder. So is the tongue only a tiny part of the body, but it can proudly claim that it does great things. Think how small a flame can set fire to a huge forest; the tongue is a flame like that. Among all the parts of the body, the tongue is a whole wicked world in itself: it infects the whole body; catching fire itself from hell, it sets fire to the whole wheel of creation. Wild animals and birds, reptiles and fish can all be tamed by man, and often are; but nobody can tame the tongue – it is a pest that will not keep still, full of deadly poison. We use it to bless the Lord and Father, but we also use it to curse men who are made in God's image: the blessing and the curse come out of the same mouth. My brothers, this must be wrong.

Psalm 11:2-5, 7-8. R. v. 8 ***It is you, O Lord, who will take us in your care.***

Mark 9:2-13

Jesus took with him Peter and James and John and led them up a high mountain where they could be alone by themselves. There in their presence he was transfigured: his clothes became dazzlingly white, whiter than any earthly bleacher could make them. Elijah appeared to them with Moses; and they were talking with Jesus. Then Peter spoke to Jesus: 'Rabbi,' he said 'it is wonderful for us to be here; so let us make three tents, one for you, one for Moses and one for Elijah.' He did not know what to say; they were so frightened. And a cloud came, covering them in shadow; and there came a voice from the cloud, 'This is my Son, the Beloved. Listen to him.' Then suddenly, when they looked round, they saw no one with them any more but only Jesus. As they came down from the mountain he warned them to tell no one what they had seen, until after the Son of Man had risen from the dead. They observed the warning faithfully, though among themselves they discussed what 'rising from the dead' could mean. And they put this question to him, 'Why do the scribes say that Elijah has to come first?' 'True,' he said 'Elijah is to come first and to see that everything is as it should be; yet how is it that the scriptures say about the Son of Man that he is to suffer grievously and be treated with contempt? However, I tell you that Elijah has come and they have treated him as they pleased, just as the scriptures say about him.'

Reflection

I am an oblate of a Benedictine abbey and at least once a year I go for a week-long retreat to the abbey, which sits on a beautiful mountain-side. As soon as I arrive, I feel the weight of the world slide off my shoulders and I very often whisper 'Lord it is good to be here'. During that week when I have no distractions, I feel especially close to God. It is something of a transfiguration experience. During the transfiguration, Jesus showed Peter, James and John a glimpse of his glory and God speaks to them. The experience is so wonderful that they want to build a tent and stay up there forever. But, as with time spent with God on retreat, we can't stay there forever. We must come back to the world so that we can share our experience of time spent with our loving God.

20
FEB SUN

SEVENTH SUNDAY IN ORDINARY TIME

Psalter Week 3

Green

1 Samuel 26:2, 7-9, 12-13, 22-23

Saul set off and went down to the wilderness of Ziph, accompanied by three thousand men chosen from Israel to search for David in the wilderness of Ziph. So in the dark David and Abishai made their way towards the force, where they found Saul asleep inside the camp, his spear stuck in the ground beside his head, with Abner and the troops lying round him. Then Abishai said to David, 'Today God has put your enemy in your power; so now let me pin him to the ground with his own spear. Just one stroke! I will not need to strike him twice.' David answered Abishai, 'Do not kill him, for who can lift his hand against the Lord's anointed and be without guilt?' David took the spear and the pitcher of water from beside Saul's head, and they made off. No one saw, no one knew, no one woke up; they were all asleep, for a deep sleep from the Lord had fallen on them. David crossed to the other side and halted on the top of the mountain a long way off; there was a wide space between them. David then called out, 'Here is the king's spear. Let one of the soldiers come across and take it. The Lord repays everyone for his uprightness and loyalty. Today the Lord put you in my power, but I would not raise my hand against the Lord's anointed.'

Psalm 102:1-4, 8, 10, 12-13. R. v. 8

The Lord is compassion and love.

1 Corinthians 15:45-49

The first man, Adam, as scripture says, became a living soul; but the last Adam has become a life-giving spirit. That is, first the one with the soul, not the spirit, and after that, the one with the spirit. The first man, being from the earth, is earthly by nature; the second man is from heaven. As this earthly man was, so are we on earth; and as the heavenly man is, so are we in heaven. And we, who have been modelled on the earthly man, will be modelled on the heavenly man.

Luke 6:27-38

Jesus said to his disciples: 'I say this to you who are listening: Love your enemies, do good to those who hate you, bless those who curse you, pray for those who treat you badly. To the man who slaps you on one cheek, present the other cheek too; to the man who takes your cloak from you, do not refuse your tunic. Give to everyone who asks you, and do not ask for your property back from the man who robs you. Treat others as you would like them to treat you. If you love those who love you, what thanks can you expect? Even sinners love those who love them. And if you do good to those who do good to you, what thanks can you expect? For even sinners do that much. And if you lend to those from whom you hope to receive, what thanks can you expect?

Even sinners lend to sinners to get back the same amount. Instead, love your enemies and do good, and lend without any hope of return. You will have a great reward, and you will be sons of the Most High, for he himself is kind to the ungrateful and the wicked.

'Be compassionate as your Father is compassionate. Do not judge, and you will not be judged yourselves; do not condemn, and you will not be condemned yourselves; grant pardon, and you will be pardoned. Give, and there will be gifts for you: a full measure, pressed down, shaken together, and running over, will be poured into your lap; because the amount you measure out is the amount you will be given back.'

Reflection

'Love your enemies, do good to those who hate you.' This is so hard to do and yet it is fundamental to Christian life. Imagine how happy our world would be if this was lived out on a global scale. And yet, this kind of attitude has to take root at the personal level before it can grow to global proportions. I have to learn to love not only my enemies, but even those who simply annoy me, those who seem to have a grudge against me, act unfairly towards me, or speak ill of me. One of our great models in learning how to do this is St Therese of Lisieux. In her 'Little Way' she showed us that doing something as simple as taking on the washing up duty for someone in our household who is annoying us can be an act of love. It may not change the person in question, but it changes us. Because when we choose to love, even through small acts of service, it opens our hearts to God's healing grace and mercy, and this can't help but overflow.

21
FEB MON

7th Week in Ordinary Time | Green
or **St Peter Damian,** *bishop, doctor* (Optional, White)

James 3:13-18
(Please see the Appendix B-5)

Psalm 18:8-10, 15. R. v. 9
The precepts of the Lord gladden the heart.

Mark 9:14-29
When Jesus, with Peter, James and John came down from the mountain and rejoined the disciples they saw a large crowd round them and some scribes arguing with them. The moment they saw him the whole crowd were struck with amazement and ran to greet him. 'What are you arguing about with them?' he asked. A man answered him from the crowd, 'Master, I have brought my son to you; there is a spirit of dumbness in him, and when it takes hold of him it throws him to the ground, and he foams at the mouth and grinds his teeth and goes rigid. And I asked your disciples to cast it out and they were unable to.' 'You faithless generation' he said to them in reply. 'How much longer must I be with you? How much longer must I put up with you? Bring him to me.' They brought the boy to him, and as soon as the spirit saw Jesus it threw the boy into convulsions, and he fell to the ground and lay writhing there, foaming at the mouth. Jesus asked the father, 'How long has this been happening to him?' 'From childhood,' he replied 'and it has often thrown him into the fire and into the water, in order to destroy him. But if you can do anything, have pity on us and help us.' 'If you can?' retorted Jesus. 'Everything is possible for anyone who has faith.' Immediately the father of the boy cried out, 'I do have faith. Help the little faith I have!' And when Jesus saw how many people were pressing round him, he rebuked the unclean spirit. 'Deaf and dumb spirit,' he said 'I command you: come out of him and never enter him again.' Then throwing the boy into violent convulsions it came out shouting, and the boy lay there so like a corpse that most of them said, 'He is dead.' But Jesus took him by the hand and helped him up, and he was able to stand. When he had gone indoors his disciples asked him privately, 'Why were we unable to cast it out?' 'This is the kind' he answered 'that can only be driven out by prayer.'

Reflection
'Lord, I believe. Help my unbelief.' This powerful little prayer is regularly voiced by those of us who live with the twin reality of faith and doubt. Some doubt is necessary for faith and trust to grow. If everything about our life in Christ was certain and set in concrete, where would be the need for faith? And how could we grow in our faith? The man in today's Gospel is a great model of faith for us. He takes his sick son to Jesus asking for healing. He affirms his faith and asks Jesus to help grow his belief further. This is all Jesus asks of us. That we go to him with our troubles, with what little faith we have, always aware of how far we fall short of perfect trust in him, and longing to believe ever more deeply. Similarly, Jesus teaches the disciples that prayer is a prerequisite for healing. We need to anchor ourselves in faith and prayer if we are to bring Jesus' healing love to those around us.

22 FEB TUE

Chair of St Peter, Apostle
Feast | White

1 Peter 5:1-4
I have something to tell your elders: I am an elder myself, and a witness to the sufferings of Christ, and with you I have a share in the glory that is to be revealed. Be the shepherds of the flock of God that is entrusted to you: watch over it, not simply as a duty but gladly, because God wants it; not for sordid money, but because you are eager to do it. Never be a dictator over any group that is put in your charge, but be an example that the whole flock can follow. When the chief shepherd appears, you will be given the crown of unfading glory.

Psalm 22. R. v. 1
The Lord is my shepherd: there is nothing I shall want.

Matthew 16:13-19
When Jesus came to the region of Caesarea Philippi he put this question to his disciples, 'Who do people say the Son of Man is?' And they said, 'Some say he is John the Baptist, some Elijah, and others Jeremiah or one of the prophets.' 'But you,' he said, 'who do you say I am?' Then Simon Peter spoke up, 'You are the Christ,' he said, 'the Son of the Living God.' Jesus replied, 'Simon son of Jonah, you are a happy man! Because it was not flesh and blood that revealed this to you but my Father in heaven. So I now say to you: You are Peter and on this rock I will build my Church. And the gates of the underworld can never hold out against it. I will give you the keys of the kingdom of heaven: whatever you bind on earth shall be considered bound in heaven; whatever you loose on earth shall be considered loosed in heaven.'

Reflection
Today we celebrate the feast of The Chair of St Peter the Apostle, an important feast day for our unity as a Church. The Gospel is Matthew's version of an incident we heard earlier this month from Mark, where Jesus asks 'Who do you say I am?' and Peter replies, 'You are the Christ, the son of the Living God.' Matthew records that Jesus then went on to tell Peter, 'You are Peter and on this rock I will build my Church … I will give you the keys to the kingdom of heaven'. Catholics understand this to be the moment that Jesus appointed Peter to lead the Church, the Body of Christ. And when Peter died, the apostles elected a new Pope and so it has gone for more than 2000 years. In a world (and often a Church) riven with discord, we can give thanks for the unity and the stability provided by the successor of Peter. *Dear Lord, please bless and protect our Pope and guide him in all his ways. Amen.*

23
FEB WED

7th Week in Ordinary Time | Green
or **St Polycarp,** *bishop, martyr* (Optional, Red)

James 4:13-17

Here is the answer for those of you who talk like this: 'Today or tomorrow, we are off to this or that town; we are going to spend a year there, trading, and make some money.' You never know what will happen tomorrow: you are no more than a mist that is here for a little while and then disappears. The most you should ever say is: 'If it is the Lord's will, we shall still be alive to do this or that.' But how proud and sure of yourselves you are now! Pride of this kind is always wicked. Everyone who knows what is the right thing to do and doesn't do it commits a sin.

Psalm 48:2-3, 6-11. R. Matthew 5:3

How happy are the poor in spirit: theirs is the kingdom of heaven.

Mark 9:38-40

John said to Jesus, 'Master, we saw a man who is not one of us casting out devils in your name; and because he was not one of us we tried to stop him.' But Jesus said, 'You must not stop him: no one who works a miracle in my name is likely to speak evil of me. Anyone who is not against us is for us.'

Reflection

Jesus never misses an opportunity to show his followers that faith in him is not reserved for 'insiders'. Today's Gospel is a classic example of this. The disciples report seeing a man casting out devils in Jesus' name, but because he wasn't one of their group, they stopped him. Jesus responds clearly: 'You must not stop him … anyone who is not against us is for us'. Jesus isn't interested in forming a club of insiders. He wants to reach out across boundaries and touch people's hearts. He wants us to seek out 'the other', those who are in some way different to us, and to invite them in to our life of faith in him. If a stranger and fellow-believer walked into my parish would they find a warm welcome, or would they feel like an outsider? *Dear Lord, help me to reach out in friendship and faith to everyone I meet. Amen.*

7th Week in Ordinary Time
Green

24
FEB THU

James 5:1-6

The answer for the rich: start crying, weep for the miseries that are coming to you. Your wealth is all rotting, your clothes are all eaten up by moths. All your gold and your silver are corroding away, and the same corrosion will be your own sentence, and eat into your body. It was a burning fire that you stored up as your treasure for the last days. Labourers mowed your fields, and you cheated them – listen to the wages that you kept back, calling out; realise that the cries of the reapers have reached the ears of the Lord of hosts. On earth you have had a life of comfort and luxury; in the time of slaughter you went on eating to your heart's content. It was you who condemned the innocent and killed them; they offered you no resistance.

Psalm 48:14-20. R. Matthew 5:3

How happy are the poor in spirit: theirs is the kingdom of heaven.

Mark 9:41-50

Jesus said to his disciples: 'If anyone gives you a cup of water to drink just because you belong to Christ, then I tell you solemnly, he will most certainly not lose his reward. 'But anyone who is an obstacle to bring down one of these little ones who have faith, would be better thrown into the sea with a great millstone round his neck. And if your hand should cause you to sin, cut it off; it is better for you to enter into life crippled, than to have two hands and go to hell, into the fire that cannot be put out. And if your foot should cause you to sin, cut it off; it is better for you to enter into life lame, than to have two feet and be thrown into hell. And if your eye should cause you to sin, tear it out; it is better for you to enter into the kingdom of God with one eye, than to have two eyes and be thrown into hell where their worm does not die nor their fire go out. For everyone will be salted with fire. Salt is a good thing, but if salt has become insipid, how can you season it again? Have salt in yourselves and be at peace with one another.'

Reflection

In today's reading, Jesus shows us again that hospitality and service are key elements of the Christian life. And hospitality doesn't have to be fancy – simply giving a cup of water in Jesus' name is enough. On the other hand, anyone whose sin forms an obstacle to those who have faith 'would be better thrown into the sea with a great millstone round his neck'. There are few things more certain to turn people off Christianity than to observe Christians living a life not in accordance with their faith. So what is Jesus' remedy? Rather graphically he illustrates for us that we have to get to the root cause of our sinful action and cut ourselves free from it. We have to be radical about it, tackle it head-on. Minor 'surgery' won't cut it. Drawing closer to Jesus in prayer, Word and sacrament will help identify for us where our sin lies and open us up to his healing love. Serving Jesus in others is also a sure channel of grace and a great practical remedy for sin.

25
FEB FRI

James 5:9-12

Do not make complaints against one another, brothers, so as not to be brought to judgement yourselves; the Judge is already to be seen waiting at the gates. For your example, brothers, in submitting with patience, take the prophets who spoke in the name of the Lord; remember it is those who had endurance that we say are the blessed ones. You have heard of the patience of Job, and understood the Lord's purpose, realising that the Lord is kind and compassionate. Above all, my brothers, do not swear by heaven or by the earth, or use any oaths at all. If you mean 'yes', you must say 'yes'; if you mean 'no', say 'no'. Otherwise you make yourselves liable to judgement.

Psalm 102:1-4, 8-9, 11-12. R. v. 8

The Lord is compassion and love.

Mark 10:1-12

Jesus came to the district of Judaea and the far side of the Jordan. And again crowds gathered round him, and again he taught them, as his custom was. Some Pharisees approached him and asked, 'Is it against the law for a man to divorce his wife?' They were testing him. He answered them, 'What did Moses command you?' 'Moses allowed us' they said 'to draw up a writ of dismissal and so to divorce.' Then Jesus said to them, 'It was because you were so unteachable that he wrote this commandment for you. But from the beginning of creation God made them male and female. This is why a man must leave father and mother, and the two become one body. They are no longer two, therefore, but one body. So then, what God has united, man must not divide.' Back in the house the disciples questioned him again about this, and he said to them, 'The man who divorces his wife and marries another is guilty of adultery against her. And if a woman divorces her husband and marries another she is guilty of adultery too.'

Reflection

Today's reading is simultaneously one of the most beautiful of Jesus' teachings and also, for some, one of the most difficult. Asked by the Pharisees whether it is against the law for a man to divorce his wife, Jesus proceeds to outline God's beautiful vision for marriage, which goes right back to the beginning of creation. The two 'become one body' and 'what God has united, man must not divide'. This teaching is the basis for our Church's doctrine that marriage is a life-long union between husband and wife, given freely to each other. Marriage is not a disposable relationship, not a transient one, but a deep union, where two become one for life. Sadly, all of us know of situations where, for various serious reasons, the marriage union has not lasted. Jesus' teaching on divorce is clear, but so is his compassion for those who suffer. *Dear Lord, bless all married couples, especially those who may be struggling. Be with them and strengthen them in love. Amen.*

7th Week in Ordinary Time
Green

26
FEB SAT

James 5:13-20

If any one of you is in trouble, he should pray; if anyone is feeling happy, he should sing a psalm. If one of you is ill, he should send for the elders of the church, and they must anoint him with oil in the name of the Lord and pray over him. The prayer of faith will save the sick man and the Lord will raise him up again; and if he has committed any sins, he will be forgiven. So confess your sins to one another, and pray for one another, and this will cure you; the heartfelt prayer of a good man works very powerfully. Elijah was a human being like ourselves – he prayed hard for it not to rain, and no rain fell for three-and-a-half years; then he prayed again and the sky gave rain and the earth gave crops. My brothers, if one of you strays away from the truth, and another brings him back to it, he may be sure that anyone who can bring back a sinner from the wrong way that he has taken will be saving a soul from death and covering up a great number of sins.

Psalm 140:1-3, 8. R. v. 2

Let my prayer come before you like incense, O Lord.

Mark 10:13-16

People were bringing little children to Jesus, for him to touch them. The disciples turned them away, but when Jesus saw this he was indignant and said to them, 'Let the little children come to me; do not stop them; for it is to such as these that the kingdom of God belongs. I tell you solemnly, anyone who does not welcome the kingdom of God like a little child will never enter it.' Then he put his arms round them, laid his hands on them and gave them his blessing.

Reflection

One of the most beautiful things about little children in a happy family life is their complete trust in their parents. In today's Gospel, Jesus is teaching the disciples that this is the correct attitude for entering the kingdom of heaven. The disciples had tried to turn the children away from Jesus, and reserve his time for the adults, the older, wiser and more entitled members of the crowd. But Jesus was having none of it: 'Let the little children come to me; do not stop them; for it is to such as these that the kingdom of God belongs.' Once again, Jesus turns things on their head. He wants nobody excluded, especially those whose faith and trust is so pure. The more we can abandon ourselves to Jesus in child-like trust, the more we come to him joyfully and without reserve, as a child to a loving father, the closer we are to the kingdom of God.

27
FEB SUN

EIGHTH SUNDAY IN ORDINARY TIME

Psalter Week 4

Green

Sirach 27:4-7

In a shaken sieve the rubbish is left behind, so too the defects of a man appear in his talk. The kiln tests the work of the potter, the test of a man is in his conversation. The orchard where the tree grows is judged on the quality of its fruit, similarly a man's words betray what he feels. Do not praise a man before he has spoken, since this is the test of men.

Psalm 91:2-3, 13-16. R. cf. v. 2

It is good to give you thanks, O Lord.

1 Corinthians 15:54-58

When this perishable nature has put on imperishability, and when this mortal nature has put on immortality, then the words of scripture will come true: Death is swallowed up in victory. Death, where is your victory? Death, where is your sting? Now the sting of death is sin, and sin gets its power from the Law. So let us thank God for giving us the victory through our Lord Jesus Christ.

Never give in then, my dear brothers, never admit defeat; keep on working at the Lord's work always, knowing that, in the Lord, you cannot be labouring in vain.

Luke 6:39-45

Jesus told a parable to his disciples. 'Can one blind man guide another? Surely both will fall into a pit? The disciple is not superior to his teacher; the fully trained disciples will always be like his teacher. Why do you observe the splinter in your brother's eye and never notice the plank in your own? How can you say to your brother, "Brother, let me take out the splinter that is in your eye," when you cannot see the plank in your own? Hypocrite! Take the plank out of your own eye first, and then you will see clearly enough to take out the splinter that is in your brother's eye.

'There is no sound tree that produces rotten fruit, nor again a rotten tree that produces sound fruit. For every tree can be told by its own fruit; people do not pick figs from thorns, nor gather grapes from brambles. A good man draws what is good from the store of goodness in his heart; a bad man draws what is bad from the store of badness. For a man's words flow out of what fills his heart.'

Reflection

Imagine if we always followed Jesus' advice to take a look at our own failings before criticising others. We would never criticise anyone, and how much happier our lives and relationships would be. Jesus reminds us that our inner spiritual health can be gauged by how we live our life, by our actions, by the fruit we bear. If we regularly display virtues such as patience, honesty and courage, there is a fair chance that this good is coming from the store of goodness in our heart. If we are prone to bad temper, impatience, dishonesty and any number of other 'rotten fruits', then, as the Scripture passage says, it is likely we are drawing from a well of badness. How do we create a store of goodness in our heart then? Through staying close to Jesus in prayer, Word and sacrament and filling ourselves with his goodness. I love to listen to Christian music in the car and around the house, because it's one small way of regularly filling myself up with Scripture-based goodness. We're still going to sin and make mistakes, but when we're drawing from the well of goodness in our heart, we're more likely to be able to share good fruits.

1 Peter 1:3-9

Blessed be God the Father of our Lord Jesus Christ, who in his great mercy has given us a new birth as his sons, by raising Jesus Christ from the dead, so that we have a sure hope and the promise of an inheritance that can never be spoilt or soiled and never fade away, because it is being kept for you in the heavens. Through your faith, God's power will guard you until the salvation which had been prepared is revealed at the end of time. This is a cause of great joy for you, even though you may for a short time have to bear being plagued by all sorts of trials; so that, when Jesus Christ is revealed, your faith will have been tested and proved like gold – only it is more precious than gold, which is corruptible even though it bears testing by fire – and then you will have praise and glory and honour. You did not see him, yet you love him; and still without seeing him, you are already filled with a joy so glorious that it cannot be described, because you believe; and you are sure of the end to which your faith looks forward, that is, the salvation of your souls.

Psalm 110:1-2, 5-6, 9-10. R. v. 5

The Lord keeps his covenant in mind.

Mark 10:17-27

Jesus was setting out on a journey when a man ran up, knelt before him and put this question to him, 'Good master, what must I do to inherit eternal life?' Jesus said to him, 'Why do you call me good? No one is good but God alone. You know the commandments: You must not kill; You must not commit adultery; You must not steal; You must not bring false witness; You must not defraud; Honour your father and mother.' And he said to him, 'Master, I have kept all these from my earliest days.' Jesus looked steadily at him and loved him, and he said, 'There is one thing you lack. Go and sell everything you own and give the money to the poor, and you will have treasure in heaven; then come, follow me.' But his face fell at these words and he went away sad, for he was a man of great wealth. Jesus looked round and said to his disciples, 'How hard it is for those who have riches to enter the kingdom of God!' The disciples were astounded by these words, but Jesus insisted, 'My children,' he said to them 'how hard it is to enter the kingdom of God! It is easier for a camel to pass through the eye of a needle than for a rich man to enter the kingdom of God.' They were more astonished than ever. 'In that case' they said to one another 'who can be saved?' Jesus gazed at them. 'For men' he said 'it is impossible, but not for God: because everything is possible for God.'

Reflection

'Jesus looked steadily at him and loved him.' Whenever I read this Gospel passage, I am stopped in my tracks by that line. What a beautiful experience that must have been for the rich young man, to have Jesus hold his eyes, look at him, and love him. This young man was doing everything right. He was keeping the commandments and the Law and he was seeking eternal life. But he wasn't prepared to give everything to follow Jesus. In his case it was his wealth and possessions he was holding back. What am I holding back from Jesus? The young man failed to understand that everything he has is a gift from God in the first place. It all belongs to him. And we are free only in the measure that we are able to return those gifts into his keeping. At the end of my life I don't want to go away sad, like this young man, because when eternal life was offered, I chose my earthly attachments instead.

8th Week in Ordinary Time
Green

01
MAR TUE

ST DAVID, BISHOP, PATRON OF WALES,
Feast – England
see Appendix A-9

1 Peter 1:10-16

It was this salvation that the prophets were looking and searching so hard for; their prophecies were about the grace which was to come to you. The Spirit of Christ which was in them foretold the sufferings of Christ and the glories that would come after them, and they tried to find out at what time and in what circumstances all this was to be expected. It was revealed to them that the news they brought of all the things which have now been announced to you, by those who preached to you the Good News through the Holy Spirit sent from heaven, was for you and not for themselves. Even the angels long to catch a glimpse of these things. Free your minds, then, of encumbrances; control them, and put your trust in nothing but the grace that will be given you when Jesus Christ is revealed. Do not behave in the way that you liked to before you learnt the truth; make a habit of obedience: be holy in all you do, since it is the Holy One who has called you, and scripture says: Be holy, for I am holy.

Psalm 97:1-4. R. v. 2

The Lord has made known his salvation.

Mark 10:28-31

'What about us?' Peter asked Jesus. 'We have left everything and followed you.' Jesus said, 'I tell you solemnly, there is no one who has left house, brothers, sisters, father, children or land for my sake and for the sake of the gospel who will not be repaid a hundred times over, houses, brothers, sisters, mothers, children and land – not without persecution – now in this present time and, in the world to come, eternal life. 'Many who are first will be last, and the last first.'

Reflection

It has been well said by one spiritual writer that 'to offer God less than everything is to settle for less than God'. This is the dilemma confronting the rich young man whose story precedes today's Gospel passage. He was not prepared, in response to Jesus' challenge, to leave all and follow him. As Jesus told Peter, this is what he expects all of his disciples to do 'for [his] sake and for the sake of the gospel'. He assures them that, having done so, they will be 'repaid a hundred times over … now in this present time' and will be blessed with eternal life 'in the world to come'. Tomorrow we begin the annual celebration of Lent. It is a good time to confront what we are clinging to unhealthily and to identify what we are withholding from God. Other than our consent to be loved by God, we have nothing to offer that has not first been God's gift to us.

02
MAR WED

Ash Wednesday
Violet

Joel 2:12-18
(Please see the Appendix B-5)

Psalm 50:3-6, 12-14, 17. R. v. 3
Have mercy on us, O Lord, for we have sinned.

2 Corinthians 5:20–6:2
We are ambassadors for Christ; it is as though God were appealing through us, and the appeal that we make in Christ's name is: be reconciled to God. For our sake God made the sinless one into sin, so that in him we might become the goodness of God. As his fellow workers, we beg you once again not to neglect the grace of God that you have received. For he says: At the favourable time, I have listened to you; on the day of salvation I came to your help. Well, now is the favourable time; this is the day of salvation.

Matthew 6:1-6, 16-18
Jesus said to his disciples: 'Be careful not to parade your good deeds before men to attract their notice; by doing this you will lose all reward from your Father in heaven. So when you give alms, do not have it trumpeted before you; this is what the hypocrites do in the synagogues and in the streets to win men's admiration. I tell you solemnly, they have had their reward. But when you give alms, your left hand must not know what your right is doing; your almsgiving must be secret, and your Father who sees all that is done in secret will reward you. 'And when you pray, do not imitate the hypocrites: they love to say their prayers standing up in the synagogues and at the street corners for people to see them. I tell you solemnly, they have had their reward. But when you pray go to your private room and, when you have shut your door, pray to your Father who is in that secret place, and your Father who sees all that is done in secret will reward you.

'When you fast do not put on a gloomy look as the hypocrites do: they pull long faces to let men know they are fasting. I tell you solemnly, they have had their reward. But when you fast, put oil on your head and wash your face, so that no one will know you are fasting except your Father who sees all that is done in secret; and your Father who sees all that is done in secret will reward you.'

Reflection
Our Lenten fast can benefit our physical health and, if accompanied by conversion of heart, our spiritual wellbeing as well. It can also serve to remind us that the whole material world is God's gift to us, to be shared and enjoyed by all people. Jesus himself fasted for forty days before he began his public ministry (Matthew 4:1-11). In today's Gospel reading Jesus links fasting with prayer, almsgiving and the practice of good works unostentatiously performed. This is completely in harmony with the word of God revealed through the prophet Isaiah: 'Is not this the sort of fast that pleases me – it is the Lord who speaks – to break unjust fetters and undo the thongs of the yoke, to let the oppressed go free, and break every yoke, to share your bread with the hungry, and shelter the homeless poor, to clothe the one you see to be naked and not turn from your own kin?' (Isaiah 58:6-7).

Thursday after Ash Wednesday
Violet

Deuteronomy 30:15-20

Moses said to the people: 'See, today I set before you life and prosperity, death and disaster. If you obey the commandments of the Lord your God that I enjoin on you today, if you love the Lord your God and follow his ways, if you keep his commandments, his laws, his customs, you will live and increase, and the Lord your God will bless you in the land which you are entering to make your own. But if your heart strays, if you refuse to listen, if you let yourself be drawn into worshipping other gods and serving them, I tell you today, you will most certainly perish; you will not live long in the land you are crossing the Jordan to enter and possess. I call heaven and earth to witness against you today: I set before you life or death, blessing or curse. Choose life, then, so that you and your descendants may live in the love of the Lord your God, obeying his voice, clinging to him; for in this your life consists, and on this depends your long stay in the land which the Lord swore to your fathers Abraham, Isaac and Jacob he would give them.

Psalm 1:1-4, 6. R. Psalm 39:5

Happy the man who has placed his trust in the Lord.

Luke 9:22-25

Jesus said to his disciples: 'The Son of Man is destined to suffer grievously, to be rejected by the elders and chief priests and scribes and to be put to death, and to be raised up on the third day.'

Then to all he said, 'If anyone wants to be a follower of mine, let him renounce himself and take up his cross every day and follow me. For anyone who wants to save his life will lose it; but anyone who loses his life for my sake, that man will save it. What gain, then, is it for a man to have won the whole world and to have lost or ruined his very self?'

Reflection

On several occasions Jesus informs his disciples that a violent death awaits him at the hands of those who reject his teaching. Twice during the Last Supper discourse, having told them that 'no servant is greater than his master' (John 13:16; 15:20), he forewarns them that they too might expect to experience suffering in his name: 'If they persecuted me, they will persecute you too' (John 15:20). Across the ages, and especially in our own time, that has been the fate of a multitude of Jesus' followers. With good reason the English Jesuit martyr Saint Robert Southwell said, 'The following of Christ is a rough profession.' While this is unlikely to be our fate, we need to accept that the practice of our Christian faith will make demands on us. Indeed, the cost of discipleship is 'not less than everything' (Fr John Dalrymple). *Help me, Lord, to be ever faithful in your service in the family home, the parish and the workplace.*

04
MAR FRI

Friday after Ash Wednesday | Violet
or **St Casimir** (Commemoration)

Isaiah 58:1-9

Thus says the Lord: Shout for all you are worth, raise your voice like a trumpet. Proclaim their faults to my people, their sins to the House of Jacob. They seek me day after day, they long to know my ways, like a nation that wants to act with integrity and not ignore the law of its God. They ask me for laws that are just, they long for God to draw near: 'Why should we fast if you never see it, why do penance if you never notice?' Look, you do business on your fastdays, you oppress all your workmen; look, you quarrel and squabble when you fast and strike the poor man with your fist. Fasting like yours today will never make your voice heard on high. Is that the sort of fast that pleases me, a truly penitential day for men? Hanging your head like a reed, lying down on sackcloth and ashes? Is that what you call fasting, a day acceptable to the Lord? Is not this the sort of fast that pleases me – it is the Lord who speaks – to break unjust fetters and undo the thongs of the yoke, to let the oppressed go free, and break every yoke, to share your bread with the hungry, and shelter the homeless poor, to clothe the man you see to be naked and not turn from your own kin? Then will your light shine like the dawn and your wound be quickly healed over. Your integrity will go before you and the glory of the Lord behind you. Cry, and the Lord will answer; call, and he will say, 'I am here.'

Psalm 50:3-6, 18-19. R. v. 19

A humbled, contrite heart, O God, you will not spurn.

Matthew 9:14-15

John's disciples came to Jesus and said, 'Why is it that we and the Pharisees fast, but your disciples do not?' Jesus replied, 'Surely the bridegroom's attendants would never think of mourning as long as the bridegroom is still with them? But the time will come for the bridegroom to be taken away from them, and then they will fast.'

Reflection

Meals featured prominently in Jesus' saving ministry. Sometimes he was a guest (as at Simon the Pharisee's house); at other times he himself was the host who generously provided for the crowds that followed him. Even after the resurrection he prepared breakfast for his disciples by the lakeside. The religious leaders criticised his dining with sinners and even described him as 'a glutton'. However, we know that Jesus fasted and assumed that, when appropriate, his followers would also fast. Believing that a teacher is answerable for the behaviour of his disciples, John the Baptist's followers asked Jesus why his approach to fasting was apparently more liberal and self-indulgent than that of the Pharisees and their own mentor. His response must have seemed rather enigmatic to them. However we may understand it, we acknowledge with Paul that 'the kingdom of God does not mean eating or drinking this or that, it means righteousness and peace and joy brought by the Holy Spirit' (Romans 14:17).

Saturday after Ash Wednesday
Violet

05
MAR SAT

Isaiah 58:9-14

The Lord says this: If you do away with the yoke, the clenched fist, the wicked word, if you give your bread to the hungry, and relief to the oppressed, your light will rise in the darkness, and your shadows become like noon. The Lord will always guide you, giving you relief in desert places. He will give strength to your bones and you shall be like a watered garden, like a spring of water whose waters never run dry. You will rebuild the ancient ruins, build up on the old foundations. You will be called 'Breach-mender', 'Restorer of ruined houses'. If you refrain from trampling the sabbath, and doing business on the holy day, if you call the sabbath 'Delightful', and the day sacred to the Lord 'Honourable', if you honour it by abstaining from travel, from doing business and from gossip, then you shall find happiness in the Lord and I will lead you triumphant over the heights of the land. I will feed you on the heritage of Jacob your father. For the mouth of the Lord has spoken.

Psalm 85:1-6. R. v. 11

Show me, Lord, your way so that I may walk in your truth.

Luke 5:27-32

Jesus noticed a tax collector, Levi by name, sitting by the customs house, and said to him, 'Follow me.' And leaving everything he got up and followed him.

In his honour Levi held a great reception in his house, and with them at table was a large gathering of tax collectors and others. The Pharisees and their scribes complained to his disciples and said, 'Why do you eat and drink with tax collectors and sinners?' Jesus said to them in reply, 'It is not those who are well who need the doctor, but the sick. I have not come to call the virtuous, but sinners to repentance.'

Reflection

One of Aesop's fables illustrates the moral lesson, 'A man is known by the company he keeps' or, otherwise expressed, 'Birds of a feather flock together'. Applying this judgement to Jesus, the Pharisees concluded that, as the friend of sinners, he himself was lacking in virtue. They were scandalised by his openness to those whose observance of the Jewish Law left much to be desired. In particular they took exception to his table fellowship with people like Levi (Matthew) and Zacchaeus, both of them tax-collectors. When scribes and Pharisees required of his disciples an explanation for this 'unacceptable' behaviour, Jesus interposed: 'It is not the healthy who need the doctor, but the sick. I did not come to call the virtuous, but sinners' (Mark 2:17). As with these self-righteous questioners, our condemnation of others is often an oblique form of self-commendation. In the words of one Pharisee we are saying, 'I thank you God, that I am not [sinful] … like the rest of mankind' (Luke 18:11).

06

MAR SUN

FIRST SUNDAY OF LENT

Psalter Week 1

Violet

Deuteronomy 26:4-10

Moses said to the people: 'The priest shall take the pannier from your hand and lay it before the altar of the Lord your God. Then, in the sight of the Lord your God, you must make this pronouncement:

"My father was a wandering Aramaean. He went down into Egypt to find refuge there, few in numbers; but there he became a nation, great, mighty, and strong. The Egyptians ill-treated us, they gave us no peace and inflicted harsh slavery on us. But we called on the Lord, the God of our fathers. The Lord heard our voice and saw our misery, our toil and our oppression; and the Lord brought us out of Egypt with mighty hand and outstretched arm, with great terror, and with signs and wonders. He brought us here and gave us this land, a land where milk and honey flow. Here then I bring the first-fruits of the produce of the soil that you, Lord, have given me." You must then lay them before the Lord your God, and bow down in the sight of the Lord your God.'

Psalm 90:1-2, 10-15. R. v. 15

Be with me, O Lord, in my distress.

Romans 10:8-13

Scripture says: The word, that is the faith we proclaim, is very near to you, it is on your lips and in your heart. If your lips confess that Jesus is Lord and if you believe in your heart that God raised him from the dead, then you will be saved. By believing from the heart you are made righteous; by confessing with your lips you are saved. When scripture says: those who believe in him will have no cause for shame, it makes no distinction between Jew and Greek: all belong to the same Lord who is rich enough, however many ask for his help, for everyone who calls on the name of the Lord will be saved.

Luke 4:1-13

Filled with the Holy Spirit, Jesus left the Jordan and was led by the Spirit through the wilderness, being tempted there by the devil for forty days. During that time he ate nothing and at the end he was hungry. Then the devil said to him, 'If you are the Son of God, tell this stone to turn into a loaf.' But Jesus replied, 'Scripture says: Man does not live on bread alone.'

Then leading him to a height, the devil showed him in a moment of time all the kingdoms of the world and said to him, 'I will give you all this power and the glory of these kingdoms, for it has been committed to me and I give it to anyone I choose. Worship me, then, and it shall all be yours.' But Jesus answered him. 'Scripture says:

You must worship the Lord your God, and serve him alone.'

Then he led him to Jerusalem and made him stand on the parapet of the Temple. 'If you are the Son of God', he said to him 'throw yourself down from here, for scripture says:

He will put his angels in charge of you to guard you,

and again:

They will hold you up on their hands
in case you hurt your foot against a stone.'

But Jesus answered him, 'It has been said:

You must not put the Lord your God to the test.'

Having exhausted all these ways of tempting him, the devil left him, to return at the appointed time.

Reflection

Later in our Eucharistic celebration we will pray, 'Father ... lead us not into temptation.' It is a plea that our loving God will strengthen and support us in the trials that inevitably confront us in our efforts to live faithful lives in accordance with God's will for his creation. In this, as in all matters related to our spiritual growth, Jesus, who was 'tempted in every way that we are, though he is without sin' (Hebrews 4:15), is our exemplar. 'Learn from me,' he says, 'and you will find rest for your souls' (Matthew 11:29-30). The dramatic account of Jesus' encounter with Satan (the adversary) occurs in all three Synoptic Gospels. It is an appropriate reading with which to introduce the penitential season of Lent. The temptations that Jesus faced at the beginning of his public ministry relate to three issues that lie at the heart of the discord and division that bedevil contemporary society – our self-centred attitudes to power, property and prestige – an unholy trinity that claims the worship of so many people. The ominous words which conclude today's reading are a reminder that the tempter is still destructively active among us and that we should be on our guard.

07
MAR MON

1st Week of Lent | Violet
or **Sts Perpetua and Felicity,** *martyrs* (Commemoration)

Leviticus 19:1-2, 11-18
(Please see the Appendix B-6)

Psalm 18:8-10, 15. R. John 6:64
Your words are spirit, Lord, and they are life.

Matthew 25:31 46
Jesus said to his disciples: 'When the Son of Man comes in his glory, escorted by all the angels, then he will take his seat on his throne of glory. All the nations will be assembled before him and he will separate men one from another as the shepherd separates sheep from goats. He will place the sheep on his right hand and the goats on his left. Then the King will say to those on his right hand, "Come, you whom my Father has blessed, take for your heritage the kingdom prepared for you since the foundation of the world. For I was hungry and you gave me food; I was thirsty and you gave me drink; I was a stranger and you made me welcome; naked and you clothed me, sick and you visited me, in prison and you came to see me." Then the virtuous will say to him in reply, "Lord, when did we see you hungry and feed you; or thirsty and give you drink? When did we see you a stranger and make you welcome; naked and clothe you; sick or in prison and go to see you?" And the King will answer, "I tell you solemnly, in so far as you did this to one of the least of these brothers of mine, you did it to me." Next he will say to those on his left hand, "Go away from me, with your curse upon you, to the eternal fire prepared for the devil and his angels. For I was hungry and you never gave me food; I was thirsty and you never gave me anything to drink; I was a stranger and you never made me welcome, naked and you never clothed me, sick and in prison and you never visited me." Then it will be their turn to ask, "Lord, when did we see you hungry or thirsty, a stranger or naked, sick or in prison, and did not come to your help?" Then he will answer, "I tell you solemnly, in so far as you neglected to do this to one of the least of these, you neglected to do it to me." And they will go away to eternal punishment, and the virtuous to eternal life.'

Reflection
The most telling word in Matthew's envisioning of the Last Judgement is the oft-repeated personal pronoun 'I'. In each case it identifies not just anybody in general who was naked, hungry, thirsty, in prison or otherwise in need of our compassionate intervention but Jesus himself. According to the evangelist, the Son of Man will say to those who have responded to this need in their daily lives: 'Truly I tell you, just as you did it to one of the least of these who are members of my family, you did it to me' (Matthew 25:40, NRSV). One who knew the truth of this and embodied it in her ministry was St Teresa of Kolkata. 'God is in every human being,' she said. 'When I wash the leper's wounds, I feel I am nursing the Lord himself. Is it not a beautiful experience?' In similar vein Rabbi Abraham Joshua Heschel wrote: 'Many things on earth are precious, some are holy, humanity is holy of holies.'

1st Week of Lent | Violet
or **St John of God,** *religious* (Commemoration)

Isaiah 55:10-11

Thus says the Lord:
As the rain and the snow come down from the heavens and do not return without watering the earth, making it yield and giving growth to provide seed for the sower and bread for the eating, so the word that goes from my mouth does not return to me empty, without carrying out my will and succeeding in what it was sent to do.

Psalm 33:4-7, 16-19. R. v. 18

The Lord rescues the just in all their distress.

Matthew 6:7-15

Jesus said to his disciples: 'In your prayers do not babble as the pagans do, for they think that by using many words they will make themselves heard. Do not be like them; your Father knows what you need before you ask him. So you should pray like this: 'Our Father in heaven, may your name be held holy, your kingdom come, your will be done, on earth as in heaven. Give us today our daily bread. And forgive us our debts, as we have forgiven those who are in debt to us. And do not put us to the test, but save us from the evil one.

'Yes, if you forgive others their failings, your heavenly Father will forgive you yours; but if you do not forgive others, your Father will not forgive your failings either.'

Reflection

In an earlier Latin version of the Mass text, we used to preface the recitation of the Lord's Prayer with the words *'audemus dicere'* ('we dare to say'). It was an appropriate introduction, given that we proceed to ask God to forgive us our sins in the same measure as we forgive those who sin against us. Where does this leave the unforgiving person? It is similarly daring on our part if we pray unthinkingly 'thy will be done' when our lives so often proclaim *'my will be done'*. In this connection Paul offers this good advice for the Lenten season: 'Do not model yourselves on the behaviour of the world around you, but let your behaviour change, modelled by your new mind' (Romans 12:2). From time to time it can be helpful for us to pray the Lord's Prayer very slowly and reflectively, dwelling on each phrase and applying it to our daily lives.

09
MAR WED

1st Week of Lent | Violet
or **St Francis of Rome,** *religious* (Commemoration)

Jonah 3:1-10

The word of the Lord was addressed to Jonah: 'Up!' he said, 'Go to Nineveh, the great city, and preach to them as I told you to.' Jonah set out and went to Nineveh in obedience to the word of the Lord. Now Nineveh was a city great beyond compare: it took three days to cross it. Jonah went on into the city, making a day's journey. He preached in these words, 'Only forty days more and Nineveh is going to be destroyed.' And the people of Nineveh believed in God; they proclaimed a fast and put on sackcloth, from the greatest to the least. The news reached the king of Nineveh, who rose from his throne, took off his robe, put on sackcloth and sat down in ashes. A proclamation was then promulgated throughout Nineveh, by decree of the king and his ministers, as follows: 'Men and beasts, herds and flocks, are to taste nothing; they must not eat, they must not drink water. All are to put on sackcloth and call on God with all their might; and let everyone renounce his evil behaviour and the wicked things he has done. Who knows if God will not change his mind and relent, if he will not renounce his burning wrath, so that we do not perish?' God saw their efforts to renounce their evil behaviour. And God relented: he did not inflict on them the disaster which he had threatened.

Psalm 50:3-4, 12-13, 18-19. R. v. 19

A humbled, contrite heart, O God, you will not spurn.

Luke 11:29-32

The crowds got even bigger and Jesus addressed them. 'This is a wicked generation; it is asking for a sign. The only sign it will be given is the sign of Jonah. For just as Jonah became a sign to the Ninevites, so will the Son of Man be to this generation. On Judgement day the Queen of the South will rise up with the men of this generation and condemn them, because she came from the ends of the earth to hear the wisdom of Solomon; and there is something greater than Solomon here. On Judgement day the men of Nineveh will stand up with this generation and condemn it, because when Jonah preached they repented; and there is something greater than Jonah here.'

Reflection

'God has created me to do him some definite service. He has committed some work to me which he has not committed to another' (St John Henry Newman). Many biblical characters (Jonah, Moses, the Old Testament prophets, Mary of Nazareth and Paul among them) could make such a claim – and so can we. No one was more conscious of this truth than Jesus himself who defined his God-given mission in many ways that are summed up in his proclamation, 'I have come so that they may have life and have it to the full' (John 10:10). His sceptical opponents demanded to know his credentials for teaching and acting as he did. When, like Herod and the jeering crowd on Calvary, they sought a sign, 'the sign of Jonah' was all that he offered them. The patent goodness and integrity of his own life, bearing God's ultimate seal of approval, was sign enough. In the poet Hopkins's words, 'What I do is me: for that I came'.

1st Week of Lent
Violet

10
MAR THU

SAINT JOHN OGILVIE, PRIEST, MARTYR, Feast
– Scotland

see Appendix A-10

Esther 4:1, 3-5, 12-14

Queen Esther took refuge with the Lord in the mortal peril which had overtaken her. She besought the Lord God of Israel in these words: 'My Lord, our King, the only one, come to my help, for I am alone and have no helper but you and am about to take my life in my hands. I have been taught from my earliest years, in the bosom of my family, that you, Lord, chose Israel out of all the nations and our ancestors out of all the people of old times to be your heritage for ever; and that you have treated them as you promised. Remember, Lord; reveal yourself in the time of our distress. As for me, give me courage, King of gods and master of all power. Put persuasive words into my mouth when I face the lion; change his feeling into hatred for our enemy, that the latter and all like him may be brought to their end. As for ourselves, save us by your hand, and come to my help, for I am alone and have no one but you, Lord.'

Psalm 137:1-3, 7-8. R. v. 3

On the day I called, you answered me, O Lord.

Matthew 7:7-12

Jesus said to his disciples; 'Ask, and it will be given to you; search, and you will find; knock, and the door will be opened to you. For the one who asks always receives; the one who searches always finds; the one who knocks will always have the door opened to him. Is there a man among you who would hand his son a stone when he asked for bread? Or would hand him a snake when he asked for a fish? If you, then, who are evil, know how to give your children what is good, how much more will your Father in heaven give good things to those who ask him! 'So always treat others as you would like them to treat you; that is the meaning of the Law and the Prophets.'

Reflection

Some people question the desirability, efficacy and authenticity of intercessory prayer. Doubtless, such prayer can be trivialised as, for example, when one prays to win the lottery or to pass an exam after study has taken second place to a riotous social life. Such aberrations aside, there is a place for intercessory prayer in our spiritual quest. How else can we interpret Jesus' words in today's Gospel reading? Jesus himself prayed in the fashion recommended there. Consider his assurance to Peter; 'I have prayed for you, Simon, that your faith may not fail …' (Luke 22:32). He prayed for his disciples collectively and 'for those also who through their words will believe in [him]' (John 17:20). He also prayed for himself in his terrifying ordeal in the Garden of Gethsemane (Luke 22:41-42); and on the cross he begged the Father's forgiveness for those responsible for his sufferings (Luke 23:34). 'The test of sincere intercession is the commitment to corresponding action' (Geoffrey Wainwright).

11
MAR FRI

1st Week of Lent
Violet

Ezekiel 18:21-28

Thus says the Lord God: 'If the wicked man renounces all the sins he has committed, respects my laws and is law-abiding and honest, he will certainly live; he will not die. All the sins he committed will be forgotten from then on; he shall live because of the integrity he has practised. What! Am I likely to take pleasure in the death of a wicked man – it is the Lord who speaks – and not prefer to see him renounce his wickedness and live? 'But if the upright man renounces his integrity, commits sin, copies the wicked man and practises every kind of filth, is he to live? All the integrity he has practised shall be forgotten from then on; but this is because he himself has broken faith and committed sin, and for this he shall die. But you object, "What the Lord does is unjust." Listen, you House of Israel: is what I do unjust? Is it not what you do that is unjust? When the upright man renounces his integrity to commit sin and dies because of this, he dies because of the evil that he himself has committed. When the sinner renounces sin to become law-abiding and honest, he deserves to live. He has chosen to renounce all his previous sins, he shall certainly live; he shall not die.'

Psalm 129. R. v. 3

If you, O Lord, should mark our guilt, Lord, who would survive?

Matthew 5:20-26

Jesus said to his disciples: 'If your virtue goes no deeper than that of the scribes and Pharisees, you will never get into the kingdom of heaven. 'You have learnt how it was said to our ancestors: You must not kill, and if anyone does kill he must answer for it before the court. But I say this to you: anyone who is angry with his brother will answer for it before the court; if a man calls his brother "Fool" he will answer for it before the Sanhedrin, and if a man calls him "Renegade" he will answer for it in hell fire. So then, if you are bringing your offering to the altar and there remember that your brother has something against you, leave your offering there before the altar, go and be reconciled with your brother first, and then come back and present your offering. Come to terms with your opponent in good time while you are still on the way to the court with him, or he may hand you over to the judge and the judge to the officer, and you will be thrown into prison. I tell you solemnly, you will not get out till you have paid the last penny.'

Reflection

Where the Old Testament prophet readily admits that he is only the mouthpiece of God ('It is the Lord who speaks'), Jesus presumes to speak in his own voice ('But I say unto you'). No wonder that the crowd listening to the discourse from which today's Gospel reading is taken were astounded at his teaching, 'because he taught them with authority, and not like their own scribes' (Matthew 7:28-29). In speaking thus Jesus does not set aside the Law and the Prophets (Matthew 5:17). Indeed he affirms them; but at the same time he stresses that outward observance of the letter of the Law counts for little if, unsupported by the right inner attitudes, it does do not proceed from a pure heart. Mindful of what Jesus said immediately before his ascension – 'All authority in heaven and on earth has been given to me' (Matthew 28:18) – let us always attend to his words; for they are 'spirit and life' (John 6:63).

12 MAR SAT

1st Week of Lent
Violet

Deuteronomy 26:16-19

Moses said to the people: 'The Lord your God today commands you to observe these laws and customs; you must keep and observe them with all your heart and with all your soul.

'You have today made this declaration about the Lord; that he will be your God, but only if you follow his ways, keep his statutes, his commandments, his ordinances, and listen to his voice. And the Lord has today made this declaration about you: that you will be his very own people as he promised you, but only if you keep all his commandments; then for praise and renown and honour he will set you high above all the nations he has made, and you will be a people consecrated to the Lord, as he promised.'

Psalm 118:1-2, 4-5, 7-8. R. v. 1

They are happy who follow God's law!

Matthew 5:43-48

Jesus said to his disciples: 'You have learnt how it was said: You must love your neighbour and hate your enemy. But I say this to you: love your enemies and pray for those who persecute you; in this way you will be sons of your Father in heaven, for he causes his sun to rise on bad men as well as good, and his rain to fall on honest and dishonest men alike. For if you love those who love you, what right have you to claim any credit? Even the tax collectors do as much, do they not? And if you save your greetings for your brothers, are you doing anything exceptional? Even the pagans do as much, do they not? You must therefore be perfect just as your heavenly Father is perfect.'

Reflection

Scripture scholars refer to the 'hard sayings' of Jesus – aspects of his teaching which may, at first glance, seem unduly demanding, even unreasonable, to his would-be disciples. In today's Gospel reading we meet one such saying: 'Love your enemies and pray for those who persecute you.' This is the lesson that Jesus taught a rich young man who claimed to live by the commandment, 'You must love … your neighbour as yourself' (Luke 10:27). By means of a parable concerning a traveller who was robbed en route to Jericho, Jesus pointed out that even enemies of the Jewish people, like the Samaritan who tended the man set upon by robbers, were included in the concept of 'neighbour'. Though authentic love worthy of a Christian does not necessarily require emotional attachment, it is all-inclusive and unconditional – without strings attached and not presuming on a positive response of benefit for oneself. This is the love that great saints embodied and of which Jesus himself is the prime exemplar.

13
MAR SUN

SECOND SUNDAY OF LENT

Psalter Week 2

Violet

Genesis 15:5-12, 17-18

Taking Abram outside the Lord said, 'Look up to heaven and count the stars if you can. Such will be your descendants' he told him. Abram put his faith in the Lord, who counted this as making him justified.

'I am the Lord' he said to him 'who brought you out of Ur of the Chaldaeans to make you heir to this land.' 'My Lord, the Lord' Abram replied 'how am I to know that I shall inherit it?' He said to him, 'Get me a three-year-old heifer, a three-year-old goat, a three-year-old ram, a turtledove and a young pigeon.' He brought him all these, cut them in half and put half on one side and half facing it on the other; but the birds he did not cut in half. Birds of prey came down on the carcasses but Abram drove them off.

Now as the sun was setting Abram fell into a deep sleep, and terror seized him. When the sun had set and darkness had fallen, there appeared a smoking furnace and a firebrand that went between the halves. That day the Lord made a Covenant with Abram in these terms:

> 'To your descendants I give this land,
> from the wadi of Egypt to the Great River.'

Psalm 26:1, 7-9, 13-14. R. v. 1

The Lord is my light and my help.

Philippians 3:17–4:1 *(Shorter form 3:20–4:1)*

My brothers, be united in following my rule of life. Take as your models everybody who is already doing this and study them as you used to study us. I have told you often, and I repeat it today with tears, there are many who are behaving as the enemies of the cross of Christ. They are destined to be lost. They make foods into their god and they are proudest of something they ought to think shameful; the things they think important are earthly things. For us, our homeland is in heaven, and from heaven comes the saviour we are waiting for, the Lord Jesus Christ, and he will transfigure these wretched bodies of ours into copies of his glorious body. He will do that by the same power with which he can subdue the whole universe.

So then, my brothers and dear friends, do not give way but remain faithful in the Lord. I miss you very much, dear friends; you are my joy and my crown.

Luke 9:28-36

Jesus took with him Peter and John and James and went up the mountain to pray. As he prayed, the aspect of his face was changed and his clothing became brilliant as lightning. Suddenly there were two men there talking to him; they were Moses and Elijah appearing in glory, and they were speaking of his passing which he was to accomplish in

Jerusalem. Peter and his companions were heavy with sleep, but they kept awake and saw his glory and the two men standing with him. As these were leaving him, Peter said to Jesus, 'Master, it is wonderful for us to be here; so let us make three tents, one for you, one for Moses and one for Elijah.' – He did not know what he was saying. As he spoke, a cloud came and covered them with shadow; and when they went into the cloud the disciples were afraid. And a voice came from the cloud saying, 'This is my Son, the Chosen One. Listen to him'. And after the voice had spoken, Jesus was found alone. The disciples kept silence and, at that time, told no one what they had seen.

Reflection

The observation of the English mystic poet, William Blake, that 'great things happen when men and mountains meet' is true of such pivotal incidents in the Hebrew and Christian Scriptures as Moses' reception of the Ten Commandments on Mt Sinai (Exodus 19:16-25; 20:1-21) and the transfiguration of Jesus 'on the mountain' (often associated with Mount Tabor). Scripture scholars point to several parallels that may be drawn between these two events. In the latter instance, as recorded in all three Synoptic Gospels and now included in the luminous mysteries of the rosary by St John Paul II, Jesus is revealed as the long-awaited Messiah. Accompanied by representatives of the Law and the Prophets (Moses and Elijah), he is transfigured in the presence of Peter, James and John – the three apostles who later are witnesses to his agony in the garden (Matthew 26:36-46). Jesus' human bodiliness becomes the vehicle through which his inner reality as God-Man shines forth. Surely, this was a source of hope to his disciples after Jesus' prediction of his death by crucifixion had become a reality. Alluding to this event Peter wrote: 'We had seen his majesty for ourselves ... when we were with him on the holy mountain' (2 Peter 1:16-18).

14
MAR MON

2nd Week of Lent
Violet

Daniel 9:4-10

O Lord, God great and to be feared, you keep the covenant and have kindness for those who love you and keep your commandments: we have sinned, we have done wrong, we have acted wickedly, we have betrayed your commandments and your ordinances and turned away from them. We have not listened to your servants the prophets, who spoke in your name to our kings, our princes, our ancestors, and to all the people of the land. Integrity, Lord, is yours; ours the look of shame we wear today, we, the people of Judah, the citizens of Jerusalem, the whole of Israel, near and far away, in every country to which you have dispersed us because of the treason we have committed against you. To us, Lord, the look of shame belongs, to our kings, our princes, our ancestors, because we have sinned against you. To the Lord our God mercy and pardon belong, because we have betrayed him, and have not listened to the voice of the Lord our God nor followed the laws he has given us through his servants the prophets.

Psalm 78:8-9, 11, 13. R. Psalm 102:10

Do not treat us according to our sins, O Lord.

Luke 6:36-38

Jesus said to his disciples: 'Be compassionate as your Father is compassionate. Do not judge, and you will not be judged yourselves; do not condemn, and you will not be condemned yourselves; grant pardon, and you will be pardoned. Give, and there will be gifts for you: a full measure, pressed down, shaken together, and running over, will be poured into your lap; because the amount you measure out is the amount you will be given back.'

Reflection

The New Testament has much to say to and about people who are judgemental. This is not to claim that passing judgement on others is always unacceptable. There is a time and place for it as anyone who has done jury service will acknowledge. Jesus himself passes judgement on those whose behaviour is manifestly unjust and hypocritical. What is wrong is the disposition, widespread in our day, to be constantly passing negative judgement on others with scant regard for truth. This reveals itself in such ways as: being supercilious or condescending, looking down on people, racial stereotyping, seeing things always in black and white, having a strong instinct for punishment and blaming the victim. In such situations, 'in judging others you condemn yourself' (Romans 2:1). The Extraordinary Jubilee of Mercy proclaimed by Pope Francis has come and gone; but the imperative to be 'merciful, just as [our] heavenly Father is merciful' remains one of the fundamental principles of following Jesus authentically.

2nd Week of Lent
Violet

15
MAR TUE

Isaiah 1:10, 16-20

Hear the word of the Lord, you rulers of Sodom; listen to the command of our God, you people of Gomorrah. 'Wash, make yourselves clean. Take your wrong-doing out of my sight. Cease to do evil. Learn to do good, search for justice, help the oppressed, be just to the orphan, plead for the widow. Come now, let us talk this over, says the Lord. Though your sins are like scarlet, they shall be as white as snow; though they are red as crimson, they shall be like wool. If you are willing to obey, you shall eat the good things of the earth. But if you persist in rebellion, the sword shall eat you instead.' The mouth of the Lord has spoken.

Psalm 49:8-9, 16-17, 21, 23. R. v. 23

I will show God's salvation to the upright.

Matthew 23:1-12

Addressing the people and his disciples Jesus said, 'The scribes and the Pharisees occupy the chair of Moses. You must therefore do what they tell you and listen to what they say; but do not be guided by what they do, since they do not practise what they preach. They tie up heavy burdens and lay them on men's shoulders, but will they lift a finger to move them? Not they! Everything they do is done to attract attention, like wearing broader phylacteries and longer tassels, like wanting to take the place of honour at banquets and the front seats in the synagogues, being greeted obsequiously in the market squares and having people call them Rabbi.

'You, however, must not allow yourselves to be called Rabbi, since you have only one Master, and you are all brothers. You must call no one on earth your father, since you have only one Father, and he is in heaven. Nor must you allow yourselves to be called teachers, for you have only one Teacher, the Christ. The greatest among you must be your servant. Anyone who exalts himself will be humbled, and anyone who humbles himself will be exalted.'

Reflection

Leading by example, Pope Francis has strongly urged bishops, priests and all holding high office in the Church to give witness to gospel values. They are to avoid ostentation in the exercise of their pastoral ministries and to live lives characterised by humility. Followers of one who 'emptied himself to assume the condition of a slave' (Philippians 2:7), they should not seek worldly status, honour and prestige. As the Holy Father's words apply to all the faithful, we need to ask ourselves where we stand in this regard. True humility involves a clear understanding and a ready acceptance of where we stand (with all our talents and all our deficiencies) before God, the source of every good gift (James 1:17). Humility is, as Simone Weil, the French mystic, observed, not just a virtue but the condition of virtue. St Peter's advice is: 'Bow down, then, before the power of God now, and he will raise you up on the appointed day' (1 Peter 5:6).

16
MAR WED

2nd Week of Lent
Violet

Jeremiah 18:18-20

'Come on,' they said 'let us concoct a plot against Jeremiah; the priest will not run short of instruction without him, nor the sage of advice, nor the prophet of the word. Come on, let us hit at him with his own tongue; let us listen carefully to every word he says.'

Listen to me, Lord, hear what my adversaries are saying. Should evil be returned for good? For they are digging a pit for me. Remember how I stood in your presence to plead on their behalf, to turn your wrath away from them.

Psalm 30:5-6, 14-16. R. v. 17

Save me in your love, O Lord.

Matthew 20:17-28

Jesus was going up to Jerusalem, and on the way he took the Twelve to one side and said to them, 'Now we are going up to Jerusalem, and the Son of Man is about to be handed over to the chief priests and scribes. They will condemn him to death and will hand him over to the pagans to be mocked and scourged and crucified; and on the third day he will rise again.'

Then the mother of Zebedee's sons came with her sons to make a request of him, and bowed low; and he said to her, 'What is it you want?' She said to him, 'Promise that these two sons of mine may one sit at your right hand and the other at your left in your kingdom.' 'You do not know what you are asking, Jesus answered. 'Can you drink the cup that I am going to drink?' They replied, 'We can.' 'Very well,' he said 'you shall drink my cup, but as for seats at my right hand and my left, these are not mine to grant; they belong to those to whom they have been allotted by my Father.'

When the other ten heard this they were indignant with the two brothers. But Jesus called them to him and said, 'You know that among the pagans the rulers lord it over them, and their great men make their authority felt. This is not to happen among you. No; anyone who wants to be great among you must be your servant, and anyone who wants to be first among you must be your slave, just as the Son of Man came not to be served but to serve, and to give his life as a ransom for many.'

Reflection

Even when Jesus' followers had ears to hear, they frequently did not hear him aright. Once again in today's Gospel reading, Jesus takes advantage of an opportunity to fine tune his disciples' understanding of the nature of his mission. Two of them, James and John, through the intervention of their mother and to the chagrin of their companions, aspire to places of honour in his kingdom. Like Peter, who will later assert his willingness to die for Jesus (John 13:37), the sons of Zebedee presumptuously proclaim their willingness to share his cup of suffering. In response, Jesus insists that the highest places in his kingdom – a kingdom not of this world (John 18:36) – will be occupied by those who follow his example of other-centred loving service and who, like him, can say, 'Here am I among you as one who serves!' (Luke 22:27). A Christian church billboard in Brisbane offers this good advice to all its parishioners and to passers-by: *Enter to Worship. Leave to Serve.*

17
MAR THU

ST PATRICK, BISHOP, Solemnity – Ireland, see Appendix A-11

Jeremiah 1:4-9

(Please see the Appendix B-6)

Psalm 116. R. Mark 16:15

Go out to the whole world; proclaim the Good News.

Acts 13:46-49

Paul and Barnabas spoke out boldly to the Jews, 'We had to proclaim the word of God to you first, but since you have rejected it, since you do not think yourselves worthy of eternal life, we must turn to the pagans. For this is what the Lord commanded us to do when he said: "I have made you a light for the nations, so that my salvation may reach the ends of the earth." ' It made the pagans very happy to hear this and they thanked the Lord for his message: all who were destined for eternal life became believers. Thus the word of the Lord spread through the whole countryside.

Luke 10:1-12, 17-20

The Lord appointed seventy-two others and sent them out ahead of him, in pairs, to all the towns and places he himself was to visit. He said to them, 'The harvest is rich but the labourers are few, so ask the Lord of the harvest to send labourers to his harvest. Start off now, but remember, I am sending you out like lambs among wolves. Carry no purse, no haversack, no sandals. Salute no one on the road. Whatever house you go into, let your first words be, "Peace to this house!" And if a man of peace lives there, your peace will go and rest on him; if not, it will come back to you. Stay in the same house, taking what food and drink they have to offer, for the labourer deserves his wages; do not move from house to house. Whenever you go into a town where they make you welcome, eat what is set before you. Cure those in it who are sick, and say, "The kingdom of God is very near to you." But whenever you enter a town and they do not make you welcome, go out into its streets and say, "We wipe the very dust of your town that clings to our feet, and leave it with you. Yet be sure of this: the kingdom of God is very near." I tell you, on that day it will not go as hard with Sodom as with that town.' The seventy-two came back rejoicing. 'Lord,' they said, 'even the devils submit to us when we use your name.' He said to them, 'I watched Satan fall like lightning from heaven. Yes, I have given you power to tread underfoot serpents and scorpions and the whole strength of the enemy; nothing shall ever hurt you. Yet do not rejoice that the spirits submit to you; rejoice rather that your names are written in heaven.'

Reflection

When, having escaped from slavery, Patrick returned to Ireland in AD 432, he did so as a man on a mission. Setting aside all the questionable folklore that has embellished the story of his life, we remember him mainly as one of the greatest missionaries in the history of the Church. With this in mind, we can see why today's Gospel reading is so appropriate for the annual celebration of his feast. It should serve to remind us that Christ's Church (read 'this congregation') has a mission or, as the Swiss theologian Wahlbert Bühlmann puts it, Christ's mission has a Church. In this spirit, let us hear Jesus' words to the seventy disciples, taken to heart by Patrick so long ago, as addressed to us today. Every Christian is called to mission in Jesus' name. 'I sense that the moment has come,' said Pope St John Paul II, 'to commit all the Church's energies to a new evangelisation' *(Redemptoris Missio #3)*.

18
MAR FRI

2nd Week of Lent | Violet
or **St Cyril of Jerusalem,** *doctor* (Commemoration)

Genesis 37:3-4, 12-13, 17-28
(Please see the Appendix B-6)

Psalm 104:16-21. R. v. 5
Remember the wonders the Lord has done.

Matthew 21:33-43, 45-46
Jesus said to the chief priests and the elders of the people: 'Listen to another parable. There was a man, a landowner, who planted a vineyard; he fenced it round, dug a winepress in it and built a tower; then he leased it to tenants and went abroad. When vintage time drew near he sent his servants to the tenants to collect his produce. But the tenants seized his servants, thrashed one, killed another and stoned a third. Next he sent some more servants, this time a larger number, and they dealt with them in the same way. Finally he sent his son to them. "They will respect my son," he said. But when the tenants saw the son, they said to each other, "This is the heir. Come on, let us kill him and take over his inheritance." So they seized him and threw him out of the vineyard and killed him. Now when the owner of the vineyard comes, what will he do to those tenants?' They answered, 'He will bring those wretches to a wretched end and lease the vineyard to other tenants who will deliver the produce to him when the season arrives.' Jesus said to them, 'Have you never read in the scriptures: It was the stone rejected by the builders that became the keystone. This was the Lord's doing and it is wonderful to see?

'I tell you, then, that the kingdom of God will be taken from you and given to a people who will produce its fruit.'

When they heard his parables, the chief priests and the scribes realised he was speaking about them, but though they would have liked to arrest him they were afraid of the crowds, who looked on him as a prophet.

Reflection
The Hebrew Scriptures speak of the Chosen People as a vineyard planted and lovingly tended by God (Isaiah 5; Psalm 80). With this in mind, we can read Matthew's parable as an allegory. God is the landowner and the vineyard (his people) is his cherished possession. However, God's sole proprietorship is challenged by murderous tenants (the religious leaders of Jesus' day) who kill his messengers (the prophets) and eventually the Son of God (Jesus himself). The harvest that God expected is denied him. The tragic conclusion is summed up in these words: 'The kingdom of God will be taken from you and given to a people who will produce its fruit' (Matthew 21:43). Matthew's audience would have interpreted this judgement in the light of the destruction of Jerusalem in AD 70. We listen attentively as Jesus says to us, 'I am the vine, you are the branches … It is to the glory of my Father that you should bear much fruit' (John 15:5, 8).

19
MAR SAT

ST JOSEPH, SPOUSE OF THE BLESSED VIRGIN MARY, Solemnity

White

2 Samuel 7:4-5, 12-14, 16

The word of the Lord came to Nathan: 'Go and tell my servant David, "Thus the Lord speaks: When your days are ended and you are laid to rest with your ancestors, I will preserve the offspring of your body after you and make his sovereignty secure. (It is he who shall build a house for my name, and I will make his royal throne secure for ever.) I will be a father to him and he a son to me. Your House and your sovereignty will always stand secure before me and your throne be established for ever." '

Psalm 88:2-5, 27, 29. R. v. 37

His dynasty shall last for ever.

Romans 4:13, 16-18, 22

The promise of inheriting the world was not made to Abraham and his descendants on account of any law but on account of the righteousness which consists in faith. That is why what fulfils the promise depends on faith, so that it may be a free gift and be available to all of Abraham's descendants, not only those who belong to the Law but also those who belong to the faith of Abraham who is the Father of all of us. As scripture says: I have made you the ancestor of many nations – Abraham is our father in the eyes of God, in whom he put his faith, and who brings the dead to life and calls into being what does not exist. Though it seemed Abraham's hope could not be fulfilled, he hoped and he believed, and through doing so he did become the father of many nations exactly as he had been promised: Your descendants will be as many as the stars. This is the faith that was 'considered as justifying him'.

Matthew 1:16, 18-21, 24 *(Alternative Gospel: Luke 2:41-51)*

Jacob was the father of Joseph the husband of Mary; of her was born Jesus who is called Christ. This is how Jesus Christ came to be born. His mother Mary was betrothed to Joseph; but before they came to live together she was found to be with child through the Holy Spirit. Her husband Joseph, being a man of honour and wanting to spare her publicity, decided to divorce her informally. He had made up his mind to do this when the angel of the Lord appeared to him in a dream and said, 'Joseph son of David, do not be afraid to take Mary home as your wife, because she has conceived what is in her by the Holy Spirit. She will give birth to a son and you must name him Jesus, because he is the one who is to save his people from their sins.' When Joseph woke up he did what the angel of the Lord had told him to do.

Reflection

It is sometimes stated that Joseph, the husband of Mary, played but a minor role in the life of Jesus. However, in his apostolic exhortation, *Redemptoris Custos* (1989), Pope St John Paul II identified and drew our attention to eight key moments in Jesus' life in which Joseph was the protagonist: the census, the circumcision, the birth and naming of Jesus and his presentation in the Temple, the Holy Family's fight into Egypt (and later return) in response to dreams, the loss and finding of Jesus in the Temple, and the paternal support and education he gave to his son in Nazareth. In a homily delivered at Casa Santa Marta on 19 March 2020 Pope Francis said that there are three important lessons that we can learn from Joseph: how to walk in darkness, how to listen to the voice of God and how to go forward in silence. We remember Joseph as 'a man of honour' (Matthew 1:19) – strong, chaste, prudent, obedient and faithful.

20
MAR SUN

THIRD SUNDAY OF LENT

Psalter Week 3

Violet

Exodus 3:1-8, 13-15

Moses was looking after the flock of Jethro, his father-in-law, priest of Midian. He led his flock to the far side of the wilderness and came to Horeb, the mountain of God. There the angel of the Lord appeared to him in the shape of a flame of fire, coming from the middle of a bush. Moses looked; there was the bush blazing but it was not being burnt up. 'I must go and look at this strange sight,' Moses said 'and see why the bush is not burnt.' Now the Lord saw him go forward to look, and God called to him from the middle of the bush. 'Moses, Moses!' he said. 'Here I am' he answered. 'Come no nearer' he said. 'Take off your shoes, for the place on which you stand is holy ground. I am the God of your father,' he said 'the God of Abraham, the God of Isaac and the God of Jacob.' At this Moses covered his face, afraid to look at God.

And the Lord said, 'I have seen the miserable state of my people in Egypt. I have heard their appeal to be free of their slave-drivers. Yes, I am well aware of their sufferings. I mean to deliver them out of the hands of the Egyptians and bring them up out of that land to a land rich and broad, a land where milk and honey flow.'

Then Moses said to God, 'I am to go, then, to the sons of Israel and say to them, "The God of your fathers has sent me to you." But if they ask me what his name is, what am I to tell them?' And God said to Moses, 'I Am who I Am. This' he added 'is what you must say to the sons of Israel: "The Lord, the God of your fathers, the God of Abraham, the God of Isaac, and the God of Jacob, has sent me to you." This is my name for all time; by this name I shall be invoked for all generations to come.'

Psalm 102:1-4, 6-8, 11. R. v. 8

The Lord is compassion and love.

1 Corinthians 10:1-6, 10-12

I want to remind you, brothers, how our fathers were all guided by a cloud above them and how they all passed through the sea. They were all baptised into Moses in this cloud and in this sea; all ate the same spiritual food and all drank the same spiritual drink, since they all drank from the spiritual rock that followed them as they went, and that rock was Christ. In spite of this, most of them failed to please God and their corpses littered the desert.

These things all happened as warnings for us, not to have the wicked lusts for forbidden things that they had. You must never complain: some of them did, and they were killed by the Destroyer. All this happened to them as a warning and it was written down to be a lesson for us who are living at the end of the age. The man who thinks he is safe must be careful that he does not fall.

Luke 13:1-9

Some people arrived and told Jesus about the Galileans whose blood Pilate had mingled with that of their sacrifices. At this he said to them, 'Do you suppose these Galileans who suffered like that were greater sinners than any other Galileans? They were not, I tell you. No; but unless you repent you will all perish as they did. Or those eighteen on whom the tower at Siloam fell and killed them? Do you suppose that they were more guilty than all the other people living in Jerusalem? They were not, I tell you. No; but unless you repent you will all perish as they did.'

He told this parable: 'A man had a fig tree planted in his vineyard and he came looking for fruit on it but found none. He said to the man who looked after the vineyard, "Look here, for three years now I have been coming to look for fruit on this fig tree and finding none. Cut it down: why should it be taking up the ground?" "Sir," the man replied "leave it one more year and give me time to dig round it and manure it: it may bear fruit next year; if not, then you can cut it down."'

Reflection

Good teachers draw on the life experience of their pupils. If they can do so by means of storytelling, the attention of their listeners will be ensured and the later recall of the lesson by them will be facilitated. In these terms Jesus was a master teacher. It was said of him, with some exaggeration, that 'he would never speak to [the crowds] except in parables' (Matthew 13:34). When Jesus related today's parable to the people (it is introduced by a call to repentance), he and his hearers were on common ground. Both were familiar with fig trees, the harvesting of their fruits and perhaps some of the more than forty references to them in their Sacred Scriptures. Such trees were of little more than decorative value if they were unproductive. Jesus has something similar to say to us, who claim to be his disciples, if, having heard his teaching, we do not put it into practice. To the gathered disciples at the Last Supper he said: 'You did not choose me, no, I chose you and I commissioned you to go out and bear fruit, fruit that will last' (John 15:16). At leisure, you might read the whole of John 15. It is an apt Lenten reading.

21
MAR MON

3rd Week of Lent
Violet

2 Kings 5:1-15

Naaman, army commander to the king of Aram, was a man who enjoyed his master's respect and favour, since through him the Lord had granted victory to the Aramaeans. But the man was a leper. Now on one of their raids, the Aramaeans had carried off from the land of Israel a little girl who had become a servant of Naaman's wife. She said to her mistress, 'If only my master would approach the prophet of Samaria. He would cure him of his leprosy.' Naaman went and told his master. 'This and this' he reported 'is what the girl from the land of Israel said.' 'Go by all means,' said the king of Aram 'I will send a letter to the king of Israel.' So Naaman left, taking with him ten talents of silver, six thousand shekels of gold and ten festal robes. He presented the letter to the king of Israel. It read: 'With this letter, I am sending my servant Naaman to you for you to cure him of his leprosy.' When the king of Israel read the letter, he tore his garments. … *(Please see the Appendix B-7)*

Psalm 41:2-3; 42:3-4. R. Psalm 41:3

My soul is thirsting for God, the God of my life: when can I enter and see the face of God?

Luke 4:24-30

Jesus came to Nazara and spoke to the people in the synagogue: 'I tell you solemnly, no prophet is ever accepted in his own country.

'There were many widows in Israel, I can assure you, in Elijah's day, when heaven remained shut for three years and six months and a great famine raged throughout the land, but Elijah was not sent to any one of these: he was sent to a widow at Zarephath, a Sidonian town. And in the prophet Elisha's time there were many lepers in Israel, but none of these was cured, except the Syrian, Naaman.'

When they heard this everyone in the synagogue was enraged. They sprang to their feet and hustled him out of the town; and they took him up to the brow of the hill their town was built on, intending to throw him down the cliff, but he slipped through the crowd and walked away.

Reflection

Like the prophets of old, Jesus was a radical critic of the conventional wisdom that shaped the social structures of his contemporaries. With the power of the Spirit in him he taught in the synagogues of Galilee where 'everyone praised him' (Luke: 4-15) – that is, until he was invited to read on a Sabbath day in the synagogue in Nazareth, his home village. Initially, his commentary on the prescribed reading from Isaiah won the approval and admiration of his hearers. However, their attitude changed when he pointed to the fact that, historically, the ministry of prophets like Elijah and Elisha sometimes favoured those who did not belong to the Chosen People. The violent reaction of Jesus' townspeople demonstrates the truth of his statement that 'no prophet is ever accepted in his own country'. This has been the experience of prophetic people in the Church in our own day. As one of them, Leonardo Boff, observed: 'No prophet ever died in his bed.'

22
MAR TUE

3rd Week of Lent
Violet

Daniel 3:25, 34-43
(Please see the Appendix B-7)

Psalm 24:4-9. R. v. 6
Remember your mercy, Lord.

Matthew 18:21-35
Peter went up to Jesus and said, 'Lord, how often must I forgive my brother if he wrongs me? As often as seven times?' Jesus answered, 'Not seven, I tell you, but seventy-seven times.

'And so the kingdom of heaven may be compared to a king who decided to settle his accounts with his servants. When the reckoning began, they brought him a man who owed ten thousand talents; but he had no means of paying, so his master gave orders that he should be sold, together with his wife and children and all his possessions, to meet the debt. At this, the servant threw himself down at his master's feet. "Give me time," he said "and I will pay the whole sum." And the servant's master felt so sorry for him that he let him go and cancelled the debt. Now as this servant went out, he happened to meet a fellow servant who owed him one hundred denarii; and he seized him by the throat and began to throttle him. "Pay what you owe me," he said. His fellow servant fell at his feet and implored him, saying, "Give me time and I will pay you." But the other would not agree; on the contrary, he had him thrown into prison till he should pay the debt. His fellow servants were deeply distressed when they saw what had happened, and they went to their master and reported the whole affair to him. Then the master sent for him. "You wicked servant," he said "I cancelled all that debt of yours when you appealed to me. Were you not bound, then, to have pity on your fellow servant just as I had pity on you?" And in his anger the master handed him over to the torturers till he should pay all his debt. And that is how my heavenly Father will deal with you unless you each forgive your brother from your heart.'

Reflection
The story is told (doubtless apocryphal) about an English village that despised a neighbouring village because, in 1069, it had failed to share with them news of the imminent invasion of marauding Danes. Such unwillingness to forgive is highlighted in Jesus' parable in the Gospel reading. Sadly, we find it today in personal relationships, perhaps in our own lives. With good reason we may sometimes judge the conduct of others towards us in such negative terms as: unconscionable, contemptible and deplorable. However, following the teaching of Jesus, there is one word that we may not apply to it – unforgiveable. That Jesus is our exemplar in this matter is clearly demonstrated in his enduring love of Peter who betrayed him and in his cry on the cross, 'Father, forgive them; they do not know what they are doing' (Luke 23:34; see too Acts 7:60 – Stephen). For Christians forgiveness is a way of life. Joy and peace cannot dwell in an unforgiving heart.

23
MAR WED

3rd Week of Lent | Violet
or **St Turibius of Mogrovejo,** *bishop* (Commemoration)

Deuteronomy 4:1, 5-9

Moses said to the people: 'And now, Israel, take notice of the laws and customs that I teach you today, and observe them, that you may have life and may enter and take possession of the land that the Lord the God of your fathers is giving you. See, as the Lord my God has commanded me, I teach you the laws and customs that you are to observe in the land you are to enter and make your own. Keep them, observe them, and they will demonstrate to the peoples your wisdom and understanding. When they come to know of all these laws they will exclaim, "No other people is as wise and prudent as this great nation." And indeed, what great nation is there that has its gods so near as the Lord our God is to us whenever we call to him? And what great nation is there that has laws and customs to match this whole Law that I put before you today?

'But take care what you do and be on your guard. Do not forget the things your eyes have seen, nor let them slip from your heart all the days of your life; rather, tell them to your children and to your children's children.'

Psalm 147:12-13, 15-16, 19-20. R. v. 12

O praise the Lord, Jerusalem.

Matthew 5:17-19

Jesus said to his disciples: 'Do not imagine that I have come to abolish the Law or the Prophets. I have come not to abolish but to complete them. I tell you solemnly, till heaven and earth disappear, not one dot, not one little stroke, shall disappear from the Law until its purpose is achieved. Therefore, the man who infringes even one of the least of these commandments and teaches others to do the same will be considered the least in the kingdom of heaven; but the man who keeps them and teaches them will be considered great in the kingdom of heaven.'

Reflection

In today's first reading Moses, at God's command, exhorts the people to observe, with wisdom and understanding, the laws and customs he teaches them. They must make them their own so that they may have life and receive God's blessings. This is the Law which Jesus himself observed – a Law he came 'not to abolish, but to complete'. Paul reminds us of this when he says to the Galatians: 'When the appointed time came, God sent his Son, born of a woman, born a subject of the Law, to redeem the subjects of the Law, and to enable us to be adopted as sons [and daughters]' (Galatians 4:4-5). In completing the Law, while respecting its spirit, Jesus rejected some of the burdensome literal interpretations of the scribes and Pharisees. In his Last Supper discourse, he said to his disciples (and says to us): 'I give you a new commandment: love one another; just as I have loved you, you must love one another' (John 13:34).

3rd Week of Lent
Violet

24
MAR THU

Jeremiah 7:23-28

These were my orders: Listen to my voice, then I will be your God and you shall be my people. Follow right to the end the way that I mark out for you, and you will prosper. But they did not listen, they did not pay attention; they followed the dictates of their own evil hearts, refused to face me, and turned their backs on me. From the day your ancestors came out of the land of Egypt until today, day after day I have persistently sent you all my servants the prophets. But they have not listened to me, have not paid attention; they have grown stubborn and behaved worse than their ancestors. You may say all these words to them: they will not listen to you; you may call them: they will not answer. So tell them this, 'Here is the nation that will not listen to the voice of the Lord its God nor take correction. Sincerity is no more, it has vanished from their mouths.'

Psalm 94:1-2. 6-9. R. v. 8

O that today you would listen to his voice! 'Harden not your hearts.'

Luke 11:14-23

Jesus was casting out a devil and it was dumb; but when the devil had gone out the dumb man spoke, and the people were amazed. But some of them said, 'It is through Beelzebul, the prince of devils, that he casts out devils.' Others asked him, as a test, for a sign from heaven; but, knowing what they were thinking, he said to them, 'Every kingdom divided against itself is heading for ruin, and a household divided against itself collapses. So too with Satan: if he is divided against himself, how can his kingdom stand? – since you assert that it is through Beelzebul that I cast out devils. Now if it is through Beelzebul that I cast out devils, through whom do your own experts cast them out? Let them be your judges, then. But if it is through the finger of God that I cast out devils, then know that the kingdom of God has overtaken you. So long as a strong man fully armed guards his own palace, his goods are undisturbed; but when someone stronger than he is attacks and defeats him, the stronger man takes away all the weapons he relied on and shares out his spoil. He who is not with me is against me; and he who does not gather with me scatters.'

Reflection

Matthew, Mark and Luke speak of Jesus' miracles as deeds of power (*dunameis*). John, who relates seven of them, describes them as signs (*semeia*). In today's Gospel reading Jesus frees a man from the demon of dumbness. Amazing as this is for many of the bystanders, it is not sign enough for some of them. They demand something more convincing – divine intervention, 'a sign from heaven' that alone can authenticate Jesus' mission. As he often does in his confrontations with the scribes and Pharisees, Jesus exposes the contradiction implicit in their stance. They are like those people of whom Abraham says in the parable of the rich man and Lazarus, 'They will not be convinced even if someone should rise from the dead' (Luke 16:31). Among our contemporaries there are people who seek in matters religious a degree of certitude that will make faith not only easy but unnecessary. 'Lord, I do have faith. Help the little faith I have!' (Mark 9:24).

25
MAR FRI

THE ANNUNCIATION OF THE LORD, Solemnity

White

Isaiah 7:10-14; 8:10

(Please see the Appendix B-8)

Psalm 39:7-11 R. vv. 8, 9

Here I am, Lord! I come to do your will.

Hebrews 10:4-10

Bulls' blood and goats' blood are useless for taking away sins, and this is what Christ said, on coming into the world: You who wanted no sacrifice or oblation, prepared a body for me. You took no pleasure in holocausts or sacrifices for sin; then I said, just as I was commanded in the scroll of the book, 'God, here I am! I am coming to obey your will.' Notice that he says first: You did not want what the Law lays down as the things to be offered, that is: the sacrifices, the oblations, the holocausts and the sacrifices for sin, and you took no pleasure in them; and then he says: Here I am! I am coming to obey your will. He is abolishing the first sort to replace it with the second. And this will was for us to be made holy by the offering of his body made once and for all by Jesus Christ.

Luke 1:26-38

The angel Gabriel was sent by God to a town in Galilee called Nazareth, to a virgin betrothed to a man named Joseph, of the House of David; and the virgin's name was Mary. He went in and said to her, 'Rejoice, so highly favoured! The Lord is with you.' She was deeply disturbed by these words and asked herself what this greeting could mean, but the angel said to her, 'Mary, do not be afraid; you have won God's favour. Listen! You are to conceive and bear a son, and you must name him Jesus. He will be great and will be called Son of the Most High. The Lord God will give him the throne of his ancestor David; he will rule over the House of Jacob for ever and his reign will have no end.' Mary said to the angel, 'But how can this come about, since I am a virgin?' 'The Holy Spirit will come upon you' the angel answered 'and the power of the Most High will cover you with its shadow. And so the child will be holy and will be called Son of God. Know this too: your kinswoman Elizabeth has, in her old age, herself conceived a son, and she whom people called barren is now in her sixth month, for nothing is impossible to God.' 'I am the handmaid of the Lord,' said Mary, 'let what you have said be done to me.' And the angel left her.

Reflection

In a homily given on today's feast in 2020 in the chapel of the Casa Santa Marta, Pope Francis acknowledged the difficulty of preaching about the Lucan account of the Annunciation. According to the Holy Father, it 'tells us the decisive moment in history, the most revolutionary. It is a turbulent situation, everything changes, history turns upside down … God enters history and does so in his original style: a surprise. The God of surprises surprises us (again).' Though today is not a Sunday, the Creed is said and the rubrics call on us to bow when we say the words 'and by the Holy Spirit was incarnate of the Virgin Mary, and became man'. The psalm response, 'Here I am Lord; I come to do your will,' is a prayer we should make our own. It has its echo in Mary's 'I am the handmaid of the Lord, let what you have said be done to me' (Luke 1:38).

3rd Week of Lent
Violet

Hosea 5:15–6:6

The Lord says this: They will search for me in their misery: 'Come, let us return to the Lord. He has torn us to pieces, but he will heal us; he has struck us down, but he will bandage our wounds; after a day or two he will bring us back to life, on the third day he will raise us and we shall live in his presence. Let us set ourselves to know the Lord; that he will come is as certain as the dawn, he will come to us as showers come, like spring rains watering the earth.' What am I to do with you, Ephraim? What am I to do with you, Judah? This love of yours is like a morning cloud, like the dew that quickly disappears. This is why I have torn them to pieces by the prophets, why I slaughtered them with the words from my mouth, his judgement will rise like the light, since what I want is love, not sacrifice; knowledge of God, not holocausts.

Psalm 50:3-4, 18-21. R. cf. Hosea 6:6

What I want is love, not sacrifice.

Luke 18:9-14

Jesus spoke the following parable to some people who prided themselves on being virtuous and despised everyone else: 'Two men went up to the Temple to pray, one a Pharisee, the other a tax collector. The Pharisee stood there and said this prayer to himself, "I thank you, God, that I am not grasping, unjust, adulterous like the rest of mankind, and particularly that I am not like this tax collector here. I fast twice a week; I pay tithes on all I get." The tax collector stood some distance away, not daring even to raise his eyes to heaven; but he beat his breast and said, "God, be merciful to me, a sinner." This man, I tell you, went home again at rights with God; the other did not. For everyone who exalts himself will be humbled, but the man who humbles himself will be exalted.'

Reflection

Richard Crashaw (1613-49), a Cambridge don who lost his position when he converted from Anglicism to Catholicism during the English Civil War, wrote a delightful poem about the parable of 'The Righteous Pharisee and the Penitent Publican': *Two went to pray? Oh, rather say / One went to brag, the other to pray; / One stands up close and treads on high / Where the other dares not send his eye; / One nearer to God's altar trod, / The other to the altar's God.* Jesus addressed this parable 'to some people who prided themselves on being virtuous and despised everyone else' (Luke 18:9). The question we need to ask ourselves is: 'Are we of their number today?' Peter and the other disciples learned this lesson well. Reiterating Jesus' teaching, he had this to say to the early Christians in his first letter: 'Wrap yourselves in humility to be servants of each other, because God refuses the proud and will always favour the humble' (1 Peter 5:5; see also Luke 1:52; Proverbs 3:34; James 4:6).

FOURTH SUNDAY OF LENT

Psalter Week 4

Violet

Joshua 5:9-12

The Lord said to Joshua, 'Today I have taken the shame of Egypt away from you.'

The Israelites pitched their camp at Gilgal and kept the Passover there on the fourteenth day of the month, at evening in the plain of Jericho. On the morrow of the Passover they tasted the produce of that country, unleavened bread and roasted ears of corn, that same day. From that time, from their first eating of the produce of that country, the manna stopped falling. And having manna no longer, the Israelites fed from that year onwards on what the land of Canaan yielded.

Psalm 33:2-7. R. v. 9

Taste and see that the Lord is good.

2 Corinthians 5:17-21

For anyone who is in Christ, there is a new creation; the old creation has gone, and now the new one is here. It is all God's work. It was God who reconciled us to himself through Christ and gave us the work of handing on his reconciliation. In other words, God in Christ was reconciling the world to himself, not holding men's faults against them, and he has entrusted to us the news that they are reconciled. So we are ambassadors for Christ; it is as though God were appealing through us, and the appeal that we make in Christ's name is: be reconciled to God. For our sake God made the sinless one into sin, so that in him we might become the goodness of God.

Luke 15:1-3, 11-32

The tax collectors and the sinners were all seeking the company of Jesus to hear what he had to say, and the Pharisees and the scribes complained. 'This man' they said 'welcomes sinners and eats with them.' So he spoke this parable to them:

'A man had two sons. The younger said to his father, "Father, let me have the share of the estate that would come to me." So the father divided the property between them. A few days later, the younger son got together everything he had and left for a distant country where he squandered his money on a life of debauchery.

'When he had spent it all, that country experienced a severe famine, and now he began to feel the pinch, so he hired himself out to one of the local inhabitants who put him on his farm to feed the pigs. And he would willingly have filled his belly with the husks the pigs were eating but no one offered him anything. Then he came to his senses and said, "How many of my father's paid servants have more food than they want, and here am I dying of hunger! I will leave this place and go to my father and say: Father, I have sinned against heaven and against you; I no longer deserve to be called your son; treat me as one of your paid servants." So he left the place and went back to his father.

'While he was still a long way off, his father saw him and was moved with pity. He ran to the boy, clasped him in his arms and kissed him tenderly. Then his son said, "Father, I have sinned against heaven and against you. I no longer deserve to be called your Son." But the father said to his servants, "Quick! Bring out the best robe and put it on him; put a ring on his finger and sandals on his feet. Bring the calf we have been fattening, and kill it; we are going to have a feast, a celebration, because this son of mine was dead and has come back to life; he was lost and is found." And they began to celebrate.

'Now the elder son was out in the fields, and on his way back, as he drew near the house, he could hear music and dancing. Calling one of the servants he asked what it was all about. "Your brother has come" replied the servant "and your father has killed the calf we had fattened because he has got him back safe and sound." He was angry then and refused to go in, and his father came out to plead with him; but he answered his father, "Look, all these years I have slaved for you and never once disobeyed your orders, yet you never offered me so much as a kid for me to celebrate with my friends. But for this son of yours, when he comes back after swallowing up your property – he and his women – you kill the calf we had been fattening."

'The father said, "My son, you are with me always and all I have is yours. But it is only right we should celebrate and rejoice, because your brother here was dead and has come to life; he was lost and is found." '

Reflection

According to Matthew, 'Jesus spoke to the crowd in parables; indeed he would never speak to them except in parables' (Matthew 13:34). We listen today to one of the most memorable of them. Responding to the accusation of the Pharisees and scribes that he welcomed and ate with sinners, Jesus told a story that could be variously entitled 'The Parable of the Prodigal Son' or 'The Parable of the Forgiving Father'. It is both challenging and reassuring to us – challenging if we have reason to see ourselves in the older brother and reassuring if, mindful of our sinfulness, we identify with his erstwhile wayward but repentant sibling. Their father receives his younger son with great love and compassion, rejoicing that he 'was lost and is found'. With reference to this parable St John Paul II wrote: '[God's love] is able to reach down to every prodigal son, to every human misery and above all to every form of moral misery, to sin. When this happens, the person who is the object of mercy does not feel humiliated, but rather found again and "restored to value"' *(Dives in Misericordia #6)*. Is there anyone whom, like the older brother, I have yet to forgive? A good Lenten question!

28
MAR MON

4th Week of Lent
Violet

Isaiah 65:17-21

Thus says the Lord: Now I create new heavens and a new earth, and the past will not be remembered, and will come no more to men's minds. Be glad and rejoice for ever and ever for what I am creating, because I now create Jerusalem 'Joy' and her people 'Gladness'. I shall rejoice over Jerusalem and exult in my people. No more will the sound of weeping or the sound of cries be heard in her; in her, no more will be found the infant living a few days only, or the old man not living to the end of his days. To die at the age of a hundred will be dying young; not to live to be a hundred will be the sign of a curse. They will build houses and inhabit them, plant vineyards and eat their fruit.

Psalm 29:2, 4-6, 11-13. R. v. 2

I will praise you, Lord, you have rescued me.

John 4:43-54

Jesus left Samaria for Galilee. He himself had declared that there is no respect for a prophet in his own country, but on his arrival the Galileans received him well, having seen all that he had done at Jerusalem during the festival which they too had attended.

He went again to Cana in Galilee, where he had changed the water into wine. Now there was a court official there whose son was ill at Capernaum and, hearing that Jesus had arrived in Galilee from Judaea, he went and asked him to come and cure his son as he was at the point of death. Jesus said, 'So you will not believe unless you see signs and portents!' 'Sir,' answered the official 'come down before my child dies.' 'Go home,' said Jesus 'your son will live.' The man believed what Jesus had said and started on his way; and while he was still on the journey back his servants met him with the news that his boy was alive. He asked them when the boy had begun to recover. 'The fever left him yesterday' they said 'at the seventh hour.' The father realised that this was exactly the time when Jesus had said, 'Your son will live'; and he and all his household believed.

This was the second sign given by Jesus, on his return from Judaea to Galilee.

Reflection

The evangelist John relates seven miracles performed by Jesus during his public ministry. For preference he calls them 'signs' because, as well as being deeds of power, they point to or reveal some aspect of Jesus' saving mission. In informing his community why he has included them in his Gospel John observes: 'These [signs] are recorded so that you may believe that Jesus is the Christ, the Son of God, and that believing this you may have life through his name' (John 20:31) – a statement which is consistent with Jesus' claim: 'I have come so that they may have life and have it to the full' (John 10:10). When the royal official from Capernaum in today's Gospel reading heard that Jesus, in response to his humble plea, had cured his son, he read the sign and 'he and all his household believed' (John 4:53). Paul's advice is: 'If there is anything you need, pray for it, asking God for it with prayer and thanksgiving' (Philippians 4:6).

4th Week of Lent
Violet

29
MAR TUE

Ezekiel 47:1-9, 12

The angel brought me to the entrance of the Temple, where a stream came out from under the Temple threshold and flowed eastwards, since the Temple faced east. The water flowed from under the right side of the Temple, south of the altar. He took me out by the north gate and led me right round outside as far as the outer east gate where the water flowed out on the right-hand side. The man went to the east holding his measuring line and measured off a thousand cubits; he then made me wade across the stream; the water reached my ankles. …*(Please see the Appendix B-8)*

Psalm 45:2-3, 5-6, 8-9. R. v. 8

The Lord of hosts is with us: the God of Jacob is our stronghold.

John 5:1-3, 5-16

There was a Jewish festival, and Jesus went up to Jerusalem. Now at the Sheep Pool in Jerusalem there is a building, called Bethzatha in Hebrew, consisting of five porticos; and under these were crowds of sick people – blind, lame, paralysed. One man there had an illness which had lasted thirty-eight years, and when Jesus saw him lying there and knew he had been in this condition for a long time, he said, 'Do you want to be well again?' 'Sir,' replied the sick man 'I have no one to put me into the pool when the water is disturbed; and while I am still on the way, someone else gets there before me.' Jesus said, 'Get up, pick up your sleeping-mat and walk.' The man was cured at once, and he picked up his mat and walked away.

Now that day happened to be the sabbath, so the Jews said to the man who had been cured, 'It is the sabbath; you are not allowed to carry your sleeping-mat.' He replied, 'But the man who cured me told me, "Pick up your mat and walk."' They asked, 'Who is the man who said to you, "Pick up your mat and walk"?' The man had no idea who it was since Jesus had disappeared into the crowd that filled the place. After a while Jesus met him in the Temple and said, 'Now you are well again, be sure not to sin any more, or something worse may happen to you.' The man went back and told the Jews that it was Jesus who had cured him. It was because he did things like this on the sabbath that the Jews began to persecute Jesus.

Reflection

When Jesus performs a miracle he is often responding to the plea of someone in need. In John's account of the restoration of health on the Sabbath to a man whose efforts to enter the potentially healing water of the Pool of Bethzatha near Jerusalem's Sheep Gate had been continually frustrated, Jesus himself takes the initiative. There is no urging from anyone else, not even the man himself. 'Do you want to be well again?', Jesus asks him – a strange question to someone who had been desperately ill for thirty-eight years. We are not told how the man reacts to his cure: he simply 'picked up his mat and walked away'. Later Jesus encounters him in the Temple and says, 'Now you are well again, be sure not to sin any more' (John 5:14; see too 8:11) – a reminder to us that we must preserve not only our physical health but also the health of the heart, our spiritual health.

Isaiah 49:8-15

(Please see the Appendix B-8)

Psalm 144:8-9, 13-14, 17-18. R. v. 8

The Lord is kind and full of compassion.

John 5:17-30

Jesus said to the Jews: 'My Father goes on working, and so do I.' But that only made the Jews even more intent on killing him, because, not content with breaking the sabbath, he spoke of God as his own Father, and so made himself God's equal. To this accusation Jesus replied: 'I tell you most solemnly, the Son can do nothing by himself; he can only do what he sees the Father doing: and whatever the Father does the Son does too. For the Father loves the Son and shows him everything he does himself, and he will show him even greater things than these, works that will astonish you. Thus, as the Father raises the dead and gives them life, so the Son gives life to anyone he chooses; for the Father judges no one; he has entrusted all judgement to the Son, so that all may honour the Son as they honour the Father. Whoever refuses honour to the Son refuses honour to the Father who sent him. I tell you most solemnly, whoever listens to my words, and believes in the one who sent me, has eternal life; without being brought to judgement he has passed from death to life. I tell you most solemnly, the hour will come – in fact it is here already – when the dead will hear the voice of the Son of God, and all who hear it will live. For the Father, who is the source of life has made the Son the source of life; and, because he is the Son of Man, has appointed him supreme judge. Do not be surprised at this, for the hour is coming when the dead will leave their graves at the sound of his voice: those who did good will rise again to life; and those who did evil, to condemnation. I can do nothing by myself; I can only judge as I am told to judge, and my judging is just, because my aim is to do not my own will, but the will of him who sent me.'

Reflection

The theme of life is central to the Good News as proclaimed by John. A word count reveals that his references to life/living exceed those of all the other evangelists combined. John's hope is that, believing in 'the signs that Jesus worked', his community 'may have life through his name' (John 20:31; see too 1 John 5:13). He alone records such sayings of Jesus as: 'I am the Way, the Truth and the Life' (14:6); 'I am the bread of life' (6:35); 'I am the resurrection and the life' (11:25 NRSV); and the consoling words in today's Gospel reading: 'I tell you most solemnly; whoever listens to my words, and believes in the one who sent me has eternal life; without being brought to judgement he has passed from death to life' (5:24). Note the use of the present tense ('has', not 'will have'). Even now, through baptism, we anticipate the life to come. 'For anyone who is in Christ, there is a new creation' (2 Corinthians 5:17).

4th Week of Lent
Violet

31 MAR THU

Exodus 32:7-14

The Lord spoke to Moses, 'Go down now, because your people whom you brought out of Egypt have apostasised. They have been quick to leave the way I marked out for them; they have made themselves a calf of molten metal and have worshipped it and offered it sacrifice. "Here is your God, Israel," they have cried, "who brought you up from the land of Egypt!" I can see how headstrong these people are! Leave me now, my wrath shall blaze out against them and devour them; of you, however, I will make a great nation.' ... *(Please see the Appendix B-9)*

Psalm 105:19-23. R. v. 4

O Lord, remember me out of the love you have for your people.

John 5:31-47

Jesus said to the Jews: 'Were I to testify on my own behalf, my testimony would not be valid; but there is another witness who can speak on my behalf, and I know that his testimony is valid. You sent messengers to John, and he gave his testimony to the truth: not that I depend on human testimony; no, it is for your salvation that I speak of this. John was a lamp alight and shining and for a time you were content to enjoy the light that he gave. But my testimony is greater than John's: the works my Father has given me to carry out, these same works of mine testify that the Father has sent me. Besides, the Father who sent me bears witness to me himself. You have never heard his voice, you have never seen his shape, and his word finds no home in you because you do not believe in the one he has sent. 'You study the scriptures, believing that in them you have eternal life; now these same scriptures testify to me, and yet you refuse to come to me for life! As for human approval this means nothing to me. Besides, I know you too well: you have no love of God in you. I have come in the name of my Father and you refuse to accept me; if someone else comes in his own name you will accept him. 'How can you believe, since you look to one another for approval and are not concerned with the approval that comes from the one God? Do not imagine that I am going to accuse you before the Father; you place your hopes on Moses, and Moses will be your accuser. If you really believed him you would believe me too, since it was I that he was writing about; but if you refuse to believe what he wrote, how can you believe what I say?'

Reflection

Throughout his public life Jesus had an abiding awareness of the divine origin of his mission. He said: 'I do nothing of myself: what the Father has taught me is what I preach ... I always do what pleases him' (John 8:28-29); 'My food is to do the will of the one who sent me, and to complete his work' (John 4:34). At Jesus' baptism (Matthew 3:17) and transfiguration, the Father set his seal of approval on his ministry: 'This is my Son, the Beloved; he enjoys my favour. Listen to him' (Matthew 17:5). Sadly, most of the people were not receptive to Jesus' teaching. 'I have come in my Father's name,' he said, 'and you do not accept me.' There is more than a note of frustration in Jesus' remonstrance: 'Are your minds closed? Have you eyes that do not see, ears that do not hear?' (Mark 8:17-18). 'Still happier are those who hear the word of God and keep it!' (Luke 11:28).

01
APR FRI

Wisdom 2:1, 12-22

The godless say to themselves, with their misguided reasoning: 'Let us lie in wait for the virtuous man, since he annoys us and opposes our way of life, reproaches us for our breaches of the law and accuses us of playing false to our upbringing. He claims to have knowledge of God, and calls himself a son of the Lord. Before us he stands, a reproof to our way of thinking, the very sight of him weighs our spirits down; his way of life is not like other men's, the paths he treads are unfamiliar. In his opinion we are counterfeit; he holds aloof from our doings as though from filth; he proclaims the final end of the virtuous as happy and boasts of having God for his father. Let us see if what he says is true, let us observe what kind of end he himself will have. If the virtuous man is God's son, God will take his part and rescue him from the clutches of his enemies. Let us test him with cruelty and with torture, and thus explore this gentleness of his and put his endurance to the proof. Let us condemn him to a shameful death since he will be looked after – we have his word for it.' This is the way they reason, but they are misled, their malice makes them blind. They do not know the hidden things of God, they have no hope that holiness will be rewarded, they can see no reward for blameless souls.

Psalm 33:16, 18, 19-21, 23. R. v. 19

The Lord is close to the broken-hearted.

John 7:1-2, 10, 25-30

Jesus stayed in Galilee; he could not stay in Judaea, because the Jews were out to kill him. As the Jewish feast of Tabernacles drew near, after his brothers had left for the festival, Jesus went up as well, but quite privately, without drawing attention to himself. Meanwhile some of the people of Jerusalem were saying, 'Isn't this the man they want to kill? And here he is, speaking freely, and they have nothing to say to him! Can it be true the authorities have made up their minds that he is the Christ? Yet we all know where he comes from, but when the Christ appears no one will know where he comes from.' Then, as Jesus taught in the Temple, he cried out: 'Yes, you know me and you know where I came from. Yet I have not come of myself: no, there is one who sent me and I really come from him, and you do not know him, but I know him because I have come from him and it was he who sent me.' They would have arrested him then, but because his time had not yet come no one laid a hand on him.

Reflection

It is ironic that sometimes we have to wait until a funeral before we realise that the person we thought we knew well had a whole different dimension to their life. As we listen to the eulogy, or read the obituary, we catch a glimpse of who they really were, their dreams and hopes and their purpose in life. Over the past four weeks of Lent we have had the opportunity to watch and listen to Jesus as he has moved around the countryside, but have we noticed that his message is getting more urgent? We have the benefit of knowing what lies ahead for him – we know who he is, where he is from and where he is going. It's all very familiar to us. The readings today invite us to pause and reflect on Jesus, and his message, and what it all means for us today. Do we truly know Jesus, or just about him? Does his message affect our lives in a significant way, or is it just more familiar words? Do we catch a glimpse of the 'hidden things of God' that Jesus is revealing? What is our response today to Jesus' question: 'Who do you say I am?'

4th Week of Lent | Violet
or **St Francis of Paola,** *hermit* (Commemoration)

02
APR SAT

Jeremiah 11:18-20

The Lord revealed it to me; I was warned. Lord, that was when you opened my eyes to their scheming. I for my part was like a trustful lamb being led to the slaughter-house, not knowing the schemes they were plotting against me, 'Let us destroy the tree in its strength, let us cut him off from the land of the living, so that his name may be quickly forgotten!'

But you, Lord of hosts, who pronounce a just sentence, who probe the loins and heart, let me see the vengeance you will take on them, for I have committed my cause to you.

Psalm 7:2-3, 9-12. R. v. 2

Lord God, I take refuge in you.

John 7:40-52

Several people who had been listening to Jesus said, 'Surely he must be the prophet,' and some said, 'He is the Christ', but others said, 'Would the Christ be from Galilee? Does not scripture say that the Christ must be descended from David and come from the town of Bethlehem?' So the people could not agree about him. Some would have liked to arrest him, but no one actually laid hands on him.

The police went back to the chief priests and Pharisees who said to them, 'Why haven't you brought him?' The police replied, 'There has never been anybody who has spoken like him.' 'So' the Pharisees answered 'you have been led astray as well? Have any of the authorities believed in him? Any of the Pharisees? This rabble knows nothing about the Law – they are damned.' One of them, Nicodemus – the same man who had come to Jesus earlier – said to them, 'But surely the Law does not allow us to pass judgement on a man without giving him a hearing and discovering what he is about?' To this they answered, 'Are you a Galilean too? Go into the matter, and see for yourself: prophets do not come out of Galilee.'

Reflection

People listened to Jesus but could not agree about who he really was. From our own experience we know that getting to the truth of a matter can be unsettling, leading us to make life-changing decisions. To some of his listeners, Jesus is a prophet, to others the Messiah. To the Pharisees he is just a despised Galilean whom no-one should believe. Nicodemus challenges his fellow Pharisees to at least listen to Jesus before passing judgement. Where are we in this crowd? Do we think we know all there is to know about Jesus? Or are we open to the surprises that we might get if we really listen to Jesus with the ears of our heart? Lent presents us with an opportunity to get to know Jesus personally, to find the truth for ourselves. We are well into the Lenten journey but there is still time to realise that 'never has anyone spoken to us like Jesus!'

03
APR SUN

FIFTH SUNDAY OF LENT

Psalter Week 1

Violet

Isaiah 43:16-21

Thus says the Lord,
who made a way through the sea,
a path in the great waters;
who put chariots and horse in the field
and a powerful army,
which lay there never to rise again,
snuffed out, put out like a wick:

No need to recall the past,
no need to think about what was done before.
See, I am doing a new deed,
even now it comes to light; can you not see it?
Yes, I am making a road in the wilderness,
paths in the wilds.

The wild beasts will honour me,
jackals and ostriches,
because I am putting water in the wilderness
(rivers in the wild)
to give my chosen people drink.
The people I have formed for myself
will sing my praises.

Psalm 125. R. v. 3

What marvels the Lord worked for us! Indeed we were glad.

Philippians 3:8-14

I believe nothing can happen that will outweigh the supreme advantage of knowing Christ Jesus my Lord. For him I have accepted the loss of everything, and I look on everything as so much rubbish if only I can have Christ and be given a place in him. I am no longer trying for perfection by my own efforts, the perfection that comes from the Law, but I want only the perfection that comes through faith in Christ, and is from God and based on faith. All I want is to know Christ and the power of his resurrection and to share his sufferings by reproducing the pattern of his death. That is the way I can hope to take my place in the resurrection of the dead. Not that I have become perfect yet: I have not yet won, but I am still running, trying to capture the prize for which Christ Jesus captured me. I can assure you my brothers, I am far from thinking that I have already won. All I can say is that I forget the past and I strain ahead for what is still to come; I am racing for the finish, for the prize to which God calls us upwards to receive in Christ Jesus.

John 8:1-11

Jesus went to the Mount of Olives. At daybreak he appeared in the Temple again; and as all the people came to him, he sat down and began to teach them.

The scribes and Pharisees brought a woman along who had been caught committing adultery; and making her stand there in full view of everybody, they said to Jesus, 'Master, this woman was caught in the very act of committing adultery, and Moses has ordered us in the Law to condemn women like this to death by stoning. What have you to say?' They asked him this as a test, looking for something to use against him. But Jesus bent down and started writing on the ground with his finger. As they persisted with their question, he looked up and said, 'If there is one of you who has not sinned, let him be the first to throw a stone at her.' Then he bent down and wrote on the ground again. When they heard this they went away one by one, beginning with the eldest, until Jesus was left alone with the woman, who remained standing there. He looked up and said, 'Woman, where are they? Has no one condemned you?' 'No one, sir,' she replied. 'Neither do I condemn you,' said Jesus 'go away, and don't sin any more.'

Reflection

The readings today are a reminder that God has done, and will continue to do, great things in our lives. Isaiah, however, reminds us that there is no gain in continually dwelling on the past; rather we are called to notice God 'doing a new deed' as God calls us into the future. The woman brought before Jesus knows she has already been judged by the crowd around her and expects the same from Jesus. Yet, in her misery she finds Jesus offering her mercy and compassion. He releases her from her past and offers her a future full of possibilities. Paul says all he wants is 'to know Christ and the power of his resurrection'. What a great mantra for this final week of Lent! We too are 'straining ahead for what is still to come … racing for the finish'. We only have a few more days with Jesus before he enters Holy Week. Can we allow him to look at us in the way he looked at the woman – to accept the mercy and compassion he offers and to be rescued from behaviours and judgements that may in the past have been harmful to others? There is still time to glimpse the *new deed* God is doing in us.

04
APR MON

5th Week of Lent | Violet
or **St Isidore,** *bishop, doctor* (Commemoration)

Daniel 13:41-62

(Longer form: 13:1-9, 15-17, 19-30, 33-62)

Susanna was condemned to death. She cried out as loud as she could 'Eternal God, you know all secrets and everything before it happens; you know that they have given false evidence against me. And now have I to die, innocent as I am of everything their malice has invented against me?'

The Lord heard her cry and, as she was being led away to die, he roused the holy spirit residing in a young boy named Daniel who began to shout, 'I am innocent of this woman's death!' At which all the people turned to him and asked, 'What do you mean by these words?' Standing in the middle of the crowd he replied, 'Are you so stupid, sons of Israel, as to condemn a daughter of Israel unheard, and without troubling to find out the truth? Go back to the scene of the trial: these men have given false evidence against her.'... *(Please see the Appendix B-9)*

Psalm 22. R. v. 4

If I should walk in the valley of darkness, no evil would I fear.

John 8:12-20

Jesus said to the people: 'I am the light of the world; anyone who follows me will not be walking in the dark; he will have the light of life.'

At this the Pharisees said to him, 'you are testifying on your own behalf; your testimony is not valid.' Jesus replied: 'It is true that I am testifying on my own behalf, but my testimony is still valid, because I know where I came from and where I am going; but you do not know where I come from or where I am going. You judge by human standards; I judge no one, but if I judge, my judgement will be sound, because I am not alone: the one who sent me is with me; and in your Law it is written that the testimony of two witnesses is valid. I may be testifying on my own behalf, but the Father who sent me is my witness too.'

They asked him, 'Where is your Father?' Jesus answered: 'You do not know me, nor do you know my Father; if you did know me, you would know my Father as well.'

He spoke these words in the Treasury, while teaching in the Temple. No one arrested him, because his time had not yet come.

Reflection

What better God-moment could there be than to watch the sun rise! To hear the birds' dawn chorus, to witness the hush that falls over all as the sky is touched by soft light and then pierced with shafts of brightness. Waiting for light to overcome the darkness puts a different perspective on starting a new day. Susanna was overcome by darkness after having been trapped by the two elders and then condemned to death. Light for her came unexpectedly when Daniel discovered the truth of the situation and, thus, gave her the chance to begin a new day. When we reflect on the dark moments of our life, how did we find the light again? Often the presence of God is mediated through others and there we experience light in our darkness. In turn, how can we be light for the darkness of others?

5th Week of Lent | Violet
or **St Vincent Ferrer,** *priest* (Commemoration)

05
APR TUE

Numbers 21:4-9

The Israelites left Mount Hor by the road to the Sea of Suph, to skirt the land of Edom. On the way the people lost patience. They spoke against God and against Moses, 'Why did you bring us out of Egypt to die in this wilderness? For there is neither bread nor water here; we are sick of this unsatisfying food.'

At this God sent fiery serpents among the people; their bite brought death to many in Israel. The people came and said to Moses, 'We have sinned by speaking against the Lord and against you. Intercede for us with the Lord to save us from these serpents.' Moses interceded for the people, and the Lord answered him, 'Make a fiery serpent and put it on a standard. If anyone is bitten and looks at it, he shall live.' So Moses fashioned a bronze serpent which he put on a standard, and if anyone was bitten by a serpent, he looked at the bronze serpent and lived.

Psalm 101:2-3, 16-21. R. v. 2

O Lord, listen to my prayer and let my cry for help reach you.

John 8:21-30

Jesus said to the Pharisees: 'I am going away; you will look for me and you will die in your sin. Where I am going, you cannot come.' The Jews said to one another, 'Will he kill himself? Is that what he means by saying, "Where I am going, you cannot come"?' Jesus went on: 'You are from below; I am from above. You are of this world; I am not of this world. I have told you already: You will die in your sins. Yes, if you do not believe that I am He, you will die in your sins.' So they said to him, 'Who are you?' Jesus answered: 'What I have told you from the outset. About you I have much to say and much to condemn; but the one who sent me is truthful, and what I have learnt from him I declare to the world.'

They failed to understand that he was talking to them about the Father. So Jesus said: 'When you have lifted up the Son of Man, then you will know that I am He and that I do nothing of myself: what the Father has taught me is what I preach; he who sent me is with me, and has not left me to myself, for I always do what pleases him.' As he was saying this, many came to believe in him.

Reflection

The Israelites lost patience with Moses and with God. They were tired and discouraged and began to complain. When they realised the consequences of their actions, they were humble enough to turn back to God and continue their journey with renewed hope. No doubt sometimes we feel overwhelmed too and are tempted to complain about the pain and brokenness of daily life – the ageing body wracked with pain, the loss of loved ones through relationship breakdown or death, the new way of living necessitated by the world pandemic, and so on. Jesus had to undergo the experience of the cross before he was lifted up, but he was willing to do this because he knew the One 'who sent me is with me and has not left me to myself'. The challenge for us, particularly during Lent, is to accept our cross and continue our journey certain that God will raise us up too. As the psalmist says, *O Lord, hear my prayer and let my cry come to you.*

06
APR WED

Daniel 3:14-20, 24-25, 28

King Nebuchadnezzar said, 'Shadrach, Meshach and Abednego, is it true that you do not serve my gods, and that you refuse to worship the golden statue I have erected? When you hear the sound of horn, pipe, lyre, trigon, harp, bagpipe, or any other instrument, are you prepared to prostrate yourselves and worship the statue I have made? If you refuse to worship it, you must be thrown straight away into the burning fiery furnace; and where is the god who could save you from my power?' …

(Please see the Appendix B-9)

Daniel 3:52-56. R. v. 52

To you glory and praise for evermore.

John 8:31-42

To the Jews who believed in him Jesus said: 'If you make my word your home you will indeed be my disciples, you will learn the truth and the truth will make you free.'

They answered, 'We are descended from Abraham and we have never been the slaves of anyone; what do you mean, "You will be made free"?' Jesus replied: 'I tell you most solemnly, everyone who commits sin is a slave. Now the slave's place in the house is not assured, but the son's place is assured. So if the Son makes you free, you will be free indeed. I know that you are descended from Abraham; but in spite of that you want to kill me because nothing I say has penetrated into you. What I, for my part, speak of is what I have seen with my Father; but you, you put into action the lessons learnt from your father.'

They repeated, 'Our father is Abraham.' Jesus said to them: 'If you were Abraham's children, you would do as Abraham did. As it is, you want to kill me when I tell you the truth as I have learnt it from God; that is not what Abraham did. What you are doing is what your father does.' 'We were not born of prostitution,' they went on 'we have one father: God.' Jesus answered: 'If God were your father, you would love me, since I have come here from God; yes, I have come from him; not that I came because I chose, no, I was sent, and by him.'

Reflection

Freedom is a value our society prizes dearly – so much so that we will rise up in protest if someone or something is seen to be impinging on our rights. By refusing to bow down to King Nebuchadnezzar's golden statue, Shadrach, Meshach and Abednego not only proclaimed their own freedom but also revealed to the king the truth of their complete faith in God. In today's Gospel Jesus tells the Jews who believed in him that making his words their own would set them free because all he said came from what he had learnt from God. The time was fast approaching when their belief in him would be put to the test. At this stage in the Lenten journey, it is timely to ask myself: How much have I made Jesus' words my own? If I was asked today to put my life on the line for those words, would I be free enough to follow the truth Jesus has revealed to me?

5th Week of Lent | Violet
or **St John Baptist de la Salle,** *priest* (Commemoration)

07
APR THU

Genesis 17:3-9

Abram bowed to the ground and God said this to him, 'Here now is my covenant with you: you shall become the father of a multitude of nations. You shall no longer be called Abram; your name shall be Abraham, for I make you father of a multitude of nations. I will make you most fruitful. I will make you into nations, and your issue shall be kings. I will establish my Covenant between myself and you, and your descendants after you, generation after generation, a Covenant in perpetuity, to be your God and the God of your descendants after you. I will give to you and to your descendants after you the land you are living in, the whole land of Canaan, to own in perpetuity, and I will be your God.'

God said to Abraham, 'You on your part shall maintain my Covenant, yourself and your descendants after you, generation after generation.'

Psalm 104:4-9. R. v. 8

The Lord remembers his covenant for ever.

John 8:51-59

Jesus said to the Jews: 'I tell you most solemnly, whoever keeps my word will never see death. 'The Jews said, 'Now we know for certain that you are possessed. Abraham is dead, and the prophets are dead, and yet you say, "Whoever keeps my word will never know the taste of death." Are you greater than our father Abraham, who is dead? The prophets are dead too. Who are you claiming to be?' Jesus answered: 'If I were to seek my own glory that would be no glory at all; my glory is conferred by the Father, by the one of whom you say, "He is our God" although you do not know him. But I know him, and if I were to say: I do not know him, I should be a liar, as you are liars yourselves. But I do know him, and I faithfully keep his word. Your father Abraham rejoiced to think that he would see my Day; he saw it and was glad.' The Jews then said, 'You are not fifty yet, and you have seen Abraham!' Jesus replied: 'I tell you most solemnly, before Abraham ever was, I Am.' At this they picked up stones to throw at him; but Jesus hid himself and left the Temple.

Reflection

Let's imagine this scene as the Jews confront Jesus. Where am I? Why am I there? What sort of response bubbles up in me as I hear Jesus' words, 'you do not know God'? Others around me are protesting. What about me? Think back over these weeks of Lent when Jesus has been inviting me into a new and deeper relationship with God. Have I given that relationship the time and commitment needed to understand what Jesus is on about here – or am I content with the way things have always been between myself and God? Am I overcome by the rhetoric/emotion of the crowd around me and ready to pick up a stone too? Relationships take time to grow – and an openness to being present to the other. Before Lent is over, do I need to be more consciously present to God so that I can truly say with Jesus, 'I faithfully keep his word'?

Jeremiah 20:10-13

Jeremiah said: 'I hear so many disparaging me, "Terror from every side!' Denounce him! Let us denounce him!" All those who used to be my friends watched for my downfall, "Perhaps he will be seduced into error. Then we will master him and take our revenge!" But the Lord is at my side, a mighty hero; my opponents will stumble, mastered, confounded by their failure; everlasting, unforgettable disgrace will be theirs. But you, Lord of hosts, you who probe with justice, who scrutinise the loins and heart, let me see the vengeance you will take on them, for I have committed my cause to you. Sing to the Lord, praise the Lord, for he has delivered the soul of the needy from the hands of evil men.'

Psalm 17:2-7. R. cf. v. 7

In my anguish I called to the Lord, and he heard my voice.

John 10:31-42

The Jews fetched stones to stone him, so Jesus said to them, 'I have done many good works for you to see, works from my Father; for which of these are you stoning me?' The Jews answered him, 'We are not stoning you for doing a good work but for blasphemy: you are only a man and you claim to be God.' Jesus answered: 'Is it not written in your Law: I said, you are gods? So the Law used the word gods of those to whom the word of God was addressed, and scripture cannot be rejected. Yet you say to someone the Father has consecrated and sent into the world, "You are blaspheming," because he says, "I am the Son of God." If I am not doing my Father's work, there is no need to believe me; but if I am doing it, then even if you refuse to believe in me, at least believe in the work I do; then you will know for sure that the Father is in me and I am in the Father.' They wanted to arrest him then, but he eluded them.

He went back again to the far side of the Jordan to stay in the district where John had once been baptising. Many people who came to him there said, 'John gave no signs, but all he said about this man was true'; and many of them believed in him.

Reflection

Sometimes it seems as if everyone and everything is contriving to make life miserable. We feel overwhelmed by political situations, climate aberrations, economic instability, pandemic uncertainty. Poverty, violence, and danger lurk around every corner. In today's readings, Jeremiah seems to feel this way; even his friends are watching for his downfall. The psalmist is feeling overcome by torrents of destruction, confronted by waves and snares and traps. Jesus, too, is facing a group of Jews ready to stone him. For them, the saying 'actions speak louder than words' is not an argument in his favour. What to do at such times? Hope comes from each turning to God in complete trust and confidence that godness will eventually prevail. Life may still be miserable but hope in a loving and merciful God enlivens us and keeps us moving forward. *Your words, Lord, are spirit and life; you have the words of everlasting life.*

5th Week of Lent
Violet

Ezekiel 37:21-28

The Lord says this: 'I am going to take the sons of Israel from the nations where they have gone. I shall gather them together from everywhere and bring them home to their own soil. I shall make them into one nation in my own land and on the mountains of Israel, and one king is to be king of them all; they will no longer form two nations, nor be two separate kingdoms. They will no longer defile themselves with their idols and their filthy practices and all their sins. I shall rescue them from all the betrayals they have been guilty of; I shall cleanse them; they shall be my people and I will be their God. My servant David will reign over them, one shepherd for all; they will follow my observances, respect my laws and practise them. They will live in the land that I gave my servant Jacob, the land in which your ancestors lived. They will live in it, they, their children, their children's children, for ever. David my servant is to be their prince for ever. I shall make a covenant of peace with them, an eternal covenant with them. I shall resettle them and increase them; I shall settle my sanctuary among them for ever. I shall make my home above them; I will be their God, they shall be my people. And the nations will learn that I am the Lord the sanctifier of Israel, when my sanctuary is with them for ever.'

Jeremiah 31:10-13. R. v. 10

The Lord will guard us as a shepherd guards his flock.

John 11:45-56

Many of the Jews who had come to visit Mary and had seen what Jesus did believed in him, but some of them went to tell the Pharisees what he had done. Then the chief priests and Pharisees called a meeting. 'Here is this man working all these signs' they said 'and what action are we taking? If we let him go on in this way everybody will believe in him, and the Romans will come and destroy the Holy Place and our nation.' One of them, Caiaphas, the high priest that year, said, 'You don't seem to have grasped the situation at all; you fail to see that it is better for one man to die for the people, than for the whole nation to be destroyed.' He did not speak in his own person, it was as high priest that he made this prophecy that Jesus was to die for the nation – and not for the nation only, but to gather together in unity the scattered children of God. From that day they were determined to kill him. So Jesus no longer went about openly among the Jews, but left the district for a town called Ephraim, in the country bordering on the desert, and stayed there with his disciples. The Jewish Passover drew near, and many of the country people who had gone up to Jerusalem to purify themselves looked out for Jesus, saying to one another as they stood about in the Temple, 'What do you think? Will he come to the festival or not?'

Reflection

We can almost feel the tension mounting here in Bethany! Jesus is at the home of Mary and Martha whose brother, Lazarus, he has raised from the dead. The Jews around him are enthralled with his presence but they are divided too: some believing in him but others going off to report him to the Pharisees. A meeting is called to talk about acting against Jesus and the decision is made that Jesus must die for the nation. Jesus' reaction is to leave the district. Imagine being with Jesus and the disciples at this critical time. What would I want to talk about with them? What questions would I want to ask Jesus? Time is running out so let's make the most of just being with Jesus and preparing for the days ahead. Let's do whatever it takes to nurture 'a new heart and a new spirit' that will give us strength to accompany Jesus to Jerusalem for the Passover.

10
APR SUN

PALM SUNDAY OF THE PASSION OF THE LORD

Psalter Week 2

Red

Isaiah 50:4-7

The Lord has given me a disciple's tongue. So that I may know how to reply to the wearied, he provides me with speech. Each morning he wakes me to hear, to listen like a disciple. The Lord has opened my ear. For my part, I made no resistance, neither did I turn away. I offered my back to those who struck me, my cheeks to those who tore at my beard; I did not cover my face against insult and spittle. The Lord comes to my help, so that I am untouched by the insults. So, too, I set my face like flint; I know I shall not be shamed.

Psalm 21:8-9, 17-20, 23-24. R. v. 2

My God, my God, why have you forsaken me?

Philippians 2:6-11

His state was divine, yet Christ Jesus did not cling to his equality with God but emptied himself to assume the condition of a slave, and became as men are; and being as all men are, he was humbler yet, even to accepting death, death on a cross. But God raised him high and gave him the name which is above all other names so that all beings in the heavens, on earth and in the underworld, should bend the knee at the name of Jesus and that every tongue should acclaim Jesus Christ as Lord, to the glory of God the Father.

Luke 22:14-23:56

(Please see the Bible for the Passion Reading)

Reflection

Most people love a parade, noisily making the most of a chance to come together with others of like mind, to celebrate an event or highlight an issue. Holy Week begins with a parade. People get really involved throwing down their garments and rejoicing at all the mighty works they have witnessed through Jesus. Jesus rides triumphant through it all and encourages his followers to praise God with loud voice. Parades can bring out the best, and worst, in people. It is hard not to get caught up in the emotion of the moment and events that were supposed to be happy and peaceful sometimes deteriorate into chaos and violence. How the parade mood changed over the course of Holy Week! In the long Gospel of the Passion we see Jesus no longer triumphant but separated from his followers, insulted, struck, spat upon, and finally carrying his cross to crucifixion on Golgotha: 'He emptied himself to assume the condition of a slave … even to accepting death on a cross.' What reaction do I have to today's readings? Has my Lenten journey prepared me to be really present during this Holy Week?

11
APR MON

Monday of Holy Week
Violet

Isaiah 42:1-7

Here is my servant whom I uphold, my chosen one in whom my soul delights. I have endowed him with my spirit that he may bring true justice to the nations. He does not cry out or shout aloud, or make his voice heard in the streets. He does not break the crushed reed, nor quench the wavering flame. Faithfully he brings true justice; he will neither waver, nor be crushed until true justice is established on earth, for the islands are awaiting his law. Thus says God, the Lord, he who created the heavens and spread them out, who gave shape to the earth and what comes from it, who gave breath to its people and life to the creatures that move in it: I, the Lord, have called you to serve the cause of right; I have taken you by the hand and formed you; I have appointed you as covenant of the people and light of the nations, to open the eyes of the blind, to free captives from prison, and those who live in darkness from the dungeon.

Psalm 26:1-3, 13-14. R. v. 1

The Lord is my light and my help.

John 12:1-11

Six days before the Passover, Jesus went to Bethany, where Lazarus was, whom he had raised from the dead. They gave a dinner for him there; Martha waited on them and Lazarus was among those at table. Mary brought in a pound of very costly ointment, pure nard, and with it anointed the feet of Jesus, wiping them with her hair; the house was full of the scent of the ointment. Then Judas Iscariot - one of his disciples, the man who was to betray him - said, 'Why wasn't this ointment sold for three hundred denarii, and the money given to the poor?' He said this, not because he cared about the poor, but because he was a thief; he was in charge of the common fund and used to help himself to the contributions. So Jesus said, 'Leave her alone; she had to keep this scent for the day of my burial. You have the poor with you always, you will not always have me.' Meanwhile a large number of Jews heard that he was there and came not only on account of Jesus but also to see Lazarus whom he had raised from the dead. Then the chief priests decided to kill Lazarus as well, since it was on his account that many of the Jews were leaving them and believing in Jesus.

Reflection

'You will not always have me …' These words of Jesus are a chilling reminder that the end of his life on earth is near. Judas has expressed his disapproval of the waste of such precious oil, but Jesus knows he does not really care about the poor. Jesus sees into the hearts of Mary of Bethany and Judas and knows their true motives. Mary is expressing her love and support, but Judas is covering up his greed and dishonesty. This leads me to ponder what Jesus sees in my heart today? Am I honest enough to admit that I, too, am capable of greed and deceit – that my words sometimes mismatch my actions? Today might be a good opportunity to open my heart to Jesus and seek God's forgiveness before I set out on the road to Calvary. Judas chose to turn away from Jesus, but can I prepare myself to 'hold firm and take heart'?

12
APR TUE

Tuesday of Holy Week
Violet

Isaiah 49:1-6

Islands, listen to me, pay attention, remotest peoples. The Lord called me before I was born, from my mother's womb he pronounced my name. He made my mouth a sharp sword, and hid me in the shadow of his hand. He made me into a sharpened arrow, and concealed me in his quiver. He said to me, 'You are my servant Israel, in whom I shall be glorified'; while I was thinking, 'I have toiled in vain, I have exhausted myself for nothing'; …
(Please see the Appendix B-10)

Psalm 70:1-6, 15, 17. R. v. 15

My lips will tell of your help.

John 13:21-33, 36-38

While at supper with his disciples, Jesus was troubled in spirit and declared, 'I tell you most solemnly, one of you will betray me.' The disciples looked at one another, wondering which he meant. The disciple Jesus loved was reclining next to Jesus; Simon Peter signed to him and said, 'Ask who it is he means', so leaning back on Jesus's breast he said, 'Who is it, Lord?' 'It is the one' replied Jesus 'to whom I give the piece of bread that I shall dip in the dish.' He dipped the piece of bread and gave it to Judas son of Simon Iscariot. At that instant, after Judas had taken the bread, Satan entered him. Jesus then said, 'What you are going to do, do quickly.' None of the others at table understood the reason he said this. Since Judas had charge of the common fund, some of them thought Jesus was telling him, 'Buy what we need for the festival', or telling him to give something to the poor. As soon as Judas had taken the piece of bread he went out. Night had fallen.

When he had gone Jesus said: 'Now has the Son of Man been glorified, and in him God has been glorified. If God has been glorified in him, God will in turn glorify him in himself, and will glorify him very soon. My little children, I shall not be with you much longer. You will look for me, and, as I told the Jews, where I am going, you cannot come.'

Simon Peter said, 'Lord, where are you going?' Jesus replied, 'Where I am going you cannot follow me now; you will follow me later.' Peter said to him, 'Why can't I follow you now? I will lay down my life for you.' 'Lay down your life for me?' answered Jesus. 'I tell you most solemnly, before the cock crows you will have disowned me three times.'

Reflection

Jesus is sharing a last meal with his friends. They have been with him through good times and bad over the past three years, but they just don't seem to understand why he is so troubled in spirit at this time. It must have been so hard for Jesus to know that one is about to betray him, and another will disown him, not only once, but three times. Night had well and truly fallen! I can quite imagine Jesus turning to his Father at this time using the words of today's psalm. In God he has trusted from his mother's womb. God has always been there teaching him the way, being a dependable source of inspiration and strength. Even if these friends desert him, he knows that God will not. In the coming days we will witness the absolute dependence that Jesus has in his Father. The words of the psalm could well become our prayer too. *It is you, O Lord, who are my hope.*

13
APR WED

Wednesday of Holy Week
Violet

Isaiah 50:4-9

The Lord has given me a disciple's tongue. So that I may know how to reply to the wearied he provides me with speech. Each morning he wakes me to hear, to listen like a disciple. The Lord has opened my ear. For my part, I made no resistance, neither did I turn away. I offered my back to those who struck me, my cheeks to those who tore at my beard; I did not cover my face against insult and spittle. The Lord comes to my help so that I am untouched by the insults. So, too, I set my face like flint; I know I shall not be shamed. My vindicator is here at hand. Does anyone start proceedings against me? Then let us go to court together. Who thinks he has a case against me? Let him approach me. The Lord is coming to my help, who dare condemn me?

Psalm 68:8-10, 21-22, 31, 33-34. R. v. 14

In your great love, O Lord, answer my prayers for your favour.

Matthew 26:14-25

One of the Twelve, the man called Judas Iscariot, went to the chief priests and said, 'What are you prepared to give me if I hand him over to you?' They paid him thirty silver pieces, and from that moment he looked for an opportunity to betray him. Now on the first day of Unleavened Bread the disciples came to Jesus to say, 'Where do you want us to make the preparations for you to eat the passover?' 'Go to so-and-so in the city' he replied 'and say to him, "The Master says: My time is near. It is at your house that I am keeping Passover with my disciples."' The disciples did what Jesus told them and prepared the Passover.

When evening came he was at table with the twelve disciples. And while they were eating he said, 'I tell you solemnly, one of you is about to betray me.' They were greatly distressed and started asking him in turn, 'Not I, Lord, surely?' He answered, 'Someone who has dipped his hand into the dish with me, will betray me. The Son of Man is going to his fate, as the scriptures say he will, but alas for that man by whom the Son of Man is betrayed! Better for that man if he had never been born!' Judas, who was to betray him, asked in his turn, 'Not I, Rabbi, surely?' 'They are your own words' answered Jesus.

Reflection

Today is the last day of Lent, the day before the action of the Easter Triduum begins. A day to look back over the past five weeks before moving into these final trying days. Isaiah's words help in looking back. The words, 'each morning God wakes me to hear, to listen like a disciple' ring true for me. During these past weeks, my morning quiet time with God has given me the strength to face whatever the day has brought. Isaiah reminds me that God has given me all I need to be a disciple, to make a difference – words to encourage others, strength in the face of adversity. Isaiah's words would no doubt have helped Jesus as he looked ahead. He could set his face towards Calvary knowing 'the Lord is coming to my help, who dare condemn me?' Judas may have betrayed him but his trust that God would be with him in the hours and days ahead gave him hope that light would eventually overcome darkness.

Holy Thursday
Evening Mass of the Lord's Supper | White

14
APR THU

Exodus 12:1-8, 11-14
(Please see the Appendix B-10)

Psalm 115:12-13, 15-18. R. cf. 1 Cor 10:16
The blessing-cup that we bless is a communion with the blood of Christ.

1 Corinthians 11:23-26
This is what I received from the Lord, and in turn passed on to you: that on the same night that he was betrayed, the Lord Jesus took some bread, and thanked God for it and broke it, and he said, 'This is my body, which is for you; do this as a memorial of me.' In the same way he took the cup after supper, and said, 'This cup is the new covenant in my blood. Whenever you drink it, do this as a memorial of me.' Until the Lord comes, therefore, every time you eat this bread and drink this cup, you are proclaiming his death.

John 13:1-15
It was before the festival of the Passover, and Jesus knew that the hour had come for him to pass from this world to the Father. He had always loved those who were his in the world, but now he showed how perfect his love was. They were at supper, and the devil had already put it into the mind of Judas Iscariot son of Simon, to betray him. Jesus knew that the Father had put everything into his hands, and that he had come from God and was returning to God, and he got up from table, removed his outer garment and, taking a towel, wrapped it round his waist; he then poured water into a basin and began to wash the disciples' feet and to wipe them with the towel he was wearing. He came to Simon Peter, who said to him, 'Lord, are you going to wash my feet?' Jesus answered, 'At the moment you do not know what I am doing, but later you will understand.' 'Never!' said Peter. 'You shall never wash my feet.' Jesus replied, 'If I do not wash you, you can have nothing in common with me.' 'Then, Lord,' said Simon Peter 'not only my feet, but my hands and my head as well!' Jesus said, 'No one who has taken a bath needs washing, he is clean all over. You too are clean, though not all of you are.' He knew who was going to betray him, that was why he said, 'though not all of you are.' When he had washed their feet and put on his clothes again he went back to the table. 'Do you understand,' he said, 'what I have done to you? You call me Master and Lord, and rightly; so I am. If I, then, the Lord and Master, have washed your feet, you should wash each other's feet. I have given you an example so that you may copy what I have done to you.'

Reflection
Tonight's readings are about *passing over*. Each year the Jews celebrated Passover, a day of festival remembering the marking of their houses with blood, the sharing of a meal and God *passing over* them, leading them to freedom. Paul *passes on* how Jesus left us a profound way of remembering him through the sharing of bread and wine with the gathered community. John describes how Jesus *passed over* to us the example of how to love one another as he had loved us – by washing the feet of others. At the time of the Passover Meal, both in Exodus and at the Last Supper, those involved did not know the significance of what was happening but later they remembered and reflected and understood. So, with us. We can read these events as they are written and move on. Or we can embed their significance in our lives as followers of Christ – a significance that sees us standing ready, sharing our lives, and humbly serving others, all because Jesus showed us what loving God really means.

15

APR FRI

Good Friday
Celebration of the Lord's Passion | Red

Isaiah 52:13–53:12

See, my servant will prosper, he shall be lifted up, exalted, rise to great heights. As the crowds were appalled on seeing him – so disfigured did he look that he seemed no longer human – so will the crowds be astonished at him, and kings stand speechless before him; for they shall see something never told and witness something never heard before: 'Who could believe what we have heard, and to whom has the power of the Lord been revealed?' Like a sapling he grew up in front of us, like a root in arid ground. Without beauty, without majesty (we saw him), no looks to attract our eyes; a thing despised and rejected by men, a man of sorrows and familiar with suffering, a man to make people screen their faces; he was despised and we took no account of him. And yet ours were the sufferings he bore, ours the sorrows he carried. …

(Please see the Appendix B-10)

Psalm 30:2, 6, 12-13, 15-17, 25. R. Luke 23:46

Father, into your hands I commend my spirit.

Hebrews 4:14-16; 5:7-9

Since in Jesus, the Son of God, we have the supreme high priest who has gone through to the highest heaven, we must never let go of the faith that we have professed. For it is not as if we had a high priest who was incapable of feeling our weaknesses with us; but we have one who has been tempted in every way that we are, though he is without sin. Let us be confident, then, in approaching the throne of grace, that we shall have mercy from him and find grace when we are in need of help.

During his life on earth, he offered up prayer and entreaty, aloud and in silent tears, to the one who had the power to save him out of death, and he submitted so humbly that his prayer was heard. Although he was Son, he learnt to obey through suffering; but having been made perfect, he became for all who obey him the source of eternal salvation.

John 18:1–19:42

(Please see the Bible for the Passion Reading)

Reflection

If we want to pray with the events of Good Friday, today's psalm provides us with just that opportunity. 'Into your hands I commend my spirit' recalls Jesus' agony in the Garden of Gethsemane, imploring God for help and coming to acceptance of what is to come. 'I am a reproach' reminds us of the scorn and fear directed at Jesus during the dark of the night as he was taken from one leader to another for judgement. 'Those who see me … run far away from me' takes us back to the loneliness that Jesus must have felt when everyone, even his friends, deserted him. 'But as for me, I trust in you, Lord' prompts us to appreciate that Jesus gave absolutely everything he had, right to his last breath. 'Be strong, let your heart take courage' is Jesus' message to those at the foot of the Cross, and to us who share this Good Friday with him two thousand years later. Can we too pray *Father, I put my life in your hands?*

Easter Vigil
White

16
APR SAT

Romans 6:3-11

When we were baptised in Christ Jesus we were baptised in his death; in other words, when we were baptised we went into the tomb with him and joined him in death, so that as Christ was raised from the dead by the Father's glory, we too might live a new life.

If in union with Christ we have imitated his death, we shall also imitate him in his resurrection. We must realise that our former selves have been crucified with him to destroy this sinful body and to free us from the slavery of sin. When a man dies, of course, he has finished with sin.

But we believe that having died with Christ we shall return to life with him: Christ, as we know, having been raised from the dead will never die again. Death has no power over him any more. When he died, he died, once for all, to sin, so his life now is life with God; and in that way, you too must consider yourselves to be dead to sin but alive for God in Christ Jesus.

Psalm 117:1-2, 16-17, 22-23

Alleluia, alleluia, alleluia!

Luke 24:1-12

On the first day of the week, at the first sign of dawn, the women went to the tomb with the spices they had prepared. They found that the stone had been rolled away from the tomb, but on entering discovered that the body of the Lord Jesus was not there. As they stood there not knowing what to think, two men in brilliant clothes suddenly appeared at their side. Terrified, the women lowered their eyes. But the two men said to them, 'Why look among the dead for someone who is alive? He is not here; he has risen. Remember what he told you when he was still in Galilee: that the Son of Man had to be handed over into the power of sinful men and be crucified, and rise again on the third day?' And they remembered his words. When the women returned from the tomb they told all this to the Eleven and to all the others. The women were Mary of Magdala, Joanna, and Mary the mother of James. The other women with them also told the apostles, but this story of theirs seemed pure nonsense, and they did not believe them. Peter, however, went running to the tomb. He bent down and saw the binding cloths, but nothing else; he then went back home, amazed at what had happened.

Reflection

Holy Saturday – a day to stay within the mystery of death, to mourn and to remember. We feel somewhat numb in our grief, emptied out after all we have witnessed these past days. There is relief perhaps that Jesus is no longer suffering, but what happens now – to him, to all of us? Jesus, who had given us such expectation for the future, is in the tomb. We feel as if we, too, have gone into the tomb with Jesus and joined him in death. 'But we believe that, having died with Christ, we shall return to life with him.' Can we dare to hope that all is not over? Is what the women are saying 'pure nonsense'? Or, like Peter, can we be amazed that 'he is not here: he has risen'. Death has no more power over him, or us. Our hearts lift as we proclaim, *I shall not die, I shall live and recount God's deeds.*

17
APR SUN

EASTER SUNDAY

Psalter Week 1

White

Acts 10:34, 37-43

Peter addressed Cornelius and his household: 'You must have heard about the recent happenings in Judaea: about Jesus of Nazareth and how he began in Galilee, after John had been preaching baptism. God had anointed him with the Holy Spirit and with power, and because God was with him, Jesus went about doing good and curing all who had fallen into the power of the devil. Now I, and those with me, can witness to everything he did throughout the countryside of Judaea and in Jerusalem itself: and also to the fact that they killed him by hanging him on a tree, yet three days afterwards God raised him to life and allowed him to be seen, not by the whole people but only by certain witnesses God had chosen beforehand. Now we are those witnesses – we have eaten and drunk with him after his resurrection from the dead – and he has ordered us to proclaim this to his people and to tell them that God has appointed him to judge everyone, alive or dead. It is to him that all the prophets bear this witness: that all who believe in Jesus will have their sins forgiven through his name.'

Psalm 117:1-2, 16-17, 22-23. R. v. 24

This day was made by the Lord: we rejoice and are glad.

Colossians 3:1-4

(Alternative Reading: 1 Corinthians 5:6-8)

Since you have been brought back to true life with Christ, you must look for the things that are in heaven, where Christ is, sitting at God's right hand. Let your thoughts be on heavenly things, not on the things that are on the earth, because you have died, and now the life you have is hidden with Christ in God. But when Christ is revealed – and he is your life – you too will be revealed in all your glory with him.

John 20:1-9

It was very early on the first day of the week and still dark, when Mary of Magdala came to the tomb. She saw that the stone had been moved away from the tomb and came running to Simon Peter and the other disciple, the one Jesus loved. 'They have taken the Lord out of the tomb' she said 'and we don't know where they have put him.'

So Peter set out with the other disciple to go to the tomb. They ran together, but the other disciple, running faster than Peter, reached the tomb first; he bent down and saw the linen cloths lying on the ground, but did not go in. Simon Peter who was following now came up, went right into the tomb, saw the linen cloths on the ground, and also the cloth that had been over his head; this was not with the linen cloths but rolled up in a place by itself. Then the other disciple who had reached the tomb first also went in; he saw and he believed. Till this moment they had failed to understand the teaching of scripture, that he must rise from the dead.

Reflection

It was still dark when Mary of Magdala came to the tomb and found the stone moved away. Her first thought was not resurrection, but that someone had taken Jesus' body, so she ran to get help. When Peter arrived, he saw the burial cloths. When John arrived, he saw the same scene, but 'he believed'. John, known as Jesus' beloved disciple, saw with the eyes of his heart and just knew that God had raised Jesus from the dead. Easter Sunday celebrates that darkness was overcome by light. But Easter is not a once-only event. We catch something of the reality of resurrection whenever we experience new life emerging from hopelessness. This transformation can be personal to our own circumstances when relationships break down or disaster of one sort or another strikes. And it can be global. What about the Good News stories that emerge from violent situations and crises such as pandemics? It is all a matter of seeing reality through the eyes of our heart. *This is the day the Lord has made; let us rejoice and be glad.*

18
APR MON

Easter Monday
White

Acts 2:14, 22-33

On the day of Pentecost, Peter stood up with the Eleven and addressed the crowd in a loud voice: 'Men of Israel, listen to what I am going to say: Jesus the Nazarene was a man commended to you by God by the miracles and portents and signs that God worked through him when he was among you, as you all know. This man, who was put into your power by the deliberate intention and foreknowledge of God, you took and had crucified by men outside the Law. You killed him, but God raised him to life, freeing him from the pangs of Hades; for it was impossible for him to be held in its power since, as David says of him: I saw the Lord before me always, for with him at my right hand nothing can shake me. So my heart was glad and my tongue cried out with joy; my body, too, will rest in the hope that you will not abandon my soul to Hades nor allow your holy one to experience corruption. …

(Please see the Appendix B-11)

Psalm 15:1-2, 5, 7-11. R. v. 1

Preserve me, Lord, I take refuge in you.

Matthew 28:8-15

Filled with awe and great joy the women came quickly away from the tomb and ran to tell the disciples.

And there, coming to meet them, was Jesus. 'Greetings' he said. And the women came up to him and, falling down before him, clasped his feet. Then Jesus said to them, 'Do not be afraid; go and tell my brothers that they must leave for Galilee; they will see me there.'

While they were on their way, some of the guard went off into the city to tell the chief priests all that had happened. These held a meeting with the elders and, after some discussion, handed a considerable sum of money to the soldiers with these instructions, 'This is what you must say, "His disciples came during the night and stole him away while we were asleep." And should the governor come to hear of this, we undertake to put things right with him ourselves and to see that you do not get into trouble.' The soldiers took the money and carried out their instructions, and to this day that is the story among the Jews.

Reflection

In the dawn light after the Sabbath, the women go to the tomb and are told by an angel that Jesus has risen from the dead. No wonder they were filled with awe and running to spread the news! 'And there, coming to meet them, was Jesus.' The women seem to have no trouble recognising Jesus, but he does not want them to linger with him. He has a message for them to deliver. This post-resurrection time was bewildering for all involved. It asked of all an openness to the mystery unfolding before them. Sometimes Jesus asks the most unlikely people to be his messengers, in this case the women, but always an encounter with Jesus sends us out on mission. During these few days of holiday perhaps we could reflect on the messengers who have come into our lives – and how we have been a messenger to others. As with the women, our encounter with Jesus gives us energy for mission. *Do not be afraid; go …*

19
APR TUE

Easter Tuesday
White

Acts 2:36-41

On the day of Pentecost, Peter spoke to the Jews: 'The whole House of Israel can be certain that God has made this Jesus whom you crucified both Lord and Christ.'

Hearing this, they were cut to the heart and said to Peter and the apostles, 'What must we do, brothers?' 'You must repent,' Peter answered 'and every one of you must be baptised in the name of Jesus Christ for the forgiveness of your sins, and you will receive the gift of the Holy Spirit. The promise that was made is for you and your children, and for all those who are far away, for all those whom the Lord our God will call to himself.' He spoke to them for a long time using many arguments, and he urged them, 'Save yourselves from this perverse generation.' They were convinced by his arguments, and they accepted what he said and were baptised. That very day about three thousand were added to their number.

Psalm 32:4-5, 18-20, 22. R. v. 5

The Lord fills the earth with his love.

John 20:11-18

Mary stayed outside near the tomb, weeping. Then, still weeping, she stooped to look inside, and saw two angels in white sitting where the body of Jesus had been, one at the head, the other at the feet. They said, 'Woman, why are you weeping?' 'They have taken my Lord away,' she replied 'and I don't know where they have put him.' As she said this she turned round and saw Jesus standing there, though she did not recognise him. Jesus said, 'Woman, why are you weeping? Who are you looking for?' Supposing him to be the gardener, she said, 'Sir, if you have taken him away, tell me where you have put him, and I will go and remove him.' Jesus said, 'Mary!' She knew him then and said to him in Hebrew, 'Rabbuni!' – which means Master. Jesus said to her, 'Do not cling to me, because I have not yet ascended to the Father. But go and find the brothers, and tell them: I am ascending to my Father and your Father, to my God and your God.' So Mary of Magdala went and told the disciples that she had seen the Lord and that he had said these things to her.

Reflection

It wasn't until Jesus called her by name that Mary recognised him. Until that moment she had been distraught, overwhelmed by grief at the realisation that Jesus was not in the tomb. It was all too much for her to understand and tears welled up from the depths of her broken heart. How many people among us could relate to this scene! Blinded by tears for the unexpected loss of a loved one, they reel from the situation, feeling only total loss and desperation for the future. Who can they turn to now? Mary turned to the gardener and discovered the one whom she loved was still with her, albeit in a new way. She ran to share this hope-filled moment. Is there someone I know who is suffering great loss and for whom I could reach out to offer hope for the future? Could I be the person through whom Jesus calls their name and allows them to see with new eyes?

20
APR WED

Easter Wednesday
White

Acts 3:1-10
(Please see the Appendix B-11)

Psalm 104:1-4, 6-9. R. v. 3
Let the hearts that seek the Lord rejoice.

Luke 24:13-35
Two of the disciples of Jesus were on their way to a village called Emmaus, seven miles from Jerusalem, and they were talking together about all that had happened. Now as they talked this over, Jesus himself came up and walked by their side; but something prevented them from recognising him. He said to them, 'What matters are you discussing as you walk along?' They stopped short, their faces downcast. Then one of them, called Cleopas, answered him, 'You must be the only person staying in Jerusalem who does not know the things that have been happening there these last few days.' 'What things?' he asked. 'All about Jesus of Nazareth' they answered 'who proved he was a great prophet by the things he said and did in the sight of God and of the whole people; and how our chief priests and our leaders handed him over to be sentenced to death, and had him crucified. Our own hope had been that he would be the one to set Israel free. And this is not all: two whole days have gone by since it all happened; and some women from our group have astounded us: they went to the tomb in the early morning, and when they did not find the body, they came back to tell us they had seen a vision of angels who declared he was alive. Some of our friends went to the tomb and found everything exactly as the women had reported, but of him they saw nothing.' Then he said to them, 'You foolish men! So slow to believe the full message of the prophets! Was it not ordained that the Christ should suffer and so enter into his glory?' Then, starting with Moses and going through all the prophets, he explained to them the passages throughout the scriptures that were about himself. When they drew near to the village to which they were going, he made as if to go on; but they pressed him to stay with them. 'It is nearly evening' they said 'and the day is almost over.' So he went in to stay with them. Now while he was with them at table, he took the bread and said the blessing; then he broke it and handed it to them. And their eyes were opened and they recognised him; but he had vanished from their sight. Then they said to each other, 'Did not our hearts burn within us as he talked to us on the road and explained the scriptures to us?' They set out that instant and returned to Jerusalem. There they found the Eleven assembled together with their companions, who said to them, 'Yes, it is true. The Lord has risen and has appeared to Simon.' Then they told their story of what had happened on the road and how they had recognised him at the breaking of bread.

Reflection
'Did not our hearts burn within us as he talked to us on the road?' Sometimes when my heart is full and I am struggling to understand a situation, I find it is good to go for a walk – alone, or with a good listening companion. The disciples' hearts and minds were certainly full of all that had happened over the past days. They talked and they listened to each other and to the stranger who joined them, but it was only when they invited this person to stay with them that they realised that Jesus was still with them and everything started to make sense. I can walk and talk and listen, but invariably it is only when I share what is in my heart with Jesus that I just know what I need to do next. I pray that I may become ever more aware of the presence of the risen Jesus with me. *Lord, open my eyes and ears, my mind and heart to you this day.*

21
APR THU

Easter Thursday
White

Acts 3:11-26

Everyone came running towards Peter and John in great excitement, to the Portico of Solomon, as it is called, where the man was still clinging to them. When Peter saw the people he addressed them, 'Why are you so surprised at this? Why are you staring at us as though we had made this man walk by our own power or holiness? You are Israelites, and it is the God of Abraham, Isaac and Jacob, the God of our ancestors, who has glorified his servant Jesus, the same Jesus you handed over and then disowned in the presence of Pilate, after Pilate had decided to release him. ...
(Please see the Appendix B-11)

Psalm 8:2, 5-9. R. v. 2

How great is your name, O Lord our God, through all the earth!

Luke 24:35-48

The disciples told their story of what had happened on the road and how they had recognised Jesus at the breaking of bread. They were still talking about this when Jesus himself stood among them and said to them, 'Peace be with you!' In a state of alarm and fright, they thought they were seeing a ghost. But he said, 'Why are you so agitated, and why are these doubts rising in your hearts? Look at my hands and feet; yes, it is I indeed. Touch me and see for yourselves; a ghost has no flesh and bones as you can see I have.' And as he said this he showed them his hands and feet. Their joy was so great that they could not believe it, and they stood there dumbfounded; so he said to them, 'Have you anything here to eat?' And they offered him a piece of grilled fish, which he took and ate before their eyes.

Then he told them, 'This is what I meant when I said, while I was still with you, that everything written about me, in the Law of Moses, in the Prophets and in the Psalms, has to be fulfilled.' He then opened their minds to understand the scriptures, and he said to them, 'So you see how it is written that the Christ would suffer and on the third day rise from the dead, and that, in his name, repentance for the forgiveness of sins would be preached to all the nations, beginning from Jerusalem. You are witnesses to this.'

Reflection

Today's Gospel is about human reactions. The disciples are alarmed and frightened at their unexpected encounter with the risen Jesus. Later, through listening to him, their minds are opened, and their fear turns to joy as they begin to understand the meaning of the events they had been experiencing. We too can experience relief when things turn out better than we anticipated. Think back to the fear and uncertainty of those first months of realisation that the world was in the grip of a pandemic. Yet, as reassuring stories started to emerge, we began to understand how to deal with this unseen threat. Like pieces of a jigsaw puzzle coming together we began to live into a 'new normal'. Today might be a good time to reflect back on the events of Holy Week that we have just celebrated. What has been my reaction to the suffering, death and now the resurrection of Jesus? Have these events affected me enough to see myself living into a 'new normal'?

Easter Friday
White

22
APR FRI

Acts 4:1-12

(Please see the Appendix B-12)

Psalm 117:1-2, 4, 22-27. R. v. 22

The stone which the builders rejected has become the corner stone.

John 21:1-14

Jesus showed himself again to the disciples. It was by the Sea of Tiberias, and it happened like this: Simon Peter, Thomas called the Twin, Nathanael from Cana in Galilee, the sons of Zebedee and two more of his disciples were together. Simon Peter said, 'I'm going fishing.' They replied, 'We'll come with you.' They went out and got into the boat but caught nothing that night.

It was light by now and there stood Jesus on the shore, though the disciples did not realise that it was Jesus. Jesus called out, 'Have you caught anything, friends?' And when they answered, 'No,' he said, 'Throw the net out to starboard and you'll find something.' So they dropped the net, and there were so many fish that they could not haul it in. The disciple Jesus loved said to Peter, 'It is the Lord.' At these words 'It is the Lord', Simon Peter, who had practically nothing on, wrapped his cloak round him and jumped into the water. The other disciples came on in the boat, towing the net and the fish; they were only about a hundred yards from land.

As soon as they came ashore they saw that there was some bread there, and a charcoal fire with fish cooking on it. Jesus said, 'Bring some of the fish you have just caught.' Simon Peter went aboard and dragged the net to the shore, full of big fish, one hundred and fifty-three of them; and in spite of there being so many the net was not broken. Jesus said to them, 'Come and have breakfast.' None of the disciples was bold enough to ask, 'Who are you?'; they knew quite well it was the Lord. Jesus then stepped forward, took the bread and gave it to them, and the same with the fish. This was the third time that Jesus showed himself to the disciples after rising from the dead.

Reflection

It is said that breakfast is the most important meal of the day – perhaps for some 'breakfast' might equate to that first cup of coffee that gets one moving! For the disciples, the breakfast of fish and bread on the beach certainly gave them the boost they needed. In their uncertainty they had gone fishing because that was something familiar and useful to do. During the long, dark night they had, no doubt, struggled with their feelings of loss and uncertainty as they waited. But, with the light everything changed. Amid their normal routine they recognised Jesus was with them, not only directing them to a huge catch of fish but also preparing and eating breakfast with them. Imagine how their spirits must have lifted! This Gospel is a good reminder to us that God is always with us where we are. Just as breakfast, or coffee, prepares us for the challenges of the day ahead, so a morning prayer time can energise our heart to face the day with confidence.

Easter Saturday
White

23
APR SAT

Acts 4:13-21

The rulers, elders and scribes were astonished at the assurance shown by Peter and John, considering they were uneducated laymen; and they recognised them as associates of Jesus; but when they saw the man who had been cured standing by their side, they could find no answer. So they ordered them to stand outside while the Sanhedrin had a private discussion. 'What are we going to do with these men?' they asked. 'It is obvious to everybody in Jerusalem that a miracle has been worked through them in public, and we cannot deny it. But to stop the whole thing spreading any further among the people, let us caution them never to speak to anyone in this name again.'

So they called them in and gave them a warning on no account to make statements or to teach in the name of Jesus. But Peter and John retorted, 'You must judge whether in God's eyes it is right to listen to you and not to God. We cannot promise to stop proclaiming what we have seen and heard.' The court repeated the warnings and then released them; they could not think of any way to punish them, since all the people were giving glory to God for what had happened.

Psalm 117:1, 14-21. R. v. 21

I will thank you, Lord, for you have given answer.

Mark 16:9-15

Having risen in the morning on the first day of the week, Jesus appeared first to Mary of Magdala from whom he had cast out seven devils. She then went to those who had been his companions, and who were mourning and in tears, and told them. But they did not believe her when they heard her say that he was alive and that she had seen him. After this, he showed himself under another form to two of them as they were on their way into the country. These went back and told the others, who did not believe them either.

Lastly, he showed himself to the Eleven themselves while they were at table. He reproached them for their incredulity and obstinacy, because they had refused to believe those who had seen him after he had risen. And he said to them, 'Go out to the whole world; proclaim the Good News to all creation.'

Reflection

Jesus reproached his disciples for their incredulity and obstinacy in not believing those who had seen him after he had risen. But, after this rebuke, Peter and John certainly took to heart Jesus' words and went out to proclaim the Good News to all creation. They were prepared to say to the authorities, 'we cannot promise to stop proclaiming what we have seen and heard'. What have we seen and heard that we want to proclaim? Perhaps today we could ponder questions such as: Who are the people in my life who have revealed Jesus to me? To whom have I proclaimed the good news about Jesus – either deliberately or by the example of my life? I pray with gratitude for those who have witnessed Jesus to me and with sincerity ask that I too may be a faithful witness to others.

24
APR SUN

SECOND SUNDAY OF EASTER (Divine Mercy Sunday)

Psalter Week 2

White

Acts 5:12-16

The faithful all used to meet by common consent in the Portico of Solomon. No one else ever dared to join them, but the people were loud in their praise and the numbers of men and women who came to believe in the Lord increased steadily. So many signs and wonders were worked among the people at the hands of the apostles that the sick were even taken out into the streets and laid on beds and sleeping-mats in the hope that at least the shadow of Peter might fall across some of them as he went past. People even came crowding in from the towns round about Jerusalem, bringing with them their sick and those tormented by unclean spirits, and all of them were cured.

Psalm 117:2-4, 22-27 R. v. 1

Give thanks to the Lord for he is good, for his love has no end.

Apocalypse 1:9-13, 17-19

My name is John, and through our union in Jesus I am your brother and share your sufferings, your kingdom, and all you endure. I was on the island of Patmos for having preached God's word and witnessed for Jesus; it was the Lord's day and the Spirit possessed me, and I heard a voice behind me, shouting like a trumpet, 'Write down all that you see in a book.' I turned round to see who had spoken to me, and when I turned I saw seven golden lamp-stands and, surrounded by them, a figure like a Son of man, dressed in a long robe tied at the waist with a golden girdle.

When I saw him, I fell in a dead faint at his feet, but he touched me with his right hand and said, 'Do not be afraid; it is I, the First and the Last; I am the Living One. I was dead and now I am to live for ever and ever, and I hold the keys of death and of the underworld. Now write down all that you see of present happenings and things that are still to come.'

John 20:19-31

In the evening of that same day, the first day of the week, the doors were closed in the room where the disciples were, for fear of the Jews. Jesus came and stood among them. He said to them, 'Peace be with you,' and showed them his hands and his side. The disciples were filled with joy when they saw the Lord, and he said to them again, 'Peace be with you.

'As the Father sent me, so am I sending you.' After saying this he breathed on them and said: 'Receive the Holy Spirit. For those whose sins you forgive, they are forgiven; for those whose sins you retain, they are retained.'

Thomas, called the Twin, who was one of the Twelve, was not with them when Jesus came. When the disciples said, 'We have seen the Lord,' he answered, 'Unless I see the holes that the nails made in his hands and can put my finger into the holes they made, and unless I can put my hand into his side, I refuse to believe.' Eight days later the disciples were in the house again and Thomas was with them. The doors were closed, but Jesus came in and stood among them. 'Peace be with you,' he said. Then he spoke to Thomas, 'Put your finger here; look, here are my hands. Give me your hand; put it into my side. Doubt no longer but believe.' Thomas replied, 'My Lord and my God!' Jesus said to him: 'You believe because you can see me. Happy are those who have not seen and yet believe.'

There were many other signs that Jesus worked and the disciples saw, but they are not recorded in this book. These are recorded so that you may believe that Jesus is the Christ, the Son of God, and that believing this you may have life through his name.

Reflection

Today, as we listen to the end of John's Gospel, maybe we recognise ourselves in the person of Thomas, wanting reassurance that the risen Jesus is really with us. Jesus says, 'happy are those who have not seen and yet believe'. It is all a matter of seeing with the eyes of faith, the eyes of our heart, noticing that 'Jesus, the Christ, the Son of God' is very much with us wherever we are. This presence brings peace, fills us with joy and sends us out on mission. Sounds easy! But just as our significant relationships take time to grow and deepen, so does our faith relationship with God. Thomas needed to see Jesus, to experience his presence, before he could believe. What do I need to do to nurture my faith? Perhaps I need look no further than to the actions, beliefs, and presence of other believers. Perhaps, like Thomas, I need to take the opportunity to 'see' Jesus for myself. If so, then there's no better day than today to start 'seeing'.

25
APR MON

St Mark, Evangelist
Feast | Red

1 Peter 5:5-14

All wrap yourselves in humility to be servants of each other, because God refuses the proud and will always favour the humble. Bow down, then, before the power of God now, and he will raise you up on the appointed day; unload all your worries on to him, since he is looking after you. Be calm but vigilant, because your enemy the devil is prowling round like a roaring lion, looking for something to eat. Stand up to him, strong in faith and in the knowledge that your brothers all over the world are suffering the same things. You will have to suffer only for a little while: the God of all grace who called you to eternal glory in Christ will see that all is well again: he will confirm, strengthen and support you. His power lasts for ever and ever. Amen.

I write these few words to you through Silvanus, who is a brother I know I can trust, to encourage you never to let go this true grace of God to which I bear witness.

Your sister in Babylon, who is with you among the chosen, sends you greetings; so does my son, Mark. Greet one another with a kiss of love. Peace to you all who are in Christ.

Psalm 88:2-3, 6-7, 16-17. R. cf. v. 2

I will sing for ever of your love, O Lord.

Mark 16:15-20

Jesus said to the Eleven, 'Go out to the whole world; proclaim the Good News to all creation. He who believes and is baptised will be saved; he who does not believe will be condemned. These are the signs that will be associated with believers: in my name they will cast out devils; they will have the gift of tongues; they will pick up snakes in their hands, and be unharmed should they drink deadly poison; they will lay their hands on the sick, who will recover.'

And so the Lord Jesus, after he had spoken to them, was taken up into heaven: there at the right hand of God he took his place, while they, going out, preached everywhere, the Lord working with them and confirming the word by signs that accompanied it.

Reflection

Jesus said to the Eleven, 'Go out to the whole world, proclaim the Good News to all creation.' This is a mission entrusted not just to the apostles but to us as well. The apostles certainly showed us how to spread the Good News throughout the world of their time. Mark, whom we especially celebrate today, took up his pen and wrote a Gospel. For two thousand years the Good News has been proclaimed in various ways by multitudes of followers of Christ. So, how am I responding to Jesus' words today? Of course, each of us has our own way, according to our own gifts. We don't have to write a gospel, but we are grateful that Mark used his gifts this way. Peter's words remind us to be humble, calm, yet vigilant disciples. We may not often be faced by devils and snakes, but we can still show by our words and actions that we are about God's work every day.

2nd Week of Easter
White

26
APR TUE

SAINT GEORGE, MARTYR, Solemnity
– England
see Appendix A-12

Acts 4:32-37
The whole group of believers was united, heart and soul; no one claimed for his own use anything that he had, as everything they owned was held in common. The apostles continued to testify to the resurrection of the Lord Jesus with great power, and they were all given great respect. None of their members was ever in want, as all those who owned land or houses would sell them, and bring the money from them, to present it to the apostles; it was then distributed to any members who might be in need. There was a Levite of Cypriot origin called Joseph whom the apostles surnamed Barnabas (which means 'son of encouragement'). He owned a piece of land and he sold it and brought the money, and presented it to the apostles.

Psalm 91:1-2,5. R. v. 1
The Lord is king, with majesty enrobed.

John 3:7-15
Jesus said to Nicodemus:

'Do not be surprised when I say: You must be born from above. The wind blows wherever it pleases; you hear its sound, but you cannot tell where it comes from or where it is going. That is how it is with all who are born of the Spirit.' 'How can that be possible?' asked Nicodemus. 'You, a teacher in Israel, and you do not know these things!' replied Jesus. 'I tell you most solemnly, we speak only about what we know and witness only to what we have seen and yet you people reject our evidence. If you do not believe me when I speak about things in this world, how are you going to believe me when I speak to you about heavenly things? No one has gone up to heaven except the one who came down from heaven, the Son of Man who is in heaven; and the Son of Man must be lifted up as Moses lifted up the serpent in the desert, so that everyone who believes may have eternal life in him.'

Reflection
Faith in Jesus is what guarantees eternal life. An apparent tendency in today's Christianity is to relegate faith to the background while upholding prosperity. Prosperity preachers seem to be "holding the mic" today. While Jesus preaches that without faith no one will see God, they hold that without riches no one will see God. The goal today is therefore to pursue riches at all costs to the detriment of one's soul. It is faith that enables us to see others as brethren in Christ. By so doing we will share our life and property with them. It is faith that helps us to begin living out our eternal life while still here. Lord, increase and deepen our faith in You!

27
APR WED

2nd Week of Easter | White
or **St Louis Grignion de Montfort,** *priest* (Optional, White)

Acts 5:17-26

The high priest intervened with all his supporters from the party of the Sadducees. Prompted by jealousy, they arrested the apostles and had them put in the common gaol. But at night the angel of the Lord opened the prison gates and said as he led them out, 'Go and stand in the Temple, and tell the people all about this new Life.' They did as they were told; they went into the Temple at dawn and began to preach. When the high priest arrived, he and his supporters convened the Sanhedrin – this was the full Senate of Israel – and sent to the gaol for them to be brought. But when the officials arrived at the prison they found they were not inside, so they went back and reported, 'We found the gaol securely locked and the warders on duty at the gates, but when we unlocked the door we found no one inside.' When the captain of the Temple and the chief priests heard this news they wondered what this could mean. Then a man arrived with fresh news. 'At this very moment,' he said 'the men you imprisoned are in the Temple. They are standing there preaching to the people.' The captain went with his men and fetched them. They were afraid to use force in case the people stoned them.

Psalm 33:2-9. R. v. 7

This poor man called and the Lord heard him.

John 3:16-21

Jesus said to Nicodemus: 'God loved the world so much that he gave his only Son, so that everyone who believes in him may not be lost but may have eternal life. For God sent his Son into the world not to condemn the world, but so that through him the world might be saved. No one who believes in him will be condemned; but whoever refuses to believe is condemned already, because he has refused to believe in the name of God's only Son. On these grounds is sentence pronounced: that though the light has come into the world men have shown they prefer darkness to the light because their deeds were evil. And indeed, everybody who does wrong hates the light and avoids it, for fear his actions should be exposed; but the man who lives by the truth comes out into the light, so that it may be plainly seen that what he does is done in God.'

Reflection

'God loved the world so much that he gave his only Son' to bring light into our darkness. The apostles spent the night in the darkness of prison but, freed at dawn, they moved back into the light and began to proclaim the new Life they were experiencing. The psalmist encourages us to 'look towards [God] and be radiant', to live in light. Jesus encourages us to come out into the light so that 'it may be plainly seen that what [we do] is done in God'. The readings today invite each of us to consider where we stand as disciples. Are we in the darkness of a prison of busyness and anxiety, finding the light outside too bright for us? Or are we being a light, albeit gentle, for others to come to know Jesus? The choice is ours.

2nd Week of Easter
St Peter Chanel, *priest, martyr,* **Memorial** | Red

28
APR THU

Acts 5:27-33

When the officials had brought the apostles in to face the Sanhedrin, the high priest demanded an explanation. 'We gave you a formal warning' he said 'not to preach in this name, and what have you done? You have filled Jerusalem with your teaching, and seem determined to fix the guilt of this man's death on us.' In reply Peter and the apostles said, 'Obedience to God comes before obedience to men; it was the God of our ancestors who raised up Jesus, but it was you who had him executed by hanging on a tree.

By his own right hand God has now raised him up to be leader and saviour, to give repentance and forgiveness of sins through him to Israel. We are witnesses to all this, we and the Holy Spirit whom God has given to those who obey him.' This so infuriated them that they wanted to put them to death.

Psalm 33:2, 9, 17-20. R. v. 7

This poor man called and the Lord heard him.

John 3:31-36

John the Baptist said to his disciples: 'He who comes from above is above all others; he who is born of the earth is earthly himself and speaks in an earthly way. He who comes from heaven bears witness to the things he has seen and heard, even if his testimony is not accepted; though all who do accept his testimony are attesting the truthfulness of God, since he whom God has sent speaks God's own words: God gives him the Spirit without reserve. The Father loves the Son and has entrusted everything to him. Anyone who believes in the Son has eternal life, but anyone who refuses to believe in the Son will never see life: the anger of God stays on him.'

Reflection

'The Lord hears the cry of the poor.' This psalm response is the same as we heard yesterday and invites us to rejoice in a God who weeps with compassion for those who are distressed, broken-hearted and crushed by life. The media certainly alerts us to easily identify these people – asylum seekers, refugees, victims of abuse, violence, mental illness, and pandemics as well as those who live in poverty and homelessness. But 'the poor' surround us every day wherever we are if we have eyes and ears open to see and hear them. God cares for 'the poor' in many ways but particularly through those who companion them in their struggles. St Peter Chanel, whom we especially commemorate today, was one such person who gave his life for 'the poor'. Martyrdom may not be asked of us, but if we listen to the whisperings of God deep in our heart, we may be surprised to hear God calling us to care in a special way for some of the people we meet incidentally as we go about our everyday activities.

29
APR FRI

2nd Week of Easter
St Catherine of Siena, *virgin, doctor,* **Feast** | White

1 John 1:5-2:2
This is what we have heard from Jesus Christ, and the message that we are announcing to you: God is light; there is no darkness in him at all. If we say that we are in union with God while we are living in darkness, we are lying because we are not living the truth. But if we live our lives in the light, as he is in the light, we are in union with one another, and the blood of Jesus, his Son, purifies us from all sin. If we say we have no sin in us, we are deceiving ourselves and refusing to admit the truth; but if we acknowledge our sins, then God who is faithful and just will forgive our sins and purify us from everything that is wrong. To say that we have never sinned is to call God a liar and to show that his word is not in us. I am writing this, my children, to stop you sinning; but if anyone should sin, we have our advocate with the Father, Jesus Christ, who is just; he is the sacrifice that takes our sins away, and not only ours, but the whole world's.

Psalm 102:1-4,8-9,13-14,17-18
My soul, give thanks to the Lord.

Matthew 11:25-30
Jesus exclaimed, 'I bless you, Father, Lord of heaven and of earth, for hiding these things from the learned and the clever and revealing them to mere children. Yes, Father, for that is what it pleased you to do. Everything has been entrusted to me by my Father; and no one knows the Son except the Father, just as no one knows the Father except the Son and those to whom the Son chooses to reveal him.

'Come to me, all you who labour and are overburdened, and I will give you rest. Shoulder my yoke and learn from me, for I am gentle and humble in heart, and you will find rest for your souls. Yes, my yoke is easy and my burden light.'

Reflection
"Take My yoke and learn from Me" (Matthew 11:28-30). Mistakes abound in life, yes. The trick, however, is to make it easier for ourselves by learning from those mistakes and not repeating them. A great advantage we have is to learn from Someone who is like us in everything except sin: Jesus Christ. He is meek and humble, even though His state is divine. Through this He attains the most exalted and glorious state in life. Isn't that wonderful? Modelling our lives after someone great is one of the greatest lessons of life. We pass through a lot because we are short of models to learn from. Look up to Jesus.

2nd Week of Easter | White
or **St Pius V,** *pope* (Optional, White)

30
APR SAT

Acts 6:1 -7

About this time, when the number of disciples was increasing, the Hellenists made a complaint against the Hebrews: in the daily distribution their own widows were being overlooked. So the Twelve called a full meeting of the disciples and addressed them 'It would not be right for us to neglect the word of God so as to give out food; you, brothers, must select from among yourselves seven men of good reputation, filled with the Spirit and with wisdom; we will hand over this duty to them, and continue to devote ourselves to prayer and to the service of the word.' The whole assembly approved of this proposal and elected Stephen, a man full of faith and of the Holy Spirit, together with Philip, Prochorus, Nicanor, Timon, Parmenas, and Nicolaus of Antioch, a convert to Judaism. They presented these to the apostles, who prayed and laid their hands on them. The word of the Lord continued to spread: the number of disciples in Jerusalem was greatly increased, and a large group of priests made their submission to the faith.

Psalm 32:1-2, 4-5, 18-19. R. v. 22

May your love be upon us, O Lord, as we place all our hope in you.

John 6:16-21

In the evening the disciples went down to the shore of the lake and got into a boat to make for Capernaum on the other side of the lake. It was getting dark by now and Jesus had still not rejoined them. The wind was strong, and the sea was getting rough. They had rowed three or four miles when they saw Jesus walking on the lake and coming towards the boat. This frightened them, but he said, 'It is I. Do not be afraid.' They were for taking him into the boat, but in no time it reached the shore at the place they were making for.

Reflection

The disciples are in a boat rowing into a storm. With the wind strengthening and the sea getting rougher they are afraid they are in serious physical danger. How will they ever reach the shore? It is only when Jesus appears walking on the water and they put their trust in his words 'do not be afraid' that suddenly they realise they are safe. In recent times there have been many storms battering what we had come to think was a normal way of living in our world. Our boats have been battered by winds and seas of uncertainty and fear. The challenge for us has been to remember to invite Jesus into our boat – to put our trust in his words 'do not be afraid'. *Jesus, we invite you into our boat this day to be light in the darkness of the confusion and doubt we so often feel. Give us the strength we need to face our challenges with increased trust and faith in you. When we feel overwhelmed, help us to be aware of you walking towards us and bringing us safely to the shore.*

01

MAY SUN

THIRD SUNDAY OF EASTER

Psalter Week 3

White

Acts 5:27-32, 40-41

The high priest demanded an explanation of the apostles. 'We gave you a formal warning,' he said 'not to preach in this name, and what have you done? You have filled Jerusalem with your teaching, and seem determined to fix the guilt of this man's death on us.' In reply Peter and the apostles said, 'Obedience to God comes before obedience to men; it was the God of our ancestors who raised up Jesus, but it was you who had him executed by hanging on a tree. By his own right hand God has now raised him up to be leader and saviour, to give repentance and forgiveness of sins through him to Israel. We are witnesses to all this, we and the Holy Spirit whom God has given to those who obey him.' They warned the apostles not to speak in the name of Jesus and released them. And so they left the presence of the Sanhedrin glad to have had the honour of suffering humiliation for the sake of the name.

Psalm 29:2, 4-6, 11-13. R. v. 2

I will praise you, Lord, you have rescued me.

Apocalypse 5:11-14

In my vision, I, John, heard the sound of an immense number of angels gathered round the throne and the animals and the elders; there were ten thousand times ten thousand of them and thousands upon thousands, shouting, 'The Lamb that was sacrificed is worthy to be given power, riches, wisdom, strength, honour, glory and blessing.' Then I heard all the living things in creation – everything that lives in the air and on the ground, and under the ground, and in the sea, crying, 'To the One who is sitting on the throne and to the Lamb, be all praise, honour, glory and power, for ever and ever.' And the four animals said, 'Amen'; and the elders prostrated themselves to worship.

John 21:1-19 *(Shorter form 21:1-14)*

Jesus showed himself again to the disciples. It was by the Sea of Tiberias, and it happened like this: Simon Peter, Thomas called the Twin, Nathanael from Cana in Galilee, the sons of Zebedee and two more of his disciples were together. Simon Peter said, 'I'm going fishing.' They replied, 'We'll come with you.' They went out and got into the boat but caught nothing that night.

It was light by now and there stood Jesus on the shore, though the disciples did not realise that it was Jesus. Jesus called out, 'Have you caught anything, friends?' And when they answered, 'No', he said, 'Throw the net out to starboard and you'll find something.' So they dropped the net, and there were so many fish that they could not haul it in. The disciple Jesus loved said to Peter, 'It is the Lord.' At these words 'It is the Lord', Simon Peter, who had practically nothing on, wrapped his cloak round him and jumped into the water. The other disciples came on in the boat, towing the net and the fish; they were only about a hundred yards from land.

As soon as they came ashore they saw that there was some bread there, and a charcoal fire with fish cooking on it. Jesus said, 'Bring some of the fish you have just caught.' Simon Peter went aboard and dragged the net to the shore, full of big fish, one hundred and fifty-three of them; and in spite of there being so many the net was not broken. Jesus said to them, 'Come and have breakfast.' None of the disciples was bold enough to ask, 'Who are you?'; they knew quite well it was the Lord. Jesus then stepped forward, took the bread and gave it to them, and the same with the fish. This was the third time that Jesus showed himself to the disciples after rising from the dead.

After the meal Jesus said to Simon Peter, 'Simon son of John, do you love me more than these others do?' He answered, 'Yes Lord, you know I love you.' Jesus said to him, 'Feed my lambs.' A second time he said to him, 'Simon son of John, do you love me?' He replied 'Yes Lord you know I love you.' Jesus said to him, 'Look after my sheep.' Then he said to him a third time, 'Simon son of John, do you love me?' Peter was upset that he asked him the third time, 'Do you love me?' and said, 'Lord, you know everything; you know I love you.' Jesus said to him, 'Feed my sheep. 'I tell you most solemnly, when you were young you put on your own belt and walked where you liked; but when you grow old you will stretch out your hands, and somebody else will put a belt round you and take you where you would rather not go.'

In these words he indicated the kind of death by which Peter would give glory to God. After this he said, 'Follow me.'

Reflection

In the Gospel reading, we are invited to reflect on the third occasion that Jesus 'shows' himself to the disciples following his resurrection. Jesus appears by the Sea of Tiberias and upon seeing the disciples struggling to catch any fish, suggests that they cast the net on the other side of the boat. When they listen to Jesus and do as he says, they catch an abundance of fish. This provokes the question – when and how does Jesus show himself in our lives? Is it through the kind word of encouragement expressed by a work colleague, or is it someone speaking truth in a difficult situation, or perhaps is it in the invitation to share a meal? Jesus shares bread and fish with the disciples, and in so doing, not only shows up, but shares something of himself – his presence and friendship. How can we show up in a similar way for others, as Jesus did for the disciples? How can we offer words of life and abundance, and give something of ourselves in the name of Jesus, today?

02
MAY MON

3rd Week of Easter
St Athanasius, *bishop, doctor,* **Memorial** | White

Acts 6:8-15

Stephen was filled with grace and power and began to work miracles and great signs among the people. But then certain people came forward to debate with Stephen, some from Cyrene and Alexandria who were members of the synagogue called the Synagogue of Freedmen, and others from Cilicia and Asia. They found they could not get the better of him because of his wisdom, and because it was the Spirit that prompted what he said. So they procured some men to say, 'We heard him using blasphemous language against Moses and against God.' Having in this way turned the people against him as well as the elders and scribes, they took Stephen by surprise, and arrested him and brought him before the Sanhedrin. There they put up false witnesses to say, 'This man is always making speeches against this Holy Place and the Law. We have heard him say that Jesus the Nazarene is going to destroy this Place and alter the traditions that Moses handed down to us.' The members of the Sanhedrin all looked intently at Stephen, and his face appeared to them like the face of an angel.

Psalm 118:23-24, 26-27, 29-30. R. v. 1

They are happy whose life is blameless.

John 6:22-29

After Jesus had fed the five thousand, his disciples saw him walking on the water. Next day, the crowd that had stayed on the other side saw that only one boat had been there, and that Jesus had not got into the boat with his disciples, but that the disciples had set off by themselves. Other boats, however, had put in from Tiberias, near the place where the bread had been eaten. When the people saw that neither Jesus nor his disciples were there, they got into those boats and crossed to Capernaum to look for Jesus. When they found him on the other side, they said to him, 'Rabbi, when did you come here?' Jesus answered: 'I tell you most solemnly, you are not looking for me because you have seen the signs but because you had all the bread you wanted to eat. Do not work for food that cannot last, but work for food that endures to eternal life, the kind of food the Son of Man is offering you, for on him the Father, God himself, has set his seal.' Then they said to him, 'What must we do if we are to do the works that God wants?' Jesus gave them this answer, 'This is working for God: you must believe in the one he has sent.'

Reflection

If our end goal is truly heaven, to be among the angels and saints, and to bask in the eternal glory of God, Jesus provides a clear directive as to what we need to do – 'do not work for the food that perishes, but for the food that endures for eternal life'. Our time on earth in a physical, bodily sense is limited. And even so, we may focus much of our attention on our bodies' ability to function, on the material goods that we can gather, and on our career or family status and how we are perceived by those who know us. And yet, Jesus reminds us clearly that we must remain focused on the spiritual and soul dimensions of our personhood – that this is what will last when we die. What decisions am I making now in my life, and what actions am I taking now, that will have an enduring impact, even after I die?

03
MAY TUE

Sts Philip and James, Apostles
Feast | Red

1 Corinthians 15:1-8

Brothers, I want to remind you of the Gospel I preached to you, the gospel that you received and in which you are firmly established; because the gospel will save you only if you keep believing exactly what I preached to you – believing anything else will not lead to anything. Well then, in the first place, I taught you what I had been taught myself, namely that Christ died for our sins, in accordance with the scriptures; that he was buried; and that he was raised to life on the third day, in accordance with the scriptures; that he appeared first to Cephas and secondly to the Twelve. Next he appeared to more than five hundred of the brothers at the same time, most of whom are still alive, though some have died; then he appeared to James, and then to all the apostles; and last of all he appeared to me too; it was as though I was born when no one expected it.

Psalm 18:2-5. R. v. 5

Their word goes forth through all the earth.

John 14:6-14

Jesus said to Thomas: 'I am the Way, the Truth and the Life. No one can come to the Father except through me. If you know me, you know my Father too. From this moment you know him and have seen him.' Philip said, 'Lord, let us see the Father and then we shall be satisfied'. 'Have I been with you all this time, Philip,' said Jesus to him 'and you still do not know me? 'To have seen me is to have seen the Father, so how can you say, "Let us see the Father?" Do you not believe that I am in the Father and the Father is in me? The words I say to you I do not speak as from myself: it is the Father, living in me, who is doing this work. You must believe me when I say that I am in the Father and the Father is in me; believe it on the evidence of this work if for no other reason. I tell you most solemnly, whoever believes in me will perform the same works as I do myself, he will perform even greater works, because I am going to the Father. Whatever you ask for in my name I will do, so that the Father may be glorified in the Son. If you ask for anything in my name, I will do it.'

Reflection

Thomas the apostle has just asked Jesus, 'How can we know the way?' It's a question that many of us might be asking ourselves at this moment. As part of his response, Jesus says, 'If you know me, you will know my Father also … I am in the Father and the Father is in me.' Jesus is providing something of a clue, or a map for each of us. God, the God who is Love, dwells in Jesus, and Jesus dwells in God, so each time we partake in an act of love, the very presence of God is alive in our hearts. And in so doing, we concretely bear witness to our belief in Jesus and in the God whose essence is Love. How can we know the way? It is the way of love, of truth, goodness and beauty. The indwelling Holy Spirit of God will lead the way. Are we listening and responding?

04
MAY WED

THE ENGLISH MARTYRS, Feast – England
see Appendix A-13

3rd Week of Easter
White

Acts 8:1-8

That day a bitter persecution started against the church in Jerusalem, and everyone except the apostles fled to the country districts of Judaea and Samaria.

There were some devout people, however, who buried Stephen and made great mourning for him.

Saul then worked for the total destruction of the Church; he went from house to house arresting both men and women and sending them to prison.

Those who had escaped went from place to place preaching the Good News. One of them was Philip who went to a Samaritan town and proclaimed the Christ to them. The people united in welcoming the message Philip preached, either because they had heard of the miracles he worked or because they saw them for themselves. There were, for example, unclean spirits that came shrieking out of many who were possessed, and several paralytics and cripples were cured. There was great rejoicing in that town as a result.

Psalm 65:1-7. R. v. 1

Cry out with joy to God, all the earth.

John 6:35-40

Jesus said to the crowd: 'I am the bread of life. He who comes to me will never be hungry; he who believes in me will never thirst. But, as I have told you, you can see me and still you do not believe. All that the Father gives me will come to me, and whoever comes to me I shall not turn him away; because I have come from heaven, not to do my own will, but to do the will of the one who sent me. Now the will of him who sent me is that I should lose nothing of all that he has given to me, and that I should raise it up on the last day. Yes, it is my Father's will that whoever sees the Son and believes in him shall have eternal life, and that I shall raise him up on the last day.'

Reflection

It is God's desire that we see Jesus, and know Jesus, deep within our hearts and souls, so that we may enjoy eternal life. Jesus is our source and compass; it is through him, that we are led to God the Father. We are invited to believe and trust Jesus' words and actions, and in so doing, we shall not be left wanting. How do we see ourselves? How do we see others? Do we see the face of Christ in the person standing opposite us? In our family members and neighbours, in our enemies? Jesus tells us, 'I am the bread of life'. Whoever sees Jesus, who is present in each one of us, and enters into relationship with him, allows the very essence of Love to enter their heart. We shall not go hungry or be thirsty. Do we choose to believe this? Do we recognise and celebrate that in so doing, we are people who have been raised up?

3rd Week of Easter
White

05
MAY THU

Acts 8:26-40

The angel of the Lord spoke to Philip saying, 'Be ready to set out at noon along the road that goes from Jerusalem down to Gaza, the desert road.' So he set off on his journey. Now it happened that an Ethiopian had been on pilgrimage to Jerusalem; he was a eunuch and an officer at the court of the kandake, or queen, of Ethiopia, and was in fact her chief treasurer. He was now on his way home; and as he sat in his chariot he was reading the prophet Isaiah. The Spirit said to Philip, 'Go up and meet that chariot.' When Philip ran up, he heard him reading Isaiah the prophet and asked, 'Do you understand what you are reading?' 'How can I' he replied 'unless I have someone to guide me?' So he invited Philip to get in and sit by his side. Now the passage of scripture he was reading was this: Like a sheep that is led to the slaughter-house, like a lamb that is dumb in front of its shearers, like these he never opens his mouth. He has been humiliated and has no one to defend him. Who will ever talk about his descendants, since his life on earth has been cut short!

The eunuch turned to Philip and said, 'Tell me, is the prophet referring to himself or someone else?' Starting, therefore, with this text of scripture Philip proceeded to explain the Good News of Jesus to him. … *(Please see the Appendix B-12)*

Psalm 65:8-9, 16-17, 20. R. v. 1

Cry out with joy to God, all the earth.

John 6:44-51

Jesus said to the crowd: 'No one can come to me unless he is drawn by the Father who sent me, and I will raise him up at the last day. It is written in the prophets: They will all be taught by God, and to hear the teaching of the Father, and learn from it, is to come to me. Not that anybody has seen the Father, except the one who comes from God: he has seen the Father. I tell you most solemnly, everybody who believes has eternal life. I am the bread of life. Your fathers ate the manna in the desert and they are dead; but this is the bread that comes down from heaven, so that a man may eat it and not die. I am the living bread which has come down from heaven. Anyone who eats this bread will live for ever; and the bread that I shall give is my flesh, for the life of the world.'

Reflection

The first reading speaks of an encouraging and inspiring encounter between two people. Philip, led by the prompting of an angel of the Lord, and filled with the Holy Spirit, approaches the Ethiopian court official and joins him in breaking open the Scripture. There is an invitation, an openness, a curiosity and a sharing. In this encounter, Philip proclaims the good news about Jesus. One can only assume that the Ethiopian was so moved by Philip's proclamation, that upon seeing water, he suggests being baptised. Something in this man's heart desired in that moment to be baptised in the name of the Father, the Son and the Holy Spirit. And he rejoiced. And so too do we rejoice each time we recall our own baptism, and what it means for each of us. We are beloved children of God – loved before all time to eternity, and the Spirit of God dwells within us. Let us rejoice!

06
MAY FRI

3rd Week of Easter
White

Acts 9:1-20

Saul was still breathing threats to slaughter the Lord's disciples. He had gone to the high priest and asked for letters addressed to the synagogues in Damascus, that would authorise him to arrest and take to Jerusalem any followers of the Way, men or women, that he could find.

Suddenly, while he was travelling to Damascus and just before he reached the city, there came a light from heaven all round him. He fell to the ground, and then he heard a voice saying, 'Saul, Saul, why are you persecuting me?' 'Who are you, Lord?' he asked, and the voice answered, 'I am Jesus, and you are persecuting me. Get up now and go into the city, and you will be told what you have to do.' The men travelling with Saul stood there speechless, for though they heard the voice they could see no one. Saul got up from the ground, but even with his eyes wide open he could see nothing at all, and they had to lead him into Damascus by the hand. For three days he was without his sight, and took neither food nor drink. ...

(Please see the Appendix B-13)

Psalm 116. R. Mark 16:15

Go out to the whole world; proclaim the Good News.

John 6:52-59

The Jews started arguing with one another: 'How can this man give us his flesh to eat?' they said. Jesus replied: 'I tell you most solemnly, if you do not eat the flesh of the Son of Man and drink his blood, you will not have life in you. Anyone who does eat my flesh and drink my blood has eternal life, and I shall raise him up on the last day. For my flesh is real food and my blood is real drink. He who eats my flesh and drinks my blood lives in me and I live in him. As I, who am sent by the living Father, myself draw life from the Father, so whoever eats me will draw life from me. This is the bread come down from heaven; not like the bread our ancestors ate: they are dead, but anyone who eats this bread will live for ever.' He taught this doctrine at Capernaum, in the synagogue.

Reflection

The story of Saul speaks of dramatic and radical transformation. Who could ever have imagined that the man responsible for killing so many who proclaimed the name of Jesus Christ, would one day be one of his most fervent and vocal supporters! This story speaks of encouragement for each one of us. Just when we think we've dug a hole so deep, or that we couldn't possibly change our hard and cruel, or selfish ways, we can take heart in Saul's transformation. How willing are we to be transformed by the love of Christ, or by the truth of the Holy Spirit? Are we prepared to allow the scales to fall from our own eyes so that we can see the reality of who we are – beloved children of God, with inherent dignity, and called to love radically, just as Jesus loves. What will it take for my heart to be radically transformed?

07
MAY SAT

3rd Week of Easter
White

Acts 9:31-42

The churches throughout Judaea, Galilee and Samaria were now left in peace, building themselves up, living in the fear of the Lord, and filled with the consolation of the Holy Spirit.

Peter visited one place after another and eventually came to the saints living down in Lydda. There he found a man called Aeneas, a paralytic who had been bedridden for eight years. Peter said to him, 'Aeneas, Jesus Christ cures you: get up and fold up your sleeping mat.' Aeneas got up immediately; everybody who lived in Lydda and Sharon saw him, and they were all converted to the Lord. ... *(Please see the Appendix B-13)*

Psalm 115:12-17. R. v. 12

How can I repay the Lord for his goodness to me?

John 6:60-69

After hearing his doctrine, many of the followers of Jesus said, 'This is intolerable language. How could anyone accept it?' Jesus was aware that his followers were complaining about it and said, 'Does this upset you? What if you should see the Son of Man ascend to where he was before?

'It is the spirit that gives life, the flesh has nothing to offer. The words I have spoken to you are spirit and they are life.

'But there are some of you who do not believe.' For Jesus knew from the outset those who did not believe, and who it was that would betray him. He went on, 'This is why I told you that no one could come to me unless the Father allows him.' After this, many of his disciples left him and stopped going with him.

Then Jesus said to the Twelve, 'What about you, do you want to go away too?' Simon Peter answered, 'Lord, who shall we go to? You have the message of eternal life, and we believe; we know that you are the Holy One of God.'

Reflection

Each day we are confronted with decisions and choices, and perhaps at times, we've grappled with the same question that Jesus posed to Simon Peter: 'Do you also wish to go away?' Indeed, there might be times when we might like to go away. We question our faith, or question how God could 'allow certain things to happen', particularly when there is so much death and destruction in the world. And yet, Simon Peter responds, 'Lord, to whom can we go?' In that decisive moment, like Simon Peter, do we choose to turn toward Christ, to embrace love and life. Do we choose to say yes to the Spirit of life that animates and moves us, bringing us ever closer to God, and to that which brings truth, beauty and goodness into the world? Today let us consider personally: Where do I find life and joy? Do I choose life over death? How am I a concrete sign of God's love in the world?

08

MAY SUN

FOURTH SUNDAY OF EASTER

Psalter Week 4

White

Acts 13:14, 43-52

Paul and Barnabas carried on from Perga till they reached Antioch in Pisidia. Here they went to synagogue on the sabbath and took their seats.

When the meeting broke up, many Jews and devout converts joined Paul and Barnabas, and in their talks with them Paul and Barnabas urged them to remain faithful to the grace God had given them.

The next sabbath almost the whole town assembled to hear the word of God. When they saw the crowds, the Jews, prompted by jealousy, used blasphemies and contradicted everything Paul said. Then Paul and Barnabas spoke out boldly, 'We had to proclaim the word of God to you first, but since you have rejected it, since you do not think yourselves worthy of eternal life, we must turn to the pagans. For this is what the Lord commanded us to do when he said: I have made you a light for the nations, so that my salvation may reach the ends of the earth.'

It made the pagans very happy to hear this and they thanked the Lord for his message; all who were destined for eternal life became believers. Thus the word of the Lord spread through the whole countryside.

But the Jews worked upon some of the devout women of the upper classes and the leading men of the city and persuaded them to turn against Paul and Barnabas and expel them from their territory. So they shook the dust from their feet in defiance and went off to Iconium; but the disciples were filled with joy and the Holy Spirit.

Psalm 99:1-3, 5. R. v. 3

We are his people, the sheep of his flock.

Apocalypse 7:9, 14-17

I, John, saw a huge number, impossible to count, of people from every nation, race, tribe and language; they were standing in front of the throne and in front of the Lamb, dressed in white robes and holding palms in their hands. One of the elders said to me, 'These are the people who have been through the great persecution, and because they have washed their robes white again in the blood of the Lamb, they now stand in front of God's throne and serve him day and night in his sanctuary; and the One who sits on the throne will spread his tent over them. They will never hunger or thirst again; neither the sun nor scorching wind will ever plague them, because the Lamb who is at the throne will be their shepherd and will lead them to springs of living water; and God will wipe away all tears from their eyes.'

John 10:27-30

Jesus said:

'The sheep that belong to me listen to my voice;
I know them and they follow me.
I give them eternal life;
they will never be lost
and no one will ever steal them from me.
The Father who gave them to me is greater than anyone,
and no one can steal from the Father.
The Father and I are one.'

Reflection

Imagine Paul and Barnabas standing tall, shaking the dust from their feet and moving out of the region filled with joy and the Holy Spirit. What a feat, considering they'd not been farewelled with good wishes and gifts. Rather, they were driven out by a group of jealous people, persecuting and protesting against the words they had been sharing. Paul and Barnabas demonstrate that they know the voice of God in their hearts. And knowing this voice, and accepting the invitation to live in God's grace, they have a clear goal to 'bring salvation to the ends of the earth'. This is their mandate, and it is ours. We too are invited to hone in to the voice of God in our hearts, to listen and act, to live in the grace of God and to be a light to all we encounter. Armed with this knowledge, in any hardship, we too can shake the dust from our feet, and move on with joy and praise, filled with the Holy Spirit. God is with us, always.

09
MAY MON

4th Week of Easter
White

Acts 11:1-18

The apostles and the brothers in Judaea heard that the pagans too had accepted the word of God, and when Peter came up to Jerusalem the Jews criticised him and said, 'So you have been visiting the uncircumcised and eating with them, have you?' Peter in reply gave them the details point by point: 'One day, when I was in the town of Jaffa,' he began 'I fell into a trance as I was praying and had a vision of something like a big sheet being let down from heaven by its four corners. This sheet reached the ground quite close to me. I watched it intently and saw all sorts of animals and wild beasts – everything possible that could walk, crawl or fly. Then I heard a voice that said to me, "Now, Peter; kill and eat!" But I answered: Certainly not, Lord; nothing profane or unclean has ever crossed my lips. And a second time the voice spoke from heaven. "What God has made clean, you have no right to call profane." This was repeated three times, before the whole of it was drawn up to heaven again. … *(Please see the Appendix B-13)*

Psalm 41:2-3; 42:3-4. R. cf. Psalm 41:3

My soul is thirsting for God, the God of my life.

John 10:1-10

Jesus said: 'I tell you most solemnly, anyone who does not enter the sheepfold through the gate, but gets in some other way, is a thief and a brigand. The one who enters through the gate is the shepherd of the flock; the gatekeeper lets him in, the sheep hear his voice, one by one he calls his own sheep and leads them out. When he has brought out his flock, he goes ahead of them, and the sheep follow because they know his voice. They never follow a stranger but run away from him: they do not recognise the voice of strangers.'

Jesus told them this parable but they failed to understand what he meant by telling it to them. So Jesus spoke to them again: 'I tell you most solemnly, I am the gate of the sheepfold. All others who have come are thieves and brigands; but the sheep took no notice of them. I am the gate. Anyone who enters through me will be safe: he will go freely in and out and be sure of finding pasture. The thief comes only to steal and kill and destroy. I have come so that they may have life and have it to the full.'

Reflection

Jesus came that I may have life and have it to the full; Abundantly! I often ponder these words: What does 'fullness' or 'abundance' look like in my life, concretely? My life is full and abundant when I experience the love of God in my heart, the source of my being. I experience abundance in the love and relationships between my family and friends, work colleagues, neighbours and sometimes even a stranger who can enliven my heart with a simple wave, smile, or warm greeting. I feel alive and full of the Holy Spirit in the presence of beauty, creativity and goodness. My heart can sing out in praise and joy upon witnessing a glorious sunset or when basking under the sun, floating in clear water. At these times, my heart is alive with the mystery, wonder and awe of life, the gift of life, that exists in relationship with God and others. This is the essence of my fullness. Where do you find abundance?

4th Week of Easter
or **St John de Avila,** *doctor* (Optional, White)

10
MAY TUE

Acts 11:19-26

Those who had escaped during the persecution that happened because of Stephen travelled as far as Phoenicia and Cyprus and Antioch, but they usually proclaimed the message only to Jews. Some of them, however, who came from Cyprus and Cyrene, went to Antioch where they started preaching to the Greeks, proclaiming the Good News of the Lord Jesus to them as well. The Lord helped them, and a great number believed and were converted to the Lord.

The church in Jerusalem heard about this and they sent Barnabas to Antioch. There he could see for himself that God had given grace, and this pleased him, and he urged them all to remain faithful to the Lord with heartfelt devotion; for he was a good man, filled with the Holy Spirit and with faith. And a large number of people were won over to the Lord.

Barnabas then left for Tarsus to look for Saul, and when he found him he brought him to Antioch. As things turned out they were to live together in that church a whole year, instructing a large number of people. It was at Antioch that the disciples were first called 'Christians'.

Psalm 86:1-7. R. Psalm 116:1

O praise the Lord, all you nations!

John 10:22-30

It was the time when the feast of Dedication was being celebrated in Jerusalem. It was winter, and Jesus was in the Temple walking up and down in the Portico of Solomon. The Jews gathered round him and said, 'How much longer are you going to keep us in suspense? If you are the Christ, tell us plainly.' Jesus replied: 'I have told you, but you do not believe. The works I do in my Father's name are my witness; but you do not believe, because you are no sheep of mine. The sheep that belong to me listen to my voice; I know them and they follow me. I give them eternal life; they will never be lost and no one will ever steal them from me. The Father who gave them to me is greater than anyone, and no one can steal from the Father. The Father and I are one.'

Reflection

It is reassuring to know that we cannot be 'snatched' out of Jesus' hands, particularly when grounded in the truth of who we are – children of God, called to live in eternal life. We are encouraged to remain steadfast in this knowledge, and to continue to listen out for, and hear, the voice of God in our life. In so doing, we can follow Jesus and be a presence of his love in the world. But how might we know the voice of God, particularly when it's often competing with so many different voices in our minds? For me, there is a sense of life-giving energy and light. And even if there is difficulty or sorrow, there is a sense of clarity and calm. I experience peace of heart and mind. Finding moments of silence in the day really helps to hone in to the voice of God whispering into my heart and consciousness: I love you, I am with you, trust me, God says. Armed with this knowledge, I move forward into my day.

11
MAY WED

4th Week of Easter
White

Acts 12:24–13:5

The word of God continued to spread and to gain followers. Barnabas and Saul completed their task and came back from Jerusalem, bringing John Mark with them.

In the church at Antioch the following were prophets and teachers: Barnabas, Simeon called Niger, and Lucius of Cyrene, Manaen, who had been brought up with Herod the tetrarch, and Saul. One day while they were offering worship to the Lord and keeping a fast, the Holy Spirit said, 'I want Barnabas and Saul set apart for the work to which I have called them.' So it was that after fasting and prayer they laid their hands on them and sent them off.

So these two, sent on their mission by the Holy Spirit, went down to Seleucia and from there sailed to Cyprus. They landed at Salamis and proclaimed the word of God in the synagogues of the Jews. John acted as their assistant.

Psalm 66:2-3, 5-6, 8. R. v. 4

Let the peoples praise you, O God; let all the peoples praise you.

John 12:44-50

Jesus declared publicly: 'Whoever believes in me believes not in me but in the one who sent me, and whoever sees me, sees the one who sent me. I, the light, have come into the world, so that whoever believes in me need not stay in the dark any more. If anyone hears my words and does not keep them faithfully, it is not I who shall condemn him, since I have come not to condemn the world, but to save the world: he who rejects me and refuses my words has his judge already: the word itself that I have spoken will be his judge on the last day. For what I have spoken does not come from myself; no, what I was to say, what I had to speak, was commanded by the Father who sent me, and I know that his commands mean eternal life. And therefore what the Father has told me is what I speak.'

Reflection

God the Father, grant me the grace to know you more deeply, to believe in your love for me and your desire to grant me eternal life. Grant me the grace to desire goodness and truth, that I may be your light in the world, leading people away from the darkness just as Jesus leads me. Lord, help me to focus my energies on loving and restoring, rather than judging and condemning. May I be a person who builds the kingdom of God here and now, through my words and deeds, and through my relationships with others. May you be at the centre of all I do. Lord, grant me the grace to love, for it is in loving that people come to know you. And may I have a joyful heart as I rest in the knowledge that you are with me always and show me the way. Amen.

12
MAY THU

4th Week of Easter | White
or **Sts Nereus and Achilleus,** *martyrs* (Optional, Red)
or **St Pancras,** *martyr* (Optional, Red)

Acts 13:13-25

Paul and his friends went by sea from Paphos to Perga in Pamphylia where John left them to go back to Jerusalem. The others carried on from Perga till they reached Antioch in Pisidia. Here they went to synagogue on the sabbath and took their seats. After the lessons from the Law and the Prophets had been read, the presidents of the synagogue sent them a message: 'Brothers, if you would like to address some words of encouragement to the congregation, please do so.' Paul stood up, held up a hand for silence and began to speak: 'Men of Israel, and fearers of God, listen! The God of our nation Israel chose our ancestors, and made our people great when they were living as foreigners in Egypt; then by divine power he led them out, and for about forty years took care of them in the wilderness. When he had destroyed seven nations in Canaan, he put them in possession of their land for about four hundred and fifty years. After this he gave them judges, down to the prophet Samuel. Then they demanded a king, and God gave them Saul son of Kish, a man of the tribe of Benjamin. After forty years, he deposed him and made David their king, of whom he approved in these words: "I have selected David son of Jesse, a man after my own heart, who will carry out my whole purpose." To keep his promise, God has raised up for Israel one of David's descendants, Jesus, as Saviour, whose coming was heralded by John when he proclaimed a baptism of repentance for the whole people of Israel. Before John ended his career he said, "I am not the one you imagine me to be; that one is coming after me and I am not fit to undo his sandal."'

Psalm 88:2-3, 21-22, 25, 27. R. cf. v. 2

I will sing for ever of your love, O Lord.

John 13:16-20

After he had washed the feet of his disciples, Jesus said to them: 'I tell you most solemnly, no servant is greater than his master, no messenger is greater than the man who sent him. 'Now that you know this, happiness will be yours if you behave accordingly. I am not speaking about all of you: I know the ones I have chosen; but what scripture says must be fulfilled: Someone who shares my table rebels against me.

'I tell you this now, before it happens, so that when it does happen you may believe that I am He. I tell you most solemnly, whoever welcomes the one I send welcomes me, and whoever welcomes me welcomes the one who sent me.'

Reflection

Jesus says to the disciples, 'whoever welcomes the one I send welcomes me; and whoever welcomes me welcomes the one who sent me'. This speaks to me of the importance of welcome. The word 'welcome' is a generous word. It speaks of open arms, warmth, care and hospitality. You are seen, acknowledged and welcomed. It is a beautiful gift to be able to welcome others, whether it be in the home, or into a conversation, or to a meal. It could be to share the space, in silence. In welcoming another, we partake in the very act of welcoming God the Father as well. We pray that God's presence receives a warm welcome in each of our hearts.

4th Week of Easter | White
or **Our Lady of Fatima** (Optional, White)

13
MAY FRI

Acts 13:26-33

Paul stood up in the synagogue at Antioch in Pisidia, held up a hand for silence and began to speak: 'My brothers, sons of Abraham's race, and all you who fear God, this message of salvation is meant for you. What the people of Jerusalem and their rulers did, though they did not realise it, was in fact to fulfil the prophecies read on every sabbath. Though they found nothing to justify his death, they condemned him and asked Pilate to have him executed. When they had carried out everything that scripture foretells about him they took him down from the tree and buried him in a tomb. But God raised him from the dead, and for many days he appeared to those who had accompanied him from Galilee to Jerusalem: and it is these same companions of his who are now his witnesses before our people.

'We have come here to tell you the Good News. It was to our ancestors that God made the promise but it is to us, their children, that he has fulfilled it, by raising Jesus from the dead. As scripture says in the first psalm: You are my son: today I have become your father.'

Psalm 2:6-11. R. v. 7

You are my Son. It is I who have begotten you this day.

John 14:1-6

Jesus said to his disciples: 'Do not let your hearts be troubled. Trust in God still, and trust in me. There are many rooms in my Father's house; if there were not, I should have told you. I am going now to prepare a place for you, and after I have gone and prepared you a place, I shall return to take you with me; so that where I am you may be too. You know the way to the place where I am going.' Thomas said, 'Lord, we do not know where you are going, so how can we know the way?' Jesus said: 'I am the Way, the Truth and the Life. No one can come to the Father except through me.'

Reflection

Like Thomas, I find myself sometimes asking Jesus the question, 'How can I know the way?' At a crossroads in my life, how can I know what the best course of action is? When a difficult choice confronts me, what is the right thing to do? Jesus consoles me: 'Do not let your hearts be troubled, believe in God, believe also in me.' He adds, 'I am the way and the truth and the life. No one comes to the Father except through me.' This is a powerful reminder to stay focused, or 'calibrated' to God's desire for me to follow his call. God desires that I live a life of love and service, filled with the Holy Spirit. My heart desires truth, beauty and goodness. I desire to stay close to Jesus and to believe more deeply. I pray for this grace to believe more deeply, to align my ways with the way of Jesus, and to speak truth as he speaks truth. With Jesus as my guide, may I too be a light to others, and help draw people closer to God the Father.

St Matthias, Apostle
Feast | Red

14
MAY SAT

Acts 1:15-17, 20-26

One day Peter stood up to speak to the brothers – there were about a hundred and twenty persons in the congregation: 'Brothers, the passage of scripture has to be fulfilled in which the Holy Spirit, speaking through David, foretells the fate of Judas, who offered himself as a guide to the men who arrested Jesus – after having been one of our number and actually sharing this ministry of ours. Now in the Book of Psalms it says: Let his camp be reduced to ruin, let there be no one to live in it. And again: Let someone else take his office.
'We must therefore choose someone who has been with us the whole time that the Lord Jesus was travelling round with us, someone who was with us right from the time when John was baptising until the day when he was taken up from us – and he can act with us as a witness to his resurrection.'
Having nominated two candidates, Joseph known as Barsabbas, whose surname was Justus, and Matthias, they prayed, 'Lord, you can read everyone's heart; show us therefore which of these two you have chosen to take over this ministry and apostolate, which Judas abandoned to go to his proper place.' They then drew lots for them, and as the lot fell to Matthias, he was listed as one of the twelve apostles.

Psalm 112:1-8. R. cf. v. 8

The Lord sets him in the company of the princes of his people.

John 15:9-17

Jesus said to his disciples: 'As the Father has loved me, so I have loved you. Remain in my love. If you keep my commandments you will remain in my love, just as I have kept my Father's commandments and remain in his love. I have told you this so that my own joy may be in you and your joy be complete. This is my commandment: love one another, as I have loved you. A man can have no greater love than to lay down his life for his friends. You are my friends, if you do what I command you. I shall not call you servants any more, because a servant does not know his master's business; I call you friends, because I have made known to you everything I have learnt from my Father. You did not choose me, no, I chose you; and I commissioned you to go out and to bear fruit, fruit that will last; and then the Father will give you anything you ask him in my name. What I command you is to love one another.'

Reflection

Remain in my love. Put another way: 'live and stay' in God's love. Jesus is inviting the disciples and each of us to dwell in and live each day from the place of God's love in our heart. How do we do this, concretely? Jesus tells us that we abide or live in God's love when we follow his commandments, particularly the command to love one another as he has loved us. Reflecting personally, am I loving others as Jesus loved? Do I welcome the stranger? Do I provide any care or show concern for those on the streets or in prison? Have I taken any time to visit someone who is ill or isolated? Am I doing my part in caring for creation and being a responsible steward of the earth? Jesus calls me friend and invites me to share in his experience of care for others. In so doing, his joy is my joy, and I rest in the knowledge that I am abiding in God's love.

15
MAY SUN

FIFTH SUNDAY OF EASTER

Psalter Week 1

White

Acts 14:21-27

Paul and Barnabas went back through Lystra and Iconium to Antioch. They put fresh heart into the disciples, encouraging them to persevere in the faith. 'We all have to experience many hardships' they said 'before we enter the kingdom of God.' In each of these churches they appointed elders, and with prayer and fasting they commended them to the Lord in whom they had come to believe.

They passed through Pisidia and reached Pamphylia. Then after proclaiming the word at Perga they went down to Attalia and from there sailed for Antioch, where they had originally been commended to the grace of God for the work they had now completed.

On their arrival they assembled the church and gave an account of all that God had done with them, and how he had opened the door of faith to the pagans.

Psalm 144:8-13. R. cf. v. 1

I will bless your name for ever, O God my King.

Apocalypse 21:1-5

I, John, saw a new heaven and a new earth; the first heaven and the first earth had disappeared now, and there was no longer any sea. I saw the holy city, and the new Jerusalem, coming down from God out of heaven, as beautiful as a bride all dressed for her husband. Then I heard a loud voice call from the throne, 'You see this city? Here God lives among men. He will make his home among them; they shall be his people, and he will be their God; his name is God-with-them. He will wipe away all tears from their eyes; there will be no more death, and no more mourning or sadness. The world of the past has gone.'

Then the One sitting on the throne spoke: 'Now I am making the whole of creation new'.

John 13:31-35

When Judas had gone Jesus said:

'Now has the Son of Man been glorified,
and in him God has been glorified.
If God has been glorified in him,
God will in turn glorify him in himself,
and will glorify him very soon.
My little children,
I shall not be with you much longer.
I give you a new commandment:
love one another;
just as I have loved you,
you also must love one another.
By this love you have for one another,
everyone will know that you are my disciples.'

Reflection

Filled with the love of God, Paul and Barnabas 'opened the door of faith' to many whom they encountered in the cities they visited. By their love, joy and zest for God, the eyes, ears and hearts of many were opened. They are clearly following Jesus' new commandment to 'love one another as I have loved you'. As Jesus did, they too spread the Good News of God among the people. They too witnessed to the love and presence of God in their hearts by their very actions. It bears reflecting, how deeply have I been impacted by the love of God? Do others know that I'm a disciple of Jesus by the love I share with others? Do people recognise Jesus in me? Do I recognise Jesus in others? I pray that I may be a living sign of God's love in the world today, that I may be one who opens the door of faith and love to those I encounter.

16
MAY MON

5th Week of Easter
White

Acts 14:5-18
With the connivance of the authorities a move was made by pagans as well as Jews to make attacks on Paul and Barnabas and to stone them. When the apostles came to hear of this, they went off for safety to Lycaonia where, in the towns of Lystra and Derbe and in the surrounding country, they preached the Good News.

A man sat there who had never walked in his life, because his feet were crippled from birth; and as he listened to Paul preaching, he managed to catch his eye. Seeing that the man had the faith to be cured, Paul said in a loud voice, 'Get to your feet – stand up,' and the cripple jumped up and began to walk. *(Please see the Appendix B-14)*

Psalm 113:1-4, 15-16. R. v. 1
Not to us, Lord, but to your name give the glory.

John 14:21-26
Jesus said to his disciples: 'Anybody who receives my commandments and keeps them will be one who loves me; and anybody who loves me will be loved by my Father, and I shall love him and show myself to him.'

Judas – this was not Judas Iscariot – said to him, 'Lord, what is all this about? Do you intend to show yourself to us and not to the world?' Jesus replied: 'If anyone loves me he will keep my word, and my Father will love him, and we shall come to him and make our home with him. Those who do not love me do not keep my word. And my word is not my own: it is the word of the one who sent me. I have said these things to you while still with you; but the Advocate, the Holy Spirit, whom the Father will send in my name, will teach you everything and remind you of all I have said to you.'

Reflection
Dear Jesus, the call to love as you love can be difficult a lot of the time. There is so much angst and division in the world, fighting and persecution among people persist, as does poverty and famine. We are plagued by natural disasters and disease. I can feel flat and defeated, unsure and lost. In these times I pray: Come Holy Spirit, helper of my heart, mind and soul. Teach me and lead me in the way of God the Father. I desire this. Move me. Lead me. Guide me. Come Holy Spirit, I desire to listen more deeply and follow you. I desire that my heart be a fertile and rich home for the love of the Father, the Son and the Holy Spirit. That this love pours forth, glorifies you for the many gifts, and leads me in all I say, do, think and dream. Come Holy Spirit, you are welcome in my heart. May the truth, beauty and goodness of God prevail today and always. And may I be a living sign of your goodness. Amen.

5th Week of Easter
White

Acts 14:19-28

Some Jews arrived from Antioch and Iconium, and turned the people against the apostles. They stoned Paul and dragged him outside the town, thinking he was dead. The disciples came crowding round him but, as they did so, he stood up and went back to the town. The next day he and Barnabas went off to Derbe.

Having preached the Good News in that town and made a considerable number of disciples, they went back through Lystra and Iconium to Antioch. They put fresh heart into the disciples, encouraging them to persevere in the faith. 'We all have to experience many hardships' they said 'before we enter the kingdom of God.' In each of these churches they appointed elders, and with prayer and fasting they commended them to the Lord in whom they had come to believe.

They passed through Pisidia and reached Pamphylia. Then after proclaiming the word at Perga they went down to Attalia and from there sailed for Antioch, where they had originally been commended to the grace of God for the work they had now completed. On their arrival they assembled the church and gave an account of all that God had done with them, and how he had opened the door of faith to the pagans. They stayed there with the disciples for some time.

Psalm 144:10-13, 21. R. cf. v. 12

Your friends, O Lord, shall make known the glorious splendour of your reign.

John 14:27-31

Jesus said to his disciples: 'Peace I bequeath to you, my own peace I give you, a peace the world cannot give, this is my gift to you. Do not let your hearts be troubled or afraid. You heard me say: I am going away, and shall return. If you loved me you would have been glad to know that I am going to the Father, for the Father is greater than I. I have told you this now before it happens, so that when it does happen you may believe. I shall not talk with you any longer, because the prince of this world is on his way. He has no power over me, but the world must be brought to know that I love the Father and that I am doing exactly what the Father told me.'

Reflection

What a gift Jesus has bestowed on each of us! Jesus is speaking to each one of us directly when he offers, 'Peace I leave with you; my peace I give to you'. This is not just any peace. Jesus is giving us his peace. And it's not as the world gives, but rather a deep, abiding, trusting and knowing peace, grounded in our identity as beloved children of God. Resting and living from this knowledge, I know who I am. I know that I am loved, and that God is with me always. I am further comforted by Jesus' words, 'Do not let your hearts be troubled and do not let them be afraid'. Life often presents me with difficult and uncertain situations, but I need not be afraid. The peace of God is with me. It flows through me. Whatever life throws at me, the deep peace of Christ abides in me. I give thanks for this life-saving gift and am prepared for whatever the day brings.

18 MAY WED

5th Week of Easter | White
or **St John I,** *pope, martyr* (Optional, Red)

Acts 15:1-6

Some men came down from Judaea and taught the brothers, 'Unless you have yourselves circumcised in the tradition of Moses you cannot be saved.' This led to disagreement, and after Paul and Barnabas had had a long argument with these men it was arranged that Paul and Barnabas and others of the church should go up to Jerusalem and discuss the problem with the apostles and elders.

All the members of the church saw them off, and as they passed through Phoenicia and Samaria they told how the pagans had been converted, and this news was received with the greatest satisfaction by the brothers. When they arrived in Jerusalem they were welcomed by the church and by the apostles and elders, and gave an account of all that God had done with them.

But certain members of the Pharisees' party who had become believers objected, insisting that the pagans should be circumcised and instructed to keep the Law of Moses. The apostles and elders met to look into the matter.

Psalm 121:1-5. R. v. 1

I rejoiced when I heard them say: 'Let us go to God's house.'

John 15:1-8

Jesus said to his disciples: 'I am the true vine, and my Father is the vinedresser. Every branch in me that bears no fruit he cuts away, and every branch that does bear fruit he prunes to make it bear even more. You are pruned already, by means of the word that I have spoken to you. Make your home in me, as I make mine in you. As a branch cannot bear fruit all by itself, but must remain part of the vine, neither can you unless you remain in me. I am the vine, you are the branches. Whoever remains in me, with me in him, bears fruit in plenty; for cut off from me you can do nothing. Anyone who does not remain in me is like a branch that has been thrown away – he withers; these branches are collected and thrown on the fire, and they are burnt. If you remain in me and my words remain in you, you may ask what you will and you shall get it. It is to the glory of my Father that you should bear much fruit, and then you will be my disciples.'

Reflection

I love a good spring clean. I pull everything out of the cupboard, or off the shelves in order to assess whether I still really need or want the items that now lie on the floor. As I hold each piece, I ask: Do I love it? Do I need this? Does this item bring life or joy? Do I feel good in this piece of clothing? In the same way, the Gospel is inviting me to do a spring clean or audit of my own heart and what I'm doing and who I'm being. Perhaps I'm called to reconsider my work: is this job bringing me life and joy, and in so doing, bring life and joy to others? Is this behaviour reflective of the love and joy of Christ in my heart, or am I dead and lifeless, like the withering vine? Jesus is reminding us that God is our trunk, the foundation from which goodness, life and love flows. Keep those branches that reflect this and discard the branches that are dead and lifeless. In so doing, we provide room for new growth to occur, life that can bear fruit.

5th Week of Easter
White

19 MAY THU

Acts 15:7-21

After the discussion had gone on a long time, Peter stood up and addressed the apostles and elders.

'My brothers,' he said 'you know perfectly well that in the early days God made his choice among you: the pagans were to learn the Good News from me and so become believers. In fact God, who can read everyone's heart, showed his approval of them by giving the Holy Spirit to them just as he had to us. God made no distinction between them and us, since he purified their hearts by faith. It would only provoke God's anger now, surely, if you imposed on the disciples the very burden that neither we nor our ancestors were strong enough to support? Remember, we believe that we are saved in the same way as they are: through the grace of the Lord Jesus.'

This silenced the entire assembly, and they listened to Barnabas and Paul describing all the signs and wonders God had worked through them among the pagans.

When they had finished it was James who spoke. 'My brothers,' he said 'listen to me. Simon has described how God first arranged to enlist a people for his name out of the pagans. This is entirely in harmony with the words of the prophets, since the scriptures say: After that I shall return and rebuild the fallen House of David; I shall rebuild it from its ruins and restore it. Then the rest of mankind, all the pagans who are consecrated to my name, will look for the Lord, says the Lord who made this known so long ago.

'I rule, then, that instead of making things more difficult for pagans who turn to God, we send them a letter telling them merely to abstain from anything polluted by idols, from fornication, from the meat of strangled animals and from blood. For Moses has always had his preachers in every town and is read aloud in the synagogues every sabbath.'

Psalm 95:1-3, 10. R. cf. v. 3

Proclaim the wonders of the Lord among all the peoples.

John 15:9-11

Jesus said to his disciples: 'As the Father has loved me, so I have loved you. Remain in my love. If you keep my commandments you will remain in my love, just as I have kept my Father's commandments and remain in his love. I have told you this so that my own joy may be in you and your joy be complete.'

Reflection

Jesus desires that his joy dwells in me. I desire this too. Deep, abiding joy, that remains even in times of difficulty and sorrow. Jesus shares his words and teachings with me so that I can dwell on them, take them to heart, and understand them more deeply, so that his joy can live in me. Today I pray for God's joy to dwell and rise in me. I know it can be hard at times to feel joyful, but I trust in God's love and providence. *Divine Joy, you are welcome in my heart. May my joyful presence be a balm to those I encounter and a witness to your presence in me. Amen.*

20

MAY FRI

5th Week of Easter | White
or **St Bernardine of Siena,** *priest* (Optional, White)

Acts 15:22-31

The apostles and elders decided to choose delegates to send to Antioch with Paul and Barnabas; the whole church concurred with this. They chose Judas known as Barsabbas and Silas, both leading men in the brotherhood, and gave them this letter to take with them:

'The apostles and elders, your brothers, send greetings to the brothers of pagan birth in Antioch, Syria and Cilicia. We hear that some of our members have disturbed you with their demands and have unsettled your minds. They acted without any authority from us, and so we have decided unanimously to elect delegates and to send them to you with Barnabas and Paul, men we highly respect who have dedicated their lives to the name of our Lord Jesus Christ. Accordingly we are sending you Judas and Silas, who will confirm by word of mouth what we have written in this letter. It has been decided by the Holy Spirit and by ourselves not to saddle you with any burden beyond these essentials: you are to abstain from food sacrificed to idols, from blood, from the meat of strangled animals and from fornication. Avoid these, and you will do what is right. Farewell.' The party left and went down to Antioch, where they summoned the whole community and delivered the letter. The community read it and were delighted with the encouragement it gave them.

Psalm 56:8-12. R. v. 10

I will thank you, Lord, among the peoples.

John 15:12-17

Jesus said to his disciples: 'This is my commandment: love one another, as I have loved you. A man can have no greater love than to lay down his life for his friends. You are my friends, if you do what I command you. I shall not call you servants any more, because a servant does not know his master's business; I call you friends, because I have made known to you everything I have learnt from my Father. You did not choose me, no, I chose you; and I commissioned you to go out and to bear fruit, fruit that will last; and then the Father will give you anything you ask him in my name. What I command you is to love one another.'

Reflection

Today we celebrate Saint Bernadine of Siena (1380-1444), who heeded the invitation of Jesus in the Gospel to love one another as Jesus loved and to go out and bear fruit that will last. At the age of 20, Bernadine spent four months nursing patients afflicted with the plague in his hometown of Siena, Italy. At 22, he entered the Franciscan order and following his ordination, lived for many years in solitude and prayer. He then took to the road, travelling on foot, to preach the Good News among the people. He is remembered as a man who attracted huge crowds. He is credited as being the creator of the insignia IHS (the first three letters of 'Jesus' in Greek) placed atop a blazing sun, which later appeared in churches, homes and public buildings. Like Saint Bernadine, may we bear fruit inspired by the love of Christ.

5th Week of Easter | White or **St Christopher Magallanes,** *priest,* **and his companions,** *martyrs* (Optional, Red)

21
MAY SAT

Acts 16:1-10

From Cilicia Paul went to Derbe, and then on to Lystra. Here there was a disciple called Timothy, whose mother was a Jewess who had become a believer; but his father was a Greek. The brothers at Lystra and Iconium spoke well of Timothy, and Paul, who wanted to have him as a travelling companion, had him circumcised. This was on account of the Jews in the locality where everyone knew his father was a Greek.

As they visited one town after another, they passed on the decisions reached by the apostles and elders in Jerusalem, with instructions to respect them.

So the churches grew strong in the faith, as well as growing daily in numbers. They travelled through Phrygia and the Galatian country, having been told by the Holy Spirit not to preach the word in Asia. When they reached the frontier of Mysia they thought to cross it into Bithynia, but as the Spirit of Jesus would not allow them, they went through Mysia and came down to Troas. One night Paul had a vision: a Macedonian appeared and appealed to him in these words, 'Come across to Macedonia and help us.' Once he had seen this vision we lost no time in arranging a passage to Macedonia, convinced that God had called us to bring them the Good News.

Psalm 99:1-3, 5. R. v. 1

Cry out with joy to the Lord, all the earth.

John 15:18-21

Jesus said to his disciples: 'If the world hates you, remember that it hated me before you. If you belonged to the world, the world would love you as its own; but because you do not belong to the world, because my choice withdrew you from the world, therefore the world hates you. Remember the words I said to you: A servant is not greater than his master. If they persecuted me, they will persecute you too; if they kept my word, they will keep yours as well. But it will be on my account that they will do all this, because they do not know the one who sent me.

Reflection

Hate is a strong word. It's one that I usually try to avoid as it leaves a bad taste in my mouth and can provoke a physical sensation of my heart shrinking and a dark cloud overcoming my soul. However, while I may say or think 'I don't hate anyone' or 'I'm not impacted by hate', Pope Francis reminds me that the opposite of love is not hate, but rather indifference. It's an attitude of 'I'm satisfied. I lack nothing. I have everything. I've assured my place in this life and the next, since I go to Mass every Sunday. I'm a good Christian. But leaving the restaurant, I look the other way [ignoring the homeless woman who lifts her hands to beg for alms].' Today I pray that I may have the courage to overcome any hate or indifference in my heart so that I can be one who reaches out and shows compassion.

22 MAY SUN

SIXTH SUNDAY OF EASTER

Psalter Week 2

White

Acts 15:1-2, 22-29

Some men came down from Judaea and taught the brothers, 'Unless you have yourselves circumcised in the tradition of Moses you cannot be saved.' This led to disagreement, and after Paul and Barnabas had had a long argument with these men it was arranged that Paul and Barnabas and others of the church should go up to Jerusalem and discuss the problem with the apostles and elders.

Then the apostles and elders decided to choose delegates to send to Antioch with Paul and Barnabas; the whole church concurred with this. They chose Judas known as Barsabbas and Silas, both leading men in the brotherhood, and gave them this letter to take with them: 'The apostles and elders, your brothers, send greetings to the brothers of pagan birth in Antioch, Syria and Cilicia. We hear that some of our members have disturbed you with their demands and have unsettled your minds. They acted without any authority from us, and so we have decided unanimously to elect delegates and to send them to you with Barnabas and Paul, men we highly respect who have dedicated their lives to the name of our Lord Jesus Christ. Accordingly we are sending you Judas and Silas, who will confirm by word of mouth what we have written in this letter. It has been decided by the Holy Spirit and by ourselves not to saddle you with any burden beyond these essentials: you are to abstain from food sacrificed to idols, from blood, from the meat of strangled animals and from fornication. Avoid these, and you will do what is right. Farewell.'

Psalm 66:2-3, 5-6, 8. R. v. 4

Let the peoples praise you, O God; let all the peoples praise you.

Apocalypse 21:10-14, 22-23

In the spirit, the angel took me to the top of an enormous high mountain and showed me Jerusalem, the holy city, coming down from God out of heaven. It had all the radiant glory of God and glittered like some precious jewel of crystal-clear diamond. The walls of it were of a great height, and had twelve gates; at each of the twelve gates there was an angel, and over the gates were written the names of the twelve tribes of Israel; on the east there were three gates, on the north three gates, on the south three gates, and on the west three gates. The city walls stood on twelve foundation stones, each one of which bore the name of one of the twelve apostles of the Lamb.

I saw that there was no temple in the city since the Lord God Almighty and the Lamb were themselves the temple, and the city did not need the sun or the moon for light, since it was lit by the radiant glory of God and the Lamb was a lighted torch for it.

John 14:23-29

Jesus said to his disciples: 'If anyone loves me he will keep my word, and my Father will love him, and we shall come to him and make our home with him. Those who do not love me do not keep my words. And my word is not my own; it is the word of the one who sent me. I have said these things to you while still with you; but the Advocate, the Holy Spirit, whom the Father will send in my name, will teach you everything and remind you of all I have said to you. Peace I bequeath to you, my own peace I give you, a peace the world cannot give, this is my gift to you. Do not let your hearts be troubled or afraid. You heard me say: I am going away, and shall return. If you loved me you would have been glad to know that I am going to the Father, for the Father is greater than I. I have told you this now before it happens, so that when it does happen you may believe.'

Reflection

I wonder how the women in Jesus' time felt. The apostles, council representatives and elders of the church were all men. Men were officially chosen as the twelve apostles and sent out as the messengers and bearers of the Good News. And yet, we know women were present in the life of Jesus. His mother, Mary; Mary Magdalene, who ran from the tomb having encountered the risen Christ; the woman at the well and the woman who was saved from being stoned to death. Women, too, knew and loved Jesus and were bearers of the Good News. They remind us that women and men are called to be living witnesses of Jesus' love in the world, to be messengers of hope, and bearers of mercy. Whether we are called to live as Religious, married, single, or in a particular profession, we are all mandated by that 'letter' of the Council of Jerusalem to announce the Good News and to live in the joy of our resurrected Christ.

23
MAY MON

6th Week of Easter
White

Acts 16:11-15

Sailing from Troas we made a straight run for Samothrace; the next day for Neapolis, and from there for Philippi, a Roman colony and the principal city of that particular district of Macedonia. After a few days in this city we went along the river outside the gates as it was the sabbath and this was a customary place for prayer. We sat down and preached to the women who had come to the meeting. One of these women was called Lydia, a devout woman from the town of Thyatira who was in the purple-dye trade. She listened to us, and the Lord opened her heart to accept what Paul was saying. After she and her household had been baptised she sent us an invitation: 'If you really think me a true believer in the Lord,' she said 'come and stay with us'; and she would take no refusal.

Psalm 149:1-6, 9. R. v. 4

The Lord takes delight in his people.

John 15:26–16:4

Jesus said to his disciples: 'When the Advocate comes, whom I shall send to you from the Father, the Spirit of truth who issues from the Father, he will be my witness. And you too will be witnesses, because you have been with me from the outset. I have told you all this so that your faith may not be shaken. They will expel you from the synagogues, and indeed the hour is coming when anyone who kills you will think he is doing a holy duty for God. They will do these things because they have never known either the Father or myself. But I have told you all this, so that when the time for it comes you may remember that I told you.'

Reflection

The gift of good friendship is such a blessing in our lives. Over time, we experience and share life's ups and downs together, the good and the bad, the joyful and sorrowful. But it takes work. Friendship and relationships by their very nature must be free, honest and reciprocal, and trust is integral. In today's Gospel, Jesus is acknowledging his friendship with the disciples, and their shared experience. Knowing that they've been through so much together, and all that the disciples have seen, Jesus trusts that they can 'testify' to who he is as they have 'been with' him from the beginning. The disciples can honestly testify to what they've experienced and witnessed – the miracles he has performed, the words of wisdom he has shared, the love and mercy he has demonstrated. Jesus entrusts each of us, too, to testify to his presence in our daily lives by the choices we make and by our words and deeds.

24
MAY TUE

6th Week of Easter
White

Acts 16:22-34

The crowd of Philippians joined in and showed their hostility to Paul and Silas, so the magistrates had them stripped and ordered them to be flogged. They were given many lashes and then thrown into prison, and the gaoler was told to keep a close watch on them. So, following his instructions, he threw them into the inner prison and fastened their feet in the stocks. Late that night Paul and Silas were praying and singing God's praises, while the other prisoners listened. Suddenly there was an earthquake that shook the prison to its foundations. All the doors flew open and the chains fell from all the prisoners. When the gaoler woke and saw the doors wide open he drew his sword and was about to commit suicide, presuming that the prisoners had escaped. But Paul shouted at the top of his voice, 'Don't do yourself any harm; we are all here.' The gaoler called for lights, then rushed in, threw himself trembling at the feet of Paul and Silas, and escorted them out, saying, 'Sirs, what must I do to be saved?' They told him, 'Become a believer in the Lord Jesus, and you will be saved, and your household too.' Then they preached the word of the Lord to him and to all his family. Late as it was, he took them to wash their wounds, and was baptised then and there with all his household. Afterwards he took them home and gave them a meal, and the whole family celebrated their conversion to belief in God.

Psalm 137:1-3,7-8. R. v. 7

You stretch out your hand and save me, O Lord.

John 16:5-11

Jesus said to his disciples: 'Now I am going to the one who sent me. Not one of you has asked, "Where are you going?" Yet you are sad at heart because I have told you this. Still, I must tell you the truth: it is for your own good that I am going because unless I go, the Advocate will not come to you; but if I do go, I will send him to you. And when he comes, he will show the world how wrong it was, about sin, and about who was in the right, and about judgement: about sin: proved by their refusal to believe in me; about who was in the right: proved by my going to the Father and your seeing me no more; about judgement: proved by the prince of this world being already condemned.'

Reflection

In a way, authentic Christians are on trial their entire lives. They are accused, tempted and abused by the world and the devil. All the lies and abuses are intended to do one thing: destroy their faith in Jesus Christ as their Saviour. Jesus knows that, left alone, we will not be able to defend ourselves, we will be lost and condemned because we not only fight against flesh and blood but against principalities and powers in the heavenly places (Eph. 6:12). That is why He sends the Holy Spirit: to defend the truth about sin, righteousness and judgment. This Holy Spirit works in our hearts and minds, to bring us to faith in Christ. Be open to the Spirit.

25
MAY WED

6th Week of Easter | White or **St Bede the Venerable,** *priest, doctor* | or **St Gregory VII,** *pope* | or **St Mary Magdalene de Pazzi,** *virgin* (Optional, White)

Acts 17:15, 22–18:1

Paul's escort took him as far as Athens, and went back with instructions for Silas and Timothy to rejoin Paul as soon as they could.

Paul stood before the whole Council of the Areopagus and made this speech: 'Men of Athens, I have seen for myself how extremely scrupulous you are in all religious matters, because I noticed, as I strolled round admiring your sacred monuments, that you had an altar inscribed: To An Unknown God. Well, the God whom I proclaim is in fact the one whom you already worship without knowing it.

'Since the God who made the world and everything in it is himself Lord of heaven and earth, he does not make his home in shrines made by human hands. Nor is he dependent on anything that human hands can do for him, since he can never be in need of anything; on the contrary, it is he who gives everything – including life and breath – to everyone. From one single stock he not only created the whole human race so that they could occupy the entire earth, but he decreed how long each nation should flourish and what the boundaries of its territory should be. And he did this so that all nations might seek the deity and, by feeling their way towards him, succeed in finding him. Yet in fact he is not far from any of us, since it is in him that we live, and move, and exist, as indeed some of your own writers have said: "We are all his children." … *(Please see the Appendix B-14)*

Psalm 148:1-2, 11-14

Your glory fills all heaven and earth.

John 16:12-15

Jesus said to his disciples: 'I still have many things to say to you but they would be too much for you now. But when the Spirit of truth comes he will lead you to the complete truth, since he will not be speaking as from himself but will say only what he has learnt; and he will tell you of the things to come. He will glorify me, since all he tells you will be taken from what is mine. Everything the Father has is mine; that is why I said: All he tells you will be taken from what is mine.'

Reflection

I praise you, Lord, for the Spirit of Truth, the Advocate who leads me to eternal life. I praise you, Lord, for the gift of faith, that my heart desires to be in deep relationship with you. I praise you, Lord, for the sun and the moon, the oceans and forests, for all elements in nature that bring beauty and sustenance to my life. I praise you, Lord, for the gift of clean air, that I may easily breathe in and out, and have life to the full. I praise you, Lord, for my family and friends, who bring such life and joy, and meaning to my existence. I praise you, Lord, for the sorrow and difficulties I face, for they remind me of my vulnerability and constant need for you. I praise you, Lord, for being by my side always, for the deep knowledge that I am loved, precious and never alone. I praise you, Lord. Amen.

26
MAY THU

THE ASCENSION OF THE LORD, Solemnity
– England, Scotland and Wales

Saint Philip Neri, Priest – Ireland
see Appendix A-14

Psalter Week 3
White

Acts 1:1-11

In my earlier work, Theophilus, I dealt with everything Jesus had done and taught from the beginning until the day he gave his instructions to the apostles he had chosen through the Holy Spirit, and was taken up to heaven. He had shown himself alive to them after his Passion by many demonstrations: for forty days he had continued to appear to them and tell them about the kingdom of God. When he had been at table with them, he had told them not to leave Jerusalem, but to wait there for what the Father had promised. 'It is' he had said 'what you have heard me speak about: John baptised with water but you, not many days from now, will be baptised with the Holy Spirit.'

Now having met together, they asked him, 'Lord, has the time come? Are you going to restore the kingdom of Israel?' He replied, 'It is not for you to know times or dates that the Father has decided by his own authority, but you will receive power when the Holy Spirit comes on you, and then you will be my witnesses not only in Jerusalem but throughout Judaea and Samaria, and indeed to the ends of the earth.' As he said this he was lifted up while they looked on, and a cloud took him from their sight. They were still staring into the sky when suddenly two men in white were standing near them and they said, 'Why are you men from Galilee standing here looking into the sky? Jesus who has been taken up from you into heaven, this same Jesus will come back in the same way as you have seen him go there.'

Psalm 46:2-3, 6-7, 8-9. R. v. 6

God goes up with shouts of joy; the Lord goes up with trumpet blast.

Hebrews 9:24-28; 10:19-23

It is not as though Christ had entered a man-made sanctuary which was only modelled on the real one; but it was heaven itself, so that he could appear in the actual presence of God on our behalf. And he does not have to offer himself again and again, like the high priest going into the sanctuary year after year with the blood that is not his own, or else he would have had to suffer over and over again since the world began. Instead of that, he has made his appearance once and for all, now at the end of the last age, to do away with sin by sacrificing himself. Since men only die once, and after that comes judgement, so Christ, too, offers himself only once to take the faults of many on himself, and when he appears a second time, it will not be to deal with sin but to reward with salvation those who are waiting for him.

In other words, brothers, through the blood of Jesus we have the right to enter the sanctuary, by a new way which he had opened for us, a living opening through the curtain, that is to say, his body. And we have the supreme high priest over all the house of God. So as we go in, let us be sincere in heart and filled with faith, our minds sprinkled and free from any trace of bad conscience and our bodies washed with pure water. Let us keep firm in the hope we profess, because the one who made the promise is faithful.

Luke 24:46-53

Jesus said to his disciples: 'You see how it is written that the Christ would suffer and on the third day rise from the dead, and that, in his name, repentance for the forgiveness of sins would be preached to all the nations, beginning from Jerusalem. You are witnesses to this.

'And now I am sending down to you what the Father has promised. Stay in the city then, until you are clothed with the power from on high.' Then he took them out as far as the outskirts of Bethany, and lifting up his hands he blessed them. Now as he blessed them, he withdrew from them and was carried up to heaven. They worshipped him and then went back to Jerusalem full of joy; and they were continually in the Temple praising God.

Reflection

I wonder what it was like for the apostles to witness Jesus' ascension into heaven. The Gospel gives a hint: 'And they worshipped him and returned to Jerusalem with great joy and they were continually in the Temple praising God'. Perhaps, too, it was the promise given by Jesus prior to his ascension, which provided deeper conviction and assurance for the disciples: 'You will receive power when the Holy Spirit has come upon you.' Luke tells us that Jesus was blessing them as he ascended. May the blessing of the ascended Christ, with the power of the Holy Spirit, lead us on. We are called to be disciples, to carry on the mission of Christ in proclaiming the kingdom of God on earth. As Christ blesses us, may we be a blessing upon all we encounter.

27
MAY FRI

SAINT AUGUSTINE OF CANTERBURY, Feast
– England

see Appendix A-15
White

6th Week of Easter | White
or **St Augustine of Canterbury,** *bishop* (Optional, White)

Acts 18:9-18

At Corinth one night the Lord spoke to Paul in a vision. 'Do not be afraid to speak out, nor allow yourself to be silenced: I am with you. I have so many people on my side in this city that no one will even attempt to hurt you.' So Paul stayed at Corinth preaching the word of God among them for eighteen months.

But while Gallio was proconsul of Achaia, the Jews made a concerted attack on Paul and brought him before the tribunal. 'We accuse this man' they said 'of persuading people to worship God in a way that breaks the Law.' Before Paul could open his mouth, Gallio said to the Jews, 'Listen, you Jews. If this were a misdemeanor or a crime, I would not hesitate to attend to you; but if it is only quibbles about words and names, and about your own Law, then you must deal with it yourselves – I have no intention of making legal decisions about things like that.' Then he sent them out of the court, and at once they all turned on Sosthenes, the synagogue president, and beat him in front of the court house. Gallio refused to take any notice at all.

After staying on for some time, Paul took leave of the brothers and sailed for Syria, accompanied by Priscilla and Aquila. At Cenchreae he had his hair cut off, because of a vow he had made.

Psalm 46:2-7. R. v. 8

God is king of all the earth.

John 16:20-23

Jesus said to his disciples: 'I tell you most solemnly, you will be weeping and wailing while the world will rejoice; you will be sorrowful but your sorrow will turn to joy. A woman in childbirth suffers, because her time has come; but when she has given birth to the child she forgets the suffering in her joy that a man has been born into the world. So it is with you: you are sad now, but I shall see you again, and your hearts will be full of joy, and that joy no one shall take from you. When that day comes, you will not ask me any questions.'

Reflection

St Augustine of Canterbury is the patron saint of England. In 596AD, about 400 monks set out from Rome to evangelise the Anglo-Saxons in England, led by Augustine. En route, stories of the ferocity of the Anglo-Saxons and the treacherous waters of the English Channel, caused the group to return. Pope Gregory the Great assured Augustine that their fears were groundless, and so they set off again. Having successfully landed in the territory of Kent, ruled by King Ethelbert, Augustine set about his work – within the year, King Ethelbert was baptised. Augustine was consecrated a bishop in France and returned to Canterbury where he founded his See. He constructed a church and monastery near where the present cathedral now stands. As the faith spread, additional Sees were established at London and Rochester. Though Augustine's work was sometimes slow and did not always meet with success, he provides an example to us of how persistence and perseverance, despite obstacles, can pay off! We must keep going, trusting in the Lord.

6th Week of Easter,
Saturday Before the Ascension, Ireland, White

28
MAY SAT

Acts 18:23-28

Paul came down to Antioch where he spent a short time before continuing his journey through the Galatian country and then through Phrygia, encouraging all the followers.

An Alexandrian Jew named Apollos now arrived in Ephesus. He was an eloquent man, with a sound knowledge of the scriptures and yet, though he had been given instruction in the Way of the Lord and preached with great earnestness and was accurate in all the details he taught about Jesus, he had only experienced the baptism of John. When Priscilla and Aquila heard him speak boldly in the synagogue, they took an interest in him and gave him further instruction about the Way.

When Apollos thought of crossing over to Achaia, the brothers encouraged him and wrote asking the disciples to welcome him. When he arrived there he was able by God's grace to help the believers considerably by the energetic way he refuted the Jews in public and demonstrated from the scriptures that Jesus was the Christ.

Psalm 46:2-3, 8-10. R. v. 8

God is king of all the earth.

John 16:23-28

Jesus said to his disciples: 'I tell you most solemnly, anything you ask for from the Father he will grant in my name. Until now you have not asked for anything in my name. Ask and you will receive, and so your joy will be complete. I have been telling you all this in metaphors; the hour is coming when I shall no longer speak to you in metaphors, but tell you about the Father in plain words. When that day comes you will ask in my name; and I do not say that I shall pray to the Father for you, because the Father himself loves you for loving me and believing that I came from God. I came from the Father and have come into the world and now I leave the world to go to the Father.'

Reflection

In Psalm 46 (47): 2 is often translated: 'For the Lord, the Most High, is awesome.' I invite you to ponder this word, 'awesome'. What does it invoke in your heart? What images come to mind? According to the dictionary, 'awesome' is an adjective which means, inspiring awe. What inspires 'awe' in your life? 'Awe' is defined as an emotion variously combining dread, veneration and wonder inspired by authority or by the sacred or sublime. Do I stand in wonder and awe before the God of all creation? When I behold a glorious sunrise or sunset, or a newborn, or good health and success, do I stand in awe at the One who created me, and everything that lies before me? Does my heart swell with awe and wonder as I contemplate the mystery of God? The mystery of life and of love? Of friendship? *Thank you, Lord, for this beautiful mystery of life. May I never cease to behold you as awesome!*

29
MAY SUN

SEVENTH SUNDAY OF EASTER
– England, Scotland and Wales, Solemnity
White

ASCENSION OF THE LORD
– Ireland, see 26 May

Acts 7:55-60

Stephen, filled with the Holy Spirit, gazed into heaven and saw the glory of God, and Jesus standing at God's right hand. 'I can see heaven thrown open' he said 'and the Son of Man standing at the right hand of God.' At this all the members of the council shouted out and stopped their ears with their hands; then they all rushed at him, sent him out of the city and stoned him. The witnesses put down their clothes at the feet of a young man called Saul. As they were stoning him, Stephen said in invocation, 'Lord Jesus, receive my spirit.' Then he knelt down and said aloud, 'Lord, do not hold this sin against them'; and with these words he fell asleep.

Psalm 96:1-2b,6-7,9. R. vv. 1.9

The Lord is king, most high above all the earth.

Apocalypse 22:12-14,16-17,20

I, John, heard a voice speaking to me: 'Very soon now, I shall be with you again, bringing the reward to be given to every man according to what he deserves. I am the Alpha and the Omega, the First and the Last, the Beginning and the End. Happy are those who will have washed their robes clean, so that they will have the right to feed on the tree of life and can come through the gates into the city.'

I, Jesus, have sent my angel to make these revelations to you for the sake of the churches. I am of David's line, the root of David and the bright star of the morning.

The Spirit and the Bride say, 'Come.' Let everyone who listens answer, 'Come.' Then let all who are thirsty come: all who want it may have the water of life, and have it free.

The one who guarantees these revelations repeats his promise: I shall indeed be with you soon. Amen; come, Lord Jesus.

John 17:20-26

Jesus raised his eyes to heaven and said:
'Holy Father,
I pray not only for these,
but for those also
who through their words will believe in me.
May they all be one.
Father, may they be one in us,
as you are in me and I am in you,
so that the world may believe it was you who sent me.
I have given them the glory you gave to me,
that they may be one as we are one.
With me in them and you in me,
may they be so completely one

that the world will realise that it was you who sent me
and that I have loved them as much as you loved me.
Father, I want those you have given me
to be with me where I am,
so that they may always see the glory you have given me
because you loved me before the foundation of the world.
Father, Righteous One,
the world has not known you,
but I have known you,
and these have known that you have sent me.
I have made your name known to them
and will continue to make it known,
so that the love with which you loved me may be in them,
and so that I may be in them.'

Reflection

What do you do when life is turned upside down? In today's First Reading we find Stephen's world being turned upside down. But that is not entirely correct. Stephen's world is ending; you might also say that Stephen is having a bad day, but that isn't true. Stephen is having the best of days. Stephen is dying to live. As he dies he has the privilege to gaze into heaven and see the glory that awaits the faithful. In the Gospel, Jesus prays for you and me. Jesus prays for everyone who will also believe in Him down through the centuries. He prays for unity, not uniformity. If Jesus is praying for our oneness then He is also recognizing and rejecting the boundaries and differences that divide us. Oneness is not about eliminating our differences; it is about love. Love God, your neighbour, yourself, and your enemy.

30
MAY MON

7th Week of Easter
White

Acts 19:1-8
While Apollos was in Corinth, Paul made his way overland as far as Ephesus, where he found a number of disciples. When he asked, 'Did you receive the Holy Spirit when you became believers?' they answered, 'No, we were never even told there was such a thing as a Holy Spirit.' 'Then how were you baptised?' he asked 'With John's baptism' they replied. 'John's baptism' said Paul 'was a baptism of repentance; but he insisted that the people should believe in the one who was to come after him – in other words Jesus.' When they heard this, they were baptised in the name of the Lord Jesus, and the moment Paul had laid hands on them the Holy Spirit came down on them, and they began to speak with tongues and to prophesy. There were about twelve of these men. He began by going to the synagogue, where he spoke out boldly and argued persuasively about the kingdom of God. He did this for three months.

Psalm 67:2-7. R. v. 33
Kingdoms of the earth, sing to God.

John 16:29-33
His disciples said to Jesus, 'Now you are speaking plainly and not using metaphors! Now we see that you know everything, and do not have to wait for questions to be put into words; because of this we believe that you came from God.' Jesus answered them:

'Do you believe at last? Listen; the time will come – in fact it has come already – when you will be scattered, each going his own way and leaving me alone. And yet I am not alone, because the Father is with me. I have told you all this so that you may find peace in me. In the world you will have trouble but be brave: I have conquered the world.'

Reflection
Take courage, Jesus has conquered the world! We are invited to have hope, despite the pain and difficulties we face in life. In the midst of darkness, we need to hold firmly onto these words of Jesus: 'Take courage, I have conquered the world'! Jesus is the light of the world, the way and the truth. He has conquered death and darkness. And by our baptism we have received the Holy Spirit, who proceeds from the Father and Son, and who is the giver of life. We are invited to practise courage each day, in the small and big acts of our daily life. Inspired by Jesus, we make decisions based on the life and love of Christ. We know what is right and wrong, and we choose life over death. Love has the last say. Christ is victorious!

The Visitation of the Blessed Virgin Mary
Feast | White

31
MAY TUE

Zephaniah 3:14-18
(Alternative Reading: Romans 12:9-16)

Shout for joy, daughter of Zion, Israel, shout aloud! Rejoice, exult with all your heart, daughter of Jerusalem! The Lord has repealed your sentence; he has driven your enemies away. The Lord, the king of Israel, is in your midst; you have no more evil to fear. When that day comes, word will come to Jerusalem; Zion, have no fear, do not let your hands fall limp. The Lord your God is in your midst, a victorious warrior. He will exult with joy over you, he will renew you by his love; he will dance with shouts of joy for you as on a day of festival.

Psalm: Isaiah 12:2-6. R. v. 6
Great in your midst is the Holy One of Israel.

Luke 1:39-56

Mary set out and went as quickly as she could to a town in the hill country of Judah. She went into Zechariah's house and greeted Elizabeth. Now as soon as Elizabeth heard Mary's greeting, the child leapt in her womb and Elizabeth was filled with the Holy Spirit. She gave a loud cry and said, 'Of all women you are the most blessed, and blessed is the fruit of your womb. Why should I be honoured with a visit from the mother of my Lord? For the moment your greeting reached my ears, the child in my womb leapt for joy. Yes, blessed is she who believed that the promise made her by the Lord would be fulfilled.'

And Mary said: 'My soul proclaims the greatness of the Lord and my spirit exults in God my saviour; because he has looked upon his lowly handmaid. Yes, from this day forward all generations will call me blessed, for the Almighty has done great things for me. Holy is his name, and his mercy reaches from age to age for those who fear him. He has shown the power of his arm, he has routed the proud of heart. He has pulled down princes from their thrones and exalted the lowly. The hungry he has filled with good things, the rich sent empty away. He has come to the help of Israel his servant, mindful of his mercy – according to the promise he made to our ancestors – of his mercy to Abraham and to his descendants for ever.'

Reflection

Like Mary, I pray: *My soul magnifies the Lord, and my spirit rejoices in God my saviour, for he has looked with favour on me, the lowliness of his servant. Surely, from now on all generations will call me blessed; For the mighty One has done great things for me, and holy is his name.* Like Mary and Elizabeth, and the child in her womb, I am filled with the Holy Spirit and my heart is full of joy. I praise the Lord for all his goodness, for the gift of life and love and joy! Like Elizabeth and Mary, I too celebrate these gifts with family and friends. I pray that I may extend the blessing to all I encounter today. And in so doing, they will know that the Holy Spirit and the love of Christ lives in me. Thank you, God, for your blessing.

01
JUN WED

7th Week of Easter
St Justin, *martyr*, **Memorial** | Red

Acts 20:28-38

Paul addressed these words to the elders of the church of Ephesus: 'Be on your guard for yourselves and for all the flock of which the Holy Spirit has made you the overseers, to feed the Church of God which he bought with his own blood. I know quite well that when I have gone fierce wolves will invade you and will have no mercy on the flock. Even from your own ranks there will be men coming forward with a travesty of the truth on their lips to induce the disciples to follow them. So be on your guard, remembering how night and day for three years I never failed to keep you right, shedding tears over each one of you. And now I commend you to God, and to the word of his grace that has power to build you up and to give you your inheritance among all the sanctified. ... *(Please see the Appendix B-14)*

Psalm 67:29-30, 33-36. R. v. 33

Kingdoms of the earth, sing to God.

John 17:11-19

Jesus raised his eyes to heaven and said: 'Holy Father, keep those you have given me true to your name, so that they may be one like us. While I was with them, I kept those you had given me true to your name. I have watched over them and not one is lost except the one who chose to be lost, and this was to fulfil the scriptures. But now I am coming to you and while still in the world I say these things to share my joy with them to the full. I passed your word on to them, and the world hated them, because they belong to the world no more than I belong to the world. I am not asking you to remove them from the world, but to protect them from the evil one. They do not belong to the world any more than I belong to the world. Consecrate them in the truth; your word is truth. As you sent me into the world, I have sent them into the world, and for their sake I consecrate myself so that they too may be consecrated in truth.'

Reflection

Jesus prays to the Father to protect the disciples since all holiness comes from the Father. The disciples are *consecrated*, that is, set apart and dedicated to keeping the name of God holy. By remaining 'consecrated in the truth', the disciples come under the protection of Jesus and the Father himself. For even as the disciples exercise their ministry in the world with authority from Jesus, they have to contend with the Evil One. But they are assured of God's protection. Jesus links his own consecration and mission to that of the disciples. As long as they are committed to keeping the truth – and not peddlers of falsehood, deceit, and lies – God's own word of truth will preserve them.

02
JUN THU

7th Week of Easter | White
or **Sts Marcellinus and Peter,** *martyrs* (Optional, Red)

Acts 22:30; 23:6-11

Since the tribune wanted to know what precise charge the Jews were bringing against Paul, he freed him and gave orders for a meeting of the chief priests and the entire Sanhedrin; then he brought Paul down and stood him in front of them.

Now Paul was well aware that one section was made up of Sadducees and the other of Pharisees, so he called out in the Sanhedrin, 'Brothers, I am a Pharisee and the son of Pharisees. It is for our hope in the resurrection of the dead that I am on trial.' ... *(Please see the Appendix B-15)*

Psalm 15:1-2, 5, 7-11. R. v. 1

Preserve me, Lord, I take refuge in you.

John 17:20-26

Jesus raised his eyes to heaven and said: 'Holy Father, I pray not only for these, but for those also who through their words will believe in me. May they all be one. Father, may they be one in us as you are in me and I am in you, so that the world may believe it was you who sent me. I have given them the glory you gave to me, that they may be one as we are one. With me in them and you in me, may they be so completely one that the world will realise that it was you who sent me and that I have loved them as much as you love me. 'Father, I want those you have given me to be with me where I am, so that they may always see the glory you have given me because you loved me before the foundation of the world. Father, Righteous One, the world has not known you, but I have known you, and these have known that you have sent me. I have made your name known to them and will continue to make it known, so that the love with which you loved me may be in them, and so that I may be in them.'

Reflection

In his prayer to the Father Jesus looks ahead to the time when many other people will believe in him through the witness of his disciples. He prays that all believers 'may be one' as he and Father are one. United with one another in love, they will give a convincing witness to the world of the intimate love of the Holy Trinity which fills their hearts. In his encyclical letter *Ut Unum Sint* ('That they may be one'), St. John Paul II calls for Christian unity. He writes, 'This unity, which the Lord has bestowed on his Church and in which he wishes to embrace all people, is not something added on, but stands at the very heart of Christ's mission ... it belongs to the very essence of this community. God wills the Church, because he wills unity, and unity is an expression of the whole depth of his agape [love]' (*art.* 9).

03

JUN FRI

7th Week of Easter | St Charles Lwanga and companions, *martyrs*, **Memorial |** Red

Acts 25:13-21

King Agrippa and Bernice arrived in Caesarea and paid their respects to Festus. Their visit lasted several days, and Festus put Paul's case before the king. 'There is a man here' he said 'whom Felix left behind in custody, and while I was in Jerusalem the chief priests and elders of the Jews laid information against him, demanding his condemnation. But I told them that Romans are not in the habit of surrendering any man, until the accused confronts his accusers and is given an opportunity to defend himself against the charge. So they came here with me, and I wasted no time but took my seat on the tribunal the very next day and had the man brought in. When confronted with him, his accusers did not charge him with any of the crimes I had expected; but they had some argument or other with him about their own religion and about a dead man called Jesus whom Paul alleged to be alive. Not feeling qualified to deal with questions of this sort, I asked him if he would be willing to go to Jerusalem, to be tried there on this issue. But Paul put in an appeal for his case to be reserved for the judgement of the august emperor, so I ordered him to be remanded until I could send him to Caesar.'

Psalm 102:1-2, 11-12, 19-20. R. v. 19

The Lord has set his sway in heaven.

John 21:15-19

Jesus showed himself to his disciples, and after they had eaten he said to Simon Peter, 'Simon son of John, do you love me more than these others do?' He answered, 'Yes Lord, you know I love you.' Jesus said to him, 'Feed my lambs.' A second time he said to him, 'Simon son of John, do you love me?' He replied, 'Yes, Lord, you know I love you.' Jesus said to him, 'Look after my sheep.' Then he said to him a third time, 'Simon son of John, do you love me?' Peter was upset that he asked him the third time, 'Do you love me?' and said, 'Lord, you know everything; you know I love you.' Jesus said to him, 'Feed my sheep.

'I tell you most solemnly, when you were young you put on your own belt and walked where you liked; but when you grow old you will stretch out your hands, and somebody else will put a belt round you and take you where you would rather not go.' In these words he indicated the kind of death by which Peter would give glory to God. After this he said, 'Follow me.'

Reflection

At the close of his Gospel, John presents Jesus giving Simon Peter a share in his mission as the Good Shepherd who knows his sheep and lays down his life for them. The foremost requirement for this responsibility is Peter's love for Jesus, the confession of which Jesus elicits from him three times. Simon is to feed Jesus' sheep through his leadership. Jesus also alludes to Simon laying down his life by signifying what kind of death Simon would glorify God. During the COVID-19 pandemic, many priests and ministers throughout the world were among those on the front lines who attended to the care of the people in their physical and spiritual needs. Many died in the line of duty. They proved to be true shepherds, like Simon Peter.

7th Week of Easter
White

04
JUN SAT

Acts 28:16-20, 30-31

On our arrival in Rome Paul was allowed to stay in lodgings of his own with the soldier who guarded him.

After three days he called together the leading Jews. When they had assembled, he said to them, 'Brothers, although I have done nothing against our people or the customs of our ancestors, I was arrested in Jerusalem and handed over to the Romans. They examined me and would have set me free, since they found me guilty of nothing involving the death penalty; but the Jews lodged an objection, and I was forced to appeal to Caesar, not that I had any accusation to make against my own nation. That is why I have asked to see you and talk to you, for it is on account of the hope of Israel that I wear this chain.'

Paul spent the whole of the two years in his own rented lodging. He welcomed all who came to visit him, proclaiming the kingdom of God and teaching the truth about the Lord Jesus Christ with complete freedom and without hindrance from anyone.

Psalm 10:4-5, 7. R. cf. v. 7

The upright shall see your face, O Lord.

John 21:20-25

Peter turned and saw the disciple Jesus loved following them – the one who had leaned on his breast at the supper and had said to him, 'Lord, who is it that will betray you?' Seeing him, Peter said to Jesus, 'What about him, Lord?' Jesus answered, 'If I want him to stay behind till I come, what does it matter to you? You are to follow me.' The rumour then went out among the brothers that this disciple would not die. Yet Jesus had not said to Peter 'He will not die,' but, 'If I want him to stay behind till I come.'

This disciple is the one who vouches for these things and has written them down, and we know that his testimony is true. There were many other things that Jesus did; if all were written down, the world itself, I suppose, would not hold all the books that would have to be written.

Reflection

An ancient tradition associates the Beloved Disciple, mentioned in the Fourth Gospel, with the Apostle John. In the Synoptic Gospels, John has a lesser role to Peter among the apostles. But in the Fourth Gospel, the Beloved Disciple is almost on a par with Simon Peter. He is the 'hero' of the Christian community that produced the Fourth Gospel – the one who testifies to the truth about Jesus. In today's Gospel passage, Simon Peter asks, 'what about him [the Beloved Disciple]? Jesus' answer led some people to think that the Beloved Disciple would not die before the Lord returned in glory. Since he had died by the time the Gospel of John had been written, the author stresses that people misinterpreted Jesus' words. Tradition holds that John [the Beloved Disciple] was the last of the Twelve to die and did not suffer martyrdom. While martyrs are always honoured within the Christian community, so too is a life of long and faithful witness to Jesus and to his new commandment to love one another as he has loved us.

05
JUN SUN

PENTECOST SUNDAY, Solemnity

Psalter Week 2

Red

Acts 2:1-11

When Pentecost day came round, the apostles had all met in one room, when suddenly they heard what sounded like a powerful wind from heaven, the noise of which filled the entire house in which they were sitting; and something appeared to them that seemed like tongues of fire; these separated and came to rest on the head of each of them. They were all filled with the Holy Spirit, and began to speak foreign languages as the Spirit gave them the gift of speech.

Now there were devout men living in Jerusalem from every nation under heaven, and at this sound they all assembled, each one bewildered to hear these men speaking his own language. They were amazed and astonished. 'Surely' they said 'all these men speaking are Galileans? How does it happen that each of us hears them in his own native language? Parthians, Medes and Elamites; people from Mesopotamia, Judaea and Cappadocia, Pontus and Asia, Phrygia and Pamphylia, Egypt and the parts of Libya round Cyrene; as well as visitors from Rome – Jews and proselytes alike – Cretans and Arabs; we hear them preaching in our own language about the marvels of God.'

Psalm 103:1, 24, 29-31, 34. R. v. 30

Send forth your spirit, O Lord, and renew the face of the earth.

Romans 8:8-17

People who are interested only in unspiritual things can never be pleasing to God. Your interests, however, are not in the unspiritual, but in the spiritual, since the Spirit of God has made his home in you. In fact, unless you possessed the Spirit of Christ you would not belong to him. Though your body may be dead it is because of sin, but if Christ is in you then your spirit is life itself because you have been justified; and if the Spirit of him who raised Jesus from the dead is living in you, then he who raised Jesus from the dead will give life to your own mortal bodies through his Spirit living in you.

So then, my brothers, there is no necessity for us to obey our unspiritual selves or to live unspiritual lives. If you do live in that way, you are doomed to die; but if by the Spirit you put an end to the misdeeds of the body you will live.

Everyone moved by the Spirit is a son of God. The spirit you received is not the spirit of slaves bringing fear into your lives again; it is the spirit of sons, and it makes us cry out, 'Abba, Father!' The Spirit himself and our spirit bear united witness that we are children of God. And if we are children we are heirs as well: heirs of God and coheirs with Christ, sharing his sufferings so as to share his glory.

John 14:15-16, 23-26

Jesus said to his disciples: 'If you love me you will keep my commandments. I shall ask the Father and he will give you another Advocate to be with you for ever. If anyone loves me he will keep my word, and my Father will love him, and we shall come to him and make our home with him. Those who do not love me do not keep my words. And my word is not my own; it is the word of the one who sent me. I have said these things to you while still with you; but the Advocate, the Holy Spirit, whom the Father will send in my name, will teach you everything and remind you of all I have said to you.

Reflection

Pentecost Sunday commemorates the descent of the Holy Spirit upon Jesus' disciples fifty days after his resurrection. This day coincides with the Jewish festival of the Harvest (Weeks), which occurs seven weeks – plus one day – after the Feast of the Unleavened Bread that commemorates the Passover meal (Exodus 23:16). Jewish pilgrims from many parts of the world had gathered in Jerusalem to celebrate the harvest feast and all could understand in their own language what the disciples were saying. That all could understand reveals the universal mission of the Christian community – to bring the Good News to all people. This event also reversed the curse of the Tower of Babel. In the ancient story, God confused the speech of the whole world because of the arrogance of humankind who had tried to build a tower reaching up to the sky, the realm of heaven. As a result, the people were scattered all over the earth (Genesis 11:1-9). With the coming of the Holy Spirit at Pentecost, people from every nation and tongue were able to understand each other, enabling them to come together. Before his departure at the arrival of the 'hour' – his passion, death, and resurrection – Jesus assured his disciples that he would not leave them orphans as he would ask the Father to send them another Advocate, the Spirit of truth, to be with them. This indwelling Spirit would be like a flame that would kindle their love for one another, thus enabling them to keep the commandments of Jesus. The Spirit is also the source of peace, who would enable the disciples to experience peace and joy while remaining in the world.

06
JUN MON

10th Week in Ordinary Time
Mary, Mother of the Church, Memorial | White

Genesis 3:9-15,20

After Adam had eaten of the tree the Lord God called to him. 'Where are you?' he asked. 'I heard the sound of you in the garden;' he replied 'I was afraid because I was naked, so I hid.' 'Who told you that you were naked?' he asked 'Have you been eating of the tree I forbade you to eat?' The man replied, 'It was the woman you put with me; she gave me the fruit, and I ate it.' Then the Lord God asked the woman, 'What is this you have done?' The woman replied, 'The serpent tempted me and I ate.' Then the Lord God said to the serpent, 'Because you have done this, 'Be accursed beyond all cattle, all wild beasts. You shall crawl on your belly and eat dust every day of your life. I will make you enemies of each other: you and the woman, your offspring and her offspring. It will crush your head and you will strike its heel.' The man named his wife 'Eve' because she was the mother of all those who live.

Psalm 86:1-2, 3, 5, 6-7. R. v. 3

Of you are told glorious things, O city of God!

John 19:25-34

Near the cross of Jesus stood his mother and his mother's sister, Mary the wife of Clopas, and Mary of Magdala. Seeing his mother and the disciple he loved standing near her, Jesus said to his mother, 'Woman, this is your son'. Then to the disciple he said, 'This is your mother'. And from that moment the disciple made a place for her in his home. After this, Jesus knew that everything had now been completed, and to fulfil the Scripture perfectly he said: 'I am thirsty'. A jar full of vinegar stood there, so putting a sponge soaked in vinegar on a hyssop stick they held it up to his mouth. After Jesus had taken the vinegar he said, 'It is finished', and bowing his head he gave up his spirit.

It was Preparation Day, and to prevent the bodies remaining on the cross during the sabbath – since the sabbath was a day of great solemnity – the Jews asked Pilate to have the legs broken and the bodies taken away. Consequently the soldiers came and broke the legs of the first man who had been crucified with him and then of the other. When they came to Jesus, they found he was already dead, so instead of breaking his legs one of the soldiers pierced his side with a lance; and immediately there came out blood and water.

Reflection

The Memorial of the Blessed Virgin Mary, Mother of the Church, was inscribed into the General Roman Calendar on the Monday after Pentecost to highlight Mary's collaboration with the mission of Jesus, and her unity with the apostles and the other disciples at the birth of the Church. As early as the fourth century, St. Ambrose of Milan had regarded Mary as a model of the Church in her faith, love, and union with Jesus from birth until his death on the cross. In his apostolic letter *Credo of the People of God* (1968), St Paul VI declares Mary as Mother of the Church, and mother of all Christians: 'Joined by a close and indissoluble bond to the Mysteries of the Incarnation and Redemption, the Blessed Virgin … Mother of the Church, continues in heaven her maternal role with regard to Christ's members, cooperating with the birth and growth of divine life in the souls of the redeemed' (*Credo*, 15).

07
JUN TUE

10th Week in Ordinary Time
Green

1 Kings 17:7-16

The stream in the place where Elijah lay hidden dried up, for the country had no rain. And then the word of the Lord came to Elijah, 'Up and go to Zarephath, a Sidonian town, and stay there. I have ordered a widow there to give you food.' So he went off to Sidon. And when he reached the city gate, there was a widow gathering sticks; addressing her he said, 'Please bring a little water in a vessel for me to drink.' She was setting off to bring it when he called after her. 'Please' he said 'bring me a scrap of bread in your hand.' 'As the Lord your God lives,' she replied 'I have no baked bread, but only a handful of meal in a jar and a little oil in a jug; I am just gathering a stick or two to go and prepare this for myself and my son to eat, and then we shall die.' But Elijah said to her, 'Do not be afraid, go and do as you have said, but first make a little scone of it for me and bring it to me, and then make some for yourself and for your son. For thus the Lord speaks, the God of Israel: "Jar of meal shall not be spent, jug of oil shall not be emptied, before the day when the Lord sends rain on the face of the earth."' The woman went and did as Elijah told her and they ate the food, she, himself and her son. The jar of meal was not spent nor the jug of oil emptied, just as the Lord had foretold through Elijah.

Psalm 4:2-5, 7-8. R. v. 7

Lift up the light of your face on us, O Lord.

Matthew 5:13-16

Jesus said to his disciples: 'You are the salt of the earth. But if salt becomes tasteless, what can make it salty again? It is good for nothing, and can only be thrown out to be trampled underfoot by men.

'You are the light of the world. A city built on a hilltop cannot be hidden. No one lights a lamp to put it under a tub; they put it on the lamp-stand where it shines for everyone in the house. In the same way your light must shine in the sight of men, so that, seeing your good works, they may give the praise to your Father in heaven.'

Reflection

In his Sermon on the Mount, Jesus calls his disciples the salt of the earth and the light of the world, The focus is on God's action in the world – not simply in the Church: In the first place Christians are to be salt of the earth. In the ancient world, salt was highly valued. The Greeks called salt divine. It serves two important functions. It is a preservative that keeps things from going bad, and it gives taste and flavour to food. Our task is to be the salt of society, preserving, reconciling, adding taste, giving meaning where there is no meaning, giving hope where there is no hope. We are also called to be the light of the world. It reminds us that we should not be preoccupied solely with the concerns of the Christian community, but we must widen our horizon to bring light to all peoples.

08
JUN WED

10th Week in Ordinary Time
Green

1 Kings 18:20-39

King Ahab called all Israel together and assembled the prophets of Baal on Mount Carmel. Elijah stepped out in front of all the people. 'How long' he said 'do you mean to hobble first on one leg then on the other? If the Lord is God, follow him; if Baal, follow him.' But the people never said a word. Elijah then said to them, 'I, I alone, am left as a prophet of the Lord, while the prophets of Baal are four hundred and fifty. Let two bulls be given us; let them choose one for themselves, dismember it and lay it on the wood, but not set fire to it. I in my turn will prepare the other bull, but not set fire to it. You must call on the name of your god, and I shall call on the name of mine; the god who answers with fire, is God indeed.' The people all answered, 'Agreed!' Elijah then said to the prophets of Baal, 'Choose one bull and begin, for there are more of you. Call on the name of your god but light no fire.' They took the bull and prepared it, and from morning to midday they called on the name of Baal. 'O Baal, answer us!' they cried, but there was no voice, no answer, as they performed their hobbling dance round the altar they had made. Midday came, and Elijah mocked them. … *(Please see the Appendix B-15)*

Psalm 15:1-2, 4-5, 8, 11. R. v. 1

Save me, Lord, I take refuge in you.

Matthew 5:17-19

Jesus said to his disciples: 'Do not imagine that I have come to abolish the Law or the Prophets. I have come not to abolish but to complete them. I tell you solemnly, till heaven and earth disappear, not one dot, not one little stroke, shall disappear from the Law until its purpose is achieved. Therefore, the man who infringes even one of the least of these commandments and teaches others to do the same will be considered the least in the kingdom of heaven; but the man who keeps them and teaches them will be considered great in the kingdom of heaven.'

Reflection

Jesus words in today's Gospel may seem to contradict his actions because, on more than one occasion, he did 'violate' the Sabbath law and other laws. What Jesus refutes in these situations is a legalistic observance of the law that disregards the spirit of the law. When a person is in need on the Sabbath day, then the spirit of the Law urges one to respond to their needs and not to refuse to give help because the law prohibits doing this or that. Jesus also combines 'the law and the prophets', that is the whole scriptures. Our moral decisions should be based on the whole message of the Bible and not on one verse viewed in isolation. May we never hide behind a particular law to avoid reaching out to someone in need.

09
JUN THU

SAINT COLUMBA (COLUM CILLE), ABBOT, FEAST
– Ireland, Scotland
see Appendix A-16

Our Lord Jesus Christ the Eternal High Priest, Feast, White

Isaiah 6:1-4,8

In the year of King Uzziah's death I saw the Lord of Hosts seated on a high throne; his train filled the sanctuary; above him stood seraphs, each one with six wings: two to cover its face, two to cover its feet, and two for flying.

And they cried out to one another in this way, 'Holy, holy, holy is the Lord of Hosts. His glory fills the whole earth.' The foundations of the threshold shook with the voice of the one who cried out, and the Temple was filled with smoke. Then I heard the voice of the Lord saying: 'Whom shall I send? Who will be our messenger?' I answered, 'Here I am, send me.'

Psalm 22:1-3a,5-6

The Lord is my shepherd; there is nothing I shall want.

John 17:1-2,9,14-24

Jesus raised his eyes to heaven and said: 'Father, the hour has come: glorify your Son so that your Son may glorify you; and, through the power over all mankind that you have given him, let him give eternal life to all those you have entrusted to him. 'I pray for them; I am not praying for the world but for those you have given me, because they belong to you. 'I passed your word on to them, and the world hated them, because they belong to the world no more than I belong to the world. I am not asking you to remove them from the world, but to protect them from the evil one. They do not belong to the world any more than I belong to the world. Consecrate them in the truth; your word is truth. As you sent me into the world, I have sent them into the world, and for their sake I consecrate myself so that they too may be consecrated in truth. 'I pray not only for these, but for those also who through their words will believe in me. May they all be one. Father, may they be one in us, as you are in me and I am in you, so that the world may believe it was you who sent me. I have given them the glory you gave to me, that they may be one as we are one. With me in them and you in me, may they be so completely one that the world will realise that it was you who sent me and that I have loved them as much as you loved me. Father, I want those you have given me to be with me where I am, so that they may always see the glory you have given me because you loved me before the foundation of the world.'

Reflection

"If you remember that your brother or sister has something against you…" – this injunction reveals the attitude and nature of God. God is an advocate of unity. His essence is unity – three Persons, one nature. He fashioned us in His image to live forever in union with Him and our brothers and sisters. Hence the bond we share is the signature of our identity as children of God. We are to sustain it and not destroy it. This is so important that God will not even accept our "offering" if we intentionally hinder our unity with those around us. As we ponder this teaching, we can recall to mind and offer in prayer those difficult relationships we are experiencing, in order to draw strength from God to love as we should.

1 Kings 19:9, 11-16

When Elijah reached Horeb, the mountain of God, he went into the cave and spent the night in it. Then he was told, 'Go out and stand on the mountain before the Lord.' Then the Lord himself went by. There came a mighty wind, so strong it tore the mountains and shattered the rocks before the Lord. But the Lord was not in the wind. After the wind came an earthquake. But the Lord was not in the earthquake. After the earthquake came a fire. But the Lord was not in the fire. And after the fire there came the sound of a gentle breeze. And when Elijah heard this, he covered his face with his cloak and went out and stood at the entrance of the cave. Then a voice came to him, which said 'What are you doing here, Elijah?' He replied, 'I am filled with jealous zeal for the Lord of hosts, because the sons of Israel have deserted you, broken down your altars and put your prophets to the sword. I am the only one left and they want to kill me.'

'Go,' the Lord said 'go back by the same way to the wilderness of Damascus. You are to go and anoint Hazael as king of Aram. You are to anoint Jehu son of Nimshi as king of Israel, and to anoint Elisha son of Shaphat, of Abel Meholah, as prophet to succeed you.'

Psalm 26:7-9, 13-14. R. v. 8

It is your face, O Lord, that I seek.

Matthew 5:27-32

Jesus said to his disciples: 'You have learnt how it was said: You must not commit adultery. But I say this to you: if a man looks at a woman lustfully, he has already committed adultery with her in his heart. If your right eye should cause you to sin, tear it out and throw it away; for it will do you less harm to lose one part of you than to have your whole body thrown into hell. And if your right hand should cause you to sin, cut if off and throw it away; for it will do you less harm to lose one part of you than to have your whole body go to hell. It has also been said: Anyone who divorces his wife must give her a writ of dismissal. But I say this to you: everyone who divorces his wife, except for the case of fornication, makes her an adulteress; and anyone who marries a divorced woman commits adultery.'

Reflection

Jesus words to tear out your eye or cut off your hand if they lead you into sin are indeed shocking, and surely, they are not meant to be taken literally. Jesus is using very strong words to shock and wake us up, urging us to recognise and root out wrong desires before they lead us into sin. Jesus knows how weak we human beings are, how we postpone difficult decisions, especially when it comes to changing our habits and seeking to be free from addictions of one form or another. Only the grace of God and decisive action on our part can free us from ways of acting that we know must stop.

10th Week in Ordinary Time
St Barnabas, *apostle,* **Memorial** | Red

11
JUN SAT

Acts 11:21-26; 13:1-3

A great number believed and were converted to the Lord. The Church in Jerusalem heard about this and they sent Barnabas to Antioch. There he could see for himself that God had given grace, and this pleased him, and he urged them all to remain faithful to the Lord with heartfelt devotion; for he was a good man, filled with the Holy Spirit and with faith. And a large number of people were won over to the Lord.

Barnabas then left for Tarsus to look for Saul, and when he found him he brought him to Antioch. As things turned out they were to live together in that church a whole year, instructing a large number of people. It was at Antioch that the disciples were first called 'Christians'.

In the church at Antioch the following were prophets and teachers: Barnabas, Simeon called Niger, and Lucius of Cyrene, Manaen, who had been brought up with Herod the tetrarch, and Saul. One day while they were offering worship to the Lord and keeping a fast, the Holy Spirit said, 'I want Barnabas and Saul set apart for the work to which I have called them.' So it was that after fasting and prayer they laid their hands on them and sent them off.

Psalm 97:1-6. R. v. 2

The Lord has shown his salvation to the nations.

Matthew 10:7-13

Jesus said to his apostles, 'As you go, proclaim that the kingdom of heaven is close at hand. Cure the sick, raise the dead, cleanse the lepers, cast out devils. You received without charge, give without charge. Provide yourselves with no gold or silver, not even with a few coppers for your purse, with no haversack for the journey or spare tunic or footwear or a staff, for the workman deserves his keep.

'Whatever town or village you go into, ask for someone trustworthy and stay with him until you leave. As you enter his house, salute it, and if the house deserves it, let your peace descend upon it; if it does not, let your peace come back to you.'

Reflection

The Gospel on this feast of St Barnabas recalls Jesus' commissioning of the Twelve. Barnabas was not one of the Twelve and probably never met Jesus personally. He was a member of the Christian community in Antioch, and he was the one who invited Paul into that community. Later he would embark with Paul on a great missionary journey. Barnabas embraced the teaching of Jesus to the Twelve, that they were to rely not on money or any earthly possessions. They were to depend solely on Jesus. We are called to be missionaries today living and sharing Christ's good news for the people of our time. We do this sometimes by our words, but most especially by living a profoundly Christian life, putting into action the values of the Gospel.

12
JUN SUN

THE MOST HOLY TRINITY, Solemnity

Psalter Week 3

White

Proverbs 8:22-31

The Wisdom of God cries aloud:
The Lord created me when his purpose first unfolded,
before the oldest of his works.
From everlasting I was firmly set,
from the beginning, before earth came into being.
The deep was not, when I was born,
there were no springs to gush with water.
Before the mountains were settled,
before the hills, I came to birth;
before he made the earth, the countryside,
or the first grains of the world's dust.
When he fixed the heavens firm, I was there,
when he drew a ring on the surface of the deep,
when he thickened the clouds above,
when he fixed fast the springs of the deep,
when he assigned the sea its boundaries
– and the waters will not invade the shore –
when he laid down the foundations of the earth,
I was by his side, a master craftsman,
delighting him day after day,
ever at play in his presence,
at play everywhere in his world,
delighting to be with the sons of men.

Psalm 8:4-9. R. v. 2

How great is your name, O Lord our God, through all the earth!

Romans 5:1-5

Through our Lord Jesus Christ, by faith we are judged righteous and at peace with God, since it is by faith and through Jesus that we have entered this state of grace in which we can boast about looking forward to God's glory. But that is not all we can boast about; we can boast about our sufferings. These sufferings bring patience, as we know, and patience brings perseverance, and perseverance brings hope, and this hope is not deceptive, because the love of God has been poured into our hearts by the Holy Spirit which has been given us.

John 16:12-15

Jesus said to his disciples:
'I still have many things to say to you
but they would be too much for you now.
But when the Spirit of truth comes
he will lead you to the complete truth,
since he will not be speaking as from himself
but will say only what he has learnt;
and he will tell you of the things to come.
He will glorify me

since all he tells you
will be taken from what is mine.
Everything the Father has is mine;
that is why I said:
All he tells you
will be taken from what is mine.'

Reflection

The feast of the Most Holy Trinity calls our attention to the great mystery of God. One way of entering into this mystery is by contemplating creation, the work of God's hands. We can look up at the moon and the stars or gaze on a panorama of mountains and valleys and be filled with wonder. Or we can look at a single tiny flower or a newborn infant and have the same sense of awe.

Such feelings engulf the author of today's responsorial psalm. What is most marvelous, and indeed most humbling and frightening, for the psalmist is the exalted place God has given to humans in the order of creation. We have been given a share in God's royal authority over creation. Our God is never a hoarder of power but One who freely delegates this power to us.

It is a great honour and an awesome responsbility to have been entrusted by God with the care of the earth. 'Sheep and cattle, yes even the wild beasts, birds of the air and fish' have all been entrusted to our stewardship. We can use our royal role to be promoters of life or agents of death.

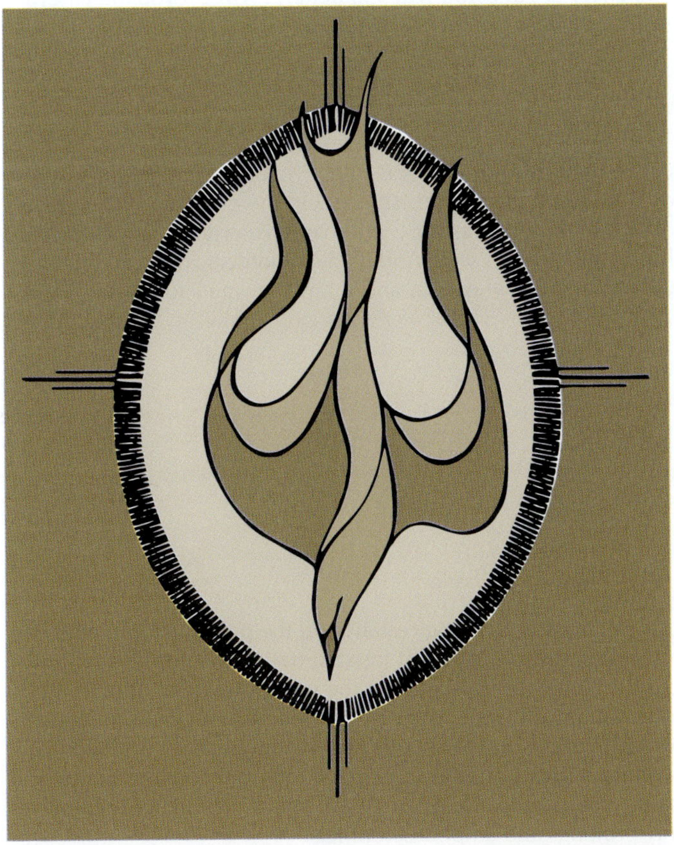

This psalm reminds us that praise of God does not mean leaving everything to God. We cannot spend all our time on our knees exclaiming, 'O Lord, our God, how wonderful you are!' At the end of every Eucharist we are sent out to love and praise the Lord by caring for our fellow human beings and for all of creation. Refreshed by the liturgy, we are called to roll up our sleeves and take up our task.

13
JUN MON

11th Week in Ordinary Time
St Anthony of Padua, *priest, doctor,* **Memorial** | White

1 Kings 21:1-16

Naboth of Jezreel had a vineyard close by the palace of Ahab king of Samaria, and Ahab said to Naboth, 'Give me your vineyard to be my vegetable garden, since it adjoins my house; I will give you a better vineyard for it or, if you prefer, I will give you its worth in money.' But Naboth answered Ahab, 'The Lord forbid that I should give you the inheritance of my ancestors!'

Ahab went home gloomy and out of temper at the words of Naboth of Jezreel, 'I will not give you the inheritance of my fathers.' He lay down on his bed and turned his face away and refused to eat. His wife Jezebel came to him. 'Why are you so dispirited' she said 'that you will not eat?' He said, 'I have been speaking to Naboth of Jezreel; I said: Give me your vineyard either for money or, if you prefer, for another vineyard in exchange. But he said, "I will not give you my vineyard."' Then his wife Jezebel said, 'You make a fine king of Israel, and no mistake! Get up and eat; cheer up, and you will feel better; I will get you the vineyard of Naboth of Jezreel myself.' ... *(Please see the Appendix B-15)*

Psalm 5:2-3, 5-7. R. v. 2

Give heed to my groaning, O Lord.

Matthew 5:38-42

Jesus said to his disciples: 'You have learnt how it was said: Eye for eye and tooth for tooth. But I say this to you: offer the wicked man no resistance. On the contrary, if anyone hits you on the right cheek, offer him the other as well; if a man takes you to law and would have your tunic, let him have your cloak as well. And if anyone orders you to go one mile, go two miles with him. Give to anyone who asks, and if anyone wants to borrow, do not turn away.'

Reflection

The Old Testament book of Leviticus was urging restraint on the part of people who had been wronged and were seeking revenge. When it insisted on 'an eye for an eye, and a tooth for a tooth' (Leviticus 24:20) it was insisting that the person wronged should do no more harm to their opponent than was done to them. Jesus, however, urges his listeners to take no revenge but to do the opposite – to treat those who offend them with kindness. This can be extremely difficult to practise but it is indeed the only path to peace and healing in relationships at a personal level or between nations. Vengeance solves nothing and only prolongs and amplifies conflicts.

11th Week in Ordinary Time
Green

14
JUN TUE

1 Kings 21:17-29

After the death of Naboth, the word of the Lord came to Elijah the Tishbite, 'Up! Go down to meet Ahab king of Israel, in Samaria. You will find him in Naboth's vineyard; he has gone down to take possession of it. You are to say this to him, "The Lord says this: You have committed murder; now you usurp as well. For this – and the Lord says this – in the place where the dogs licked the blood of Naboth, the dogs will lick your blood too."' Ahab said to Elijah, 'So you have found me out, O my enemy!' Elijah answered, 'I have found you out. For your double dealing, and since you have done what is displeasing to the Lord, I will now bring disaster down on you; I will sweep away your descendants, and wipe out every male belonging to the family of Ahab, fettered or free in Israel. I will treat your House as I treated the House of Jeroboam son of Nebat and of Baasha son of Ahijah, for provoking my anger and leading Israel into sin. (Against Jezebel too the Lord spoke these words: The dogs will eat Jezebel in the Field of Jezreel.) Those of Ahab's family who die in the city, the dogs will eat; and those who die in the open country, the birds of the air will eat.' ... *(Please see the Appendix B-16)*

Psalm 50:3-6, 11, 16. R. cf. v. 3

Have mercy on us, Lord, for we have sinned.

Matthew 5:43-48

Jesus said to his disciples: 'You have learnt how it was said: You must love your neighbour and hate your enemy. But I say this to you: love your enemies and pray for those who persecute you; in this way you will be sons of your Father in heaven, for he causes his sun to rise on bad men as well as good, and his rain to fall on honest and dishonest men alike. For if you love those who love you, what right have you to claim any credit? Even the tax collectors do as much, do they not? And if you save your greetings for your brothers, are you doing anything exceptional? Even the pagans do as much, do they not? You must therefore be perfect just as your heavenly Father is perfect.'

Reflection

How can we be perfect as God is perfect? We know well that we are only human. We often excuse ourselves for making mistakes and even for doing wrong by saying, 'I'm not perfect'. So, what does it mean to be perfect as God is perfect? The perfection of God lies in God's boundless love and compassion, exemplified in the life and death of Jesus. We are called to reflect God's love and compassion in our own lives. How often has God forgiven me? How often have I experienced God's infinite love and mercy? Imitating this, I slowly become 'perfect' as the heavenly Father is perfect, able even to forgive my enemies.

15
JUN WED

11th Week in Ordinary Time
Green

2 Kings 2:1, 6-14

This is what happened when the Lord took Elijah up to heaven in the whirlwind: Elijah and Elisha set out from Gilgal. Elijah said, 'Elisha, please stay here, the Lord is only sending me to the Jordan.' But he replied, 'As the Lord lives and as you yourself live, I will not leave you!' And they went on together. ... *(Please see the Appendix B-16)*

Psalm 30:20, 21, 24. R. v. 25

Let your heart take courage, all who hope in the Lord.

Matthew 6:1-6, 16-18

Jesus said to his disciples: 'Be careful not to parade your good deeds before men to attract their notice; by doing this you will lose all reward from your Father in heaven. So when you give alms, do not have it trumpeted before you; this is what the hypocrites do in the synagogues and in the streets to win men's admiration. I tell you solemnly, they have had their reward. But when you give alms, your left hand must not know what your right is doing; your almsgiving must be secret, and your Father who sees all that is done in secret will reward you.

'And when you pray, do not imitate the hypocrites: they love to say their prayers standing up in the synagogues and at the street corners for people to see them. I tell you solemnly, they have had their reward. But when you pray, go to your private room and when you have shut your door, pray to your Father who is in that secret place, and your Father who sees all that is done in secret will reward you.

'When you fast do not put on a gloomy look as the hypocrites do: they pull long faces to let men know they are fasting. I tell you solemnly, they have had their reward. But when you fast, put oil on your head and wash your face, so that no one will know you are fasting except your Father who sees all that is done in secret; and your Father who sees all that is done in secret will reward you.'

Reflection

Jesus speaks of the three penitential acts performed by Jews – prayer, fasting and almsgiving. With all three, there is a danger of doing them for show, to win the admiration of people. As Jesus notes, image building is its own reward, but true recompense comes from the Father who is generous, merciful, and just – and 'who sees all that is done in secret'. What is important is not the quantity or showiness of our prayer, but its quality, that we seek to hear God's word to us. Fasting signifies our desire to empty ourselves that we may be filled with the life of God. And almsgiving reminds us of the social dimension of our faith. The ultimate barometer for the genuineness of our Christian life lies in the way we respond to the needs of our brothers and sisters, especially those who are much less fortunate than we are.

11th Week in Ordinary Time
Green

16
JUN THU

Sirach 48:1-14

The prophet Elijah arose like a fire, his word flaring like a torch. It was he who brought famine on them, and who decimated them in his zeal. By the word of the Lord, he shut up the heavens, he also, three times, brought down fire. How glorious you were in your miracles, Elijah! Has anyone reason to boast as you have? – rousing a corpse from death, from Sheol by the word of the Most High; dragging kings down to destruction, and high dignitaries from their beds; hearing reproof on Sinai, and decrees of punishment on Horeb; anointing kings as avengers, and prophets to succeed you; taken up in the whirlwind of fire, in a chariot with fiery horses; designated in the prophecies of doom to allay God's wrath before the fury breaks, to turn the hearts of fathers towards their children, and to restore the tribes of Jacob. Happy shall they be who see you, and those who have fallen asleep in love; for we too will have life. Elijah was shrouded in the whirlwind, and Elisha was filled with his spirit; throughout his life no ruler could shake him, and no one could subdue him. No task was too hard for him, and even in death his body prophesied. In his lifetime he performed wonders, and in death his works were marvellous.

Psalm 96:1-7. R. v. 12

Rejoice, you just, in the Lord.

Matthew 6:7-15

Jesus said to his disciples: 'In your prayers do not babble as the pagans do, for they think that by using many words they will make themselves heard. Do not be like them; your Father knows what you need before you ask him. So you should pray like this: Our Father in heaven, may your name be held holy, your kingdom come, your will be done, on earth as in heaven. Give us today our daily bread. And forgive us our debts, as we have forgiven those who are in debt to us. And do not put us to the test, but save us from the evil one.

'Yes, if you forgive others their failings, your heavenly Father will forgive you yours; but if you do not forgive others, your Father will not forgive your failings either.'

Reflection

The Lord's Prayer is a summary of a long prayer the Jews pray every day, called the 18 Benedictions. A prayer leader proclaims, 'Glorified and sanctified be God's great name throughout the world which he has created according to his will. May he establish his kingdom in your lifetime and during your days.' And the assembly responds, 'May his great name be blessed forever to all eternity.' In the Lord's Prayer, Jesus injects something new: his disciples are to address God with a familial term *Abba*, the Aramaic equivalent of 'Daddy' or 'Papa'. Jesus tells his disciples to maintain this special relationship with the Father, which is consistent with the Christian belief that in Jesus we have become God's adopted children. St Paul reiterates this special privilege: 'As proof that you are children, God sent the spirit of his Son into our hearts, crying out, "*Abba*, Father!"'(Galatians 4:6).

17
JUN FRI

11th Week in Ordinary Time
Green

2 Kings 11:1-4, 9-18, 20

When Athaliah the mother of Ahaziah learned that her son was dead, she promptly did away with all those of royal stock. But Jehosheba, daughter of King Jehoram and sister of Ahaziah, secretly took away Jehoash, her brother's son, from among the sons of the king who were being murdered, and put him with his nurse in the sleeping quarters; in this way she hid him from Athaliah, and he was not put to death. He stayed with her for six years, hidden in the Temple of the Lord, while Athaliah governed the country. In the seventh year, Jehoiada sent for the commanders of hundreds of the Carians and of the guards, and had them brought to him in the Temple of the Lord. He made a pact with them and, putting them under oath, showed them the king's son. The commanders of hundreds did everything as Jehoiada the priest had ordered. They brought their men, those coming off duty on the sabbath together with those mounting guard on the sabbath, and came to Jehoiada the priest. The priests equipped the commanders of hundreds with King David's spears and shields which were in the Temple of the Lord. The guards formed up, each man with his weapon in his hand, from the south corner to the north corner of the Temple, surrounding the altar and the Temple. Then Jehoiada brought out the king's son, put the crown and armlets on him, and he anointed him king. They clapped their hands and shouted, 'Long live the king!' ... *(Please see the Appendix B-16)*

Psalm 131:11-14, 17-18. R. v. 13

The Lord has chosen Zion; he has desired it for his dwelling.

Matthew 6:19-23

Jesus said to his disciples: 'Do not store up treasures for yourselves on earth, where moths and woodworms destroy them and thieves can break in and steal. But store up treasures for yourselves in heaven, where neither moth or woodworms destroy them and thieves cannot break in and steal. For where your treasure is, there will your heart be also. The lamp of the body is the eye. It follows that if your eye is sound, your whole body will be filled with light. But if your eye is diseased, your whole body will be all darkness. If then, the light inside you is darkness, what darkness that will be!'

Reflection

A treasure is something or someone we hold dear. In Jesus' words, it is where our heart lies. On earth, treasures can come in the form of gold or jewelry, property and other possessions, physical strength and beauty. Persons who are dear to us are also treasures. Italians call someone very dear to them *Tesoro mio* ('my treasure'). Jesus teaches that true wealth does not consist in material abundance and earthly securities all of which are transitory; the real treasures, which he calls 'treasure in heaven', are the ones that last, even beyond our life on this earth. We can include here our love for God, our union with Jesus our Lord, our faith and confidence that God that will not abandon us, and our love for our family and friends. These are not subject to decay nor can they be stolen by thieves. During the COVID-19 pandemic, many came to realise that in life our best protection is God, our best refuge is our home, our best company is our family, and our real time is today. These are the true treasures to be safeguarded.

18 JUN SAT

11th Week in Ordinary Time
Green

2 Chronicles 24:17-25

After the death of Jehoiada, the officials of Judah came to pay court to the king, and the king now turned to them for advice. The Judaeans abandoned the Temple of the Lord, the God of their ancestors, for the worship of sacred poles and idols. Because of their guilt, God's anger fell on Judah and Jerusalem. He sent them prophets to bring them back to the Lord, but when these gave their message, they would not listen. The spirit of God took possession of Zechariah son of Jehoiada the priest. He stood up before the people and said, 'God says this, "Why do you transgress the commandments of the Lord to no good purpose? You have deserted the Lord, now he deserts you."' They then plotted against him and by order of the king stoned him in the court of the Temple of the Lord. ...
(Please see the Appendix B-17)

Psalm 88:4-5, 29-34. R. v. 29

I will keep my love for him always.

Matthew 6:24-34

Jesus said to his disciples: 'No one can be the slave of two masters: he will either hate the first and love the second, or treat the first with respect and the second with scorn. You cannot be the slave both of God and of money. That is why I am telling you not to worry about your life and what you are to eat, nor about your body and how you are to clothe it. Surely life means more than food, and the body more than clothing! Look at the birds in the sky. They do not sow or reap or gather into barns; yet your heavenly Father feeds them. Are you not worth much more than they are? Can any of you, for all his worrying, add one single cubit to his span of life? And why worry about clothing? Think of the flowers growing in the fields; they never have to work or spin; yet I assure you that not even Solomon in all his regalia was robed like one of these. Now if that is how God clothes the grass in the field which is there today and thrown into the furnace tomorrow, will he not much more look after you, you men of little faith? So do not worry; do not say, "What are we to eat? What are we to drink? How are we to be clothed?" It is the pagans who set their hearts on all these things. Your heavenly Father knows you need them all. Set your hearts on his kingdom first, and on his righteousness, and all these other things will be given you as well. So do not worry about tomorrow: tomorrow will take care of itself. Each day has enough trouble of its own.'

Reflection

It is natural for human beings to worry about many things. A wise person once wrote that 90 per cent of the things we worry about never happen, and the other 10 per cent would have happened whether we worried about them or not. Jesus urges us not to carry tomorrow's burdens today. When we reach tomorrow, Jesus will be there, with us, ready to help us deal with them. He expresses this basic call to live in the present in the prayer he taught us, 'Give us this day our daily bread'. So, let us take one day at a time, trusting in Jesus to help us this day, rather than constantly worrying about what tomorrow may hold. If we seek to do well what we must do today, the future will take care of itself.

19
JUN SUN

THE MOST HOLY BODY & BLOOD OF CHRIST (CORPUS CHRISTI), Solemnity

Psalter Week 4

White

Genesis 14:18-20

Melchizedek king of Salem brought bread and wine; he was a priest of God Most High. He pronounced this blessing:

'Blessed be Abraham by God Most High,
creator of heaven and earth,
and blessed be God Most High for handing over
your enemies to you.'

And Abraham gave him a tithe of everything.

Psalm 109:1-4. R. v. 4

You are a priest for ever, a priest like Melchizedek of old.

1 Corinthians 11:23-26

This is what I received from the Lord, and in turn passed on to you: that on the same night that he was betrayed, the Lord Jesus took some bread, and thanked God for it and broke it, and he said, 'This is my body, which is for you; do this as a memorial of me.' In the same way he took the cup after supper, and said, 'This cup is the new covenant in my blood. Whenever you drink it, do this as a memorial of me.' Until the Lord comes, therefore, every time you eat this bread and drink this cup, you are proclaiming his death.

Luke 9:11-17

Jesus made the crowds welcome and talked to them about the kingdom of God; and he cured those who were in need of healing.

It was late afternoon when the Twelve came to him and said, 'Send the people away, and they can go to the villages and farms round about to find lodging and food; for we are in a lonely place here.' He replied, 'Give them something to eat yourselves.' But they said, 'We have no more than five loaves and two fish, unless we are to go ourselves and buy food for all these people.' For there were about five thousand men. But he said to his disciples, 'Get them to sit down in parties of about fifty.' They did so and made them all sit down. Then he took the five loaves and the two fish, raised his eyes to heaven, and said the blessing over them; then he broke them and handed them to his disciples to distribute among the crowd. They all ate as much as they wanted, and when the scraps remaining were collected they filled twelve baskets.

Reflection

There are very few recorded instances in history of one person being both a king and a priest. Today's first reading tells of one such person, the mysterious Melchisedek, king of Salem, who fulfilled a priestly role by blessing Abraham. David and Solomon, two kings of Israel, also performed some priestly functions.

Another person who is both priest and king is Jesus Christ. As king, Christ is the lawgiver and protector. His law is contained in the Sermon on the Mount (see Matthew, chapters 5–7) and summed up in his command, 'love one another as I have loved you' (John 13:34). As priest, Christ offers his life on the cross, reconciling all of creation to God.

Through baptism we participate in Christ's priestly and kingly roles. We share in the kingship of Christ by serving one another, protecting the most vulnerable among us and giving our wise counsel. We share in Christ's priestly role when we take part in worship, interceding on behalf of humanity and mediating the life and blessings of God to our world. We are both priests and kings when we fulfil the instruction of Jesus in today's Gospel: 'give them something to eat yourselves'.

20 JUN MON

12th Week in Ordinary Time
Green

2 Kings 17:5-8, 13-15, 18

The king of Assyria invaded the whole country and, coming to Samaria, laid siege to it for three years. In the Ninth year of Hoshea, the king of Assyria captured Samaria and deported the Israelites to Assyria. He settled them in Halah on the Habor, a river of Gozan, and in the cities of the Medes.

This happened because the Israelites had sinned against the Lord their God who had brought them out of the land of Egypt, out of the grip of Pharaoh, king of Egypt. They worshipped other gods, they followed the practices of the nations that the Lord had dispossessed for them.

And yet through all the prophets and all the seers, the Lord had given Israel and Judah this warning, 'Turn from your wicked ways and keep my commandments and my law in accordance with the entire Law I laid down for your fathers and delivered to them through my servants the prophets.' But they would not listen, they were more stubborn than their ancestors had been who had no faith in the Lord their God. They despised his laws and the covenant he had made with their ancestors, and the warnings he had given them. For this, the Lord was enraged with Israel and thrust them away from him. There was none left but the tribe of Judah only.

Psalm 59:3-5, 12-13. R. v. 7

Hear us, O Lord, and help us.

Matthew 7:1-5

Jesus said to his disciples: 'Do not judge, and you will not be judged; because the judgements you give are the judgements you will get, and the amount you measure out is the amount you will be given. Why do you observe the splinter in your brother's eye and never notice the plank in your own? How dare you say to your brother, "Let me take the splinter out of your eye", when all the time there is a plank in your own? Hypocrite! Take the plank out of your own eye first, and then you will see clearly enough to take the splinter out of your brother's eye.'

Reflection

Human judgement, even at its best, has its limitations and imperfections. It is very hard to be objective when we cannot fathom the subjective motivations, feelings and emotions behind human actions. According to the Johari Window, there are areas to be considered: known to me and known to another (arena); unknown to me but known to another (blind spot); known to me but unknown to another (façade); unknown to me and unknown to another (unknown). Human standards are flawed; only God can make a perfect judgement. Legal judgement is necessary for the ordering of society, and Jesus does not prohibit it. What he wants us to do is to proceed cautiously in our judgements. We may fall into the ridiculous mistake of pointing out the splinter in someone else's eye yet failing to perceive the wooden beam in our own. Let us remember that when we point a finger at someone, the rest of our fingers are pointing back at us.

12th Week in Ordinary Time
St Aloysius Gonzaga, *religious,* **Memorial |** White

21
JUN TUE

2 Kings 19:9-11, 14-21, 31-36

Sennacherib, King of the Assyrians, sent messengers to Hezekiah saying, 'Tell this to Hezekiah king of Judah, "Do not let your God on whom you are relying deceive you, when he says: Jerusalem shall not fall into the power of the king of Assyria. You have learnt by now what the kings of Assyria have done to every country, putting them all under the ban. Are you likely to be spared?"'

Hezekiah took the letter from the hands of the messenger and read it; he then went up to the Temple of the Lord and spread it out before the Lord. Hezekiah said this prayer in the presence of the Lord, 'Lord of hosts, God of Israel, enthroned on the cherubs, you alone are God of all the kingdoms of the earth, you have made heaven and earth.

'Give ear, Lord, and listen. Open your eyes, Lord, and see. Hear the words of Sennacherib who has sent to insult the living God.

'It is true, Lord, that the kings of Assyria have exterminated all the nations, they have thrown their gods on the fire, for these were not gods but the work of men's hands, wood and stone, and hence they have destroyed them. But now, Lord our God, save us from his hand, I pray you, and let all the kingdoms of the earth know that you alone are God, Lord.' ... *(Please see the Appendix B-17)*

Psalm 47:2-4, 10-11. R. cf. v. 9

God upholds his city for ever.

Matthew 7:6, 12-14

Jesus said to his disciples: 'Do not give dogs what is holy; and do not throw your pearls in front of pigs, or they may trample them and then turn on you and tear you to pieces. So always treat others as you would like them to treat you; that is the meaning of the Law and the Prophets. Enter by the narrow gate, since the road that leads to perdition is wide and spacious, and many take it; but it is a narrow gate and a hard road that leads to life, and only a few find it.'

Reflection

A Gentile once challenged the famous Jewish teacher, Hillel the Elder (died about AD 10), to explain the Torah (the five books of Moses) to him while standing on one foot. Hillel replied: 'What is hateful to you, do not do to your fellow: this is the whole Torah; the rest is the explanation; go and learn.' Jesus spoke in similar vein in his Sermon on the Mount: 'So always treat others as you would like them to treat you; that is the meaning of the Law and the Prophets.' This 'golden rule' (the ethic of reciprocity) is to be found in many ancient cultures and religions. Its non-observance in contemporary politics and economics leaves us a long way from achieving the 'civilisation of love' that both Pope St Paul VI and Pope St John Paul II spoke about. Can I truthfully say that this rule is a guiding principal of my moral life?

22
JUN WED

12th Week in Ordinary Time | Sts John Fisher, *bishop*, and **Thomas More,** *martyrs*, **Memorial** | Red

SAINTS JOHN FISHER, BISHOP, AND THOMAS MORE, MARTYRS, Feast – England
see Appendix A-17

2 Kings 22:8-13; 23:1-3

The high priest Hilkiah said to Shaphan the secretary, 'I have found the Book of the Law in the Temple of the Lord.' And Hilkiah gave the book to Shaphan, who read it. Shaphan the secretary went to the king and reported to him as follows. 'Your servants' he said 'have melted down the silver which was in the Temple and have handed it over to the masters of works attached to the Temple of the Lord.' Then Shaphan the secretary informed the king, 'Hilkiah the priest has given me a book'; and Shaphan read it aloud in the king's presence. On hearing the contents of the Book of the Law, the king tore his garments, and gave the following order to Hilkiah the priest, Ahikam son of Shaphan, Achbor son of Micaiah, Shaphan the secretary and Asaiah the king's minister: 'Go and consult the Lord, on behalf of me and the people, about the contents of this book that has been found. Great indeed must be the anger of the Lord blazing out against us because our ancestors did not obey what this book says by practising everything written in it.' The king then had all the elders of Judah and of Jerusalem summoned to him, and the king went up to the Temple of the Lord with all the men of Judah and all the inhabitants of Jerusalem, priests, prophets and all the people, of high or low degree. In their hearing he read out everything that was said in the book of the covenant found in the Temple of the Lord. The king stood beside the pillar, and in the presence of the Lord he made a covenant to follow the Lord and keep his commandments and decrees and laws with all his heart and soul, in order to enforce the terms of the covenant as written in that book. All the people gave their allegiance to the covenant.

Psalm 118:33-37, 40. R. v. 33

Lord, teach me your statutes.

Matthew 7:15-20

Jesus said to his disciples: 'Beware of false prophets who come to you disguised as sheep but underneath are ravenous wolves. You will be able to tell them by their fruits. Can people pick grapes from thorns, or figs from thistles? In the same way, a sound tree produces good fruit but a rotten tree bad fruit. A sound tree cannot bear bad fruit, nor a rotten tree bear good fruit. Any tree that does not produce good fruit is cut down and thrown on the fire. I repeat, you will be able to tell them by their fruits.'

Reflection

Already in the Old Testament, false prophets were common. In general, false prophets say what people like to hear. A true prophet speaks the Word of God whether it is welcome or unwelcome, pleasant or unpleasant. False prophets also claim to have all the answers. But, as Pope Francis has said, 'if a person claims to have the answers to all the questions – that is proof that God is not with them. It means the person is a false prophet using religion for personal gain. The great leaders of the people of God, like Moses, have always left room for doubt. We too must leave room for the Lord, not for our certainties; we must be humble.'

23 JUN THU

THE NATIVITY OF SAINT JOHN THE BAPTIST (MASS DURING THE DAY)**, Solemnity | ** White

Isaiah 49:1-6

Islands, listen to me, pay attention, remotest peoples. The Lord called me before I was born, from my mother's womb he pronounced my name. He made my mouth a sharp sword, and hid me in the shadow of his hand. He made me into a sharpened arrow, and concealed me in his quiver. He said to me, 'You are my servant Israel, in whom I shall be glorified'; while I was thinking, 'I have toiled in vain, I have exhausted myself for nothing'; and all the while my cause was with the Lord, my reward with my God. I was honoured in the eyes of the Lord, my God was my strength. And now the Lord has spoken, he who formed me in the womb to be his servant, to bring Jacob back to him, to gather Israel to him: 'It is not enough for you to be my servant, to restore the tribes of Jacob and bring back the survivors of Israel; I will make you the light of the nations so that my salvation may reach to the ends of the earth.'

Psalm 138:1-3, 13-15. R. v. 14 ***I thank you for the wonder of my being.***

Acts 13:22-26

Paul said: 'God made David the king of our ancestors, of whom he approved in these words, "I have selected David son of Jesse, a man after my own heart, who will carry out my whole purpose." To keep his promise, God has raised up for Israel one of David's descendants, Jesus, as Saviour, whose coming was heralded by John when he proclaimed a baptism of repentance for the whole people of Israel. Before John ended his career he said, "I am not the one you imagine me to be; that one is coming after me and I am not fit to undo his sandal." 'My brothers, sons of Abraham's race, and all you who fear God, this message of salvation is meant for you.'

Luke 1:57-66, 80

The time came for Elizabeth to have her child, and she gave birth to a son; and when her neighbours and relations heard that the Lord had shown her so great a kindness, they shared her joy. Now on the eighth day when they came to circumcise the child, they were going to call him Zechariah after his father, but his mother spoke up. 'No,' she said 'he is to be called John.' They said to her 'But no one in your family has that name', and made signs to his father to find out what he wanted him called. The father asked for a writing tablet and wrote, 'His name is John.' And they were all astonished. At that instant his power of speech returned and he spoke and praised God. All their neighbours were filled with awe and the whole affair was talked about throughout the hill country of Judaea. All those who heard of it treasured it in their hearts. 'What will this child turn out to be?' they wondered. And indeed the hand of the Lord was with him. The child grew up and his spirit matured. And he lived out in the wilderness until the day he appeared openly to Israel.

Reflection

Israelite priesthood is reserved to the sons of Levi, and John, the son of the priest Zechariah, was expected to become a priest like his father. Instead, he grew up in desert surroundings in tune with his vocation as a prophet of the Lord – and more, as the precursor of the one who was coming, the Messiah. The mysterious events that accompanied his birth – the annunciation to Zechariah and his loss of speech, his birth to elderly infertile parents, and his being named John, all pointed to the hand of the Lord being with him. It is not surprising that the townspeople wondered, 'what will this child turn out to be.'

24

JUN FRI

THE MOST SACRED HEART OF JESUS, Solemnity

White

Ezekiel 34:11-16

The Lord God says this: I am going to look after my flock myself and keep all of it in view. As a shepherd keeps all his flock in view when he stands up in the middle of his scattered sheep, so shall I keep my sheep in view. I shall rescue them from wherever they have been scattered during the mist and darkness. I shall bring them out of the countries where they are; I shall gather them together from foreign countries and bring them back to their own land. I shall pasture them on the mountains of Israel, in the ravines and in every inhabited place in the land. I shall feed them in good pasturage; the high mountains of Israel will be their grazing ground. There they will rest in good grazing ground: they will browse in rich pastures on the mountains of Israel: I myself will pasture my sheep, I myself will show them where to rest – it is the Lord who speaks. I shall look for the lost one; bring back the stray, bandage the wounded and make the weak strong. I shall watch over the fat and healthy. I shall be a true shepherd to them.

Psalm 22. R. v. 1

The Lord is my shepherd: there is nothing I shall want.

Romans 5:5-11

The love of God has been poured into our hearts by the Holy Spirit which has been given us. We were still helpless when at his appointed moment Christ died for sinful men. It is not easy to die even for a good man – though of course for someone really worthy, a man might be prepared to die – but what proves that God loves us is that Christ died for us while we were still sinners. Having died to make us righteous, is it likely that he would now fail to save us from God's anger? When we were reconciled to God by the death of his Son, we were still enemies; now that we have been reconciled, surely we may count on being saved by the life of his Son? Not merely because we have been reconciled but because we are filled with joyful trust in God, through our Lord Jesus Christ, through whom we have already gained our reconciliation.

Luke 15:3-7

Jesus spoke this parable to the scribes and Pharisees: 'What man among you with a hundred sheep, losing one; would not leave the ninety-nine in the wilderness and go after the missing one till he found it? And when he found it, would he not joyfully take it on his shoulders and then, when he got home, call together his friends and neighbours? 'Rejoice with me,' he would say '! have found my sheep that was lost.' In the same way, I tell you, there will be more rejoicing in heaven over one repentant sinner than over ninety-nine virtuous men who have no need of repentance.'

Reflection

'Rejoice with me. I have found my sheep that was lost!' The Most Sacred Heart of Jesus is compared to the heart of a shepherd who goes out in search of the sheep that was lost and when he finds it, carries it back on his shoulders to the sheepfold. As *shepherd* (the 'Good Shepherd' in John), Jesus guides his flock along the right path through his teaching and example. He nourishes them with material food and with the bread come down from heaven, gives them comfort and security, and renews their strength. As *companion*, Jesus protects them with his 'staff' against those who would do them harm. As *host*, Jesus leads his followers to the 'house of the Lord' to enjoy goodness and mercy in the heavenly banquet. Moreover, the heart of the shepherd is revealed in his readiness to lay down his life for his sheep.

25
JUN SAT

THE IMMACULATE HEART OF MARY
White

Lamentations 2:2,10-14,18-19

The Lord has pitilessly destroyed all the homes of Jacob; in his displeasure he has shattered the strongholds of the daughter of Judah; he has thrown to the ground, he has left accursed the kingdom and its rulers. Mutely they sit on the ground, the elders of the daughter of Zion; they have put dust on their heads, and wrapped themselves in sackcloth. The virgins of Jerusalem hang their heads down to the ground. My eyes wasted away with weeping, my entrails shuddered, my liver spilled on the ground at the ruin of the daughters of my people, as children, mere infants, fainted in the squares of the Citadel. They kept saying to their mothers, 'Where is the bread?' as they fainted like wounded men in the squares of the City, as they poured out their souls on their mothers' breasts. How can I describe you, to what compare you, daughter of Jerusalem? Who can rescue and comfort you, virgin daughter of Zion? For huge as the sea is your affliction; who can possibly cure you? The visions your prophets had on your behalf were delusive, tinsel things, they never pointed out your sin, to ward off your exile. The visions they proffered you were false, fallacious, misleading. Cry aloud, then, to the Lord, groan, daughter of Zion; let your tears flow like a torrent, day and night; give yourself no relief, grant your eyes no rest. Up, cry out in the night-time, in the early hours of darkness; pour your heart out like water before the Lord. Stretch out your hands to him for the lives of your children who faint with hunger at the entrance to every street.

Psalm 73:1-7,20-21

Do not forget your poor servants for ever.

Luke 2:41-51

Every year the parents of Jesus used to go to Jerusalem for the feast of the Passover. When he was twelve years old, they went up for the feast as usual. When they were on their way home after the feast, the boy Jesus stayed behind in Jerusalem without his parents knowing it. They assumed he was with the caravan, and it was only after a day's journey that they went to look for him among their relations and acquaintances. When they failed to find him they went back to Jerusalem looking for him everywhere.

Three days later, they found him in the Temple, sitting among the doctors, listening to them, and asking them questions; and all those who heard him were astounded at his intelligence and his replies. They were overcome when they saw him, and his mother said to him, 'My child, why have you done this to us? See how worried your father and I have been, looking for you.' 'Why were you looking for me?' he replied. 'Did you not know that I must be busy with my Father's affairs?' But they did not understand what he meant. He then went down with them and came to Nazareth and lived under their authority. His mother stored up all these things in her heart.

Reflection

The feast of the Immaculate Heart of Mary, which we celebrate in today's liturgy, honours Mary's profound love for God and humanity. Today's feast places Mary in front of us as an inspiration and support in our daily struggle. She stands before us as a source of consolation, hope, and encouragement. Mary challenges us to fall in love with God.

26

JUN SUN

THIRTEENTH SUNDAY IN ORDINARY TIME

Psalter Week 1

Green

1 Kings 19:16, 19-21

The Lord said to Elijah: 'Go, you are to anoint Elisha son of Shaphat, of Abel Meholah, as prophet to succeed you.' Leaving there, Elijah came on Elisha son of Shaphat as he was ploughing behind twelve yoke of oxen, he himself being with the twelfth. Elijah passed near to him and threw his cloak over him. Elisha left his oxen and ran after Elijah. 'Let me kiss my father and mother, then I will follow you' he said. Elijah answered, 'Go, go back; for have I done anything to you?' Elisha turned away, took the pair of oxen and slaughtered them. He used the plough for cooking the oxen, then gave to his men, who ate. He then rose, and followed Elijah and became his servant.

Psalm 15:1-2, 5, 7-11. R. cf. v. 5

O Lord, it is you who are my portion.

Galatians 5:1, 13-18

When Christ freed us, he meant us to remain free. Stand firm, therefore, and do not submit again to the yoke of slavery. My brothers, you were called, as you know, to liberty; but be careful, or this liberty will provide an opening for self-indulgence. Serve one another, rather, in works of love, since the whole of the Law is summarised in a single command: Love your neighbour as yourself. If you go snapping at each other and tearing each other to pieces, you had better watch or you will destroy the whole community.

Let me put it like this: if you are guided by the Spirit you will be in no danger of yielding to self-indulgence, since self-indulgence is the opposite of the Spirit, the Spirit is totally against such a thing, and it is precisely because the two are so opposed that you do not always carry out your good intentions. If you are led by the Spirit, no law can touch you.

Luke 9:51-62

As the time drew near for him to be taken up to heaven, Jesus resolutely took the road for Jerusalem and sent messengers ahead of him. These set out, and they went into a Samaritan village to make preparations for him, but the people would not receive him because he was making for Jerusalem. Seeing this, the disciples James and John said, 'Lord, do you want us to call down fire from heaven to burn them up?' But he turned and rebuked them, and they went off to another village.

As they travelled along they met a man on the road who said to him, 'I will follow you wherever you go.' Jesus answered, 'Foxes have holes and the birds of the air have nests, but the Son of Man has nowhere to lay his head.'

Another to whom he said, 'Follow me,' replied, 'Let me go and bury my father first.' But he answered, 'Leave the dead to bury their dead; your duty is to go and spread the news of the kingdom of God.'

Another said, 'I will follow you, sir, but first let me go and say good-bye to my people at home.' Jesus said to him, 'Once the hand is laid on the plough, no one who looks back is fit for the kingdom of God.'

Reflection

The call to follow Jesus is always a grace and a privilege. However, today's liturgy alerts us to what the Lutheran theologian and martyr of the Nazi regime, Dietrich Bonhoeffer, called 'the cost of discipleship'.

Jesus himself embraced the suffering and death by which he was to redeem his brothers and sisters. Luke writes: 'Jesus resolutely took the road for Jerusalem'. Mark: Resolutely. He had already twice prophesied that he was destined to suffer grievously, be rejected and put to death (Luke 9:22; 9:44-45) and would do so again on the road (Luke 18:31-34). In that context he emphasised the condition of following: 'If anyone wants to be a follower of mine, let him renounce himself and take up his cross every day' (Luke 9:23-26). Today's three calls make the same demand.

We are called. We are called to follow the Crucified. We are called to share his lot, to shoulder our cross daily. This comes from fidelity to Christ and his values in daily living.

13th Week in Ordinary Time | Green
or **St Cyril of Alexandria,** *bishop, doctor* (Optional, White)

27
JUN MON

Amos 2:6-10, 13-16

Thus says the Lord: For the three crimes, the four crimes, of Israel I have made my decree and will not relent: because they have sold the virtuous man for silver and the poor man for a pair of sandals, because they trample on the heads of ordinary people and push the poor out of their path, because father and son have both resorted to the same girl, profaning my holy name, because they stretch themselves out by the side of every altar on clothes acquired as pledges, and drink the wine of the people they have fined in the house of their god... Yet it was I who overthrew the Amorites when they attacked, men tall as cedars and strong as oaks, I who destroyed them, both fruit above ground and root below. It was I who brought you out of the land of Egypt and for forty years led you through the wilderness to take possession of the Amorite's country. See then how I am going to crush you into the ground as the threshing-sledge crushes when clogged by straw; flight will not save even the swift, the strong man will find his strength useless, the mighty man will be powerless to save himself. The bowman will not stand his ground, the fast runner will not escape, the horse-man will not save himself, the bravest warriors will run away naked that day. It is the Lord who speaks.

Psalm 49:16-23. R. v. 22

Mark this, you who never think of God.

Matthew 8:18-22

When Jesus saw the great crowds all about him he gave orders to leave for the other side. One of the scribes then came up and said to him, 'Master, I will follow you wherever you go.' Jesus replied, 'Foxes have holes and the birds of the air have nests, but the Son of Man has nowhere to lay his head.' Another man, one of his disciples, said to him, 'Sir, let me go and bury my father first.' But Jesus replied, 'Follow me, and leave the dead to bury their dead.'

Reflection

'Master, I will follow you wherever you go.' It is easy for us to say this in a burst of fervour and enthusiasm. But, as Jesus points, out there is a cost to following him that we must think about. If we start with each letter in the word DISCIPLESHIP we get an idea of what is required: (D) *divine calling,* (I) *interior life* and prayer, (S) *service and sacrifice* in love (C) *commitment* to the call, (I) *integrity* of one's witness, (P) *pursuit of* truth and righteousness, (L) *listening heart,* (E) *empowerment* by the Holy Spirit, (S) *stewardship* of God's grace and blessings, (H) *hope* in the midst of adversity, (I) *intuitiveness* to read the signs of the times, and (P) *perseverance* in order to accomplish the mission of evangelisation.

13th Week in Ordinary Time
St Irenaeus, *bishop, martyr,* **Memorial** | Red

28
JUN TUE

Amos 3:1-8; 4:11-12

Listen, sons of Israel, to this oracle the Lord speaks against you, against the whole family I brought out of the land of Egypt: You alone, of all the families of earth, have I acknowledged, therefore it is for all your sins that I mean to punish you.

Do two men take the road together
if they have not planned to do so?
Does the lion roar in the jungle
if no prey has been found?
Does the young lion growl in his lair
if he has captured nothing?
Does the bird fall to the ground
if no trap has been set?
Does the snare spring up from the ground
if nothing has been caught?
Does the trumpet sound in the city
without the populace becoming alarmed?
Does misfortune come to a city
if the Lord has not sent it?

No more does the Lord do anything without revealing his plans to his servants the prophets. The lion roars: who can help feeling afraid? The Lord speaks: who can refuse to prophesy? I overthrew you as God overthrew Sodom and Gomorrah, and you were like a brand snatched from the blaze; and yet you never came back to me. It is the Lord who speaks. This therefore, Israel, is what I plan to do to you, and because I am going to do this to you, Israel, prepare to meet your God!

Psalm 5:5-8. R. v. 9 *Lead me, O Lord, in your justice.*

Matthew 8:23-27

Jesus got into the boat followed by his disciples. Without warning a storm broke over the lake, so violent that the waves were breaking right over the boat. But he was asleep. So they went to him and woke him saying, 'Save us, Lord, we are going down!' And he said to them, 'Why are you so frightened, you men of little faith?' And with that he stood up and rebuked the winds and the sea; and all was calm again. The men were astounded and said, 'Whatever kind of man is this? Even the winds and the sea obey him.'

Reflection

Pope Francis has compared our experience of the COVID pandemic with the disciples' experience in the boat during a violent storm. Like the disciples we have found ourselves afraid and lost, caught off guard by the sudden unexpected emergence of this pandemic. Like them, we may feel that Jesus is doing nothing to help us. In the boat, Jesus reproves the disciples for their lack of faith. He is always there with them; they have nothing to fear. We also need to have faith in him in the most difficult of times. Like the disciples – Pope Francis adds – we will experience that with Jesus on board our ship there will be no shipwreck. Because this is God's strength: turning to the good everything that happens to us, even the bad things. God brings serenity into our storms because, with God, life never dies.

29

JUN WED

STS PETER AND PAUL, APOSTLES, (MASS DURING THE DAY),

Solemnity

Red

Acts 12:1-11

(Please see the Appendix B-17)

Psalm 33:2-9. R. v. 5

From all my terrors the Lord set me free.

2 Timothy 4:6-8, 17-18

My life is already being poured away as a libation, and the time has come for me to be gone. I have fought the good fight to the end; I have run the race to the finish; I have kept the faith; all there is to come now is the crown of righteousness reserved for me, which the Lord, the righteous judge, will give to me on that Day; and not only to me but to all those who have longed for his Appearing. The Lord stood by me and gave me power, so that through me the whole message might be proclaimed for all the pagans to hear; and so I was rescued from the lion's mouth. The Lord will rescue me from all evil attempts on me, and bring me safely to his heavenly kingdom. To him be glory for ever and ever. Amen.

Matthew 16:13-19

When Jesus came to the region of Caesarea Philippi he put this question to his disciples. 'Who do people say the Son of Man is?' And they said, 'Some say he is John the Baptist, some Elijah, and others Jeremiah or one of the prophets.' 'But you,' he said 'who do you say I am?' Then Simon Peter spoke up, 'You are the Christ,' he said 'the Son of the living God.' Jesus replied, 'Simon son of Jonah, you are a happy man! Because it was not flesh and blood that revealed this to you but my Father in heaven. So I now say to you: You are Peter and on this rock I will build my Church. And the gates of the underworld can never hold out against it. I will give you the keys of the kingdom of heaven: whatever you bind on earth shall be considered bound in heaven; whatever you loose on earth shall be considered loosed in heaven.'

Reflection

Simon Peter was first in the list of the Twelve Apostles. Along with James and John, he was witness to significant moments in the life of Jesus such as the transfiguration (Matthew 17:1), the raising up of the daughter of Jairus (Mark 5:37), and the agony in the garden (Matthew 26:37). In today's Gospel he is revealed as the rock on which Jesus will build his Church. Peter's primacy was recognised by the early Christian community and his martyrdom and burial in Rome helped to make the eternal city a place of great religious significance. The apostle Paul brought the Good News to the nations, to the Gentile world. Many of the letters he wrote are included in the New Testament. As his life drew close, he took comfort in knowing that he had devoted his life to the spreading of the Gospel and that 'the crown of righteousness' awaited him. Like Peter, he suffered martyrdom. He was buried just outside the walls of Rome.

13th Week in Ordinary Time | Green
or **The First Martyrs of the Holy Roman Church** (Opt., Red)

30
JUN THU

Amos 7:10-17

Amaziah the priest of Bethel sent word to Jeroboam king of Israel as follows. 'Amos is plotting against you in the heart of the House of Israel; the country can no longer tolerate what he keeps saying. For this is what he says, "Jeroboam is going to die by the sword, and Israel go into exile far from its country."' To Amos, Amaziah said, 'Go away, seer; get back to the land of Judah; earn your bread there, do your prophesying there. We want no more prophesying in Bethel; this is the royal sanctuary, the national temple.' 'I was no prophet, neither did I belong to any of the brotherhoods of prophets,' Amos replied to Amaziah. 'I was a shepherd, and looked after sycamores: but it was the Lord who took me from herding the flock, and the Lord who said, "Go, prophesy to my people Israel." So listen to the word of the Lord. You say: "Do not prophesy against Israel, utter no oracles against the House of Isaac." 'Very well, this is what the Lord says, "Your wife will be forced to go on the streets, your sons and daughters will fall by the sword, your land will be parcelled out by measuring line, and you yourself die on unclean soil and Israel will go into exile far distant from its own land."'

Psalm 18:8-11. R. v. 10

The decrees of the Lord are truth and all of them just.

Matthew 9:1-8

Jesus got back in the boat, crossed the water and came to his own town. Then some people appeared, bringing him a paralytic stretched out on a bed. Seeing their faith, Jesus said to the paralytic, 'Courage, my child, your sins are forgiven.' And at this some scribes said to themselves, 'This man is blaspheming.' Knowing what was in their minds Jesus said, 'Why do you have such wicked thoughts in your hearts? Now, which of these is easier: to say, "Your sins are forgiven", or to say, "Get up and walk"? But to prove to you that the Son of Man has authority on earth to forgive sins,' – he said to the paralytic – 'get up, and pick up your bed and go off home.' And the man got up and went home. A feeling of awe came over the crowd when they saw this, and they praised God for giving such power to men.

Reflection

Jesus surprises those around him, including some scribes, by declaring to the paralytic, 'Your sins are forgiven'. They say of Jesus, 'This man is blaspheming' – that is, he is usurping the power that belongs to God alone. Jesus then proves his power to forgive sins by curing the paralytic. If his word is effective to cure physical illness, his claim to have power on earth to forgive sins is likewise true. After his resurrection, Jesus passed on to his disciples and their successors the power to forgive sins in his name. In the evening of the first day of the week, he appeared to his disciples, breathed on them and said, 'Receive the Holy Spirit. Whose sins you forgive are forgiven them, and whose sins you retain are retained' (John 20:22-23). Forgiveness of sin is accomplished through the Sacrament of Reconciliation.

01
JUL FRI

13th Week in Ordinary Time
Saint Oliver Plunket, Bishop, Martyr | Green

Saint Oliver Plunket, Bishop, Martyr, Memorial
– Ireland
see Appendix A-18

Amos 8:4-6, 9-12

Listen to this, you who trample on the needy and try to suppress the poor people of the country, you who say, 'When will New Moon be over so that we can sell our corn, and sabbath, so that we can market our wheat? Then by lowering the bushel, raising the shekel, by swindling and tampering with the scales, we can buy up the poor for money, and the needy for a pair of sandals, and get a price even for the sweepings of the wheat.'

That day – it is the Lord who speaks – I will make the sun go down at noon and darken the earth in broad daylight. I am going to turn your feasts into funerals, and your singing into lamentation; I will have your loins all in sackcloth, your heads all shaved.

I will make it a mourning like the mourning for an only son, as long as it lasts I will make it a day of bitterness. See what days are coming – it is the Lord who speaks – days when I will bring famine on the country, a famine not of bread, a drought not of water, but of hearing the word of the Lord. They will stagger from sea to sea, wander from north to east, seeking the word of the Lord and failing to find it.'

Psalm 118:2, 10, 20, 30, 40, 131. R. Matthew 4:4

Man does not live on bread alone but on every word that comes from the mouth of God.

Matthew 9:9-13

As Jesus was walking on he saw a man named Matthew sitting by the customs house, and he said to him, 'Follow me.' And he got up and followed him.

While he was at dinner in the house it happened that a number of tax collectors and sinners came to sit at the table with Jesus and his disciples. When the Pharisees saw this, they said to his disciples, 'Why does your master eat with tax collectors and sinners?' When he heard this he replied, 'It is not the healthy who need the doctor, but the sick. Go and learn the meaning of the words: What I want is mercy, not sacrifice. And indeed I did not come to call the virtuous, but sinners.

Reflection

We often hear stories of how Jesus gives the command, 'Follow me', and people like Matthew get up and follow him. Remember, there are many ways to follow Jesus. How do you hear his words today? 'Follow me…' Do you start thinking about all the things you might have to sacrifice? Or as the psalm suggests, do you seek God with all your heart? Jesus reminds us in today's Gospel of the importance of the will of God, the commandment to love, and how we might live it in mercy, that is in loving kindness to all. We might not have to look too far to find the tax collectors and sinners in our lives who are waiting eagerly for our merciful love, for an ear that might listen and a voice that might soothe. Surprise yourself today and see what happens when you take up this invitation with all your heart.

13th Week in Ordinary Time
Green

02
JUL SAT

Amos 9:11-15

It is the Lord who speaks: 'That day I will re-erect the tottering hut of David, make good the gaps in it, restore its ruins and rebuild it as it was in the days of old, so that they can conquer the remnant of Edom and all the nations that belonged to me.'

It is the Lord who speaks, and he will carry this out. 'The days are coming now – it is the Lord who speaks – when harvest will follow directly after ploughing, the treading of grapes soon after sowing, when the mountains will run with new wine and the hills all flow with it. I mean to restore the fortunes of my people Israel; they will rebuild the ruined cities and live in them, plant vineyards and drink their wine, dig gardens and eat their produce. I will plant them in their own country, never to be rooted up again out of the land I have given them, says the Lord, your God.'

Psalm 84:9, 11-14. R. v. 9

The Lord speaks peace to his people.

Matthew 9:14-17

John's disciples came to Jesus and said, 'Why is it that we and the Pharisees fast, but your disciples do not?' Jesus replied, 'Surely the bridegroom's attendants would never think of mourning as long as the bridegroom is still with them? But the time will come for the bridegroom to be taken away from them, and then they will fast. No one puts a piece of unshrunken cloth on to an old cloak, because the patch pulls away from the cloak and the tear gets worse. Nor do people put new wine into old wineskins, if they do, the skins burst, the wine runs out, and the skins are lost. No; they put new wine into fresh skins and both are preserved.'

Reflection

Our ideas about time, the past and the future have a strong impact on our actions now. The people in Amos' time waited as the Lord said to Amos, 'The days are coming now…' outlining a promise of peace and plenty in contrast to the earlier threats of punishment. Jesus linked time to action when he said that there was little point in fasting when the bridegroom was present. 'The time will come for the bridegroom to be taken away and then they will fast.' Both situations speak of future possibilities. Yet the psalmist recalls the voice of peace that we will hear *when we turn to God in our hearts*. Jesus, Immanuel, teaches that God is with us *now*, always, as an indwelling presence. We don't have to wait for a prophet's reminder. We simply pause, turn our attention inwards, and then find Jesus' peace already in our hearts.

03
JUL SUN

FOURTEENTH SUNDAY IN ORDINARY TIME

Psalter Week 2

Green

Isaiah 66:10-14

Rejoice, Jerusalem,
be glad for her, all you who love her!
Rejoice, rejoice for her,
all you who mourned her!

That you may be suckled, filled,
from her consoling breast,
that you may savour with delight
her glorious breasts.

For thus says the Lord:
Now towards her I send flowing
peace, like a river,
and like a stream in spate
the glory of the nations.

At her breast will her nurslings be carried
and fondled in her lap.
Like a son comforted by his mother
will I comfort you.
And by Jerusalem you will be comforted.

At the sight your heart will rejoice,
and your bones flosurish like the grass.
To his servants the Lord will reveal his hand.

Psalm 65:1-7, 16, 20. R. v. 1

Cry out with joy to God, all the earth.

Galatians 6:14-18

The only thing I can boast about is the cross of our Lord Jesus Christ, through whom the world is crucified to me, and I to the world. It does not matter if a person is circumcised or not; what matters is for him to become an altogether new creature. Peace and mercy to all who follow this rule, who form the Israel of God.

I want no more trouble from anybody after this; the marks on my body are those of Jesus. The grace of our Lord Jesus Christ be with your spirit, my brothers. Amen.

Luke 10:1-12, 17-20

The Lord appointed seventy-two others and sent them out ahead of him, in pairs, to all the towns and places he himself was to visit. He said to them, 'The harvest is rich but the labourers are few, so ask the Lord of the harvest to send labourers to his harvest. Start off now, but remember, I am sending you out like lambs among wolves. Carry no purse, no haversack, no sandals. Salute no one on the road. Whatever house you go into, let your first words be, "Peace to this house!" And if a man of peace lives there, your peace will go and rest on him; if not, it will come back to you. Stay in the same house, taking what food and drink they have to offer, for the labourer deserves his wages; do not move from house to house. Whenever you go into a town where they make you welcome, eat what is set before you. Cure those in it who are sick, and say, "The kingdom of God is very near to you." But whenever you enter a town and they do not make you welcome, go out into its streets and say, "We wipe off the very dust of your town that clings to our feet, and leave it with you. Yet be sure of this: the kingdom of God is very near." I tell you, that on that day it will not go as hard with Sodom as with that town.'

The seventy-two came back rejoicing. 'Lord', they said, 'even the devils submit to us when we use your name.' He said to them, 'I watched Satan fall like lightning from heaven. Yes, I have given you power to tread underfoot serpents and scorpions and the whole strength of the enemy; nothing shall ever hurt you. Yet do not rejoice that the spirits submit to you; rejoice rather that your names are written in heaven.'

Reflection

If we look deeply into today's Gospel, the focus seems to be on peace as a key to healing, and our acceptance of peace as a way of knowing the nearness of the kingdom of God. In fact, to get his message across, Luke asserts twice that the kingdom of God is very near to you! Paul reiterates the same theme to the Galatians. In your being healed, you will become altogether a new creation – peace and mercy to all! This peace though is a peace that does not ignore the marks of Jesus' crucifixion. It is a peace that embraces the cross, that does not shy away from those times in our lives when our commitment to following the rule of love is put to the test. It is then that we will know the grace of this peace. God's love will not be withheld, says the psalmist. The prophet Isaiah too portrays this so beautifully in the images of peace flowing like a river, and the suckling infant consoled at the mother's breast. So, might we be comforted this week in the lap of our God, carried by peace, nourished by peace, becoming peace for our world.

04
JUL MON

14th Week in Ordinary Time | Green
or **St Elizabeth of Portugal** (Optional, White)

Hosea 2:16-18, 21-22

It is the Lord who speaks: I am going to lure her and lead her out into the wilderness and speak to her heart. There she will respond to me as she did when she was young, as she did when she came out of the land of Egypt. When that day comes – it is Lord who speaks – she will call me, 'My husband', no longer will she call me, 'My Baal'. I will betroth you to myself for ever, betroth you with integrity and justice, with tenderness and love; I will betroth you to myself with faithfulness, and you will come to know the Lord.

Psalm 144:2-9. R. v. 8

The Lord is kind and full of compassion.

Matthew 9:18-26

While Jesus was speaking, up came one of the officials, who bowed low in front of him and said, 'My daughter has just died, but come and lay your hand on her and her life will be saved.' Jesus rose and, with his disciples, followed him.

Then from behind him came a woman, who had suffered from a haemorrhage for twelve years, and she touched the fringe of his cloak, for she said to herself, 'If I can only touch his cloak I shall be well again.' Jesus turned round and saw her; and he said to her, 'Courage, my daughter, your faith has restored you to health.' And from that moment the woman was well again.

When Jesus reached the official's house, and saw the flute players, with the crowd making a commotion he said, 'Get out of here; the little girl is not dead, she is asleep.' And they laughed at him. But when the people had been turned out he went inside and took the little girl by the hand; and she stood up. And the news spread all round the countryside.

Reflection

The Gospel today gives us stories of two daughters – one, the death of a little daughter of an official, and the other the illness of an older woman. Interestingly, when Jesus notices this woman touching his cloak, he addresses her saying, 'Courage, my daughter…' What an incredible statement of kinship and intimacy for someone he has not even met! Then hearing that she belongs, as daughter, she becomes well again. Isn't this true? When we know we belong, something in us is brought alive. Hope is born anew and then purpose returns to our days. Is there someone in your life who needs reassuring that they belong? Belonging to a family, to a friendship, to a cause; belonging to Love! The psalm reminds us that God is good to all. Can we too extend our compassion to all creatures and let them know they belong?

14th Week in Ordinary Time | Green
or **St Anthony Zaccaria,** *priest* (Optional, White)

05
JUL TUE

Hosea 8:4-7, 11-13

Thus says the Lord: They have set up kings, but not with my consent, and appointed princes, but without my knowledge. Out of their own silver and gold they have made idols, which are doomed to destruction. I spurn your calf, Samaria, my anger blazes against it. (How long will it be before they purge themselves of this, the sons of Israel?) A workman made the thing, this cannot be God!

Yes, the calf of Samaria shall go up in flames. They sow the wind, they will reap the whirlwind; their wheat will yield no ear, the ear will yield no flour, or, if it does, foreigners will swallow it. Ephraim has built altar after altar, they have only served him as occasion for sin. Were I to write out the thousand precepts of my Law for him, they would be paid no more attention than those of a stranger. They love sacrificing; right, let them sacrifice! They love meat; right, let them eat it! The Lord takes no pleasure in these. He is now going to remember their iniquity and punish their sins; they will have to go back to Egypt.

Psalm 113:3-10. R. v. 9

Sons of Israel, trust in the Lord.

Matthew 9:32-38

A man was brought to Jesus, a dumb demoniac. And when the devil was cast out, the dumb man spoke and the people were amazed. 'Nothing like this has ever been seen in Israel' they said. But the Pharisees said, 'It is through the prince of devils that he casts out devils.'

Jesus made a tour through all the towns and villages, teaching in their synagogues, proclaiming the Good News of the kingdom and curing all kinds of diseases and sickness. And when he saw the crowds he felt sorry for them because they were harassed and dejected, like sheep without a shepherd. Then he said to his disciples, 'The harvest is rich but the labourers are few, so ask the Lord of the harvest to send labourers to his harvest.'

Reflection

Today we continue to reflect on belonging. When we feel like sheep without a shepherd, we feel lost. We don't know who we are or where we belong. There can be many reasons for this – sickness, despair, our sin in seeking false idols which only leads to further separation from God. The more we focus on our plight, the more we can't see, hear, speak, or sense the truth. We give up and feel like we might have to go back to Egypt. Such bleak times are exactly the times to practise trust. Jesus, when he sees us lost like this, reminds us, as he did his disciples, that there *is* a harvest, and it is a rich one. All is not lost! The Good News is that we do have a shepherd and we do belong to this shepherd. We can be cured of all kinds of reasons for feeling lost.

06
JUL WED

14th Week in Ordinary Time | Green
or **St Maria Goretti,** *virgin, martyr* (Optional, Red)

Hosea 10:1-3, 7-8, 12

Israel was a luxuriant vine yielding plenty of fruit. The more his fruit increased, the more altars he built; the richer his land became, the richer he made the sacred stones. Their heart is a divided heart; very well, they must pay for it; the Lord is going to break their altars down and destroy their sacred stones. Then they will say, 'We have no king because we have not feared the Lord.' But what can a king do for us?

Samaria has had her day. Her king is like a straw drifting on the water. The idolatrous high places shall be destroyed – that sin of Israel; thorn and thistle will grow on their altars. Then they will say to the mountains, 'Cover us!' and to the hills, 'Fall on us!'

Sow integrity for yourselves, reap a harvest of kindness, break up your fallow ground: it is time to go seeking the Lord until he comes to rain salvation on you.

Psalm 104:2-7. R. v. 4

Constantly seek the face of the Lord.

Matthew 10:1-7

Jesus summoned his twelve disciples, and gave them authority over unclean spirits with power to cast them out and to cure all kinds of diseases and sickness.

These are the names of the twelve apostles: first, Simon who is called Peter, and his brother Andrew; James the son of Zebedee, and his brother John; Philip and Bartholomew; Thomas, and Matthew the tax collector; James the son of Alphaeus, and Thaddaeus; Simon the Zealot and Judas Iscariot, the one who was to betray him. These twelve Jesus sent out, instructing them as follows:

'Do not turn your steps to pagan territory, and do not enter any Samaritan town; go rather to the lost sheep of the House of Israel. And as you go, proclaim that the kingdom of heaven is close at hand.'

Reflection

In today's Gospel Jesus clearly instructs the apostles where to put their focus: don't go to pagan territory but to the lost sheep of the House of Israel. Of course, we know that Jesus came for all, but here he is reminding us to first attend to the ones who should be doing the right thing and have gone astray. The message they are to take is that the kingdom of heaven is close at hand. If we dare to call ourselves Christian, how attentive are we to this closeness of the kingdom? Do we know it? Do we proclaim it through our lives? The first reading from Hosea gives us a few clues. If we have a divided heart like that of Israel, then it is time to sow some integrity, to reap a harvest of kindness and keep seeking the Lord. Do others see in your life, the kingdom Jesus proclaimed?

07
JUL THU

14th Week in Ordinary Time | Green
or **Blessed Peter To Rot,** *martyr* (Optional, Red)

Hosea 11:1-4, 8-9

Thus says the Lord: When Israel was a child I loved him, and I called my son out of Egypt. But the more I called to them, the further they went from me; they have offered sacrifice to the Baals and set their offerings smoking before the idols. I myself taught Ephraim to walk, I took them in my arms; yet they have not understood that I was the one looking after them. I led them with reins of kindness, with leading-strings of love. I was like someone who lifts an infant close against his cheek; stooping down to him I gave him his food. My heart recoils from it, my whole being trembles at the thought. I will not give rein to my fierce anger, I will not destroy Ephraim again, for I am God, not man: I am the Holy One in your midst and have no wish to destroy.

Psalm 79:2-3, 15-16. R. v. 4

Let your face shine on us, O Lord, and we shall be saved.

Matthew 10:7-15

Jesus instructed the Twelve as follows: 'As you go, proclaim that the kingdom of heaven is close at hand. Cure the sick, raise the dead, cleanse the lepers, cast out devils. You received without charge, give without charge. Provide yourselves with no gold or silver, not even with a few coppers for your purses, with no haversack for the journey or spare tunic or footwear or a staff, for the workman deserves his keep.

'Whatever town or village you go into, ask for someone trustworthy and stay with him until you leave. As you enter his house, salute it, and if the house deserves it, let your peace descend upon it; if it does not, let your peace come back to you. And if anyone does not welcome you or listen to what you have to say, as you walk out of the house or town shake the dust from your feet. I tell you solemnly, on the day of Judgement it will not go as hard with the land of Sodom and Gomorrah as with that town.'

Reflection

As we go about proclaiming the kingdom through our lives, the Gospel reminds us that the key ingredient must be peace. You would think that no one would reject such an offer. Jesus knows that is not always the case and he wisely reminds the apostles of a Jewish custom, to shake the dust from their feet and leave if not welcomed. While rejection is never easy, Hosea's words of loving devotion to Israel can be great encouragement for us today. Let's hear them addressed by God to ourselves: 'I myself taught you to walk, I took you in my arms, I led you with reins of kindness, with leading-strings of love. I was like someone who lifts an infant close against their cheek; stooping down to you I gave you your food … I am the Holy One in your midst and have no wish to destroy.' *We thank you loving God!*

08
JUL FRI

Hosea 14:2-10

The Lord says this: Israel, come back to the Lord your God; your iniquity was the cause of your downfall. Provide yourself with words and come back to the Lord. Say to him, 'Take all iniquity away so that we may have happiness again and offer you our words of praise. Assyria cannot save us, we will not ride horses any more, or say, "Our God!" to what our own hands have made, for you are the one in whom orphans find compassion.' – I will heal their disloyalty, I will love them with all my heart for my anger has turned from them. I will fall like dew on Israel. ...
(Please see the Appendix B-18)

Psalm 50:3-4, 8-9, 12-14, 17. R. v. 17

My mouth shall declare your praise.

Matthew 10:16-23

Jesus instructed the Twelve as follows: 'Remember, I am sending you out like sheep among wolves; so be cunning as serpents and yet as harmless as doves.

'Beware of men: they will hand you over to sanhedrins and scourge you in their synagogues. You will be dragged before governors and kings for my sake, to bear witness before them and the pagans. But when they hand you over, do not worry about how to speak or what to say; what you are to say will be given to you when the time comes; because it is not you who will be speaking; the Spirit of your Father will be speaking in you.

'Brother will betray brother to death, and the father his child; children will rise against their parents and have them put to death. You will be hated by all men on account of my name; but the man who stands firm to the end will be saved. If they persecute you in one town, take refuge in the next; and if they persecute you in that, take refuge in another. I tell you solemnly, you will not have gone the round of the towns of Israel before the Son of Man comes.'

Reflection

Hosea speaks of the Lord calling Israel to come back and reassuring them, 'I will love them with all my heart … it is I who hear their prayer and care for them.' Jesus reiterates this same deep trust in God when he warns the twelve of the difficulties to come. Jesus tells them that even the words they are to say will be given by the Spirit of the Father speaking in them. St Paul picks this up in 1 Corinthians 1:16 – 'Who has ever known the mind of the Lord, to be his counsellor? But we have the mind of Christ.' If we let the mind of Jesus live in us, then not only can we trust deeply, but we will not even have to worry about what to say. What would it be like to let the Spirit of God speak this way in you today?

14th Week in Ordinary Time | Green or **St Augustine Zhao Rong and companions,** *martyrs* (Optional, Red)

09
JUL SAT

OUR LADY OF ABERDEEN, Feast
– Scotland
see Appendix A-19

Isaiah 6:1-8

In the year of King Uzziah's death I saw the Lord seated on a high throne; his train filled the sanctuary; above him stood seraphs, each one with six wings: two to cover its face, two to cover its feet and two for flying.

And they cried out to one another in this way, 'Holy, holy, holy is the Lord of hosts. His glory fills the whole earth.' ...
(Please see the Appendix B-18)

Psalm 92:1-2, 5. R. v. 1

The Lord is king, with majesty enrobed.

Matthew 10:24-33

Jesus said to his apostles: 'The disciple is not superior to his teacher, nor the slave to his master. It is enough for the disciple that he should grow to be like his teacher, and the slave like his master. If they have called the master of the house Beelzebul, what will they not say of his household?

'Do not be afraid of them therefore. For everything that is now covered will be uncovered, and everything now hidden will be made clear. What I say to you in the dark, tell in the daylight; what you hear in whispers, proclaim from the housetops.

'Do not be afraid of those who kill the body but cannot kill the soul; fear him rather who can destroy both body and soul in hell. Can you not buy two sparrows for a penny? And yet not one falls to the ground without your Father knowing. Why, every hair on your head has been counted. So there is no need to be afraid; you are worth more than hundreds of sparrows.

'So if anyone declares himself for me in the presence of men, I will declare myself for him in the presence of my Father in heaven. But the one who disowns me in the presence of men, I will disown in the presence of my Father in heaven.'

Reflection

We can waste so much time worrying about how to act and what to say to prove a point or justify a position. Just in case we are still doubting that the Spirit of God can speak in us, today Isaiah tells us one way in which this can happen in the story of the seraph touching his mouth and purging his sin. All we need do is remember who we are and allow the Spirit to live fully and unimpeded in our every thought and action. Perhaps this is what Jesus meant when he said that it is enough for the disciple to grow to be like the teacher. The only way we can do this is to trust more and more in the Spirit rather than in our own, often selfish, motives. Then everything will be made clear and there will be no need to be afraid.

10
JUL SUN

FIFTEENTH SUNDAY IN ORDINARY TIME

Psalter Week 3

Green

Deuteronomy 30:10-14

Moses said to the people: 'Obey the voice of the Lord your God, keeping those commandments and laws of his that are written in the Book of this Law, and you shall return to the Lord your God with all your heart and soul.

'For this Law that I enjoin on you today is not beyond your strength or beyond your reach. It is not in heaven, so that you need to wonder, "Who will go up to heaven for us and bring it down to us, so that we may hear it and keep it?" Nor is it beyond the seas, so that you need to wonder, "Who will cross the seas for us and bring it back to us, so that we may hear it and keep it?" No, the Word is very near to you, it is in your mouth and in your heart for your observance.'

Psalm 68:14, 17, 30-31, 33-34, 36-37. R. cf. v. 33

Seek the Lord, you who are poor, and your hearts will revive.

Colossians 1:15-20

Christ Jesus is the image of the unseen God
and the first-born of all creation,
for in him were created
all things in heaven and on earth:
everything visible and everything invisible,
Thrones, Dominations, Sovereignties, Powers –
all things were created through him and for him.
Before anything was created, he existed,
and he holds all things in unity.
Now the Church is his body,
he is its head.
As he is the Beginning,
he was first to be born from the dead,
so that he should be first in every way;
because God wanted all perfection
to be found in him
and all things to be reconciled through him and for him,
everything in heaven and everything on earth,
when he made peace
by his death on the cross.

Luke 10:25-37

There was a lawyer who, to disconcert Jesus, stood up and said to him, 'Master, what must I do to inherit eternal life?' He said to him, 'What is written in the law? What do you read there?' He replied, 'You must love the Lord your God with all your heart, with all your soul, with all your strength, and with all your mind, and your neighbour as yourself.' 'You have answered right,' said Jesus, 'do this and life is yours.'

But the man was anxious to justify himself and said to Jesus, 'And who is my neighbour?' Jesus replied, 'A man was once on his way down from Jerusalem to Jericho and fell into the hands of brigands; they took all he had, beat him and then made off, leaving him half dead. Now a priest happened to be travelling down the same road, but when he saw the man, he passed by on the other side. In the same way a Levite who came to the place saw him, and passed by on the other side. But a Samaritan traveller who came upon him was moved with compassion when he saw him. He went up and bandaged his wounds, pouring oil and wine on them. He then lifted him on to his own mount, carried him to the inn and looked after him. Next day, he took out two denarii and handed them to the innkeeper. "Look after him," he said "and on my way back I will make good any extra expense you have." Which of these three, do you think, proved himself a neighbour to the man who fell into the brigands' hands?' 'The one, who took pity on him' he replied. Jesus said to him, 'Go, and do the same yourself.'

Reflection

We all want to live 'eternal life', life *in* God, as the lawyer in today's Gospel puts it. Jesus tells the lawyer we can have such life if we love God wholeheartedly and love our neighbour as ourself. Similarly, in the passage from Deuteronomy, we hear that it is through keeping the commandments that we return to God with all our heart and soul. We can take heart too that this law is not beyond our strength or our reach. In fact it is very close, in our mouths and in our hearts! The lawyer is taught that Jesus is this law brought to perfection. As Paul tells us in his letter to the Colossians, now the Church, of which we are a part, is Christ's body and Christ is its head. Christ Jesus who lives so closely in us is the image of the unseen God. As we reflect on our life over this past week, and endeavour to live more fully in Christ in the week to come, let's pray with the psalmist, 'In your great love, answer me, O God, with your help that never fails: Lord, answer, for your love is kind; in your compassion, turn towards me.'

11
JUL MON

St Benedict, *abbot,* **Co-Patron of Europe,**
Feast | White

Proverbs 2:1-9

My son, if you take my words to heart, if you set store by my commandments, tuning your ear to wisdom, and applying your heart to truth: yes, if your plea is for clear perception, if you cry out for discernment, if you look for it as if it were silver, and search for it as for buried treasure, you will then understand what the fear of the Lord is, and discover the knowledge of God. For the Lord himself is giver of wisdom, from his mouth issue knowledge and discernment. He keeps his help for honest men, he is the shield of those whose ways are honourable; he stands guard over the paths of justice, he keeps watch on the way of his devoted ones. Then you will understand what virtue is, justice, and fair dealing, all paths that lead to happiness.

Psalm 33:2-11. R. v. 2

I will bless the Lord at all times.

Matthew 19:27-29

Peter spoke to Jesus. 'What about us?' he said. 'We have left everything and followed you. What are we to have, then?' Jesus said to him, 'I tell you solemnly, when all is made new and the Son of Man sits on his throne of glory, you will yourselves sit on twelve thrones to judge the twelve tribes of Israel. And everyone who has left houses, brothers, sisters, father, mother, children or land for the sake of my name will be repaid a hundred times over, and also inherit eternal life.'

Reflection

Jesus promises a hundredfold of all that one has given up for the kingdom of God. This hundredfold is possible if the giving up is with a true sense of detachment. Jesus also adds persecution as part of the reward for such renunciation. Am I attached to God or to wealth and the pleasures of this life?

15th Week in Ordinary Time
Green

12
JUL TUE

Isaiah 7:1-9

In the reign of Ahaz son of Jotham, son of Uzziah, king of Judah, Razon the king of Aram went up against Jerusalem with Pekah son of Remaliah, king of Israel, to lay siege to it; but he was unable to capture it.

The news was brought to the House of David. 'Aram,' they said 'has reached Ephraim.' Then the heart of the king and the hearts of the people shuddered as the trees of the forest shudder in front of the wind. The Lord said to Isaiah, 'Go with your son Shear-jashub, and meet Ahaz at the end of the conduit of the upper pool on the Fuller's Field road, and say to him: "Pay attention, keep calm, have no fear, do not let your heart sink because of these two smouldering stumps of firebrands, or because Aram, Ephraim and the son of Remaliah have plotted to ruin you, and have said: Let us invade Judah and terrorise it and seize it for ourselves, and set up a king there, the son of Tabeel. The Lord says this: It shall not come true; it shall not be. The capital of Aram is Damascus, the head of Damascus, Razon; the capital of Ephraim, Samaria, the head of Samaria, the son of Remaliah. Six or five years more and shattered Ephraim shall no longer be a people. But if you do not stand by me, you will not stand at all."'

Psalm 47:2-8. R. v. 9

God upholds his city for ever.

Matthew 11:20-24

Jesus began to reproach the towns in which most of his miracles had been worked, because they refused to repent.

'Alas for you, Chorazin! Alas for you, Bethsaida! For if the miracles done in you had been done in Tyre and Sidon, they would have repented long ago in sackcloth and ashes. And still, I tell you that it will not go as hard on Judgement day with Tyre and Sidon as with you. And as for you, Capernaum, did you want to be exalted as high as heaven? You shall be thrown down to hell. For if the miracles done in you had been done in Sodom, it would have been standing yet. And still, I tell you it will not go as hard with the land of Sodom on Judgement day as with you.'

Reflection

Jesus calls out the people in various towns for their failed response to his miracles. They still have not turned to God. King Ahaz was warned, 'If you do not stand by me, you will not stand at all.' Jesus similarly warns the Jewish people that if the miracles had been done in the towns where the people repented, those towns would still be standing. The instruction Isaiah is told to give King Ahaz begins with advice that is good for us to remember when we are hesitant in doing the right thing. Isaiah tells him, 'Pay attention, keep calm, have no fear, do not let your heart sink.' Can we heed such advice? It will be much easier to do so if we turn back to God. Then with the psalmist we can sing, 'The Lord is great and worthy to be praised in the city of our God.'

13
JUL WED

15th Week in Ordinary Time | Green
or **St Henry** (Optional, White)

Isaiah 10:5-7, 13-16

Thus says the Lord: 'Woe to Assyria, the rod of my anger, the club brandished by me in my fury! I sent him against a godless nation; I gave him commission against a people that provokes me, to pillage and to plunder freely and to stamp down like the mud in the streets. But he did not intend this, his heart did not plan it so. No, in his heart was to destroy, to go on cutting nations to pieces without limit.' For he has said: 'By the strength of my own arm I have done this and by my own intelligence, for understanding is mine; I have pushed back the frontiers of peoples and plundered their treasures. I have brought their inhabitants down to the dust. As if they were a bird's nest, my hand has seized the riches of the peoples. As people pick up deserted eggs I have picked up the whole earth, with not a wing fluttering, not a beak opening, not a chirp.' Does the axe claim more credit than the man who wields it, or the saw more strength than the man who handles it? It would be like the cudgel controlling the man who raises it, or the club moving what is not made of wood! And so the Lord of hosts is going to send a wasting sickness on his stout warriors; beneath his plenty, a burning will burn like a consuming fire.

Psalm 93:5-10, 14-15. R. v. 14

The Lord will not abandon his people.

Matthew 11:25-27

Jesus exclaimed, 'I bless you, Father, Lord of heaven and earth, for hiding these things from the learned and the clever and revealing them to mere children. Yes, Father, for that is what it pleased you to do. Everything has been entrusted to me by my Father; and no one knows the Son except the Father, just as no one knows the Father except the Son and those to whom the Son chooses to reveal him.'

Reflection

In the reading from Isaiah we hear about the heart of Assyria, who not only exceeded the commission given by the Lord, but took the credit for its conquests instead of giving credit to the Lord. How different this is from Jesus' gratitude to the Lord for revealing everything to children! The hearts of children are simple and undivided, with full trust in their parents. Jesus knows this in his relationship with the Lord of heaven and earth whom he calls 'Father'. He knows this unconditional love and mercy so deeply that his very being, his whole life, reflects it. He lives what the psalmist sings, 'The Lord will not abandon his people … for judgement shall again be just and all true hearts shall uphold it.' Let's give thanks for the Lord who doesn't abandon us, and live this day, as Jesus did, with the true heart of a child.

15th Week in Ordinary Time | Green
or **St Camillus de Lellis,** *priest* (Optional, White)

14
JUL THU

Isaiah 26:7-9, 12, 16-19

The path of the upright man is straight, you smooth the way of the upright. Following the path of your judgements, we hoped in you, Lord, your name, your memory are all my soul desires.

At night my soul longs for you and my spirit in me seeks for you; when your judgements appear on earth the inhabitants of the world learn the meaning of integrity.

Lord, you are giving us peace, since you treat us as our deeds deserve.

Distressed, we search for you, Lord; the misery of oppression was your punishment for us. As a woman with child near her time writhes and cries out in her pangs, so are we, O Lord, in your presence: we have conceived, we writhe as if we were giving birth; we have not given the spirit of salvation to the earth, no more inhabitants of the world are born.

Your dead will come to life, their corpses will rise; awake, exult, all you who lie in the dust, for your dew is a radiant dew and the land of ghosts will give birth.

Psalm 101:13-21. R. v. 20

The Lord looked down from heaven to the earth.

Matthew 11:28-30

Jesus said, 'Come to me, all you who labour and are overburdened, and I will give you rest. Shoulder my yoke and learn from me, for I am gentle and humble in heart, and you will find rest for your souls. Yes, my yoke is easy and my burden light.'

Reflection

Today Isaiah speaks of hope and a new birth for all who lie in the dust. For those who hope in the Lord, 'your name, your memory are all my soul desires … At night my soul longs for you and my spirit in me seeks for you.' Isaiah knows that the Lord will give us peace, treating us as our deeds deserve. In the psalmist's response we hear that the Lord will arise and have mercy. Then we see this mercy in Jesus who lovingly calls all who are weary and overburdened to come to him. In this beautiful Gospel passage, Jesus tenderly gives us a glimpse of his own gentle and humble heart. If only we too can gentle our souls, be humble in our dealings with others and honestly admit when we need help, then we will find true rest in the company of Jesus.

15 JUL FRI

15th Week in Ordinary Time
St Bonaventure, *bishop, doctor,* **Memorial** | White

Isaiah 38:1-6, 21-22, 7-8

Hezekiah fell ill and was at the point of death. The prophet Isaiah son of Amoz came and said to him, 'The Lord says this, "Put your affairs in order, for you are going to die, you will not live."' Hezekiah turned his face to the wall and addressed this prayer to the Lord, 'Ah, Lord, remember, I beg you, how I have behaved faithfully and with sincerity of heart in your presence and done what is right in your eyes.' And Hezekiah shed many tears. Then the word of the Lord came to Isaiah, 'Go and say to Hezekiah, "The Lord, the God of David your ancestor, says this: I have heard your prayer and seen your tears. I will cure you: in three days' time you shall go up to the Temple of the Lord. I will add fifteen years to your life. I will save you from the hands of the king of Assyria, I will protect this city."' 'Bring a fig poultice,' Isaiah said. 'Apply it to the ulcer and he will recover.' Hezekiah said, 'What is the sign to tell me that I shall be going up to the Temple of the Lord?' 'Here' Isaiah replied 'is the sign from the Lord that he will do what he has said. Look, I shall make the shadow cast by the declining sun go back ten steps on the steps of Ahaz.' And the sun went back the ten steps by which it had declined.

Isaiah 38:10-12, 16. R. cf. v. 27

You have held back my life, O Lord, from the pit of doom.

Matthew 12:1-8

Jesus took a walk one sabbath day through the cornfields. His disciples were hungry and began to pick ears of corn and eat them. The Pharisees noticed it and said to him, 'Look, your disciples are doing something that is forbidden on the sabbath.' But he said to them, 'Have you not read what David did when he and his followers were hungry – how he went into the house of God and how they ate the loaves of offering which neither he nor his followers were allowed to eat, but which were for the priests alone? Or again, have you not read in the Law that on the sabbath day the Temple priests break the sabbath without being blamed for it? Now here, I tell you, is something greater than the Temple. And if you had understood the meaning of the words: What I want is mercy, not sacrifice, you would not have condemned the blameless. For the Son of Man is master of the sabbath.'

Reflection

The presence of God is an extraordinary healing power. Jesus sums this up when he says 'Now here, I tell you, is something greater than the Temple.' The dying Hezekiah is told to apply a fig poultice to his ulcer. Interestingly, *The Epistle of Privy Counsel*, a medieval text, uses the image of a poultice, a remedy laid on a festering wound to draw out the poison, to describe the healing encounter with God: 'Take good and gracious God, just as he is … lay him on your sick self just as you are, for all the world as if he were a poultice. For touching God is eternal health.' When next you are about to receive the Eucharist and pray, 'Only say the word and I shall be healed,' 'lay him' on your wounded self, and allow him to draw from you all that is not life-giving, all that is not of him.

16 JUL SAT

15th Week in Ordinary Time | Green
or **Our Lady of Mount Carmel** (Optional, White)

Micah 2:1-5

Woe to those who plot evil, who lie in bed planning mischief! No sooner is it dawn than they do it – their hands have the strength for it. Seizing the fields that they covet, they take over houses as well, owner and house they confiscate together, taking both man and inheritance. So the Lord says this: Now it is I who plot such mischief against this breed as your necks will not escape; nor will you be able to walk proudly, so evil will the time be. On that day they will make a satire on you, sing a dirge and say, 'We are stripped of everything; my people's portion is measured out and shared, no one will give it back to them, our fields are awarded to our despoiler.' Therefore you will have no one to measure out a share in the community of the Lord.

Psalm 9B: 1-4, 7-8, 14. R. v. 12

Lord, do not forget the poor.

Matthew 12:14-21

The Pharisees went out and began to plot against Jesus, discussing how to destroy him.

Jesus knew this and withdrew from the district. Many followed him and he cured them all, but warned them not to make him known. This was to fulfil the prophecy of Isaiah: Here is my servant whom I have chosen, my beloved, the favourite of my soul. I will endow him with my spirit, and he will proclaim the true faith to the nations. He will not brawl or shout, nor will anyone hear his voice in the streets. He will not break the crushed reed, nor put out the smouldering wick till he has led the truth to victory: in his name the nations will put their hope.

Reflection

On this Optional Memorial of Our Lady of Mt Carmel, the patroness of the Carmelite Order, we remember that Mt Carmel has traditionally been seen as the meeting place of God and the people. In Mary too, not only do we see a patroness and protector, but we see most clearly a meeting place of God in the human, in her son Jesus. We hear in the Gospel today of the many followers of Jesus who came to meet God in his healing presence. Matthew then quotes Isaiah's prophecy of this beloved servant to teach just how close Jesus was to God. He was so close that he was called the 'favourite of my soul' and he was endowed with God's spirit. So where will you go today, to whom will you go today, to find your meeting place with God? Give yourself the time and space to do so.

17

JUL SUN

SIXTEENTH WEEK IN ORDINARY TIME

Psalter Week 4

Green

Genesis 18:1-10

The Lord appeared to Abraham at the Oak of Mamre while he was sitting by the entrance of the tent during the hottest part of the day. He looked up, and there he saw three men standing near him. As soon as he saw them he ran from the entrance of the tent to meet them, and bowed to the ground. 'My Lord,' he said 'I beg you, if I find favour with you, kindly do not pass your servant by. A little water shall be brought; you shall wash your feet and lie down under the tree. Let me fetch a little bread and you shall refresh yourselves before going further. That is why you have come in your servant's direction.' They replied, 'Do as you say.'

Abraham hastened to the tent to find Sarah. 'Hurry,' he said 'knead three bushels of flour and make loaves.' Then running to the cattle Abraham took a fine and tender calf and gave it to the servant, who hurried to prepare it. Then taking cream, milk and the calf he had prepared, he laid all before them, and they ate while he remained standing near them under the tree. 'Where is your wife Sarah? they asked him. 'She is in the tent' he replied. Then his guest said, 'I shall visit you again next year without fail and your wife will then have a son.'

Psalm 14:2-5. R. v. 1

The just will live in the presence of the Lord.

Colossians 1:24-28

It makes me happy to suffer for you, as I am suffering now, and in my body to do what I can to make up all that has still to be undergone by Christ for the sake of his body, the Church. I became the servant of the Church when God made me responsible for delivering God's message to you, the message which was a mystery hidden for generations and centuries and has now been revealed to his saints. It was God's purpose to reveal it to them and to show all the rich glory of this mystery to pagans. The mystery is Christ among you, your hope of glory: this is the Christ we proclaim, this is the wisdom in which we thoroughly train everyone and instruct everyone, to make them all perfect in Christ.

Luke 10:38-42

Jesus came to a village, and a woman named Martha welcomed him into her house. She had a sister called Mary, who sat down at the Lord's feet and listened to him speaking. Now Martha who was distracted with all the serving said, 'Lord, do you not care that my sister is leaving me to do the serving all by myself? Please tell her to help me.' But the Lord answered: 'Martha, Martha,' he said 'you worry and fret about so many things, and yet few are needed, indeed only one. It is Mary who has chosen the better part; it is not to be taken from her.'

Reflection

Do you wonder how Abraham knew straight away that his three visitors represented God? He runs to meet them and addresses them as 'My Lord'. Somehow, he knew that in their presence he was in the presence of God. Abraham and Sarah were no strangers to suffering and neither was Paul. Just as Abraham is happy to show hospitality to his visitors, Paul is happy to unite his suffering with that of the Christ. Somehow Paul knew that God's presence was *in* the suffering, and that this hidden mystery was now being revealed in Christ. The mystery *is* Christ *among* you! Mary and Martha also came to learn this in a particular way. As it was for Abraham and Paul, Jesus teaches them that all serving must be grounded in a deep relationship of love with God. The presence of God is already with us, in the mystery of Christ. We just need to be open to knowing it, in all that we do. Just for today then, what would it be like to run to serve a stranger as if you were meeting God? How will you sit at the feet of Jesus?

18
JUL MON

16th Week in Ordinary Time
Green

Micah 6:1-4, 6-8

Listen to what the Lord is saying: Stand up and let the case begin in the hearing of the mountains and let the hills hear what you say. Listen, you mountains, to the Lord's accusation, give ear, you foundations of the earth, for the Lord is accusing his people, pleading against Israel: My people, what have I done to you, how have I been a burden to you? Answer me. I brought you out of the land of Egypt, I rescued you from the house of slavery; I sent Moses to lead you, with Aaron and Miriam.

'With what gift shall I come into the Lord's presence and bow down before God on high? Shall I come with holocausts, with calves one year old? Will he be pleased with rams by the thousand, with libations of oil in torrents? Must I give my first-born for what I have done wrong, the fruit of my body for my own sin?'

What is good has been explained to you, man; this is what the Lord asks of you: only this, to act justly, to love tenderly and to walk humbly with your God.

Psalm 49:5-6, 8-9, 16-17, 21, 23. R. v. 23

I will show God's salvation to the upright.

Matthew 12:38-42

Some of the scribes and Pharisees spoke up. 'Master,' they said 'we should like to see a sign from you.' Jesus replied, 'It is an evil and unfaithful generation that asks for a sign! The only sign it will be given is the sign of the prophet Jonah. For as Jonah was in the belly of the sea-monster for three days and three nights, so will the Son of Man be in the heart of the earth for three days and three nights. On Judgement day the men of Nineveh will stand up with this generation and condemn it, because when Jonah preached they repented; and there is something greater than Jonah here. On Judgement day the Queen of the South will rise up with this generation and condemn it, because she came from the ends of the earth to hear the wisdom of Solomon; and there is something greater than Solomon here.'

Reflection

In today's Gospel the scribes and Pharisees ask Jesus for a sign. A sign is something external and physical that we can see and touch and feel. Jesus however, exasperated, tells them that the only sign will be that of a person, the life of the prophet Jonah. Similarly in the reading from Micah, we hear of the people wanting to offer God physical gifts in return for God's covenant love. Yet all that God wants is a real life, a life of conversion, a life that shows justice, tenderness and a true devotion to God. Isn't this what it means to love, to give one's life, not expensive offerings? Of course, the one sign we really want is the life of Jesus living in each one of us. Nothing could be better, for his life is not only something greater than Jonah, but even greater than the wisdom of Solomon.

16th Week in Ordinary Time
Green

19
JUL TUE

Micah 7:14-15, 18-20

With shepherd's crook, O Lord, lead your people to pasture, the flock that is your heritage, living confined in a forest with meadow land all around. Let them pasture in Bashan and Gilead as in the days of old. As in the days when you came out of Egypt grant us to see wonders. What god can compare with you: taking fault away, pardoning crime, not cherishing anger for ever but delighting in showing mercy? Once more have pity on us, tread down our faults, to the bottom of the sea throw all our sins. Grant Jacob your faithfulness, and Abraham your mercy, as you swore to our fathers from the days of long ago.

Psalm 84:2-8. R. v. 8

Let us see, O Lord, your mercy.

Matthew 12:46-50

Jesus was speaking to the crowds when his mother and his brothers appeared; they were standing outside and were anxious to have a word with him. But to the man who told him this Jesus replied, 'Who is my mother? Who are my brothers?' And stretching out his hand towards his disciples he said, 'Here are my mother and my brothers. Anyone who does the will of my Father in heaven is my brother and sister and mother.'

Reflection

We all want to belong. In Micah's time, the people, the flock that is the heritage of God, prayed for forgiveness to a God they knew was merciful, a God who treads down faults all the way to the bottom of the sea! Jesus expands the notion of belonging. He likens it to the powerful bonds of family and gives it just one condition – doing the will of God. Note how the Gospel says he stretches out his hand towards his disciples when he explains this. No longer is there family and disciples. To be a brother or sister in the kingdom of God means to be a disciple and do the will of God. And what is this will? The will of God is to love, to be forgiven, and to forgive and then live as the psalmist sings, with life again restored and rejoicing in God our helper.

20 JUL WED

16th Week in Ordinary Time | Green
or **St Apollinaris,** *bishop, martyr* (Optional, Red)

Jeremiah 1:1, 4-10

The words of Jeremiah son of Hilkiah, of a priestly family living at Anathoth in the territory of Benjamin.

The word of the Lord was addressed to me, saying, 'Before I formed you in the womb I knew you; before you came to birth I consecrated you; I have appointed you as prophet to the nations.'

I said, 'Ah, Lord; look, I do not know how to speak: I am a child!' But the Lord replied, 'Do not say, "I am a child." Go now to those to whom I send you and say whatever I command you. Do not be afraid of them, for I am with you to protect you – it is the Lord who speaks!'

Then the Lord put out his hand and touched my mouth and said to me: 'There! I am putting my words into your mouth. Look, today I am setting you over nations and over kingdoms, to tear up and to knock down, to destroy and to overthrow, to build and to plant.'

Psalm 70:1-6, 15, 17. R. cf. v. 15

My lips will tell of your justice, O Lord.

Matthew 13:1-9

Jesus left the house and sat by the lakeside, but such crowds gathered round him that he got into a boat and sat there. The people all stood on the beach, and he told them many things in parables.

He said, 'Imagine a sower going out to sow. As he sowed some seeds fell on the edge of the path, and the birds came and ate them up. Others fell on patches of rock where they found little soil and sprang up straight away, because there was no depth of earth; but as soon as the sun came up they were scorched and, not having any roots, they withered away. Others fell among thorns, and the thorns grew up and choked them. Others fell on rich soil and produced their crop, some a hundredfold, some sixty, some thirty. Listen, anyone who has ears!'

Reflection

Todays' parable might leave us a little disheartened at first. Seeds sown in the wrong place, with all manner of obstacles to growth: birds, rocky ground, scorching sun and thorny bushes! And yet, some seed did manage to fall into rich soil and produce a marvellous crop. The parable begins, 'Imagine a sower going out to sow.' So let's imagine today that you are that sower. Like Jeremiah, known to the Lord before he was formed in the womb, consecrated before birth and appointed as prophet to the nations, can you go about this day, knowing that it is God who protects you and God who will even put the words you need in your mouth. What hope and trust will you hold in your heart as you sow seeds of love today? Be confident and pray, 'It is you, O Lord, who are my hope, my trust, O Lord since my youth!'

16th Week in Ordinary Time | Green
or **St Lawrence of Brindisi,** *priest, doctor* (Optional, White)

21
JUL THU

Jeremiah 2:1-3, 7-8, 12-13

The word of the Lord was addressed to me saying, 'Go and shout this in the hearing of Jerusalem: "The Lord says this: I remember the affection of your youth, the love of your bridal days: you followed me through the wilderness, through a land unsown. Israel was sacred to the Lord, the first-fruits of his harvest; anyone who ate of this had to pay for it, misfortune came to them – it is the Lord who speaks."

'I brought you to a fertile country to enjoy its produce and good things; but no sooner had you entered than you defiled my land, and made my heritage detestable. The priests have never asked, "Where is the Lord?" Those who administer the Law have no knowledge of me. The shepherds have rebelled against me; the prophets have prophesied in the name of Baal, following things with no power in them. 'You heavens, stand aghast at this, stand stupefied, stand utterly appalled – it is the Lord who speaks – since my people have committed a double crime: they have abandoned me, the fountain of living water, only to dig cisterns for themselves, leaky cisterns that hold no water.'

Psalm 35:6-11. R. v. 10

In you, Lord, is the source of life.

Matthew 13:10-17

The disciples went up to Jesus and asked, 'Why do you talk to the crowds in parables?' 'Because' he replied, 'the mysteries of the kingdom of heaven are revealed to you, but they are not revealed to them. For anyone who has will be given more, and he will have more than enough; but from anyone who has not, even what he has will be taken away. The reason I talk to them in parables is that they look without seeing and listen without hearing or understanding. So in their case this prophecy of Isaiah is being fulfilled: You will listen and listen again, but not understand, see and see again, but not perceive. For the heart of this nation has grown coarse, their ears are dull of hearing and they have shut their eyes for fear they should see with their eyes, hear with their ears, understand with their heart, and be converted and be healed by me. But happy are your eyes because they see, your ears because they hear! I tell you solemnly, many prophets and holy men longed to see what you see, and never saw it; to hear what you hear, and never heard it.'

Reflection

The psalm speaks of the Lord as source of life. 'Your love, Lord, reaches to heaven, your truth to the skies. Your justice is like God's mountain, your judgements like the deep.' What an expansive picture of God's precious love we are given. Jesus describes this mystery in a more challenging way: anyone who has will be given more, anyone who has not, even what they have will be taken away. The only answer here is Love. There is no limit to love. The more we love, the more love creates for us. But if we turn away from love, we risk losing everything. The people in Jeremiah's time abandoned God and their continual access to the fountain of living water. Their selfish hoarding in cisterns of their own making ended up leaking away. Let's make sure we are listening to Jesus, our one true source of life.

22
JUL FRI

St Mary Magdalene
Feast | White

Song 3:1-4 *(Alternative Reading: 2 Corinthians 5:14-17)*
The bride says this: On my bed, at night, I sought him whom my heart loves. I sought but did not find him. So I will rise and go through the City; in the streets and the squares I will seek him whom my heart loves. I sought but did not find him. The watchmen came upon me on their rounds in the City: 'Have you seen him whom my heart loves?' Scarcely had I passed them than I found him whom my heart loves.

Psalm 62:2-6, 8-9. R. v. 2
For you my soul is thirsting, O Lord my God.

John 20:1-2, 11-18
It was very early on the first day of the week and still dark, when Mary of Magdala came to the tomb. She saw that the stone had been moved away from the tomb and came running to Simon Peter and the other disciple, the one Jesus loved. 'They have taken the Lord out of the tomb' she said 'and we don't know where they have put him.'

Mary stayed outside near the tomb, weeping. Then, still weeping, she stooped to look inside, and saw two angels in white sitting where the body of Jesus had been, one at the head, the other at the feet. They said, 'Woman, why are you weeping?' 'They have taken my Lord away' she replied 'and I don't know where they have put him.' As she said this she turned round and saw Jesus standing there, though she did not recognise him. Jesus said, 'Woman, why are you weeping? Who are you looking for?' Supposing him to be the gardener, she said, 'Sir, if you have taken him away, tell me where you have put him, and I will go and remove him.' Jesus said, 'Mary!' She knew him then and said to him in Hebrew, 'Rabbuni!' – which means Master. Jesus said to her, 'Do not cling to me, because I have not yet ascended to the Father. But go and find the brothers, and tell them: I am ascending to my Father and your Father, to my God and your God.' So Mary of Magdala went and told the disciples that she had seen the Lord and that he had said these things to her.

Reflection
Today we have the opportunity to remember the wonderful witness of St Mary Magdalene, one of the women who remained faithful to Jesus through his passion, death, and resurrection. It is she whom Jesus instructs to tell the other apostles that the Lord has risen. As such, she is known as Apostle to the Apostles. She is a faithful witness at the tomb and then she is entrusted with the news of Jesus' resurrection. It is not difficult therefore to imagine the depth of the relationship between them. What might her example of faithfulness and trustworthiness teach each one of us about our relationship with Jesus? We might ask ourselves: 'Am I faithful to him in the death moments of life? How will I respond when I hear Jesus call my name? Is my heart ready to be entrusted with a special mission from Jesus?'

23
JUL SAT

St Bridget of Sweden, Patroness of Europe
Feast | White

Galatians 2:19-20

Through the Law I am dead to the Law, so that now I can live with God. I have been crucified with Christ, and I live now not with my own life but with the life of Christ who lives in me. The life I now live in this body I live in faith: faith in the Son of God who loved me and who sacrificed himself for my sake.

Psalm 33:2-11. R. v. 2

I will bless the Lord at all times.

John 15:1-8

Jesus said to his disciples: 'I am the true vine, and my Father is the vinedresser. Every branch in me that bears no fruit he cuts away, and every branch that does bear fruit he prunes to make it bear even more. You are pruned already, by means of the word that I have spoken to you. Make your home in me, as I make mine in you. As a branch cannot bear fruit all by itself, but must remain part of the vine, neither can you unless you remain in me. I am the vine, you are the branches. Whoever remains in me, with me in him, bears fruit in plenty; for cut off from me you can do nothing. Anyone who does not remain in me is like a branch that has been thrown away – he withers; these branches are collected and thrown on the fire, and they are burnt. If you remain in me and my words remain in you, you may ask what you will and you shall get it. It is to the glory of my Father that you should bear much fruit, and then you will be my disciples.'

Reflection

The picture of the vine and the branches is a powerful metaphor for our relationship with Jesus. Just as the branches bear fruit only if they are joined to the vine, so we will bear the fruits of the Holy Spirit only if we are united with Jesus. As branches can bear more fruits if they are pruned, we, too, must be pruned regularly of anything that is not of God to bear fruits in abundance. Pruning is painful, yet it is vital for our spiritual progress. As St Brigid has demonstrated, it is our oneness with Jesus as well as our commitment to hearing his voice and doing his will that will make us his true disciples.

24
JUL SUN

SEVENTEENTH SUNDAY IN ORDINARY TIME

Psalter Week 1

Green

Genesis 18:20-32

The Lord said, 'How great an outcry there is against Sodom and Gomorrah! How grievous is their sin! I propose to go down and see whether or not they have done all that is alleged in the outcry against them that has come up to me. I am determined to know.'

The men left there and went to Sodom while Abraham remained standing before the Lord. Approaching him he said, 'Are you really going to destroy the just man with the sinner? Perhaps there are fifty just men in the town. Will you really overwhelm them, will you not spare the place for the fifty just men in it? Do not think of doing such a thing: to kill the just man with the sinner, treating just and sinner alike! Do not think of it! Will the judge of the whole earth not administer justice?' The Lord replied, 'If at Sodom I find fifty just men in the town, I will spare the whole place because of them.'

Abraham replied, 'I am bold indeed to speak like this to my Lord, I who am dust and ashes. But perhaps the fifty just men lack five: will you destroy the whole city for five?' 'No', he replied, 'I will not destroy it if I find forty-five just men there.' Again Abraham said to him, 'Perhaps there will only be forty there.' 'I will not do it' he replied 'for the sake of the forty.'

Abraham said, 'I trust my Lord will not be angry, but give me leave to speak: perhaps there will only be thirty there.' 'I will not do it' he replied 'if I find thirty there.' He said, 'I am bold indeed to speak like this, but perhaps there will only be twenty there.' 'I will not destroy it' he replied 'for the sake of the twenty.' He said, 'I trust my Lord will not be angry if I speak once more: perhaps there will only be ten.' 'I will not destroy it' he replied 'for the sake of the ten.'

Psalm 137:1-3, 6-8. R. v. 3

On the day I called, you answered me, O Lord.

Colossians 2:12-14

You have been buried with Christ, when you were baptised; and by baptism, too, you have been raised up with him through your belief in the power of God who raised him from the dead. You were dead, because you were sinners and had not been circumcised: he has brought you to life with him, he has forgiven us all our sins.

He has overridden the Law, and cancelled every record of the debt that we had to pay; he has done away with it by nailing it to the cross.

Luke 11:1-13

Once Jesus was in a certain place praying, and when he had finished, one of his disciples said, 'Lord, teach us to pray, just as John taught his disciples.' He said to them, 'Say this when you pray: "Father, may your name be held holy, your kingdom come; give us each day our daily bread, and forgive us our sins, for we ourselves forgive each one who is in debt to us. And do not put us to the test." '

He also said to them, 'Suppose one of you has a friend and goes to him in the middle of the night to say, "My friend, lend me three loaves because a friend of mine on his travels has just arrived at my house and I have nothing to offer him"; and the man answers from inside the house, "Do not bother me. The door is bolted now, and my children and I are in bed; I cannot get up to give it to you," I tell you, if the man does not get up and give it him for friendship's sake, persistence will be enough to make him get up and give his friend all he wants.

'So I say to you: Ask, and it will be given to you; search, and you will find; knock, and the door will be opened to you. For the one who asks always receives; the one who searches always finds; the one who knocks will always have the door opened to him. What father among you would hand his son a stone when he asked for bread? Or hand him a snake instead of a fish? Or hand him a scorpion if he asked for an egg? If you then, who are evil, know how to give your children what is good, how much more will the heavenly Father give the Holy Spirit to those who ask him!'

Reflection

Today's readings highlight for us that however we define prayer, it is ultimately about relationship. They show us an uncompromising level of intimacy with God. Abraham dares to bargain with God, and God in return does not hesitate to keep forgiving the people of Sodom for the sake of the just. Jesus too uses examples of great human intimacy, asking help from a friend in the middle of the night, and a little boy asking his Dad for food. The psalmist sums it up so well in saying: You stretch out your hand and save me ... Lord, on the day I called for help, you answered me. We might ask ourselves: how intimate am I in my relationship with God? Do I willingly spend time in prayer? Do I honestly present my needs before God in prayer? Am I humble enough to call for help in my prayer? The great saint, Teresa of Avila, reminds us that 'prayer is ... nothing else than an intimate sharing between friends, frequently spending time alone with the one whose love for us is beyond doubt (*Life*, 8).' May our prayer this week be grounded in this love beyond doubt.

25
JUL MON

St James, Apostle
Feast | Red

2 Corinthians 4:7-15

We are only the earthenware jars that hold this treasure, to make it clear that such an overwhelming power comes from God and not from us. We are in difficulties on all sides, but never cornered; we see no answer to our problems, but never despair; we have been persecuted, but never deserted; knocked down, but never killed; always wherever we may be, we carry with us in our body the death of Jesus, so that the life of Jesus, too, may always be seen in our body. Indeed, while we are still alive, we are consigned to our death every day, for the sake of Jesus, so that in our mortal flesh the life of Jesus, too, may be openly shown. So death is at work in us, but life in you.

But as we have the same spirit of faith that is mentioned in scripture – I believed, and therefore I spoke – we too believe and therefore we too speak, knowing that he who raised the Lord Jesus to life will raise us with Jesus in our turn, and put us by his side and you with us. You see, all this is for your benefit, so that the more grace is multiplied among people, the more thanksgiving there will be, to the glory of God.

Psalm 125. R. v. 5

Those who are sowing in tears will sing when they reap.

Matthew 20:20-28

The mother of the sons of Zebedee came to Jesus with her sons to make a request of him, and bowed low; and he said to her, 'What is it you want?' She said to him, 'Promise that these two sons of mine may sit one at your right hand and the other at your left in your kingdom.' 'You do not know what you are asking' Jesus answered. 'Can you drink the cup that I am going to drink?' They replied, 'We can.' 'Very well' he said 'you shall drink my cup, but as for seats at my right hand and my left, these are not mine to grant; they belong to those to whom they have been allotted by my Father.' When the other ten heard this they were indignant with the two brothers. But Jesus called them to him and said, 'You know that among the pagans the rulers lord it over them, and their great men make their authority felt. This is not to happen among you. No; anyone who wants to be great among you must be your servant, and anyone who wants to be first among you must be your slave, just as the Son of Man came not to be served but to serve, and to give his life as a ransom for many.'

Reflection

It is worth noting that James and John, sons of Zebedee, were with their mother when she put her request to Jesus. They must have wanted those positions too. This mother knew what it was like to sow in tears – imagine her shock and sadness the day Zebedee came home without her sons! Perhaps her request to Jesus is a sign of her wanting to know that her sacrifice had been worthwhile. Jesus is willing to let them join him in all his works, but he tells them that there is more to the kingdom. Greatness is redefined in the kingdom. It encompasses a service that requires the total sacrifice of self. James in his martyrdom was to learn all this. Such kingdom living is not easy. Yet Paul reassures us that if we carry with us the death of Jesus, then his life too will be seen in us.

26
JUL TUE

17th Week in Ordinary Time | Sts Joachim and Anne,
parents of Blessed Virgin Mary, **Memorial** | White

Jeremiah 14:17-22

The Lord said to me: Say this word to the people: 'Tears flood my eyes night and day, unceasingly, since a crushing blow falls on the daughter of my people, a most grievous injury. If I go into the countryside, there lie men killed by the sword; if I go into the city, I see people sick with hunger; even prophets and priests plough the land: they are at their wit's end.'

'Have you rejected Judah altogether? Does your very soul revolt at Zion? Why have you struck us down without hope of cure? We were hoping for peace – no good came of it! For the moment of cure – nothing but terror! Lord, we do confess our wickedness and our fathers' guilt: we have indeed sinned against you. For your name's sake do not reject us, do not dishonour the throne of your glory. Remember us; do not break your covenant with us. Can any of the pagan Nothings make it rain? Can the heavens produce showers? No, it is you, Lord. O our God, you are our hope, since it is you who do all this.'

Psalm 78:8-9, 11, 13. R. v. 9

Rescue us, O Lord, for the glory of your name.

Matthew 13:36-43

Leaving the crowds, Jesus went to the house, and his disciples came to him and said, 'Explain the parable about the darnel in the field to us.' He said in reply, 'The sower of the good seed is the Son of Man. The field is the world; the good seed is the subjects of the kingdom; the darnel, the subjects of the evil one; the enemy who sowed them, the devil; the harvest is the end of the world; the reapers are the angels. Well then, just as the darnel is gathered up and burnt in the fire, so it will be at the end of time. The Son of Man will send his angels and they will gather out of his kingdom all things that provoke offences and all who do evil, and throw them into the blazing furnace, where there will be weeping and grinding of teeth. Then the virtuous will shine like the sun in the kingdom of their Father. Listen, anyone who has ears!'

Reflection

Listen, anyone who has ears! At first this might seem a strange statement. Of course, ears are for hearing. Jesus, however, is calling us to take heed of what has been said and let it have an impact on our life. It is interesting to note that the letters that make up the word 'listen' also make up the word 'silent'. We have to listen carefully is we are to hear the silence of God. Remember St John of the Cross says that God's first language is silence. It is only when we are silent that we can listen for the soft whisperings of God in our heart. What do you need to do today to nurture your listening heart? If you are in the midst of a difficult situation, do you keep pestering God? Or can you take a deep breath, wait in silence, and trust God's covenant love?

27
JUL WED

17th Week in Ordinary Time
Green

Jeremiah 15:10, 16-21

Woe is me, my mother, for you have borne me to be a man of strife and of dissension for all the land. I neither lend nor borrow, yet all of them curse me, and avenge me on my persecutors. Your anger is very slow: do not let me be snatched away. Realise that I suffer insult for your sake. When your words came, I devoured them: your word was my delight and the joy of my heart; for I was called by your name, Lord, God of hosts.

I never took pleasure in sitting in scoffers' company; with your hand on me I held myself aloof, since you had filled me with indignation. Why is my suffering continual, my wound incurable, refusing to be healed? Do you mean to be for me a deceptive stream with inconstant waters? To which the Lord replied,

'If you come back, I will take you back into my service; and if you utter noble, not despicable, thoughts, you shall be as my own mouth. They will come back to you, but you must not go back to them. I will make you a bronze wall fortified against this people.

They will fight against you but they will not overcome you, because I am with you to save you and to deliver you – it is the Lord who speaks. I mean to deliver you from the hands of the wicked and redeem you from the clutches of the violent.'

Psalm 58:2-5, 10-11, 17-18. R. v. 17

O God, you have been a refuge in the day of my distress.

Matthew 13:44-46

Jesus said to the crowds: 'The kingdom of heaven is like treasure hidden in a field which someone has found; he hides it again, goes off happy, sells everything he owns and buys the field.

'Again, the kingdom of heaven is like a merchant looking for fine pearls; when he finds one of great value he goes and sells everything he owns and buys it.'

Reflection

Jesus gives us some enticing images of the kingdom today. They evoke great joy and satisfaction and absolute commitment, selling everything we own in exchange. Jeremiah too, in the midst of his lament, remembers the great delight the word of God brought to him and the joy in his heart, knowing he was called by the name of God. We do know this, yet how often do we let ourselves be overcome by trials and negativity? The Lord says he will take Jeremiah back if he utters noble, not despicable thoughts. He adds, that persecutors will come back but you must not go back to them. Isn't it so with our thoughts? There will always be something that triggers a negative thought, but it we stay with the noble thoughts, the word of God, then joy will remain in our heart and we will find the treasure of the kingdom.

28
JUL THU

17th Week in Ordinary Time
Green

Jeremiah 18:1-6

The word that was addressed to Jeremiah by the Lord, 'Get up and make your way down to the potter's house; there I shall let you hear what I have to say.' So I went down to the potter's house, and there he was, working at the wheel. And whenever the vessel he was making came out wrong, as happens with the clay handled by potters, he would start afresh and work it into another vessel, as potters do. Then this word of the Lord was addressed to me, 'House of Israel, can not I do to you what this potter does? – it is the Lord who speaks. Yes, as the clay is in the potter's hand, so you are in mine, House of Israel.'

Psalm 145:2-6. R. v. 5

He is happy who is helped by Jacob's God.

Matthew 13:47-53

Jesus said to crowds: 'The kingdom of heaven is like a dragnet cast into the sea that brings in a haul of all kinds. When it is full, the fishermen haul it ashore; then, sitting down, they collect the good ones in a basket and throw away those that are no use. This is how it will be at the end of time; the angels will appear and separate the wicked from the just to throw them into the blazing furnace where there will be weeping and grinding of teeth.

'Have you understood all this?' They said, 'Yes.' And he said to them, 'Well then, every scribe who becomes a disciple of the kingdom of heaven is like a householder who brings out from his storeroom things both new and old.' When Jesus had finished these parables he left the district.

Reflection

Are you fearful of making mistakes? Sometimes our fear can turn into an anxiety so great that we are too scared even to begin a task. We make excuses and procrastinate over and over again. Today's well-known story of the potter should be very encouraging for us if we fall into this category. Here is a story of great patience, of nothing being wasted, of making the most of new opportunities, and of untiring hope! It almost makes you want to be a lump of clay so that you can be so lovingly moulded into a beautiful vessel. This makes sense too of the words from the psalm, 'They are happy who are helped by Jacob's God, whose hope is in the Lord their God.' What would it be like to let the God of Love fashion you into a new vessel today?

29 JUL FRI

17th Week in Ordinary Time
Sts Martha, Mary and Lazarus, Memorial | White

1 John 4:7-16

My dear people, let us love one another since love comes from God and everyone who loves is begotten by God and knows God. Anyone who fails to love can never have known God, because God is love. God's love for us was revealed when God sent into the world his only Son so that we could have life through him; this is the love I mean: not our love for God, but God's love for us when he sent his Son to be the sacrifice that takes our sins away. My dear people, since God has loved us so much, we too should love one another. No one has ever seen God; but as long as we love one another God will live in us and his love will be complete in us. We can know that we are living in him and he is living in us because he lets us share his Spirit. We ourselves saw and we testify that the Father sent his Son as saviour of the world. If anyone acknowledges that Jesus is the Son of God, God lives in him, and he in God. We ourselves have known and put our faith in God's love towards ourselves. God is love and anyone who lives in love lives in God, and God lives in him.

Psalm 33:2-11. R. v. 2. Alt. R. v. 9

I will bless the Lord at all times.

John 11:19-27 *(Alternative Gospel: Luke 10:38-42)*

Many Jews had come to Martha and Mary to sympathise with them over their brother. When Martha heard that Jesus had come she went to meet him. Mary remained sitting in the house. Martha said to Jesus, 'If you had been here, my brother would not have died, but I know that, even now, whatever you ask of God, he will grant you.' 'Your brother' said Jesus to her 'will rise again.' Martha said, 'I know he will rise again at the resurrection on the last day.' Jesus said: 'I am the resurrection and the life. If anyone believes in me, even though he dies he will live, and whoever lives and believes in me will never die. Do you believe this?'

'Yes, Lord,' she said 'I believe that you are the Christ, the Son of God, the one who was to come into this world.'

Reflection

We often remember Martha for all her worrying and activity, but she also knew the power of Jesus' relationship with God. Not only did she believe that if Jesus had been there her brother would not have died, but perhaps even more importantly, 'I know that even now, whatever you ask of God, he will grant you.' She then witnesses to the fruits of her deep friendship and knowledge of Jesus as she confidently professes her faith, 'Yes, Lord. I believe that you are the Christ, the Son of God the one who was to come into this world.' Did she and Peter, who also proclaimed his faith in these words, ever compare notes? How different things might be if we remembered her first for her great witness to Jesus as the resurrection and the life, rather than just as the one who was busy with many things.

30 JUL SAT

17th Week in Ordinary Time | Green
or **St Peter Chrysologus,** *bishop, doctor* (Optional, White)

Jeremiah 26:11-16, 24

The priests and prophets addressed the officials and all the people, 'This man deserves to die, since he has prophesied against this city, as you have heard with your own ears.' Jeremiah, however, replied to the people as follows, 'The Lord himself sent me to say all the things you have heard against this Temple and this city. So now amend your behaviour and actions, listen to the voice of the Lord your God: if you do, he will relent and not bring down on you the disaster he has pronounced against you. For myself, I am as you see in your hands. Do whatever you please or think right with me. But be sure of this, that if you put me to death, you will be bringing innocent blood on yourselves, on this city and on its citizens, since the Lord has truly sent me to you to say all these words in your hearing.' The officials and all the people then said to the priests and prophets, 'This man does not deserve to die: he has spoken to us in the name of the Lord our God.' And Jeremiah had a protector in Ahikam son of Shaphan, so he was not handed over to the people to be put to death.

Psalm 68:15-16, 30-31, 33-34. R. cf. v. 14

In your great love, answer me, O God.

Matthew 14:1-12

Herod the tetrarch heard about the reputation of Jesus, and said to his court, 'This is John the Baptist himself; he has risen from the dead, and that is why miraculous powers are at work in him.' Now it was Herod who had arrested John, chained him up and put him in prison because of Herodias, his brother Philip's wife. For John had told him, 'It is against the Law for you to have her.' He had wanted to kill him but was afraid of the people, who regarded John as a prophet. Then, during the celebrations for Herod's birthday, the daughter of Herodias danced before the company, and so delighted Herod that he promised on oath to give her anything she asked. Prompted by her mother she said, 'Give me John the Baptist's head, here, on a dish.' The king was distressed but, thinking of the oaths he had sworn and of his guests, he ordered it to be given her, and sent and had John beheaded in the prison. The head was brought in on a dish and given to the girl who took it to her mother. John's disciples came and took the body and buried it; then they went off to tell Jesus.

Reflection

Here we have two stories. One is of Jeremiah who did not deserve to die because he had spoken in the name of the Lord, and is not handed over to be put to death. The other is of John, who people thought was risen from the dead in the person of Jesus. Jeremiah, of course, is prophesying the destruction of the Temple as Jesus did also. John, on the other hand, always said he was only the forerunner, not fit to even untie the straps of Jesus' sandals. The lives of both Jeremiah and John pointed to something greater – the person of Jesus. We can imagine both of them praying the words of today's psalm. Whatever today brings us, let us pray with them, 'Let your help, O God, lift me up. I will praise God's name with a song; I will glorify God with thanksgiving. Lord, in your great love, answer me.'

31

JUL SUN

EIGHTEENTH SUNDAY IN ORDINARY TIME

Psalter Week 2

Green

Ecclesiastes 1:2; 2:21-23

Vanity of vanities, the Preacher says. Vanity of vanities. All is vanity!

For so it is that a man who has laboured wisely, skilfully and successfully must leave what is his own to someone who has not toiled for it at all. This, too, is vanity and great injustice; for what does he gain for all the toil and strain that he has undergone under the sun? What of all his laborious days, his cares of office, his restless nights? This, too, is vanity.

Psalm 89:3-6, 12-14, 17. R. v. 1

O Lord, you have been our refuge from one generation to the next.

Colossians 3:1-5, 9-11

Since you have been brought back to true life with Christ, you must look for the things that are in heaven, where Christ is, sitting at God's right hand. Let your thoughts be on heavenly things, not on the things that are on the earth, because you have died, and now the life you have is hidden with Christ in God. But when Christ is revealed – and he is your life – you too will be revealed in all your glory with him.

That is why you must kill everything in you that belongs only to earthly life: fornication, impurity, guilty passion, evil desires and especially greed, which is the same thing as worshipping a false god; and never tell each other lies. You have stripped off your old behaviour with your old self, and you have put on a new self which will progress towards true knowledge the more it is renewed in the image of its creator; and in that image there is no room for distinction between Greek and Jew, between the circumcised or the uncircumcised, or between barbarian and Scythian, slave and free man. There is only Christ: he is everything and he is in everything.

Luke 12:13-21

A man in the crowd said to Jesus, 'Master, tell my brother to give me a share of our inheritance.' 'My friend,' he replied 'who appointed me your judge, or the arbitrator of your claims?' Then he said to them, 'Watch, and be on your guard against avarice of any kind, for a man's life is not made secure by what he owns, even when he has more than he needs.'

Then he told them a parable: 'There was once a rich man who, having had a good harvest from his land, thought to himself, "What am I to do? I have not enough room to store my crops." Then he said, "This is what I will do: I will pull down my barns and build bigger ones, and store all my grain and my goods in them, and I will say to my soul: My soul, you have plenty of good things laid by for many years to come; take things easy, eat, drink, have a good time." But God said to him, "Fool! This very night the demand will be made for your soul; and this hoard of yours, whose will it be then?" So it is when a man stores up treasure for himself in place of making himself rich in the sight of God.'

Reflection

We began this month reflecting on the many ways to follow Jesus, with love, mercy and kindness to all. At the end of the month, and indeed past the halfway mark of the year, we can look again at our life and take stock of the treasures we are storing up. Our purpose in life is not to hoard riches in a barn but to keep seeking heavenly, that is, Godly riches, in our heart. Paul's letter to the Colossians puts it clearly. Our life must be a true life in Christ. There is only Christ who is everything and in everything and our task must be to let him be revealed more and more in us each day. When there is greed of any kind in us, and it can slip in very easily, our focus becomes wholly caught up in ourself. That is why Jesus says to watch and be on your guard against avarice of any kind, because this is what takes us away from Jesus, our one true security. There is only one thing we need to fill our hearts with – Love. 'In the morning, fill us with your love; we shall exult and rejoice all our days.'

01
AUG MON

18th Week in Ordinary Time
St Alphonsus Liguori, *bishop, doctor,* **Memorial** | White

Jeremiah 28:1-17

At the beginning of the reign of Zedekiah king of Judah in the fifth month of the fourth year, the prophet Hananiah son of Azzur, a Gibeonite, spoke as follows to Jeremiah in the Temple of the Lord in the presence of the priests and of all the people. ... *(Please see the Appendix B-18).*

Psalm 118:29, 43, 79-80, 95, 102. R. v. 68

Lord, teach me your statutes.

Matthew 14:13-21

When Jesus received the news of John the Baptist's death he withdrew by boat to a lonely place where they could be by themselves. But the people heard of this and, leaving the towns, went after him on foot. So as he stepped ashore he saw a large crowd; and he took pity on them and healed their sick. When evening came, the disciples went to him and said, 'This is a lonely place, and the time has slipped by; so send the people away, and they can go to the villages to buy themselves some food.' Jesus replied, 'There is no need for them to go: give them something to eat yourselves.' But they answered, 'All we have with us is five loaves and two fish.' 'Bring them here to me,' he said. He gave orders that the people were to sit down on the grass; then he took the five loaves and the two fish, raised his eyes to heaven and said the blessing. And breaking the loaves he handed them to his disciples who gave them to the crowds. They all ate as much as they wanted, and they collected the scraps remaining, twelve baskets full. Those who ate numbered about five thousand men, to say nothing of women and children.

Reflection

The resounding message of Jesus in the Gospels is, 'come to me all of you, follow me'. So, it is somewhat strange to hear the disciples say to Jesus in today's Gospel, 'send the people away, so they can buy some food.' The disciples' intention was probably good, but their suggestion was never going to be taken up by Jesus. 'There is no need for them to go away', he immediately replies, and he adds the challenging words, 'give them something to eat yourselves'. Sometimes in life we can find ourselves in a lonely or deserted place like the people in today's Gospel. Our every inclination may be to flee to a more comfortable place where our needs can be met. Perhaps this is possible, perhaps it is not. Let us not forget, however, that Jesus is with us in that lonely place and that if we remain with him, we will find nourishment beyond all our expectations, a nourishment we can never hope to find in the more comfortable places of our lives.

02
AUG TUE

18th Week in Ordinary Time | Green
or **St Eusebius of Vercelli,** *bishop* (Optional, White)
or **St Peter Julian Eymard,** *priest* (Optional, White)

Jeremiah 30:1-2, 12-15, 18-22

The word addressed to Jeremiah by the Lord: The Lord, the God of Israel says this: Write all the words I have spoken to you in a book. ... *(Please see the Appendix B-19).*

Psalm 101:16-21, 29, 22-23. R. v. 17

The Lord shall build up Zion again and appear in all his glory.

Matthew 14:22-36

When the crowds had eaten their fill Jesus made the disciples get into the boat and go on ahead to the other side while he would send the crowds away. After sending the crowds away he went up into the hills by himself to pray. When evening came, he was there alone, while the boat, by now far out on the lake, was battling with a heavy sea, for there was a head-wind. In the fourth watch of the night he went towards them, walking on the lake, and when the disciples saw him walking on the lake they were terrified.

'It is a ghost' they said, and cried out in fear. But at once Jesus called out to them, saying, 'Courage! It is I! Do not be afraid.' It was Peter who answered. 'Lord,' he said 'if it is you, tell me to come to you across the water.' 'Come' said Jesus. Then Peter got out of the boat and started walking towards Jesus across the water, but as soon as he felt the force of the wind, he took fright and began to sink. 'Lord! Save me!' he cried. Jesus put out his hand at once and held him. 'Man of little faith,' he said 'why did you doubt?' And as they got into the boat the wind dropped. The men in the boat bowed down before him and said, 'Truly, you are the Son of God.'

Having made the crossing, they came to land at Gennesaret. When the local people recognised him they spread the news through the whole neighbourhood and took all that were sick to him, begging him just to let them touch the fringe of his cloak. And all those who touched it were completely cured.

Reflection

For some of you, today's first reading is not simply describing the experience of the Israelites during the time of exile but your own present experience. Perhaps you have learned in recent times that 'your wound is incurable, your injury past healing, that there is no medicine to make you well again.' The wound may refer to a terminal illness or to an emotional trauma from which no recovery seems possible. In this most wretched time of your life, Jesus will come to you, as he came to the disciples trapped on the lake during a dreadful storm. He will say to you, 'courage, it is I, do not be afraid.' What is important is to keep your gaze on him. Don't look at what is engulfing you but look at him, reach out and grab his outstretched hand. The terminal situation may not go away, but hopefully the inner gale will quieten, peace will return, and you will be able to face the future with hope. And know that many readers of *God's Word* are praying for you today.

03
AUG WED

18th Week in Ordinary Time
St Dominic, *priest,* **Memorial** | White

Jeremiah 31:1-7

I will be the God of all the clans of Israel – it is the Lord who speaks – they shall be my people.

The Lord says this: They have found pardon in the wilderness, those who have survived the sword. Israel is marching to his rest. The Lord has appeared to him from afar: I have loved you with an everlasting love, so I am constant in my affection for you. I build you once more; you shall be rebuilt, virgin of Israel. Adorned once more, and with your tambourines, you will go out dancing gaily. You will plant vineyards once more on the mountains of Samaria (the planters have done their planting: they will gather the fruit). Yes, a day will come when the watchmen shout on the mountains of Ephraim, 'Up! Let us go up to Zion, to the Lord our God!' For the Lord says this: Shout with joy for Jacob! Hail the chief of nations! Proclaim! Praise! Shout: 'The Lord has saved his people, the remnant of Israel!'

Jeremiah 31:10-13. R. cf. v. 10

The Lord will guard us, as a shepherd guards his flock.

Matthew 15:21-28

Jesus left Gennesaret and withdrew to the region of Tyre and Sidon. Then out came a Canaanite woman from that district and started shouting, 'Sir, Son of David, take pity on me. My daughter is tormented by a devil.' But he answered her not a word. And his disciples went and pleaded with him. 'Give her what she wants,' they said 'because she is shouting after us.' He said in reply, 'I was sent only to the lost sheep of the House of Israel.' But the woman had come up and was kneeling at his feet. 'Lord,' she said 'help me.' He replied, 'It is not fair to take the children's food and throw it to the house-dogs.' She retorted, 'Ah yes, sir; but even house-dogs can eat the scraps that fall from their master's table.' Then Jesus answered her, 'Woman, you have great faith. Let your wish be granted.' And from that moment her daughter was well again.

Reflection

Have you ever been asked to do something and said in reply 'I'm sorry but this is not my job; you have to ask someone else!' But the person replies that there is no-one else. We need you to help us. You may perhaps grumble at the unfairness of the situation and pout that everything gets left to you, but you know you must do it. And remarkably, when you do, you find you are rewarded in unexpected ways – you learn something, you enjoy the task, you feel better about yourself, you see goodness and faith in others. In today's Gospel, the Canaanite woman refuses to accept Jesus' retort that healing her daughter was not his job. In her persistence she reveals her great love for her daughter, for whom she will bear any insult, and her faith in Jesus' power to heal. In response Jesus grants her prayer and all present are rewarded as they witness the healing of Jesus and the woman's remarkable faith and love for her daughter.

18th Week in Ordinary Time
St John Vianney, *priest,* **Memorial** | White

04
AUG THU

Jeremiah 31:31-34

See, the days are coming – it is the Lord who speaks – when I will make a new covenant with the House of Israel and the House of Judah, but not a covenant like the one I made with their ancestors on the day I took them by the hand to bring them out of the land of Egypt. They broke that covenant of mine, so I had to show them who was master. It is the Lord who speaks. No, this is the covenant I will make with the House of Israel when those days arrive – it is the Lord who speaks. Deep within them I will plant my Law, writing it on their hearts. Then I will be their God and they shall be my people. There will be no further need for neighbour to try to teach neighbour, or brother to say to brother, 'Learn to know the Lord!' No, they will all know me, the least no less than the greatest – it is the Lord who speaks – since I will forgive their iniquity and never call their sin to mind.

Psalm 50:12-15, 18-19. R. v. 12

A pure heart create for me, O God.

Matthew 16:13-23

When Jesus came to the region of Caesarea Philippi he put this question to his disciples, 'Who do people say the Son of Man is?' And they said, 'Some say he is John the Baptist, some Elijah, and others Jeremiah or one of the prophets.' 'But you,' he said 'who do you say I am?' Then Simon Peter spoke up, 'You are the Christ,' he said 'the Son of the living God.' Jesus replied, 'Simon son of Jonah, you are a happy man! Because it was not flesh and blood that revealed this to you but my Father in heaven. So I now say to you: You are Peter and on this rock I will build my Church. And the gates of the underworld can never hold out against it. I will give you the keys of the kingdom of heaven; whatever you bind on earth shall be considered bound in heaven; whatever you loose on earth shall be considered loosed in heaven.' Then he gave the disciples strict orders not to tell anyone that he was the Christ. From that time Jesus began to make it clear to his disciples that he was destined to go to Jerusalem and suffer grievously at the hands of the elders and chief priests and scribes, to be put to death and to be raised up on the third day. Then, taking him aside, Peter started to remonstrate with him. 'Heaven preserve you, Lord,' he said 'this must not happen to you.' But he turned and said to Peter, 'Get behind me, Satan! You are an obstacle in my path, because the way you think is not God's way but man's.'

Reflection: On two occasions in today's Gospel Jesus calls Peter a rock, once to commend him and once to criticise him. Responding to Peter's wonderful profession of faith, Jesus says, 'You are Peter and on this rock, I will build my Church.' Later, in response to Peter's rejection of Jesus' words, Jesus says to him, 'get behind me, Satan, you are an obstacle [a stumbling block, a rock] in my path.' The stability and immoveable nature of rock is wonderful if we need a foundation on which to build a house (or a church); but those same qualities in another situation are negatives. A rock blocking a path can prevent further movement. We need the humility to appreciate that our greatest personal strengths in some situations are, in other situations, our greatest liabilities. There are moments when we need to step up and other moments when we need to step back and let others take the lead, to ensure that we don't become an obstacle in the path of healing and growth.

05

AUG FRI

18th Week in Ordinary Time | Green or
Dedic. of Basilica of St Mary Major (Optional, White)

Nahum 2:1, 3; 3:1-3, 6-7

See, over the mountains the messenger hurries! 'Peace!' he proclaims. Judah, celebrate your feasts, carry out your vows, for Belial will never pass through you again; he is utterly annihilated. Yes, the Lord is restoring the vineyard of Jacob and the vineyard of Israel. For the plunderers had plundered them, they had broken off their branches. Woe to the city soaked in blood, full of lies, stuffed with booty, whose plunderings know no end! The crack of the whip! The rumble of wheels! Galloping horse, jolting chariot, charging cavalry, flash of swords, gleam of spears ... a mass of wounded, hosts of dead, countless corpses; they stumble over the dead. I am going to pelt you with filth, shame you, make you a public show. And all who look on you will turn their backs on you and say, 'Nineveh is a ruin.' Could anyone pity her? Where can I find anyone to comfort her?

Deuteronomy 32:35-36, 39, 41. R. v. 39

It is the Lord who deals death and life.

Matthew 16:24-28

Jesus said to his disciples, 'If anyone wants to be a follower of mine, let him renounce himself and take up his cross and follow me. For anyone who wants to save his life will lose it; but anyone who loses his life for my sake will find it. What, then, will a man gain if he wins the whole world and ruins his life? Or what has a man to offer in exchange for his life?

'For the Son of Man is going to come in the glory of his Father with his angels, and, when he does, he will reward each one according to his behaviour. I tell you solemnly, there are some of these standing here who will not taste death before they see the Son of Man coming with his kingdom.'

Reflection

I once read that the Greek word that we usually translate as 'take up' can also be translated as 'embrace'. Jesus is inviting us not just to take up our cross and carry it wearily on our backs where it weighs us down and bends us over. He wants us to embrace our cross, to hug it, to carry it close to our heart, to befriend it. Why? Because somehow it is through the crosses in our lives that we grow as human beings, that we become more compassionate people, and more deeply aware of our need for God. Ita Buttrose once wrote that 'Mary MacKillop has been declared a Saint, but who knows, had she not made a conscious decision to trust in her God-given journey and to love the obstacles with the same fervour as she loved the straight roads, we may not even be hearing about her now. '

Transfiguration of the Lord
Feast | White

06
AUG SAT

Daniel 7:9-10, 13-14
(Please see the Appendix B-19).

Psalm 96:1-2, 5-6, 9. R. vv. 1, 9
The Lord is king, most high above all the earth.

2 Peter 1:16-19
It was not any cleverly invented myths that we were repeating when we brought you the knowledge of the power and the coming of our Lord Jesus Christ; we had seen his majesty for ourselves. He was honoured and glorified by God the Father, when the Sublime Glory itself spoke to him and said, 'This is my Son, the Beloved; he enjoys my favour.' We heard this ourselves, spoken from heaven, when we were with him on the holy mountain. So we have confirmation of what was said in prophecies; and you will be right to depend on prophecy and take it as a lamp for lighting a way through the dark until the dawn comes and the morning star rises in your minds.

Luke 9:28-36
Jesus took with him Peter and John and James and went up the mountain to pray. As he prayed, the aspect of his face was changed and his clothing became brilliant as lightning. Suddenly there were two men there talking to him; they were Moses and Elijah appearing in glory, and they were speaking of his passing which he was to accomplish in Jerusalem. Peter and his companions were heavy with sleep, but they kept awake and saw his glory and the two men standing with him. As these were leaving him, Peter said to Jesus, 'Master, it is wonderful for us to be here; so let us make three tents, one for you, one for Moses and one for Elijah.' – He did not know what he was saying. As he spoke, a cloud came and covered them with shadow; and when they went into the cloud the disciples were afraid. And a voice came from the cloud, saying, 'This is my son, the Chosen One. Listen to him.' And after the voice had spoken, Jesus was found alone. The disciples kept silence and, at that time, told no one what they had seen.

Reflection
Luke begins his account of the Transfiguration with the words: 'Jesus took with him Peter, John and James and went up the mountain to pray.' Later Jesus will take these same three disciples with him into the garden of Gethsemane to pray just before his arrest. In the Transfiguration episode they saw him in his glory as the Son of God. His face shone like the sun and his clothes became brilliant as lightning; in the garden of Gethsemane they will see him in the fullness of his humanity as in agony his sweat becomes like great drops of blood and he prays to the Father to let this cup pass him by. The two events are linked: He revealed his glory in the Transfiguration to strengthen his disciples for the scandal of the cross. May the transfiguration moments in our life – moments of grace when we catch a glimpse of the sacred in the ordinary – strengthen us for the 'agony' moments we all experience, enabling us to pray to the Father with Jesus, 'not my will, but thine be done.'

07

AUG SUN

NINETEENTH SUNDAY IN ORDINARY TIME

Psalter Week 3

Green

Wisdom 18:6-9

That night had been foretold to our ancestors, so that, once they saw what kind of oaths they had put their trust in they would joyfully take courage.

This was the expectation of your people, the saving of the virtuous and the ruin of their enemies; for by the same act with which you took vengeance on our foes you made us glorious by calling us to you.

The devout children of worthy men offered sacrifice in secret and this divine pact they struck with one accord: that the saints would share the same blessings and dangers alike; and forthwith they had begun to chant the hymns of the fathers.

Psalm 32:1, 12, 18-20, 22. R. v. 12

Happy are the people the Lord has chosen as his own.

Hebrews 11:1-2, 8-12 *(Longer form 11:1-2, 8-19)*

Only faith can guarantee the blessings that we hope for, or prove the existence of the realities that at present remain unseen. It was for faith that our ancestors were commended.

It was by faith that Abraham obeyed the call to set out for a country that was the inheritance given to him and his descendants, and that he set out without knowing where he was going. By faith he arrived, as a foreigner, in the Promised Land, and lived there as if in a strange country, with Isaac and Jacob, who were heirs with him of the same promise. They lived there in tents while he looked forward to a city founded, designed and built by God.

It was equally by faith that Sarah, in spite of being past the age, was made able to conceive, because she believed that he who had made the promise would be faithful to it. Because of this, there came from one man, and one who was already as good as dead himself, more descendants than could be counted, as many as the stars of heaven or the grains of sand on the seashore.

Luke 12:32-48 *(Shorter form 12:35-40)*

Jesus said to his disciples: 'There is no need to be afraid, little flock, for it has pleased your Father to give you the kingdom. 'Sell your possessions and give alms. Get yourselves purses that do not wear out, treasure that will not fail you, in heaven where no thief can reach it and no moth destroy it. For where your treasure is, there will your heart be also.

'See that you are dressed for action and have your lamps lit. Be like men waiting for their master to return from the wedding feast, ready to open the door as soon as he comes and knocks. Happy those servants whom the master finds awake when he comes. I tell you solemnly, he will put on an apron, sit them down at table and wait on them. It may be in the second watch he comes, or in the third, but happy those servants if he finds them ready. You may be quite sure of this, that if the householder had known at what hour the burglar would come, he would not have let anyone break through the wall of his house. You too must stand ready, because the Son of Man is coming at an hour you do not expect.'

Peter said, 'Lord, do you mean this parable for us, or for everyone?' The Lord replied, 'What sort of steward, then, is faithful and wise enough for the master to place him over his household to give them their allowance of food at the proper time? Happy that servant if his master's arrival finds him at this employment. I tell you truly, he will place him over everything he owns. But as for the servant who says to himself, "My master is taking his time coming", and sets about beating the menservants and the maids, and eating and drinking and getting drunk, his master will come on a day he does not expect and at an hour he does not know. The master will cut him off and send him to the same fate as the unfaithful.

'The servant who knows what his master wants, but has not even started to carry out those wishes, will receive very many strokes of the lash. The one who did not know, but deserves to be beaten for what he has done, will receive fewer strokes. When a man has had a great deal given him, a great deal will be demanded of him; when a man has had a great deal given him on trust, even more will be expected of him.'

Reflection

We experience many things that can make us fearful – pandemics, loss of employment, violence, financial and relationship stresses, and so on. In the face of such challenges it is easy to develop a self-protective stance towards life, to do what we can to be in control of our situation, to protect ourselves from dangers. Yet, the simple fact is that we can never have complete control over our situation. We always remain vulnerable to unexpected difficulties. Ultimately the uncertainties of life, unpleasant as they can be, remind us that we are on this earth as pilgrims, journeying towards a better homeland, our heavenly homeland. If, like Abraham and Sarah, we can put our faith in God's promises, we will find comfort in the words of Jesus in today's Gospel, 'There is no need to be afraid, little flock, for it has pleased your Father to give you the kingdom.' We will be generous with what we have, not focused on our own security but on the well-being of our brothers and sisters. We will hold our possessions lightly.

08
AUG MON

Saint Dominic, Priest
| White

Ezekiel 1:2-5,24-28

On the fifth of the month – it was the fifth year of exile for King Jehoiachin – the word of the Lord was addressed to the priest Ezekiel son of Buzi, in the land of the Chaldaeans, on the bank of the river Chebar. There the hand of the Lord came on me. I looked; a stormy wind blew from the north, a great cloud with light around it, a fire from which flashes of lightning darted, and in the centre a sheen like bronze at the heart of the fire. In the centre I saw what seemed four animals. They looked like this. They were of human form. I heard the noise of their wings as they moved; it sounded like rushing water, like the voice of Shaddai, a noise like a storm, like the noise of a camp; when they halted, they folded their wings, and there was a noise. Above the vault over their heads was something that looked like a sapphire; it was shaped like a throne and high up on this throne was a being that looked like a man. I saw him shine like bronze, and close to and all around him from what seemed his loins upwards was what looked like fire; and from what seemed his loins downwards I saw what looked like fire, and a light all round like a bow in the clouds on rainy days; that is how the surrounding light appeared. It was something that looked like the glory of the Lord. I looked, and prostrated myself.

Psalm 148:1-2,11-14

Your glory fills all heaven and earth.

Matthew 17:22-27

One day when they were together in Galilee, Jesus said to his disciples, 'The Son of Man is going to be handed over into the power of men; they will put him to death, and on the third day he will be raised to life again.' And a great sadness came over them.

When they reached Capernaum, the collectors of the half-shekel came to Peter and said, 'Does your master not pay the half-shekel?' 'Oh yes' he replied, and went into the house. But before he could speak, Jesus said, 'Simon, what is your opinion? From whom do the kings of the earth take toll or tribute? From their sons or from foreigners?' And when he replied, 'From foreigners', Jesus said, 'Well then, the sons are exempt. However, so as not to offend these people, go to the lake and cast a hook; take the first fish that bites, open its mouth and there you will find a shekel; take it and give it to them for me and for you.'

Reflection

Jesus warns the disciples once more that he will be delivered to his foes. He will die, but he will be raised to life on the third day. Even after knowing what was in store for him, Jesus encourages Peter to pay the Temple tax when the collectors approach him. He tells Peter to go fishing, and in the mouth of the first fish he catches, he will find a silver coin sufficient to pay their Temple taxes. Even when he disagreed with those in positions of authority, civil or religious, Jesus always respected them. In the Gospel of Mark, Jesus says, 'Give to the emperor the things that are the emperor's and to God the things that are God's' (Mark 12:17).

09
AUG TUE

19th Week in Ordinary Time | Green or **St Theresa Benedicta of the Cross,** *virgin, martyr***, Feast**, | Red

Hosea 2:16,17,21-22

The Lord says this:

I am going to lead her out into the wilderness and speak to her heart. There she will respond to me as she did when she was young, as she did when she came out of the land of Egypt. I will betroth you to myself for ever, betroth you with integrity and justice, with tenderness and love; I will betroth you to myself with faithfulness, and you will come to know the Lord.

Psalm 44:11-12,14-17

Listen, O daughter, give ear to my words.

Matthew 25:1-13

Jesus told this parable to his disciples: 'The kingdom of heaven will be like this: Ten bridesmaids took their lamps and went to meet the bridegroom. Five of them were foolish and five were sensible: the foolish ones did take their lamps, but they brought no oil, whereas the sensible ones took flasks of oil as well as their lamps. The bridegroom was late, and they all grew drowsy and fell asleep. But at midnight there was a cry, "The bridegroom is here! Go out and meet him." At this, all those bridesmaids woke up and trimmed their lamps, and the foolish ones said to the sensible ones, "Give us some of your oil: our lamps are going out." But they replied, "There may not be enough for us and for you; you had better go to those who sell it and buy some for yourselves." They had gone off to buy it when the bridegroom arrived. Those who were ready went in with him to the wedding hall and the door was closed. The other bridesmaids arrived later. "Lord, Lord," they said "open the door for us." But he replied, "I tell you solemnly, I do not know you." So stay awake, because you do not know either the day or the hour.'

Reflection

Like the five wise bridesmaids in the Gospel parable, let us keep the fire of holiness burning bright in our lives. It would be foolish to let this fire burn out for lack of prayer. Because, when the fire of God's love is quenched by our carelessness, then the fire of lust and immorality will arise and destroy us.

10
AUG WED

St Lawrence, *deacon, martyr*
Feast | Red

2 Corinthians 9:6-10

Thin sowing means thin reaping; the more you sow, the more you reap. Each one should give what he has decided in his own mind, not grudgingly or because he is made to, for God loves a cheerful giver. And there is no limit to the blessings which God can send you – he will make sure that you will always have all you need for yourselves in every possible circumstance, and still have something to spare for all sorts of good works. As scripture says: He was free in almsgiving, and gave to the poor: his good deeds will never be forgotten.

The one who provides seed for the sower and bread for food will provide you with all the seed you want and make the harvest of your good deeds a larger one.

Psalm 111:1-2. 5-9. R. v. 5

Happy the man who takes pity and lends.

John 12:24-26

Jesus said to his disciples: 'I tell you, most solemnly, unless a wheat grain falls on the ground and dies, it remains only a single grain; but if it dies, it yields a rich harvest. Anyone who loves his life loses it; anyone who hates his life in this world will keep it for the eternal life. If a man serves me, he must follow me, wherever I am, my servant will be there too. If anyone serves me, my Father will honour him.'

Reflection

St Lawrence was a deacon in Rome in the third century, when Christians were being persecuted under the Emperor, Valerian. He was responsible for the material goods of the community and the distribution of alms to the poor. The Prefect of Rome demanded that Lawrence hand over all the treasures of the Church to the Roman authorities. Lawrence happily agreed and on the day of the handover, he brought with him all the poor and sick of the Christian community, and said, 'here is the treasure of the Church'. How true are his words! The Church's riches can never be counted in gold or silver, but in the faith-filled lives of those who willingly share in the cross of Christ. Not surprisingly, the Prefect was unimpressed by Lawrence's gesture, and ordered him to be burned over hot coals on a kind of grille. After experiencing this tortuous treatment for some time, Lawrence said, 'I'm well done on this side. Turn me over!' He epitomises the 'cheerful giver' that Paul praises in today's first reading.

19th Week in Ordinary Time
St Clare, *virgin,* **Memorial** | White

11
AUG THU

Ezekiel 12:1-12

(Please see the Appendix B-20)

Psalm 77:56-59, 61-62. R. cf. v. 7

Never forget the deeds of the Lord.

Matthew 18:21–19:1

Peter went up to Jesus and said, 'Lord, how often must I forgive my brother if he wrongs me? As often as seven times?' Jesus answered, 'Not seven, I tell you, but seventy-seven times.

'And so the kingdom of heaven may be compared to a king who decided to settle his accounts with his servants. When the reckoning began, they brought him a man who owed ten thousand talents; but he had no means of paying, so his master gave orders that he should be sold, together with his wife and children and all his possessions, to meet the debt. At this, the servant threw himself down at his master's feet. "Give me time" he said "and I will pay the whole sum." And the servant's master felt so sorry for him that he let him go and cancelled the debt. Now as this servant went out, he happened to meet a fellow servant who owed him one hundred denarii; and he seized him by the throat and began to throttle him. "Pay what you owe me" he said. His fellow servant fell at his feet and implored him, saying, "Give me time and I will pay you." But the other would not agree; on the contrary, he had him thrown into prison till he should pay the debt. His fellow servants were deeply distressed when they saw what had happened, and they went to their master and reported the whole affair to him. Then the master sent for him. "You wicked servant," he said. "I cancelled all that debt of yours when you appealed to me. Were you not bound, then, to have pity on your fellow servant just as I had pity on you?" And in his anger the master handed him over to the torturers till he should pay all his debt. And that is how my heavenly Father will deal with you unless you each forgive your brother from your heart.' Jesus had now finished what he wanted to say, and he left Galilee and came into the part of Judaea which is on the far side of the Jordan.

Reflection

There is much we can say about forgiveness, as we reflect on Jesus' teaching in today's Gospel. Something that is not always mentioned is that human beings generally are very forgiving. And thank goodness for this. We forgive 99 per cent of the wrongs done to us either individually or as communities. But at times we encounter the 1 per cent that we find truly unforgiveable and we learn the truth of the saying that 'to err is human, to forgive divine.' I think it is helpful to see forgiveness as a process, rather than something accomplished in an instant. Sometimes we must explore with someone, 'what steps do we have to take to bring healing and forgiveness to this situation?' These steps are never easy but always worth the effort. Forgiveness cannot change the past, but it makes a future possible.

12
AUG FRI

19th Week In Ordinary Time | Green or **St Jane Frances De Chantal,** *religious* (Optional, White)

Ezekiel 16:59-63 *(Alternative Reading 16:1-15, 60-63)*

'The Lord says this: "Jerusalem, I will treat you as you deserve, you who have despised your oath even to the extent of breaking a covenant, but I will remember the covenant that I made with you when you were a girl, and I will conclude a covenant with you that shall last for ever. And you for your part will remember your past behaviour and be covered with shame when I take your elder and younger sisters and make them your daughters, although this was not included in this covenant. I am going to renew my covenant with you; and you will learn that I am the Lord, and so remember and be covered with shame, and in your confusion be reduced to silence, when I have pardoned you for all that you have done – it is the Lord who speaks."'

Isaiah 12:2-6. R. v. 1

Your anger has passed, O Lord, and you give me comfort.

Matthew 19:3-12

Some Pharisees approached Jesus, and to test him they said, 'Is it against the Law for a man to divorce his wife on any pretext whatever?' He answered, 'Have you not read that the creator from the beginning made them male and female and that he said: This is why a man must leave father and mother, and cling to his wife, and the two become one body? They are no longer two, therefore, but one body. So then, what God has united, man must not divide.'

They said to him, 'Then why did Moses command that a writ of dismissal should be given in cases of divorce?' 'It was because you were so unteachable' he said 'that Moses allowed you to divorce your wives, but it was not like this from the beginning. Now I say this to you: the man who divorces his wife – I am not speaking of fornication – and marries another, is guilty of adultery.' The disciples said to him, 'If that is how things are between husband and wife, it is not advisable to marry.' But he replied, 'It is not everyone who can accept what I have said, but only those to whom it is granted. There are eunuchs born that way from their mother's womb, there are eunuchs made so by men and there are eunuchs who have made themselves that way for the sake of the kingdom of heaven. Let anyone accept this who can.'

Reflection

In today's Gospel Jesus gives to the relationship of husband and wife a position of the highest dignity, something it didn't enjoy in his day and doesn't always enjoy today. He also affirms the equality of husband and wife in a marriage – the two become one body. In Jewish Law the husband could divorce his wife but the wife couldn't divorce her husband. Jesus takes this 'privilege' away from the husband. Today we pray for all married couples as they journey together through the joys and struggles of married life. We also pray for those who have experienced the pain of a marriage breakdown. No one wants their marriage to break down but at times it happens. May they always know the infinte love of God for them in their journey to recovery and wholeness.

19th Week in Ordinary Time | Green or **Sts Pontian,** *pope,* **and Hippolytus,** *priest, martyrs* (Optional, Red)

13
AUG SAT

Ezekiel 18:1-10, 13, 30-32

The word of the Lord was addressed to me as follows, 'Why do you keep repeating this proverb in the land of Israel: The fathers have eaten unripe grapes; and the children's teeth are set on edge? 'As I live – it is the Lord who speaks – there will no longer be any reason to repeat this proverb in Israel. See now: all life belongs to me; the father's life and the son's life, both alike belong to me. The man who has sinned, he is the one who shall die.

'The upright man is law-abiding and honest; he does not eat on the mountains or raise his eyes to the idols of the House of Israel, does not seduce his neighbour's wife or sleep with a woman during her periods. He oppresses no one, returns pledges, never steals, gives his own bread to the hungry, his clothes to the naked. He never charges usury on loans, takes no interest, abstains from evil, gives honest judgement between man and man, keeps my laws and sincerely respects my observances – such a man is truly upright. It is the Lord who speaks.

'But if anyone has a son prone to violence and bloodshed, who commits one of these misdeeds, then this son shall certainly not live; having committed all these appalling crimes he will have to die, and his blood be on his own head. 'House of Israel, in future I mean to judge each of you by what he does – it is the Lord who speaks. Repent, renounce all your sins, avoid all occasions of sin! Shake off all the sins you have committed against me, and make yourselves a new heart and a new spirit! Why are you so anxious to die, House of Israel? I take no pleasure in the death of anyone – it is the Lord who speaks. Repent and live!'

Psalm 50:12-15, 18-19. R. v. 12

A pure heart create for me, O God.

Matthew 19:13-15

People brought little children to Jesus, for him to lay his hands on them and say a prayer. The disciples turned them away, but Jesus said, 'Let the little children alone, and do not stop them coming to me; for it is to such as these that the kingdom of heaven belongs.' Then he laid his hands on them and went on his way.

Reflection

Parents have many anxieties concerning their children. They naturally want the best for them and sometimes worry that this is not possible for financial reasons. Today's Gospel reminds us that the most wonderful thing parents can do for their children is to bring them to Jesus for his blessing. And this costs nothing! Jesus always has time for children. 'Let the children come to me', he says. Let us also remember that we are all God's children, whether we are 6-years-old, or 16 or 60! Today you may like to go to Jesus for a blessing. In quiet, allow him to lay his hands on you and bless you.

14
AUG SUN

TWENTIETH SUNDAY IN ORDINARY TIME
– Ireland
Psalter Week 4

Green

THE ASSUMPTION OF THE BLESSED VIRGIN MARY
– England, Wales and Scotland

see Monday,

August 15

Jeremiah 38:4-6, 8-10

The king's leading men spoke to the king. 'Let Jeremiah be put to death: he is unquestionably disheartening the remaining soldiers in the city, and all the people too, by talking like this. The fellow does not have the welfare of this people at heart so much as its ruin.' 'He is in your hands as you know,' King Zedekiah answered 'for the king is powerless against you.' So they took Jeremiah and threw him into the well of Prince Malchiah in the Court of the Guard, letting him down with ropes. There was no water in the well, only mud, and into the mud Jeremiah sank.

Ebed-melech came out from the palace and spoke to the king, 'My lord king,' he said 'these men have done a wicked thing by treating the prophet Jeremiah like this: they have thrown him into the well where he will die.' At this the king gave Ebed-melech the Cushite the following order: 'Take three men with you from here and pull Jeremiah out of the well before he dies.'

Psalm 39:2-4, 18. R. v. 14

Lord, come to my aid!

Hebrews 12:1-4

With so many witnesses in a great cloud on every side of us, we too, then, should throw off everything that hinders us, especially the sin that clings so easily, and keep running steadily in the race we have started. Let us not lose sight of Jesus, who leads us in our faith and brings it to perfection: for the sake of the joy which was still in the future, he endured the cross, disregarding the shamefulness of it, and from now on has taken his place at the right of God's throne. Think of the way he stood such opposition from sinners and then you will not give up for want of courage. In the fight against sin, you have not yet had to keep fighting to the point of death.

Luke 12:49-53

Jesus said to his disciples: 'I have come to bring fire to the earth, and how I wish it were blazing already! There is a baptism I must still receive, and how great is my distress till it is over!

'Do you suppose that I am here to bring peace on earth? No, I tell you, but rather division. For from now on a household of five will be divided: three against two and two against three; the father divided against the son, son against father, mother against daughter, daughter against mother, mother-in-law against daughter-in-law, daughter-in-law against mother-in-law.'

Reflection

Today's Gospel passage would have been a source of great consolation to the community for which Luke was writing his Gospel. You might wonder how Jesus' words that he has come to bring not peace but rather division to the earth, and that there will be conflicts within families, could be a source of consolation for Luke's community? Well, this was a community that was experiencing conflicts and family divisions, and its members were wondering if they were doing something wrong. Surely everything in the Christian community should be lovely and full of peace and joy. But Luke is saying, 'no, it is normal for Christian communities to experience conflicts and struggles.' Jesus saved us by walking the way of the cross, and for us also, there is no other way to glory than the way of the cross. Be strong, be faithful, that is what is most important. The author of the Letter to the Hebrews makes a similar point: in the fight against sin, we must keep fighting to the point of death. We should be sorry for our failures but not discouraged by them. We must humbly acknowledge that the battle against sin is a lifelong battle.

15
AUG MON

THE ASSUMPTION OF THE BLESSED VIRGIN MARY (MASS DURING THE DAY), **Solemnity** – Ireland

White

Monday of Twentieth Week in Ordinary Time
– England, Wales and Scotland
see Appendix A-20

Apocalypse 11:19; 12:1-6, 10
(Please see the Appendix B-20)

Psalm 44:10-12, 16. R. v. 10
On your right stands the queen, in garments of gold.

1 Corinthians 15:20-26
(Please see the Appendix B-20)

Luke 1:39-56
Mary set out at that time and went as quickly as she could to a town in the hill country of Judah. She went into Zechariah's house and greeted Elizabeth. Now as soon as Elizabeth heard Mary's greeting, the child leapt in her womb and Elizabeth was filled with the Holy Spirit. She gave a loud cry and said, 'Of all women you are the most blessed, and blessed is the fruit of your womb. Why should I be honoured with a visit from the mother of my Lord? For the moment your greeting reached my ears, the child in my womb leapt for joy. Yes, blessed is she who believed that the promise made her by the Lord would be fulfilled.'

And Mary said: 'My soul proclaims the greatness of the Lord and my spirit exults in God my saviour; because he has looked upon his lowly handmaid. Yes, from this day forward all generations will call me blessed, for the Almighty has done great things for me. Holy is his name, and his mercy reaches from age to age for those who fear him. He has shown the power of his arm, he has routed the proud of heart. He has pulled down princes from their thrones and exalted the lowly. The hungry he has filled with good things, the rich sent empty away. He has come to the help of Israel his servant, mindful of his mercy – according to the promise he made to our ancestors – of his mercy to Abraham and to his descendants for ever.'

Mary stayed with Elizabeth about three months and then went back home.

Reflection
The feast of the Assumption of Mary into heaven dates from the 5th century. It has been celebrated in both the East and the West in an unbroken tradition for some 1500 years. So, it was surprising that in 1950, Pope Pius XII declared ex-cathedra, that is infallibly, the doctrine of Mary's Assumption. To understand why the Pope did this we need to reflect on the events that occurred in the years before 1950, most especially the Second World War in which millions of people in Europe, Asia and other parts of the world were brutally killed. Massive atrocities such as the holocaust degraded and devalued human life. By declaring the Assumption of Mary into heaven to be a dogma, Pope Pius XII affirmed the sacredness and eternal destiny of human life at a time when the world most needed to hear this. While the dogma of the Assumption is an important teaching about Mary, it is also an important affirmation of the dignity of all human life. As with Mary, the eternal destiny of every human being is to be with God in the beatific vision of heaven.

16 AUG TUE

20th Week in Ordinary Time | Green
or **St Stephen of Hungary** (Optional, White)

Ezekiel 28:1-10

The word of the Lord was addressed to me as follows, 'Son of man, tell the ruler of Tyre, "The Lord says this: Being swollen with pride, you have said: I am a god; I am sitting on the throne of God, surrounded by the seas. Though you are a man and not a god, you consider yourself the equal of God. You are wiser now than Daniel; there is no sage as wise as you. By your wisdom and your intelligence you have amassed great wealth; you have piles of gold and silver inside your treasure-houses. Such is your skill in trading, your wealth has continued to increase, and with this your heart has grown more arrogant. And so, the Lord says this: Since you consider yourself the equal of God, very well, I am going to bring foreigners against you, the most barbarous of the nations. They will draw sword against your fine wisdom, they will defile your glory; they will throw you down into the pit and you will die a violent death surrounded by the seas. Are you still going to say: I am a god, when your murderers confront you? No, you are a man and not a god in the clutches of your murderers! You will die like the uncircumcised at the hand of foreigners. For I have spoken – it is the Lord who speaks."'

Deuteronomy 32:26-28, 30, 35-36. R. v. 39

It is the Lord who deals death and life.

Matthew 19:23-30

Jesus said to his disciples, 'I tell you solemnly, it will be hard for a rich man to enter the kingdom of heaven. Yes, I tell you again, it is easier for a camel to pass through the eye of a needle than for a rich man to enter the kingdom of heaven.' When the disciples heard this they were astonished. 'Who can be saved, then?' they said. Jesus gazed at them. 'For men' he told them 'this is impossible; for God everything is possible.'

Then Peter spoke. 'What about us?' he said to him. 'We have left everything and followed you. What are we to have, then?' Jesus said to him, 'I tell you solemnly, when all is made new and the Son of Man sits on his throne of glory, you will yourselves sit on twelve thrones to judge the twelve tribes of Israel. And everyone who has left houses, brothers, sisters, father, mother, children or land for the sake of my name will be repaid a hundred times over, and also inherit eternal life. 'Many who are first will be last, and the last, first.'

Reflection

In biblical times people saw riches as a sign of God's blessing, and so they were shocked to hear Jesus exclaim, 'how hard it is for the rich to enter the kingdom of heaven.' If that is the case, they respond, 'who can be saved?' The key sentence in the whole episode is Jesus' reply: 'For men this is impossible; but for God everything is possible.' None of us can save ourself; it is Jesus who does the saving by his death on the cross. A danger with wealth is that we can forget our need for a saviour and find our security on our riches. The poor are more blessed. In their difficult circumstances they know their need for God. Whether we are rich or poor, a good life lived in trustful dependance on God reveals our acceptance of God's offer of salvation.

17
AUG WED

20th Week in Ordinary Time or **Our Lady of Knock, Memorial, Ireland** | Green

Ezekiel 34:1-11
(Please see the Appendix B-21)

Psalm 22. R. v. 1
The Lord is my shepherd: there is nothing I shall want.

Matthew 20:1-16
Jesus told this parable to his disciples: 'The kingdom of heaven is like a landowner going out at daybreak to hire workers for his vineyard. He made an agreement with the workers for one denarius a day, and sent them to his vineyard. Going out at about the third hour he saw others standing idle in the market place and said to them, "You go to my vineyard too and I will give you a fair wage." So they went. At about the sixth hour and again at about the ninth hour, he went out and did the same. Then at about the eleventh hour he went out and found more men standing round, and he said to them, "Why have you been standing here idle all day?" "Because no one has hired us" they answered. He said to them, "You go into my vineyard too." In the evening, the owner of the vineyard said to his bailiff, "Call the workers and pay them their wages, starting with the last arrivals and ending with the first." So those who were hired at about the eleventh hour came forward and received one denarius each. When the first came, they expected to get more, but they too received one denarius each. They took it, but grumbled at the landowner. "The men who came last" they said "have done only one hour, and you have treated them the same as us, though we have done a heavy day's work in all the heat." He answered one of them and said, "My friend, I am not being unjust to you; did we not agree on one denarius? Take your earnings and go. I choose to pay the last-comer as much as I pay you. Have I no right to do what I like with my own? Why be envious because I am generous?" Thus the last will be first, and the first, last.'

Reflection
Among the people who suffered the most economically during the COVID-19 pandemic were day workers – people who don't have a regular or permanent job but survive on getting casual work here and there. In poorer countries work dried up very quickly for these day workers and, without government support, they had no money to feed themselves or their families. In Jesus' time, day workers would go to the marketplace and wait until someone hired them. Sometimes they were lucky and got a full day's work. Often it was only half a day's work or even no work at all. How boring and anxious it must have been as they waited in the hot sun hoping for work. Fortunately, the owner of the vineyard mentioned in today's Gospel parable was kind and gave all the workers a living wage, including those who through no fault of their own had worked for just a short time. May we show a similar generosity – or is it justice? – to our fellow citizens in their times of difficulty.

18 AUG THU

20th Week in Ordinary Time
Green

Ezekiel 36:23-28

The word of the Lord was addressed to me as follows: I mean to display the holiness of my great name, which has been profaned among the nations, which you have profaned among them. And the nations will learn that I am the Lord – it is the Lord who speaks – when I display my holiness for your sake before their eyes. Then I am going to take you from among the nations and gather you together from all the foreign countries, and bring you home to your own land. ... *(Please see the Appendix B-21)*

Psalm 50:12-15, 18-19. R. Ezekiel 36:25

I shall pour clean water over you and all your sins will be washed away.

Matthew 22:1-14

Jesus began to speak in parables once again to the chief priests and elders of the people: 'The kingdom of heaven may be compared to a king who gave a feast for his son's wedding. He sent his servants to call those who had been invited, but they would not come. Next he sent some more servants. "Tell those who have been invited" he said "that I have my banquet all prepared, my oxen and fattened cattle have been slaughtered, everything is ready. Come to the wedding." But they were not interested: one went off to his farm, another to his business, and the rest seized his servants, maltreated them and killed them. The king was furious. He despatched his troops, destroyed those murderers and burnt their town. Then he said to his servants, "The wedding is ready; but as those who were invited proved to be unworthy, go to the crossroads in the town and invite everyone you can find to the wedding." So these servants went out on to the roads and collected together everyone they could find, bad and good alike; and the wedding hall was filled with guests. When the king came in to look at the guests he noticed one man who was not wearing a wedding garment, and said to him, "How did you get in here, my friend, without a wedding garment?" And the man was silent. Then the king said to the attendants, "Bind him hand and foot and throw him out into the dark, where there will be weeping and grinding of teeth." For many are called, but few are chosen.'

Reflection

There are times in life when we come close to exhaustion, when we feel that we cannot keep giving of ourselves, and yet we know we must keep going. We have responsibilities and people need us. In such moments it is helpful to hear the words of God spoken through the prophet Ezekiel in today's first reading: 'I will put my spirit in you! I will give you a new heart!' Too often we think that it's all up to us. We forget that the great work is God's. In fact God is inviting us to come to the banquet prepared for us. Sadly we sometimes say, 'sorry, I'm too busy. I have too much to do.' We may even get angry with those who mediate the invitation. If we can say 'yes' to the invitation of God – to let God be God for us – we can experience a renewal of spirit. Our feelings of exhaustion diminish, replaced by strength and hope.

19
AUG FRI

20th Week in Ordinary Time | Green or
St John Eudes, *priest* (Optional, White)

Ezekiel 37:1-14

The hand of the Lord was laid on me, and he carried me away by the spirit of the Lord and set me down in the middle of a valley, a valley full of bones. He made me walk up and down among them. There were vast quantities of these bones on the ground the whole length of the valley; and they were quite dried up. He said to me, 'Son of man, can these bones live?' I said, 'You know, Lord.' He said, 'Prophesy over these bones. Say, "Dry bones, hear the word of the Lord. The Lord says this to these bones: I am now going to make the breath enter you, and you will live. I shall put sinews on you, I shall make flesh grow on you, I shall cover you with skin and give you breath, and you will live; and you will learn that I am the Lord."' I prophesied as I had been ordered. While I was prophesying, there was a noise, a sound of clattering; and the bones joined together. I looked, and saw that they were covered with sinews; flesh was growing on them and skin was covering them, but there was no breath in them. He said to me, 'Prophesy to the breath; prophesy, son of man. Say to the breath, "The Lord says this: Come from the four winds, breath; breathe on these dead; let them live!"' I prophesied as he had ordered me, and the breath entered them; they came to life again and stood up on their feet, a great, an immense army. Then he said, 'Son of man, these bones are the whole House of Israel. … *(Please see the Appendix page B-21)*

Psalm 106:2-9. R. v. 1

O give thanks to the Lord for he is good, for his love has no end.

Matthew 22:34-40

When the Pharisees heard that Jesus had silenced the Sadducees they got together and, to disconcert him, one of them put a question, 'Master, which is the greatest commandment of the Law?' Jesus said, 'You must love the Lord your God with all your heart, with all your soul, and with all your mind. This is the greatest and the first commandment. The second resembles it: You must love your neighbour as yourself. On these two commandments hang the whole Law, and the Prophets also.'

Reflection

In a sermon shortly before his death in 2020, Colomban priest, Fr Noel Connolly, shared his experience of diminishment as the cancer in his body was preventing him from doing many of the tasks he would normally do: 'I was with some former Columban lay missionaries and clearly needed help but was trying to do something for myself when they said to me something I have thought about ever since, "Noel, let us love you" ... We need to be humble and confident enough to let people love us. We need to trust in God when we are weak, because being weak is also part of being human, part of the Incarnation, part of being like Jesus. We are not only like God when we are loving others. It is a beautiful thing to love. It is perhaps an even more gracious and beautiful thing to be loved. Then we are releasing the lover in others.'

20 AUG SAT

20th Week in Ordinary Time
St Bernard, *abbot, doctor,* **Memorial** | White

Ezekiel 43:1-7

The angel took me to the gate, the one facing east. I saw the glory of the God of Israel approaching from the east. A sound came with it, like the sound of the ocean, and the earth shone with his glory. This vision was like the one I had seen when I had come for the destruction of the city, and like the one I had seen on the bank of the river Chebar. Then I prostrated myself. The glory of the Lord arrived at the Temple by the east gate. The spirit lifted me up and brought me into the inner court; I saw the glory of the Lord fill the Temple. And I heard someone speaking to me from the Temple while the man stood beside me. The voice said, 'Son of man, this is the dais of my throne, the step on which I rest my feet. I shall live here among the sons of Israel for ever.'

Psalm 84:9-14. R. cf. v. 10

The glory of the Lord will dwell in our land.

Matthew 23:1-12

Addressing the people and his disciples Jesus said, 'The scribes and the Pharisees occupy the chair of Moses. You must therefore do what they tell you and listen to what they say; but do not be guided by what they do: since they do not practise what they preach. They tie up heavy burdens and lay them on men's shoulders, but will they lift a finger to move them? Not they! Everything they do is done to attract attention, like wearing broader phylacteries and longer tassels, like wanting to take the place of honour at banquets and the front seats in the synagogues, being greeted obsequiously in the market squares and having people call them Rabbi. 'You, however, must not allow yourselves to be called Rabbi, since you have only one Master, and you are all brothers. You must call no one on earth your father, since you have only one Father, and he is in heaven. Nor must you allow yourselves to be called teachers, for you have only one Teacher, the Christ. The greatest among you must be your servant. Anyone who exalts himself will be humbled, and anyone who humbles himself will be exalted.'

Reflection

There is a sharp contrast between the prophet Ezekiel in today's first reading and the scribes and Pharisees mentioned in the Gospel. In a vision the prophet Ezekiel sees the glory of the Lord enter and then fill the temple. He hears the voice of God saying, 'I will live here among the people of Israel forever'. Most importantly, Ezekiel communicates this vision to the people. His message would have given them great heart with its assurance that God is with them. By contrast the scribes and Pharisees don't point to God but to themselves. Everything they do is done to attract attention. They wear magnificent clothes and want the front seats in the synagogues and have the people bow before them. Most terribly, they do nothing to lift the spirits of the people but lay heavy burdens on them. May the prophet Ezekiel inspire us this day. May we reveal the presence of God among us by humbly and joyfully serving our brothers and sisters.

21
AUG SUN

TWENTY-FIRST SUNDAY IN ORDINARY TIME

Psalter Week 1

Green

Isaiah 66:18-21

The Lord says this: I am coming to gather the nations of every language. They shall come to witness my glory. I will give them a sign and send some of their survivors to the nations: to Tarshish, Put, Lud, Moshech, Rosh, Tubal, and Javan, to the distant islands that have never heard of me or seen my glory. They will proclaim my glory to the nations. As an offering to the Lord they will bring all your brothers, on horses, in chariots, in litters, on mules, on dromedaries, from all the nations to my holy mountain in Jerusalem, says the Lord, like Israelites bringing oblations in clean vessels to the Temple of the Lord. And of some of them I will make priests and Levites, says the Lord.

Psalm 116. R. Mark 16:15

Go out to the whole world; proclaim the Good News.

Hebrews 12:5-7, 11-13

Have you forgotten that encouraging text in which you are addressed as sons? My son, when the Lord corrects you, do not treat it lightly; but do not get discouraged when he reprimands you. For the Lord trains the ones that he loves and he punishes all those that he acknowledges as his sons. Suffering is part of your training; God is treating you as his sons. Has there ever been any son whose father did not train him? Of course, any punishment is most painful at the time, and far from pleasant; but later, in those on whom it has been used, it bears fruit in peace and goodness. So hold up your limp arms and steady your trembling knees and smooth out the path you tread; then the injured limb will not be wrenched, it will grow strong again.

Luke 13:22-30

Through towns and villages Jesus went teaching, making his way to Jerusalem. Someone said to him, 'Sir, will there be only a few saved?' He said to them, 'Try your best to enter by the narrow door, because I tell you, many will try to enter and will not succeed.

'Once the master of the house has got up and locked the door, you may find yourself knocking on the door, saying, "Lord, open to us" but he will answer, "I do not know where you come from." Then you will find yourself saying, "We once ate and drank in your company; you taught in our streets" but he will reply, "I do not know where you come from. Away from me, all you wicked men!"

'Then there will be weeping and grinding of teeth, when you see Abraham and Isaac and Jacob and all the prophets in the kingdom of God, and yourselves turned outside. And men from east and west, from north and south, will come to take their places at the feast in the kingdom of God.

'Yes, there are those now last who will be first, and those now first who will be last.'

Reflection

It was terrible for the Jewish people when Jerusalem was destroyed and its citizens were taken into exile in Babylon. But the exile proved an eye-opening experience of other peoples and cultures and ways of doing things. Not all Jews returned to Israel after the exile. Many remained in the diaspora. In time some Jews came to see that the love of God is for all peoples and that the people of Israel were chosen by God to be a light to the nations, to reveal to them the one true God. In today's first reading, the prophet Isaiah foresees a time when people from all nations will come to Jerusalem to worship the Lord. In today's Gospel Jesus declares that people 'from east and west, from north and south, will come to take their places at the feast in the kingdom of God.' He also stresses that, while the kingdom is open to all, the gateway to the kingdom is narrow. A broadminded love and compassion for all peoples is demanded of those who wish to enter. The Rule of the St Vincent de Paul Society states that 'The Society serves those in need regardless of creed, ethnic or social background, health, gender, or political opinions.' It is a rule we must all adopt if we are to enter by the narrow gate.

22
AUG MON

21st Week in Ordinary Time | Queenship of the Blessed Virgin Mary, Memorial | White

2 Thessalonians 1:1-5, 11-12

From Paul, Silvanus and Timothy, to the Church in Thessalonika which is in God our Father and the Lord Jesus Christ; wishing you grace and peace from God the Father and the Lord Jesus Christ. We feel we must be continually thanking God for you, brothers; quite rightly, because your faith is growing so wonderfully and the love that you have for one another never stops increasing; and among the churches of God we can take special pride in you for your constancy and faith under all the persecutions and troubles you have to bear. It all shows that God's judgement is just, and the purpose of it is that you may be found worthy of the kingdom of God; it is for the sake of this that you are suffering now. We pray continually that our God will make you worthy of his call, and by his power fulfil all your desires for goodness and complete all that you have been doing through faith; because in this way the name of our Lord Jesus Christ will be glorified in you and you in him, by the grace of our God and the Lord Jesus Christ.

Psalm 95:1-5. R. v. 3

Proclaim the wonders of the Lord among all the peoples.

Matthew 23:13-22

Jesus said: 'Alas for you, scribes and Pharisees, you hypocrites! You who shut up the kingdom of heaven in men's faces, neither going in yourselves nor allowing others to go in who want to.

'Alas for you, scribes and Pharisees, you hypocrites! You who travel over sea and land to make a single proselyte, and when you have him you make him twice as fit for hell as you are. Alas for you, blind guides! You who say, "If a man swears by the Temple, it has no force; but if a man swears by the gold of the Temple, he is bound." Fools and blind! For which is of greater worth, the gold or the Temple that makes the gold sacred? Or else, "If a man swears by the altar it has no force; but if a man swears by the offering that is on the altar, he is bound." You blind men! For which is of greater worth, the offering or the altar that makes the offering sacred? Therefore, when a man swears by the altar he is swearing by that and by everything on it. And when a man swears by the Temple he is swearing by that and by the One who dwells in it. And when a man swears by heaven he is swearing by the throne of God and by the One who is seated there.'

Reflection

In his second letter to the Thessalonians, which we begin to hear today, St Paul offers words of thanksgiving and encouragement to the community. The comforting tone of this letter is so different to the tone of Jesus in the Gospels we will hear this week in which he vehemently attacks the scribes and Pharisees for their hypocrisy. (We should note that in other passages of the New Testament we find Jesus offering words of comfort and Paul expressing anger.) We need to recognise that both comfort and righteous anger can be expressions of love. There is a time for every purpose under heaven. Sometimes love demands that we speak strongly to someone and sometimes it demands that we are gentle and comforting towards them. Let us pray for the wisdom to know how best to act in love on every occasion.

21st Week in Ordinary Time | Green
or **St Rose of Lima,** *virgin* (Optional, White)

23
AUG TUE

2 Thessalonians 2:1-3, 14-17

To turn, brothers, to the coming of our Lord Jesus Christ and how we shall all be gathered round him: please do not get excited too soon or alarmed by any prediction or rumour or any letter claiming to come from us, implying that the Day of the Lord has already arrived. Never let anyone deceive you in this way.

Through the Good News that we brought God called you so that you should share the glory of our Lord Jesus Christ. Stand firm, then, brothers, and keep the traditions that we taught you, whether by word of mouth or by letter. May our Lord Jesus Christ himself, and God our Father who has given us his love and, through his grace, such inexhaustible comfort and such sure hope, comfort you and strengthen you in everything good that you do or say.

Psalm 95:10-13. R. v. 13

The Lord comes to rule the earth.

Matthew 23:23-26

Jesus said, 'Alas for you, scribes and Pharisees, you hypocrites! You who pay your tithe of mint and dill and cummin and have neglected the weightier matters of the Law – justice, mercy, good faith! These you should have practised, without neglecting the others. You blind guides! Straining out gnats and swallowing camels!

'Alas for you, scribes and Pharisees, you hypocrites! You who clean the outside of cup and dish and leave the inside full of extortion and intemperance. Blind Pharisee! Clean the inside of cup and dish first so that the outside may become clean as well.'

Reflection

In today's first reading St Paul tells the Christians of Thessalonika not to get excited or to be alarmed by rumors that the Day of the Lord is imminent or has already arrived. He prays instead that the Lord will bestow on them inexhaustible comfort and sure hope. Today very few people get excited or alarmed that the world is coming to an end. But there are many other things that can trouble and alarm us greatly such as the COVID-19 pandemic and a whole range of national, international and personal matters. In every one of these situations the prayer of comfort Paul uttered for the Thessalonians is still relevant: 'May our Lord Jesus Christ, and God our Father who has given us his love and, through his grace, such inexhaustible comfort and sure hope, comfort you and strengthen you in everything good that you do or say.'

24
AUG WED

St Bartholomew, Apostle
Feast | Red

Apocalypse 21:9-14

The angel came to speak to me, and said, 'Come here and I will show you the bride that the Lamb has married.' In the spirit he took me to the top of an enormous high mountain and showed me Jerusalem, the holy city, coming down from God out of heaven. It had all the radiant glory of God and glittered like some precious jewel of crystal-clear diamond. The walls of it were of a great height, and had twelve gates; at each of the twelve gates there was an angel, and over the gates were written the names of the twelve tribes of Israel; on the east there were three gates, on the north three gates, on the south three gates, and on the west three gates. The city walls stood on twelve foundation stones, each one of which bore the name of one of the twelve apostles of the Lamb.

Psalm 144:10-13, 17-18. R. cf. v. 12

Your friends, O Lord, make known the glorious splendour of your reign.

John 1:45-51

Philip found Nathanael and said to him, 'We have found the one Moses wrote about in the Law, the one about whom the prophets wrote: he is Jesus son of Joseph, from Nazareth,' 'From Nazareth?' said Nathanael. 'Can anything good come from that place?' 'Come and see' replied Philip. When Jesus saw Nathanael coming he said of him, 'There is an Israelite who deserves the name, incapable of deceit.' 'How do you know me?' said Nathanael. 'Before Philip came to call you,' said Jesus 'I saw you under the fig tree.' Nathanael answered, 'Rabbi, you are the Son of God, you are the King of Israel.' Jesus replied, 'You believe that just because I said: I saw you under the fig tree. You will see greater things than that.' And then he added, 'I tell you most solemnly, you will see heaven laid open and, above the Son of Man, the angels of God ascending and descending.'

Reflection

There is an ancient tradition which identifies Bartholomew, who is mentioned among the twelve apostles in the Synoptic Gospels, with Nathanael who is mentioned in the Gospel of John. Today's Gospel describes Nathanael's first meeting with Jesus. From being prejudiced against him – 'can anything good come from Nazareth?' – Nathanael suddenly exclaims, 'Rabbi, you are the Son of God, you are the King of Israel.' We can only imagine what Nathanael experienced in the presence of Jesus. It was life-transforming for him. May the Lord open our eyes also that we may recognise his presence among us, often in places and people where we least expect to find him, blinded as we often are by our prejudices. May we be blessed with good friends, like Philip, who simply say, 'come and see'.

21st Week in Ordinary Time | Green
or **St Louis |** or **St Joseph Calasanz,** *priest* (Optional, White)

25
AUG THU

1 Corinthians 1:1-9

I, Paul, appointed by God to be an apostle, together with brother Sosthenes, send greetings to the church of God in Corinth, to the holy people of Jesus Christ, who are called to take their place among all the saints everywhere who pray to our Lord Jesus Christ; for he is their Lord no less than ours. May God our Father and the Lord Jesus Christ send you grace and peace. I never stop thanking God for all the graces you have received through Jesus Christ. I thank him that you have been enriched in so many ways, especially in your teachers and preachers; the witness to Christ has indeed been strong among you so that you will not be without any of the gifts of the Spirit while you are waiting for our Lord Jesus Christ to be revealed; and he will keep you steady and without blame until the last day, the day of our Lord Jesus Christ, because God by calling you has joined you to his Son, Jesus Christ; and God is faithful.

Psalm 144:2-7. R. cf. v. 1

I will bless your name for ever, O Lord.

Matthew 24:42-51

Jesus said to his disciples: 'Stay awake, because you do not know the day when your master is coming. You may be quite sure of this, that if the householder had known at what time of the night the burglar would come, he would have stayed awake and would not have allowed anyone to break the wall of his house. Therefore, you too must stand ready because the Son of Man is coming at an hour you do not expect. 'What sort of servant, then, is faithful and wise enough for the master to place him over his household to give them their food at the proper time? Happy that servant if his master's arrival finds him at this employment. I tell you solemnly, he will place him over everything he owns. But as for the dishonest servant who says to himself, "My master is taking his time," and sets about beating his fellow servants and eating and drinking with drunkards, his master will come on a day he does not expect and at an hour he does not know. The master will cut him off and send him to the same fate as the hypocrites, where there will be weeping and grinding of teeth.'

Reflection

The readings today invite us to be grateful for the past and prepared for the future. St Paul invites us to remember all of the graces we have received through Jesus Christ. In a special way to be thankful for our teachers and preachers (and that includes our parents and so many others) whose help and care have enriched us so greatly. So often, we see only our troubles and forget the blessings we have received. In the Gospel Jesus urges us to be prepared for the future when the Son of Man will come in glory. How can we do this? By living this day as well and as fully and faithfully as we can, doing the tasks assigned to us. If we do, tomorrow will take care of itself. The challenge is not to focus on the future when the Lord will come in glory but to recognise that the Lord is with us now. If we respond to him in the present we will have no difficulties welcoming him when he comes in glory.

26
AUG FRI

21st Week in Ordinary Time
Green

1 Corinthians 1:17-25

Christ did not send me to baptise, but to preach the Good News, and not to preach that in the terms of philosophy in which the crucifixion of Christ cannot be expressed. The language of the cross may be illogical to those who are not on the way to salvation, but those of us who are on the way see it as God's power to save. As scripture says: I shall destroy the wisdom of the wise and bring to nothing all the learning of the learned. Where are the philosophers now? Where are the scribes? Where are any of our thinkers today? ... *(Please see the Appendix B-21)*

Psalm 32:1-2, 4-5, 10-11. R. v. 5

The Lord fills the earth with his love.

Matthew 25:1-13

Jesus said to his disciples: 'The kingdom of heaven will be like this: Ten bridesmaids took their lamps and went to meet the bridegroom. Five of them were foolish and five were sensible: the foolish ones did take their lamps, but they brought no oil, whereas the sensible ones took flasks of oil as well as their lamps. The bridegroom was late, and they all grew drowsy and fell asleep. But at midnight there was a cry, "The bridegroom is here! Go out and meet him." At this, all those bridesmaids woke up and trimmed their lamps, and the foolish ones said to the sensible ones, "Give us some of your oil: our lamps are going out." But they replied, "There may not be enough for us and for you; you had better go to those who sell it and buy some for yourselves." They had gone off to buy it when the bridegroom arrived. Those who were ready went in with him to the wedding hall and the door was closed. The other bridesmaids arrived later. "Lord, Lord," they said, "open the door for us." But he replied, "I tell you solemnly, I do not know you." So stay awake, because you do not know either the day or the hour.'

Reflection

One of the values that the Gospels present is that of sharing our goods with others. For instance, in the Sermon on the Mount Jesus says: 'if someone asks for your tunic, give them your cloak as well' (Matthew 5:40). But in today's Gospel parable, the five wise bridesmaids refuse to share their oil with the other bridesmaids, and Jesus seems to applaud them for their action. So, what is going on here? I think the answer is simple. There are certain things in life that we cannot give to others no matter how much we may want to. They must acquire them for themselves. For instance, I cannot give you my relationship with God. You must develop your own relationship with God and cultivate your own spiritual life. Similarly, wisdom is not something that can be given to us gift-wrapped. It is something that we can acquire only through slow and sometimes painful reflection on our experience.

21st Week in Ordinary Time
St Monica, Memorial | White

27
AUG SAT

1 Corinthians 1:26-31
(Please see the Appendix B-22)

Psalm 32:12-13, 18-21. R. cf. v. 12
Happy the people the Lord has chosen as his own.

Matthew 25:14-30
Jesus told his disciples this parable: 'A man on his way abroad summoned his servants and entrusted his property to them. To one he gave five talents, to another two, to a third one; each in proportion to his ability. Then he set out. The man who had received the five talents promptly went and traded with them and made five more. The man who had received two made two more in the same way. But the man who had received one went off and dug a hole in the ground and hid his master's money. Now a long time after, the master of those servants came back and went through his accounts with them. The man who had received the five talents came forward bringing five more. "Sir," he said "you entrusted me with five talents; here are five more that I have made." His master said to him, "Well done, good and faithful servant; you have shown you can be faithful in small things, I will trust you with greater; come and join in your master's happiness."

Next the man with the two talents came forward. "Sir," he said "you entrusted me with two talents; here are two more that I have made." His master said to him, "Well done, good and faithful servant; you have shown you can be faithful in small things, I will trust you with greater; come and join in your master's happiness." Last came forward the man who had the one talent. "Sir," said he "I had heard you were a hard man, reaping where you have not sown and gathering where you have not scattered; so I was afraid, and I went off and hid your talent in the ground. Here it is; it was yours, you have it back." But his master answered him, "You wicked and lazy servant! So you knew that I reap where I have not sown and gather where I have not scattered? Well then, you should have deposited my money with the bankers, and on my return I would have recovered my capital with interest. So now, take the talent from him and give it to the man who has the five talents. For to everyone who has will be given more, and he will have more than enough; but from the man who has not, even what he has will be taken away. As for this good-for-nothing servant, throw him out into the dark, where there will be weeping and grinding of teeth."'

Reflection
'Our soul is waiting for Lord', the psalmist writes. Generally, in our modern world, we are not very good at waiting. We crave instant gratification, and instant solutions to our problems. St Monica, whose feast we celebrate today, models Christian waiting to a remarkable degree. For many years she poured out tears and prayers for the conversion of her son, Augustine. For many years it seemed that her prayers were futile. But she never gave up and in faith waited for her prayers to be answered. Eventually they were answered in abundance. Not only did Augustine become a Christian but one of the greatest Christian thinkers of all time and eventually a saint. In her faithfulness and willingness to wait, Monica proved to be one of the little ones chosen by God to show up those who have everything.

28

AUG SUN

TWENTY-SECOND SUNDAY IN ORDINARY TIME

Psalter Week 2

Green

Sirach 3:17-20, 28-29

My son, be gentle in carrying out your business, and you will be better loved than a lavish giver. The greater you are, the more you should behave humbly, and then you will find favour with the Lord; for great though the power of the Lord is, he accepts the homage of the humble.

There is no cure for the proud man's malady, since an evil growth has taken root in him. The heart of a sensible man will reflect on parables, an attentive ear is the sage's dream.

Psalm 67:4-7, 10-11. R. cf. v. 11

In your goodness, O God, you prepared a home for the poor.

Hebrews 12:18-19, 22-24

What you have come to is nothing known to the senses: not a blazing fire, or a gloom turning to total darkness, or a storm; or trumpeting thunder or the great voice speaking which made everyone that heard it beg that no more should be said to them. But what you have come to is Mount Zion and the city of the living God, the heavenly Jerusalem where the millions of angels have gathered for the festival, with the whole Church in which everyone is a 'first-born son' and a citizen of heaven. You have come to God himself, the supreme Judge, and been placed with spirits of the saints who have been made perfect; and to Jesus, the mediator who brings a new covenant.

Luke 14:1, 7-14

On a sabbath day Jesus had gone for a meal to the house of one of the leading Pharisees; and they watched him closely. He then told the guests a parable, because he had noticed how they picked the places of honour. He said this, 'When someone invites you to a wedding feast, do not take your seat in the place of honour. A more distinguished person than you may have been invited, and the person who invited you both may come and say, "Give up your place to this man." And then, to your embarrassment, you would have to go and take the lowest place. No; when you are a guest, make your way to the lowest place and sit there, so that, when your host comes, he may say, "My friend, move up higher." In that way, everyone with you at the table will see you honoured. For everyone who exalts himself will be humbled, and the man who humbles himself will be exalted.'

Then he said to his host, 'When you give a lunch or a dinner, do not ask your friends, brothers, relations or rich neighbours, for fear they repay your courtesy by inviting you in return. No; when you have a party, invite the poor, the crippled, the lame, the blind; that they cannot pay you back means that you are fortunate, because repayment will be made to you when the virtuous rise again.'

Reflection

I remember the best Christmas I ever had as a child. I suppose I was 8 or 9 years old. My dad invited a man called Jack to join us for lunch. Jack had returned to Australia after the Second World War not physically injured but severely damaged mentally. An alcoholic, he worked as a labourer for the council, and lived in a room in a boarding house.

Jack was so moved to be invited to have Christmas lunch with us that he arrived sober and cleaned up and in his best clothes, and his joy in being with us was visible throughout the meal. After the meal my dad gave him a suit he had and Jack wept tears of joy. I was so happy too. Our decision to share Christmas with him enriched our own Christmas in ways I could never imagine.

When Jesus urges us in today's Gospel to invite the poor, the crippled, the lame and the blind to have a meal with us, he is not recommending it purely as an act of charity, as a corporal work of mercy. He is thinking not only about the poor but also about us. They will not be able to repay us in money or by returning the invitation. But they will enrich us in ways we cannot imagine. We will be the most fortunate of people to have had the courage to make this invitation.

29
AUG MON

22nd Week in Ordinary Time
The Passion of St John the Baptist, Memorial | Red

Jeremiah 1:17-19

The word of the Lord was addressed to me, saying: 'Brace yourself for action. Stand up and tell them all I command you. Do not be dismayed at their presence, or in their presence I will make you dismayed. I, for my part, today will make you into a fortified city, a pillar of iron, and a wall of bronze to confront all this land: the kings of Judah, its princes, its priests and the country people. They will fight against you but shall not overcome you, for I am with you to deliver you – it is the Lord who speaks.'

Psalm 70:1-6, 15, 17. R. v. 15

My lips will tell of your help.

Mark 6:17-29

Herod had sent to have John arrested, and had him chained up in prison because of Herodias, his brother Philip's wife whom he had married. For John had told Herod, 'It is against the law for you to have your brother's wife.' As for Herodias, she was furious with him and wanted to kill him; but she was not able to, because Herod was afraid of John, knowing him to be a good and holy man, and gave him his protection. When he had heard him speak he was greatly perplexed, and yet he liked to listen to him.

An opportunity came on Herod's birthday when he gave a banquet for the nobles of his court, for his army officers and for the leading figures in Galilee. When the daughter of this same Herodias came in and danced, she delighted Herod and his guests; so the king said to the girl, 'Ask me anything you like and I will give it you.' And he swore her an oath, 'I will give you anything you ask, even half my kingdom.' She went out and said to her mother, 'What shall I ask for?' She replied, 'The head of John the Baptist.' The girl hurried straight back to the king and made her request, 'I want you to give me John the Baptist's head, here and now, on a dish.' The king was deeply distressed, but thinking of the oaths he had sworn and of his guests, he was reluctant to break his word to her. So the king at once sent one of the bodyguard with orders to bring John's head. The man went off and beheaded him in prison; then he brought the head on a dish and gave it to the girl, and the girl gave it to her mother. When John's disciples heard about this, they came and took his body and laid it in a tomb.

Reflection

John the Baptist was imprisoned by Herod because he had the courage to speak up and criticise Herod for his marriage to his brother's wife. Sometimes we can find ourselves in situations where we feel the need to speak up about a situation that is wrong but lack the courage to do so. Perhaps we fear for our own safety, or just for our own comfort. 'Why rock the boat?' we may ask. The late Cardinal Martini once wrote that 'fraternal correction is one of the ordinary ingredients of the life of a Christian community. On the contrary, however, it is one of the most neglected elements.' Let us pray for the courage we need to speak the truth in love when necessary, whether it be to civil authorities or to our brothers and sisters in the community. And may we have the humility to listen in love when others speak the truth to us.

30
AUG TUE

22nd Week in Ordinary Time
Green

1 Corinthians 2:10-16

The Spirit reaches the depths of everything, even the depths of God. After all, the depths of a man can only be known by his own spirit, not by any other man, and in the same way the depths of God can only be known by the Spirit of God. Now instead of the spirit of the world, we have received the Spirit that comes from God, to teach us to understand the gifts that he has given us. Therefore we teach, not in the way in which philosophy is taught, but in the way that the Spirit teaches us: we teach spiritual things spiritually. An unspiritual person is one who does not accept anything of the Spirit of God: he sees it all as nonsense; it is beyond his understanding because it can only be understood by means of the Spirit. A spiritual man, on the other hand, is able to judge the value of everything, and his own value is not to be judged by other men. As scripture says: Who can know the mind of the Lord, so who can teach him? But we are those who have the mind of Christ.

Psalm 144:8-14. R. v. 17

The Lord is just in all his ways.

Luke 4:31-37

Jesus went down to Capernaum, a town in Galilee, and taught them on the sabbath. And his teaching made a deep impression on them because he spoke with authority.

In the synagogue there was a man who was possessed by the spirit of an unclean devil, and it shouted at the top of its voice, 'Ha! What do you want with us, Jesus of Nazareth? Have you come to destroy us? I know who you are: the Holy One of God.' But Jesus said sharply, 'Be quiet! Come out of him!' And the devil, throwing the man down in front of everyone, went out of him without hurting him at all. Astonishment seized them and they were all saying to one another, 'What teaching! He gives orders to unclean spirits with authority and power and they come out.' And reports of him went all through the surrounding countryside.

Reflection

Often in the Gospels it is the person considered 'crazy' or 'possessed' who recognises that Jesus is the Holy One of God, while the people considered 'normal' cannot see it. I think that Paul has been saying something similar in his letter to the Corinthians when he says that human wisdom cannot know God. God's wisdom is foolishness and somehow we have to be foolish to understand the ways of God. I find this all very encouraging. I think the majority of human beings, myself included, are mostly sane but there is a little part in each of us that could be described as 'broken' or 'crazy'. And that part is so precious. It is the part that recognises and welcomes the Holy One of God; that, in a sense, introduces God to our whole being, even the 'normal' bits.

31
AUG WED

22nd Week in Ordinary Time
Green

1 Corinthians 3:1-9

Brothers, I myself was unable to speak to you as people of the Spirit: I treated you as sensual men, still infants in Christ. What I fed you with was milk, not solid food, for you were not ready for it; and indeed, you are still not ready for it since you are still unspiritual. Isn't that obvious from all the jealousy and wrangling that there is among you, from the way that you go on behaving like ordinary people? What could be more unspiritual than your slogans, 'I am for Paul' and 'I am for Apollos'?

After all, what is Apollos and what is Paul? They are servants who brought the faith to you. Even the different ways in which they brought it were assigned to them by the Lord. I did the planting, Apollos did the watering, but God made things grow. Neither the planter nor the waterer matters: only God, who makes things grow. It is all one who does the planting and who does the watering, and each will duly be paid according to his share in the work. We are fellow workers with God; you are God's farm, God's building.

Psalm 32:12-15, 20-21. R. v. 12

Happy the people the Lord has chosen as his own.

Luke 4:38-44

Leaving the synagogue Jesus went to Simon's house. Now Simon's mother-in-law was suffering from a high fever and they asked him to do something for her. Leaning over her he rebuked the fever and it left her. And she immediately got up and began to wait on them.

At sunset all those who had friends suffering from diseases of one kind or another brought them to him, and laying his hands on each he cured them. Devils too came out of many people, howling, 'You are the Son of God.' But he rebuked them and would not allow them to speak because they knew that he was the Christ.

When daylight came he left the house and made his way to a lonely place. The crowds went to look for him, and when they had caught up with him they wanted to prevent him leaving them, but he answered, 'I must proclaim the Good News of the kingdom of God to the other towns too, because that is what I was sent to do.' And he continued his preaching in the synagogues of Judaea.

Reflection

In today's Gospel we observe Jesus healing many people. We too stand in need of healing in one way or another, whether it be physical, emotional or spiritual. Let us come to Jesus today seeking healing for ourself or maybe for someone else. This Gospel also reminds us that healing is always for service. We are not only 'healed from' but 'healed for'. We pray for healing not just to be rid of our pains and ailments but, like Peter's mother-in-law, that we can resume our service to the community.

22nd Week in Ordinary Time | Green
Saint Giles, Abbot, Memorial, Scotland

01
SEP THU

1 Corinthians 3:18-23

Make no mistake about it: if any one of you thinks of himself as wise, in the ordinary sense of the word, then he must learn to be a fool before he really can be wise. Why? Because the wisdom of this world is foolishness to God. As scripture says: The Lord knows wise men's thoughts: he knows how useless they are; or again: God is not convinced by the arguments of the wise. So there is nothing to boast about in anything human: Paul, Apollos, Cephas, the world, life and death, the present and the future, are all your servants; but you belong to Christ and Christ belongs to God.

Psalm 23:1-6. R. v. 1

The Lord's is the earth and its fullness.

Luke 5:1-11

Jesus was standing one day by the lake of Gennesaret, with the crowd pressing round him listening to the word of God, when he caught sight of two boats close to the bank. The fishermen had gone out of them and were washing their nets. He got into one of the boats – it was Simon's – and asked him to put out a little from the shore. Then he sat down and taught the crowds from the boat. When he had finished speaking he said to Simon, 'Put out into deep water and pay out your nets for a catch.' 'Master,' Simon replied 'we worked hard all night long and caught nothing, but if you say so, I will pay out the nets.' And when they had done this they netted such a huge number of fish that their nets began to tear, so they signalled to their companions in the other boat to come and help them; when these came, they filled the two boats to sinking point. When Simon Peter saw this he fell at the knees of Jesus saying, 'Leave me, Lord; I am a sinful man.' For he and all his companions were completely overcome by the catch they had made; so also were James and John, sons of Zebedee, who were Simon's partners. But Jesus said to Simon, 'Do not be afraid; from now on it is men you will catch.' Then, bringing their boats back to land, they left everything and followed him.

Reflection

None of us likes to be called a fool. We are all guilty of doing silly things on occasions but in our hearts we genuinely seek wisdom and mostly we try to learn from our mistakes. Paradoxically, as St Paul tells us in today's first reading, the greatest wisdom is to accept the foolishness of God. Peter, and Andrew, James and John, were very foolish by this world's standards to leave their boats and secure incomes to follow Jesus, and to do so on the spur of the moment when they were 'overcome by the catch they had made'. Wait and think it over, may have been the wise thing to do. But their foolish act in choosing to follow Jesus would over time be greatly rewarded as they would come to see him not only as a prophet and teacher but indeed 'the Son of God'. Are we foolish enough to entrust our lives totally to Jesus?

02
SEP FRI

1 Corinthians 4:1-5

People must think of us as Christ's servants, stewards entrusted with the mysteries of God. What is expected of stewards is that each one should be found worthy of his trust. Not that it makes the slightest difference to me whether you, or indeed any human tribunal, find me worthy or not. I will not even pass judgement on myself. True, my conscience does not reproach me at all, but that does not prove that I am acquitted: the Lord alone is my judge. There must be no passing of premature judgement. Leave that until the Lord comes: he will light up all that is hidden in the dark and reveal the secret intentions of men's hearts. Then will be the time for each one to have whatever praise he deserves, from God.

Psalm 36:3-6, 27-28, 39-40. R. v. 39

The salvation of the just comes from the Lord.

Luke 5:33-39

The Pharisees and the scribes said to Jesus, 'John's disciples are always fasting and saying prayers, and the disciples of the Pharisees too, but yours go on eating and drinking.' Jesus replied, 'Surely you cannot make the bridegroom's attendants fast while the bridegroom is still with them? But the time will come, the time for the bridegroom to be taken away from them; that will be the time when they will fast.'

He also told them this parable, 'No one tears a piece from a new cloak to put it on an old cloak; if he does, not only will he have torn the new one, but the piece taken from the new will not match the old.

'And nobody puts new wine into old skins; if he does, the new wine will burst the skins and then run out, and the skins will be lost. No; new wine must be put into fresh skins. And nobody who has been drinking old wine wants new. "The old is good" he says.'

Reflection

We live in a culture that oftentimes values success more than failure, the end more than the means and profits more than people. Many of us struggle with feelings of being unworthy and not good enough as society pressures us to be the best. Competitiveness can drive our life decisions and quite often expose us to the harsh judgements of others. God however does not judge us according to these standards. We are Christ's servants, entrusted with the mysteries of God. God sees not only our external acts but also the inner intentions of our hearts. He wants us to be the best shining light of his love to ourselves and others.

St Gregory the Great, *pope, doctor,*
Memorial | White

03
SEP SAT

ST GREGORY THE GREAT, POPE, DOCTOR, Feast
– England
see Appendix A-21

1 Corinthians 4:6-15

Take Apollos and myself as an example and remember the maxim: 'Keep to what is written.' It is not for you, so full of your own importance, to go taking sides for one man against another. In any case, brother, has anybody given you some special right? What do you have that was not given to you? And if it was given, how can you boast as though it were not? Is it that you have everything you want – that you are rich already, in possession of your kingdom, with us left outside? Indeed I wish you were really kings, and we could be kings with you! But instead, it seems to me, God has put us apostles at the end of his parade, with the men sentenced to death; it is true – we have been put on show in front of the whole universe, angels as well as men. Here we are, fools for the sake of Christ, while you are the learned men in Christ; we have no power, but you are influential; you are celebrities, we are nobodies. To this day, we go without food and drink and clothes; we are beaten and have no homes; we work for our living with our own hands. When we are cursed, we answer with a blessing; when we are hounded, we put up with it; we are insulted and we answer politely. We are treated as the offal of the world, still to this day, the scum of the earth.

I am saying all this not just to make you ashamed but to bring you, as my dearest children, to your senses. You might have thousands of guardians in Christ, but not more than one father and it was I who begot you in Christ Jesus by preaching the Good News.

Psalm 144:17-21

The Lord is close to all who call him.

Luke 6:1-5

One sabbath Jesus happened to be taking a walk through the cornfields, and his disciples were picking ears of corn, rubbing them in their hands and eating them. Some of the Pharisees said, 'Why are you doing something that is forbidden on the sabbath day?' Jesus answered them, 'So you have not read what David did when he and his followers were hungry how he went into the house of God, took the loaves of offering and ate them and gave them to his followers, loaves which only the priests are allowed to eat?' And he said to them, 'The Son of Man is master of the sabbath.'

Reflection

As we continue to reflect on the letter of St Paul to the Corinthians, we experience Paul's passion for Christ and his concern with the faithful in Corinth who are so hard to be formed in true missionary discipleship. Paul talks with honesty, patience and determination, asking them to prioritise God. From his own experience of Christ, he knows the truthfulness of the psalmist's words that 'the Lord is near to all who call him'. In the Gospel Jesus also gives a lesson in priorities. He makes it clear that we will never fully follow the law of love if we forget to prioritise God. The teaching of Jesus and Paul is important for us. We too must prioritise God and the divine law of love. This is important for us and for the credibility of the Church.

04
SEP SUN

TWENTY-THIRD SUNDAY IN ORDINARY TIME

Psalter Week 3

Green

Wisdom 9:13-18

'What man can know the intentions of God? Who can divine the will of the Lord? The reasonings of mortals are unsure and our intentions unstable; for a perishable body presses down the soul, and this tent of clay weighs down the teeming mind. It is hard enough for us to work out what is on earth, laborious to know what lies within our reach; who, then, can discover what is in the heavens. As for your intention, who could have learnt it, had you not granted Wisdom and sent your holy spirit from above?

Thus have the paths of those on earth been straightened and men been taught what pleases you, and saved, by Wisdom.'

Psalm 89:3-6, 12-14, 17. R. v. 1

O Lord, you have been our refuge from one generation to the next.

Philemon 9-10, 12-17

This is Paul writing, an old man now and, what is more, still a prisoner of Christ Jesus. I am appealing to you for a child of mine, whose father I became while wearing these chains: I mean Onesimus. I am sending him back to you, and with him – I could say – a part of my own self. I should have liked to keep him with me; he could have been a substitute for you, to help me while I am in the chains that the Good News has brought me. However, I did not want to do anything without your consent; it would have been forcing your act of kindness, which should be spontaneous. I know you have been deprived of Onesimus for a time, but it was only so that you could have him back for ever, not as a slave any more, but something much better than a slave, a dear brother; especially dear to me, but how much more to you, as a blood-brother as well as a brother in the Lord. So if all that we have in common means anything to you, welcome him as you would me.

Luke 14:25-33

Great crowds accompanied Jesus on his way and he turned and spoke to them. 'If any man comes to me without hating his father, mother, wife, children, brothers, sisters, yes and his own life too, he cannot be my disciple. Anyone who does not carry his cross and come after me cannot be my disciple.

'And indeed, which of you here, intending to build a tower, would not first sit down and work out the cost to see if he had enough to complete it? Otherwise, if he laid the foundation and then found himself unable to finish the work, the onlookers would all start making fun of him and saying, 'Here is a man who started to build and was unable to finish.' Or again, what king marching to war against another king would not first sit down and consider whether with ten thousand men he could stand up to the other who advanced against him with twenty thousand? If not, then while the other king was still a long way off, he would send envoys to sue for peace. So in the same way, none of you can be my disciple unless he gives up all his possessions.'

Reflection

'Who can know the intentions of God?' (Wisdom 9:13). This question often arises when we cannot understand or have difficulty accepting our life experiences or situations.

Sometimes, the uncertainties we face here on earth strengthen our desire to be with God for ever. At other times they raise more questions about heaven's reality. But we can take courage from God's reassurance and our experience that God has been our refuge from generation to generation (Psalm 89). Saint Paul writes his letter to Philemon from prison, having lived through many challenges and hardships. He asks Philemon to accept back the slave, Onesimus, not as a slave but as a dear brother in Christ, and with him a part of Paul's own self.

The attitude of welcoming is also fostered in the Gospel, despite the statement about hating 'mother and father' which usually shocks us when we read it. Jesus is using a kind of reverse psychology. He is stressing that our primary commitment must be to him. This will ensure that we don't have an undue attachment to others in order to meet our own needs, but that our relationships with others are welcoming, and our hearts are open for everyone. Let us make this a priority in the upcoming week.

05
SEP MON

23rd Week in Ordinary Time
Green

1 Corinthians 5:1-8

I have been told as an undoubted fact that one of you is living with his father's wife. This is a case of sexual immorality among you that must be unparalleled even among pagans. How can you be so proud of yourselves? You should be in mourning. A man who does a thing like that ought to have been expelled from the community. Though I am far away in body, I am with you in spirit, and have already condemned the man who did this thing as if I were actually present. When you are assembled together in the name of the Lord Jesus, and I am spiritually present with you, then with the power of our Lord Jesus he is to be handed over to Satan so that his sensual body may be destroyed and his spirit saved on the day of the Lord. The pride that you take in yourselves is hardly to your credit. You must know how even a small amount of yeast is enough to leaven all the dough, so get rid of all the old yeast, and make yourselves into a completely new batch of bread, unleavened as you are meant to be. Christ, our passover, has been sacrificed; let us celebrate the feast, then, by getting rid of all the old yeast of evil and wickedness, having only the unleavened bread of sincerity and truth.

Psalm 5:5-7, 12. R. v. 9

Lead me, Lord, in your justice.

Luke 6:6-11

On the sabbath Jesus went into the synagogue and began to teach, and a man was there whose right hand was withered. The scribes and the Pharisees were watching him to see if he would cure a man on the sabbath, hoping to find something to use against him. But he knew their thoughts; and he said to the man with the withered hand, 'Stand up! Come out into the middle.' And he came out and stood there. Then Jesus said to them, 'I put it to you: is it against the law on the sabbath to do good, or to do evil; to save life, or to destroy it?' Then he looked round at them all and said to the man, 'Stretch out your hand.' He did so, and his hand was better. But they were furious, and began to discuss the best way of dealing with Jesus.

Reflection

People who like cooking may wonder what St Paul means when he uses the example of new and old yeast. He is encouraging us to think about our relationship with God and one another. As old yeast affects the whole batch of bread, so our wrongdoing has a negative impact on others. On the other hand, our good deeds, like fresh yeast in bread-making, can have a very positive effect, helping to build up the Body of Christ, our Church. The challenge sometimes is to determine if the yeast is still fresh. In the Gospel Jesus does not condemn the law of not working on the Sabbath. But he makes it clear that situations will arise where the greater law of love must take precedence. In these situations, choosing to help someone is choosing the best ingredient. Do we have the courage to follow Jesus in choosing new, life-giving ways, or do we prefer to stay with the old, safe recipes?

23rd Week in Ordinary Time
Green

1 Corinthians 6:1-11

How dare one of your members take up a complaint against another in the law courts of the unjust instead of before the saints? As you know, it is the saints who are to 'judge the world'; and if the world is to be judged by you, how can you be unfit to judge trifling cases? Since we are also to judge angels, it follows that we can judge matters of everyday life; but when you have had cases of that kind, the people you appointed to try them were not even respected in the Church. You should be ashamed: is there really not one reliable man among you to settle differences between brothers and so one brother brings a court case against another in front of unbelievers? It is bad enough for you to have lawsuits at all against one another: oughtn't you let yourselves be wronged, and let yourselves be cheated? But you are doing the wronging and the cheating, and to your own brothers. ... *(Please see the Appendix B-22)*

Psalm 149:1-6, 9. R. v. 4

The Lord takes delight in his people.

Luke 6:12-19

Jesus went out into the hills to pray; and he spent the whole night in prayer to God. When day came he summoned his disciples and picked out twelve of them; he called them 'apostles': Simon whom he called Peter, and his brother Andrew; James, John, Philip, Bartholomew, Matthew, Thomas, James son of Alphaeus, Simon called the Zealot, Judas son of James, and Judas Iscariot who became a traitor. He then came down with them and stopped at a piece of level ground where there was a large gathering of his disciples with a great crowd of people from all parts of Judaea and from Jerusalem and from the coastal region of Tyre and Sidon who had come to hear him and to be cured of their diseases. People tormented by unclean spirits were also cured, and everyone in the crowd was trying to touch him because power came out of him that cured them all.

Reflection

The story of humankind is one of great achievements and great failures. God was delighted when Adam and Eve came into being, but it did not take long for them to choose their own interests and turn away from God. And the story continues over the ages. In his First Letter to the Corinthians, St Paul names and condemns the wrongdoings of the people and reminds them that following Christ entails choosing God above themselves. Most amazing to us is that, despite our failures, God continuously gives us new chances to be like him. You and I can see ourselves in the twelve apostles chosen by Jesus in the Gospel reading of today. You and I are entrusted with continuing to follow him. You and I are summoned to be instruments of his healing. God takes delight in you and in me. Isn't that 'Good News'?

07
SEP WED

23rd Week in Ordinary Time
Green

1 Corinthians 7:25-31

About remaining celibate, I have no directions from the Lord but give my own opinion as one who, by the Lord's mercy, has stayed faithful. Well then, I believe that in these present times of stress this is right: that it is good for a man to stay as he is. If you are tied to a wife, do not look for freedom; if you are free of a wife, then do not look for one. But if you marry, it is no sin, and it is not a sin for a young girl to get married. They will have their troubles, though, in their married life, and I should like to spare you that.

Brothers, this is what I mean: our time is growing short. Those who have wives should live as though they had none, and those who mourn should live as though they had nothing to mourn for; those who are enjoying life should live as though there were nothing to laugh about; those whose life is buying things should live as though they had nothing of their own; and those who have to deal with the world should not become engrossed in it. I say this because the world as we know it is passing away.

Psalm 44:11-12, 14-17. R. v. 11

Listen, O daughter, give ear to my words.

Luke 6:20-26

Fixing his eyes on his disciples Jesus said: 'How happy are you who are poor: yours is the kingdom of God. Happy you who are hungry now: you shall be satisfied. Happy you who weep now: you shall laugh. Happy are you when people hate you, drive you out, abuse you, denounce your name as criminal, on account of the Son of Man. Rejoice when that day comes and dance for joy, for then your reward will be great in heaven. This was the way their ancestors treated the prophets. 'But alas for you who are rich: you are having your consolation now. Alas for you who have your fill now: you shall go hungry. Alas for you who laugh now: you shall mourn and weep. Alas for you when the world speaks well of you! This was the way their ancestors treated the false prophets.'

Reflection

At times in our life, perhaps especially when we are children, we may dream of being members of royalty. Perhaps we envy people who marry a prince or princess and live 'happily ever after'. Today's responsorial psalm is a royal psalm that describes the daughter of the king being led into the palace of the king amid gladness and joy. In the Gospel Jesus also speaks of a kingdom, the kingdom of God, to which we are all invited. How happy we will be in this kingdom, Jesus assures us. But here our imagination is challenged as the reasons Jesus gives for happiness are so different from those we dream about. Blessed are the poor, the hungry, those who weep, those insulted, etc. They are the ones following the true path to happiness. Are we ready to enter his palace?

The Nativity of the Blessed Virgin Mary
Feast | White

08
SEP THU

Micah 5:1-4
The Lord says this:

But you, Bethlehem Ephrathah, the least of the clans of Judah, out of you will be born for me the one who is to rule over Israel; his origin goes back to the distant past, to the days of old. The Lord is therefore going to abandon them till the time when she who is to give birth gives birth. Then the remnant of his brothers will come back to the sons of Israel. He will stand and feed his flock with the power of the Lord, with the majesty of the name of his God. They will live secure, for from then on he will extend his power to the ends of the land. He himself will be peace.

Psalm 12:6-7. R. Isaiah 61:10
I exult for joy in the Lord.

Matthew 1:18-23 *(Longer form, Matthew 1:1-16, 18-23)*
This is how Jesus Christ came to be born. His mother Mary was betrothed to Joseph; but before they came to live together she was found to be with child through the Holy Spirit. Her husband Joseph, being a man of honour and wanting to spare her publicity, decided to divorce her informally. He had made up his mind to do this when the angel of the Lord appeared to him in a dream and said, 'Joseph, son of David, do not be afraid to take Mary home as your wife, because she has conceived what is in her by the Holy Spirit. She will give birth to a son and you must name him Jesus, because he is the one who is to save his people from their sins.' Now all this took place to fulfil the words spoken by the Lord through the prophet: The virgin will conceive and give birth to a son and they will call him Emmanuel, a name which means 'God-is-with-us.'

Reflection
Family matters. The popularity of websites and institutions through which we can research our ancestors proves how important to us are our roots and the places to which we belong. The knowledge about our family history can be both reassuring and disturbing. Not all stories are the most encouraging or bring us pride, but the acceptance of who we are and where we came from brings us peace and makes our life more meaningful. Although the birth of Blessed Mary is not narrated in the Bible, we know that she was blessed in her parents and ancestors, and that her coming into the world was planned by God. Through the intercession of Blessed Mary, let us pray with thanksgiving for our own families today.

09
SEP FRI

23rd Week in Ordinary Time | Green
or **St Peter Claver,** *priest* (Optional, White)

1 Corinthians 9:16-19, 22-27
I do not boast of preaching the gospel, since it is a duty which has been laid on me; I should be punished if I did not preach it! If I had chosen this work myself, I might have been paid for it, but as I have not, it is a responsibility which has been put into my hands. Do you know what my reward is? It is this: in my preaching, to be able to offer the Good News free, and not insist on the rights which the gospel gives me.

So though I am not a slave of any man I have made myself the slave of everyone so as to win as many as I could. I made myself all things to all men in order to save some at any cost; and I still do this, for the sake of the gospel, to have a share in its blessing.

All the runners at the stadium are trying to win, but only one of them gets the prize. You must run in the same way, meaning to win. All the fighters at the games go into strict training; they do this just to win a wreath that will wither away, but we do it for a wreath that will never wither. That is how I run, intent on winning; that is how I fight, not beating the air. I treat my body hard and make it obey me, for, having been an announcer myself, I should not want to be disqualified.

Psalm 83:3-6, 12. R. v. 2
How lovely is your dwelling-place, Lord, God of hosts.

Luke 6:39-42
Jesus told a parable to the disciples, 'Can one blind man guide another? Surely both will fall into a pit? The disciple is not superior to his teacher; the fully trained disciple will always be like his teacher. Why do you observe the splinter in your brother's eye and never notice the plank in your own? How can you say to your brother, "Brother, let me take out the splinter that is in your eye," when you cannot see the plank in your own? Hypocrite! Take the plank out of your own eye first, and then you will see clearly enough to take out the splinter that is in your brother's eye.'

Reflection
We live in a very competitive world. The desire for instant gratification for everything we do and an expectation to be the best makes people self-centred and less sensitive to each other's needs. This is not what Jesus teaches us in the Gospel. He asks us to reflect on our own actions before seeing or commenting on what someone else does. We all tend to criticise and point out people's shortcomings much faster than seeing our own. St Paul reminds us today that our competitive spirit should be used only in spreading the Good News. We should never get tired in our efforts to live the values in the Gospel in our daily life. Through our actions, people will recognise that we are longing for God and the reward to be closer to him. Let's make it our goal for today.

23rd Week in Ordinary Time
Green

10
SEP SAT

1 Corinthians 10:14-22

My dear brothers, you must keep clear of idolatry. I say to you as sensible people: judge for yourselves what I am saying. The blessing-cup that we bless is a communion with the blood of Christ, and the bread that we break is a communion with the body of Christ. The fact that there is only one loaf means that, though there are many of us, we form a single body because we all have a share in this one loaf. Look at the other Israel, the race, where those who eat the sacrifices are in communion with the altar. Does this mean that the food sacrificed to idols has a real value, or that the idol itself is real? Not at all. It simply means that the sacrifices that they offer they sacrifice to demons who are not God. I have no desire to see you in communion with demons. You cannot drink the cup of the Lord and the cup of demons. You cannot take your share at the table of the Lord and the table of demons. Do we want to make the Lord angry; are we stronger than he is?

Psalm 115:12-13, 17-18. R. v. 17

A thanksgiving sacrifice I make to you, O Lord.

Luke 6:43-49

Jesus said to his disciples: 'There is no sound tree that produces rotten fruit, nor again a rotten tree that produces sound fruit. For every tree can be told by its own fruit: people do not pick figs from thorns, nor gather grapes from brambles. A good man draws what is good from the store of goodness in his heart; a bad man draws what is bad from the store of badness. For a man's words flow out of what fills his heart.

'Why do you call me, "Lord, Lord" and not do what I say?

'Everyone who comes to me and listens to my words and acts on them – I will show you what he is like. He is like the man who when he built his house dug, and dug deep, and laid the foundations on rock; when the river was in flood it bore down on that house but could not shake it, it was so well built. But the one who listens and does nothing is like the man who built his house on soil, with no foundations: as soon as the river bore down on it, it collapsed; and what a ruin that house became!'

Reflection

Today's readings are very confronting. One of the words that stands out is 'sacrifice'. St Paul challenges the Corinthians and us to be honest and realise that if we bring despair to others and disturb communion among believers, our sacrifice is not real and is not the one desired by God. What is real sacrifice, then? Jesus gives us two simple parables taken from everyday experience. If you are a good tree, you will produce good fruit. If you build your house on a strong foundation, your house will not collapse. It is simple indeed. The only real sacrifice on which God looks with favour is the one made with a genuine heart. And this cannot happen through our own efforts. We need to call upon the Lord's name, as the psalmist says today, and offer our good intentions, asking God to turn them into good deeds.

11
SEP SUN

TWENTY-FOURTH SUNDAY IN ORDINARY TIME

Psalter Week 4

Green

Exodus 32:7-11, 13-14

The Lord spoke to Moses, 'Go down now, because your people whom you brought out of Egypt have apostasised. They have been quick to leave the way I marked out for them; they have made themselves a calf of molten metal and have worshipped it and offered it sacrifice. "Here is your God, Israel," they have cried "who brought you up from the land of Egypt!" I can see how headstrong these people are! Leave me, now, my wrath shall blaze out against them and devour them; of you, however, I will make a great nation.' But Moses pleaded with the Lord his God. 'Lord,' he said, 'why should your wrath blaze out against this people of yours whom you brought out of the land of Egypt with arm outstretched and mighty hand? Remember Abraham, Isaac and Jacob, your servants to whom by your own self you swore and made this promise: I will make your offspring as many as the stars of heaven, and all this land which I promised I will give to your descendants, and it shall be their heritage for ever.' So the Lord relented and did not bring on the people the disaster he had threatened.

Psalm 50:3-4, 12-13, 17, 19. R. Luke 15:18

I will leave this place and go to my father.

1 Timothy 1:12-17

I thank Christ Jesus our Lord, who has given me strength, and who judged me faithful enough to call into his service even though I used to be a blasphemer and did all I could to injure and discredit the faith. Mercy, however, was shown me, because until I became a believer I had been acting in ignorance; and the grace of our Lord filled me with faith and with the love that is in Christ Jesus. Here is a saying that you can rely on and nobody should doubt: that Christ Jesus came into the world to save sinners. I myself am the greatest of them; and if mercy has been shown to me, it is because Jesus Christ meant to make me the greatest evidence of his inexhaustible patience for all the other people who would later have to trust in him to come to eternal life. To the eternal King, the undying, invisible and only God, be honour and glory for ever and ever. Amen.

Luke 15:1-2, 8-11 *(Longer form Luke 15:1-32)*

The tax collectors and the sinners were all seeking the company of Jesus to hear what he had to say, and the Pharisees and the scribes complained. 'This man' they said 'welcomes sinners and eats with them.' So he spoke this parable to them: 'What man among you with a hundred sheep, losing one, would not leave the ninety-nine in the wilderness and go after the missing one till he found it? And when he found it, would he not joyfully take it on his shoulders and then, when he got home, call together his friends, and neighbours? "Rejoice with me," he would say "I have found my sheep that was lost." In the same way, I tell you, there will be more rejoicing in heaven over one repentant sinner than over ninety-nine virtuous men who have no need of repentance. Or again, what woman with ten drachmas would not, if she lost one, light a lamp and sweep out the house and search thoroughly till she found it? And then, when she had found it, call together her friends and neighbours? "Rejoice with me," she would say "I have found the drachma I lost." In the same way, I tell you, there is rejoicing among the angels of God over one repentant sinner.'

Reflection

Our readings this Sunday are a handbook for learning about God. We read the words which, in the different contexts of the Old and New Testament stories, seem to say the same thing: God is merciful! Our reflection starts with a very well-known story about the people of Israel. Their action in replacing the Covenant of Love with worship of a golden calf shows both human weakness and the endless patience of God. Despite the chosen people disappointing their leader, Moses, by offending God, God is patient and does not bring on them any punishment. Similarly, what we learn in the responsorial psalm is that God is kind and forgiving. He can purify our hearts and make them his own again. There is even more reassurance about the extent of God's forgiveness for us, who have been sinners, in the letter of Saint Paul to Timothy. The parables in today's Gospel also highlight the mercy of God who searches for all who are lost until they are found. The focus in this story is not on how they came to be lost but on God who celebrates their return and shows even more clearly that his love is unconditional and endless. What if the focus of our week to come will be to mirror in some small way God's attitude? What if, this week, we try to find something good in every person we meet, despite our natural reaction to their wrongdoings? What if, this week, we try to be a little bit more merciful to ourselves? What if...?

12
SEP MON

24th Week in Ordinary Time | Green
or **The Most Holy Name of Mary** (Optional, White)

1 Corinthians 11:17-26, 33

On the subject of instructions, I cannot say that you have done well in holding meetings that do you more harm than good. In the first place, I hear that when you all come together as a community, there are separate factions among you, and I half believe it – since there must no doubt be separate groups among you, to distinguish those who are to be trusted. The point is, when you hold these meetings, it is not the Lord's Supper that you are eating, since when the time comes to eat, everyone is in such a hurry to start his own supper that one person goes hungry while another is getting drunk. ... *(Please see the Appendix B-22)*

Psalm 39:7-10, 17. R. v. 1 Corinthians 11:26

Proclaim the death of the Lord, until he comes.

Luke 7:1-10

When Jesus had come to the end of all he wanted the people to hear, he went into Capernaum. A centurion there had a servant, a favourite of his, who was sick and near death. Having heard about Jesus he sent some Jewish elders to him to ask him to come and heal his servant. When they came to Jesus they pleaded earnestly with him. 'He deserves this of you' they said 'because he is friendly towards our people; in fact, he is the one who built the synagogue. So Jesus went with them, and was not very far from the house when the centurion sent word to him by some friends: 'Sir,' he said 'do not put yourself to trouble; because I am not worthy to have you under my roof; and for this same reason I did not presume to come to you myself; but give the word and let my servant be cured. For I am under authority myself, and have soldiers under me; and I say to one man: Go, and he goes; to another: Come here, and he comes; to my servant: 'Do this, and he does it.' When Jesus heard these words he was astonished at him and, turning round, said to the crowd following him, 'I tell you, not even in Israel have I found faith like this.' And when the messengers got back to the house they found the servant in perfect health.

Reflection

We all like to be called by our name. It identifies us and highlights our uniqueness. In some languages and cultures, the name is chosen to describe the attributes the family hopes to see in the person. Quite often names are given to newborns out of respect for their ancestors. Jesus is a man of his own time and culture. Jewish people will never say out loud the name of God. God's name is Holy. Today, on this Optional Memorial of the Most Holy Name of Mary, we are reminded that Jesus's mother was part of this respectful and special culture that honoured a person's name. Of course, as Jesus points out, saying a person's name it is not enough to show respect. Our actions are also important. 'Why do you call me, "Lord, Lord" and not do what I say?' he asks his disciples. Perhaps we also need to ponder this question.

24th Week in Ordinary Time
St John Chrysostom, *bishop, doctor,* **Memorial** | White

13
SEP TUE

1 Corinthians 12:12-14, 27-31

Just as a human body, though it is made up of many parts, is a single unit because all these parts, though many, make one body, so it is with Christ. In the one Spirit we were all baptised, Jews as well as Greeks, slaves as well as citizens, and one Spirit was given to us all to drink. Nor is the body to be identified with any one of its many parts. Now you together are Christ's body; but each of you is a different part of it. In the Church, God has given the first place to apostles, the second to prophets, the third to teachers; after them, miracles, and after them the gift of healing; helpers, good leaders, those with many languages. Are all of them apostles, or all of them prophets, or all of them teachers? Do they all have the gift of miracles, or all have the gift of healing? Do all speak strange languages, and all interpret them? Be ambitious for the higher gifts.

Psalm 99. R. v. 3

We are his people, the sheep of his flock.

Luke 7:11-17

Jesus went to a town called Nain, accompanied by his disciples and a great number of people. When he was near the gate of the town it happened that a dead man was being carried out for burial, the only son of his mother, and she was a widow.

And a considerable number of the townspeople were with her. When the Lord saw her he felt sorry for her. 'Do not cry' he said. Then he went up and put his hand on the bier and the bearers stood still, and he said, 'Young man, I tell you to get up.' And the dead man sat up and began to talk, and Jesus gave him to his mother. Everyone was filled with awe and praised God saying, 'A great prophet has appeared among us; God has visited his people.' And this opinion of him spread throughout Judaea and all over the countryside.

Reflection

It amazes me how little we believe in ourselves at times and how easily we come to the conclusion that who we are and what we do is not 'good enough'. The readings of today encourage us to name our gifts and use them for the benefits of others, and also to be 'ambitious for the higher gifts'. This sentence makes me curious. What are the higher gifts which the Apostle Paul encourages the Corinthians to long for? Today's Gospel story gives some insight. We see Jesus showing empathy and compassion to a mother who just lost her son. The ultimate gift he gives to this woman is the gift of life, given to her son for the second time. This validates the actions of Jesus, and the message 'God has visited his people' spreads rapidly by word-of-mouth. Will anyone be able to say this on account of my actions today? How do I bring myself and others to God?

14
SEP WED

The Exaltation of the Holy Cross
Feast | Red

Numbers 21:4-9

On the way through the wilderness the people lost patience. They spoke against God and against Moses, 'Why did you bring us out of Egypt to die in this wilderness? For there is neither bread nor water here: we are sick of this unsatisfying food.' At this God sent fiery serpents among the people; their bite brought death to many in Israel. The people came and said to Moses, 'We have sinned by speaking against the Lord and against you. Intercede for us with the Lord to save us from these serpents.' Moses interceded for the people, and the Lord answered him, 'Make a fiery serpent and put it on a standard. If anyone is bitten and looks at it, he shall live.' So Moses fashioned a bronze serpent which he put on a standard, and if anyone was bitten by a serpent, he looked at the bronze serpent and lived.

Psalm 77:1-2, 34-38. R. v. 7

Never forget the deeds of the Lord.

Philippians 2:6-11

The state of Jesus Christ was divine, yet he did not cling to his equality with God but emptied himself to assume the condition of a slave, and became as men are: and being as all men are, he was humbler yet, even to accepting death, death on a cross. But God raised him high and gave him the name which is above all other names so that all beings in the heavens, on earth and in the underworld, should bend the knee at the name of Jesus and that every tongue should acclaim Jesus Christ as Lord, to the glory of God the Father.

John 3:13-17

Jesus said to Nicodemus: 'No one has gone up to heaven except the one who came down from heaven, the Son of Man who is in heaven; and the Son of Man must be lifted up as Moses lifted up the serpent in the desert, so that everyone who believes may have eternal life in him. Yes, God loved the world so much that he gave his only Son, so that everyone who believes in him may not be lost but may have eternal life. For God sent his Son into the world not to condemn the world, but so that through him the world might be saved.'

Reflection

The Feast of the Exaltation of the Holy Cross recalls three historical events: the finding of the Cross of Calvary by Saint Helena; the dedication of the churches built by Constantine on the site of the Holy Sepulchre on Mount Calvary; and the restoration of the True Cross to Jerusalem by the emperor Heraclius II. These reasons help us to acknowledge the historical site of our faith. However, the true reason to commemorate this day is the One who died on the cross – Jesus. Today's Gospel lists the reasons why we reverence the cross. It is the supreme expression of God's saving love for humanity and the true source of our forgiveness and healing. It is truly the instrument of our salvation. Let us be attentive every time we bless ourselves with the sign of the cross, thanking Jesus for his love for us.

24th Week in Ordinary Time
Our Lady of Sorrows, Memorial | White

15
SEP THU

Hebrews 5:7-9
During his life on earth, Christ offered up prayer and entreaty, aloud and in silent tears, to the one who had the power to save him out of death, and he submitted so humbly that his prayer was heard. Although he was Son, he learnt to obey through suffering; but having been made perfect, he became for all who obey him the source of eternal salvation.

Psalm 30:2-6, 15-16, 20. R. v. 17
Save me, O Lord, in your love.

John 19:25-27 *(Alternative Reading Luke 2:33-35)*
Near the cross of Jesus stood his mother and his mother's sister, Mary the wife of Clopas, and Mary of Magdala. Seeing his mother and the disciple he loved standing near her, Jesus said to his mother, 'Woman, this is your son.' Then to the disciple he said, 'This is your mother.' And from that moment the disciple made a place for her in his home.

Reflection
Some years ago, I received a set of prayer beads which looked like a rosary. When I started to pray, I realised that there are seven sets of seven beads which left me confused about how to use them. Little did I know that I had been given the Rosary of the Seven Sorrows. This prayer has now become close to my heart. Based on the Scriptures, the mysteries of this chaplet recall the Sorrows the Virgin Mother of God endured in love during the life, suffering and death of her son, Jesus. Meditating on these sorrows has helped me on many occasions when I was experiencing life's tribulations. Today's scene from the Gospel describes the ultimate moment of the sorrow of Mary – the death of her Son on the cross. Let us thank Jesus for giving us a Mother who feels our hurts and sorrows and is there for us when we need her the most.

16
SEP FRI

ST NINIAN, BISHOP
Feast – Scotland
see Appendix A-22
White

24th Week in Ordinary Time | Sts Cornelius, *pope,* **and Cyprian,** *bishop, martyrs,* **Memorial** | Red

1 Corinthians 15:12-20

If Christ raised from the dead is what has been preached, how can some of you be saying that there is no resurrection of the dead? If there is no resurrection of the dead, Christ himself cannot have been raised and if Christ has not been raised then our preaching is useless and your believing it is useless; indeed, we are shown up as witnesses who have committed perjury before God, because we swore in evidence before God that he had raised Christ to life. For if the dead are not raised, Christ has not been raised, and if Christ has not been raised, you are still in your sins. And what is more serious, all who have died in Christ have perished. If our hope in Christ has been for this life only, we are the most unfortunate of all people.

But Christ has in fact been raised from the dead, the first-fruits of all who have fallen asleep.

Psalm 16:1, 6-8, 15. R. v. 15

I shall be filled, when I awake, with the sight of your glory, O Lord.

Luke 8:1-3

Jesus made his way through towns and villages preaching, and proclaiming the Good News of the kingdom of God. With him went the Twelve, as well as certain women, who had been cured of evil spirits and ailments: Mary surnamed the Magdalene, from whom seven demons had gone out, Joanna the wife of Herod's steward Chuza, Susanna, and several others who provided for them out of their own resources.

Reflection

Today's Gospel is very short. Every time I read it, however, many thoughts spring to mind. Firstly, we learn that Jesus made his way through towns and villages, preaching and proclaiming the Good News about the kingdom of God. As I listen to these words, I ask myself: as I make my way through the day at work and home, do my words and actions point to the kingdom of God? Secondly, we learn that Jesus was accompanied by his disciples. This makes me think, as a disciple of Jesus, how well I am following him and his teaching in my daily routine. Finally, the Gospel lists the names of women who were supporting Jesus in his mission from their own resources. This statement makes me ponder on my own generosity and eagerness in supporting Jesus' mission in his Church community.

24th Week in Ordinary Time | Green
or **St Robert Bellarmine,** *bishop, doctor* (Optional, White)
or **St Hildegard of Bingen,** *doctor* (Optional, White)

17
SEP SAT

1 Corinthians 15:35-37, 42-49
(Please see the Appendix B-22)

Psalm 55:10-14. R. cf. v. 14
I shall walk in the presence of God in the light of the living.

Luke 8:4-15
With a large crowd gathering and people from every town finding their way to him, Jesus used this parable: 'A sower went out to sow his seed. As he sowed, some fell on the edge of the path and was trampled on; and the birds of the air ate it up. Some seed fell on rock, and when it came up it withered away, having no moisture. Some seed fell amongst thorns and the thorns grew with it and choked it. And some seed fell into rich soil and grew and produced its crop a hundredfold.' Saying this he cried, 'Listen, anyone who has ears to hear!'

The disciples asked him what this parable might mean, and he said, 'The mysteries of the kingdom of God are revealed to you; for the rest there are only parables, so that they may see but not perceive, listen but not understand.

'This, then, is what the parable means: the seed is the word of God. Those on the edge of the path are people who have heard it, and then the devil comes and carries away the word from their hearts in case they should believe and be saved. Those on the rock are people who, when they first hear it, welcome the word with joy. But these have no root; they believe for a while, and in time of trial they give up. As for the part that fell into thorns, this is people who have heard, but as they go on their way they are choked by the worries and riches and pleasures of life and do not reach maturity. As for the part in the rich soil, this is people with a noble and generous heart who have heard the word and take it to themselves and yield a harvest through their perseverance.'

Reflection
It fascinates me how down to earth Jesus was when talking to his various audiences. He spoke differently to fishermen than to those working in the fields. He carefully chose his words, using examples that each group would understand. To explain the various responses of people to the word of God, Jesus took the image of seed that is sown in a field. The seed (the Word of God) is good, but its fruitfulness depends on the condition of the soil in which the seed is sown. The people would have immediately understood what he was saying. Some realities, like the resurrection of the body that Paul speaks about in today's first reading, are more difficult to understand. We give thanks for great theologians and teachers like St Robert Bellarmine and St Hildegard, whom we remember today, who throughout the centuries have continued to explore and shed greater light on the mysteries of our faith.

18
SEP SUN

TWENTY-FIFTH SUNDAY IN ORDINARY TIME

Psalter Week 1

Green

Amos 8:4-7

Listen to this, you who trample on the needy and try to suppress the poor people of the country, you who say, 'When will New Moon be over so that we can sell our corn, and sabbath, so that we can market our wheat? Then by lowering the bushel, raising the shekel, by swindling and tampering with the scales, we can buy up the poor for money, and the needy for a pair of sandals, and get a price even for the sweeping of the wheat.' The Lord swears it by the pride of Jacob, 'Never will I forget a single thing you have done.'

Psalm 112:1-2, 4-8. R. cf. vv. 1, 7

Praise the Lord, who raises the poor.

1 Timothy 2:1-8

My advice is that, first of all, there should be prayers offered for everyone – petitions, intercessions and thanksgiving – and especially for kings and others in authority, so that we may be able to live religious and reverent lives in peace and quiet. To do this is right, and will please God our saviour: he wants everyone to be saved and reach full knowledge of the truth. For there is only one God, and there is only one mediator between God and humankind, himself a man, Christ Jesus, who sacrificed himself as a ransom for them all. He is the evidence of this, sent at the appointed time, and I have been named a herald and apostle of it and – I am telling the truth and no lie – a teacher of the faith and the truth to the pagans.

In every place, then, I want the men to lift their hands up reverently in prayer, with no anger or argument.

Luke 16:1-13

Jesus said to his disciples, 'There was a rich man and he had a steward who was denounced to him for being wasteful with his property. He called for the man and said, "What is this I hear about you? Draw me up an account of your stewardship because you are not to be my steward any longer." Then the steward said to himself, "Now that my master is taking the stewardship from me, what am I to do? Dig? I am not strong enough. Go begging? I should be too ashamed. Ah, I know what I will do to make sure that when I am dismissed from office there will be some to welcome me into their homes."

'Then he called his master's debtors one by one. To the first he said, "How much do you owe my master?" "One hundred measures of oil" was the reply. The steward said, "Here, take your bond; sit down straight away and write fifty." To another he said, "And you, sir, how much do you owe?" "One hundred measures of wheat" was the reply. The steward said, "Here, take your bond and write eighty."

'The master praised the dishonest steward for his astuteness. For the children of this world are more astute in dealing with their own kind than are the children of light.

'And so I tell you this: use money, tainted as it is, to win you friends, and thus make sure that when it fails you, they will welcome you into the tents of eternity. The man who can be trusted in little things can be trusted in great; the man who is dishonest in little things can be dishonest in great. If then you cannot be trusted with money, that tainted thing, who will trust you with genuine riches? And if you cannot be trusted with what is not yours, who will give you what is your very own? 'No servant can be the slave of two masters: he will either hate the first and love the second, or treat the first with respect and the second with scorn. You cannot be the slave both of God and of money.'

Reflection

From our earliest days we have been told that people in authority shouldn't have favourites. If someone receives 'special treatment' others will complain about unfairness and prejudice. But the readings of this Sunday show that God very clearly 'favours' one group of people. All those who are poor, needy, lonely and disadvantaged will be the ones whose prayers are answered first. God never forgets those who help his favoured people and encourages us to praise the Lord in all of life's circumstances. It is eye-opening to realise that God, whom we may think of as being 'up-high', takes an interest in the lives of those who are 'low down'. All the promises about the kingdom of God, which were fulfilled in the person of Jesus, become clear and visible. Only those who, like Jesus, are willing to do what they can to help others, live according to God's plans. But to choose God instead of fame, money or any other possession is not only an act of our will. God encourages us to rely on him, to draw our energy and enthusiasm from his power and use every possible opportunity to bring people to him. Our astuteness should be expressed in our eagerness to choose the good over bad and others over ourselves. This is a much greater challenge than working out how to spend our money responsibly.

19
SEP MON

25th Week in Ordinary Time | Green
or **St Januarius,** *bishop, martyr* (Optional, Red)

Proverbs 3:27-34

My son, do not refuse a kindness to anyone who begs it, if it is in your power to perform it. Do not say to your neighbour, 'Go away! Come another time! I will give it tomorrow,' if you can do it now. Do not plot harm against your neighbour as he lives unsuspecting next door. Do not pick a groundless quarrel with a man who has done you no harm. Do not emulate the man of violence, never model your conduct on his; for the wilful wrong-doer is abhorrent to the Lord, who confides only in honest men.

The Lord's curse lies on the house of the wicked, but he blesses the home of the virtuous. He mocks those who mock, but accords his favour to the humble.

Psalm 14:2-5. R. v. 1

The just will live in the presence of the Lord.

Luke 8:16-18

Jesus said to his disciples: 'No one lights a lamp to cover it with a bowl or to put it under a bed. No, he puts it on a lamp-stand so that people may see the light when they come in. For nothing is hidden but it will be made clear, nothing secret but it will be known and brought to light. So take care how you hear; for anyone who has will be given more; from anyone who has not, even what he thinks he has will be taken away.'

Reflection

Today's reading from the book of Proverbs reminds me of the many motivational, inspirational quotes we can find on social media. The positive words of the sacred writer encouraging us to act now and help those in need are timeless. The time to do good for the sake of others is every day and every time. This is what Jesus expects of we who are the light of the world. Those who want to follow Jesus' call cannot be shy and stay in a dark corner, unsure of their values and what they must do. If we are disciples of Christ, our only choice is to stay faithful to being virtuous. This is a tough call, but we are not alone in living it. God empowers us and always wants to give us more.

25th Week in Ordinary Time | Sts Andrew Kim Tae-gŏn, *priest, martyr,* **and Paul Chŏng Ha-sang and companions,** *martyrs,* **Memorial** | Red

20 SEP TUE

Proverbs 21:1-6, 10-13

Like flowing water is the heart of the king in the hand of the Lord, who turns it where he pleases. A man's conduct may strike him as upright, the Lord, however, weighs the heart. To act virtuously and with justice is more pleasing to the Lord than sacrifice. Haughty eye, proud heart, lamp of the wicked, nothing but sin. The hardworking man is thoughtful, and all is gain; too much haste, and all that comes of it is want. To make a fortune with the help of a lying tongue, such the idle fantasy of those who look for death. The wicked man's soul is intent on evil, he looks on his neighbour with dislike. When a mocker is punished, the ignorant man grows wiser, when a wise man is instructed he acquires more knowledge. The Just One watches the house of the wicked: he hurls the wicked to destruction. He who shuts his ear to the poor man's cry shall himself plead and not be heard.

Psalm 118:1, 27, 30, 34-35, 44. R. v. 35

Guide me, Lord, in the path of your commands.

Luke 8:19-21

The mother and the brothers of Jesus came looking for him, but they could not get to him because of the crowd. He was told, 'Your mother and brothers are standing outside and want to see you.' But he said in answer, 'My mother and my brothers are those who hear the word of God and put it into practice.'

Reflection

The book of Proverbs contains a collection of sayings by various people. We do not know their names but clearly, they were people of wisdom who were able to draw valuable lessons from their experience of life. Through succinct 'wise sayings' (proverbs) they were able to pass on these lessons to future generations. Today's responsorial psalm, which also comes from the Bible's wisdom tradition, reassures us that God's way brings happiness and peace. Today's Gospel episode may disturb us because of the way Jesus responds when told that his mother and relatives are waiting outside. His words seem to be sharp and insensitive. But there is wisdom in his words that 'my mother and brothers are those who hear the word of God and keep it'. He is expanding the concept of family not rejecting it. Mary is his mother not only by virtue of giving birth to him but above all by being someone who heard God's word and put it into practice in her life.

21
SEP WED

St Matthew, Apostle and Evangelist
Feast | Red

Ephesians 4:1-7, 11-13

I, the prisoner in the Lord, implore you to lead a life worthy of your vocation. Bear with one another charitably, in complete selflessness, gentleness and patience. Do all you can to preserve the unity of the Spirit by the peace that binds you together. There is one Body, one Spirit, just as you were all called into one and the same hope when you were called. There is one Lord, one faith, one baptism, and one God who is Father of all, over all, through all and within all.

Each one of us, however, has been given his own share of grace, given as Christ allotted it. And to some, his gift was that they should be apostles; to some, prophets; to some, evangelists; to some, pastors and teachers; so that the saints together make a unity in the work of service, building up the body of Christ. In this way we are all to come to unity in our faith and in our knowledge of the Son of God, until we become the perfect Man, fully mature with the fullness of Christ himself.

Psalm 18:2-5. R. v. 5

Their word goes forth through all the earth.

Matthew 9:9-13

As Jesus was walking on he saw a man named Matthew sitting by the customs house, and he said to him, 'Follow me.' And he got up and followed him.

While he was at dinner in the house it happened that a number of tax collectors and sinners came to sit at the table with Jesus and his disciples. When the Pharisees saw this, they said to his disciples, 'Why does your master eat with tax collectors and sinners?' When he heard this he replied, 'It is not the healthy who need the doctor, but the sick. Go and learn the meaning of the words: What I want is mercy, not sacrifice. And indeed I did not come to call the virtuous, but sinners.'

Reflection

The verb 'to follow' has taken on a very different meaning in the age of social media. Today we 'follow' people on Facebook, Twitter, Instagram and other platforms. Quite often we measure our popularity by how many people 'follow' us and are interested in updates about our activities and ideas. This is certainly not how St Matthew, whose feast we celebrate today, understood the invitation of Jesus to follow him. Being a tax collector, the last thing he would have expected was to be called to follow a rabbi. In the history of Christianity, some very unlikely people have heard the call of Jesus to follow him and their positive response has produced new and very effective ways of spreading the Good News throughout the earth. Let us try our best to follow Jesus intentionally in both word and deed that those who follow us may experience the true love of God.

25th Week in Ordinary Time
Green

22
SEP THU

Ecclesiastes 1:2-11

Vanity of vanities, the Preacher says. Vanity of vanities. All is vanity! For all his toil, his toil under the sun, what does man gain by it?

A generation goes, a generation comes, yet the earth stands firm for ever. The sun rises, the sun sets; then to its place it speeds and there it rises. Southward goes the wind, then turns to the north; it turns and turns again; back then to its circling goes the wind. Into the sea all the rivers go, and yet the sea is never filled, and still to their goal the rivers go. All things are wearisome. No man can say that eyes have not had enough of seeing, ears their fill of hearing. What was will be again; what has been done will be done again; and there is nothing new under the sun. Take anything of which it may be said, 'Look now, this is new.' Already, long before our time, it existed. Only no memory remains of earlier times, just as in times to come next year itself will not be remembered.

Psalm 89:3-6, 12-14, 17. R. v. 1

O Lord, you have been our refuge from one generation to the next.

Luke 9:7-9

Herod the tetrarch had heard about all that was being done by Jesus; and he was puzzled, because some people were saying that John had risen from the dead, others that Elijah had reappeared, still others that one of the ancient prophets had come back to life. But Herod said, 'John? I beheaded him. So who is this I hear such reports about?' And he was anxious to see him.

Reflection

Today's reading from the book Ecclesiastes is quoted by many in various life situations. Our life passes so quickly. We do not know how long or short our time is on earth. As we grow older, we tend to gain much more understanding of those things that truly matter and those we need to let go. But it is always easier to say than to do. Life's tribulations and our insecurities make us feel anxious like Herod, who in today's Gospel felt afraid of both St John the Baptist and Jesus. The unknown, or things we think are too much to cope with, sometimes make us feel hopeless or depressed. Our most important task is well described in the responsorial psalm: to be close to God in every age and to find refuge in Him. This is the best and the most fulfilling way to live.

23
SEP FRI

25th Week in Ordinary Time
St Pius of Pietrelcina, *priest,* **Memorial** | White

Ecclesiastes 3:1-11

There is a season for everything, a time for every occupation under heaven: A time for giving birth, a time for dying; a time for planting, a time for uprooting what has been planted. A time for killing, a time for healing; a time for knocking down, a time for building. A time for tears, a time for laughter; a time for mourning, a time for dancing. A time for throwing stones away, a time for gathering them up; a time for embracing, a time to refrain from embracing. A time for searching, a time for losing; a time for keeping, a time for throwing away. A time for tearing, a time for sewing; a time for keeping silent, a time for speaking. A time for loving, a time for hating; a time for war, a time for peace.

What does a man gain for the efforts that he makes? I contemplate the task that God gives mankind to labour at. All that he does is apt for its time; but though he has permitted man to consider time in its wholeness, man cannot comprehend the work of God from beginning to end.

Psalm 143:1-4. R. v. 1

Blessed be the Lord, my rock.

Luke 9:18-22

One day when Jesus was praying alone in the presence of his disciples he put this question to them, 'Who do the crowds say I am?' And they answered, 'John the Baptist; others Elijah; and others say one of the ancient prophets come back to life.' 'But you,' he said 'who do you say I am?' It was Peter who spoke up. 'The Christ of God' he said. But he gave them strict orders not to tell anyone anything about this. 'The Son of Man' he said 'is destined to suffer grievously, to be rejected by the elders and chief priests and scribes and to be put to death, and to be raised up on the third day.'

Reflection

We all desire to love God the best we can. There are times when we proclaim our love joyously, repeating the words of the psalmist: 'The Lord is my rock, my love and my fortress'. We lean on him in times of tribulation and praise him on happy occasions. We see the Lord's greatness in comparison to our own littleness. Sometimes we struggle with see his loving presence and perhaps at times complain about being abandoned by him. To recognise that he is with us can be a challenge. In today's Gospel, Jesus puts a difficult but important question to his disciples: Who do you say I am? Peter had the courage and the spiritual insight to declare, 'You are the Christ, the son of the Living God.' It seems the other disciples were still unsure, and their faith was shaken further by Jesus' words that he was destined to suffer grievously, be put to death and be raised on the third day. Today Jesus asks each of us: Who am I for you? Reflect honestly and give him your answer.

25th Week in Ordinary Time
Green

24
SEP SAT

Ecclesiastes 11:9–12:8

Rejoice in your youth, you who are young; let your heart give you joy in your young days. Follow the promptings of your heart and the desires of your eyes. But this you must know: for all these things God will bring you to judgement. Cast worry from your heart, shield your flesh from pain. Yet youth, the age of dark hair, is vanity. And remember your creator in the days of your youth, before evil days come and the years approach when you say, 'These give me no pleasure', before sun and light and moon and stars grow dark, and the clouds return after the rain; the day when those who keep the house tremble and strong men are bowed; when the women grind no longer at the mill, because day is darkening at the windows and the street doors are shut; when the sound of the mill is faint, when the voice of the bird is silenced, and song notes are stilled, when to go uphill is an ordeal and a walk is something to dread. Yet the almond tree is in flower, the grasshopper is heavy with food and the caper bush bears its fruit, while man goes to his everlasting home. And the mourners are already walking to and fro in the street before the silver cord has snapped, or the golden lamp been broken, or the pitcher shattered at the spring, or the pulley cracked at the well, or before the dust returns to the earth as it once came from it, and the breath of God who gave it.

Vanity of vanities, the Preacher says. All is vanity.

Psalm 89:3-6, 12-14, 17. R. v. 1

O Lord, you have been our refuge from one generation to the next.

Luke 9:43-45

At a time when everyone was full of admiration for all he did, Jesus said to his disciples, 'For your part, you must have these words constantly in your mind: The Son of Man is going to be handed over into the power of men.' But they did not understand him when he said this; it was hidden from them so that they should not see the meaning of it, and they were afraid to ask him about what he had just said.

Reflection

I like talking to the people in our aged care home. It is always interesting to hear the stories of their youth and to learn about the joys, challenges and accomplishments of their life. Even those who have lived long and full lives, and are still active, agree on one thing: life is short and passes so quickly. Today's first reading describes this in beautiful yet melancholic detail. Life is a great and wonderful gift, and while we can enjoy the gifts that come to us, we must always recognise their temporary character. The shortness of life should not, however, lead us to discouragement or inactivity. Whatever our age, we have the precious gift of this day. Like the psalmist, let us ask the Lord's blessing on the work we will do today, whatever that may be. May we say 'yes' for all that will come our way this day. And may we be encouraged by our faith that at the end of our life on this earth we will be raised to a new and glorious life with God.

25
SEP SUN

TWENTY-SIXTH SUNDAY IN ORDINARY TIME

Psalter Week 2

Green

Amos 6:1, 4-7

The almighty Lord says this:

Woe to those ensconced so snugly in Zion
and those who feel so safe on the mountain of Samaria.
Lying on ivory beds
and sprawling on their divans,
they dine on lambs from the flock,
and stall-fattened veal;
they bawl to the sound of the harp,
they invent new instruments of music like David,
they drink wine by the bowlful,
and use the finest oil for anointing themselves,
but about the ruin of Joseph they do not care at all.
That is why they will be the first to be exiled;
the sprawlers' revelry is over.

Psalm 145:6-10. R. v. 2

My soul, give praise to the Lord.

1 Timothy 6:11-16

As a man dedicated to God, you must aim to be saintly and religious, filled with faith and love, patient and gentle. Fight the good fight of the faith and win for yourself the eternal life to which you were called when you made your profession and spoke up for the truth in front of many witnesses. Now, before God the source of all life and before Jesus Christ, who spoke up as a witness for the truth in front of Pontius Pilate, I put to you the duty of doing all that you have been told, with no faults or failures, until the Appearing of our Lord Jesus Christ,

who at the due time will be revealed
by God, the blessed and only Ruler of all,
the King of kings and the Lord of lords,
who alone is immortal,
whose home is in inaccessible light,
whom no man has seen and no man is able to see:
to him be honour and everlasting power. Amen.

Luke 16:19-31

Jesus said to the Pharisees: 'There was a rich man who used to dress in purple and fine linen and feast magnificently every day. And at his gate there lay a poor man called Lazarus, covered with sores, who longed to fill himself with the scraps that fell from the rich man's table. Dogs even came and licked his sores. Now the poor man died and was carried away by the angels to the bosom of Abraham. The rich man also died and was buried.

'In his torment in Hades he looked up and saw Abraham a long way off with Lazarus in his bosom. So he cried out, "Father Abraham, pity me and send Lazarus to dip the tip of his finger in water and cool my tongue, for I am in agony in these flames." "My son," Abraham replied "remember that during your life good things came your way, just as bad things came the way of Lazarus. Now he is being comforted here while you are in agony. But that is not all: between us and you a great gulf has been fixed, to stop any crossing from your side to ours."

'The rich man replied, "Father, I beg you then to send Lazarus to my father's house, since I have five brothers, to give them warning so that they do not come to this place of torment too." "They have Moses and the prophets," said Abraham "let them listen to them." "Ah no, father Abraham," said the rich man "but if someone comes to them from the dead, they will repent." Then Abraham said to him, "If they will not listen either to Moses or to the prophets, they will not be convinced even if someone should rise from the dead." '

Reflection

Our journey through the Gospel of Luke in our Sunday readings continues to explore human weaknesses. This week's topic encourages us to reflect on the consequences of our life's choices and the values we live by. We meet two symbolic characters, a wealthy man and a poor man, who both face God and are sent to the places they deserve. For Lazarus, this brings relief from the pain and suffering which he experienced on earth. For the rich man it brings the suffering in Hades that he did not expect while living his self-absorbed life. These stories have a common thread, which St Paul highlights in his letter to Timothy, when he encourages him to fight the good fight to win for himself eternal life. While we recognise the weakness of our human nature and how easily we fail, we also see that God accepts us with our shortcomings and his faithful love helps us to refocus, to see the lonely, hungry and abandoned. Let us make an intentional choice this week to stay focused on the needs of others, not on our own. Let us aspire to be saintly – loving, patient and gentle.

26
SEP MON

26th Week in Ordinary Time | Green
or **Sts Cosmas and Damian,** *martyrs* (Optional, White)

Job 1:6-22

One day the Sons of God came to attend on the Lord, and among them was Satan. So the Lord said to Satan, 'Where have you been?' 'Round the earth,' he answered 'roaming about.' So the Lord asked him, 'Did you notice my servant Job? There is no one like him on the earth: a sound and honest man who fears God and shuns evil.' 'Yes,' Satan said 'but Job is not God-fearing for nothing, is he? Have you not put a wall round him and his house and all his domain? You have blessed all he undertakes, and his flocks throng the countryside. But stretch out your hand and lay a finger on his possessions: I warrant you, he will curse you to your face.' 'Very well,' the Lord said to Satan 'all he has is in your power. But keep your hands off his person.' So Satan left the presence of the Lord.

On the day when Job's sons and daughters were at their meal and drinking wine at their eldest brother's house, a messenger came to Job. 'Your oxen' he said 'were at the plough, with the donkeys grazing at their side, when the Sabaeans swept down on them and carried them off. Your servants they put to the sword: I alone escaped to tell you.' He had not finished speaking when another messenger arrived. … *(Please see the Appendix B-23)*

Psalm 16:1-3, 6-7. R. v. 6

Turn your ear to me, O Lord; hear my words.

Luke 9:46-50

An argument started between the disciples about which of them was the greatest. Jesus knew what thoughts were going through their minds, and he took a little child and set him by his side and then said to them, 'Anyone who welcomes this little child in my name welcomes me; and anyone who welcomes me welcomes the one who sent me. For the least among you all, that is the one who is great.' John spoke up. 'Master,' he said 'we saw a man casting out devils in your name, and because he is not with us we tried to stop him.' But Jesus said to him, 'You must not stop him: anyone who is not against you is for you.'

Reflection

Situations arise in all our lives that can test our faith in God and in ourselves. Sudden news about a terminal illness, the loss of employment, a broken relationship or some other tragic event may lead us to get angry with God and ask him where he is or was in our time of trouble. Or we can blame ourselves for what has happened and try to identify what we have done wrong. When we read the story of Job, which we start today, we see that oftentimes neither God nor ourselves are to blame. Even the most faithful servant of God can go through tribulations that have no reasonable explanation. Though it is difficult, we are often being invited to have a childlike trust in God in these situations, to have faith that God is close to us and hears our prayer. We can be sure that Christ is present in the people who welcome us and support us in those difficult moments. Let us pray today for those whose faith is being tested at this time.

27 SEP TUE

26th Week in Ordinary Time
St Vincent de Paul, *priest,* **Memorial** | White

Job 3:1-3, 11-17, 20-23

Job broke the silence and cursed the day of his birth. This is what he said: May the day perish when I was born, and the night that told of a boy conceived. Why did I not die new-born, not perish as I left the womb? Why were there two knees to receive me, two breasts for me to suck? Had there not been, I should now be lying in peace, wrapped in a restful slumber, with the kings and high viziers of earth who build themselves vast vaults, or with princes who have gold and to spare and houses crammed with silver. Or put away like a still-born child that never came to be, like unborn babes that never see the light. Down there, bad men bustle no more, there the weary rest. Why give light to a man of grief? Why give life to those bitter of heart, who long for a death that never comes, and hunt for it more than for a buried treasure? They would be glad to see the grave-mound and shout with joy if they reached the tomb. Why make this gift of light to a man who does not see his way, whom God baulks on every side?

Psalm 87:2-8. R. v. 3

Let my prayer come into your presence, O Lord.

Luke 9:51-56

As the time drew near for him to be taken up to heaven, Jesus resolutely took the road for Jerusalem and sent messengers ahead of him. These set out, and they went into a Samaritan village to make preparations for him, but the people would not receive him because he was making for Jerusalem. Seeing this, the disciples James and John said, 'Lord, do you want us to call down fire from heaven to burn them up?' But he turned and rebuked them, and they went off to another village.

Reflection

In our lives we seek to avoid rejection and loss at any cost. At the same time, we often reject others and leave them feeling abandoned and not supported. The story of Job shows in a very dramatic and extreme way that despite our right choices, life can take from us almost everything that we think we deserve. Our natural reaction to rejection and injustice is defence and avoidance. Hearing that some Samaritans did not accept Jesus, James and John came up with the idea of burning this village. But Jesus firmly rebuked them. Like Job, who in the misery of his situation turns to God, we too are invited to turn to God in prayer and cry for help. We have nothing to fear! He has conquered the devil and death – he will help us in our life's challenges.

28
SEP WED

26th Week in Ordinary Time | Green
or **St Wenceslaus,** *martyr* (Optional, Red)
or **St Lawrence Ruiz and companions,** *martyrs* (Opt., Red)

Job 9:1-12, 14-16

Job spoke to his friends. Indeed, I know it is as you say: how can man be in the right against God? If any were so rash as to challenge him for reasons, one in a thousand could be more than they could answer. His heart is wise, and his strength is great: who then can successfully defy him? He moves the mountains, though they do not know it; he throws them down when he is angry. He shakes the earth, and moves it from its place, making all its pillars tremble. The sun, at his command, forbears to rise, and on the stars he sets a seal. He and no other stretched out the skies, and trampled the Sea's tall waves. The Bear, Orion too, are of his making, the Pleiades and the Mansions of the South. His works are great, beyond all reckoning, his marvels, past all counting. Were he to pass me, I should not see him, nor detect his stealthy movement. Were he to snatch a prize, who could prevent him, or dare to say, 'What are you doing?' How dare I plead my cause, then, or choose arguments against him? Suppose I am in the right, what use is my defence? For he whom I must sue is judge as well. If he deigned to answer my citation, could I be sure that he would listen to my voice?

Psalm 87:10-15. R. v. 3

Let my prayer come into your presence, O Lord.

Luke 9:57-62

As Jesus and his disciples travelled along they met a man on the road who said to him, 'I will follow you wherever you go.' Jesus answered, 'Foxes have holes and the birds of the air have nests, but the Son of Man has nowhere to lay his head.'

Another to whom he said, 'Follow me', replied, 'Let me go and bury my father first.' But he answered, 'Leave the dead to bury their dead; your duty is to go and spread the news of the kingdom of God.'

Another said, 'I will follow you, sir, but first let me go and say good-bye to my people at home.' Jesus said to him, 'Once the hand is laid on the plough, no one who looks back is fit for the kingdom of God.'

Reflection

It could be argued that the people in today's Gospel have good reasons for delaying their acceptance of Jesus' invitation to follow him. What is important however is to see what should have the highest priority and that must be to follow Jesus wholeheartedly. When we do that, somehow the other important matters in our lives are also attended to. If we are delaying following Jesus, we are quite possibly neglecting other tasks as well. As we reach the middle of this working week, let us ask ourselves: am I prioritising the Word of God in my life? How much effort am I putting into spreading his kingdom in my daily tasks? A test may be whether I am attending well to my daily chores and responsibilities.

Sts Michael, Gabriel, Raphael, Archangels
Feast | White

29
SEP THU

Daniel 7:9-10, 13-14

(Alternative Reading: Apocalypse 12:7-12)

As I watched: Thrones were set in place and one of great age took his seat. His robe was white as snow, the hair of his head as pure as wool. His throne was a blaze of flames, its wheels were a burning fire. A stream of fire poured out, issuing from his presence. A thousand thousand waited on him, ten thousand times ten thousand stood before him. A court was held and the books were opened. I gazed into the visions of the night. And I saw, coming on the clouds of heaven, one like a son of man. He came to the one of great age and was led into his presence. On him was conferred sovereignty, glory and kingship, and men of all peoples, nations and languages became his servants. His sovereignty is an eternal sovereignty which shall never pass away, nor will his empire ever be destroyed.

Psalm 137:1-5. R. v. 1

In the presence of the angels I will bless you, O Lord.

John 1:47-51

When Jesus saw Nathanael coming he said of him, 'There is an Israelite who deserves the name, incapable of deceit.' 'How do you know me?' said Nathanael. 'Before Philip came to call you,' said Jesus, 'I saw you under the fig tree.' Nathanael answered, 'Rabbi, you are the Son of God, you are the King of Israel.' Jesus replied, 'You believe that just because I said: I saw you under the fig tree. You will see greater things than that.' And then he added, 'I tell you most solemnly, you will see heaven laid open and, above the Son of Man, the angels of God ascending and descending.'

Reflection

Many of us, whether we are religious or not, are fascinated by angels. They are often portrayed as heavenly creatures who have connections with the mighty powers. Angels and archangels quite often symbolise our desire for spiritual gifts which we believe they possess. They are also expressions of our deepest desires to be better and to be present to others whenever they need us. The very special patrons of today, Saints Michael, Raphael and Gabriel, fulfil their assigned tasks very efficiently. The Bible shows Saint Michael as the one who fights the devil (Revelation 12:7-10). He reveals the protection of God. Saint Raphael reveals the healing of God and guides the people of God on their journey (Book of Tobit). Saint Gabriel, who brought the good news of the incarnation to Mary, is God's messenger (Luke 1:26-38). Let us take some time today to read more about their stories in the Bible. What would be one quality we desire that we could learn from these heavenly intercessors?

30
SEP FRI

26th Week in Ordinary Time
St Jerome, *priest, doctor,* **Memorial** | White

2 Timothy 3:14-17

You must keep to what you have been taught and know to be true; remember who your teachers were, and how, ever since you were a child, you have known the holy scriptures – from these you can learn the wisdom that leads to salvation through faith in Christ Jesus. All scripture is inspired by God and can profitably be used for teaching, for refuting error, for guiding people's lives and teaching them to be holy. This is how the man who is dedicated to God becomes fully equipped and ready for any good work.

Psalm 118:9-14

Lord, teach me your statutes.

Matthew 13:47-52

Jesus said to the crowds: 'The kingdom of heaven is like a dragnet cast into the sea that brings in a haul of all kinds. When it is full, the fishermen haul it ashore; then, sitting down, they collect the good ones in a basket and throw away those that are no use. This is how it will be at the end of time: the angels will appear and separate the wicked from the just to throw them into the blazing furnace where there will be weeping and grinding of teeth.

'Have you understood all this?' They said, 'Yes.' And he said to them, 'Well then, every scribe who becomes a disciple of the kingdom of heaven is like a householder who brings out from his storeroom things both new and old.'

Reflection

Today we celebrate the memorial of St Jerome, priest and doctor of the church. He dedicated the major part of his life translating the Bible from the Greek and Hebrew languages into Latin, which was the language spoken by many Christians at the time. His translation came to be called the Vulgate (meaning, 'in the common vernacular'). He also wrote many commentaries on the Gospels in Latin. His work marked a significant breakthrough. For the first time, people could hear the texts and stories of the Bible in their own language. Perhaps we today take for granted the fact that we can read the Bible in our native tongue. Let us say a prayer of thanks today for St Jerome and the many biblical scholars throughout the ages who have worked, and continue to work, to provide us with the very best translations and explanations of the foundational text of our faith.

26th Week in Ordinary Time
St Therese of the Child Jesus, *virgin, doctor,* **Memorial** | White

01
OCT SAT

Job 42:1-3, 5-6, 12-17

This was the answer Job gave to the Lord: I know that you are all-powerful: what you conceive, you can perform. I am the man who obscured your designs with my empty-headed words. I have been holding forth on matters I cannot understand, on marvels beyond me and my knowledge. I knew you then only by hearsay; but now, having seen you with my own eyes, I retract all I have said, and in dust and ashes I repent. *(Please see the Appendix B-23)*

Psalm 118:66, 71, 75, 91, 125, 130. R. v. 135

Let your face shine on your servant, O Lord.

Luke 10:17-24

The seventy-two came back rejoicing. 'Lord,' they said 'even the devils submit to us when we use your name.' Jesus said to them, 'I watched Satan fall like lightning from heaven. Yes, I have given you power to tread underfoot serpents and scorpions and the whole strength of the enemy; nothing shall ever hurt you. Yet do not rejoice that the spirits submit to you; rejoice rather that your names are written in heaven.'

It was then that, filled with joy by the Holy Spirit, he said, 'I bless you, Father, Lord of heaven and of earth, for hiding these things from the learned and the clever and revealing them to mere children. Yes, Father, for that is what it pleased you to do. Everything has been entrusted to me by my Father; and no one knows who the Son is except the Father, and who the Father is except the Son and those to whom the Son chooses to reveal him.'

Then turning to his disciples he spoke to them in private, 'Happy the eyes that see what you see, for I tell you that many prophets and kings wanted to see what you see, and never saw it; to hear what you hear, and never heard it.'

Reflection

The seventy-two disciples who returned after their first mission experience share a high sense of job-satisfaction because they were effective in their work, delighted that even the evil spirits submitted to them! Like a true leader, Jesus allows them to rejoice, to savour this moment of victory before reminding them that the real fruit of their work, the real victory is when God's name is glorified in the Spirit. Their success was not the result of their personal effort, but because they opened their hearts in humility and simplicity to God's plan for them. If we open our hearts to God in docility, we too shall experience success in our efforts. Saint Thérèse of Lisieux reminds us that the struggle and size of our actions are entirely irrelevant if we do not do them out of love. *Lord, give me the grace to be your witness through word and deed.*

02
OCT SUN

TWENTY-SEVENTH SUNDAY IN ORDINARY TIME

Psalter Week 3

Green

Habakkuk 1:2-3; 2:2-4

How long, Lord, am I to cry for help while you will not listen; to cry 'Oppression!' in your ear and you will not save? Why do you set injustice before me, why do you look on where there is tyranny? Outrage and violence, this is all I see, all is contention, and discord flourishes. Then the Lord answered and said,

> 'Write the vision down,
> inscribe it on tablets
> to be easily read,
> since this vision is for its own time only:
> eager for its own fulfilment, it does not deceive;
> if it comes slowly, wait,
> for come it will, without fail.
> See how he flags, he whose soul is not at rights,
> but the upright man will live by his faithfulness.'

Psalm 94:1-2, 6-9. R. v. 8

O that today you would listen to his voice! 'Harden not your hearts.'

2 Timothy 1:6-8, 13-14

I am reminding you to fan into a flame the gift that God gave you when I laid my hands on you. God's gift was not a spirit of timidity, but the Spirit of power, and love, and self-control. So you are never to be ashamed of witnessing to the Lord, or ashamed of me for being his prisoner; but with me, bear the hardships for the sake of the Good News, relying on the power of God.

Keep as your pattern the sound teaching you have heard from me, in the faith and love that are in Christ Jesus. You have been trusted to look after something precious; guard it with the help of the Holy Spirit who lives in us.

Luke 17:5-10

The Apostles said to the Lord, 'Increase our faith.' The Lord replied, 'Were your faith the size of a mustard seed you could say to this mulberry tree, "Be uprooted and planted in the sea," and it would obey you.

'Which of you, with a servant ploughing or minding sheep, would say to him when he returned from the fields, "Come and have your meal immediately?" Would he not be more likely to say, "Get my supper laid; make yourself tidy and wait on me while I eat and drink. You can eat and drink yourself afterwards?" Must he be grateful to the servant for doing what he was told? So with you: when you have done all you have been told to do, say, "We are merely servants: we have done no more than our duty." '

Reflection

Today's readings caution us not to discount small things as insignificant and clamour for big and more. What we need is not more things, more money, a bigger house or car, but enough of everything to live a good Christian life. Jesus shows us the creative miracle locked in faith as tiny as a mustard seed. Every good deed, backed by genuine faith, takes us further ahead in our journey towards God. There is immense value even in a small deed if done in faith. Just like the tiny mustard seed that could be lost if not handled carefully, faith too, if not nurtured carefully, can be lost. As today's second reading advises, we each need to 'fan into a flame the gift that God gave (us)' and guard this precious gift with the help of the Holy Spirit who lives in us. What small things can you do to help others? How big could those small things become? *Lord, give me the grace to do small acts of kindness that help others and keep aflame my faith.*

27th Week in Ordinary Time
Green

Galatians 1:6-12
(Please see the Appendix B-23)

Psalm 110:1-2, 7-10. R. v. 5
The Lord keeps his covenant ever in mind.

Luke 10:25-37
There was a lawyer who, to disconcert Jesus, stood up and said to him, 'Master, what must I do to inherit eternal life?' He said to him, 'What is written in the Law? What do you read there?' He replied, 'You must love the Lord your God with all your heart, with all your soul, with all your strength, and with all your mind, and your neighbour as yourself.' 'You have answered right,' said Jesus 'do this and life is yours.'

But the man was anxious to justify himself and said to Jesus, 'And who is my neighbour?' Jesus replied, 'A man was once on his way down from Jerusalem to Jericho and fell into the hands of brigands; they took all he had, beat him and then made off, leaving him half dead. Now a priest happened to be travelling down the same road, but when he saw the man, he passed by on the other side. In the same way a Levite who came to the place saw him, and passed by on the other side. But a Samaritan traveller who came upon him was moved with compassion when he saw him. He went up and bandaged his wounds, pouring oil and wine on them. He then lifted him on to his own mount, carried him to the inn and looked after him. Next day, he took out two denarii and handed them to the innkeeper. "Look after him," he said "and on my way back I will make good any extra expense you have." Which of these three, do you think, proved himself a neighbour to the man who fell into the brigands' hands?' 'The one who took pity on him' he replied. Jesus said to him, 'Go, and do the same yourself.'

Reflection
The parable of the Good Samaritan was a fitting reply from Jesus to the lawyer who thought he could 'inherit' or 'earn' eternal life. Jesus expands the definition of 'neighbour' by cutting to the roots of the world's prejudices based on religion, ethnicity, etc. Eternal life is a gift from God which we, by our daily actions, become worthy to receive. Through small acts of kindness, we teach ourselves to be sensitive to the needs of those around us, empathise with the marginalised and act on behalf of the suffering, serving one another without counting the cost. We might fool ourselves into thinking that we love God with all our heart and all our soul. But love not translated into service of neighbour renders worship of God false. *Lord, give me a heart to love you present in the faces of others.*

27th Week in Ordinary Time
St Francis of Assisi, Memorial | White

04
OCT TUE

Galatians 1:13-24

You must have heard of my career as a practising Jew, how merciless I was in persecuting the Church of God, how much damage I did to it, how I stood out among other Jews of my generation, and how enthusiastic I was for the traditions of my ancestors.

Then God, who had specially chosen me while I was still in my mother's womb, called me through his grace and chose to reveal his Son in me, so that I might preach the Good News about him to the pagans. I did not stop to discuss this with any human being, nor did I go up to Jerusalem to see those who were already apostles before me, but I went off to Arabia at once and later went straight back from there to Damascus. Even when after three years I went up to Jerusalem to visit Cephas and stayed with him for fifteen days, I did not see any of the other apostles; I only saw James, the brother of the Lord, and I swear before God that what I have just written is the literal truth. After that I went to Syria and Cilicia, and was still not known by sight to the churches of Christ in Judaea, who had heard nothing except that their one-time persecutor was now preaching the faith he had previously tried to destroy; and they gave glory to God for me.

Psalm 138:1-3, 13-15. R. v. 24

Lead me, O Lord, in the path of life eternal.

Luke 10:38-42

Jesus came to a village, and a woman named Martha welcomed him into her house. She had a sister called Mary, who sat down at the Lord's feet and listened to him speaking. Now Martha who was distracted with all the serving said, 'Lord, do you not care that my sister is leaving me to do the serving all by myself? Please tell her to help me.' But the Lord answered: 'Martha, Martha,' he said 'you worry and fret about so many things, and yet few are needed, indeed only one. It is Mary who has chosen the better part; it is not to be taken from her.'

Reflection

'Choose the right things in life and they will not be taken away from you', Jesus promises. What are these right things? Often, we are busy doing great things for God – or so we think! – without really finding out if this is what God wants of us. The first right thing to do is to follow what Mary did: spend time with the Lord whose work we are called to carry out. The more we work, the greater our need to contemplate the Lord. Like St Paul after his conversion, we need to seek first the approval of God and not the approval of other human beings. St Francis of Assisi advised us to 'start by doing what is necessary, then what is possible, and suddenly you are doing the impossible!' Are my activities a fruit of my time with God? *Lord, bless me with comfort and peace in time spent in your presence.*

05
OCT WED

27th Week in Ordinary Time | Green
or **St Faustina Kowalska,** *religious* (Optional, White)

Galatians 2:1-2, 7-14

It was not till fourteen years had passed that I went up to Jerusalem again. I went with Barnabas and took Titus with me. I went there as the result of a revelation, and privately I laid before the leading men the Good News as I proclaim it among the pagans; I did so for fear the course I was adopting or had already adopted would not be allowed. On the contrary, they recognised that I had been commissioned to preach the Good News to the uncircumcised just as Peter had been commissioned to preach it to the circumcised. The same person whose action had made Peter the apostle of the circumcised had given me a similar mission to the pagans. So, James, Cephas and John, these leaders, these pillars, shook hands with Barnabas and me as a sign of partnership: we were to go to the pagans and they to the circumcised. The only thing they insisted on was that we should remember to help the poor, as indeed I was anxious to do. ... *(Please see the Appendix B-24)*

Psalm 116. R. Mark 16:15

Go out to the whole world and proclaim the Good News.

Luke 11:1-4

Once Jesus was in a certain place praying, and when he had finished, one of his disciples said, 'Lord, teach us to pray, just as John taught his disciples.' He said to them, 'Say this when you pray: "Father, may your name be held holy, your kingdom come; give us each day our daily bread, and forgive us our sins, for we ourselves forgive each one who is in debt to us. And do not put us to the test."'

Reflection

The Lord's Prayer expresses the interconnectedness of our life, inspiring us to draw strength from above (God) to build a 'civilisation of love' where fraternal communion and mutual forgiveness reign supreme. Our life as Christians will bear lasting fruit and bring us a sense of fulfilment only when we communicate and relate to one another as members of one family. It is this desire for fraternal communion that prompts Paul and Barnabas to connect with the apostles in Jerusalem and mutually plan their future activities (first reading). The power from above will supply us with 'the daily bread' we need to face the challenges and problems of this day. Does my care for others match my love for God? *Lord, make me a channel of your forgiveness and peace in my family, workplace and community.*

06
OCT THU

27th Week in Ordinary Time | Green
or **St Bruno,** *priest* (Optional, White)

Galatians 3:1-5

Are you people in Galatia mad? Has someone put a spell on you, in spite of the plain explanation you have had of the crucifixion of Jesus Christ? Let me ask you one question: was it because you practised the Law that you received the Spirit, or because you believed what was preached to you? Are you foolish enough to end in outward observances what you began in the Spirit? Have all the favours you received been wasted? And if this were so, they would most certainly have been wasted. Does God give you the Spirit so freely and work miracles among you because you practise the Law, or because you believed what was preached to you?

Luke 1:69-75. R. cf. v. 68

Blessed be the Lord, the God of Israel! He has visited his people and redeemed them.

Luke 11:5-13

Jesus said to his disciples: 'Suppose one of you has a friend and goes to him in the middle of the night to say, "My friend, lend me three loaves, because a friend of mine on his travels has just arrived at my house and I have nothing to offer him"; and the man answers from inside the house, "Do not bother me. The door is bolted now, and my children and I are in bed; I cannot get up to give it you." I tell you, if the man does not get up and give it him for friendship's sake, persistence will be enough to make him get up and give his friend all he wants.

'So I say to you: Ask, and it will be given to you; search, and you will find; knock, and the door will be opened to you. For the one who asks always receives; the one who searches always finds; the one who knocks will always have the door opened to him. What father among you would hand his son a stone when he asked for bread? Or hand him a snake instead of a fish? Or hand him a scorpion if he asked for an egg? If you then, who are evil, know how to give your children what is good, how much more will the heavenly Father give the Holy Spirit to those who ask him!'

Reflection

We usually pray fervently before commencing a new project or new initiative. We humbly acknowledge that without God's intervention our efforts will be futile. But do we pray as fervently throughout the duration of the project? Normally, NO! The intensity of our prayer decreases, as our confidence grows that we can manage on our own. Our efforts and hard work start taking precedence over God's grace! Saint Paul points out how foolish we are to begin with the Spirit but end with the flesh. Fervent prayer is necessary not just when things go wrong but also when we experience success. It is God who opens for us new vistas for creative expression of our mission in the world. Do I remember God in good times? *Lord, in all simplicity I seek faith and trust that I may depend entirely on you rather than my abilities for success in my activities.*

07
OCT FRI

27th Week in Ordinary Time
Our Lady of the Rosary, Memorial | White

Galatians 3:7-14

Don't you see that it is those who rely on faith who are the sons of Abraham? Scripture foresaw that God was going to use faith to justify the pagans, and proclaimed the Good News long ago when Abraham was told: In you all the pagans will be blessed. Those therefore who rely on faith receive the same blessing as Abraham, the man of faith. ...
(Please see the Appendix B-24)

Psalm 110:1-6. R. v. 5

The Lord keeps his covenant ever in mind.

Luke 11:15-26

When Jesus had cast out a devil, some of the people said, 'It is through Beelzebul, the prince of devils, that he casts out devils.' Others asked Jesus, as a test, for a sign from heaven; but, knowing what they were thinking, he said to them, 'Every kingdom divided against itself is heading for ruin, and a household divided against itself collapses. So too with Satan: if he is divided against himself, how can his kingdom stand? – since you assert that it is through Beelzebul that I cast out devils. Now if it is through Beelzebul that I cast out devils, through whom do your own experts cast them out? Let them be your judges, then. But if it is through the finger of God that I cast out devils, then know that the kingdom of God has overtaken you. So long as a strong man fully armed guards his own palace, his goods are undisturbed; but when someone stronger than he is attacks and defeats him, the stronger man takes away all the weapons he relied on and shares out his spoil.

'He who is not with me is against me; and he who does not gather with me scatters.

'When an unclean spirit goes out of a man it wanders through waterless country looking for a place to rest, and not finding one it says, "I will go back to the home I came from." But on arrival, finding it swept and tidied, it then goes off and brings seven other spirits more wicked than itself, and they go in and set up house there, so that the man ends up by being worse than he was before.'

Reflection

Jesus wasn't in the least perturbed when the Jewish leaders accused him of being an agent of Beelzebul or asked for a sign from God, despite the many miracles he had performed for them. He knew that their hearts were so tightly closed that they would not be able to recognise the loving power of God at work in him. If we do not watch over our hearts and feelings, safeguarding the presence of the Holy Spirit within us, the influence of the evil one can take over. We must make a deliberate choice for God, to gather with him and not to scatter. On this Memorial of Our Lady of the Rosary, may Mary our mother be our example in keeping our hearts open to God's actions in our life. *Lord, help me to be aware of your continual presence in my life.*

27th Week in Ordinary Time
Green

08
OCT SAT

Galatians 3:22-29

Scripture makes no exceptions when it says that sin is master everywhere. In this way the promise can only be given through faith in Jesus Christ and can only be given to those who have this faith.

Before faith came, we were allowed no freedom by the Law; we were being looked after till faith was revealed. The Law was to be our guardian until the Christ came and we could be justified by faith. Now that that time has come we are no longer under that guardian, and you are, all of you, sons of God through faith in Christ Jesus. All baptised in Christ, you have all clothed yourselves in Christ, and there are no more distinctions between Jew and Greek, slave and free, male and female, but all of you are one in Christ Jesus. Merely by belonging to Christ you are the posterity of Abraham, the heirs he was promised.

Psalm 104:2-7. R. v. 8

The Lord remembers his covenant for ever.

Luke 11:27-28

As Jesus was speaking, a woman in the crowd raised her voice and said, 'Happy the womb that bore you and the breasts you sucked!' But he replied, 'Still happier those who hear the word of God and keep it!'

Reflection

Was Jesus really dismissive of his mother? Not at all! Jesus was reiterating the truth that his mother was more blessed for receiving the Word of God in her life and living by it, than being the physical mother of Jesus. She believed in God's promises. By listening to God's word and obeying it unquestioningly, she made the birth of Jesus possible. As St Augustine says, 'Mary conceived the Word in her heart before she conceived it in her womb.' This blessing in the life of Mary will ours be too when we surrender ourselves to God's will. We will then bear Christ in the womb of our hearts to give birth to him in the daily events of our life. How much time do I spend to receive the word of God in my life? *Lord, open my heart to receive your Word and live by it.*

09
OCT SUN

TWENTY-EIGHTH SUNDAY IN ORDINARY TIME

Psalter Week 4
Green

2 Kings 5:14-17

Naaman the leper went down and immersed himself seven times in the Jordan, as Elisha had told him to do. And his flesh became clean once more like the flesh of a little child.

Returning to Elisha with his whole escort, he went in and stood before him. 'Now I know' he said 'that there is no God in all the earth except in Israel. Now, please, accept a present from your servant.' But Elisha replied, 'As the Lord lives, whom I serve, I will accept nothing.' Naaman pressed him to accept, but he refused. Then Naaman said, 'Since your answer is "No," allow your servant to be given as much earth as two mules may carry, because your servant will no longer offer holocaust or sacrifice to any god except the Lord.'

Psalm 97:1-4. R. cf. v. 2

The Lord has shown his salvation to the nations.

2 Timothy 2:8-13

Remember the Good News that I carry, 'Jesus Christ risen from the dead, sprung from the race of David'; it is on account of this that I have my own hardships to bear, even to being chained like a criminal – but they cannot chain up God's news. So I bear it all for the sake of those who are chosen, so that in the end they may have the salvation that is in Christ Jesus and the eternal glory that comes with it.

Here is a saying that you can rely on:
If we have died with him, then we shall live with him.
If we hold firm, then we shall reign with him.
If we disown him, then he will disown us.
We may be unfaithful, but he is always faithful,
for he cannot disown his own self.

Luke 17:11-19

On the way to Jerusalem Jesus travelled along the border between Samaria and Galilee. As he entered one of the villages, ten lepers came to meet him. They stood some way off and called to him, 'Jesus! Master! Take pity on us.' When he saw them he said, 'Go and show yourselves to the priests.' Now as they were going away they were cleansed. Finding himself cured, one of them turned back praising God at the top of his voice and threw himself at the feet of Jesus and thanked him. The man was a Samaritan. This made Jesus say, 'Were not all ten made clean? The other nine, where are they? It seems that no one has come back to give praise to God, except this foreigner.' And he said to the man, 'Stand up and go on your way. Your faith has saved you.'

Reflection

Like the nine lepers who didn't think it necessary to thank Jesus for the healing received, many of us take for granted our innumerable everyday blessings! We seem to move about with a sense of entitlement convinced we are deserving of the blessings received. True happiness lies not in what we receive, but in how we receive. As is evident from Jesus' commendation, 'your faith has saved you', the thankful Samaritan had understood the full meaning of what he had experienced. St Ignatius of Loyola says, 'Gratitude is an attitude that keeps us aware of how we are blessed and who it is that blesses us.' No doubt, all ten lepers had cried out in faith, 'Jesus, Master, take pity on us'. But only one felt inclined to show gratitude. When in trouble or pain we, like the lepers, desperately seek God and when help does come, be it through family, neighbour or friend, do we bother to thank God and that person? Or do we simply take it for granted, saying, 'Oh! He or she was just doing their duty'. Today let us take the time to recall gratefully ten miracles God has wrought in our lives! *Lord, let your touch warm us and heal us.*

10
OCT MON

28th Week in Ordinary Time
Green

Galatians 4:22-24, 26-27, 31–5:1

The Law says, if you remember, that Abraham had two sons, one by the slave-girl, and one by his free-born wife. The child of the slave-girl was born in the ordinary way; the child of the free woman was born as the result of a promise. This can be regarded as an allegory: the women stand for the two covenants. The first who comes from Mount Sinai, and whose children are slaves, is Hagar. The Jerusalem above, however, is free and is our mother, since scripture says: Shout for joy, you barren women who bore no children! Break into shouts of joy and gladness, you who were never in labour. For there are more sons of the forsaken one than sons of the wedded wife. So, my brothers, we are the children, not of the slave-girl, but of the free-born wife.

When Christ freed us, he meant us to remain free. Stand firm, therefore, and do not submit again to the yoke of slavery.

Psalm 112:1-7. R. v. 2

May the name of the Lord be blessed for evermore!

Luke 11:29-32

The crowds got even bigger and Jesus addressed them, 'This is a wicked generation; it is asking for a sign. The only sign it will be given is the sign of Jonah. For just as Jonah became a sign to the Ninevites, so will the Son of Man be to this generation. On Judgement day the Queen of the South will rise up with the men of this generation and condemn them, because she came from the ends of the earth to hear the wisdom of Solomon, and there is something greater than Solomon here. On Judgement day the men of Nineveh will stand up with this generation and condemn it, because when Jonah preached they repented; and there is something greater than Jonah here.'

Reflection

The Queen of Sheba and the Ninevites, both foreigners, were open enough to recognise God's actions in their respective milieu. The Israelites of Jesus' time may have had a robust sense of religious identity as the chosen people of God, but perhaps pride got in the way of their recognition of God's presence in the person of Jesus. They seek more earth-shattering 'spectacular' signs, while shutting themselves to the signs of God's presence in their daily lives. We all look for signs from time to time to provide greater certainty in what we believe. However, there cannot be a better sign from God than becoming one like us. Where do I see signs of God's activity in my life? *Lord, give me eyes to see your presence and action in my life.*

28th Week in Ordinary Time | Green
or **St John XXIII,** *pope* (Optional, White)

11
OCT TUE

Galatians 5:1-6

When Christ freed us, he meant us to remain free. Stand firm, therefore, and do not submit again to the yoke of slavery. It is I, Paul, who tell you this: if you allow yourselves to be circumcised, Christ will be of no benefit to you at all. With all solemnity I repeat my warning: Everyone who accepts circumcision is obliged to keep the whole Law. But if you do look to the Law to make you justified, then you have separated yourselves from Christ, and have fallen from grace. Christians are told by the Spirit to look to faith for those rewards that righteousness hopes for, since in Christ Jesus whether you are circumcised or not makes no difference – what matters is faith that makes its power felt through love.

Psalm 118:41, 43-45, 47-48. R. v. 41

Lord, let your love come upon me.

Luke 11:37-41

Jesus had just finished speaking when a Pharisee invited him to dine at his house. He went in and sat down at the table. The Pharisee saw this and was surprised that he had not first washed before the meal. But the Lord said to him, 'Oh, you Pharisees! You clean the outside of cup and plate, while inside yourselves you are filled with extortion and wickedness. Fools! Did not he who made the outside make the inside too? Instead, give alms from what you have and then indeed everything will be clean for you.'

Reflection

The Pharisee who invited Jesus expected him to wash himself before he sat down to eat. This was nothing unusual. Every Jew meticulously followed this ritual of washing before eating. Jesus intentionally skips this ritual to remind his host that what counts as beautiful in the eyes of God is our inner cleanliness and our generosity to understand and serve one another. Without cultivating a good heart, religious practices are meaningless. It's only from the abundance of our hearts that we can reach out and live the Eucharist we celebrate. As Pope Francis says, 'When we stop living for ourselves, for success, to gain something or to become someone, but live for Jesus and, like him, live for others, we assume his mentality.' *Lord, you know my heart. Cleanse it and fill it with an inclination towards your heart.*

12
OCT WED

Galatians 5:18-25

If you are led by the Spirit, no law can touch you. When self-indulgence is at work the results are obvious: fornication, gross indecency and sexual irresponsibility; idolatry and sorcery; feuds and wrangling, jealousy, bad temper and quarrels; disagreements, factions, envy; drunkenness, orgies and similar things. I warn you now, as I warned you before: those who behave like this will not inherit the kingdom of God. What the Spirit brings is very different: love, joy, peace, patience, kindness, goodness, trustfulness, gentleness and self-control. There can be no law against things like that, of course. You cannot belong to Christ Jesus unless you crucify all self-indulgent passions and desires. Since the Spirit is our life, let us be directed by the Spirit.

Psalm 1:1-4, 6. R. cf. John 8:12

Anyone who follows you, O Lord, will have the light of life.

Luke 11:42-46

The Lord said to the Pharisees: 'Alas for you Pharisees! You who pay your tithe of mint and rue and all sorts of garden herbs and overlook justice and the love of God! These you should have practised, without leaving the others undone. Alas for you Pharisees who like taking the seats of honour in the synagogues and being greeted obsequiously in the market squares! Alas for you, because you are like the unmarked tombs that men walk on without knowing it!'

A lawyer then spoke up. 'Master,' he said 'when you speak like this you insult us too.' 'Alas for you lawyers also,' he replied 'because you load on men burdens that are unendurable, burdens that you yourselves do not move a finger to lift.'

Reflection

Don't we get annoyed when civic and religious authorities impose some restrictions on us which they themselves appear to avoid? Do I repeat this behaviour in the small world of my family or workplace? Jesus reminds us that he expects honesty, integrity, justice and love from all his disciples. An increased number of pious observances will not absolve us of our insensitive acts of injustice and indifference towards others. Conforming to others' expectations may ensure a trouble-free life. However, silence and indifference are alien to Jesus' spirituality. What do I do to ease the burdens of those around me? *Lord, unburden me of my needless preoccupations and infuse in my heart a spirit of love and justice.*

28th Week in Ordinary Time
Green

13
OCT THU

Ephesians 1:1-10

From Paul, appointed by God to be an apostle of Christ Jesus, to the saints who are faithful to Christ Jesus: Grace and peace to you from God our Father and from the Lord Jesus Christ. Blessed be God the Father of our Lord Jesus Christ, who has blessed us with all the spiritual blessings of heaven in Christ. Before the world was made, he chose us, chose us in Christ, to be holy and spotless, and to live through love in his presence, determining that we should become his adopted sons, through Jesus Christ for his own kind purposes, to make us praise the glory of his grace, his free gift to us in the Beloved, in whom, through his blood, we gain our freedom, the forgiveness of our sins. … *(Please see the Appendix B-24)*

Psalm 97:1-6. R. v. 2

The Lord has shown his salvation.

Luke 11:47-54

Jesus said: 'Alas for you who build the tombs of the prophets, the men your ancestors killed! In this way you both witness what your ancestors did and approve it; they did the killing, you do the building.

'And that is why the Wisdom of God said, "I will send them prophets and apostles; some they will slaughter and persecute, so that this generation will have to answer for every prophet's blood that has been shed since the foundation of the world, from the blood of Abel to the blood of Zechariah, who was murdered between the altar and the sanctuary." Yes, I tell you, this generation will have to answer for it all.

'Alas for you lawyers who have taken away the key of knowledge! You have not gone in yourselves, and have prevented others going in who wanted to.'

When he left the house, the scribes and the Pharisees began a furious attack on him and tried to force answers from him on innumerable questions, setting traps to catch him out in something he might say.

Reflection

It is obvious that Jesus hated the hypocritical attitudes of the scribes and Pharisees and never minced words to denounce them publicly. As Pope Francis says, 'hypocrisy is the language of the devil'. Examining ourselves, we can all find shades of hypocritical behaviour in our daily life and activities. In such moments we are giving the devil his opportunity to reign evil in our midst. We are happy to condemn and sign online petitions against violence, injustice, cruelty and oppression perpetrated by others, while sometimes silently perpetuating the same in our homes, neighbourhood and community. Am I trapped by my own hypocritical behaviour? *Lord, help me live a life of love.*

14
OCT FRI

28th Week in Ordinary Time | Green
or **St Callistus I,** *pope, martyr* (Optional, Red)

Ephesians 1:11-14

It is in Christ that we were claimed as God's own, chosen from the beginning, under the predetermined plan of the one who guides all things as he decides by his own will; chosen to be, for his greater glory, the people who would put their hopes in Christ before he came. Now you too, in him, have heard the message of the truth and the good news of your salvation, and have believed it; and you too have been stamped with the seal of the Holy Spirit of the Promise, the pledge of our inheritance which brings freedom for those whom God has taken for his own, to make his glory praised.

Psalm 32:1-2, 4-5, 12-13. R. v. 12

Happy the people the Lord has chosen as his own.

Luke 12:1-7

The people had gathered in their thousands so that they were treading on one another. And Jesus began to speak, first of all to his disciples. 'Be on your guard against the yeast of the Pharisees – that is, their hypocrisy. Everything that is now covered will be uncovered, and everything now hidden will be made clear. For this reason, whatever you have said in the dark will be heard in the daylight, and what you have whispered in hidden places will be proclaimed on the housetops.

'To you my friends I say: Do not be afraid of those who kill the body and after that can do no more. I will tell you whom to fear: fear him who, after he has killed, has the power to cast into hell. Yes, I tell you, fear him. Can you not buy five sparrows for two pennies? And yet not one is forgotten in God's sight. Why, every hair on your head has been counted. There is no need to be afraid: you are worth more than hundreds of sparrows.'

Reflection

Our lives are often conditioned by societal, religious and cultural traditions. It takes tremendous courage to give up set patterns of behaviour and tread new paths. Fear of criticism and alienation can prevent us from living out our true selves. We think a little bit of hypocrisy is fine if it brings some material benefit or social status or if it helps save us from trouble. Do we realise that it only takes a little hypocrisy to undermine the best of intentions? Jesus demands courage and genuineness from his followers. The author of today's first reading urges us not to be afraid, for 'we are stamped with the seal of the Holy Spirit'. Is there something in my life that I indulge in out of fear? *Lord, give me the courage to face up to my fears and thus realise my true worth.*

28th Week in Ordinary Time
St Teresa of Jesus, *virgin, doctor,* **Memorial** | White

15
OCT SAT

Ephesians 1:15-23

I, having once heard about your faith in the Lord Jesus, and the love that you show towards all the saints, have never failed to remember you in my prayers and to thank God for you. May the God of our Lord Jesus Christ, the Father of glory, give you a spirit of wisdom and perception of what is revealed, to bring you to full knowledge of him. May he enlighten the eyes of your mind so that you can see what hope his call holds for you, what rich glories he has promised the saints will inherit and how infinitely great is the power that he has exercised for us believers. This you can tell from the strength of his power at work in Christ, when he used it to raise him from the dead and to make him sit at his right hand, in heaven, far above every Sovereignty, Authority, Power or Domination, or any other name that can be named, not only in this age but also in the age to come. He has put all things under his feet, and made him, as the ruler of everything, the head of the Church; which is his body, the fullness of him who fills the whole creation.

Psalm 8:2-7. R. cf. v. 7

You gave your Son power over the works of your hand.

Luke 12:8-12

Jesus said to his disciples: 'I tell you, if anyone openly declares himself for me in the presence of men, the Son of Man will declare himself for him in the presence of God's angels. But the man who disowns me in the presence of men will be disowned in the presence of God's angels. 'Everyone who says a word against the Son of Man will be forgiven, but he who blasphemes against the Holy Spirit will not be forgiven. 'When they take you before synagogues and magistrates and authorities, do not worry about how to defend yourselves or what to say, because when the time comes, the Holy Spirit will teach you what you must say.'

Reflection

Jesus assures all who publicly declare their loyalty to him that they belong to him. This belongingness is nurtured by living the values of Christ and thereby influencing every fabric of society around us. When we choose to live honest and incorrupt lives, preferring to counter those who oppose us not with revenge but with love and forgiveness, we manifest our fidelity to Christ. When we behave arrogantly towards others, when we follow the crowd and remain silent amidst injustice, we reject Christ and breach our loyalty to him. The Holy Spirit is our guide in living Gospel values. Let St Teresa of Avila, who courageously allowed the Spirit to lead her in her efforts to promote spiritual renewal in the Carmelite order, be our inspiration in our personal spiritual renewal as witnesses of Christ. *Lord, may I stand up for what is true and right.*

16
OCT SUN

TWENTY-NINTH SUNDAY IN ORDINARY TIME

Psalter Week 1

Green

Exodus 17:8-13

The Amalekites came and attacked Israel at Rephidim. Moses said to Joshua, 'Pick out men for yourself, and tomorrow morning march out to engage Amalek. I, meanwhile, will stand on the hilltop, the staff of God in my hand.' Joshua did as Moses told him and marched out to engage Amalek, while Moses and Aaron and Hur went up to the top of the hill. As long as Moses kept his arms raised, Israel had the advantage; when he let his arms fall, the advantage went to Amalek. But Moses' arms grew heavy, so they took a stone and put it under him and on this he sat, Aaron and Hur supporting his arms, one on one side, one on the other; and his arms remained firm till sunset. With the edge of the sword Joshua cut down Amalek and his people.

Psalm 120. R. cf. v. 2

Our help is in the name of the Lord, who made heaven and earth.

2 Timothy 3:14–4:2

You must keep to what you have been taught and know to be true; remember who your teachers were, and how, ever since you were a child, you have known the holy scriptures – from these you can learn the wisdom that leads to salvation through faith in Christ Jesus. All scripture is inspired by God and can profitably be used for teaching, for refuting error, for guiding people's lives and teaching them to be holy. This is how the man who is dedicated to God becomes fully equipped and ready for any good work.

Before God and before Christ Jesus who is to be judge of the living and the dead, I put this duty to you, in the name of his Appearing and of his kingdom: proclaim the message and, welcome or unwelcome, insist on it. Refute falsehood, correct error, call to obedience – but do all with patience and with the intention of teaching.

Luke 18:1-8

Jesus told his disciples a parable about the need to pray continually and never lose heart. 'There was a judge in a certain town' he said 'who had neither fear of God nor respect for man. In the same town there was a widow who kept on coming to him and saying, "I want justice from you against my enemy!" For a long time he refused, but at last he said to himself, "Maybe I have neither fear of God nor respect for man, but since she keeps pestering me I must give this widow her just rights, or she will persist in coming and worry me to death." '

And the Lord said, 'You notice what the unjust judge has to say? Now will not God see justice done to his chosen who cry to him day and night even when he delays to help them? I promise you, he will see justice done to them, and done speedily. But when the Son of Man comes, will he find any faith on earth?'

Reflection

We all believe in the power of prayer to influence the outcome of events and help change the lives of people. Yet, many a time we feel that our prayers fall on deaf ears. This is when we look for tangible evidence to reassure ourselves that our prayers are answered. If we cannot find such evidence, we lose heart. Jesus challenges us keep our faith alive and never lose heart. Our God doesn't take pleasure in seeing us struggle through life. At the same time, we cannot manipulate God into granting us our requests. It is only through self-surrender that we can experience his help. Today's first reading emphasises the importance of praying for one another. The Israelites were able to defeat the Amalekites because Moses kept his hands raised in prayer. So also on our faith journey, we need others to raise their hands in prayer for us as we do for them. The parable of the wicked judge reminds us that those who plead with God for a just cause will not be disappointed. The widow pleaded for justice. What do we ask of God? Do we pray for a just cause or do we ask for things that will make our already comfortable lives more comfortable? *Lord, rekindle my confidence in your providence.*

17
OCT MON

29th Week in Ordinary Time
St Ignatius of Antioch, *bishop, martyr,* **Memorial** | Red

Ephesians 2:1-10

You were dead, through the crimes and the sins in which you used to live when you were following the way of this world, obeying the ruler who governs the air, the spirit who is at work in the rebellious. We all were among them too in the past, living sensual lives, ruled entirely by our own physical desires and our own ideas; so that by nature we were as much under God's anger as the rest of the world. But God loved us with so much love that he was generous with his mercy: when we were dead through our sins, he brought us to life with Christ – it is through grace that you have been saved – and raised us up with him and gave us a place with him in heaven, in Christ Jesus. ... *(Please see the Appendix B-24)*

Psalm 99. R. v. 3

He made us, we belong to him.

Luke 12:13-21

A man in the crowd said to Jesus, 'Master, tell my brother to give me a share of our inheritance.' 'My friend,' he replied, 'who appointed me your judge, or the arbitrator of your claims?' Then he said to them, 'Watch, and be on your guard against avarice of any kind, for a man's life is not made secure by what he owns, even when he has more than he needs.'

Then he told them a parable: 'There was once a rich man who, having had a good harvest from his land, thought to himself, "What am I to do? I have not enough room to store my crops." Then he said, "This is what I will do: I will pull down my barns and build bigger ones, and store all my grain and my goods in them, and I will say to my soul: My soul, you have plenty of good things laid by for many years to come; take things easy, eat, drink, have a good time." But God said to him, "Fool! This very night the demand will be made for your soul; and this hoard of yours, whose will it be then?" So it is when a man stores up treasure for himself in place of making himself rich in the sight of God.'

Reflection

The parable of the rich fool underlines that while providing for our physical needs we shouldn't lose our capacity to be concerned about others. The rich man does not come across as evil but as greedy and self-centred. Similarly, we may not be trampling over others to accumulate more material things in an unjust way. But, as we look for security in our own life, we also need to be sensitive to the needs of others. The goodwill and gratitude we receive from people are like rich treasures invested for the future. That is how we make ourselves rich in the sight of God. The life of St Ignatius of Antioch teaches that we are made for something – Someone – infinitely greater and higher than created things. What are we living for? *Lord Jesus, free my heart from all possessiveness and enrich me with your love.*

18
OCT TUE

St Luke, Evangelist
Feast | Red

2 Timothy 4:10-17

Demas has deserted me for love of this life and gone to Thessalonika, Crescens has gone to Galatia and Titus to Dalmatia; only Luke is with me. Get Mark to come and bring him with you; I find him a useful helper in my work. I have sent Tychicus to Ephesus. When you come, bring the cloak I left with Carpus in Troas, and the scrolls, especially the parchment ones. Alexander the coppersmith has done me a lot of harm; the Lord will repay him for what he has done. Be on your guard against him yourself, because he has been bitterly contesting everything that we say.

The first time I had to present my defence, there was not a single witness to support me. Everyone of them deserted me – may they not be held accountable for it. But the Lord stood by me and gave me power, so that through me the whole message might be proclaimed for all the pagans to hear.

Psalm 144:10-13, 17-18. R. v. 12

Your friends, O Lord, shall make known the glorious splendour of your reign.

Luke 10:1-9

The Lord appointed seventy-two others and sent them out ahead of him, in pairs, to all the towns and places he himself was to visit. He said to them, 'The harvest is rich but the labourers are few, so ask the Lord of the harvest to send labourers to his harvest. Start off now, but remember, I am sending you out like lambs among wolves. Carry no purse, no haversack, no sandals. Salute no one on the road. Whatever house you go into, let your first words be, "Peace to this house!" And if a man of peace lives there, your peace will go and rest on him; if not, it will come back to you. Stay in the same house, taking what food and drink they have to offer, for the labourer deserves his wages; do not move from house to house. Whenever you go into a town where they make you welcome, eat what is set before you. Cure those in it who are sick, and say, "The kingdom of God is very near to you."'

Reflection

On the feast of St Luke, Jesus invites us to widen our understanding of mission and salvation to embrace an inclusive, pluralistic and universal vision in our journey as his disciples. The message of the Gospel is not our private possession but one that needs to be shared and multiplied in the concrete situations of our daily life. In this sense, though our mission is urgent and ongoing, it does not depend upon our own resources. The only reliable resource is the assurance of the one who has sent us that the labourer 'deserves his reward' (1 Timothy 5:18). We will receive a reward in proportion to the effort we put in to make his presence known to all. Do I come across to people as someone who carries the good news of Christ? *Lord, help me spread the joy of the Gospel wherever I am.*

19
OCT WED

29th Week in Ordinary Time | Green or **Sts John of Brebeuf and Isaac Jogues,** *priests,* **and Companions,** *martyrs* | or **St Paul of the Cross,** *priest* (Optional, Red/White)

Ephesians 3:2-12

You have probably heard how I have been entrusted by God with the grace he meant for you, and that it was by a revelation that I was given the knowledge of the mystery, as I have just described it very shortly. If you read my words, you will have some idea of the depths that I see in the mystery of Christ. … *(Please see the Appendix B-24)*

Isaiah 12:2-6. R. cf. v. 3

With joy you will draw water from the wells of salvation.

Luke 12:39-48

Jesus said to his disciples: 'You may be quite sure of this, that if the householder had known at what hour the burglar would come, he would not have let anyone break through the wall of his house. You too must stand ready, because the Son of Man is coming at an hour you do not expect.'

Peter said, 'Lord, do you mean this parable for us, or for everyone?' The Lord replied, 'What sort of steward, then, is faithful and wise enough for the master to place him over his household to give them their allowance of food at the proper time? Happy that servant if his master's arrival finds him at this employment. I tell you truly, he will place him over everything he owns. But as for the servant who says to himself, "My master is taking his time coming," and sets about beating the menservants and the maids, and eating and drinking and getting drunk, his master will come on a day he does not expect and at an hour he does not know. The master will cut him off and send him to the same fate as the unfaithful.

'The servant who knows what his master wants, but has not even started to carry out those wishes, will receive very many strokes of the lash. The one who did not know, but deserves to be beaten for what he has done, will receive fewer strokes. When a man has had a great deal given him, a great deal will be demanded of him; when a man has had a great deal given him on trust, even more will be expected of him.'

Reflection

St Teresa of Calcutta once said, 'God has not called me to be successful, but to be faithful.' As stewards of God's household, we are rewarded not for our efficiency, academic qualification or for the number of gifts and talents we possess but for our faithfulness to the duties of our life. When we are faithful, God qualifies us, making us efficient through the use of our gifts and talents. One dimension of faithfulness is our ability to discern what the master expects of us and to act accordingly. Whatever truly builds up the community of believers will receive God's reward. Do I realise the seriousness of my responsibility as God's steward? Do I misuse my gifts and talents for my personal gain and glory? *Lord, instil in me a sense of responsibility in the execution of my daily activities.*

20 OCT THU

29th Week in Ordinary Time

Green

Ephesians 3:14-21

This is what I pray, kneeling before the Father, from whom every family, whether spiritual or natural, takes its name:

Out of his infinite glory, may he give you the power through his Spirit for your hidden self to grow strong, so that Christ may live in your hearts through faith, and then, planted in love and built on love, you will with all the saints have strength to grasp the breadth and the length, the height and the depth; until, knowing the love of Christ, which is beyond all knowledge, you are filled with the utter fullness of God.

Glory be to him whose power, working in us, can do infinitely more than we can ask or imagine; glory be to him from generation to generation in the Church and in Christ Jesus for ever and ever. Amen.

Psalm 32:1-2, 4-5, 11-12, 18-19. R. v. 5

The Lord fills the earth with his love.

Luke 12:49-53

Jesus said to his disciples: 'I have come to bring fire to the earth, and how I wish it were blazing already! There is a baptism I must still receive, and how great is my distress till it is over!

'Do you suppose that I am here to bring peace on earth? No, I tell you, but rather division. For from now on a household of five will be divided: three against two and two against three; the father divided against the son, son against father, mother against daughter, daughter against mother, mother-in-law against daughter-in-law, daughter-in-law against mother-in-law.'

Reflection

St Paul shares with the Ephesians his personal conviction about what God can do in the lives of those who walk hand in hand with him. His realisation that God 'can do infinitely more than we can ask or imagine' was born out of his personal encounter with the risen Christ. A 'God-experience' is a kind of cleansing by fire. It will disturb us, shake us out of our complacency and make our hearts burn within us. Our Christian commitment is tested in moments of suffering, rejection and loneliness. While God provides the graces necessary to stay afloat, we have to make a conscious decision to choose God's side and tread along courageously. Often, a call to a decision is a call for division. We cannot say 'yes' to God and live by worldly values. How am I living my faith today? *Lord, rekindle the fire of my faith!*

21
OCT FRI

29th Week in Ordinary Time
Green

Ephesians 4:1-6

I, the prisoner in the Lord, implore you to lead a life worthy of your vocation. Bear with one another charitably, in complete selflessness, gentleness and patience. Do all you can to preserve the unity of the Spirit by the peace that binds you together. There is one Body, one Spirit, just as you were all called into one and the same hope when you were called. There is one Lord, one faith, one baptism, and one God who is Father of all, over all, through all and within all.

Psalm 23:1-6. R. cf. v. 6

Such are the men who seek your face, O Lord.

Luke 12:54-59

Jesus said to the crowds, 'When you see a cloud looming up in the west you say at once that rain is coming, and so it does. And when the wind is from the south you say it will be hot, and it is. Hypocrites! You know how to interpret the face of the earth and the sky. How is it you do not know how to interpret these times?

'Why not judge for yourselves what is right? For example: when you go to court with your opponent, try to settle with him on the way, or he may drag you before the judge and the judge hand you over to the bailiff and the bailiff have you thrown into prison. I tell you, you will not get out till you have paid the very last penny.'

Reflection

St Paul invites us to 'live a life worthy of our calling' by practising the essential Christian qualities of 'humility, kindness, patience and bearing with one another in love.' These qualities will enable us to see the miracles of God happening around us. Sometimes we can be so full of ourselves that we are unable to see the good in others, as happened with most of the crowd in Jesus' time. While Jesus went about doing good, people were fooled by the false propaganda of the Pharisees. Do we overlook the good in others and disown our responsibility by refusing to stand up against injustice when we can speak out? We cannot allow ourselves to be complacent. A simple question to ask is: how would Jesus respond if he were living now? *Lord, help me recognise what is evil and to always take the side of justice and mercy.*

29th Week in Ordinary Time | Green
or **St John Paul II,** *pope* (Optional, White)

Ephesians 4:7-16

Each one of us has been given his own share of grace, given as Christ allotted it. It was said that he would: When he ascended to the height, he captured prisoners, he gave gifts to men.

When it says, 'he ascended', what can it mean if not that he descended right down to the lower regions of the earth? The one who rose higher than all the heavens to fill all things is none other than the one who descended. ... *(Please see the Appendix B-25)*

Psalm 121:1-5. R. v. 1

I rejoiced when I heard them say: 'Let us go to God's house.'

Luke 13:1-9

Some people arrived and told Jesus about the Galileans whose blood Pilate had mingled with that of their sacrifices. At this he said to them, 'Do you suppose these Galileans who suffered like that were greater sinners than any other Galileans? They were not, I tell you. No; but unless you repent you will all perish as they did. Or those eighteen on whom the tower at Siloam fell and killed them? Do you suppose that they were more guilty than all the other people living in Jerusalem? They were not, I tell you. No; but unless you repent you will all perish as they did.'

He told this parable: 'A man had a fig tree planted in his vineyard, and he came looking for fruit on it but found none. He said to the man who looked after the vineyard, "Look here, for three years now I have been coming to look for fruit on this fig tree and finding none. Cut it down: why should it be taking up the ground?" "Sir," the man replied "leave it one more year and give me time to dig round it and manure it: it may bear fruit next year; if not, then you can cut it down."'

Reflection

Jesus says, 'Unless you change your ways, you will all perish'. It is a warning to all of us who feel satisfied with our ways of living our Christian call. The fig tree was meant to produce fruit. If not, why should it occupy the ground? Each of us is given our own share of grace by Christ in order to 'build up the body of Christ', as St Paul teaches in today's first reading. Depending on our state of life, we have to fulfil our role as God's visible sign in this world. Of course, God does not leave us to fend for ourselves. He provides us with everything that is needed to bear fruit. Am I producing the desired fruit or am I merely using up the ground? *Lord, you know my frailties. Let the seeds of change bear fruit in me.*

23

OCT SUN

THIRTIETH SUNDAY IN ORDINARY TIME

Psalter Week 2

Green

Sirach 35:12-14, 16-19

The Lord is a judge who is no respecter of personages. He shows no respect of personages to the detriment of a poor man, he listens to the plea of the injured party. He does not ignore the orphan's supplication, nor the widow's as she pours out her story. The man who with his whole heart serves God will be accepted, his petitions will carry to the clouds. The humble man's prayer pierces the clouds, until it arrives he is inconsolable, nor will he desist until the Most High takes notice of him, acquits the virtuous and delivers judgement. And the Lord will not be slow, nor will he be dilatory on their behalf.

Psalm 32:2-3, 17-19, 23. R. v. 7

This poor man called; the Lord has heard him.

2 Timothy 4:6-8, 16-18

My life is already being poured away as a libation, and the time has come for me to be gone. I have fought the good fight to the end; I have run the race to the finish; I have kept the faith; all there is to come now is the crown of righteousness reserved for me, which the Lord, the righteous judge, will give to me on that Day; and not only to me but to all those who have longed for his Appearing.

The first time I had to present my defence, there was not a single witness to support me. Every one of them deserted me – may they not be held accountable for it. But the Lord stood by me and gave me power, so that through me the whole message might be proclaimed for all the pagans to hear; and so I was rescued from the lion's mouth. The Lord will rescue me from all evil attempts on me, and bring me safely to his heavenly kingdom. To him be glory for ever and ever. Amen.

Luke 18:9-14

Jesus spoke the following parable to some people who prided themselves on being virtuous and despised everyone else. 'Two men went up to the Temple to pray, one a Pharisee, the other a tax collector. The Pharisee stood there and said this prayer to himself, "I thank you, God, that I am not grasping, unjust, adulterous like the rest of mankind, and particularly that I am not like this tax collector here. I fast twice a week; I pay tithes on all I get." The tax collector stood some distance away, not daring even to raise his eyes to heaven; but he beat his breast and said, "God, be merciful to me, a sinner." This man, I tell you, went home again at rights with God; the other did not. For everyone who exalts himself will be humbled, but the man who humbles himself will be exalted.'

Reflection

Today's first reading is a perfect companion piece to the Gospel parable. In one striking image, the writer says that 'the prayer of the humble person pierces the clouds'. Such a prayer is heard because it comes from the heart. Both the Pharisee and the tax collector believed in the same God, belonged to the same religion and worshipped in the same temple, yet only one went home at peace with God. Why? The tax collector was conscious that he needed God to move forward; the Pharisee, however, seemed so self-sufficient as to merely desire God's approval. Such a belief in God saves nobody. What really matters is how our faith in God affects our view of ourselves and of others. We behave like the God we believe in. The Pharisee believed in a discriminating God who loves good people and hates the bad. The tax collector trusted not in himself or in anything he had done but only in God's mercy. In our daily prayer, do we try to impress God with our achievements, or do we humbly acknowledge God's blessings? *Lord, be merciful to me, a sinner!*

24
OCT MON

30th Week in Ordinary Time | Green
or **St Anthony Mary Claret,** *bishop* (Optional, White)

Ephesians 4:32–5:8

Be friends with one another, and kind, forgiving each other as readily as God forgave you in Christ. Try, then, to imitate God, as children of his that he loves, and follow Christ by loving as he loved you, giving himself up in our place as a fragrant offering and a sacrifice to God. Among you there must be not even a mention of fornication or impurity in any of its forms, or promiscuity: this would hardly become the saints! ...
(Please see the Appendix B-25)

Psalm 1:1-4, 6. R. cf. Ephesians 5:1

Try to imitate God, as children of his that he loves.

Luke 13:10-17

One sabbath day Jesus was teaching in one of the synagogues, and a woman was there who for eighteen years had been possessed by a spirit that left her enfeebled; she was bent double and quite unable to stand upright. When Jesus saw her he called her over and said, 'Woman, you are rid of your infirmity' and he laid his hands on her. And at once she straightened up, and she glorified God. But the synagogue official was indignant because Jesus had healed on the sabbath, and he addressed the people present. 'There are six days' he said 'when work is to be done. Come and be healed on one of those days and not on the sabbath.' But the Lord answered him. 'Hypocrites!' he said. 'Is there one of you who does not untie his ox or his donkey from the manger on the sabbath and take it out for watering? And this woman, a daughter of Abraham whom Satan has held bound these eighteen years – was it not right to untie her bonds on the sabbath day?' When he said this, all his adversaries were covered with confusion, and all the people were overjoyed at all the wonders he worked.

Reflection

For the leader of the synagogue, the healing of the crippled woman was merely a 'favour' that merited no urgency. So, he tells people to come on days other than a Sabbath. Jesus saw in that woman a 'daughter of Abraham' awaiting liberation from 'bondage', physical and spiritual. God's actions cannot be controlled by humans. Neither time nor space nor season can determine his actions. Reaching out in service and compassion – living in solidarity – are not time and space dependent activities but dynamic and ongoing attitudes that characterise the life of the Christian. St Paul exhorts us to 'behave as children of light'. The crowd rejoiced on seeing whatever Jesus did. Do people rejoice in seeing what we, his followers, do? Do we sometimes avoid doing good, giving legalistic and uncharitable excuses? *Lord, heal my prejudices and rationalising attitudes and restore me to the fullness of life.*

30th Week in Ordinary Time
Green

25
OCT TUE

THE SIX WELSH MARTYRS AND THEIR COMPANIONS, Feast

– Wales

see Appendix A-23

Ephesians 5:21-33

Give way to one another in obedience to Christ. Wives should regard their husbands as they regard the Lord, since as Christ is head of the Church and saves the whole body, so is a husband the head of his wife; and as the Church submits to Christ, so should wives to their husbands, in everything. Husbands should love their wives just as Christ loved the Church and sacrificed himself for her to make her holy. He made her clean by washing her in water with a form of words, so that when he took her to himself she would be glorious, with no speck or wrinkle or anything like that, but holy and faultless. In the same way, husbands must love their wives as they love their own bodies; for a man to love his wife is for him to love himself. A man never hates his own body, but he feeds it and looks after it; and that is the way Christ treats the Church, because it is the body – and we are its living parts. For this reason, a man must leave his father and mother and be joined to his wife, and the two will become one body. This mystery has many implications; but I am saying it applies to Christ and the Church. To sum up; you too, each one of you, must love his wife as he loves himself; and let every wife respect her husband.

Psalm 127:1-5. R. cf. v. 1

O blessed are those who fear the Lord.

Luke 13:18-21

Jesus said, 'What is the kingdom of God like? What shall I compare it with? It is like a mustard seed which a man took and threw into his garden: it grew and became a tree, and the birds of the air sheltered in its branches.'

Another thing he said, 'What shall I compare the kingdom of God with? It is like the yeast a woman took and mixed in with three measures of flour till it was leavened all through.'

Reflection

Those of us who feel discouraged and hopeless, asking whether Gospel values can really make a difference in the modern world, have an answer in today's Gospel. The work of God often begins small but ends with a huge impact. There is an old saying, 'Little is much if God is in it', that should calm all our temptations to give up when we go through struggles in life. When the world shouts 'size matters', Jesus responds, 'What matters is not size but the potential within us as designed and willed by God who invites us to think big and to go beyond the limiting appearances around us to discover the infinite possibilities we can create. Kingdom values may penetrate slowly in society but will gradually reach everyone. *Lord, forgive my faint heart and help me see the big picture!*

26
OCT WED

30th Week in Ordinary Time
Green

Ephesians 6:1-9

Children, be obedient to your parents in the Lord – that is your duty. The first commandment that has a promise attached to it is: Honour your father and mother; and the promise is: and you will prosper and have a long life in the land. And parents, never drive your children to resentment but in bringing them up correct them and guide them as the Lord does. ... *(Please see the Appendix B-25)*

Psalm 144:10-14. R. v. 13

The Lord is faithful in all his words.

Luke 13:22-30

Through towns and villages Jesus went teaching, making his way to Jerusalem. Someone said to him, 'Sir, will there be only a few saved?' He said to them, 'Try your best to enter by the narrow door, because, I tell you, many will try to enter and will not succeed.

'Once the master of the house has got up and locked the door, you may find yourself knocking on the door, saying, "Lord, open to us" but he will answer, "I do not know where you come from." Then you will find yourself saying, "We once ate and drank in your company; you taught in our streets" but he will reply, "I do not know where you come from. Away from me, all you wicked men!"

'Then there will be weeping and grinding of teeth, when you see Abraham and Isaac and Jacob and all the prophets in the kingdom of God, and yourselves turned outside. And men from east and west, from north and south, will come to take their places at the feast in the kingdom of God. 'Yes, there are those now last who will be first, and those now first who will be last.'

Reflection

Jesus' message was simple yet radical and demanding. As he went about preaching, people thought not many could follow his way of life. Probably only a few would be saved. When questioned, Jesus did not give a direct answer. He reminded them that following his way of life was similar to entering through a narrow door. We have to be alert and proceed with caution and confidence in the Lord. We cannot afford to be complacent, with a false sense of entitlement. God goes by the size of our heart, our love, our generosity and the quality of our character. To enter through this narrow gate we will have to consciously struggle to resist the values of the world. Does my life reveal that I 'know' Jesus and follow his way? *Lord, open my ears to your word!*

30th Week in Ordinary Time
Green

27
OCT THU

Ephesians 6:10-20

Grow strong in the Lord, with the strength of his power. Put God's armour on so as to be able to resist the devil's tactics. For it is not against human enemies that we have to struggle, but against the Sovereignties and the Powers who originate the darkness of this world, the spiritual army of evil in the heavens. That is why you must rely on God's armour, or you will not be able to put up any resistance when the worst happens, or have enough resources to hold your ground. ...
(Please see the Appendix B-25)

Psalm 143:1-2, 9-10. R. v. 1

Blessed be the Lord, my rock.

Luke 13:31-35

Some Pharisees came up to Jesus. 'Go away' they said. 'Leave this place, because Herod means to kill you.' He replied, 'You may go and give that fox this message: Learn that today and tomorrow I cast out devils and on the third day attain my end. But for today and tomorrow and the next day I must go out, since it would not be right for a prophet to die outside Jerusalem.

'Jerusalem, Jerusalem, you that kill the prophets and stone those who are sent to you! How often have I longed to gather your children, as a hen gathers her brood under her wings, and you refused! So be it! Your house will be left to you. Yes, I promise you, you shall not see me till the time comes when you say: Blessings on him who comes in the name of the Lord!'

Reflection

Jesus sets a perfect example of courage and self-respect, two qualities that we should have in plenty if we are to carry out our mission in the modern world confronting corruption in society and hypocritical attitudes. Without courage and a strong sense of personal integrity we will not be effective in our work or be able to instil these qualities in others. Jesus' integrity was his strength against those who sought to obstruct his mission. Unfortunately, many of us suffer from fear and insecurity due to hostility from political and secular forces. As a result, we can silently make compromises at the cost of our self-respect and dignity. We may even stop doing good works that provoke criticism from others, avoiding situations to protect ourselves and our reputations. *Lord, when I face such situations, instil in me a deep sense of integrity.*

28
OCT FRI

Sts Simon and Jude, Apostles
Feast | Red

Ephesians 2:19-22

You are no longer aliens or foreign visitors: you are citizens like all the saints, and part of God's household. You are part of a building that has the apostles and prophets for its foundations, and Christ Jesus himself for its main cornerstone. As every structure is aligned on him, all grow into one holy temple in the Lord; and you too, in him, are being built into a house where God lives, in the Spirit.

Psalm 18:2-5. R. v. 5

Their word goes forth through all the earth.

Luke 6:12-19

Jesus went out into the hills to pray; and he spent the whole night in prayer to God. When day came he summoned his disciples and picked out twelve of them; he called them 'apostles': Simon whom he called Peter, and his brother Andrew; James, John, Philip, Bartholomew, Matthew, Thomas, James son of Alphaeus, Simon called the Zealot, Judas son of James, and Judas Iscariot who became a traitor.

He then came down with them and stopped at a piece of level ground where there was a large gathering of his disciples with a great crowd of people from all parts of Judaea and from Jerusalem and from the coastal region of Tyre and Sidon who had come to hear him and to be cured of their diseases. People tormented by unclean spirits were also cured, and everyone in the crowd was trying to touch him because power came out of him that cured them all.

Reflection

Jesus makes a well discerned choice of his apostles in consultation with his Father. Then he brings these apostles into the midst of the crowd to let them know the 'smell of the sheep' (Remember Pope Francis' exhortation?) Jesus' mission can be carried out meaningfully only if we know the smell of sheep, that is, we need to come close to people and their life situations. We need to come down and stand on the same level as the people we wish to serve. Jesus let people touch him, and they found him infused with the power of God. The feast of the Apostles Simon and Jude reminds us to reflect on our missionary spirit and fervour. What do people find in us? Are we able to draw closer to Jesus and thus stay closer to the people, too? Or are we comfortable with armchair service, avoiding the real needs and the 'smell' of the people? *Lord, rekindle my missionary fervour.*

30th Week in Ordinary Time
Green

29
OCT SAT

Philippians 1:18-26

Christ is proclaimed; and that makes me happy; and I shall continue being happy, because I know this will help to save me, thanks to your prayers and to the help which will be given to me by the Spirit of Jesus. My one hope and trust is that I shall never have to admit defeat, but that now as always I shall have the courage for Christ to be glorified in my body, whether by my life or by my death. Life to me, of course, is Christ, but then death would bring me something more; but then again, if living in this body means doing work which is having good results – I do not know what I should choose. I am caught in this dilemma: I want to be gone and be with Christ, which would be very much the better, but for me to stay alive in this body is a more urgent need for your sake. This weighs with me so much that I feel sure I shall survive and stay with you all, and help you to progress in the faith and even increase your joy in it; and so you will have another reason to give praise to Christ Jesus on my account when I am with you again.

Psalm 41:2-3, 5. R. v. 3

My soul is thirsting for God, the God of my life.

Luke 14:1, 7-11

Now on a sabbath day Jesus had gone for a meal to the house of one of the leading Pharisees; and they watched him closely. He then told the guests a parable, because he had noticed how they picked the places of honour. He said this, 'When someone invites you to a wedding feast, do not take your seat in the place of honour. A more distinguished person than you may have been invited, and the person who invited you both may come and say, "Give up your place to this man." And then, to your embarrassment, you would have to go and take the lowest place. No; when you are a guest, make your way to the lowest place and sit there, so that, when your host comes, he may say, "My friend, move up higher." In that way, everyone with you at the table will see you honoured. For everyone who exalts himself will be humbled, and the man who humbles himself will be exalted.'

Reflection

A keen observer of social behaviour, Jesus, noticing how people chose places of honour to prove their self-importance, affirms that anyone who tries to make themself great will be humbled. Our efforts at being acknowledged and honoured can often end up in self-humiliation. The greatest honour we can ever achieve lies in how we fare in the eyes of God. Jesus says, '(let people) see your good deeds and give glory to God' (Matthew 5:16). St Paul exhorts us to have the courage for Christ to be glorified in our body. Instead of seeking honour and respect from others, let our lives bring us honour in the eyes of God. As Christ's disciples we need to make a realistic assessment of our daily conduct to avoid putting on a façade to look good. Am I living a transparent life, devoid of a craving for appreciation and honour? *Lord, teach me to be happy with myself.*

30
OCT SUN

THIRTY-FIRST SUNDAY IN ORDINARY TIME

Psalter Week 3

Green

Wisdom 11:22–12:2

In your sight, Lord, the whole world is like a grain of dust that tips the scales, like a drop of morning dew falling on the ground. Yet you are merciful to all, because you can do all things and overlook men's sins so that they can repent.

Yes, you love all that exists, you hold nothing of what you have made in abhorrence, for had you hated anything, you would not have formed it. And how, had you not willed it, could a thing persist, how be conserved if not called forth by you?

You spare all things because all things are yours, Lord, lover of life, you whose imperishable spirit is in all. Little by little, therefore, you correct those who offend, you admonish and remind them of how they have sinned, so that they may abstain from evil and trust in you, Lord.

Psalm 144:1-2, 8-11, 13-14. R. cf. v. 1

I will bless your name for ever, O God my King.

2 Thessalonians 1:11–2:2

We pray continually that our God will make you worthy of his call, and by his power fulfil all your desires for goodness and complete all that you have been doing through faith; because in this way the name of our Lord Jesus Christ will be glorified in you and you in him, by the grace of our God and the Lord Jesus Christ.

To turn now, brothers, to the coming of our Lord Jesus Christ and how we shall all be gathered round him: please do not get excited too soon or alarmed by any prediction or rumour or any letter claiming to come from us, implying that the Day of the Lord has already arrived.

Luke 19:1-10

Jesus entered Jericho and was going through the town when a man whose name was Zacchaeus made his appearance; he was one of the senior tax collectors and a wealthy man. He was anxious to see what kind of man Jesus was, but he was too short and could not see him for the crowd; so he ran ahead and climbed a sycamore tree to catch a glimpse of Jesus who was to pass that way. When Jesus reached the spot he looked up and spoke to him: 'Zacchaeus, come down. Hurry, because I must stay at your house today.' And he hurried down and welcomed him joyfully. They all complained when they saw what was happening. 'He has gone to stay at a sinner's house' they said. But Zacchaeus stood his ground and said to the Lord, 'Look, sir, I am going to give half my property to the poor, and if I have cheated anybody I will pay him back four times the amount.' And

Jesus said to him, 'Today salvation has come to this house, because this man too is a son of Abraham; for the Son of Man has come to seek out and save what was lost.'

Reflection

Zacchaeus wanted to 'see' Jesus, while Jesus wanted to 'meet and stay' with Zacchaeus. The subtle difference in intent between Jesus and Zacchaeus has implications for our relationship with God. God wants to be engaged in our lives, to meet and stay with us where we are, sharing his forgiving love and presence. If we let him into our lives, we will go through a Zacchaeus-experience: everything I have, I am willing to share, to give up everything to receive the giver of all things into my life! From a mere desire to see, Zacchaeus takes Jesus home, regardless of what others think. Without being asked, he declares that he will share his wealth with the poor, not out of selfish motives but obviously moved by Jesus' love. His life's priorities straightened out, money was no longer the driving force. All he cared about was to follow Jesus. We can learn much from Zacchaeus in our daily life. An effort to catch a glimpse of Jesus will have him waiting for us, inviting himself into our hearts. When we take one step towards God, he takes several towards us. Do we still only want to 'see' Jesus or to 'meet' and be transformed by him forever? *Lord, I leave the doors of my heart open, please enter in.*

31
OCT MON

Philippians 2:1-4

If our life in Christ means anything to you, if love can persuade at all, or the Spirit that we have in common, or any tenderness and sympathy, then be united in your convictions and united in your love, with a common purpose and a common mind. That is the one thing which would make me completely happy. There must be no competition among you, no conceit; but everybody is to be self-effacing. Always consider the other person to be better than yourself, so that nobody thinks of his own interests first but everybody thinks of other people's interests instead.

Psalm 130

Keep my soul in peace before you, O Lord.

Luke 14:12-14

Jesus said to his host, one of the leading Pharisees, 'When you give a lunch or a dinner, do not ask your friends, brothers, relations or rich neighbours, for fear they repay your courtesy by inviting you in return. No; when you have a party, invite the poor, the crippled, the lame, the blind; that they cannot pay you back means that you are fortunate, because repayment will be made to you when the virtuous rise again.'

Reflection

Living as we do in a society that always asks, 'What's in it for me?', Jesus proposes a new vision of life where selfless love supersedes selfish love. So often our relationships, be it in the family or workplace or in a community, are barter-based rather than love-rooted. We keep a record of the good that we have done to others and we expect them to do likewise for us. Our choices and conduct of life can also be influenced by the expectations and behaviours of others. Jesus challenges us to give freely, even as we ourselves have received freely! As Jesus' disciples, we must be on our feet to do the unexpected, the unobvious, the extraordinary. When was the last time you did something without expecting anything in return? Will you attempt such an act today? *Lord, may I be as generous towards others as you are with me!*

01

NOV TUE

All Saints Day

Solemnity

White

Apocalypse 7:2-4, 9-14

I, John, saw another angel rising where the sun rises, carrying the seal of the living God; he called in a powerful voice to the four angels whose duty was to devastate land and sea, 'Wait before you do any damage on land or at sea or to the trees, until we have put the seal on the foreheads of the servants of our God.' Then I heard how many were sealed: a hundred and forty-four thousand, out of all the tribes of Israel. *(Please see the Appendix B-26)*

Psalm 23:1-6. R. cf. v. 6

Such are the men who seek your face, O Lord.

1 John 3:1-3

Think of the love that the Father has lavished on us, by letting us be called God's children; and that is what we are. Because the world refused to acknowledge him, therefore it does not acknowledge us. My dear people, we are already the children of God but what we are to be in the future has not yet been revealed; all we know is, that when it is revealed we shall be like him because we shall see him as he really is. Surely everyone who entertains this hope must purify himself, must try to be as pure as Christ.

Matthew 5:1-12

Seeing the crowds, Jesus went up the hill. There he sat down and was joined by his disciples. Then he began to speak. This is what he taught them: 'How happy are the poor in spirit; theirs is the kingdom of heaven. Happy the gentle: they shall have the earth for their heritage; Happy those who mourn: they shall be comforted; Happy those who hunger and thirst for what is right: they shall be satisfied; Happy the merciful: they shall have mercy shown them; Happy the pure in heart: they shall see God; Happy the peacemakers: they shall be called sons of God; Happy those who are persecuted in the cause of right: theirs is the kingdom of heaven.

'Happy are you when people abuse you and persecute you and speak all kinds of calumny against you on my account. Rejoice and be glad, for your reward will be great in heaven.'

Reflection

As we honour all the saints, Jesus shares what it means to be God's children. This is God's way: gently comforting, showing mercy, bringing peace and goodness into concrete situations. Like Jesus and the saints, we are to be merciful, pure in heart, poor enough in spirit to know our need for God. Living this way, we are happy, blessed. Attuned to the Spirit, we become poor like Jesus and our favourite saints. God brings about, unexpectedly and wonderfully, the grace we seek in prayer. God's love, at the heart of our lives, is the source of the Beatitudes. Jesus' promise, well-known to the saints, encourages us: 'Come to me, all you that labour and are burdened, and I will give you rest'.

02
NOV WED

The Commemoration of all the Faithful Departed

(All Souls Day) | Violet

Isaiah 25:6-9

(Please see the Appendix B-26)

Psalm 22. R. v. 1

The Lord is my shepherd; there is nothing I shall want.

Romans 5:5-11

Hope is not deceptive, because the love of God has been poured into our hearts by the Holy Spirit which has been given to us. We were still helpless when at his appointed moment Christ died for sinful men. It is not easy to die even for a good man – though of course for someone really worthy, a man might be prepared to die – but what proves that God loves us is that Christ died for us while we were still sinners. Having died to make us righteous, is it likely that he would now fail to save us from God's anger? When we were reconciled to God by the death of his Son, we were still enemies; now that we have been reconciled, surely we may count on being saved by the life of his Son? Not merely because we have been reconciled but because we are filled with joyful trust in God, through our Lord Jesus Christ, through whom we have already gained our reconciliation.

Luke 7:11-17

Jesus went to a town called Nain, accompanied by his disciples and a great number of people. When he was near the gate of the town it happened that a dead man was being carried out for burial, the only son of his mother, and she was a widow. And a considerable number of the townspeople were with her. When the Lord saw her he felt sorry for her. 'Do not cry' he said. Then he went up and put his hand on the bier and the bearers stood still, and he said, 'Young man, I tell you to get up.' And the dead man sat up and began to talk, and Jesus gave him to his mother. Everyone was filled with awe and praised God saying, 'A great prophet has appeared among us; God has visited his people.' And this opinion of him spread throughout Judaea and all over the countryside.

Reflection

Today's hope-filled readings state that Jesus died for our loved ones for whom we are praying, and for each of us, while we were sinners. Jesus' purpose, obeying the Father, reflects the Father's own will and purpose: that Jesus should lose nothing of all that the Father has given him. And we are part of the 'all' that the Father has given him. Jesus, the Lamb of God, is our Shepherd, leading us. In Jesus we are one with the faithful departed, with 'all souls'. May we experience God's loving compassion today, helping us to recognise more deeply the love God has poured into our hearts by the Spirit. With the faithful departed we will dwell in the Lord's own house. Goodness and kindness shall follow us for in God, the God of the banquet, Jesus of Nazareth was crucified and is risen.

31st Week in Ordinary Time | Green
St Malachy, Bishop, Memorial – Ireland | White

03
NOV THU

Philippians 3:3-8

We are the real people of the circumcision, we who worship in accordance with the Spirit of God; we have our own glory from Christ Jesus without having to rely on a physical operation. If it came to relying on physical evidence, I should be fully qualified myself. Take any man who thinks he can rely on what is physical: I am even better qualified. I was born of the race of Israel and of the tribe of Benjamin, a Hebrew born of Hebrew parents, and I was circumcised when I was eight days old. As for the Law, I was a Pharisee; as for working for religion, I was a persecutor of the Church; as far as the Law can make you perfect, I was faultless. But because of Christ, I have come to consider all the advantages that I had as disadvantages. Not only that, but I believe nothing can happen that will outweigh the supreme advantage of knowing Christ Jesus my Lord.

Psalm 104:2-7. R. v. 3

Let the hearts that seek the Lord rejoice.

Luke 15:1-10

The tax collectors and the sinners were all seeking the company of Jesus to hear what he had to say, and the Pharisees and the scribes complained. 'This man' they said 'welcomes sinners and eats with them.' So he spoke this parable to them: 'What man among you with a hundred sheep, losing one, would not leave the ninety-nine in the wilderness and go after the missing one till he found it? And when he found it, would he not joyfully take it on his shoulders and then, when he got home, call together his friends and neighbours? "Rejoice with me," he would say "I have found my sheep that was lost." In the same way, I tell you, there will be more rejoicing in heaven over one repentant sinner than over ninety-nine virtuous men who have no need of repentance. "Or again, what woman with ten drachmas would not, if she lost one, light a lamp and sweep out the house and search thoroughly till she found it? And then, when she had found it, call together her friends and neighbours? "Rejoice with me," she would say "I have found the drachma I lost." In the same way, I tell you, there is rejoicing among the angels of God over one repentant sinner.'

Reflection

Some people complain that Jesus welcomes the tax collectors and sinners who seek his company. He responds, from his heart, to this complaint by pointing to the shepherd searching for his missing sheep; finding it, he 'joyfully' takes it on his shoulders, calling friends and neighbours to rejoice with him. Jesus also speaks of the woman energetically searching till she finds the drachma. The Pharisees and scribes are 'on about' excluding people they consider to be outsiders. Here is God, energetically seeking each one of us, bringing us into the family, rejoicing with friends and neighbours. God is 'on about' being family and rejoicing together. The inviting God, whom the tax collectors and sinners recognise in Jesus, welcomes everyone. The psalm sets the scene of rejoicing, searching, seeking God's face, remembering wonders. The reality that 'He the Lord, is our God' is made flesh in Jesus.

04
NOV FRI

31st Week in Ordinary Time
St Charles Borromeo, *bishop,* **Memorial** | White

Philippians 3:17–4:1
My brothers, be united in following my rule of life. Take as your models everybody who is already doing this and study them as you used to study us. I have told you often, and I repeat it today with tears, there are many who are behaving as the enemies of the cross of Christ. They are destined to be lost. They make foods into their god and they are proudest of something they ought to think shameful; the things they think important are earthly things. For us, our homeland is in heaven, and from heaven comes the saviour we are waiting for, the Lord Jesus Christ, and he will transfigure these wretched bodies of ours into copies of his glorious body. He will do that by the same power with which he can subdue the whole universe. So then, my brothers and dear friends, do not give way but remain faithful in the Lord. I miss you very much, dear friends; you are my joy and my crown.

Psalm 121:1-5. R. v. 1
Let us go rejoicing to the house of the Lord.

Luke 16:1-8
Jesus said to his disciples: 'There was a rich man and he had a steward who was denounced to him for being wasteful with his property. He called for the man and said, "What is this I hear about you? Draw me up an account of your stewardship because you are not to be my steward any longer." Then the steward said to himself, "Now that my master is taking the stewardship from me, what am I to do? Dig? I am not strong enough. Go begging? I should be too ashamed. Ah, I know what I will do to make sure that when I am dismissed from office there will be some to welcome me into their homes." 'Then he called his master's debtors one by one. To the first he said, "How much do you owe my master?" "One hundred measures of oil" was the reply. The steward said, "Here, take your bond; sit down straight away and write fifty." To another he said, "And you, sir, how much do you owe?" "One hundred measures of wheat" was the reply. The steward said, "Here, take your bond and write eighty." 'The master praised the dishonest steward for his astuteness. For the children of this world are more astute in dealing with their own kind than are the children of light.'

Reflection
Jesus wants us to be people of light, astute and alert in using our talents and gifts, sharing the light Jesus brings into the world of our daily living. This is not always an easy task. The steward is described as 'wasteful' and we are urged to use, not waste, our individual gifts. We can be wasteful, even indirectly, 'behaving as the enemies of the cross of Christ', as Paul says in the first reading, by idolising what is less than God, making the means with which we are gifted an end in themselves. Paul pleads with us to 'remain faithful in the Lord' calling his listeners, and us, 'dear friends'. We are very dear to Jesus who enlightens us through his Spirit at work in us, enabling us to bring his light – to bring him – to countless others who are also his very dear sisters and brothers.

31st Week in Ordinary Time
Green

05
NOV SAT

Philippians 4:10-19

It is a great joy to me, in the Lord, that at last you have shown some concern for me again; though of course you were concerned before, and only lacked an opportunity. I am not talking about shortage of money: I have learnt to manage on whatever I have, I know how to be poor and I know how to be rich too. I have been through my initiation and now I am ready for anything anywhere: full stomach or empty stomach, poverty or plenty. There is nothing I cannot master with the help of the One who gives me strength. All the same, it was good of you to share with me in my hardships. ... *(Please see the Appendix B-26)*

Psalm 111:1-2, 5-6, 8, 9. R. v. 1

Happy are those who fear the lord.

Luke 16:9-15

Jesus said to his disciples, 'I tell you this: use money, tainted as it is, to win you friends, and thus make sure that when it fails you, they will welcome you into the tents of eternity. The man who can be trusted in little things can be trusted in great; the man who is dishonest in little things will be dishonest in great. If then you cannot be trusted with money, that tainted thing, who will trust you with genuine riches? And if you cannot be trusted with what is not yours, who will give you what is your very own?

'No servant can be the slave of two masters: he will either hate the first and love the second, or treat the first with respect and the second with scorn. You cannot be the slave both of God and of money.' The Pharisees, who loved money, heard all this and laughed at him. He said to them, 'You are the very ones who pass yourselves off as virtuous in people's sight, but God knows your hearts. For what is thought highly of by men is loathsome in the sight of God.'

Reflection

There is an urgency in Jesus' words about choosing to live God's way, 'in the sight of God' who knows, and lives in, our hearts. If money or another idol is our priority, there is no place for such true living. Following Jesus is about allowing God to fill our hearts with divine love. The Gospel acclamation says: 'Jesus Christ was rich but he became poor'. Why? To make us, 'rich out of his poverty', to share the inner wealth which enables us to be 'open-handed' towards others. The person who seeks God, says the psalmist, is one who 'takes delight in all his commands', 'with a steadfast heart' that is trustful, able to give to others from the 'poverty' – the true riches – they live with Jesus. We know people like this; they will be 'remembered for ever'.

06
NOV SUN

THIRTY-SECOND SUNDAY IN ORDINARY TIME

Psalter Week 4
Green

2 Maccabees 7:1-2, 9-14

There were seven brothers who were arrested with their mother. The king tried to force them to taste pig's flesh, which the Law forbids, by torturing them with whips and scourges. One of them, acting as spokesman for the others, said, 'What are you trying to find out from us? We are prepared to die rather than break the Law of our ancestors.'

With his last breath the second brother exclaimed, 'Inhuman fiend, you may discharge us from this present life, but the King of the world will raise us up, since it is for his laws that we die, to live again for ever.'

After him, they amused themselves with the third, who on being asked for his tongue promptly thrust it out and boldly held out his hands, with these honourable words, 'It was heaven that gave me these limbs; for the sake of his laws I disdain them; from him I hope to receive them again.' The king and his attendants were astounded at the young man's courage and his utter indifference to suffering.

When this one was dead they subjected the fourth to the same savage torture. When he neared his end he cried, 'Ours is the better choice, to meet death at men's hands, yet relying on God's promise that we shall be raised up by him; whereas for you there can be no resurrection, no new life.'

Psalms 16:1, 5-6, 8, 15. R. v. 15

I shall be filled, when I awake, with the sight of your glory, O Lord.

2 Thessalonians 2:16–3:5

May our Lord Jesus Christ himself, and God our Father who has given us his love and, through his grace, such inexhaustible comfort and such sure hope, comfort you and strengthen you in everything good that you do or say.

Finally, brothers, pray for us; pray that the Lord's message may spread quickly, and be received with honour as it was among you; and pray that we may be preserved from the interference of bigoted and evil people, for faith is not given to everyone. But the Lord is faithful, and he will give you strength and guard you from the evil one, and we, in the Lord, have every confidence that you are doing and will go on doing all that we tell you. May the Lord turn your hearts towards the love of God and the fortitude of Christ.

Luke 20:27-38 *(Shorter form 20:27, 34-38)*

Some Sadducees – those who say that there is no resurrection – approached Jesus and they put this question to him, 'Master, we have it from Moses in writing, that if a man's married brother dies childless, the man must marry the widow to raise up children for his brother. Well, then, there were seven brothers. The first, having married a wife, died childless. The second and then the third married the widow. And the same with all the seven, they died leaving no children. Finally the woman herself died. Now, at the resurrection, to which of them will she be wife since she had been married to all seven?' Jesus replied, 'The children of this world take wives and husbands, but those who are judged worthy of a place in the other world and in the resurrection from the dead do not marry because they can no longer die, for they are the same as the angels, and being children of the resurrection they are sons of God. And Moses himself implies that the dead rise again, in the passage about the bush where he calls the Lord the God of Abraham, the God of Isaac and the God of Jacob. Now he is God, not of the dead, but of the living; for to him all are in fact alive.'

Reflection

Today's readings speak strongly about 'new life', 'resurrection'. As children of God, we are people of the resurrection. Jesus refers to Moses' experience of God at the burning bush; Jesus, our new Moses, states that this same God who spoke to Moses is 'God of the living; for to him all are in fact alive'.

The seven brothers mentioned in today's first reading from the Second Book of Maccabees, died 'relying on God's promise that (they) shall be raised up by him'. In the psalm we proclaim that God will 'fill us with the sight of (God's) glory' when we 'awake' after our death. The Gospel acclamation proclaims that 'Jesus Christ is the firstborn of the dead'. In wonder and awe, with strong hope, trust and joy we proclaim: 'glory and kingship be his for ever and ever'. Every Sunday, like Easter Sunday, celebrates the resurrection of the Lord, in which our own resurrection is assured because God is not a God 'of the dead but of the living, for to him all are, in fact, alive.'

32nd Week in Ordinary Time
Green

Titus 1:1-9

From Paul, servant of God, an apostle of Jesus Christ to bring those whom God has chosen to faith and to the knowledge of the truth that leads to true religion; and to give them the hope of the eternal life that was promised so long ago by God. He does not lie and so, at the appointed time, he revealed his decision, and, by the command of God our saviour, I have been commissioned to proclaim it. To Titus, true child of mine in the faith that we share, wishing you grace and peace from God the Father and from Christ Jesus our saviour. The reason I left you behind in Crete was for you to get everything organised there and appoint elders in every town, in the way that I told you: that is, each of them must be a man of irreproachable character: he must not have been married more than once and his children must be believers and not uncontrollable or liable to be charged with disorderly conduct. Since, as president, he will be God's representative, he must be irreproachable: never an arrogant or hot-tempered man, nor a heavy drinker or violent, nor out to make money; but a man who is hospitable and a friend of all that is good; sensible, moral, devout and self-controlled; and he must have a firm grasp of the unchanging message of the tradition, so that he can be counted on for both expounding the sound doctrine and refuting those who argue against it.

Psalm 23:1-6. R. cf. v.6

Such are the men who seek your face, O Lord.

Luke 17:1-6

Jesus said to his disciples, 'Obstacles are sure to come, but alas for the one who provides them! It would be better for him to be thrown into the sea with a millstone put round his neck than that he should lead astray a single one of these little ones. Watch yourselves!

'If your brother does something wrong, reprove him and, if he is sorry forgive him. And if he wrongs you seven times a day and seven times comes back to you and says, "I am sorry," you must forgive him.' The apostles said to the Lord, 'Increase our faith.' The Lord replied, 'Were your faith the size of a mustard seed you could say to this mulberry tree, "Be uprooted and planted in the sea," and it would obey you.'

Reflection

Following Jesus' words about human difficulties, forgiveness and the need to 'watch' ourselves, the disciples say to him, 'Lord, increase our faith'. They understand that what Jesus is asking of them is very demanding and they will need a strong faith in him to live by his words. Prayer will be important. With the psalmist we pray, 'Lord, this is the people that longs to see your face'. We pray this prayer as a community attuned to God to whom belongs 'the world and all its peoples'. It is not just my prayer; it is our prayer. We pray it on behalf of our sisters and brothers that we may all experience the presence and grace of God in our daily situations.

32nd Week in Ordinary Time Green,
Blessed John Duns Scotus, Priest, Memorial – Scotland

08
NOV TUE

ALL SAINTS OF WALES, Feast – Wales
see Appendix A-24

Titus 2:1-8, 11-14

It is for you to preach the behaviour which goes with healthy doctrine. The older men should be reserved, dignified, moderate, sound in faith and love and constancy. Similarly, the older women should behave as though they were religious, with no scandal-mongering and no habitual wine-drinking – they are to be the teachers of the right behaviour and show the younger women how they should love their husbands and love their children, how they are to be sensible and chaste, and how to work in their homes, and be gentle, and do as their husbands tell them, so that the message of God is never disgraced. In the same way, you have got to persuade the younger men to be moderate and in everything you do make yourself an example to them of working for good: when you are teaching, be an example to them in your sincerity and earnestness and in keeping all that you say so wholesome that nobody can make objections to it; and then any opponent will be at a loss, with no accusation to make against us. ... *(Please see the Appendix B-26)*

Psalm 36:3-4, 18, 23, 27, 29. R. v. 39

The salvation of the just comes from the Lord.

Luke 17:7-10

Jesus said to his disciples: 'Which of you, with a servant ploughing or minding sheep, would say to him when he returned from the fields, "Come and have your meal immediately"? Would he not be more likely to say, "Get my supper laid; make yourself tidy and wait on me while I eat and drink. You can eat and drink yourself afterwards"? Must he be grateful to the servant for doing what he was told? So with you: when you have done all you have been told to do, say, "We are merely servants: we have done no more than our duty."'

Reflection

What's wrong with being a mere servant? We are not alone in our task of being 'merely servants', doing our 'duty'. We hear that 'the Lord guides' our steps through the workings of the Spirit within us. To be a servant is our call, knowing that salvation 'comes from the Lord'; we are not told that it may come; very clearly it comes, says the psalm response; we experience it in the present, each day, as we serve God in the people among whom he has placed us. Jesus draws our attention to the Master we serve, the same Master Jesus himself served as one of us. And Paul says, 'God's grace has been revealed' in Jesus the Servant who obeyed the Master, the Father, with whom he is one, for our salvation.

09
NOV WED

The Dedication of the Lateran Basilica

Feast | White

Ezekiel 47:1-2, 8-9, 12

The angel brought me to the entrance of the Temple, where a stream came out from under the Temple threshold and flowed eastwards, since the Temple faced east. The water flowed from under the right side of the Temple, south of the altar. … *(Please see the Appendix B-27)*

Psalm 45:2-3, 5-6, 8-9. R. v. 5

The waters of a river give joy to God's city, the holy place where the Most High dwells.

1 Corinthians 3:9-11, 16-17

You are God's building. By the grace God gave me, I succeeded as an architect and laid the foundations, on which someone else is doing the building. Everyone doing the building must work carefully. For the foundation, nobody can lay any other than the one which has already been laid, that is, Jesus Christ. Didn't you realise that you were God's temple and that the Spirit of God was living among you? If anybody should destroy the temple of God, God will destroy him, because the temple of God is sacred; and you are that temple.

John 2:13-22

Just before the Jewish Passover Jesus went up to Jerusalem, and in the Temple he found people selling cattle and sheep and pigeons, and the money changers sitting at their counters there. Making a whip out of some cord, he drove them all out of the Temple, cattle and sheep as well, scattered the money changers' coins, knocked their tables over and said to the pigeon-sellers, 'Take all this out of here and stop turning my Father's house into a market.' Then his disciples remembered the words of scripture: Zeal for your house will devour me. The Jews intervened and said, 'What sign can you show us to justify what you have done?' Jesus answered, 'Destroy this sanctuary, and in three days I will raise it up.' The Jews replied, 'It has taken forty-six years to build this sanctuary: are you going to raise it up in three days?' But he was speaking of the sanctuary that was his body, and when Jesus rose from the dead, his disciples remembered that he had said this, and they believed the scripture and the words he had said.

Reflection

It was David who first thought of building a temple for God in Jerusalem, but he was a warrior, 'a man of blood'. It fell to his son Solomon, who lived at a time of peace, to proceed with the project. Solomon's temple lasted until 587 BC, when it was destroyed by the Babylonians. The inhabitants of Judah who returned from exile in Babylon commenced building the 'second' temple in 537 BC. Extended by Herod the Great, this is the temple that Jesus 'cleanses' in his zeal for the holiness of God's house. But it will cost him his life, just as the prophets committed to the honour of God were persecuted. Today's feast reminds us that 'the temple of God' has a variety of meanings: the house where we worship, our body, the community, the Church, the Body of Christ. How do you keep God's temple holy?

32nd Week in Ordinary Time
St Leo the Great, *pope, doctor,* **Memorial** | White

10 NOV THU

Philemon 7-20

I am so delighted, and comforted, to know of your love; they tell me, brother, how you have put new heart into the saints. Now, although in Christ I can have no diffidence about telling you to do whatever is your duty, I am appealing to your love instead, reminding you that this is Paul writing, an old man now and, what is more, still a prisoner of Christ Jesus. I am appealing to you for a child of mine, whose father I became while wearing these chains: I mean Onesimus. He was of no use to you before, but he will be useful to you now, as he has been to me. I am sending him back to you, and with him – I could say – a part of my own self. I should have liked to keep him with me; he could have been a substitute for you, to help me while I am in the chains that the Good News has brought me. However, I did not want to do anything without your consent; it would have been forcing your act of kindness, which should be spontaneous. … *(Please see the Appendix B-27)*

Psalm 145:7-10. R. v. 5

He is happy who is helped by Jacob's God.

Luke 17:20-25

Asked by the Pharisees when the kingdom of God was to come, Jesus gave them this answer, 'The coming of the kingdom of God does not admit of observation and there will be no one to say, "Look here! Look there!" For, you must know, the kingdom of God is among you.'

He said to the disciples, 'A time will come when you will long to see one of the days of the Son of Man and will not see it. They will say to you, "Look there!" or, "Look here!" Make no move; do not set off in pursuit; for as the lightning flashing from one part of heaven lights up the other, so will be the Son of Man when his day comes. But first he must suffer grievously and be rejected by this generation.'

Reflection

Jesus tells us that the kingdom of God is among us. It does not admit of observation, but it is real. The source of the kingdom is the presence of Jesus, the vine, among us. 'I am the vine, you are the branches', he tells us. To bear the fruits of the kingdom, to live Jesus' way, we need to remain attached to him. With the Spirit as our helper and guide, as we face the challenges of each day, we find in tangible, and often unexpected, ways that the appropriate fruit of the Spirit is at work: love, joy, peace, patience, kindness, goodness, gentleness, trustfulness and self-control, to name some. The Spirit knows which one is needed in each moment.

11
NOV FRI

32nd Week in Ordinary Time
St Martin of Tours, *bishop,* **Memorial** | White

2 John 4-9

It has given me great joy to find that your children have been living the life of truth as we were commanded by the Father. I am writing now, dear lady, not to give you any new commandment, but the one which we were given at the beginning, and to plead: let us love one another. To love is to live according to his commandments: this is the commandment which you have heard since the beginning, to live a life of love. There are many deceivers about in the world, refusing to admit that Jesus Christ has come in the flesh. They are the Deceiver; they are the Antichrist. Watch yourselves, or all our work will be lost and not get the reward it deserves. If anybody does not keep within the teaching of Christ but goes beyond it, he cannot have God with him: only those who keep to what he taught can have the Father and the Son with them.

Psalm 118:1-2, 10-11, 17-18. R. v. 1

They are happy who follow God's law.

Luke 17:26-37

Jesus said to the disciples: 'As it was in Noah's day, so will it also be in the days of the Son of Man. People were eating and drinking, marrying wives and husbands, right up to the day Noah went into the ark, and the Flood came and destroyed them all. It will be the same as it was in Lot's day: people were eating and drinking, buying and selling, planting and building, but the day Lot left Sodom, God rained fire and brimstone from heaven and it destroyed them all. It will be the same when the day comes for the Son of Man to be revealed.

'When that day comes, anyone on the housetop, with his possessions in the house, must not come down to collect them, nor must anyone in the fields turn back either. Remember Lot's wife. Anyone who tries to preserve his life will lose it; and anyone who loses it will keep it safe. I tell you, on that night two will be in one bed: one will be taken, the other left; two women will be grinding corn together: one will be taken, the other left.' The disciples interrupted. 'Where Lord?' they asked. He said, 'Where the body is, there too will the vultures gather.'

Reflection

We are used to being alerted when severe weather patterns are forming or a health crisis is emerging. In today's Gospel, Jesus speaks of looming hard times and our need to be alert. His words remind us of the fragile nature of human life and the losses that occur. In his letter, St John helps us to prepare for such eventualities: 'let us love one another' and keep living 'the life of truth'. How can we live like this? By seeking God with all our heart, says the psalm, treasuring God's promise, and asking God to open our eyes to see the wonders of his law. God's wonders are not in short supply, as we follow the law of the Lord, written in the heart of each of us. We discover the utter kindness at the heart of life, for the Spirit is with us and in us.

32nd Week in Ordinary Time
St Josaphat, *bishop, martyr,* **Memorial** | Red

12 NOV SAT

3 John 5-8

My friend, you have done faithful work in looking after these brothers, even though they were complete strangers to you. They are a proof to the whole Church of your charity and it would be a very good thing if you could help them on their journey in a way that God would approve. It was entirely for the sake of the name that they set out, without depending on the pagans for anything; it is our duty to welcome men of this sort and contribute our share to their work for the truth.

Psalm 111:1-6. R. v. 1

Happy the man who fears the Lord.

Luke 18:1-8

Jesus told his disciples a parable about the need to pray continually and never lose heart. 'There was a judge in a certain town' he said 'who had neither fear of God nor respect for man. In the same town there was a widow who kept on coming to him and saying, "I want justice from you against my enemy!" For a long time he refused, but at last he said to himself, "Maybe I have neither fear of God nor respect for man, but since she keeps pestering me I must give this widow her just rights, or she will persist in coming and worry me to death."'

And the Lord said, 'You notice what the unjust judge has to say? Now will not God see justice done to his chosen who cry to him day and night even when he delays to help them? I promise you, he will see justice done to them, and done speedily. But when the Son of Man comes, will he find any faith on earth?'

Reflection

There is a poignancy in Jesus' final words in today's Gospel, about whether he will find any faith on earth. He contrasts the actions of God with those of an unjust judge who takes a long time to respond to the pleas of the widow for justice; the judge finally responds not because he cares about the widow but for his own comfort – so that she will stop pestering him. God, on the other hand, is not only aware of the cries of his chosen but will see justice done to them and done speedily. We who matter so much to God 'need to pray continually and never lose heart'. Let us take heart in knowing that God has called us with the Gospel to share in the glory of our Lord Jesus Christ.

13
NOV SUN

THIRTY-THIRD SUNDAY IN ORDINARY TIME

Psalter Week 1

Green

Malachi 3:19-20

The day is coming now, burning like a furnace; and all the arrogant and the evil-doers will be like stubble. The day that is coming is going to burn them up, says the Lord of hosts, leaving them neither root nor stalk. But for you who fear my name, the sun of righteousness will shine out with healing in its rays.

Psalm 97:5-9. R. cf. v. 9

The Lord comes to rule the peoples with fairness.

2 Thessalonians 3:7-12

You know how you are supposed to imitate us: now we were not idle when we were with you, nor did we ever have our meals at anyone's table without paying for them; no, we worked night and day, slaving and straining, so as not to be a burden on any of you. This was not because we had no right to be, but in order to make ourselves an example for you to follow.

We gave you a rule when we were with you: not to let anyone have any food if he refused to do any work. Now we hear that there are some of you who are living in idleness, doing no work themselves but interfering with everyone else's. In the Lord Jesus Christ, we order and call on people of this kind to go on quietly working and earning the food that they eat.

Luke 21:5-19

When some were talking about the Temple, remarking how it was adorned with fine stonework and votive offerings, Jesus said, 'All these things you are staring at now – the time will come when not a single stone will be left on another: everything will be destroyed.' And they put to him this question: 'Master', they said 'when will this happen, then, and what sign will there be that this is about to take place?'

'Take care not to be deceived', he said 'because many will come using my name and saying, "I am he", and, "The time is near at hand." Refuse to join them. And when you hear of wars and revolutions, do not be frightened, for this is something that must happen but the end is not so soon.' Then he said to them, 'Nation will fight against nation, and kingdom against kingdom. There will be great earthquakes and plagues and famines here and there; there will be fearful sights and great signs from heaven. 'But before all this happens, men will seize you and persecute you; they will hand you over to the synagogues and to imprisonment, and bring you before kings and governors because of my name – and that will be your opportunity to bear witness. Keep this carefully in mind: you are not to prepare your defence, because I myself shall give you an eloquence and a wisdom that none of your opponents will be able to resist or contradict. You will be betrayed even by parents and brothers, relations and friends; and some of you will be put to death. You will be hated by all men on account of my name, but not a hair of your head will be lost. Your endurance will win you your lives.'

Reflection

What is the source of our hoping, our believing? It is the reality that 'the Lord comes' according to today's psalm. Whatever the situation we find ourselves in, the Lord comes into it with us. Jesus experienced betrayal, even by those close to him; he knew hatred. From his experience of human reality, which is also our reality, he asks us to trust in him when we experience betrayal or hatred of whatever kind. Today he calls us for he 'comes' and is always coming, to encourage us towards a new spirit of endurance, believing that with him we 'win' our lives.

The end is near, Jesus points out, reminding us of the temporary nature of our life on earth, and all the things that make up our lives. The Communion antiphon captures the essence of today's readings and liturgy: 'To be near God is my happiness, to place my hope in God the Lord.' Whatever you ask in prayer, believe that you will receive, and it shall be given to you', says the Lord, for I come, helping you to live joyfully and endure with me.

14 NOV MON

33rd Week in Ordinary Time
Green

Apocalypse 1:1-4; 2:1-5

This is the revelation given by God to Jesus Christ so that he could tell his servants about the things which are now to take place very soon; he sent his angel to make it known to his servant John, and John has written down everything he saw and swears it is the word of God guaranteed by Jesus Christ. Happy the man who reads this prophecy, and happy those who listen to him, if they treasure all that it says, because the Time is close. From John, to the seven churches of Asia: grace and peace to you from him who is, who was, and who is to come, from the seven spirits in his presence before his throne. I heard the Lord saying to me: 'Write to the angel of the church in Ephesus and say, "Here is the message of the one who holds the seven stars in his right hand and who lives surrounded by the seven golden lampstands: I know all about you: how hard you work and how much you put up with. I know you cannot stand wicked men, and how you tested the impostors who called themselves apostles and proved they were liars. I know, too, that you have patience, and have suffered for my name without growing tired. Nevertheless, I have this complaint to make; you have less love now than you used to. Think where you were before you fell; repent, and do as you used to at first."'

Psalm 1:1-4, 6. R. Apocalypse 2:7

Those who prove victorious I will feed from the tree of life.

Luke 18:35-43

As Jesus drew near to Jericho there was a blind man sitting at the side of the road begging. When he heard the crowd going past he asked what it was all about, and they told him that Jesus the Nazarene was passing by. So he called out, 'Jesus, Son of David, have pity on me.' The people in front scolded him and told him to keep quiet, but he shouted all the louder, 'Son of David, have pity on me.' Jesus stopped and ordered them to bring the man to him, and when he came up, asked him, 'What do you want me to do for you?' 'Sir,' he replied 'let me see again.' Jesus said to him, 'Receive your sight. Your faith has saved you.' And instantly his sight returned and he followed him praising God, and all the people who saw it gave praise to God for what had happened.

Reflection

The blind beggar hears the commotion, he asks what is happening. When he hears that Jesus of Nazareth is passing by he cries out to Jesus for help. Told to be quiet, he shouts all the louder, and Jesus wastes no time in asking him, 'What do you want me to do for you?' 'Sir, let me see again.' Instantly his sight returns and he follows Jesus, praising God. In fact, all who see what has happened praise God, for they 'see' the reality of God at work, so simply, unexpectedly, promptly. We are also invited to follow and praise God for what is happening in so many of our daily moments. May we, like the man, have the inner sight to confidently implore Jesus to take pity on us and give us the help we need. In faith, let us see him approaching us and asking, 'What do you want me to do for you?' What answer do you give him?

15 NOV TUE

33rd Week in Ordinary Time | Green
or **St Albert the Great,** *bishop, doctor* (Optional, White)

Apocalypse 3:1-6, 14-22

I, John, heard the Lord saying to me: 'Write to the angel of the church in Sardis and say, "Here is the message of the one who holds the seven spirits of God and the seven stars: I know all about you: how you are reputed to be alive and yet are dead. Wake up; revive what little you have left: it is dying fast. So far I have failed to notice anything in the way you live that my God could possibly call perfect, and yet do you remember how eager you were when you first heard the message? Hold on to that. Repent. If you do not wake up, I shall come to you like a thief, without telling you at what hour to expect me. There are a few in Sardis, it is true, who have kept their robes from being dirtied, and they are fit to come with me, dressed in white. ... *(Please see the Appendix B-27)*

Psalm 14:2-5. R. Apocalypse 3:21

Those who prove victorious I will allow to share my throne.

Luke 19:1-10

Jesus entered Jericho and was going through the town when a man whose name was Zacchaeus made his appearance; he was one of the senior tax collectors and a wealthy man. He was anxious to see what kind of man Jesus was, but he was too short and could not see him for the crowd; so he ran ahead and climbed a sycamore tree to catch a glimpse of Jesus who was to pass that way. When Jesus reached the spot he looked up and spoke to him: 'Zacchaeus, come down. Hurry, because I must stay at your house today.' And he hurried down and welcomed him joyfully. They all complained when they saw what was happening. 'He has gone to stay at a sinner's house' they said. But Zacchaeus stood his ground and said to the Lord, 'Look, sir, I am going to give half my property to the poor, and if I have cheated anybody I will pay him back four times the amount.' And Jesus said to him, 'Today salvation has come to this house, because this man too is a son of Abraham; for the Son of Man has come to seek out and save what was lost.'

Reflection

Zacchaeus is a wealthy man, but he knows that much is lacking in his life and he believes that Jesus will provide what he seeks. Responding with characteristic generous acceptance of the person, Jesus has no interest in Zacchaeus' reputation and tells him that he 'must stay' at his house 'today'. How eagerly Jesus responds to Zacchaeus, inviting himself to his house, seizing the moment to honour the seeking man. Jesus' readiness to be with Zacchaeus is a clear lesson for each of us to welcome and be with those who are lost in any way, to share what is of God, recognising that they too are children of Abraham and of the God we worship.

33rd Week in Ordinary Time | Green
or **St Gertude,** *virgin* (Optional, White)

16
NOV WED

ST MARGARET OF SCOTLAND, Feast
– Scotland

see Appendix A-25

Apocalypse 4:1-11

(Please see the Appendix B-28)

Psalm 150. R. Apocalypse 4:8

Holy, Holy, Holy is the Lord God, the Almighty.

Luke 19:11-28

While the people were listening, Jesus went on to tell a parable, because he was near Jerusalem and they imagined that the kingdom of God was going to show itself then and there. Accordingly he said, 'A man of noble birth went to a distant country to be appointed king and afterwards return. He summoned ten of his servants and gave them ten pounds. "Do business with these" he told them "until I get back." But his compatriots detested him and sent a delegation to follow him with this message, "We do not want this man to be our king." 'Now on his return, having received his appointment as king, he sent for those servants to whom he had given the money, to find out what profit each had made. The first came in and said, "Sir, your one pound has brought in ten." "Well done, my good servant!" he replied. "Since you have proved yourself faithful in a very small thing, you shall have the government of ten cities." Then came the second and said, "Sir, your one pound has made five." To this one also he said, "And you shall be in charge of five cities." Next came the other and said, "Sir, here is your pound. I put it away safely in a piece of linen because I was afraid of you; for you are an exacting man: you pick up what you have not put down and reap what you have not sown." "You wicked servant!" he said. "Out of your own mouth I condemn you. So you knew I was an exacting man, picking up what I have not put down and reaping what I have not sown? Then why did you not put my money in the bank? On my return I could have drawn it out with interest." And he said to those standing by, "Take the pound from him and give it to the man who has ten pounds." And they said to him, "But, sir, he has ten pounds . . ." "I tell you, to everyone who has will be given more; but from the man who has not, even what he has will be taken away. '"But as for my enemies who did not want me for their king, bring them here and execute them in my presence."' When he had said this he went on ahead, going up to Jerusalem.

Reflection

The third servant mentioned in today's Gospel parable, who failed to make good use of his gifts, is very different to the two servants who used their gifts fruitfully. The story reminds us of the words of Jesus in John's Gospel where he commissions his disciples to go out and bear fruit, fruit that will last (John 15:16). In the parable the master praises the servants who produced good results from the little they had and puts them in charge of cities. May we be productive servants today, from our littleness working for the fruit Jesus seeks, affirming others' efforts and supportive in various needs.

33rd Week in Ordinary Time
St Elizabeth of Hungary, *religious,* **Memorial** | White

17
NOV THU

Apocalypse 5:1-10

I, John, saw that in the right hand of the One sitting on the throne there was a scroll that had writing on back and front and was sealed with seven seals. Then I saw a powerful angel who called with a loud voice, 'Is there anyone worthy to open the scroll and break the seals of it?' But there was no one, in heaven or on the earth or under the earth, who was able to open the scroll and read it. I wept bitterly because there was nobody fit to open the scroll and read it, but one of the elders said to me, 'There is no need to cry: the Lion of the tribe of Judah, the Root of David, has triumphed, and he will open the scroll and the seven seals of it.' Then I saw, standing between the throne with its four animals and the circle of the elders, a Lamb that seemed to have been sacrificed; it had seven horns, and it had seven eyes, which are the seven Spirits God has sent out all over the world. The Lamb came forward to take the scroll from the right hand of the One sitting on the throne, and when he took it, the four animals prostrated themselves before him and with them the twenty-four elders; each one of them was holding a harp and had a golden bowl full of incense made of the prayers of the saints. They sang a new hymn: 'You are worthy to take the scroll and break the seals of it, because you were sacrificed, and with your blood you bought men for God of every race, language, people and nation and made them a line of kings and priests, to serve our God and to rule the world.'

Psalm 149:1-6, 9. R. Apocalypse 5:10

You made us a line of kings and priests to serve our God.

Luke 19:41-44

As Jesus drew near Jerusalem and came in sight of the city he shed tears over it and said, 'If you in your turn had only understood on this day the message of peace! But, alas, it is hidden from your eyes! Yes, a time is coming when your enemies will raise fortifications all round you, when they will encircle you and hem you in on every side; they will dash you and the children inside your walls to the ground; they will leave not one stone standing on another within you – and all because you did not recognise your opportunity when God offered it!'

Reflection

Today's psalm calls us to be ready for something new, to 'sing a new song'. These words can comfort us even if, at this time, we are shedding tears of disappointment over something that has happened. Jesus knew what it was like to shed tears and he can identify with what we are feeling. An open-hearted listening in prayer enables us to recognise the opportunity of the moment, however difficult, for relating with others and, in quiet moments, growing more deeply aware of God presence in the nitty-gritty of life. In the gentleness of God's presence, we can rejoice in our heart, 'shout for joy and take our rest' as the psalm celebrates. Over and over, we are offered opportunities to live fully like Jesus. Today let us turn to him as dear friends.

18
NOV FRI

33rd Week in Ordinary Time | Green
or **Dedication of the Basilicas of Sts Peter and Paul, Apostles** (Optional, White)

Apocalypse 10:8-11

I, John, heard the voice I had heard from heaven speaking to me again. 'Go,' it said 'and take that open scroll out of the hand of the angel standing on sea and land.' I went to the angel and asked him to give me the small scroll, and he said, 'Take it and eat it; it will turn your stomach sour, but in your mouth it will taste as sweet as honey.' So I took it out of the angel's hand, and swallowed it; it was as sweet as honey in my mouth, but when I had eaten it my stomach turned sour. Then I was told, 'You are to prophesy again, this time about many different nations and countries and languages and emperors.'

Psalm 118:14, 24, 72, 103, 111, 131. R. v. 103

Your promise is sweet to my taste, O Lord.

Luke 19:45-48

Jesus went into the Temple and began driving out those who were selling. 'According to scripture,' he said 'my house will be a house of prayer. But you have turned it into a robbers' den.'

He taught in the Temple every day. The chief priests and the scribes, with the support of the leading citizens, tried to do away with him, but they did not see how they could carry this out because the people as a whole hung on his words.

Reflection

In today's Gospel we hear that the people 'as a whole' are listening closely to Jesus as he teaches in the temple, while the chief priests and scribes are on the lookout for 'a way to do away with him.' They see Jesus as a threat because many people are welcoming his words. Because of his support among the people, they don't know how they can do away with him. Jesus wants his house to be a house of prayer; his listeners, including each of us today, are his 'sheep' who listen to his voice and follow him. In the turmoil of life which threatens to turn the inner temple of our hearts into 'a robber's den', robbing us of true peace, the sweetness and sureness of God's promise, alive in us, is our nourishment and deep hope. We discover that God is the joy of our heart.

33rd Week in Ordinary Time
Green

19 NOV SAT

Apocalypse 11:4-12

I, John, heard a voice saying: 'These, my two witnesses, are the two olive trees and the two lamps that stand before the Lord of the world. Fire can come from their mouths and consume their enemies if anyone tries to harm them; and if anybody does try to harm them he will certainly be killed in this way. They are able to lock up the sky so that it does not rain as long as they are prophesying; they are able to turn water into blood and strike the whole world with any plague as often as they like. …*(Please see the Appendix B-28)*

Psalm 143:1-2, 9-10. R. v. 1

Blessed be the Lord, my rock.

Luke 20:27-40

Some Sadducees – those who say that there is no resurrection – approached Jesus and they put this question to him, 'Master, we have it from Moses in writing, that if a man's married brother dies childless, the man must marry the widow to raise up children for his brother. Well then, there were seven brothers. The first, having married a wife, died childless. The second and then the third married the widow. And the same with all seven, they died leaving no children. Finally the woman herself died. Now, at the resurrection, to which of them will she be wife since she had been married to all seven?'

Jesus replied, 'The children of this world take wives and husbands, but those who are judged worthy of a place in the other world and in the resurrection from the dead do not marry because they can no longer die, for they are the same as the angels, and being children of the resurrection they are sons of God. And Moses himself implies that the dead rise again, in the passage about the bush where he calls the Lord the God of Abraham, the God of Isaac and the God of Jacob. Now he is God, not of the dead, but of the living; for to him all men are in fact alive.'

Some scribes then spoke up. 'Well put, Master' they said – because they would not dare to ask him any more questions.

Reflection

A seemingly petty question is put to Jesus about which husband the woman will have 'at the resurrection'. Jesus speaks of children of the resurrection as children of God, calling on Moses' words about Abraham, Isaac and Jacob to show that God 'is God of the living.' In our resurrected life we will relate differently to our present ways. Resurrection will transform us, freeing us to love as God loves, including all people. The goodness and wholeness we now experience in relating are a foretaste of the love awaiting us in God, which we sense at times, even now. For 'Our Saviour Jesus Christ has brought us life through his gospel'. There will be a totally new song to sing to the God we know as our 'place of refuge', 'our stronghold, our saviour'.

20
NOV SUN

OUR LORD JESUS CHRIST, KING OF THE UNIVERSE, Solemnity
Psalter
Week 2
White

2 Samuel 5:1-3
All the tribes of Israel came to David at Hebron. 'Look' they said 'we are your own flesh and blood. In days past when Saul was our king, it was you who led Israel in all their exploits; and the Lord said to you, "You are the man who shall be shepherd of my people Israel, you shall be the leader of Israel."' So all the elders of Israel came to the king at Hebron, and King David made a pact with them at Hebron in the presence of the Lord, and they anointed David king of Israel.

Psalm 121:1-5. R. cf. v. 2
I rejoiced when I heard them say: 'Let us go to God's house.'

Colossians 1:12-20
We give thanks to the Father who has made it possible for you to join the saints and with them to inherit the light.

Because that is what he has done: he has taken us out of the power of darkness and created a place for us in the kingdom of the Son that he loves, and in him, we gain our freedom, the forgiveness of our sins.

He is the image of the unseen God
and the first-born of all creation,
for in him were created
all things in heaven and on earth:
everything visible and everything invisible,
Thrones, Dominations, Sovereignties, Powers –
all things were created through him and for him.
Before anything was created, he existed,
and he holds all things in unity.
Now the Church is his body,
he is its head.

As he is the Beginning,
he was first to be born from the dead,
so that he should be first in every way;
because God wanted all perfection
to be found in him
and all things to be reconciled through him and for him,
everything in heaven and everything on earth,
when he made peace
by his death on the cross.

Luke 23:35-43
The people stayed there before the cross watching Jesus. As for the leaders, they jeered at him. 'He saved others', they said 'let him save himself if he is the Christ of God, the Chosen One'. The soldiers mocked him too, and when they approached to offer him vinegar they said, 'If you are the king of the Jews, save yourself'. Above him there was an inscription: 'This is the King of the Jews.'

One of the criminals hanging there abused him. 'Are you not the Christ?' he said. 'Save yourself and us as well.' But the other spoke up and rebuked him. 'Have you no fear of God at all?' he said, 'You got the same sentence as he did, but in our case we deserved it: we are paying for what we did. But this man has done nothing wrong. Jesus,' he said 'remember me when you come into your kingdom.' 'Indeed, I promise you,' he replied 'today you will be with me in paradise.'

Reflection

Today's readings speak about God restoring all things, all people, in Jesus, the King of the universe. And so we come rejoicing to the house of the Lord, whether physically or in spirit, aware of the mystery of God our Creator who goes on creating his kingdom, right where we are. What does Jesus say to the thief beside him, who asks to be remembered when Jesus comes into his 'kingdom'? '... today you will be with me in paradise.' This is Jesus, our King – his throne a wooden cross, present today wherever there are criminals and outcasts. The attitude he teaches us to have towards our sisters and brothers, whatever their situation, is to include them and be with them in their struggles, as he is with us in our struggles. We are called to share with each one the gifts of unity and peace, that Jesus, our King for ever, has bestowed on us. With the repentant thief, may we take heart in Jesus' assurance that we will be with him for ever.

21
NOV MON

34th Week in Ordinary Time | The Presentation of the Blessed Virgin Mary, Memorial | White

Apocalypse 14:1-5

In my vision I, John, saw Mount Zion, and standing on it a Lamb who had with him a hundred and forty-four thousand people, all with his name and his Father's name written on their foreheads. I heard a sound coming out of the sky like the sound of the ocean or the roar of thunder; it seemed to be the sound of harpists playing their harps. There in front of the throne they were singing a new hymn in the presence of the four animals and the elders, a hymn that could only be learnt by the hundred and forty-four thousand who had been redeemed from the world; they follow the Lamb wherever he goes; they have been redeemed from amongst men to be the first-fruits for God and for the Lamb. They never allowed a lie to pass their lips and no fault can be found in them.

Psalm 23:1-6. R. cf. v. 6

Such are the men who seek your face, O Lord.

Luke 21:1-4

As Jesus looked up he saw rich people putting their offerings into the Treasury; then he happened to notice a poverty-stricken widow putting in two small coins and he said, 'I tell you truly, this poor widow has put in more than any of them; for they have all contributed money they had over, but she from the little she had has put in all she had to live on.'

Reflection

While Jesus is praising the widow for her generosity, he is also criticising a religious system that pressured a poor widow into giving all she had rather than helping her in her need. We may think that situation is remote from us if we confine ourselves to thinking of monetary giving. But there are other ways in which we are called to give. Often in families or communities, the burden of caring for people with difficulties or disability falls on a few or one. It is important that we don't miss they signs that they are giving everything and expect them to give more. Rather we need to learn to be like Jesus, seeing the real situation of people, recognising where some are being called to give more than they can, and offering our help or even just doing our fair share.

22 NOV TUE

34th Week in Ordinary Time
St Cecilia, *virgin, martyr,* **Memorial** | Red

Apocalypse 14:14-19

In my vision I, John, saw a white cloud and, sitting on it, one like a son of man with a gold crown on his head and a sharp sickle in his hand. Then another angel came out of the sanctuary, and shouted aloud to the one sitting on the cloud, 'Put your sickle in and reap: harvest time has come and the harvest of the earth is ripe.' Then the one sitting on the cloud set his sickle to work on the earth, and the earth's harvest was reaped. Another angel, who also carried a sharp sickle, came out of the temple in heaven, and the angel in charge of the fire left the altar and shouted aloud to the one with sharp sickle, 'Put your sickle in and cut all the bunches off the vine of the earth; all its grapes are ripe'. So the angel set his sickle to work on the earth and harvested the whole vintage of the earth and put it into a huge winepress, the winepress of God's anger.

Psalm 95:10-13. R. v. 13

The Lord comes to rule the earth.

Luke 21:5-11

When some were talking about the Temple, remarking how it was adorned with fine stonework and votive offerings, Jesus said, 'All these things you are staring at now – the time will come when not a single stone will be left on another: everything will be destroyed.' And they put to him this question: 'Master,' they said 'when will this happen, then, and what sign will there be that this is about to take place?' 'Take care not to be deceived,' he said 'because many will come using my name and saying, "I am he" and, "The time is near at hand." Refuse to join them. And when you hear of wars and revolutions, do not be frightened, for this is something that must happen but the end is not so soon.' Then he said to them, 'Nation will fight against nation, and kingdom against kingdom. There will be great earthquakes and plagues and famines here and there; there will be fearful sights and great signs from heaven.'

Reflection

Jesus is helping us to realise that the material goods we admire have their day and then are no more. Jesus wants us to be alert, living as we are in an environment in which it is easy to be 'deceived'. Despite this sense of gloom, the psalm calls on 'the land and all it bears' to 'rejoice at the presence of the Lord for he comes'. How can we be this 'land' rejoicing in the Lord's presence? St Cecilia, whom we celebrate today, gives an insight into the answer. She is 'a wise bridesmaid whom the Lord found waiting at his coming; she went with him to the wedding feast'. St Cecilia sang in her heart during her martyrdom. Our 'martyrdom' may not be as intense as Cecilia's; like her, though, we can sing in our hearts as we notice the wonders Jesus works in us and even proclaim these wonders, right where we are.

23
NOV WED

34th Week in Ordinary Time
or **St Clement I,** *pope, martyr* (Optional, Red)
or **St Columban,** *abbot* (Optional, White)

Apocalypse 15:1-4

What I, John, saw in heaven was a great and wonderful sign: seven angels were bringing the seven plagues that are the last of all, because they exhaust the anger of God. I seemed to see a glass lake suffused with fire, and standing by the lake of glass, those who had fought against the beast and won, and against his statue and the number which is his name. They all had harps from God, and they were singing the hymn of Moses, the servant of God, and of the Lamb: 'How great and wonderful are all your works, Lord God Almighty; just and true are all your ways, King of nations. Who would not revere and praise your name, O Lord? You alone are holy, and all the pagans will come and adore you for the many acts of justice you have shown.'

Psalm 97:1-3, 7-9. R. Apocalypse 15:3

How great and wonderful are all your works, Lord God almighty.

Luke 21:12-19

Jesus said to his disciples: 'Men will seize you and persecute you; they will hand you over to the synagogues and to imprisonment, and bring you before kings and governors because of my name – and that will be your opportunity to bear witness. Keep this carefully in mind: you are not to prepare your defence, because I myself shall give you an eloquence and a wisdom that none of your opponents will be able to resist or contradict. You will be betrayed even by parents and brothers, relations and friends; and some of you will be put to death. You will be hated by all men on account of my name, but not a hair of your head will be lost. Your endurance will win you your lives.'

Reflection

'Endurance' is not a popular word. Jesus uses it today, encouraging us to remember that 'not a hair of our head will be lost'. With this healthy Christian attitude, we can celebrate today's psalm because God has 'brought salvation', 'has shown God's justice to the nations', 'remembered God's truth and love for the house of Israel'. He has done all this for us, the new 'house of Israel' in Jesus our saviour and brother. Today as we call on the rivers to 'clap their hands', and the hills 'to sing out their joy at the presence of the Lord', let us ask God to make our faith and love stronger, so that, right here, we do our best to 'be faithful until death', looking forward to receiving 'the crown of life', confident that 'not a hair of our head will be lost'. We will be given what we need.

34th Week in Ordinary Time | St Andrew Dung-Lac, priest and Companions, *martyrs,* **Memorial** | Red

24
NOV THU

Apocalypse 18:1-2, 21-23; 19:1-3, 9

I, John, saw an angel come down from heaven, with great authority given to him; the earth was lit up with his glory. At the top of his voice he shouted, 'Babylon has fallen, Babylon the Great has fallen, and has become the haunt of devils and a lodging for every foul spirit and dirty, loathsome bird.' Then a powerful angel picked up a boulder like a great millstone, and as he hurled it into the sea, he said, 'That is how the great city of Babylon is going to be hurled down, never to be seen again. 'Never again in you, Babylon, will be heard the song of harpists and minstrels, the music of flute and trumpet; never again will craftsmen of every skill be found or the sound of the mill be heard; never again will shine the light of the lamp, never again will be heard the voices of bridegroom and bride. Your traders were the princes of the earth, all the nations were under your spell.' ... *(Please see the Appendix B-28)*

Psalm 99:2-5. R. Apocalypse 19:9

Happy are those who are invited to the wedding-feast of the Lamb.

Luke 21:20-28

Jesus said to his disciples: 'When you see Jerusalem surrounded by armies, you must realise that she will soon be laid desolate. Then those in Judaea must escape to the mountains, those inside the city must leave it, and those in country districts must not take refuge in it. For this is the time of vengeance when all that scripture says must be fulfilled. Alas for those with child, or with babies at the breast, when those days come! 'For great misery will descend on the land and wrath on this people. They will fall by the edge of the sword and be led captive to every pagan country; and Jerusalem will be trampled down by the pagans until the age of the pagans is completely over.

'There will be signs in the sun and moon and stars; on earth nations in agony, bewildered by the clamour of the ocean and its waves; men dying of fear as they await what menaces the world, for the powers of heaven will be shaken. And then they will see the Son of Man coming in a cloud with power and great glory. When these things begin to take place, stand erect, hold your heads high, because your liberation is near at hand.'

Reflection

Our response to today's psalm reminds us that we are being called to the 'wedding feast of the Lamb'. How mind-blowing a gift: our happiness is in being 'invited to the wedding feast of the Lamb'. Beforehand we will experience agony and bewilderment because of 'what menaces the world', Jesus tells us in the Gospel. But the time will come when people see the Son of Man coming in glory. We do not know when this will happen but, believing that it will happen, enables us live now in joy as we wait in faith and trust. This enables us to 'stand erect', holding our 'heads high', because our 'liberation is near at hand' in the person of Jesus.

25
NOV FRI

Apocalypse 20:1-4, 11–21:2

I, John, saw an angel come down from heaven with the key of the Abyss in his hand and an enormous chain. He overpowered the dragon, the primeval serpent which is the devil and Satan, and chained him up for a thousand years. He threw him into the Abyss, and shut the entrance and sealed it over him, to make sure he would not deceive the nations again until the thousand years had passed. At the end of that time he must be released, but only for a short while.

Then I saw thrones, and I saw those who are given the power to be judges take their seats on them. I saw the souls of all who had been beheaded for having witnessed for Jesus and for having preached God's word, and those who refused to worship the beast or his statue and would not have the brand-mark on their foreheads or hands; they came to life, and reigned with Christ for a thousand years.

Then I saw a great white throne and the One who was sitting on it. In his presence, earth and sky vanished, leaving no trace. I saw the dead, both great and small, standing in front of his throne, while the book of life was opened, and other books opened which were the record of what they had done in their lives, by which the dead were judged. ...
(Please see the Appendix B-29)

Psalm 83:3-6, 8. R. Apocalypse 21:3

Here God lives among men.

Luke 21:29-33

Jesus told his disciples a parable, 'Think of the fig tree and indeed every tree. As soon as you see them bud, you know that summer is now near. So with you when you see these things happening: know that the kingdom of God is near. I tell you solemnly, before this generation has passed away all will have taken place. Heaven and earth will pass away, but my words will never pass away.'

Reflection

Jesus tells his listeners, and us, that summer and figs go together. Similarly, there are signs to help us to 'know that the kingdom of God is near'. Jesus promises us that his words 'will never pass away'. The first reading speaks of 'the new Jerusalem'; the psalm says that this reality is where God lives among his people. How amazingly reassuring to know that we dwell in God's house, that our strength is in God. Whatever the difficulty or hardship, let us 'walk with ever-growing strength' for our 'redemption is near at hand'; just as summer and figs go together, each one of us belong in this reality: 'my heart and my soul ring out their joy to God, the living God'.

34th Week in Ordinary Time
Green

26
NOV SAT

Apocalypse 22:1-7

The angel showed me, John, the river of life, rising from the throne of God and of the Lamb and flowing crystal-clear down the middle of the city street. On either side of the river were the trees of life, which bear twelve crops of fruit in a year, one in each month, and the leaves of which are the cure for the pagans.

The ban will be lifted. The throne of God and of the Lamb will be in its place in the city; his servants will worship him, they will see him face to face, and his name will be written on their foreheads. It will never be night again and they will not need lamplight or sunlight, because the Lord God will be shining on them. They will reign for ever and ever.

The angel said to me, 'All that you have written is sure and will come true: the Lord God who gives the spirit to the prophets has sent his angel to reveal to his servants what is soon to take place. Very soon now, I shall be with you again.' Happy are those who treasure the prophetic message of this book.

Psalm 94:1-7. R. 1 Corinthians 16:22; Apocalypse 22:20

Marana tha! Come, Lord Jesus!

Luke 21:34-36

Jesus said to his disciples: 'Watch yourselves, or your hearts will be coarsened with debauchery and drunkenness and the cares of life, and that day will be sprung on you suddenly, like a trap. For it will come down on every living man on the face of the earth. Stay awake, praying at all times for the strength to survive all that is going to happen, and to stand with confidence before the Son of Man.'

Reflection

To pray constantly takes some getting used to as we learn to live in the now, in the present moment, aware of God's gracious presence wherever we are. We are urged, today, to be watchful; it is easy to focus only on 'the cares of life' of which Jesus speaks, whereas we need to pray, whatever our 'cares', for the strength to survive all that is going to happen, and 'to stand with confidence before the Son of Man'. Like a tender parent and dearest friend, Jesus advises and encourages us. The psalm speaks of coming before the God who made us, for he is our God and we are the people who belong to his pasture, the flock that is led by his hand. We belong in God as his very dear flock, each one precious, led by his own hand! Today! Now!

27
NOV SUN

FIRST SUNDAY OF ADVENT (YEAR A)

Psalter Week 1

Violet

Isaiah 2:1-5

The vision of Isaiah son of Amoz, concerning Judah and Jerusalem.

In the days to come
the mountain of the Temple of the Lord
shall tower above the mountains
and be lifted higher than the hills.
All the nations will stream to it,
peoples without number will come to it;
and they will say:

'Come, let us go up to the mountain of the Lord,
to the Temple of the God of Jacob
that he may teach us his ways
so that we may walk in his paths;
since the Law will go out from Zion,
and the oracle of the Lord from Jerusalem.'

He will wield authority over the nations
and adjudicate between many peoples;
these will hammer their swords into ploughshares,
their spears into sickles.
Nation will not lift sword against nation,
there will be no more training for war.
O House of Jacob, come,
let us walk in the light of the Lord.

Psalm 121:1-2, 4-5, 6-9. R. cf. v. 1

I rejoiced when I heard them say: 'Let us go to God's house.'

Romans 13:11-14

You know 'the time' has come: you must wake up now: our salvation is even nearer than it was when we were converted. The night is almost over, it will be daylight soon – let us give up all the things we prefer to do under cover of the dark; let us arm ourselves and appear in the light. Let us live decently as people do in the daytime: no drunken orgies, no promiscuity or licentiousness, and no wrangling or jealousy. Let your armour be the Lord Jesus Christ.

Matthew 24:37-44

Jesus said to his disciples: 'As it was in Noah's day, so will it be when the Son of Man comes. For in those days before the Flood people were eating, drinking, taking wives, taking husbands, right up to the day Noah went into the ark, and they suspected nothing till the Flood came and swept all away. It will be like this when the Son of Man comes. Then of two men in the fields one is taken, one left; of two women at the millstone grinding, one is taken, one left.

'So stay awake, because you do not know the day when your master is coming. You may be quite sure of this that if the householder had known at what time of night the burglar would come, he would have stayed awake and would not have allowed anyone to break through the wall of his house. Therefore, you too must stand ready because the Son of Man is coming at an hour you do not expect.'

Reflection

Jesus is speaking about the ordinary things of our lives like eating and drinking, and in faith we know that in the ordinary moments of our day God is with us. To help us 'stay awake', and pay attention to what is going on, today's Gospel acclamation expresses trustfully this prayer: 'Lord, show us your mercy and love, and grant us your salvation'. We gradually learn how much we need God's mercy, love and salvation; praying this prayer gives us light and direction in our daily living. The psalm tells us of the peace which is enduring, calling on us, the 'house of the Lord', living in God's kingdom, our home. We continue to pray: 'Thy kingdom come'. Taking up Isaiah's Advent cue, 'O house of Jacob, come, let us walk in the light of the Lord', we relate with God and one another in the ordinariness, the sacredness, of each day, enlightened and loved.

28
NOV MON

Isaiah 4:2-6

That day, the branch of the Lord shall be beauty and glory, and the fruit of the earth shall be the pride and adornment of Israel's survivors. Those who are left of Zion and remain of Jerusalem shall be called holy and those left in Jerusalem, noted down for survival. When the Lord has washed away the filth of the daughter of Zion and cleansed Jerusalem of the blood shed in her with the blast of judgement and the blast of destruction the Lord will come and rest on the whole stretch of Mount Zion and on those who are gathered there, a cloud by day, and smoke, and by night the brightness of a flaring fire. For, over all, the glory of the Lord will be a canopy and a tent to give shade by day from the heat, refuge and shelter from the storm and the rain.

Psalm 121:1-2, 4-5, 6-9. R. cf. v. 1

I rejoiced when I heard them say: 'Let us go to God's house.'

Matthew 8:5-11

When Jesus went into Capernaum a centurion came up and pleaded with him. 'Sir,' he said 'my servant is lying at home paralysed, and in great pain.' 'I will come myself and cure him' said Jesus. The centurion replied, 'Sir, I am not worthy to have you under my roof; just give the word and my servant will be cured. For I am under authority myself, and have soldiers under me; and I say to one man: Go, and he goes; to another: Come here, and he comes; to my servant: Do this, and he does it.' When Jesus heard this he was astonished and said to those following him, 'I tell you solemnly, nowhere in Israel have I found faith like this. And I tell you that many will come from east and west to take their places with Abraham and Isaac and Jacob at the feast in the kingdom of heaven.'

Reflection

We are called today to confidently grow in our faith in the reality of God saving us. We can learn from the centurion who astonished Jesus: 'nowhere in Israel' has Jesus 'found such faith'. As we prepare to celebrate God's unfailing presence in Jesus' birth, we hear Jesus' words that 'many will come'. They will join us 'at the feast in the kingdom of heaven' to which Advent points. Jesus responds to the centurion's faith, rejoicing that one of God's children, a foreigner, represents the many who will come 'from east and west to take their places with Abraham and Isaac and Jacob at the feast in the kingdom'. Jesus, descended from these patriarchs, born into God's world, into our hearts, as into the centurion's faith-filled heart, so that, together, we journey as one family 'rejoicing to the house of the Lord'.

1st Week of Advent
Violet

29
NOV TUE

Isaiah 11:1-10

A shoot springs from the stock of Jesse, a scion thrusts from his roots: on him the spirit of the Lord rests, a spirit of wisdom and insight, a spirit of counsel and power, a spirit of knowledge and of the fear of the Lord. (The fear of the Lord is his breath.) He does not judge by appearances, he gives no verdict on hearsay, but judges the wretched with integrity, and with equity gives a verdict for the poor of the land. His word is a rod that strikes the ruthless, his sentences bring death to the wicked. Integrity is the loincloth round his waist, faithfulness the belt about his hips.

The wolf lives with the lamb, the panther lies down with the kid, calf and lion cub feed together with a little boy to lead them. The cow and the bear make friends, their young lie down together. The lion eats straw like the ox. The infant plays over the cobra's hole; into the viper's lair the young child puts his hand. They do not hurt, no harm, on all my holy mountain, for the country is filled with the knowledge of the Lord as the waters swell the sea. That day, the root of Jesse shall stand as a signal to the peoples. It will be sought out by the nations and its home will be glorious.

Psalm 71:1-2, 7-8, 12-13, 17. R. cf. v. 7

In his days justice shall flourish, and peace till the moon fails.

Luke 10:21-24

Filled with joy by the Holy Spirit, Jesus said, 'I bless you, Father, Lord of heaven and of earth, for hiding these things from the learned and the clever and revealing them to mere children. Yes, Father, for that is what it pleased you to do. Everything has been entrusted to me by my Father; and no one knows who the Son is except the Father, and who the Father is except the Son and those to whom the Son chooses to reveal him.'

Then turning to his disciples he spoke to them in private, 'Happy the eyes that see what you see, for I tell you that many prophets and kings wanted to see what you see, and never saw it; to hear what you hear, and never heard it.'

Reflection

Isaiah's poetic words encourage us to look forward to the flourishing of God's justice, for God 'does not judge by appearances'. Instead God 'gives a verdict for the poor of the land' in the person of Jesus to whom 'everything has been entrusted' by his Father. Jesus chooses to reveal to us his Father; with the Spirit's gift of wisdom we can 'judge the things of earth and hold firm to the things of heaven'. In Advent hope we eagerly await God's Word and believe that God will 'enlighten the eyes of his servants'. The simplicity of children prepares us to receive 'these things' of which Jesus speaks and makes available to us with the grace of wisdom. Like Jesus, may we be 'filled with joy by the Holy Spirit', joining 'with all nations' to 'bless God's name'.

30
NOV WED

St Andrew, *apostle*
Feast | Red

ST ANDREW, Solemnity
– Scotland

see Appendix A-27

Romans 10:9 18

If your lips confess that Jesus is Lord and if you believe in your heart that God raised him from the dead, then you will be saved. By believing from the heart you are made righteous; by confessing with your lips you are saved. When scripture says: those who believe in him will have no cause for shame, it makes no distinction between Jew and Greek: all belong to the same Lord who is rich enough however many ask his help, for everyone who calls on the name of the Lord will be saved.

But they will not ask his help unless they believe in him, and they will not believe in him unless they have heard of him, and they will not hear of him unless they get a preacher, and they will never have a preacher unless one is sent, but as scripture says: The footsteps of those who bring good news are a welcome sound. Not everyone, of course, listens to the Good News. As Isaiah says: Lord, how many believed what we proclaimed? So faith comes from what is preached, and what is preached comes from the word of Christ. Let me put the question: is it possible that they did not hear? Indeed they did; in the words of the psalm, their voice has gone out through all the earth, and their message to the ends of the world.

Psalm 18:2-5. R. v. 5

Their word goes forth through all the earth.

Matthew 4:18-22

As Jesus was walking by the Sea of Galilee he saw two brothers, Simon, who was called Peter, and his brother Andrew; they were making a cast in the lake with their net, for they were fishermen. And he said to them, 'Follow me and I will make you fishers of men.' And they left their nets at once and followed him. Going on from there he saw another pair of brothers, James son of Zebedee and his brother John; they were in their boat with their father Zebedee, mending their nets, and he called them. At once, leaving the boat and their father, they followed him.

Reflection

'Follow me' says Jesus to Andrew, Peter, James and John. Following 'at once' they gradually become 'fishers' of people, on mission with Jesus. Their readiness has a beauty of openness as well as a sense of mystery. Like ourselves in our personal call, they have no idea of what is ahead. St Paul speaking of 'believing from the heart' tells us what kind of faith the apostles, like ourselves, are called into: an outreaching faith because 'all belong to the same Lord who is rich enough however many ask his help'. Seeking God's help follows belief in God, which firstly requires hearing of God. Andrew's preaching ensured countless people heard of God and we believe today through the apostles' living witness as Jesus' followers. Jesus' call to 'follow me' continues to have an urgency requiring our open response.

01
DEC THU

1st Week of Advent
Violet

Isaiah 26:1-6

That day, this song will be sung in the land of Judah: We have a strong city; to guard us he has set wall and rampart about us. Open the gates! Let the upright nation come in, she, the faithful one whose mind is steadfast, who keeps the peace, because she trusts in you. Trust in the Lord for ever, for the Lord is the everlasting Rock; he has brought low those who lived high up in the steep citadel; he brings it down, brings it down to the ground, flings it down in the dust: the feet of the lowly, the footsteps of the poor trample on it.

Psalm 117:1, 8-9, 19-21, 25-27. R. v. 26

Blessed in the name of the Lord is he who comes.

Matthew 7:21, 24-27

Jesus said to his disciples: 'It is not those who say to me, "Lord, Lord", who will enter the kingdom of heaven, but the person who does the will of my Father in heaven.

'Therefore, everyone who listens to these words of mine and acts on them will be like a sensible man who built his house on rock. Rain came down, floods rose, gales blew and hurled themselves against that house, and it did not fall: it was founded on rock. But everyone who listens to these words of mine and does not act on them will be like a stupid man who built his house on sand. Rain came down, floods rose, gales blew and struck that house, and it fell; and what a fall it had!'

Reflection

For the first two weeks of Advent, all the first readings are taken from the prophet Isaiah. One beautiful Advent exercise is to read them all. They will take you into a sense of what 'Trust in the Lord' means. Today's reading is the second of two parts of Isaiah's vision. In the first part (Isaiah 25:6-10) he saw God's people returning in procession into a re-built Jerusalem. God has prepared a feast for all peoples, destroyed death forever, opened the city to the poor and needy and wiped away every tear from every eye. Today sees the exiles sing as they enter the gates of the city. They can at last say, God is our 'everlasting rock'. In the meantime, Jesus tells us of our entry, not into Jerusalem, but into the kingdom of heaven. We need to listen to his Word. There we will learn God's will and put our faith into action.

02
DEC FRI

1st Week of Advent
Violet

Isaiah 29:17-24

The Lord says this: In a short time, a very short time, shall not Lebanon become fertile land and fertile land turn into forest? The deaf, that day, will hear the words of a book and, after shadow and darkness, the eyes of the blind will see. But the lowly will rejoice in the Lord even more and the poorest exult in the Holy One of Israel; for tyrants shall be no more, and scoffers vanish, and all be destroyed who are disposed to do evil: those who gossip to incriminate others, those who try at the gate to trip the arbitrator and get the upright man's case dismissed for groundless reasons. Therefore the Lord speaks, the God of the House of Jacob, Abraham's redeemer: No longer shall Jacob be ashamed, no more shall his face grow pale, for he shall see what my hands have done in his midst, he shall hold my name holy. They will hallow the Holy One of Jacob, stand in awe of the God of Israel. Erring spirits will learn wisdom and murmurers accept instruction.

Psalm 26:1, 4, 13-14. R. v. 1

The Lord is my light and my help.

Matthew 9:27-31

As Jesus went on his way two blind men followed him shouting, 'Take pity on us, Son of David.' And when Jesus reached the house the blind men came up with him and he said to them, 'Do you believe I can do this?' They said, 'Sir, we do.' Then he touched their eyes saying, 'Your faith deserves it, so let this be done for you.' And their sight returned. Then Jesus sternly warned them, 'Take care that no one learns about this.' But when they had gone, they talked about him all over the countryside.

Reflection

Isaiah's 'the eyes of the blind shall see' invite us to look at the link between faith and sight. Who first spoke about faith to you? Whose word started you off? Identify yourself with the two blind men as you ponder the Gospel. They first hear about this Jesus. Someone has told them that he is the Son of David – shorthand for the promised Messiah. They respond with faith in that word and call out to him. The second word they hear is Jesus' own voice: do they believe he can heal? Remember, they cannot see. Now, they respond to his word with faith. Then Jesus touches their eyes. Imagine what it means to be blind and to experience this touch from this person whom they know only by faith. Accompanying the touch is Jesus' spoken word, affirming their faith and bringing healing and recognition of Jesus. They are truly Advent people!

1st Week of Advent
St Francis Xavier, *priest,* **Memorial** | White

03
DEC SAT

Isaiah 30:19-21, 23-26

Thus says the Lord God, the Holy One of Israel: People of Zion, you will live in Jerusalem and weep no more. He will be gracious to you when he hears your cry; when he hears he will answer. When the Lord has given you the bread of suffering and the water of distress, he who is your teacher will hide no longer, and you will see your teacher with your own eyes. Whether you turn to right or left, your ears will hear these words behind you, 'This is the way, follow it.' He will send rain for the seed you sow in the ground, and the bread that the ground provides will be rich and nourishing. Your cattle will graze, that day, in wide pastures. Oxen and donkeys that till the ground will eat a salted fodder, winnowed with shovel and fork. On every lofty mountain, on every high hill there will be streams and watercourses, on the day of the great slaughter when the strongholds fall. Then moonlight will be bright as sunlight and sunlight itself be seven times brighter – like the light of seven days in one – on the day the Lord dresses the wound of his people and heals the bruises his blows have left.

Psalm 146:1-6. R. Isaiah 30:18

Happy are all who hope in the Lord.

Matthew 9:35–10:1, 6-8

Jesus made a tour through all the towns and villages, teaching in their synagogues, proclaiming the Good News of the kingdom and curing all kinds of diseases and sickness. And when he saw the crowds he felt sorry for them because they were harassed and dejected, like sheep without a shepherd. Then he said to his disciples, 'The harvest is rich but the labourers are few, so ask the Lord of the harvest to send labourers to his harvest.' He summoned his twelve disciples, and gave them authority over unclean spirits with power to cast them out and to cure all kinds of diseases and sickness. These twelve Jesus sent out, instructing them as follows: 'Go rather to the lost sheep of the House of Israel. And as you go, proclaim that the kingdom of heaven is close at hand. Cure the sick, raise the dead, cleanse the lepers, cast out devils. You received without charge, give without charge.'

Reflection

Our prayer today might well be wonder of Jesus. We see an 'outer' description of his ministry: Jesus proclaims the good news of God's very different kingdom, and he heals many as he visits towns and villages in Galilee. But we also see a wonderful description of Jesus' inner life: compassion. At the very depths of his being, he is the Compassionate One who sees the lost-ness of his people and reaches out in compassion and love! He calls his twelve disciples and sends them out to continue his mission. They can only do so if they in their turn discover God's loving compassion within themselves. Only then can they hand on a healing and passion for God's kingdom. In what ways do mission and compassion describe your life? In your prayer today, why not invite Jesus to join his compassion to yours?

04
DEC SUN

SECOND SUNDAY OF ADVENT

Psalter Week 2

Violet

Isaiah 11:1-10

A shoot springs from the stock of Jesse, a scion thrusts from his roots: on him the spirit of the Lord rests, a spirit of wisdom and insight, a spirit of counsel and power, a spirit of knowledge and of the fear of the Lord. (The fear of the Lord is his breath.) He does not judge by appearances, he gives no verdict on hearsay, but judges the wretched with integrity, and with equity gives a verdict for the poor of the land. His word is a rod that strikes the ruthless; his sentences bring death to the wicked. Integrity is the loincloth round his waist, faithfulness the belt about his hips. The wolf lives with the lamb, the panther lies down with the kid, calf and lion cub feed together with a little boy to lead them. The cow and the bear make friends, their young lie down together. The lion eats straw like the ox. The infant plays over the cobra's hole; into the viper's lair the young child puts his hand. They do no hurt, no harm, on all my holy mountain, for the country is filled with the knowledge of the Lord as the waters swell the sea. That day, the root of Jesse shall stand as signal to the peoples. It will be sought out by the nations and its home will be glorious.

Psalm 71:1-2, 7-8, 12-13, 17. R. cf. v. 7

In his days justice shall flourish, and peace till the moon fails.

Romans 15:4-9

Everything that was written long ago in the scriptures was meant to teach us something about hope from the examples scripture gives of how people who did not give up were helped by God. And may he who helps us when we refuse to give up, help you all to be tolerant with each other, following the example of Christ Jesus, so that united in mind and voice you may give glory to the God and Father of our Lord Jesus Christ.

It can only be to God's glory, then, for you to treat each other in the same friendly way as Christ treated you. The reason Christ became the servant of circumcised Jews was not only so that God could faithfully carry out the promises made to the patriarchs, it was also to get the pagans to give glory to God for his mercy, as scripture says in one place: For this I shall praise you among the pagans and sing your name.

Matthew 3:1-12

In due course John the Baptist appeared; he preached in the wilderness of Judaea and this was his message: 'Repent, for the kingdom of heaven is close at hand.' This was the man the prophet Isaiah spoke of when he said:

> A voice cries in the wilderness:
> Prepare a way for the Lord,
> make his paths straight.

This man John wore a garment made of camel-hair with a leather belt round his waist, and his food was locusts and wild honey. Then Jerusalem and all Judaea and the whole Jordan district made their way to him, and as they were baptised by him in the river Jordan they confessed their sins. But when he saw a number of Pharisees and Sadducees coming for baptism he said to them, 'Brood of vipers, who warned you to fly from the retribution that is coming? But if you are repentant, produce the appropriate fruit, and do not presume to tell yourselves, "We have Abraham for our father," because, I tell you, God can raise children for Abraham from these stones. Even now the axe is laid to the roots of the trees, so that any tree which fails to produce good fruit will be cut down and thrown on the fire. I baptise you in water for repentance, but the one who follows me is more powerful than I am, and I am not fit to carry his sandals; he will baptise you with the Holy Spirit and fire. His winnowing-fan is in his hand; he will clear his threshing-floor and gather his wheat into the barn; but the chaff he will burn in a fire that will never go out.'

Reflection

What is the significance of Jesus? What did he come for? In Advent we try to understand Jesus through the lens of the Gospel accounts of John the Baptist. His relationship with Jesus slowly helps us clarify who this Messiah Jesus is. The second reading takes us immediately to the heart of the Gospel: He came for the salvation of all. We await the fulfilment of this salvation: it is part of our life-long Advent. Two prophets help us on our journey. Isaiah foresees the Messiah as a king on whom the Spirit of God rests. In him, God's reign comes and creation is itself made new. John is another Elijah, crying in the wilderness and baptising in the Jordan river. There the people come and wash, in order to reclaim their identity with their ancestors, and their readiness to welcome the Messiah, Jesus, who will baptise with the Holy Spirit and with fire. In your prayer, attend to this double awaiting: the coming of your Saviour, and signs of God's universal reign emerging even now in your daily life.

05
DEC MON

2nd Week of Advent
Violet

Isaiah 35:1-10

Let the wilderness and the dry-lands exult, let the wasteland rejoice and bloom, let it bring forth flowers like the jonquil, let it rejoice and sing for joy. The glory of Lebanon is bestowed on it, the splendour of Carmel and Sharon; they shall see the glory of the Lord, the splendour of our God. ...
(Please see the Appendix B-29)

Psalm 84:9-14. R. Isaiah 35:4

Look, our God is coming to save us.

Luke 5:17-26

Jesus was teaching one day, and among the audience there were Pharisees and doctors of the Law who had come from every village in Galilee, from Judaea and from Jerusalem. And the Power of the Lord was behind his works of healing. Then some men appeared, carrying on a bed a paralysed man whom they were trying to bring in and lay down in front of him. But as the crowd made it impossible to find a way of getting him in, they went up on to the flat roof and lowered him and his stretcher down through the tiles into the middle of the gathering, in front of Jesus. Seeing their faith he said, 'My friend, your sins are forgiven you.' The scribes and the Pharisees began to think this over. 'Who is this man talking blasphemy? Who can forgive sins but God alone?' But Jesus, aware of their thoughts, made them this reply, 'What are these thoughts you have in your hearts? Which of these is easier: to say, "Your sins are forgiven you" or to say, "Get up and walk"? But to prove to you that the Son of Man has authority on earth to forgive sins,' – he said to the paralysed man – 'I order you: get up, and pick up your stretcher and go home.' And immediately before their very eyes he got up, picked up what he had been lying on and went home praising God.

They were all astounded and praised God, and were filled with awe, saying, 'We have seen strange things today.'

Reflection

Isaiah invites us to enter into a wonderful vision of the return of the people from exile in Babylon to Mount Zion in Jerusalem. On the way, there is salvation both for humans and for all the earth's ecosystems. In your prayer, just be with the travellers on their journey, and make connections with your own life's journey on this earth. The four men who bring a paralysed man to Jesus are the patron saints of all the wonderful people who work with people with disabilities. They clearly have a disinterested love and care for this man; they are creative and persistent; they will not be put off by crowds or difficulties. Jesus honours them: 'Seeing their faith, Jesus said to the man ...' It seems this man has physical disabilities, and a deep guilt. As he walks away whole: healing, forgiveness and praise of God walk hand in hand with him.

06 DEC TUE

2nd Week of Advent | Violet
or **St Nicholas,** *bishop* (Optional, White)

Isaiah 40:1-11

'Console my people, console them' says your God. 'Speak to the heart of Jerusalem and call to her that her time of service is ended, that her sin is atoned for, that she has received from the hand of the Lord double punishment for all her crimes.' A voice cries, 'Prepare in the wilderness a way for the Lord. Make a straight highway for our God across the desert. Let every valley be filled in, every mountain and hill be laid low, let every cliff become a plain, and the ridges a valley; then the glory of the Lord shall be revealed and all mankind shall see it; for the mouth of the Lord has spoken.' A voice commands: 'Cry!' and I answered, 'What shall I cry?' – 'All flesh is grass and its beauty like the wild flower's. The grass withers, the flower fades when the breath of the Lord blows on them. (The grass is without doubt the people.) The grass withers, the flower fades, but the word of our God remains for ever.' Go up on a high mountain, joyful messenger to Zion. Shout with a loud voice, joyful messenger to Jerusalem. Shout without fear, say to the towns of Judah, 'Here is your God.' Here is the Lord coming with power, his arms subduing all things to him. The prize of his victory is with him, his trophies all go before him. He is like a shepherd feeding his flock, gathering lambs in his arms, holding them against his breast and leading to their rest the mother ewes.

Psalm 95:1-3, 10-13. R. cf. Isaiah 40:9-10

Here is our God coming with power.

Matthew 18:12-14

Jesus said to his disciples: 'Tell me. Suppose a man has a hundred sheep and one of them strays; will he not leave the ninety-nine on the hillside and go in search of the stray? I tell you solemnly, if he finds it, it gives him more joy than do the ninety-nine that did not stray at all. Similarly, it is never the will of your Father in heaven that one of these little ones should be lost.'

Reflection

God tells Isaiah to 'speak tenderly' to Jerusalem. Isaiah's vision today sees the ultimate in landscape engineering, where mountains, valleys, cliffs are all re-made! – a Way for our God in the wilderness, a way that leads some thousands of kilometres from slavery to Jerusalem, city of peace. God goes with them on the journey. Isaiah pictures God both as a triumphant king, and as a shepherd who feeds and holds the flock with tender, loving care. You may like to pray with Jesus' parable of searching and finding. The shepherd has a huge flock of sheep – all valuable! But he still focuses on searching out the lost one. His care is measured by his joy in finding it. For Matthew, 'little ones' is a code word for the least members of his community. He links this parable with the pastoral care of the community, especially those who are lost.

07
DEC WED

2nd Week of Advent
St Ambrose, *bishop, doctor,* **Memorial** | White

Isaiah 40:25-31

'To whom could you liken me and who could be my equal?' says the Holy One. Lift your eyes and look. Who made these stars if not he who drills them like an army, calling each one by name? So mighty is his power, so great his strength, that not one fails to answer.

How can you say, Jacob, how can you insist, Israel, 'My destiny is hidden from the Lord, my rights are ignored by my God'? Did you not know? Had you not heard?

The Lord is an everlasting God, he created the boundaries of the earth. He does not grow tired or weary, his understanding is beyond fathoming. He gives strength to the wearied, he strengthens the powerless. Young men may grow tired and weary, youths may stumble, but those who hope in the Lord renew their strength, they put out wings like eagles. They run and do not grow weary, walk and never tire.

Psalm 102:1-4, 8, 10. R. v. 1

My soul, give thanks to the Lord.

Matthew 11:28-30

Jesus exclaimed, 'Come to me, all you who labour and are overburdened, and I will give you rest. Shoulder my yoke and learn from me, for I am gentle and humble in heart, and you will find rest for your souls. Yes, my yoke is easy and my burden light.'

Reflection

'Come to me ...' This invitation of the Compassionate Christ has echoed down the ages until it comes to us today. Come with your truth, your burdens, without pretensions, without demands. Come just as you truly are. That may be enough for your prayer today. But you may like to reflect further. Jesus does not promise a magical healing of present suffering but opens up a journey into a future with him. It is with him, on this journey, that he promises that 'I will give you rest.' Compare the journey of the exiles in Isaiah today: they travel, walking, running with eagles' wings, and the Lord renews their strength. For those who lose hope and see no way through their present situation, this is a gentle invitation to begin to move forward with him and claim hope again.

08

DEC THU

THE IMMACULATE CONCEPTION OF THE BLESSED VIRGIN MARY

Solemnity

White

Genesis 3:9-15, 20

(Please see the Appendix B-29)

Psalm 97:1-4. R. v. 1

Sing a new song to the Lord for he has worked wonders.

Ephesians 1:3-6, 11-12

Blessed be God the Father of our Lord Jesus Christ, who has blessed us with all the spiritual blessings of heaven in Christ. Before the world was made, he chose us, chose us in Christ, to be holy and spotless, and to live through love in his presence, determining that we should become his adopted sons, through Jesus Christ for his own kind purposes, to make us praise the glory of his grace, his free gift to us in the Beloved. And it is in him that we were claimed as God's own, chosen from the beginning, under the predetermined plan of the one who guides all things as he decides by his own will; chosen to be, for his greater glory, the people who would put their hopes in Christ before he came.

Luke 1:26-38

The angel Gabriel was sent by God to a town in Galilee called Nazareth, to a virgin betrothed to a man named Joseph, of the House of David; and the virgin's name was Mary. He went in and said to her, 'Rejoice, so highly favoured! The Lord is with you.' She was deeply disturbed by these words and asked herself what this greeting could mean, but the angel said to her, 'Mary, do not be afraid; you have won God's favour. Listen! You are to conceive and bear a son, and you must name him Jesus. He will be great and will be called Son of the Most High. The Lord God will give him the throne of his ancestor David; he will rule over the House of Jacob for ever and his reign will have no end.' Mary said to the angel, 'But how can this come about, since I am a virgin?' 'The Holy Spirit will come upon you,' the angel answered, 'and the power of the Most High will cover you with its shadow. And so the child will be holy and will be called Son of God. Know this too: your kinswoman Elizabeth has, in her old age, herself conceived a son, and she whom people called barren is now in her sixth month, for nothing is impossible to God.' I am the handmaid of the Lord,' said Mary, 'let what you have said be done to me.' And the angel left her.

Reflection

This feast is not recounted in the Bible. The Bible does tell us the story of the Annunciation, that Jesus is virginally conceived. This feast honours the dogma that Mary was immaculately conceived, and thus did not share, from the first moment of her existence, in the sin of Adam and Eve. The deeper reason is that, as Jesus' mother, she needed to hand on to her Son a perfect, sinless humanity. This was her special gift, given her 'in advance', as it were, by her Son. Hence our feast. Let us step back from this heady theology, and simply pray with two beautiful thoughts. The first from the second reading: like Mary, God chose us in Christ. Blessed are we! The second: Mary's 'Yes' to the angel in the Annunciation story of today's Gospel, invites us to spend some time with Mary, and, like her, say 'yes' to God in the challenges of our life.

09
DEC FRI

2nd Week of Advent | Violet
or **St Juan Diego Cuauhtlatoatzin** (Optional, White)

Isaiah 48:17-19

Thus says the Lord, your redeemer, the Holy One of Israel: I, the Lord, your God, teach you what is good for you, I lead you in the way that you must go. If only you had been alert to my commandments, your happiness would have been like a river, your integrity like the waves of the sea. Your children would have been numbered like the sand, your descendants as many as its grains. Never would your name have been cut off or blotted out before me.

Psalm 1:1-4, 6. R. cf. John 8:12

Anyone who follows you, Lord, will have the light of life.

Matthew 11:16-19

Jesus spoke to the crowds: 'What description can I find for this generation? It is like children shouting to each other as they sit in the market place: "We played the pipes for you, and you wouldn't dance; we sang dirges, and you wouldn't be mourners."

'For John came, neither eating nor drinking, and they say, "He is possessed." The Son of Man came, eating and drinking, and they say, "Look, a glutton and a drunkard, a friend of tax collectors and sinners." Yet wisdom has been proved right by her actions.'

Reflection

How have you handled disappointment in your life? Spend some time with Isaiah on this issue, or with Jesus in the Gospel. He is described in truly insulting language: 'a glutton and a drunkard, a friend of tax collectors and sinners.' We compare John the Baptist and his austere ministry in the desert, and Jesus, with his ministry in the towns. Jesus enters a town with his message of the nearness of the reign of God, with healing, forgiveness, exorcisms, prayer, and inclusion. In particular, he reaches out to those rejected because they cannot keep the whole law (sinners) and those who are truly hated. At the end of the day, all sit down together with Jesus at a meal unlike any other. Imagine the joy for that town! Then Jesus moves on, leaving that village to reflect on what they have experienced: God among them, truly compassionate to all. Thank God the accusation is not without foundation – Jesus is the friend of tax collectors and sinners!

10 DEC SAT

2nd Week of Advent | Violet
or **Our Lady of Loreto** (Optional, White)

Sirach 48:1-4, 9-11

The prophet Elijah arose like a fire, his word flaring like a torch. It was he who brought famine on them, and who decimated them in his zeal. By the word of the Lord, he shut up the heavens, he also, three times, brought down fire. How glorious you were in your miracles, Elijah! Has anyone reason to boast as you have? – taken up in the whirlwind of fire, in a chariot with fiery horses; designated in the prophecies of doom to allay God's wrath before the fury breaks, to turn the hearts of fathers towards their children, and to restore the tribes of Jacob. Happy shall they be who see you, and those who have fallen asleep in love.

Psalm 79:2-3, 15-16, 18-19. R. v. 4

God of hosts, bring us back; let your face shine on us and we shall be saved.

Matthew 17:10-13

As they came down from the mountain the disciples put this question to Jesus, 'Why do the scribes say that Elijah has to come first?' 'True', he replied; 'Elijah is to come to see that everything is once more as it should be; however, I tell you that Elijah has come already and they did not recognise him but treated him as they pleased; and the Son of Man will suffer similarly at their hands.' The disciples understood then that he had been speaking of John the Baptist.

Reflection

We continue to compare Jesus, John the Baptist and the prophet Elijah. The first reading summarises many stories of Elijah's life, 'a prophet like fire, and his word burned like a torch.' In particular, we hear the story of the end of Elijah's earthly life: 'a chariot of fire and horses of fire separated the two of them (Elijah and his disciple Elisha), and Elijah ascended in a whirlwind into heaven' (2 Kings 2:11). These wonderful stories form the background to the tradition that he is the greatest prophet, that he did not die, that he was expected to return before the Messiah comes (today's reading and Malachi 4:5). And if Elijah has already come, then the awaited Messiah is near! There is a good Advent 'waiting' note for our prayer today.

11
DEC SUN

THIRD SUNDAY OF ADVENT

Psalter Week 3

Violet (or Rose)

Isaiah 35:1-6, 10

Let the wilderness and the dry-lands exult,
let the wasteland rejoice and bloom,
let it bring forth flowers like the jonquil,
let it rejoice and sing for joy.

The glory of Lebanon is bestowed on it,
the splendour of Carmel and Sharon;
they shall see the glory of the Lord,
the splendour of our God.

Strengthen all weary hands,
steady all trembling knees
and say to all faint hearts,
'Courage! Do not be afraid.

'Look your God is coming,
vengeance is coming,
the retribution of God;
he is coming to save you.'

Then the eyes of the blind shall be opened,
the ears of the deaf unsealed,
then the lame shall leap like a deer
and the tongues of the dumb sing for joy,
for those the Lord has ransomed shall return.

They will come to Zion shouting for joy,
everlasting joy in their faces;
joy and gladness will go with them
and sorrow and lament be ended.

Psalm 145:6-10. R. cf. Isaiah 35:4

Come, Lord, and save us.

James 5:7-10

Be patient, brothers, until the Lord's coming. Think of a farmer: how patiently he waits for the precious fruit of the ground until it has had the autumn rains and the spring rains! You too have to be patient; do not lose heart, because the Lord's coming will be soon. Do not make complaints against one another, brothers, so as not to be brought to judgement yourselves; the Judge is already to be seen waiting at the gates. For your example, brothers, in submitting with patience, take the prophets who spoke in the name of the Lord.

Matthew 11:2-11

John in his prison had heard what Christ was doing and he sent his disciples to ask him, 'Are you the one who is to come, or have we got to wait for someone else?' Jesus answered, 'Go back and tell John what you hear and see; the blind see again, and the lame walk, lepers are cleansed, and the deaf hear, and the dead are raised to life and the Good News is proclaimed to the poor; and happy is the man who does not lose faith in me.'

As the messengers were leaving, Jesus began to talk to the people about John: 'What did you go out into the wilderness to see? A reed swaying in the breeze? No? Then what did you go out to see? A man wearing fine clothes? Oh no, those who wear fine clothes are to be found in palaces. Then what did you go out for? To see a prophet? Yes, I tell you, and much more than a prophet: he is the one of whom scripture says: Look, I am going to send my messenger before you; he will prepare your way before you. I tell you solemnly, of all the children born of women, a greater than John the Baptist has never been seen; yet the least in the kingdom of heaven is greater than he is.'

Reflection

Isaiah's wonderful vision sings of the journey home to his enslaved people in Babylon. The sacred highway is lined with nature made new and luxuriant: nature itself sings for joy! And as they travel, people are given sight, hearing, speech – healing – and sing for joy! The image of growth underlies the second reading, as the farmer patiently awaits his crop. Be patient! And John himself continues to await the Messiah. He sends messengers to ask Jesus, but Jesus points them to the Kingdom and its fruits, and asks them to make the identification for themselves. Jesus' praise of John is extraordinary: even more extraordinary is his praise of the least in the kingdom of heaven. What does this say about your relationship with Jesus this Advent? A great question to take to your prayer!

12
DEC MON

3rd Week of Advent | Violet
or **Our Lady of Guadalupe** (Optional, White)

Numbers 24:2-7, 15-17

Raising his eyes Balaam saw Israel, encamped by tribes; the spirit of God came on him and he declaimed his poem. He said: 'The oracle of Balaam son of Beor, the oracle of the man with far-seeing eyes, the oracle of one who hears the word of God. He sees what Shaddai makes him see, receives the divine answer, and his eyes are opened. How fair are your tents, O Jacob! How fair your dwellings, Israel! Like valleys that stretch afar, like gardens by the banks of a river, like aloes planted by the Lord, like cedars beside the waters! A hero arises from their stock, he reigns over countless peoples. His king is greater than Agag, his majesty is exalted.' Then Balaam declaimed his poem again. He said: 'The oracle of Balaam son of Beor, the oracle of the man with far-seeing eyes, the oracle of the one who hears the word of God, of one who knows the knowledge of the Most High. He sees what Shaddai makes him see, receives the divine answer, and his eyes are opened. I see him – but not in the present, I behold him – but not close at hand: a star from Jacob takes the leadership, a sceptre arises from Israel.'

Psalm 24:4-9. R. v. 4

Lord, make me know your ways.

Matthew 21:23-27

Jesus had gone into the Temple and was teaching, when the chief priests and the elders of the people came to him and said, 'What authority have you for acting like this? And who gave you this authority?' 'And I' replied Jesus 'will ask you a question, only one; if you tell me the answer to it, I will then tell you my authority for acting like this. John's baptism: where did it come from: heaven or man?' And they argued it out this way among themselves, 'If we say from heaven, he will retort, "Then why did you refuse to believe him?"; but if we say from man, we have the people to fear, for they all hold that John was a prophet.' So their reply to Jesus was, 'We do not know.' And he retorted, 'Nor will I tell you my authority for acting like this.'

Reflection

On Friday we had the memorial of St Juan Diego. Today we bring him and the Mother of Jesus together, and reflect on the feast of Our Lady of Guadalupe, patroness of Mexico, of the Americas and of the Philippines. Mary's appearance to this poor indigenous man in Tepeyac, the image she left on his cloak, and her statement to this poor man, ('am I, your mother, not here?'), have set in train a world-wide devotion. We take the opportunity to focus our Advent prayer on the poverty of the Americas – their peoples' Advent prayers would surely include prayers for food, fresh water, education for their children, a fair share in the wealth of their countries and an end to political and criminal corruption. Let us bring them into our Advent praying of Mary's prayer, The Magnificat, in St Luke's Gospel (1:46-55).

3rd Week of Advent
St Lucy, *virgin, martyr,* **Memorial** | Red

13
DEC TUE

Zephaniah 3:1-2, 9-13

Trouble is coming to the rebellious, the defiled, the tyrannical city! She would never listen to the call, would never learn the lesson; she has never trusted in the Lord, never drawn near to her God. Yes, I will then give the peoples lips that are clean, so that all may invoke the name of the Lord and serve him under the same yoke. From beyond the banks of the rivers of Ethiopia my suppliants will bring me offerings. When that day comes you need feel no shame for all the misdeeds you have committed against me, for I will remove your proud boasters from your midst; and you will cease to strut on my holy mountain. In your midst I will leave a humble and lowly people, and those who are left in Israel will seek refuge in the name of the Lord. They will do no wrong, will tell no lies; and the perjured tongue will no longer be found in their mouths. But they will be able to graze and rest with no one to disturb them.

Psalm 33:2-3, 6-7, 16, 18-19, 23. R. v. 7

This poor man called; the Lord heard him.

Matthew 21:28-32

Jesus said to the chief priests and the elders of the people, 'What is your opinion? A man had two sons. He went and said to the first, "My boy, you go and work in the vineyard today." He answered, "I will not go," but afterwards thought better of it and went. The man then went and said the same thing to the second who answered, "Certainly, sir," but did not go. Which of the two did the father's will? 'The first' they said. Jesus said to them, 'I tell you solemnly, tax collectors and prostitutes are making their way into the kingdom of God before you. For John came to you, a pattern of true righteousness, but you did not believe him, and yet the tax collectors and prostitutes did. Even after seeing that, you refused to think better of it and believe in him.'

Reflection

Zephaniah proclaims the importance of hope as one waits. He first chastises his people for their infidelity – they never trusted in the Lord, never drew near – and then he proclaims God's promise: after the devastation of Jerusalem, 'I will leave in your midst a people humble and lowly. They shall seek refuge in the name of the Lord,' and constitute a faithful 'remnant of Israel'. Similarly, Jesus offers a devastating critique of Israel's religious leaders. His question: which son did the will of his father, implies that they were not doing God's will. Instead, he lifts up the hated tax collectors and the prostitutes who have listened to his words as examples of true kingdom virtue. Do we do God's will? Let us pray for similar conversion for our whole church and for ourselves.

14
DEC WED

3rd Week of Advent
St John of the Cross, *priest, doctor,* **Memorial** | White

Isaiah 45:6-8, 18, 21-26

Apart from me, all is nothing. I am the Lord, unrivalled, I form the light and create the dark. I make good fortune and create calamity, it is I, the Lord, who do all this. Send victory like a dew, you heavens, and let the clouds rain it down. Let the earth open for salvation to spring up. Let deliverance, too, bud forth which I, the Lord, shall create. Yes, thus says the Lord, creator of the heavens, who is God, who formed the earth and made it, who set it firm, created it no chaos, but a place to be lived in: 'I am the Lord, unrivalled. There is no other god besides me, a God of integrity and a saviour; there is none apart from me. Turn to me and be saved, all the ends of the earth, for I am God unrivalled. By my own self I swear it; what comes from my mouth is truth, a word irrevocable; before me every knee shall bend, by me every tongue shall swear, saying, "From the Lord alone come victory and strength." To him shall come, ashamed, all who raged against him. Victorious and glorious through the Lord shall be all the descendants of Israel.'

Psalm 84:9-14. R. cf. Isaiah 45:8

Send victory like a dew, you heavens, and let the clouds rain it down.

Luke 7:19-23

John, summoning two of his disciples, sent them to the Lord to ask, 'Are you the one who is to come, or must we wait for someone else?' When the men reached Jesus they said, 'John the Baptist has sent us to you, to ask, "Are you the one who is to come or have we to wait for someone else?"' It was just then that he cured many people of diseases and afflictions and of evil spirits, and gave the gift of sight to many who were blind. Then he gave the messengers their answer, 'Go back and tell John what you have seen and heard: the blind see again, the lame walk, lepers are cleansed, and the deaf hear, the dead are raised to life, the Good News is proclaimed to the poor and happy is the man who does not lose faith in me.'

Reflection

Many mothers whose children have disappeared in war or in a foreign country, never give up their belief, and continue to wait in hope for the day their child will return. Last Sunday we heard Matthew's version of John's sending his disciples to Jesus to ask if he is the expected Messiah. 'Are we to wait for another?' Steadfast faith and hope in difficult times are a challenge we all know. Yet in some sense they constitute who we really are. Today, Luke invites us to ponder on John, and ask that question: Who am I, that I believe and hope? Perhaps we can bring into our prayer those for whom faith and hope are just too much – those with mental difficulties, those who have 'given up', those who have chosen other philosophies of life. God does not lose faith or hope either in them or us.

15 DEC THU

3rd Week of Advent
Violet

Isaiah 54:1-10

Shout for joy, you barren women who bore no children! Break into cries of joy and gladness, you who were never in labour! For the sons of the foresaken one are more in number than the sons of the wedded wife, says the Lord. Widen the space of your tent, stretch out your hangings freely, lengthen your ropes, make your pegs firm; for you will burst out to right and to left. Your race will take possession of the nations, and people the abandoned cities. Do not be afraid, you will not be put to shame, do not be dismayed, you will not be disgraced; for you will forget the shame of your youth and no longer remember the curse of your widowhood. ... *(Please see the Appendix B-29)*

Psalm 29:2, 4-6, 11-13. R. v. 2

I will praise you, Lord, you have rescued me.

Luke 7:24-30

When John's messengers had gone Jesus began to talk to the people about John, 'What did you go out into the wilderness to see? A reed swaying in the breeze? No? Then what did you go out to see? A man dressed in fine clothes? Oh no, those who go in for fine clothes and live luxuriously are to be found at court! Then what did you go out to see? A prophet? Yes, I tell you, and much more than a prophet: he is the one of whom scripture says: See, I am going to send my messenger before you; he will prepare the way before you. I tell you, of all the children born of women, there is no greater than John; yet the least in the kingdom of God is greater than he is. All the people who heard him, and the tax collectors too, acknowledged God's plan by accepting baptism from John; but by refusing baptism from him the Pharisees and the lawyers had thwarted what God had in mind for them.'

Reflection

Isaiah precedes this magnificent song with another song – that of the Suffering Servant, who was despised, struck down, who bore the sins of his people. Because he has made such atonement, Israel is at peace with God. Thus Isaiah encourages his people to see their sufferings and slavery through the image of a once broken marriage covenant, restored because of God's faithful, compassionate love. 'For a moment I hid my face from you, but with everlasting love I will have compassion on you, says the LORD, your Redeemer.' Thanks to this Servant, hope is possible; salvation lies ahead. In the Gospel, let us ponder Jesus' words about John, then bring to our prayer the immense privilege of being a member of God's kingdom. There the least is the greatest.

16
DEC FRI

Isaiah 56:1-3, 6-8

Thus says the Lord: Have a care for justice, act with integrity, for soon my salvation will come and my integrity be manifest. Blessed is the man who does this and the son of man who clings to it: observing the sabbath, not profaning it, and keeping his hand from every evil deed. Let no foreigner who has attached himself to the Lord say, 'The Lord will surely exclude me from his people.' Foreigners who have attached themselves to the Lord to serve him and to love his name and be his servants – all who observe the sabbath, not profaning it, and cling to my covenant – these I will bring to my holy mountain. I will make them joyful in my house of prayer. Their holocausts and their sacrifices will be accepted on my altar, for my house will be called a house of prayer for all the peoples. It is the Lord God who speaks, who gathers the outcasts of Israel: there are others I will gather besides those already gathered.

Psalm 66:2-3, 5, 7-8. R. v. 4

Let the peoples praise you, O God, let all the peoples praise you.

John 5:33-36

Jesus said to the Jews: You sent messengers to John, and he gave his testimony to truth: not that I depend on human testimony; no, it is for your salvation that I speak of this. John was a lamp alight and shining and for a time you were content to enjoy the light that he gave. But my testimony is greater than John's: the works my Father has given me to carry out, these same works of mine testify that the Father has sent me.

Reflection

What do you witness to by your life? Witness is a key part of all human life. While John is a witness to the truth, a lamp alight and shining, Jesus is also a witness. He witnesses to the transcendent mystery of God, whom he calls 'my Father'. His whole life and 'works' witness both to the salvation he brings ('that you may be saved') and to his identity, that he is 'sent from the Father'. It is by responding to his witness that we enter into the mystery of God, the mystery of Christ and his resurrection, and into the salvation he brings. The key is that our deeds must be the first witness. Isaiah hints at universal salvation, which we believe Christ brings. Spend some time with the last verse of the first reading.

17
DEC SAT

3rd Week of Advent
Violet

Genesis 49:2, 8-10
(Please see the Appendix B-30)

Psalm 71:1-4, 7-8, 17. R. cf. v. 7
In his days justice shall flourish, and peace till the moon fails.

Matthew 1:1-17
A genealogy of Jesus Christ, son of David, son of Abraham: Abraham was the father of Isaac, Isaac the father of Jacob, Jacob the father of Judah and his brothers, Judah was the father of Perez and Zerah, Tamar being their mother, Perez was the father of Hezron, Hezron the father of Ram, Ram was the father of Amminadab, Amminadab the father of Nahshon, Nahshon the father of Salmon, Salmon was the father of Boaz, Rahab being his mother, Boaz was the father of Obed, Ruth being his mother, Obed was the father of Jesse; and Jesse was the father of King David. David was the father of Solomon, whose mother had been Uriah's wife, Solomon was the father of Rehoboam, Rehoboam the father of Abijah, Abijah the father of Asa, Asa was the father of Jehoshaphat, Jehoshaphat the father of Joram, Joram the father of Azariah, Azariah was the father of Jotham, Jotham the father of Ahaz, Ahaz the father of Hezekiah, Hezekiah was the father of Manasseh, Manasseh the father of Amon, Amon the father of Josiah; and Josiah was the father of Jechoniah and his brothers. Then the deportation to Babylon took place. After the deportation to Babylon: Jechoniah was the father of Shealtiel, Shealtiel the father of Zerubbabel, Zerubbabel was the father of Abiud, Abiud the father of Eliakim, Eliakim the father of Azor, Azor was the father of Zadok, Zadok the father of Achim, Achim the father of Eliud, Eliud was the father of Eleazar, Eleazar the father of Matthan, Matthan the father of Jacob; and Jacob was the father of Joseph the husband of Mary; of her was born Jesus who is called Christ. The sum of generations is therefore: fourteen from Abraham to David; fourteen from David to the Babylonian deportation; and fourteen from the Babylonian deportation to Christ.

Reflection
Who are you? Who are we? Our indigenous brothers and sisters have something to teach us as we seek to answer these questions. We have our identity in and through our relationships with God, with people, with our land. Like us, Jesus too has these three relationships. His genealogy is a partial one, beginning with Abraham (and Sarah), moving to David and his kingly line, through to Joseph, who marries Mary and provides Jesus with his kingly identity, thus fulfilling God's promise of a Messiah king. Note how few women are mentioned! The Land is the place of God's promise. He is born in Bethlehem, the kingly town of David, his home is Nazareth in Galilee. Note the many agricultural parables and images he uses to open up the mystery of God and God's dealing with us. And he prays … In these final Advent days, we too have lots to bring into our prayer!

18
DEC SUN

FOURTH SUNDAY OF ADVENT

Psalter Week 4

Violet

Isaiah 7:10-14

The Lord spoke to Ahaz and said, 'Ask the Lord your God for a sign for yourself coming either from the depths of Sheol or from the heights above.' 'No,' Ahaz answered 'I will not put the Lord to the test.' Then Isaiah said: 'Listen now, House of David: are you not satisfied with trying the patience of men without trying the patience of God, too? The Lord himself, therefore, will give you a sign. It is this: the maiden is with child and will soon give birth to a son whom she will call Emmanuel, a name which means "God-is-with-us".'

Psalm 23:1-6. R. cf. vv. 7. 10

Let the Lord enter! He is the king of glory.

Romans 1:1-7

From Paul, a servant of Christ Jesus who has been called to be an apostle, and specially chosen to preach the Good News that God promised long ago through his prophets in the scriptures. This news is about the Son of God, who, according to the human nature he took, was a descendant of David: it is about Jesus Christ our Lord who, in the order of the spirit, the spirit of holiness that was in him, was proclaimed Son of God in all his power through his resurrection from the dead. Through him we received grace and our apostolic mission to preach the obedience of faith to all pagan nations in honour of his name. You are one of these nations, and by his call belong to Jesus Christ. To you all, then, who are God's beloved in Rome, called to be saints, may God our Father and the Lord Jesus Christ send grace and peace.

Matthew 1:18-24

This is how Jesus Christ came to be born. His mother Mary was betrothed to Joseph; but before they came to live together she was found to be with child through the Holy Spirit. Her husband Joseph, being a man of honour and wanting to spare her publicity, decided to divorce her informally. He had made up his mind to do this when the angel of the Lord appeared to him in a dream, and said 'Joseph son of David, do not be afraid to take Mary home as your wife, because she has conceived what is in her by the Holy Spirit. She will give birth to a son and you must name him Jesus, because he is the one who is to save his people from their sins.' Now all this took place to fulfil the words spoken by the Lord through the prophet: The virgin will conceive and give birth to a son and they will call him Emmanuel, a name which means 'God-is-with-us'. When Joseph woke up he did what the angel of the Lord had told him to do: he took his wife to his home.

Reflection

Joseph is the main actor in our Gospel today. On learning that Mary is pregnant, he is faced with three choices. He can expose her 'infidelity' and have her put to death under the Law: this is one form of righteousness. Or he can send her back quietly to her people before the marriage contract is completed. This is another, more compassionate form of righteousness. The Gospel today says that he had decided to do this, when the angel appeared and announced the Gospel message to him: the child is of divine origin, and Joseph is to marry Mary, and name him 'Jesus' (God saves). Joseph, like Mary, says 'Yes' to the angel's Word and becomes husband to Mary and Father to her son. This third form of righteousness before God embodies a faith that transcends mere observance, a love and generosity that transcend justice, an acceptance of, and commitment to, a future which gives us our saviour. Truly a just ('righteous') man! Bring before God all those who have suffered trauma at the hands of church members, the church as a whole, single parents ... the list goes on. Mary had her Joseph. May they have her and your compassionate help.

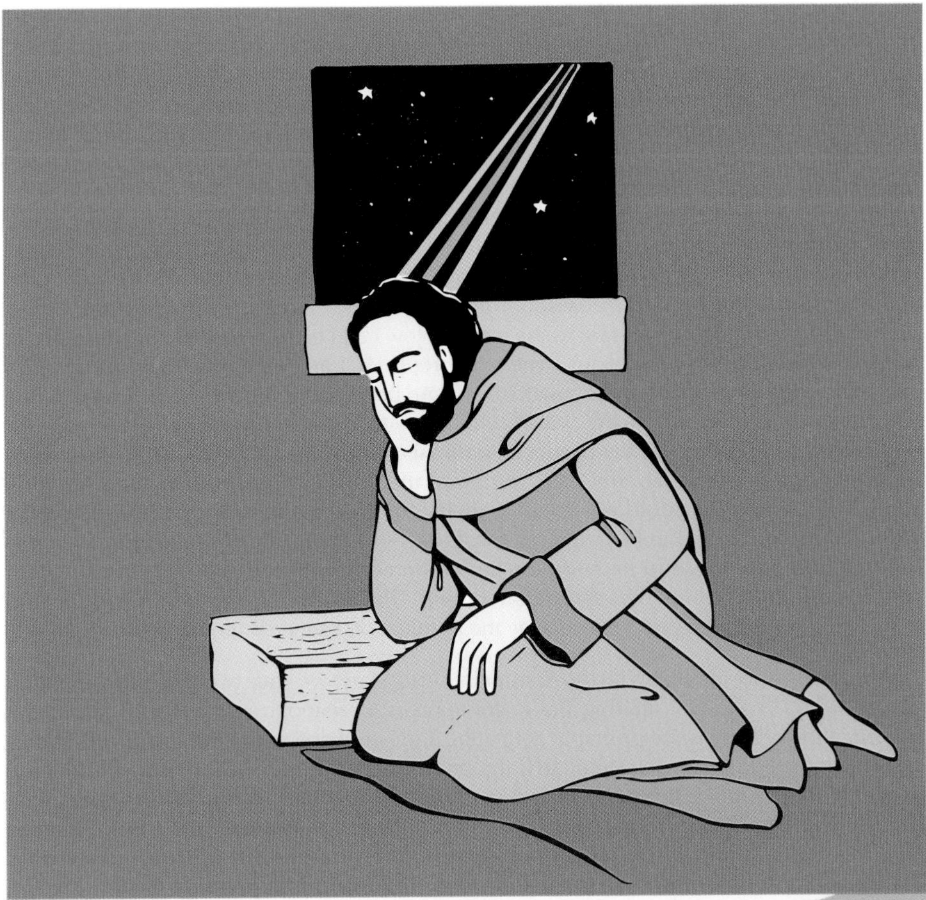

19
DEC MON

4th Week of Advent
Violet

Judges 13:2-7, 24-25
(Please see the Appendix B-30)

Psalm 70:3-6, 16-17. R. cf. v. 8
My lips are filled with your praise, with your glory all the day long.

Luke 1:5-25
In the days of King Herod of Judaea there lived a priest called Zechariah who belonged to the Abijah section of the priesthood, and he had a wife, Elizabeth by name, who was a descendant of Aaron. Both were worthy in the sight of God, and scrupulously observed all the commandments and observances of the Lord. But they were childless: Elizabeth was barren and they were both getting on in years. Now it was the turn of Zechariah's section to serve, and he was exercising his priestly office before God when it fell to him by lot, as the ritual custom was, to enter the Lord's sanctuary and burn incense there. And at the hour of incense the whole congregation was outside, praying. Then there appeared to him the angel of the Lord, standing on the right of the altar of incense. The sight disturbed Zechariah and he was overcome with fear. But the angel said to him, 'Zechariah, do not be afraid, your prayer has been heard. Your wife Elizabeth is to bear you a son and you must name him John. He will be your joy and delight and many will rejoice at his birth, for he will be great in the sight of the Lord; he must drink no wine, no strong drink. Even from his mother's womb he will be filled with the Holy Spirit, and he will bring back many of the sons of Israel to the Lord their God. With the spirit and power of Elijah, he will go before him to turn the hearts of fathers towards their children and the disobedient back to the wisdom that the virtuous have, preparing for the Lord a people fit for him.' Zechariah said to the angel, 'How can I be sure of this? I am an old man and my wife is getting on in years.' The angel replied, 'I am Gabriel who stand in God's presence, and I have been sent to speak to you and bring you this good news. Listen! Since you have not believed my words, which will come true at their appointed time, you will be silenced and have no power of speech until this has happened.' Meanwhile the people were waiting for Zechariah and were surprised that he stayed in the sanctuary so long. When he came out he could not speak to them, and they realised that he had received a vision in the sanctuary. But he could only make signs to them, and remained dumb. When his time of service came to an end he returned home. Some time later his wife Elizabeth conceived, and for five months she kept to herself. 'The Lord has done this for me' she said 'now that it has pleased him to take away the humiliation I suffered among men.'

Reflection: We are familiar with the Annunciation to Mary: we have two more annunciation stories today. In the first reading the angel appears to Manoah's wife. Sadly, she is not named, although she is the principal actor. She and her husband believe the angel's Word, and have their son, Samson. Similarly, the priest Zechariah receives a message from the angel of God. Unlike the woman and her husband Manoah, Zechariah responds with disbelief. Nonetheless, God blesses Elizabeth with her son. Between now and Christmas Eve, we will follow this wonderful woman. Zechariah finally will obey the angel's Word, name their son John, and close our Advent with praise of God.

4th Week of Advent
Violet

20
DEC TUE

Isaiah 7:10-14

The Lord spoke to Ahaz and said, 'Ask the Lord your God for a sign for yourself coming either from the depths of Sheol or from the heights above.' 'No,' Ahaz answered, 'I will not put the Lord to the test.' Then Isaiah said: 'Listen now, House of David: are you not satisfied with trying the patience of men without trying the patience of my God, too? The Lord himself, therefore, will give you a sign. It is this: the maiden is with child and will soon give birth to a son whom she will call Emmanuel, a name which means "God-is-with-us"'.

Psalm 23:1-6. R. cf. v. 7, 10

Let the Lord enter! He is the king of glory.

Luke 1:26-38

The angel Gabriel was sent by God to a town in Galilee called Nazareth, to a virgin betrothed to a man named Joseph, of the House of David; and the virgin's name was Mary. He went in and said to her, 'Rejoice, so highly favoured! The Lord is with you.' She was deeply disturbed by these words and asked herself what this greeting could mean, but the angel said to her, 'Mary, do not be afraid; you have won God's favour. Listen! You are to conceive and bear a son, and you must name him Jesus. He will be great and will be called Son of the Most High. The Lord God will give him the throne of his ancestor David; he will rule over the House of Jacob for ever and his reign will have no end.' Mary said to the angel, 'But how can this come about, since I am a virgin?' 'The Holy Spirit will come upon you,' the angel answered, 'and the power of the Most High will cover you with its shadow. And so the child will be holy and will be called Son of God. Know this too: your kinswoman Elizabeth has, in her old age, herself conceived a son, and she whom people called barren is now in her sixth month, for nothing is impossible to God.' 'I am the handmaid of the Lord,' said Mary, 'let what you have said be done to me.' And the angel left her.

Reflection

Today, let us stay with the Gospel, the Annunciation. Let two thoughts guide us. First, what a dangerous and terrifying invitation the angel Gabriel brings. This young woman Mary is to become pregnant while betrothed, not married. In her pregnancy, she will have to face Joseph, her family, – and most frightening of all, if this becomes known, she will face the penalty of the Law: death for adultery. She hears this frightening Word, and in complete faith and obedience, without reflecting on the consequences, says 'Yes'. The second thought comes from her hearing of the rest of the message. Her son is to be king in the line of David, he will have a kingdom which has no end. Her faith-filled 'Yes' is thus also expressed in commitment to her child, whom she, as his Mother, must raise to be king. What are your 'Yes-es'? Bring them to your prayer, in the light of Mary's faith and faith-filled commitment.

21
DEC WED

4th Week of Advent | Violet
or **St Peter Canisius,** *priest, doctor* (Commemoration)

Song 2:8-14

(Alternative Reading: Zephaniah 3:14-18)

I hear my Beloved. See how he comes leaping on the mountains, bounding over the hills. My Beloved is like a gazelle, like a young stag. See where he stands behind our wall. He looks in at the window, he peers through the lattice. My Beloved lifts up his voice, he says to me, 'Come then, my love, my lovely one, come. For see, winter is past, the rains are over and gone. The flowers appear on the earth. The season of glad songs has come, the cooing of the turtledove is heard in our land. The fig tree is forming its first figs and the blossoming vines give out their fragrance. Come then, my love, my lovely one, come. My dove, hiding in the clefts of the rock, in the coverts of the cliff, show me your face, let me hear your voice; for your voice is sweet and your face is beautiful.'

Psalm 32:2-3, 11-12, 20-21. R. vv. 1, 3

Ring out your joy to the Lord, O you just; O sing him a song that is new.

Luke 1:39-45

Mary set out and went as quickly as she could to a town in the hill country of Judah. She went into Zechariah's house and greeted Elizabeth. Now as soon as Elizabeth heard Mary's greeting, the child leapt in her womb and Elizabeth was filled with the Holy Spirit. She gave a loud cry and said, 'Of all women you are the most blessed, and blessed is the fruit of your womb. Why should I be honoured with a visit from the mother of my Lord? For the moment your greeting reached my ears, the child in my womb leapt for joy. Yes, blessed is she who believed that the promise made her by the Lord would be fulfilled.'

Reflection

In our prayer today, let us stay with this wonderful encounter between these two pregnant women. Mother meets mother. In their wombs, son meets Son. Elizabeth – and her child – without the benefit of the angel's message to Mary, recognise exactly who is coming to visit them. Elizabeth is the very first prophet of the New Testament, the first in Luke's Gospel to publicly welcome Mary's Son. Like Mary at the Annunciation, now Elizabeth is filled with the Holy Spirit. Inspired by the Spirit, she blesses Mary with wonderful words – blessed are you amongst women, and blessed is your child, the 'fruit' of your womb. The whole mystery of the Incarnation is captured here.

4th Week of Advent
Violet

22
DEC THU

1 Samuel 1:24-28

When Hannah had weaned Samuel, she took him up with her together with a three-year old bull, an ephah of flour and a skin of wine, and she brought him to the temple of the Lord at Shiloh; and the child was with them. They slaughtered the bull and the child's mother came to Eli. She said, 'If you please, my lord. As you live, my lord, I am the woman who stood here beside you, praying to the Lord. This is the child I prayed for, and the Lord granted me what I asked him. Now I make him over to the Lord for the whole of his life. He is made over to the Lord.' There she left him, for the Lord.

1 Samuel 2:1, 4-8. R. v. 1

My heart exults in the Lord my Saviour.

Luke 1:46-56

Mary said: 'My soul proclaims the greatness of the Lord and my spirit exults in God my saviour; because he has looked upon his lowly handmaid. Yes, from this day forward all generations will call me blessed, for the Almighty has done great things for me. Holy is his name, and his mercy reaches from age to age for those who fear him.

'He has shown the power of his arm, he has routed the proud of heart. He has pulled down princes from their thrones and exalted the lowly. The hungry he has filled with good things, the rich sent empty away. He has come to the help of Israel his servant, mindful of his mercy – according to the promise he made to our ancestors – of his mercy to Abraham and to his descendants for ever.'

Mary stayed with Elizabeth about three months and then went back home.

Reflection

I love Mary's prayer! It takes us to the real Mary. She captures the moment of her encounter with Elizabeth: she sings, proclaiming and exulting in God her saviour. Her delight and joy are obvious. She knows her scripture, bringing Miriam and Hannah, her forebears who also sang in faith, into her song. No false humility here, but the joy and hope in God of one who delights to be God's handmaid. She sings of God's holiness and endless mercy and looks forward to the future, as she proclaims in her prayer a reversal, where the powerless, the hungry and the suffering will finally know God's mercy, and rejoice, as she does, in the child of her womb. Her passion is to change the world. Join Mary in prayer as we approach our Christmas feast.

4th Week of Advent | Violet
or **St John of Kanty,** *priest* (Commemoration)

Malachi 3:1-4, 23-24

The Lord God says this: Look, I am going to send my messenger to prepare a way before me. And the Lord you are seeking will suddenly enter his Temple; and the angel of the covenant whom you are longing for, yes, he is coming, says the Lord of hosts. Who will be able to resist the day of his coming? Who will remain standing when he appears? For he is like the refiner's fire and the fullers' alkali. He will take his seat as refiner and purifier; he will purify the sons of Levi and refine them like gold and silver, and then they will make the offering to the Lord as it should be made. The offering of Judah and Jerusalem will be welcomed by the Lord as in former days, as in the years of old. Know that I am going to send you Elijah the prophet before my day comes, that great and terrible day. He shall turn the hearts of fathers towards their children and the hearts of the children towards their fathers, lest I come and strike the land with a curse.

Psalm 24:4-5, 8-9, 10, 14. R. Luke 21:28

Stand erect, hold your heads high, because your liberation is near at hand.

Luke 1:57-66

The time came for Elizabeth to have her child, and she gave birth to a son; and when her neighbours and relations heard that the Lord had shown her so great a kindness, they shared her joy. Now on the eighth day they came to circumcise the child; they were going to call him Zechariah after his father, but his mother spoke up. 'No,' she said 'he is to be called John.' They said to her, 'But no one in your family has that name,' and made signs to his father to find out what he wanted him called. The father asked for a writing-tablet and wrote, 'His name is John.' And they were all astonished. At that instant his power of speech returned and he spoke and praised God. All their neighbours were filled with awe and the whole affair was talked about throughout the hill country of Judaea. All those who heard of it treasured it in their hearts. 'What will this child turn out to be?' they wondered. And indeed the hand of the Lord was with him.

Reflection

Today we are invited to reflect as hearers who are called to obey the Word of God both as individuals and, for some, as a married couple. There are two roles Elizabeth plays: she is the first New Testament prophet to recognise Jesus; and in challenging circumstances she helps her husband, despite his disobedience, to name their son John as the angel said. They are then joined in their obedience. Mary and Joseph and Elizabeth and Zechariah are two married couples joined not only by their sons, but by their shared obedience to the Word of God as conveyed by an angel. Let us pray that in our unique personal and family situations, we may hear God's word and follow it.

4th Week of Advent
Violet

24
DEC SAT

2 Samuel 7:1-5, 8-12, 14, 16

Once David had settled into his house and the Lord had given him rest from all the enemies surrounding him, the king said to the prophet Nathan, 'Look, I am living in a house of cedar while the ark of God dwells in a tent.' Nathan said to the king, 'Go and do all that is in your mind, for the Lord is with you.'

But that very night the word of the Lord came to Nathan: 'Go and tell my servant David, "Thus the Lord speaks: Are you the man to build me a house to dwell in? … *(Please see the Appendix B-30)*

Psalm 88:2-5, 27, 29. R. cf. v. 2

I will sing for ever of your love, O Lord.

Luke 1:67-79

John's father Zechariah was filled with the Holy Spirit and spoke this prophecy: 'Blessed be the Lord, the God of Israel, for he has visited his people, he has come to their rescue and he has raised up for us a power for salvation in the House of his servant David, even as he proclaimed, by the mouth of his holy prophets from ancient times, that he would save us from our enemies and from the hands of all who hate us. Thus he shows mercy to our ancestors, thus he remembers his holy covenant, the oath he swore to our father Abraham that he would grant us, free from fear, to be delivered from the hands of our enemies, to serve him in holiness and virtue in his presence, all our days. And you, little child, you shall be called Prophet of the Most High, for you will go before the Lord to prepare the way for him. To give his people knowledge of salvation through the forgiveness of their sins, this by the tender mercy of our God who from on high will bring the rising Sun to visit us, to give light to those who live in darkness and the shadow of death, and to guide our feet into the way of peace.'

Reflection

Zechariah completes our Advent journey to Christmas in a spirit of praise. His obedience to the angel fulfilled, his muteness is healed. He is 'filled with the Holy Spirit', and he bursts into a song of blessing and praise of God, who remains true to the promise made to Abraham. Note that Zechariah knows the whole story: his prayer presupposes the visit of Mary, and that he knows Mary's own story and the significance of her son. He then turns to his own son and gives the best summary of John the Baptist's future ministry and significance that we have. Complete your Advent journey with your prayer, and perhaps finish with praise of God similar to that of Zechariah.

25 DEC SUN

THE NATIVITY OF THE LORD (MASS DURING THE DAY), **Solemnity**

White

Isaiah 52:7-10

How beautiful on the mountains, are the feet of one who brings good news, who heralds peace, brings happiness, proclaims salvation, and tells Zion, 'Your God is king!' Listen! Your watchmen raise their voices, they shout for joy together, for they see the Lord face to face, as he returns to Zion. Break into shouts of joy together, you ruins of Jerusalem; for the Lord is consoling his people, redeeming Jerusalem. The Lord bares his holy arm in the sight of all the nations, and all the ends of the earth shall see the salvation of our God.

Psalm 97:1-6. R. v. 3

All the ends of the earth have seen the salvation of our God.

Hebrews 1:1-6

At various times in the past and in various different ways, God spoke to our ancestors through the prophets; but in our own time, the last days, he has spoken to us through his Son, the Son that he has appointed to inherit everything and through whom he made everything there is. He is the radiant light of God's glory and the perfect copy of his nature, sustaining the universe by his powerful command; and now that he has destroyed the defilement of sin, he has gone to take his place in heaven at the right hand of divine Majesty. So he is now as far above the angels as the title which he has inherited is higher than their own name.

God has never said to any angel: You are my Son, today I have become your father, or: I will be a father to him and he a son to me. Again, when he brings the First-born into the world, he says: Let all the angels of God worship him.

John 1:1-18 *(Shorter form 1:1-5, 9-14)*

In the beginning was the Word: the Word was with God and the Word was God. He was with God in the beginning. Through him all things came to be, not one thing had its being but through him. All that came to be had life in him and that life was the light of men, a light that shines in the dark, a light that darkness could not overpower.

A man came, sent by God. His name was John. He came as a witness, as a witness to speak for the light, so that everyone might believe through him. He was not the light, only a witness to speak for the light. The Word was the true light that enlightens all men; and he was coming into the world. He was in the world that had its being through him, and the world did not know him. He came to his own domain and his own people did not accept him. But to all who did accept him he gave power to become children of God, to all who believe in the name of him who was born not out of human stock or urge of the flesh or will of man but of God himself. The Word was made flesh, he lived among us, and we saw his glory, the glory that is his as the only Son of the Father, full of grace and truth.

John appears as his witness. He proclaims: 'This is the one of whom I said: He who comes after me ranks before me because he existed before me.' Indeed, from his fullness we have, all of us, received – yes, grace in return for grace, since, though the Law was given through Moses, grace and truth have come through Jesus Christ. No one has ever seen God; it is the only Son, who is nearest to the Father's heart, who has made him known.

Reflection

'The Word became flesh and lived among us, and we have seen his glory ... From his fullness we have all received, grace upon grace.' This is the Gospel for Christmas morning. It invites us to move from contemplating the baby in the manger to contemplating the full depth of the Christian mystery of Christmas: Jesus Christ in his birth, life, death, and resurrection. It is the fully human Jesus, the eternal Word of God become flesh like us, who reveals to us the true nature of God – God is love. The further part of the mystery is the 'Why'? We contemplate a future life of mutual love with God, a life beyond our present imagining. In our prayer, let us contemplate the child in the manger, Jesus Christ in all his glory, our pain-filled suffering world and the light of hope shining upon all. Enjoy a blessed Christmas Feast.

26
DEC MON

St Stephen, First Martyr
Feast | Red

Acts 6:8-10; 7:54-59

Stephen was filled with grace and power and began to work miracles and great signs among the people. But then certain people came forward to debate with Stephen, some from Cyrene and Alexandria who were members of the synagogue called the Synagogue of Freedmen, and others from Cilicia and Asia. They found they could not get the better of him because of his wisdom and because it was the Spirit that prompted what he said. They were infuriated when they heard what he said, and ground their teeth at him. But Stephen, filled with the Holy Spirit, gazed into heaven and saw the glory of God, and Jesus standing at God's right hand. 'I can see heaven thrown open' he said 'and the Son of Man standing at the right hand of God.' At this all the members of the council shouted out and stopped their ears with their hands; then they all rushed at him, sent him out of the city and stoned him. The witnesses put down their clothes at the feet of a young man called Saul. As they were stoning him, Stephen said in invocation, 'Lord Jesus, receive my spirit.' Then he knelt down and said aloud, 'Lord, do not hold this sin against them'; and with these words he fell asleep. Saul entirely approved of the killing.

Psalm 30:3-4, 6, 8, 16-17. R. v. 6

IInto your hands, O Lord, I commend my spirit.

Matthew 10:17-22

Jesus said to his apostles: 'Beware of men: they will hand you over to sanhedrins and scourge you in their synagogues. You will be dragged before governors and kings for my sake, to bear witness before them and the pagans. But when they hand you over, do not worry about how to speak or what to say; what you are to say will be given to you when the time comes; because it is not you who will be speaking; the Spirit of your Father will be speaking in you. 'Brother will betray brother to death, and the father his child; children will rise against their parents and have them put to death. You will be hated by all men on account of my name; but the man who stands firm to the end will be saved.'

Reflection

St Stephen is the first martyr in the Jerusalem Church. The conflict between the birth of the Son, and resistance to God's love – yes, even in the first Christian community – become immediately apparent. Greek-speaking widows were going hungry! Read Acts 6:1-5 to get the full story. Stephen was chosen as a 'diakonos', a man who spoke Greek could thus tend to their practical needs. The Twelve, contrary to Jesus' command, set themselves above the rest: 'It is not right that we should neglect the word of God in order to wait on tables' (Acts 6:2). Very soon, however, we see Stephen preaching the Word of God to the Greek-speaking people of Jerusalem, for which he was martyred. Can I recognise and accept the new in the Church?

St John, Apostle and Evangelist
Feast | White

27 DEC TUE

1 John 1:1-4

Something which has existed since the beginning, that we have heard, and we have seen with our own eyes; that we have watched and touched with our hands: the Word, who is life – this is our subject. That life was made visible: we saw it and we are giving our testimony, telling you of the eternal life which was with the Father and has been made visible to us. What we have seen and heard we are telling you so that you too may be in union with us, as we are in union with the Father and with his Son Jesus Christ. We are writing this to you to make our own joy complete.

Psalm 96:1-2. 5-6. 11-12. R. v. 12

Rejoice, you just, in the Lord.

John 20:2-8

On the first day of the week Mary of Magdala came running to Simon Peter and the other disciple, the one Jesus loved. 'They have taken the Lord out of the tomb' she said 'and we don't know where they have put him.' So Peter set out with the other disciple to go to the tomb. They ran together, but the other disciple, running faster than Peter, reached the tomb first; he bent down and saw the linen cloths lying on the ground, but did not go in. Simon Peter who was following now came up, went right into the tomb, saw the linen cloths on the ground, and also the cloth that had been over his head; this was not with the linen cloths but rolled up in a place by itself. Then the other disciple who had reached the tomb first also went in; he saw and he believed.

Reflection

What a gift to us is John, the beloved disciple, apostle and evangelist. He gave us his Gospel and his three letters. We are invited in our prayer to contemplate what was the source of his wonderful ministry and gift to us. Close friendship, a reflective and faithful sharing of Jesus' ministry right until the Last Supper and the cross, where Jesus entrusted his mother to his care, his presence at the tomb – all tell us something of the kind of person he was. 'He saw and he believed.' Add to that his magnificent Book of Signs (his Gospel) and his affirmation of the real meaning of the Gospel: God is love, and whoever abides in love abides in God and God in them. Do I so abide? We give thanks for those we know who so abide.

28
DEC WED

The Holy Innocents, Martyrs
Feast | Red

1 John 1:5–2:2

This is what we have heard from Jesus Christ, and the message that we are announcing to you: God is light; there is no darkness in him at all. If we say that we are in union with God while we are living in darkness, we are lying because we are not living the truth. But if we live our lives in the light, as he is in the light, we are in union with one another, and the blood of Jesus, his Son, purifies us from all sin. If we say we have no sin in us, we are deceiving ourselves and refusing to admit the truth; but if we acknowledge our sins, then God who is faithful and just will forgive our sins and purify us from everything that is wrong. To say that we have never sinned is to call God a liar and to show that his word is not in us. I am writing this, my children, to stop you sinning; but if anyone should sin, we have our advocate with the Father, Jesus Christ, who is just; he is the sacrifice that takes our sins away, and not only ours, but the whole world's.

Psalm 123:2-5, 7-8. R. v. 7

Our life, like a bird, has escaped from the snare of the fowler.

Matthew 2:13-18

After the wise men had left, the angel of the Lord appeared to Joseph in a dream and said, 'Get up, take the child and his mother with you, and escape into Egypt, and stay there until I tell you, because Herod intends to search for the child and do away with him.' So Joseph got up and, taking the child and his mother with him, left that night for Egypt, where he stayed until Herod was dead. This was to fulfil what the Lord had spoken through the prophet: I called my son out of Egypt. Herod was furious when he realised that he had been outwitted by the wise men, and in Bethlehem and its surrounding district he had all the male children killed who were two years old or under, reckoning by the date he had been careful to ask the wise men. It was then that the words spoken through the prophet Jeremiah were fulfilled: A voice was heard in Ramah, sobbing and loudly lamenting: it was Rachel weeping for her children, refusing to be comforted because they were no more.

Reflection

Only Matthew tells this story of Herod's horrific infanticide. The joy of the birth of the Messiah is here linked with the cries of the mothers (and fathers) weeping for their children. Jeremiah once lamented another death: the exile of Jacob and Rachel's children, the people of Israel, in Babylon. Matthew adds to this story of mass murder, the flight of Joseph, Mary and Jesus to Egypt, where they know what it is to be refugees. Sadly, these situations and crimes abound today. As for Matthew, so we need a realistic assessment of the personal, political and financial injustices – sin – that hold our world captive today. Then we can join Matthew in his proclamation of the healing mystery of Christ and his very different kingdom. Let us bring all who know such pain before God today.

29
DEC THU

5th Day within the Octave of Christmas | White
or **St Thomas Becket,** *bishop, martyr* (Commemoration)

SAINT THOMAS BECKET, BISHOP, MARTYR, Feast
– England

see Appendix A-28

1 John 2:3-11

We can be sure that we know Jesus only by keeping his commandments. Anyone who says, 'I know him', and does not keep his commandments, is a liar, refusing to admit the truth. But when anyone does obey what he has said, God's love comes to perfection in him. … *(Please see the Appendix B-30)*

Psalm 95:1-3, 5-6. R. v. 11

Let the heavens rejoice and earth be glad.

Luke 2:22-35

When the day came for them to be purified as laid down by the Law of Moses, the parents of Jesus took him up to Jerusalem to present him to the Lord – observing what stands written in the Law of the Lord: Every first-born male must be consecrated to the Lord – and also to offer in sacrifice, in accordance with what is said in the Law of the Lord, a pair of turtledoves or two young pigeons. Now in Jerusalem there was a man named Simeon. He was an upright and devout man; he looked forward to Israel's comforting and the Holy Spirit rested on him. It had been revealed to him by the Holy Spirit that he would not see death until he had set eyes on the Christ of the Lord. Prompted by the Spirit he came to the Temple: and when the parents brought in the child Jesus to do for him what the Law required, he took him into his arms and blessed God; and he said: 'Now, Master, you can let your servant go in peace, just as you promised; because my eyes have seen the salvation which you have prepared for all the nations to see, a light to enlighten the pagans and the glory of your people Israel.'

As the child's father and mother stood there wondering at the things that were being said about him, Simeon blessed them and said to Mary his mother, 'You see this child: he is destined for the fall and for the rising of many in Israel, destined to be a sign that is rejected – and a sword will pierce your own soul too – so that the secret thoughts of many may be laid bare.'

Reflection

St John's blunt and practical words to us invite us to ponder two ongoing Gospel challenges: our integrity, and second, do I commit to constantly ponder Jesus' Gospel, and put him and what he teaches first – a kind of lifestyle very different from, and more challenging than, just living 'good values'. Today we see Mary and Joseph faithfully fulfilling their obligations under the Law. We also we meet another faithful Advent person, Simeon. In our prayer we may contemplate Simeon: His waiting is over, his life is complete, and his passion for the future is all-encompassing. Or we can contemplate Mary, who, as Jesus' mother, is asked to support the messianic destiny of her son, her own pain notwithstanding. As Luke says, she 'treasured all these words and pondered them in her heart' (Luke 2:19).

30
DEC FRI

The Holy Family of Jesus, Mary and Joseph

Feast | White

Sirach 3:2-6, 12-14

The Lord honours the father in his children, and upholds the rights of a mother over her sons. Whoever respects his father is atoning for his sins, he who honours his mother is like someone amassing a fortune. Whoever respects his father will be happy with children of his own, he shall be heard on the day when he prays. Long life comes to him who honours his father, he who sets his mother at ease is showing obedience to the Lord. My son, support your father in his old age, do not grieve him during his life. Even if his mind should fail, show him sympathy, do not despise him in your health and strength; for kindness to a father shall not be forgotten but will serve as reparation for your sins.

Psalm 127:1-5. R. cf. v. 1

O blessed are those who fear the Lord and walk in his ways!

Matthew 2:13-15, 19-23

After the wise men had left, the angel of the Lord appeared to Joseph in a dream and said, 'Get up, take the child and his mother with you, and escape into Egypt, and stay there until I tell you, because Herod intends to search for the child and do away with him.' So Joseph got up and, taking the child and his mother with him, left that night for Egypt, where he stayed until Herod was dead. This was to fulfil what the Lord had spoken through the prophet: I called my son out of Egypt. After Herod's death, the angel of the Lord appeared in a dream to Joseph in Egypt and said, 'Get up, take the child and his mother with you and go back to the land of Israel, for those who wanted to kill the child are dead'. So Joseph got up and, taking the child and his mother with him, went back to the land of Israel. But when he learnt that Archelaus had succeeded his father Herod as ruler of Judaea he was afraid to go there, and being warned in a dream he left for the region of Galilee. There he settled in a town called Nazareth. In this way the words spoken through the prophets were to be fulfilled: He will be called a Nazarene.

Reflection

In the cultural world of Jesus' day, family, land, patriarchy and the institution of arranged marriage, were inseparable. Today, Jesus, Mary and Joseph are held up as the Holy Family. They flee from violence into Egypt, where they live as refugees, before returning to 'normal' life at home. What does a Christ-like 'holy' family look like today? We also need to bring into our prayer the single, the divorced, the re-married, single parents, the fatherless, the motherless, victims of physical, psychological and sexual violence. They belong to us if we are to be holy like Mary and Joseph's Son.

31
DEC SAT

7th Day within the Octave of Christmas | White
or **St Sylvester I,** pope (Commemoration)

1 John 2:18-21
(Please see the Appendix B-31)

Psalm 95:1-2, 11-13. R. v. 11
Let the heavens rejoice and earth be glad.

John 1:1-18
In the beginning was the Word: the Word was with God and the Word was God. He was with God in the beginning. Through him all things came to be, not one thing had its being but through him. All that came to be had life in him and that life was the light of men, a light that shines in the dark, a light that darkness could not overpower. A man came, sent by God. His name was John. He came as a witness, as a witness to speak for the light, so that everyone might believe through him. He was not the light, only a witness to speak for the light.

The Word was the true light that enlightens all men; and he was coming into the world. He was in the world that had its being through him, and the world did not know him. He came to his own domain and his own people did not accept him. But to all who did accept him he gave power to become children of God, to all who believe in the name of him who was born not out of human stock or urge of the flesh or will of man but of God himself. The Word was made flesh, he lived among us, and we saw his glory, the glory that is his as the only Son of the Father, full of grace and truth. John appears as his witness. He proclaims: 'This is the one of whom I said: He who comes after me ranks before me because he existed before me.' Indeed, from his fullness we have, all of us, received – yes, grace in return for grace, since, though the Law was given through Moses, grace and truth have come through Jesus Christ. No one has ever seen God; it is the only Son, who is nearest to the Father's heart, who has made him known.

Reflection
We conclude our Octave of Christmas with the Gospel of Christmas morning. John's wonderful prologue leaves behind the stories surrounding Jesus's birth, and invites us to explore the all-encompassing wonder, the meaning, the mystery, of the total life of Christ. He is the Word of God – God, active in creation, now made flesh among us, full of grace and truth. He shares our humanity completely and is God's very self-revelation. It is a wonderful opportunity for us to look back on our Christmas season, and in the light of this Gospel, to move in prayer to explore our own relationship with him and our perception of his 'light', his glory, and the sheer giftedness of our life. 'From his fulness we have all received grace upon grace'. In this pain-filled world sometimes shrouded in darkness, how can we make his healing love, wisdom, and light a permanent part of our own life?

03

JAN MON

MONDAY AFTER EPIPHANY
– Scotland

1 John 3:22–4:6

Whatever we ask God, we shall receive, because we keep his commandments and live the kind of life that he wants. His commandments are these: that we believe in the name of his Son Jesus Christ and that we love one another as he told us to. Whoever keeps his commandments lives in God and God lives in him. We know that he lives in us by the Spirit that he has given us. It is not every spirit, my dear people, that you can trust; test them, to see if they come from God, there are many false prophets, now, in the world. You can tell the spirits that come from God by this: every spirit which acknowledges that Jesus the Christ has come in the flesh is from God; but any spirit which will not say this of Jesus is not from God, but is the spirit of Antichrist, whose coming you were warned about. Well, now he is here, in the world. Children, you have already overcome these false prophets, because you are from God and you have in you one who is greater than anyone in this world; as for them, they are of the world, and so they speak the language of the world and the world listens to them. But we are children of God, and those who know God listen to us; those who are not of God refuse to listen to us. This is how we can tell the spirit of truth from the spirit of falsehood.

Psalm 2:7-8, 10-11. R. v. 8

I will give you all the nations for your heritage.

Matthew 4:12-17, 23-25

Hearing that John had been arrested, Jesus went back to Galilee, and leaving Nazareth he went and settled in Capernaum, a lakeside town on the borders of Zebulun and Naphtali. In this way the prophecy of Isaiah was to be fulfilled: Land of Zebulun! Land of Naphtali! Way of the sea on the far side of Jordan, Galilee of the nations! The people that lived in darkness has seen a great light; on those who dwell in the land and shadow of death a light has dawned. From that moment Jesus began his preaching with the message, 'Repent, for the kingdom of heaven is close at hand.' He went round the whole of Galilee teaching in their synagogues, proclaiming the Good News of the kingdom and curing all kinds of diseases and sickness among the people. His fame spread throughout Syria, and those who were suffering from diseases and painful complaints of one kind or another, the possessed, epileptics, the paralysed, were all brought to him, and he cured them. Large crowds followed him, coming from Galilee, the Decapolis, Jerusalem, Judaea and Transjordania.

04
JAN TUE

TUESDAY AFTER EPIPHANY
– Scotland

1 John 4:7-10

My dear people, let us love one another since love comes from God and everyone who loves is begotten by God and knows God. Anyone who fails to love can never have known God, because God is love. God's love for us was revealed when God sent into the world his only Son so that we could have life through him; this is the love I mean: not our love for God, but God's love for us when he sent his Son to be the sacrifice that takes our sins away.

Psalm 71:1-4, 7-8. R. cf. v. 11

All nations shall fall prostrate before you, O Lord.

Mark 6:34-44

As Jesus stepped ashore he saw a large crowd; and he took pity on them because they were like sheep without a shepherd, and he set himself to teach them at some length. By now it was getting very late, and his disciples came up to him and said, 'This is a lonely place and it is getting very late, so send them away, and they can go to the farms and villages round about, to buy themselves something to eat.' He replied, 'Give them something to eat yourselves.' They answered, 'Are we to go and spend two hundred denarii on bread for them to eat?' 'How many loaves have you?' he asked. 'Go and see.' And when they had found out they said, 'Five, and two fish.' Then he ordered them to get all the people together in groups on the green grass, and they sat down on the ground in squares of hundreds and fifties. Then he took the five loaves and the two fish, raised his eyes to heaven and said the blessing; then he broke the loaves and handed them to his disciples to distribute among the people. He also shared out the two fish among them all. They all ate as much as they wanted. They collected twelve basketfuls of scraps of bread and pieces of fish. Those who had eaten the loaves numbered five thousand men.

05
JAN WED

WEDNESDAY AFTER EPIPHANY
– Scotland

1 John 4:11-18

My dear people, since God has loved us so much, we too should love one another. No one has ever seen God; but as long as we love one another God will live in us and his love will be complete in us. We can know that we are living in him and he is living in us because he lets us share his Spirit. We ourselves saw and we testify that the Father sent his Son as saviour of the world. If anyone acknowledges that Jesus is the Son of God, God lives in him, and he in God. We ourselves have known and put our faith in God's love towards ourselves. God is love and anyone who lives in love lives in God, and God lives in him. Love will come to its perfection in us when we can face the day of Judgement without fear; because even in this world we have become as he is. In love there can be no fear, but fear is driven out by perfect love: because to fear is to expect punishment, and anyone who is afraid is still imperfect in love.

Psalm 71:1-2, 10-13. R. cf. v. 11

All nations shall fall prostrate before you, O Lord.

Mark 6:45-52

After the five thousand had eaten and were filled, Jesus made his disciples get into the boat and go on ahead to Bethsaida, while he himself sent the crowd away. After saying good-bye to them he went off into the hills to pray. When evening came, the boat was far out on the lake, and he was alone on the land. He could see they were worn out with rowing, for the wind was against them; and about the fourth watch of the night he came towards them, walking on the lake. He was going to pass them by, but when they saw him walking on the lake they thought it was a ghost and cried out, for they had all seen him and were terrified. But he at once spoke to them, and said, 'Courage! It is I! Do not be afraid.' Then he got into the boat with them, and the wind dropped. They were utterly and completely dumbfounded, because they had not seen what the miracle of the loaves meant; their minds were closed.

06

JAN THU

THURSDAY AFTER EPIPHANY – Scotland

1 John 4:19—5:4

We are to love, because God loved us first. Anyone who says, 'I love God', and hates his brother, is a liar, since a man who does not love the brother that he can see cannot love God, whom he has never seen. So this is the commandment that he has given us, that anyone who loves God must also love his brother. Whoever believes that Jesus is the Christ has been begotten by God, and whoever loves the Father that begot him loves the child whom he begets. We can be sure that we love God's children if we love God himself and do what he has commanded us; this is what loving God is – keeping his commandments; and his commandments are not difficult, because anyone who has been begotten by God has already overcome the world; this is the victory over the world – our faith.

Psalm 71:1-2, 14-15, 17. R. cf. v. 11

All nations shall fall prostrate before you, O Lord.

Luke 4:14-22

Jesus, with the power of the Spirit in him, returned to Galilee; and his reputation spread throughout the countryside. He taught in their synagogues and everyone praised him. He came to Nazara, where he had been brought up, and went into the synagogue on the sabbath day as he usually did. He stood up to read, and they handed him the scroll of the prophet Isaiah. Unrolling the scroll he found the place where it is written: The spirit of the Lord has been given to me, for he has anointed me. He has sent me to bring the good news to the poor, to proclaim liberty to captives and to the blind new sight, to set the downtrodden free, to proclaim the Lord's year of favour.

He then rolled up the scroll, gave it back to the assistant and sat down. And all eyes in the synagogue were fixed on him. Then he began to speak to them, 'This text is being fulfilled today even as you listen.' And he won the approval of all, and they were astonished by the gracious words that came from his lips.

07

JAN FRI

FRIDAY AFTER EPIPHANY
– Scotland

1 John 5:5-13

Who can overcome the world? Only the man who believes that Jesus is the Son of God: Jesus Christ who came by water and blood, not with water only, but with water and blood; with the Spirit as another witness – since the Spirit is the truth – so that there are three witnesses, the Spirit, the water and the blood, and all three of them agree. We accept the testimony of human witnesses, but God's testimony is much greater, and this is God's testimony, given as evidence for his Son. Everybody who believes in the Son of God has this testimony inside him; and anyone who will not believe God is making God out to be a liar, because he has not trusted the testimony God has given about his Son. This is the testimony: God has given us eternal life and this life is in his Son; anyone who has the Son has life, anyone who does not have the Son does not have life. I have written all this to you so that you who believe in the name of the Son of God may be sure that you have eternal life.

Psalm 147:12-15, 19-20. R. v. 12

O Praise the Lord, Jerusalem!

Luke 5:12-16

Jesus was in one of the towns when a man appeared, covered with leprosy. Seeing Jesus he fell on his face and implored him. 'Sir,' he said 'If you want to, you can cure me.' Jesus stretched out his hand, touched him and said, 'Of course I want to! Be cured!' And the leprosy left him at once. He ordered him to tell no one, 'But go and show yourself to the priest and make the offering for your healing as Moses prescribed it, as evidence for them.'

His reputation continued to grow, and large crowds would gather to hear him and to have their sickness cured, but he would always go off to some place where he could be alone and pray.

08
JAN SAT

SATURDAY AFTER EPIPHANY
– Scotland

1 John 5:14-21

We are quite confident that if we ask the Son of God for anything, and it is in accordance with his will, he will hear us; and, knowing that whatever we may ask, he hears us, we know that we have already been granted what we asked of him. If anybody sees his brother commit a sin that is not a deadly sin, he has only to pray, and God will give life to the sinner – not those who commit a deadly sin; for there is a sin that is death, and I will not say that you must pray about that. Every kind of wrong-doing is sin, but not all sin is deadly.

We know that anyone who has been begotten by God does not sin, because the begotten Son of God protects him, and the Evil One does not touch him. We know that we belong to God, but the whole world lies in the power of the Evil One. We know, too, that the Son of God has come, and has given us the power to know the true God. We are in the true God, as we are in his Son, Jesus Christ. This is the true God, this is eternal life. Children, be on your guard against false gods.

Psalm 149:1-6,9. R. v.4

The Lord takes delight in his people.

John 3:22-30

Jesus went with his disciples into the Judaean countryside and stayed with them there and baptised. At the same time John was baptising at Aenon near Salim, where there was plenty of water, and people were going there to be baptised. This was before John had been put in prison.

Now some of John's disciples had opened a discussion with a Jew about purification, so they went to John and said, 'Rabbi, the man who was with you on the far side of the Jordan, the man to whom you bore witness, is baptising now; and everyone is going to him.'

John replied:

'A man can lay claim only to what is given him from heaven. 'You yourselves can bear me out: I said: I myself am not the Christ; I am the one who has been sent in front of him.

'The bride is only for the bridegroom; and yet the bridegroom's friend, who stands there and listens, is glad when he hears the bridegroom's voice. This same joy I feel, and now it is complete. He must grow greater, I must grow smaller.'

13
JAN THU

Saint Kentigern (Mungo), Bishop, Feast – Scotland

Isaiah 52:7-10

How beautiful on the mountains, are the feet of one who brings good news, who heralds peace, brings happiness, proclaims salvation, and tells Zion, 'Your God is king!' Listen! Your watchmen raise their voices, they shout for joy together, for they see the Lord face to face, as he returns to Zion. Break into shouts of joy together, you ruins of Jerusalem; for the Lord is consoling his people, redeeming Jerusalem. The Lord bares his holy arm in the sight of all the nations, and all the ends of the earth shall see the salvation of our God.

Psalm 95(96):1-3,7-8,10

Proclaim the wonders of the Lord among all the peoples.

2 Timothy 4:1-5

Before God and before Christ Jesus who is to be judge of the living and the dead, I put this duty to you, in the name of his Appearing and of his kingdom: proclaim the message and, welcome or unwelcome, insist on it. Refute falsehood, correct error, call to obedience – but do all with patience and with the intention of teaching. The time is sure to come when, far from being content with sound teaching, people will be avid for the latest novelty and collect themselves a whole series of teachers according to their own tastes; and then, instead of listening to the truth, they will turn to myths. Be careful always to choose the right course; be brave under trials; make the preaching of the Good News your life's work, in thoroughgoing service.

Luke 5:1-11

Jesus was standing one day by the Lake of Gennesaret, with the crowd pressing round him listening to the word of God, when he caught sight of two boats close to the bank. The fishermen had gone out of them and were washing their nets. He got into one of the boats – it was Simon's – and asked him to put out a little from the shore. Then he sat down and taught the crowds from the boat.

When he had finished speaking he said to Simon, 'Put out into deep water and pay out your nets for a catch.' 'Master,' Simon replied, 'we worked hard all night long and caught nothing, but if you say so, I will pay out the nets.' And when they had done this they netted such a huge number of fish that their nets began to tear, so they signalled to their companions in the other boat to come and help them; when these came, they filled the two boats to sinking point.

When Simon Peter saw this he fell at the knees of Jesus saying, 'Leave me, Lord; I am a sinful man.' For he and all his companions were completely overcome by the catch they had made; so also were James and John, sons of Zebedee, who were Simon's partners. But Jesus said to Simon, 'Do not be afraid; from now on it is men you will catch.' Then, bringing their boats back to land, they left everything and followed him.

01

FEB TUE

SAINT BRIGID, ABBESS, SECONDARY PATRON OF IRELAND

Job 31:16-20,24-25,31-32

Have I been insensible to poor men's needs,
 or let a widow's eyes grow dim?
Or taken my share of bread alone,
 not giving a share to the orphan?
I, whom God has fostered father-like, from childhood,
 and guided since I left my mother's womb.
Have I ever seen a wretch in need of clothing,
 or a beggar going naked,
without his having cause to bless me from his heart,
 as he felt the warmth of the fleece from my lambs?
Have I put all my trust in gold,
 from finest gold sought my security?
Have I ever gloated over my great wealth,
 or the riches that my hands have won?
The people of my tent, did they not say,
 'Is there a man he has not filled with meat'?
No stranger ever had to sleep outside,
 my door was always open to the traveller.

Psalm 106:35-38, 41-42

Give thanks to the Lord for he is good; for his love has no end.

Luke 6:32-38

Jesus said to his disciples:

'If you love those who love you, what thanks can you expect? Even sinners love those who love them. And if you do good to those who do good to you, what thanks can you expect? For even sinners do that much. And if you lend to those from whom you hope to receive, what thanks can you expect? Even sinners lend to sinners to get back the same amount. Instead, love your enemies and do good, and lend without any hope of return. You will have a great reward, and you will be sons of the Most High, for he himself is kind to the ungrateful and the wicked.

'Be compassionate as your Father is compassionate. Do not judge, and you will not be judged yourselves; do not condemn, and you will not be condemned yourselves; grant pardon, and you will be pardoned. Give, and there will be gifts for you: a full measure, pressed down, shaken together, and running over, will be poured into your lap; because the amount you measure out is the amount you will be given back.'

01
MAR TUE

ST DAVID, BISHOP, PATRON OF WALES,
Feast – England

Philippians 3:8-14

I believe nothing can happen that will outweigh the supreme advantage of knowing Christ Jesus my Lord. For him I have accepted the loss of everything, and I look on everything as so much rubbish if only I can have Christ and be given a place in him. I am no longer trying for perfection by my own efforts, the perfection that comes from the Law, but I want only the perfection that comes through faith in Christ, and is from God and based on faith. All I want is to know Christ and the power of his resurrection and to share his sufferings by reproducing the pattern of his death. That is the way I can hope to take my place in the resurrection of the dead. Not that I have become perfect yet: I have not yet won, but I am still running, trying to capture the prize for which Christ Jesus captured me. I can assure you my brothers, I am far from thinking that I have already won. All I can say is that I forget the past and I strain ahead for what is still to come; I am racing for the finish, for the prize to which God calls us upwards to receive in Christ Jesus.

Psalm 1:1-4,6

Happy the man who has placed his trust in the Lord.

Matthew 5:13-16

Jesus said to his disciples: 'You are the salt of the earth. But if salt becomes tasteless, what can make it salty again? It is good for nothing, and can only be thrown out to be trampled underfoot by men.

'You are the light of the world. A city built on a hill-top cannot be hidden. No one lights a lamp to put it under a tub; they put it on the lamp-stand where it shines for everyone in the house. In the same way your light must shine in the sight of men, so that, seeing your good works, they may give the praise to your Father in heaven.'

10

MAR THU

SAINT JOHN OGILVIE, PRIEST, MARTYR, Feast

– Scotland

Isaiah 50:5-9

The Lord has opened my ear. For my part, I made no resistance, neither did I turn away. I offered my back to those who struck me, my cheeks to those who tore at my beard; I did not cover my face against insult and spittle. The Lord comes to my help, so that I am untouched by the insults. So, too, I set my face like flint; I know I shall not be shamed. My vindicator is here at hand. Does anyone start proceedings against me? Then let us go to court together. Who thinks he has a case against me? Let him approach me. The Lord is coming to my help, who will dare to condemn me?

Psalm 76:12-16,21

I remember the deeds of the Lord.

1 Corinthians 1:3-7

May God our Father and the Lord Jesus Christ send you grace and peace.

I never stop thanking God for all the graces you have received through Jesus Christ. I thank him that you have been enriched in so many ways, especially in your teachers and preachers; the witness to Christ has indeed been strong among you so that you will not be without any of the gifts of the Spirit while you are waiting for our Lord Jesus Christ to be revealed.

John 12:24-26

Jesus said to his disciples: 'I tell you, most solemnly, unless a wheat grain falls on the ground and dies, it remains only a single grain; but if it dies, it yields a rich harvest. Anyone who loves his life loses it; anyone who hates his life in this world will keep it for the eternal life. If a man serves me, he must follow me, wherever I am, my servant will be there too. If anyone serves me, my Father will honour him.'

17
MAR THU

ST PATRICK, BISHOP,
Solemnity – Ireland

Amos 7:12-15

Amaziah, the priest of Bethel, said to Amos, 'Go away, seer;' get back to the land of Judah; earn your bread there, do your prophesying there. We want no more prophesying in Bethel; this is the royal sanctuary, the national temple.' 'I was no prophet, neither did I belong to any of the brotherhoods of prophets,' Amos replied to Amaziah 'I was a shepherd, and looked after sycamores: but it was the Lord who took me from herding the flock, and the Lord who said, "Go, prophesy to my people Israel."'

Psalm 138:1-3,7-10,13-14

If I dwell at the sea's furthest end, even there you watch over me.

1 Thessalonians 2:2-8

It was our God who gave us the courage to proclaim his Good News to you in the face of great opposition. We have not taken to preaching because we are deluded, or immoral, or trying to deceive anyone; it was God who decided that we were fit to be entrusted with the Good News, and when we are speaking, we are not trying to please men but God, who can read our inmost thoughts. You know very well, and we can swear it before God, that never at any time have our speeches been simply flattery, or a cover for trying to get money; nor have we ever looked for any special honour from men, either from you or anybody else, when we could have imposed ourselves on you with full weight, as apostles of Christ.

Instead, we were unassuming. Like a mother feeding and looking after her own children, we felt so devoted and protective towards you, and had come to love you so much, that we were eager to hand over to you not only the Good News but our whole lives as well.

Luke 5:1-11

Jesus was standing one day by the Lake of Gennesaret, with the crowd pressing round him listening to the word of God, when he caught sight of two boats close to the bank. The fishermen had gone out of them and were washing their nets. He got into one of the boats – it was Simon's – and asked him to put out a little from the shore. Then he sat down and taught the crowds from the boat.

When he had finished speaking he said to Simon, 'Put out into deep water and pay out your nets for a catch.' 'Master,' Simon replied, 'we worked hard all night long and caught nothing, but if you say so, I will pay out the nets.' And when they had done this they netted such a huge number of fish that their nets began to tear, so they signalled to their companions in the other boat to come and help them; when these came, they filled the two boats to sinking point.

When Simon Peter saw this he fell at the knees of Jesus saying, 'Leave me, Lord; I am a sinful man.' For he and all his companions were completely overcome by the catch they had made; so also were James and John, sons of Zebedee, who were Simon's partners. But Jesus said to Simon, 'Do not be afraid; from now on it is men you will catch.' Then, bringing their boats back to land, they left everything and followed him.

26

APR TUE

SAINT GEORGE, MARTYR, Solemnity
– England

Apocalypse 12:10-12

I, John, heard a voice shout from heaven, 'Victory and power and empire for ever have been won by our God, and all authority for his Christ, now that the persecutor, who accused our brothers day and night before our God, has been brought down. They have triumphed over him by the blood of the Lamb and by the witness of their martyrdom, because even in the face of death they would not cling to life. Let the heavens rejoice and all who live there.'

Psalm 125 R. v. 5

Those who are sowing in tears will sing when they reap.

Romans 5:1-5

Through our Lord Jesus Christ, by faith we are judged righteous and at peace with God, since it is by faith and through Jesus that we have entered this state of grace in which we can boast about looking forward to God's glory. But that is not all we can boast about; we can boast about our sufferings. These sufferings bring patience, as we know, and patience brings perseverance, and perseverance brings hope, and this hope is not deceptive, because the love of God has been poured into our hearts by the Holy Spirit which has been given us.

John 15:18-21

Jesus said to his disciples:

'If the world hates you,
remember that it hated me before you.
If you belonged to the world,
the world would love you as its own;
but because you do not belong to the world,
because my choice withdrew you from the world,
therefore the world hates you.
Remember the words I said to you: A servant is not greater than his master.
If they persecuted me, they will persecute you too;
if they kept my word, they will keep yours as well.
But it will be on my account that they will do all this,
because they do not know the one who sent me.'

04
MAY WED

THE ENGLISH MARTYRS,
Feast – England

Acts 7:55-60

Stephen, filled with the Holy Spirit, gazed into heaven and saw the glory of God, and Jesus standing at God's right hand. 'I can see heaven thrown open' he said 'and the Son of Man standing at the right hand of God.' At this all the members of the council shouted out and stopped their ears with their hands; then they all rushed at him, sent him out of the city and stoned him. The witnesses put down their clothes at the feet of a young man called Saul. As they were stoning him, Stephen said in invocation, 'Lord Jesus, receive my spirit.' Then he knelt down and said aloud, 'Lord, do not hold this sin against them'; and with these words he fell asleep.

Psalm 30:3-4,6,8,17,21

Into your hands, O Lord, I commend my spirit.

Matthew 10:17-20

Jesus said to his disciples: 'Beware of men: they will hand you over to sanhedrins and scourge you in their synagogues. You will be dragged before governors and kings for my sake, to bear witness before them and the pagans. But when they hand you over, do not worry about how to speak or what to say; what you are to say will be given to you when the time comes; because it is not you who will be speaking; the Spirit of your Father will be speaking in you.'

'Brother will betray brother to death, and the father his child; children will rise against their parents and have them put to death. You will be hated by all men on account of my name; but the man who stands firm to the end will be saved.'

26
MAY THU

SAINT PHILIP NERI, PRIEST, Memorial
– Ireland

Acts 18:1-8

Paul left Athens and went to Corinth, where he met a Jew called Aquila whose family came from Pontus. He and his wife Priscilla had recently left Italy because an edict of Claudius had expelled all the Jews from Rome. Paul went to visit them, and when he found they were tentmakers, of the same trade as himself, he lodged with them, and they worked together. Every sabbath he used to hold debates in the synagogues, trying to convert Jews as well as Greeks.

After Silas and Timothy had arrived from Macedonia, Paul devoted all his time to preaching, declaring to the Jews that Jesus was the Christ. When they turned against him and started to insult him, he took his cloak and shook it out in front of them, saying, 'Your blood be on your own heads; from now on I can go to the pagans with a clear conscience.' Then he left the synagogue and moved to the house next door that belonged to a worshipper of God called Justus. Crispus, president of the synagogue, and his whole household, all became believers in the Lord. A great many Corinthians who had heard him became believers and were baptised.

Psalm 97:1-4

The Lord has shown his salvation to the nations.

John 16:16-20

Jesus said to his disciples:

'In a short time you will no longer see me, and then a short time later you will see me again.'

Then some of his disciples said to one another, 'What does he mean, "In a short time you will no longer see me, and then a short time later you will see me again" and, "I am going to the Father"? What is this "short time"? We do not know what he means.' Jesus knew that they wanted to question him, so he said, 'You are asking one another what I meant by saying: In a short time you will no longer see me, and then a short time later you will see me again.

'I tell you most solemnly, you will be weeping and wailing while the world will rejoice; you will be sorrowful, but your sorrow will turn to joy.'

27
MAY FRI

SAINT AUGUSTINE OF CANTERBURY, Feast
– England

1 Thessalonians 2:2-8

It was our God who gave us the courage to proclaim his Good News to you in the face of great opposition. We have not taken to preaching because we are deluded, or immoral, or trying to deceive anyone; it was God who decided that we were fit to be entrusted with the Good News, and when we are speaking, we are not trying to please men but God, who can read our inmost thoughts. You know very well, and we can swear it before God, that never at any time have our speeches been simply flattery, or a cover for trying to get money; nor have we ever looked for any special honour from men, either from you or anybody else, when we could have imposed ourselves on you with full weight, as apostles of Christ.

Instead, we were unassuming. Like a mother feeding and looking after her own children, we felt so devoted and protective towards you, and had come to love you so much, that we were eager to hand over to you not only the Good News but our whole lives as well.

Psalm 116

Go out to the whole world; proclaim the Good News.

Luke 10:1-9

The Lord appointed seventy-two others and sent them out ahead of him, in pairs, to all the towns and places he himself was to visit. He said to them, 'The harvest is rich but the labourers are few, so ask the Lord of the harvest to send labourers to his harvest. Start off now, but remember, I am sending you out like lambs among wolves. Carry no purse, no haversack, no sandals. Salute no one on the road. Whatever house you go into, let your first words be, "Peace to this house!" And if a man of peace lives there, your peace will go and rest on him; if not, it will come back to you. Stay in the same house, taking what food and drink they have to offer, for the labourer deserves his wages; do not move from house to house. Whenever you go into a town where they make you welcome, eat what is set before you. Cure those in it who are sick, and say, "The kingdom of God is very near to you."'

09
JUN THU

SAINT COLUMBA (COLUM CILLE), ABBOT, Feast

– Ireland, Scotland

Romans 12:1-2,9-13

Think of God's mercy, my brothers, and worship him, I beg you, in a way that is worthy of thinking beings, by offering your living bodies as a holy sacrifice, truly pleasing to God. Do not model yourselves on the behaviour of the world around you, but let your behaviour change, modelled by your new mind. This is the only way to discover the will of God and know what is good, what it is that God wants, what is the perfect thing to do.

Do not let your love be a pretence, but sincerely prefer good to evil. Love each other as much as brothers should, and have a profound respect for each other. Work for the Lord with untiring effort and with great earnestness of spirit. If you have hope, this will make you cheerful. Do not give up if trials come; and keep on praying. If any of the saints are in need you must share with them; and you should make hospitality your special care.

Psalm 33:2-3,10-15

Taste and see that the Lord is good.

Matthew 8:18-27

When Jesus saw the great crowds all about him he gave orders to leave for the other side. One of the scribes then came up and said to him, 'Master, I will follow you wherever you go.' Jesus replied, 'Foxes have holes and the birds of the air have nests, but the Son of Man has nowhere to lay his head.'

Another man, one of his disciples, said to him, 'Sir, let me go and bury my father first.' But Jesus replied, 'Follow me, and leave the dead to bury their dead.'

Jesus got into the boat followed by his disciples. Without warning a storm broke over the lake, so violent that the waves were breaking right over the boat. But he was asleep. So they went to him and woke him saying, 'Save us, Lord, we are going down!' And he said to them, 'Why are you so frightened, you men of little faith?' And with that he stood up and rebuked the winds and the sea; and all was calm again. The men were astounded and said, 'Whatever kind of man is this? Even the winds and the sea obey him.'

22
JUN WED

SAINTS JOHN FISHER, BISHOP, AND THOMAS MORE, MARTYRS,
Feast – England

2 Maccabees 6:18,21,24-31

Eleazar, one of the foremost teachers of the Law, a man already advanced in years and of most noble appearance, was being forced to open his mouth wide to swallow pig's flesh. Those in charge of the impious banquet, because of their long-standing friendship with him, took him aside and privately urged him to have meat brought of a kind he could properly use, prepared by himself, and only pretend to eat the portions of sacrificial meat as prescribed by the king.

'Such pretence' he said 'does not square with our time of life; many young people would suppose that Eleazar at the age of ninety had conformed to the foreigners' way of life, and because I had played this part for the sake of a paltry brief spell of life might themselves be led astray on my account; I should only bring defilement and disgrace on my old age. Even though for the moment I avoid execution by man, I can never, living or dead, elude the grasp of the Almighty. Therefore if I am man enough to quit this life here and now I shall prove myself worthy of my old age, and I shall have left the young a noble example of how to make a good death, eagerly and generously, for the venerable and holy laws.'

With these words he went straight to the block. His escorts, so recently well disposed towards him, turned against him after this declaration, which they regarded as sheer madness. Just before he died under the blows, he groaned aloud and said, 'The Lord whose knowledge is holy sees clearly that, though I might have escaped death, whatever agonies of body I now endure under this bludgeoning, in my soul I am glad to suffer, because of the awe which he inspires in me.'

This was how he died, leaving his death as an example of nobility and a record of virtue not only for the young but for the great majority of the nation.

Psalm 30:2,6,12-13,15-17,25

Father, into your hands I commend my spirit.

Matthew 24:4-13

Jesus said to his disciples: 'Take care that no one deceives you; because many will come using my name and saying, "I am the Christ," and they will deceive many. You will hear of wars and rumours of wars; do not be alarmed, for this is something that must happen, but the end will not be yet. For nation will fight against nation, and kingdom against kingdom. There will be famines and earthquakes here and there. All this is only the beginning of the birth-pangs.

'Then they will hand you over to be tortured and put to death; and you will be hated by all the nations on account of my name. And then many will fall away; men will betray one another and hate one another. Many false prophets will arise; they will deceive many, and with the increase of lawlessness, love in most men will grow cold; but the man who stands firm to the end will be saved.'

1
JUL FRI

St Oliver Plunkett, Memorial
– Ireland

Amos 8:4-6,9-12

Listen to this, you who trample on the needy and try to suppress the poor people of the country, you who say, 'When will New Moon be over so that we can sell our corn, and sabbath, so that we can market our wheat? Then by lowering the bushel, raising the shekel, by swindling and tampering with the scales, we can buy up the poor for money, and the needy for a pair of sandals, and get a price even for the sweepings of the wheat.' That day – it is the Lord who speaks – I will make the sun go down at noon, and darken the earth in broad daylight. I am going to turn your feasts into funerals, all your singing into lamentation; I will have your loins all in sackcloth, your heads all shaved. I will make it a mourning like the mourning for an only son, as long as it lasts it will be like a day of bitterness. See what days are coming – it is the Lord who speaks – days when I will bring famine on the country, a famine not of bread, a drought not of water, but of hearing the word of the Lord. They will stagger from sea to sea, wander from north to east, seeking the word of the Lord and failing to find it.

Psalm 118:2,10,20,30,40,131

Man does not live on bread alone but on every word that comes from the mouth of God.

Matthew 9:9-13

As Jesus was walking on, he saw a man named Matthew sitting by the customs house, and he said to him, 'Follow me.' And he got up and followed him.

While he was at dinner in the house it happened that a number of tax collectors and sinners came to sit at the table with Jesus and his disciples. When the Pharisees saw this, they said to his disciples, 'Why does your master eat with tax collectors and sinners?' When he heard this he replied, 'It is not the healthy who need the doctor, but the sick. Go and learn the meaning of the words: What I want is mercy, not sacrifice. And indeed I did not come to call the virtuous, but sinners.'

09

JUL SAT

OUR LADY OF ABERDEEN, Feast
– Scotland

Genesis 3:9-15,20

After Adam had eaten of the tree the Lord God called to him. 'Where are you?' he asked. 'I heard the sound of you in the garden;' he replied 'I was afraid because I was naked, so I hid.' 'Who told you that you were naked?' he asked 'Have you been eating of the tree I forbade you to eat?' The man replied, 'It was the woman you put with me; she gave me the fruit, and I ate it.' Then the Lord God asked the woman, 'What is this you have done?' The woman replied, 'The serpent tempted me and I ate.'

Then the Lord God said to the serpent, 'Because you have done this, 'Be accursed beyond all cattle, all wild beasts. You shall crawl on your belly and eat dust every day of your life.

I will make you enemies of each other: you and the woman, your offspring and her offspring. It will crush your head and you will strike its heel.'

The man named his wife 'Eve' because she was the mother of all those who live.

Psalm 1 Samuel 2:1,4-8

My heart exults in the Lord my Saviour.

Matthew 1:18-23

This is how Jesus Christ came to be born. His mother Mary was betrothed to Joseph; but before they came to live together she was found to be with child through the Holy Spirit. Her husband Joseph; being a man of honour and wanting to spare her publicity, decided to divorce her informally. He had made up his mind to do this when the angel of the Lord appeared to him in a dream and said, 'Joseph son of David, do not be afraid to take Mary home as your wife, because she has conceived what is in her by the Holy Spirit. She will give birth to a son and you must name him Jesus, because he is the one who is to save his people from their sins.' Now all this took place to fulfil the words spoken by the Lord through the prophet:

The virgin will conceive and give birth to a son and they will call him Emmanuel, a name which means 'God-is-with-us.'

15
AUG MON

Monday of Twentieth Week in Ordinary Time
– England, Wales and Scotland

Ezekiel 24:15-24

The word of the Lord was addressed to me as follows, 'Son of man, I am about to deprive you suddenly of the delight of your eyes. But you are not to lament, not to weep, not to let your tears run down. Groan in silence, do not go into mourning for the dead, knot your turban round your head, put your sandals on your feet, do not cover your beard, do not eat common bread.' I told this to the people in the morning, and my wife died in the evening, and the next morning I did as I had been ordered.

The people then said to me, 'Are you not going to explain what meaning these actions have for us?'

I replied, 'The word of the Lord has been addressed to me as follows, "Say to the House of Israel: The Lord says this. I am about to profane my sanctuary, the pride of your strength, the delight of your eyes, the passion of your souls. Those of your sons and daughters whom you have left behind will fall by the sword. And you are to do as I have done; you must not cover your beards or eat common bread; you must keep your turbans on your heads and your sandals on your feet; you must not lament or weep. You shall waste away owing to your sins and groan among yourselves. Ezekiel is to be a sign for you. You are to do just as he has done. And when this happens, you will learn that I am the Lord."'

Psalm Deuteronomy 32:18-21

You forget the God who fathered you.

Matthew 19:16-22

There was a man who came to Jesus and asked, 'Master, what good deed must I do to possess eternal life?' Jesus said to him, 'Why do you ask me about what is good? There is one alone who is good. But if you wish to enter into life, keep the commandments.' He said, 'Which?' 'These:' Jesus replied 'You must not kill. You must not commit adultery. You must not bring false witness. Honour your father and mother, and: you must love your neighbour as yourself.' The young man said to him, 'I have kept all these. What more do I need to do?' Jesus said, 'If you wish to be perfect, go and sell what you own and give the money to the poor, and you will have treasure in heaven; then come, follow me.' But when the young man heard these words he went away sad, for he was a man of great wealth.

03
SEP SAT

ST GREGORY THE GREAT, POPE, DOCTOR, Feast
– England

1 Thessalonians 2:2-8

It was our God who gave us the courage to proclaim his Good News to you in the face of great opposition. We have not taken to preaching because we are deluded, or immoral, or trying to deceive anyone; it was God who decided that we were fit to be entrusted with the Good News, and when we are speaking, we are not trying to please men but God, who can read our inmost thoughts. You know very well, and we can swear it before God, that never at any time have our speeches been simply flattery, or a cover for trying to get money; nor have we ever looked for any special honour from men, either from you or anybody else, when we could have imposed ourselves on you with full weight, as apostles of Christ.

Instead, we were unassuming. Like a mother feeding and looking after her own children, we felt so devoted and protective towards you, and had come to love you so much, that we were eager to hand over to you not only the Good News but our whole lives as well.

Psalm 95:1-3,7-8,10

Proclaim the wonders of the Lord among all the peoples.

Matthew 16:13-19

When Jesus came to the region of Caesarea Philippi he put this question to his disciples, 'Who do people say the Son of Man is?' And they said, 'Some say he is John the Baptist, some Elijah, and others Jeremiah or one of the prophets.' 'But you,' he said 'who do you say I am?' Then Simon Peter spoke up, 'You are the Christ,' he said 'the Son of the living God.' Jesus replied, 'Simon son of Jonah, you are a happy man! Because it was not flesh and blood that revealed this to you but my Father in heaven. So I now say to you: You are Peter and on this rock I will build my Church. And the gates of the underworld can never hold out against it. I will give you the keys of the kingdom of heaven: whatever you bind on earth shall be considered bound in heaven; whatever you loose on earth shall be considered loosed in heaven.'

16
SEP FRI

ST NINIAN, BISHOP,
Feast – Scotland

Exodus 32:7-14

The Lord spoke to Moses, 'Go down now, because your people whom you brought out of Egypt have apostatised. They have been quick to leave the way I marked out for them; they have made themselves a calf of molten metal and have worshipped it and offered it sacrifice. "Here is your God, Israel," they have cried "who brought you up from the land of Egypt!"' the Lord said to Moses, 'I can see how headstrong these people are! Leave me, now, my wrath shall blaze out against them and devour them; of you, however, I will make a great nation.'

But Moses pleaded with the Lord his God. 'Lord,' he said 'why should your wrath blaze out against this people of yours whom you brought out of the land of Egypt with arm outstretched and mighty hand? Why let the Egyptians say, "Ah, it was in treachery that he brought them out, to do them to death in the mountains and wipe them off the face of the earth"? Leave your burning wrath; relent and do not bring this disaster on your people. Remember Abraham, Isaac and Jacob, your servants to whom by your own self you swore and made this promise: I will make your offspring as many as the stars of heaven, and all this land which I promised I will give to your descendants, and it shall be their heritage for ever.'

So the Lord relented and did not bring on his people the disaster he had threatened.

Psalm 88:2-5,21-22,25,27

I will sing for ever of your love, O Lord.

Matthew 9:35-37

Jesus made a tour through all the towns and villages, teaching in their synagogues, proclaiming the Good News of the kingdom and curing all kinds of diseases and sickness.

And when he saw the crowds he felt sorry for them because they were harassed and dejected, like sheep without a shepherd. Then he said to his disciples, 'The harvest is rich but the labourers are few, so ask the Lord of the harvest to send labourers to his harvest.'

25

OCT TUE

THE SIX WELSH MARTYRS AND THEIR COMPANIONS, Feast

– Wales

Hebrews 11:33-40

Gideon, Barak, Samson, Jephthah, David, Samuel and the prophets – these were men who through faith conquered kingdoms, did what is right and earned the promises. They could keep a lion's mouth shut, put out blazing fires and emerge unscathed from battle. They were weak people who were given strength, to be brave in war and drive back foreign invaders. Some came back to their wives from the dead, by resurrection; and others submitted to torture, refusing release so that they would rise again to a better life. Some had to bear being pilloried and flogged, or even chained up in prison. They were stoned, or sawn in half, or beheaded; they were homeless, and dressed in the skins of sheep and goats; they were penniless and were given nothing but ill-treatment. They were too good for the world and they went out to live in deserts and mountains and in caves and ravines. These are all heroes of faith, but they did not receive what was promised, since God had made provision for us to have something better, and they were not to reach perfection except with us.

Psalm 15:1-2,5,7-11

You are my inheritance, O Lord.

John 12:24-26

Jesus said to his disciples:

'I tell you, most solemnly, unless a wheat grain falls on the ground and dies, it remains only a single grain; but if it dies, it yields a rich harvest. Anyone who loves his life loses it; anyone who hates his life in this world will keep it for the eternal life. If a man serves me, he must follow me, wherever I am, my servant will be there too. If anyone serves me, my Father will honour him.'

Apocalypse 7:2-4,9-14

I, John, saw another angel rising where the sun rises, carrying the seal of the living God; he called in a powerful voice to the four angels whose duty was to devastate land and sea, 'Wait before you do any damage on land or at sea or to the trees, until we have put the seal on the foreheads of the servants of our God.' Then I heard how many were sealed: a hundred and forty-four thousand, out of all the tribes of Israel. After that I saw a huge number, impossible to count, of people from every nation, race, tribe and language; they were standing in front of the throne and in front of the Lamb, dressed in white robes and holding palms in their hands. They shouted aloud, 'Victory to our God, who sits on the throne, and to the Lamb!' And all the angels who were standing in a circle round the throne, surrounding the elders and the four animals, prostrated themselves before the throne, and touched the ground with their foreheads, worshipping God with these words, 'Amen. Praise and glory and wisdom and thanksgiving and honour and power and strength to our God for ever and ever. Amen.' One of the elders then spoke, and asked me, 'Do you know who these people are, dressed in white robes, and where they have come from?' I answered him, 'You can tell me, my lord.' Then he said, 'These are the people who have been through the great persecution, and they have washed their robes white again in the blood of the Lamb.'

Psalm 23:1-6

Such are the men who seek your face, O Lord.

Matthew 5:1-12a

Seeing the crowds, Jesus went up the hill. There he sat down and was joined by his disciples. Then he began to speak. This is what he taught them:

'How happy are the poor in spirit; theirs is the kingdom of heaven. Happy the gentle: they shall have the earth for their heritage. Happy those who mourn: they shall be comforted. Happy those who hunger and thirst for what is right: they shall be satisfied. Happy the merciful: they shall have mercy shown them. Happy the pure in heart: they shall see God. Happy the peacemakers: they shall be called sons of God. Happy those who are persecuted in the cause of right: theirs is the kingdom of heaven. 'Happy are you when people abuse you and persecute you and speak all kinds of calumny against you on my account. Rejoice and be glad, for your reward will be great in heaven.'

ALL SAINTS OF WALES,
Feast – Wales

16
NOV WED

ST MARGARET OF SCOTLAND, Feast

– Scotland

Proverbs 31:10-13,19-20,30-31

A perfect wife – who can find her? She is far beyond the price of pearls. Her husband's heart has confidence in her, from her he will derive no little profit. Advantage and not hurt she brings him all the days of her life. She is always busy with wool and with flax, she does her work with eager hands. She sets her hands to the distaff, her fingers grasp the spindle. She holds out her hand to the poor, she opens her arms to the needy. Charm is deceitful, and beauty empty; the woman who is wise is the one to praise. Give her a share in what her hands have worked for, and let her works tell her praises at the city gates.

Psalm 127:1-5

O blessed are those who fear the Lord.

1 Corinthians 12:31-13:13

Be ambitious for the higher gifts. And I am going to show you a way that is better than any of them.

If I have all the eloquence of men or of angels, but speak without love, I am simply a gong booming or a cymbal clashing. If I have the gift of prophecy, understanding all the mysteries there are, and knowing everything, and if I have faith in all its fullness, to move mountains, but without love, then I am nothing at all. If I give away all that I possess, piece by piece, and if I even let them take my body to burn it, but am without love, it will do me no good whatever.

Love is always patient and kind; it is never jealous; love is never boastful or conceited; it is never rude or selfish; it does not take offence, and is not resentful. Love takes no pleasure in other people's sins but delights in the truth; it is always ready to excuse, to trust, to hope, and to endure whatever comes.

Love does not come to an end. But if there are gifts of prophecy, the time will come when they must fail; or the gift of languages, it will not continue for ever; and knowledge – for this, too, the time will come when it must fail. For our knowledge is imperfect and our prophesying is imperfect; but once perfection comes, all imperfect things will disappear. When I was a child, I used to talk like a child, and think like a child, and argue like a child, but now I am a man, all childish ways are put behind me. Now we are seeing a dim reflection in a mirror; but then we shall be seeing face to face. The knowledge that I have now is imperfect; but then I shall know as fully as I am known.

In short, there are three things that last: faith, hope and love; and the greatest of these is love.

Matthew 25:31-46

Jesus said to his disciples: 'When the Son of Man comes in his glory, escorted by all the angels, then he will take his seat on his throne of glory. All the nations will be assembled before him and he will separate men one from another as the shepherd separates sheep from goats. He will place the sheep on his right hand and the goats on his left.

'Then the King will say to those on his right hand, "Come, you whom my Father has blessed, take for your heritage the kingdom prepared for you since the foundation of the world. For I was hungry and you gave me food; I was thirsty and you gave me drink; I was a stranger and you made me welcome; naked and you clothed me, sick and you visited me, in prison and you came to see me." Then the virtuous will say to him in reply, "Lord, when did we see you hungry and feed you; or thirsty and give you drink? When did we see you a stranger and make you welcome; naked and clothe you; sick or in prison and go to see you?" And the King will answer, "I tell you solemnly, in so far as you did this to one of the least of these brothers of mine, you did it to me."

'Next he will say to those on his left hand, "Go away from me, with your curse upon you, to the eternal fire prepared for the devil and his angels. For I was hungry and you never gave me food; I was thirsty and you never gave me anything to drink; I was a stranger and you never made me welcome, naked and you never clothed me, sick and in prison and you never visited me." Then it will be their turn to ask, "Lord, when did we see you hungry or thirsty, a stranger or naked, sick or in prison, and did not come to your help?" Then he will answer, "I tell you solemnly, in so far as you neglected to do this to one of the least of these, you neglected to do it to me."

And they will go away to eternal punishment, and the virtuous to eternal life.'

30

NOV WED

ST ANDREW, Solemnity

– Scotland

Wisdom 3:1-9

The souls of the virtuous are in the hands of God, no torment shall ever touch them. In the eyes of the unwise, they did appear to die, their going looked like a disaster, their leaving us, like annihilation; but they are in peace. If they experienced punishment as men see it, their hope was rich with immortality; slight was their affliction, great will their blessings be. God has put them to the test and proved them worthy to be with him; he has tested them like gold in a furnace, and accepted them as a holocaust. When the time comes for his visitation they will shine out; as sparks run through the stubble, so will they. They shall judge nations, rule over peoples, and the Lord will be their king for ever. They who trust in him will understand the truth, those who are faithful will live with him in love; for grace and mercy await those he has chosen.

Psalm 30:3-4,6,8,17,21

Into your hands, O Lord, I commend my spirit.

Romans 10:9-18

If your lips confess that Jesus is Lord and if you believe in your heart that God raised him from the dead, then you will be saved. By believing from the heart you are made righteous; by confessing with your lips you are saved. When scripture says: those who believe in him will have no cause for shame, it makes no distinction between Jew and Greek: all belong to the same Lord who is rich enough, however many ask his help, for everyone who calls on the name of the Lord will be saved.

But they will not ask his help unless they believe in him, and they will not believe in him unless they have heard of him, and they will not hear of him unless they get a preacher, and they will never have a preacher unless one is sent, but as scripture says: The footsteps of those who bring good news are a welcome sound. Not everyone, of course, listens to the Good News. As Isaiah says: Lord, how many believed what we proclaimed? So faith comes from what is preached, and what is preached comes from the word of Christ. Let me put the question: is it possible that they did not hear? Indeed they did; in the words of the psalm, their voice has gone out through all the earth, and their message to the ends of the world.

Matthew 4:18-22

As Jesus was walking by the Sea of Galilee, he saw two brothers, Simon, who was called Peter, and his brother Andrew; they were making a cast in the lake with their net, for they were fishermen. And he said to them, 'Follow me and I will make you fishers of men.' And they left their nets at once and followed him. Going on from there he saw another pair of brothers, James son of Zebedee and his brother John; they were in their boat with their father Zebedee, mending their nets, and he called them. At once, leaving the boat and their father, they followed him.

29
DEC THU

SAINT THOMAS BECKET, BISHOP, MARTYR, Feast
– England

Colossians 1:24-29

It makes me happy to suffer for you, as I am suffering now, and in my own body to do what I can to make up all that has still to be undergone by Christ for the sake of his body, the Church. I became the servant of the Church when God made me responsible for delivering God's message to you, the message which was a mystery hidden for generations and centuries and has now been revealed to his saints. It was God's purpose to reveal it to them and to show all the rich glory of this mystery to pagans. The mystery is Christ among you, your hope of glory: this is the Christ we proclaim, this is the wisdom in which we thoroughly train everyone and instruct everyone, to make them all perfect in Christ. It is for this I struggle wearily on, helped only by his power driving me irresistibly.

Psalm 22

The Lord is my shepherd: there is nothing I shall want.

Luke 22:24-30

A dispute arose between the disciples about which should be reckoned the greatest, but Jesus said to them:

'Among pagans it is the kings who lord it over them, and those who have authority over them are given the title Benefactor. This must not happen with you. No; the greatest among you must behave as if he were the youngest, the leader as if he were the one who serves. For who is the greater: the one at table or the one who serves? The one at table, surely? Yet here am I among you as one who serves!

'You are the men who have stood by me faithfully in my trials; and now I confer a kingdom on you, just as my Father conferred one on me: you will eat and drink at my table in my kingdom, and you will sit on thrones to judge the twelve tribes of Israel.'

January 14 Friday: 1st Week in Ordinary Time
1 Samuel 8:4-7, 10-22

... All that the Lord has said Samuel repeated to the people who were asking him for a king. He said, 'These will be the rights of the king who is to reign over you. He will take your sons and assign them to his chariotry and cavalry, and they will run in front of his chariot. He will use them as leaders of a thousand and leaders of fifty; he will make them plough his ploughland and harvest his harvest and make his weapons of war and the gear for his chariots. He will also take your daughters as perfumers, cooks and bakers. He will take the best of your fields, of your vineyards and olive groves and give them to his officials. He will tithe your crops and vineyards to provide for his eunuchs and his officials. He will take the best of your manservants and maidservants, of your cattle and your donkeys, and make them work for him. He will tithe your flocks, and you yourselves will become his slaves. When that day comes, you will cry out on account of the king you have chosen for yourselves, but on that day God will not answer you.'

The people refused to listen to the words of Samuel. They said, 'No! We want a king, so that we in our turn can be like the other nations; our king shall rule us and be our leader and fight our battles.' Samuel listened to all that the people had to say and repeated it in the ears of the Lord. The Lord then said to Samuel, 'Obey their voice and give them a king.'

January 18 Tuesday: 2nd Week in Ordinary Time
1 Samuel 16:1-13

... When they arrived, he caught sight of Eliab and thought, 'Surely the Lord's anointed one stands there before him,' but the Lord said to Samuel, 'Take no notice of his appearance or his height for I have rejected him; God does not see as man sees; man looks at appearances but the Lord looks at the heart.' Jesse then called Abinadab and presented him to Samuel, who said, 'The Lord has not chosen this one either'. Jesse then presented Shammah, but Samuel said, 'The Lord has not chosen this one either.' Jesse presented his seven sons to Samuel, but Samuel said to Jesse, 'The Lord has not chosen these.' He then asked Jesse, 'Are these all the sons you have?' He answered, 'There is still one left, the youngest; he is out looking after the sheep.' Then Samuel said to Jesse, 'Send for him; we will not sit down to eat until he comes.' Jesse had him sent for, a boy of fresh complexion, with fine eyes and pleasant bearing. The Lord said, 'Come, anoint him, for this is the one.' At this, Samuel took the horn of oil and anointed him where he stood with his brothers; and the spirit of the Lord seized on David and stayed with him from that day on. As for Samuel, he rose and went to Ramah.

January 19 Wednesday: 2nd Week in Ordinary Time
1 Samuel 17:32-33, 37, 40-51

... The Philistine said to David, 'Come over here and I will give your flesh to the birds of the air and the beasts of the field.' But David answered the Philistine, 'You come against me with sword and spear and javelin, but I come against you in the name of the Lord of hosts, the God of the armies of Israel that you have dared to insult. Today the Lord will deliver you into my hand and I shall kill you; I will cut off your head, and this very day I will give your dead body and the bodies of the Philistine army to the birds of the air and the wild beasts of the earth, so that all the earth may know that there is a God in Israel, and that all this assembly may know that it is not by sword or by spear that the Lord gives the victory, for he is lord of the battle and he will deliver you into our power.'

No sooner had the Philistine started forward to confront David than David left the line of battle and ran to meet the Philistine. Putting his hand in his bag, he took out a stone and slung it and struck the Philistine on the forehead; the stone penetrated his forehead and he fell on his face to the ground. Thus David triumphed over the Philistine with a sling and a stone and struck the Philistine down and killed him. David had no sword in his hand. Then David ran and, standing over the Philistine, seized his sword and drew it from the scabbard, and with this he killed him, cutting off his head. The Philistines saw that their champion was dead and took to flight.

January 21 Friday: 2nd Week in Ordinary Time
1 Samuel 24:3-21

... Why, your own eyes have seen today how the Lord put you in my power in the cave and how I refused to kill you, but spared you. "I will not raise my hand against my lord," I said, "for he is the anointed of the Lord." O my father, see, look at the border of your cloak in my hand. Since I cut off the border of your cloak, yet did not kill you, you must acknowledge frankly that there is neither malice nor treason in my mind. I have not offended against you, yet you hunt me down to take my life. May the Lord be judge between me and you, and may the Lord avenge me on you; but my hand shall not be laid on you. (As the old proverb says: Wickedness goes out from the wicked, and my hand will not be laid on you.) On whose trail has the king of Israel set out? On whose trail are you in hot pursuit? On the trail of a dead dog! On the trail of a single flea! May the Lord be the judge and decide between me and you; may he take up my cause and defend it and give judgement for me, freeing me from your power.'

When David had finished saying these words to Saul, Saul said, 'Is that your voice, my son David?' And Saul wept aloud. 'You are a more upright man than I,' he said to David 'for you have repaid me with good while I have repaid you with evil. Today you have crowned your goodness towards me since the Lord had put me in your power yet you did not kill me. When a man comes on his enemy, does he let him go unmolested? May the Lord reward you for the goodness you have shown me today. Now I know you will indeed reign and that the sovereignty in Israel will be secure in your hands.'

January 26 Wednesday: 3rd Week in Ordinary Time
2 Timothy 1:1-8

From Paul, appointed by God to be an apostle of Christ Jesus in his design to promise life in Christ Jesus; to Timothy, dear child of mine, wishing you grace, mercy and peace from God the Father and from Christ Jesus our Lord.

Night and day I thank God, keeping my conscience clear and remembering my duty to him as my ancestors did, and always I remember you in my prayers; I remember your tears and long to see you again to complete my happiness. Then I am reminded of the sincere faith which you have; it came first to live in your grandmother Lois, and your mother Eunice, and I have no doubt that it is the same faith in you as well.

That is why I am reminding you now to fan into a flame the gift that God gave you when I laid my hands on you. God's gift was not a spirit of timidity, but the Spirit of power, and love, and self-control. So you are never to be ashamed of witnessing to the Lord, or ashamed of me for being his prisoner; but with me, bear the hardships for the sake of the Good News, relying on the power of God who has saved us and called us to be holy.

January 28 Friday: 3rd Week in Ordinary Time
2 Samuel 11:1-10, 13-17

... Then David sent messengers and had her brought. She came to him, and he slept with her. She then went home again. The woman conceived and sent word to David, 'I am with child.' Then David sent Joab a message, 'Send me Uriah the Hittite,' whereupon Joab sent Uriah to David. When Uriah came into his presence, David asked after Joab and the army and how the war was going. David then said to Uriah, 'Go down to your house and enjoy yourself.' Uriah left the palace, and was followed by a present from the king's table. Uriah however slept by the palace door with his master's bodyguard and did not go down to his house.

This was reported to David 'Uriah' they said 'did not go down to his house.' The next day David invited him to eat and drink in his presence and made him drunk. In the evening Uriah went out and lay on his couch with his master's bodyguard, but he did not go down to his house. Next morning David wrote a letter to Joab and sent it by Uriah. In the letter he wrote, 'Station Uriah in the thick of the fight and then fall back behind him so that he may be struck down and die.' Joab, then besieging the town, posted Uriah in a place where he knew there were fierce fighters. The men of the town sallied out and engaged Joab; the army suffered casualties, including some of David's bodyguard; and Uriah the Hittite was killed too.

January 29 Saturday: 3rd Week in Ordinary Time
2 Samuel 12:1-7, 10-17

... Then Nathan said to David, 'You are the man. So now the sword will never be far from your House, since you have shown contempt for me and taken the wife of Uriah the Hittite to be your wife. 'Thus the Lord speaks, "I will stir up evil for you out of your own House. Before your very eyes I will take your wives and give them to your neighbour, and he shall lie with your wives in the sight of this sun. You worked in secret, I will work this in the face of all Israel and in the face of the sun."'

David said to Nathan, 'I have sinned against the Lord.' Then Nathan said to David, 'The Lord, for his part, forgives your sin; you are not to die. Yet because you have outraged the Lord by doing this, the child that is born to you is to die.' Then Nathan went home. The Lord struck the child that Uriah's wife had borne to David and it fell gravely ill. David pleaded with the Lord for the child; he kept a strict fast and went home and spent the night on the bare ground, covered with sacking. The officials of his household came and stood round him to get him to rise from the ground, but he refused, nor would he take food with them.

January 31 Monday: 4th Week in Ordinary Time
2 Samuel 15:13-14, 30; 16:5-13

A messenger came to tell David, 'The hearts of the men of Israel are now with Absalom.' So David said to all his officers who were with him in Jerusalem, 'Let us be off, let us fly, or we shall never escape from Absalom. Leave as quickly as you can in case he mounts a surprise attack and worsts us and puts the city to the sword.' David then made his way up the Mount of Olives, weeping as he went, his head covered and his feet bare. And all the people with him had their heads covered and made their way up, weeping as they went.

As David was reaching Bahurim, out came a man of the same clan as Saul's family. His name was Shimei son of Gera, and as he came he uttered curse after curse and threw stones at David and at all King David's officers, though the whole army and all the champions flanked the king right and left. The words of his curse were these, 'Be off, be off, man of blood, scoundrel! The Lord has brought on you all the blood of the

House of Saul whose sovereignty you have usurped; and the Lord has transferred that same sovereignty to Absalom your son. Now your doom has overtaken you, man of blood that you are.' Abishai son of Zeruiah said to the king, 'Is this dead dog to curse my lord the king? Let me go over and cut his head off.' But the king replied, 'What business is it of mine and yours, son of Zeruiah? Let him curse. If the Lord said to him, "Curse David," what right has anyone to say, "Why have you done this?"' David said to Abishai and all his officers, 'Why, my own son, sprung from my body, is now seeking my life; so now how much the more this Benjaminite? Let him curse on if the Lord has told him to. Perhaps the Lord will look on my misery and repay me with good for his curse today.' So David and his men went on their way.

February 1 Tuesday: 4th Week in Ordinary Time
2 Samuel 18:9-10, 14, 24-25, 30–19:3

Absalom happened to run into some of David's followers. Absalom was riding a mule and the mule passed under the thick branches of a great oak. Absalom's head caught fast in the oak and he was left hanging between heaven and earth, while the mule he was riding went on. Someone saw this and told Joab. 'I have just seen Absalom' he said 'hanging from an oak.' And Joab took three lances in his hand and thrust them into Absalom's heart while he was still alive there in the oak tree.

David was sitting between the two gates. The look-out had gone up to the roof of the gate, on the ramparts; he looked up and saw a man running all by himself. The watch called out to the king and told him. The king said, 'Move aside and stand there.' He moved aside and stood waiting.

Then the Cushite arrived. 'Good news for my lord the king!' cried the Cushite. 'The Lord has vindicated your cause today by ridding you of all who rebelled against you.' 'Is all well with young Absalom?' the king asked the Cushite. 'May the enemies of my Lord the King' the Cushite answered 'and all who rebelled against you to your hurt, share the lot of that young man.'

The king shuddered. He went up to the room over the gate and burst into tears, and weeping said, 'My son Absalom! My son! My son Absalom! Would I had died in your place! Absalom, my son, my son!' Word was brought to Joab, 'The king is now weeping and mourning for Absalom.' And the day's victory was turned to mourning for all the troops, because they learned that the king was grieving for his son. And the troops returned stealthily that day to the town, as troops creep back ashamed when routed in battle.

February 4 Friday: 4th Week in Ordinary Time
Sirach 47:2-11

As the fat is set apart from the communion sacrifice, so David was chosen out of all the sons of Israel. He played with lions as though with kids, and with bears as though with lambs of the flock. While still a boy, did he not slay the giant, and relieve the people of their shame, by putting out a hand to sling a stone which brought down the arrogance of Goliath? For he called on the Lord Most High, who gave strength to his right arm to put a mighty warrior to death, and lift up the horn of his people. Hence they gave him credit for ten thousand, and praised him while they blessed the Lord, by offering him a crown of glory; for he massacred enemies on every side, he annihilated his foes the Philistines, and crushed their horn to this very day. In all his activities he gave thanks to the Holy One, the Most High, in words of glory; he put all his heart into his songs out of love for his Maker. He placed harps before the altar to make the singing sweeter with their music; he gave the feasts their splendour, the festivals their solemn pomp, causing the Lord's holy name to be praised and the sanctuary to resound from dawn. The Lord took away his sins, and exalted his horn for ever; he gave him a royal covenant, and a glorious throne in Israel.

February 8 Tuesday: 5th Week in Ordinary Time
1 Kings 8:22-23, 27-30

In the presence of the whole assembly of Israel, Solomon stood before the altar of the Lord and, stretching out his hands towards heaven, said, 'Lord God of Israel, not in heaven above nor on earth beneath is there such a God as you, true to your covenant and your kindness towards your servants when they walk wholeheartedly in your way. Yet will God really live with men on the earth? Why, the heavens and their own heavens cannot contain you. How much less this house that I have built! Listen to the prayer and entreaty of your servant, Lord my God; listen to the cry and to the prayer your servant makes to you today. Day and night let your eyes watch over this house, over this place of which you have said, "My name shall be there." Listen to the prayer that your servant will offer in this place.

'Hear the entreaty of your servant and of Israel your people as they pray in this place. From heaven where your dwelling is, hear; and as you hear, forgive.'

February 18 Friday: 6th Week in Ordinary Time
James 2:14-24, 26

... Do realise, you senseless man, that faith without good deeds is useless. You surely know that Abraham our father was justified by his deed, because he offered his son Isaac on the altar? There you see it: faith and deeds were working together; his faith became perfect by what he did. This is what scripture really means when it says: Abraham put his faith in God, and this was counted as making him justified; and that is why he was called 'the friend of God.'

You see now that it is by doing something good, and not only by believing, that a man is justified. A body dies when it is separated from the spirit, and in the same way faith is dead if it is separated from good deeds.

February 21 Monday: 7th Week in Ordinary Time
James 3:13-18

If there are any wise or learned men among you, let them show it by their good lives, with humility and wisdom in their actions. But if at heart you have the bitterness of jealousy, or a self-seeking ambition, never make any claims for yourself or cover up the truth with lies – principles of this kind are not the wisdom that comes down from above: they are only earthly, animal and devilish. Wherever you find jealousy and ambition, you find disharmony, and wicked things of every kind being done; whereas the wisdom that comes down from above is essentially something pure; it also makes for peace, and is kindly and considerate; it is full of compassion and shows itself by doing good; nor is there any trace of partiality or hypocrisy in it. Peacemakers, when they work for peace, sow the seeds which will bear fruit in holiness.

March 2 Wednesday: Ash Wednesday
Joel 2:12-18

'Now, now – it is the Lord who speaks – come back to me with all your heart, fasting, weeping, mourning.' Let your hearts be broken not your garments torn, turn to the Lord your God again, for he is all tenderness and compassion, slow to anger, rich in graciousness, and ready to relent. Who knows if he will not turn again, will not relent, will not leave a blessing as he passes, oblation and libation for the Lord your God? Sound the trumpet in Zion! Order a fast, proclaim a solemn assembly, call the people together, summon the community, assemble the elders, gather the children, even the infants at the breast. Let the bridegroom leave his bedroom and the bride her alcove. Between vestibule and altar let the priests, the ministers of the Lord, lament. Let them say, 'Spare your people, Lord! Do not make your heritage a thing of shame, a byword for the nations. Why should it be said among the nations, "Where is their God?"' Then the Lord, jealous on behalf of his land, took pity on his people.

March 7 Monday: 1st Week of Lent
Leviticus 19:1-2, 11-18

The Lord spoke to Moses; he said: 'Speak to the whole community of the sons of Israel and say to them: "Be holy, for I, the Lord your God, am holy.

"You must not steal nor deal deceitfully or fraudulently with your neighbour. You must not swear falsely by my name, profaning the name of your God. I am the Lord. You must not exploit or rob your neighbour. You must not keep back the labourer's wage until next morning. You must not curse the dumb, nor put an obstacle in the blind man's way, but you must fear your God. I am the Lord.

"You must not be guilty of unjust verdicts. You must neither be partial to the little man nor overawed by the great; you must pass judgement on your neighbour according to justice. You must not slander your own people, and you must not jeopardise your neighbour's life. I am the Lord. You must not bear hatred for your brother in your heart. You must openly tell him, your neighbour, of his offence; this way you will not take a sin upon yourself. You must not exact vengeance, nor must you bear a grudge against the children of your people. You must love your neighbour as yourself. I am the Lord."'

March 17 Thursday: St Patrick, Patron of Ireland
Jeremiah 1:4-9

The word of the Lord was addressed to me, saying: 'Before I formed you in the womb I knew you; before you came to birth I consecrated you; I have appointed you as prophet to the nations.' I said, 'Ah, Lord; look, I do not know how to speak: I am a child!' But the Lord replied, 'Do not say, "I am a child." Go now to those to whom I send you and say whatever I command you. Do not be afraid of them for I am with you to protect you – it is the Lord who speaks!'

Then the Lord put out his hand and touched my mouth and said to me: 'There! I am putting my words into your mouth.'

March 18 Friday: 2nd Week of Lent
Genesis 37:3-4, 12-13, 17-28

Israel loved Joseph more than all his other sons, for he was the son of his old age, and he had a coat with long sleeves made for him. But his brothers, seeing how his father loved him more than all his other sons, came to hate him so much that they could not say a civil word to him.

His brothers went to pasture their father's flock at Shechem. Then Israel said to Joseph, 'Are not your brothers with the flock at Shechem? Come, I am going to send you to them.' So Joseph went after his brothers and found them at Dothan.

They saw him in the distance, and before he reached them they made a plot among themselves to put him to death. 'Here comes the man of dreams' they said to one another. 'Come on, let us kill him and throw him into some well; we can say that a wild beast devoured him. Then we shall see what becomes of his dreams.'

But Reuben heard, and he saved him from their violence. 'We must not take his life' he said. 'Shed no blood,' said Reuben to them 'throw him into this well in the wilderness, but do not lay violent hands on him' – intending to save him from them and to restore him to his father. So, when Joseph reached his brothers, they pulled off his coat, the coat with long sleeves that he was wearing, and catching hold of him they threw him into the well, an empty well with no water in it. They then sat down to eat.

Looking up they saw a group of Ishmaelites who were coming from Gilead, their camels laden with gum, tragacanth, balsam and resin, which they were taking down into Egypt. Then Judah said to his brothers, 'What do we gain by killing our brother and covering up his blood? Come, let us sell him to the Ishmaelites, but let us not do any harm to him. After all, he is our brother, and our own flesh.' His brothers agreed.

Now some Midianite merchants were passing, and they drew Joseph up out of the well. They sold Joseph to the Ishmaelites for twenty silver pieces, and these men took Joseph to Egypt.

March 21 Monday: 3rd Week of Lent
2 Kings 5:1-15

... 'Am I a god to give death and life,' he said 'that he sends a man to me and asks me to cure him of his leprosy? Listen to this, and take note of it and see how he intends to pick a quarrel with me.'

When Elisha heard that the king of Israel had torn his garments he sent word to the king, 'Why did you tear your garments? Let him come to me, and he will find there is a prophet in Israel.' So Naaman came with his team and chariot and drew up at the door of Elisha's house. And Elisha sent him a messenger to say, 'Go and bathe seven times in the Jordan, and your flesh will become clean once more.' But Naaman was indignant and went off, saying, 'Here was I thinking he would be sure to come out to me, and stand there, and call on the name of the Lord his God, and wave his hand over the spot and cure the leprous part. Surely Abana and Pharpar, the rivers of Damascus, are better than any water in Israel? Could I not bathe in them and become clean?' And he turned round and went off in a rage. But his servants approached him and said, 'My father, if the prophet had asked you to do something difficult, would you not have done it? All the more reason, then, when he says to you, "Bathe, and you will become clean."' So he went down and immersed himself seven times in the Jordan, as Elisha had told him to do. And his flesh became clean once more like the flesh of a little child.

Returning to Elisha with his whole escort, he went in and stood before him. 'Now I know' he said 'that there is no God in all the earth except in Israel.'

March 22 Tuesday: 3rd Week of Lent
Daniel 3:25. 34-43

Azariah stood in the heart of the fire, and he began to pray: Oh! Do not abandon us for ever, for the sake of your name; do not repudiate your covenant, do not withdraw your favour from us, for the sake of Abraham, your friend, of Isaac your servant, and of Israel your holy one, to whom you promised descendants as countless as the stars of heaven and as the grains of sand on the seashore. Lord, now we are the least of all the nations, now we are despised throughout the world, today because of our sins. We have at this time no leader, no prophet, no prince, no holocaust, no sacrifice, no oblation, no incense, no place where we can offer you the first-fruits and win your favour. But may the contrite soul, the humbled spirit be as acceptable to you as holocausts of rams and bullocks, as thousands of fattened lambs: such let our sacrifice be to you today, and may it be your will that we follow you wholeheartedly, since those who put their trust in you will not be disappointed. And now we put our whole heart into following you, into fearing you and seeking your face once more. Do not disappoint us: treat us gently, as you yourself are gentle and very merciful. Grant us deliverance worthy of your wonderful deeds, let your name win glory, Lord.

March 25 Friday: The Annunciation of the Lord
Isaiah 7:10-14; 8:10

The Lord spoke to Ahaz and said, 'Ask the Lord your God for a sign for yourself coming either from the depths of Sheol or from the heights above.' 'No,' Ahaz answered 'I will not put the Lord to the test.' Then Isaiah said: 'Listen now, House of David: are you not satisfied with trying the patience of men without trying the patience of God, too? The Lord himself, therefore, will give you a sign. It is this: the maiden is with child and will soon give birth to a son whom she will call Emmanuel, a name which means "God-is-with-us".'

March 29 Tuesday: 4th Week of Lent
Ezekiel 47:1-9, 12

… He measured off another thousand and made me wade across the stream again; the water reached my knees. He measured off another thousand and made me wade across again; the water reached my waist. He measured off another thousand; it was now a river which I could not cross; the stream had swollen and was now deep water, a river impossible to cross. He then said, 'Do you see, son of man?' He took me further, then brought me back to the bank of the river. When I got back, there were many trees on each bank of the river. He said, 'This water flows east down to the Arabah and to the sea; and flowing into the sea it makes its waters wholesome. Whenever the river flows, all living creatures teeming in it will live. Fish will be very plentiful, for wherever the water goes it brings health, and life teems wherever the river flows. Along the river, on either bank, will grow every kind of fruit tree with leaves that never wither and fruit that never fails; they will bear new fruit every month, because this water comes from the sanctuary. And their fruit will be good to eat and the leaves medicinal.'

March 30 Wednesday: 4th Week of Lent
Isaiah 49:8-15

Thus says the Lord: At the favourable time I will answer you, on the day of salvation I will help you. (I have formed you and have appointed you as covenant of the people.) I will restore the land and assign you the estates that lie waste. I will say to the prisoners, 'Come out', to those who are in darkness, 'Show yourselves'.

On every roadway they will graze, and each bare height shall be their pasture. They will never hunger or thirst, scorching wind and sun shall never plague them; for he who pities them will lead them and guide them to springs of water. I will make a highway of all the mountains and the high roads shall be banked up. Some are on their way from afar, others from the north and the west, others from the land of Sinim. Shout for joy, you heavens; exult, you earth! You mountains, break into happy cries! For the Lord consoles his people and takes pity on those who are afflicted.

For Zion was saying, 'The Lord has abandoned me, the Lord has forgotten me.' Does a woman forget her baby at the breast or fail to cherish the son of her womb? Yet even if these forget, I will never forget you.

March 31 Thursday: 4th Week of Lent
Exodus 32:7-14
... But Moses pleaded with the Lord his God. 'Lord,' he said 'why should your wrath blaze out against this people of yours whom you brought out of the land of Egypt with arm outstretched and mighty hand? Why let the Egyptians say, "Ah, it was in treachery that he brought them out, to do them to death in the mountains and wipe them off the face of the earth"? Leave your burning wrath; relent and do not bring this disaster on your people. Remember Abraham, Isaac and Jacob, your servants to whom by your own self you swore and made this promise: I will make your offspring as many as the stars of heaven, and all this land which I promised I will give to your descendants, and it shall be their heritage for ever.' So the Lord relented and did not bring on his people the disaster he had threatened.

April 4 Monday: 5th Week of Lent
Daniel 13:41-62
... All the people hurried back, and the elders said to Daniel, 'Come and sit with us and tell us what you mean, since God has given you the gifts that elders have.' Daniel said, 'Keep the men well apart from each other for I want to question them.' When the men had been separated, Daniel had one of them brought to him. 'You have grown old in wickedness,' he said 'and now the sins of your earlier days have overtaken you, you with your unjust judgements, your condemnation of the innocent, your acquittal of guilty men, when the Lord has said, "You must not put the innocent and the just to death." Now then, since you saw her so clearly, tell me what tree you saw them lying under?' He replied, 'Under a mastic tree.' Daniel said, 'True enough! Your lie recoils on your own head: the angel of God has already received your sentence from him and will slash you in half.' He dismissed the man, ordered the other to be brought and said to him, 'Spawn of Canaan, not of Judah, beauty has seduced you, lust has led your heart astray! This is how you have been behaving with the daughters of Israel and they were too frightened to resist; but here is a daughter of Judah who could not stomach your wickedness! Now then, tell me what tree you surprised them under?' He replied, 'Under a holm oak.' Daniel said, 'True enough! Your lie recoils on your own head: the angel of God is waiting, with a sword to drive home and split you, and destroy the pair of you.'

Then the whole assembly shouted, blessing God, the saviour of those who trust in him. And they turned on the two elders whom Daniel had convicted of false evidence out of their own mouths. As prescribed in the Law of Moses, they sentenced them to the same punishment as they had intended to inflict on their neighbour. They put them to death; the life of an innocent woman was spared that day.

April 6 Wednesday: 5th Week of Lent
Daniel 3:14-20, 24-25, 28
... Shadrach, Meshach and Abednego replied to King Nebuchadnezzar, 'Your question hardly requires an answer: if our God, the one we serve, is able to save us from the burning fiery furnace and from your power, O king, he will save us; and even if he does not, then you must know, O king, that we will not serve your god or worship the statue you have erected.' These words infuriated King Nebuchadnezzar; his expression was very different now as he looked at Shadrach, Meshach and Abednego. He gave

orders for the furnace to be made seven times hotter than usual, and commanded certain stalwarts from his army to bind Shadrach, Meshach and Abednego and throw them into the burning fiery furnace.

Then King Nebuchadnezzar sprang to his feet in amazement. He said to his advisers, 'Did we not have these three men thrown bound into the fire?' They replied, 'Certainly, O king.' 'But,' he went on 'I can see four men walking about freely in the heart of the fire without coming to any harm. And the fourth looks like a son of the gods.'

Nebuchadnezzar exclaimed, 'Blessed be the God of Shadrach, Meshach and Abednego: he has sent his angel to rescue his servants who, putting their trust in him, defied the order of the king, and preferred to forfeit their bodies rather than serve or worship any god but their own.'

April 12 Tuesday: Tuesday of Holy Week
Isaiah 49:1-6

... and all the while my cause was with the Lord, my reward with my God. I was honoured in the eyes of the Lord, my God was my strength. And now the Lord has spoken, he who formed me in the womb to be his servant, to bring Jacob back to him, to gather Israel to him: 'It is not enough for you to be my servant, to restore the tribes of Jacob and bring back the survivors of Israel; I will make you the light of the nations so that my salvation may reach to the ends of the earth.'

April 14 Thusday: Holy Thursday
Exodus 12:1-8, 11-14

The Lord said to Moses and Aaron in the land of Egypt, 'This month is to be the first of all the others for you, the first month of your year. Speak to the whole community of Israel and say, "On the tenth day of this month each man must take an animal from the flock, one for each family: one animal for each household. If the household is too small to eat the animal, a man must join with his neighbour, the nearest to his house, as the number of persons requires. You must take into account what each can eat in deciding the number for the animal. It must be an animal without blemish, a male one year old; you may take it from either sheep or goats. You must keep it till the fourteenth day of the month when the whole assembly of the community of Israel shall slaughter it between the two evenings. Some of the blood must then be taken and put on the two doorposts and the lintel of the houses where it is eaten. That night, the flesh is to be eaten, roasted over the fire; it must be eaten with unleavened bread and bitter herbs. You shall eat it like this: with a girdle round your waist, sandals on your feet, a staff in your hand. You shall eat it hastily: it is a passover in honour of the Lord. That night, I will go through the land of Egypt and strike down all the first-born in the land of Egypt, man and beast alike, and I shall deal out punishment to all the gods of Egypt, I am the Lord. The blood shall serve to mark the houses that you live in. When I see the blood I will pass over you and you shall escape the destroying plague when I strike the land of Egypt. This day is to be a day of remembrance for you, and you must celebrate it as a feast in the Lord's honour. For all generations you are to declare it a day of festival, for ever."'

April 15 Friday: Good Friday
Isaiah 52:13–53:12

... But we, we thought of him as someone punished, struck by God, and brought low. Yet he was pierced through for our faults, crushed for our sins. On him lies a punishment that brings us peace, and through his wounds we are healed. We had all gone astray like sheep, each taking his own way, and the Lord burdened him with the sins of all of us. Harshly dealt with, he bore it humbly, he never opened his mouth, like a lamb that is led to the slaughter-house, like a sheep that is dumb before its shearers never opening its mouth. By force and by law he was taken; would anyone plead his cause? Yes, he was torn away from the land of the living; for our faults struck down in death. They gave him a grave with the wicked, a tomb with the rich, though he had done no wrong and there had been no perjury in his mouth. The Lord has been pleased to crush him with suffering. If he offers his life in atonement, he shall see his heirs, he shall have a long life and through him what the Lord wishes will be done. His soul's anguish over he shall see the light and be content. By his sufferings shall my servant justify many, taking their faults on himself. Hence I will grant whole hordes for his tribute, he shall divide the spoil with the mighty, for surrendering himself to death and letting himself be taken for a sinner, while he was bearing the faults of many and praying all the time for sinners.

April 18 Monday: Easter Monday
Acts 2:14, 22-33

... You have made known the way of life to me, you will fill me with gladness through your presence. Brothers, no one can deny that the patriarch David himself is dead and buried: his tomb is still with us. But since he was a prophet, and knew that God had sworn him an oath to make one of his descendants succeed him on the throne, what he foresaw and spoke about was the resurrection of the Christ: he is the one who was not abandoned to Hades, and whose body did not experience corruption. God raised this man Jesus to life, and all of us are witnesses to that. Now raised to the heights by God's right hand, he has received from the Father the Holy Spirit, who was promised, and what you see and hear is the outpouring of that Spirit.'

April 20 Wednesday: Easter Wednesday
Acts 3:1-10

Once, when Peter and John were going up to the Temple for the prayers at the ninth hour, it happened that there was a man being carried past. He was a cripple from birth; and they used to put him down every day near the Temple entrance called the Beautiful Gate so that he could beg from the people going in. When this man saw Peter and John on their way into the Temple he begged from them. Both Peter and John looked straight at him and said, 'Look at us.' He turned to them expectantly, hoping to get something from them, but Peter said, 'I have neither silver nor gold, but I will give you what I have: in the name of Jesus Christ the Nazarene, walk!' Peter then took him by the hand and helped him to stand up. Instantly his feet and ankles became firm, he jumped up, stood, and began to walk, and he went with them into the Temple, walking and jumping and praising God. Everyone could see him walking and praising God, and they recognised him as the man who used to sit begging at the Beautiful Gate of the Temple. They were all astonished and unable to explain what had happened to him.

April 21 Thursday: Easter Thursday
Acts 3:11-2

... 'It was you who accused the Holy One, the Just One, you who demanded the reprieve of a murderer while you killed the prince of life. God, however, raised him from the dead, and to that fact we are the witnesses; and it is the name of Jesus which, through our faith in it, has brought back the strength of this man whom you see here and who is well known to you. It is faith in that name that has restored this man to health, as you can all see.

'Now I know, brothers, that neither you nor your leaders had any idea what you were really doing; this was the way God carried out what he had foretold, when he said through all his prophets that Christ would suffer. Now you must repent and turn to God, so that your sins may be wiped out, and so that the Lord may send the time of comfort. Then he will send you the Christ he has predestined, that is Jesus, whom heaven must keep till the universal restoration comes which God proclaimed, speaking through his holy prophets. Moses, for example, said: The Lord God will raise up a prophet like myself for you, from among your own brothers; you must listen to whatever he tells you. The man who does not listen to that prophet is to be cut off from the people. In fact, all the prophets that have ever spoken, from Samuel onwards, have predicted these days.

'You are the heirs of the prophets, the heirs of the covenant God made with our ancestors when he told Abraham: in your offspring all the families of the earth will be blessed. It was for you in the first place that God raised up his servant and sent him to bless you by turning every one of you from your wicked ways.'

April 22 Friday: Easter Friday
Acts 4:1-12

While Peter and John were talking to the people the priests came up to him, accompanied by the captain of the Temple and the Sadducees. They were extremely annoyed at their teaching the people the doctrine of the resurrection from the dead by proclaiming the resurrection of Jesus. They arrested them, but as it was already late, they held them till the next day. But many of those who had listened to their message became believers, the total number of whom had now risen to something like five thousand.

The next day the rulers, elders and scribes had a meeting in Jerusalem with Annas the high priest, Caiaphas, Jonathan, Alexander and all the members of the high-priestly families. They made the prisoners stand in the middle and began to interrogate them, 'By what power, and by whose name have you men done this?' Then Peter, filled with the Holy Spirit, addressed them, 'Rulers of the people, and elders! If you are questioning us today about an act of kindness to a cripple, and asking us how he was healed, then I am glad to tell you all, and would indeed be glad to tell the whole people of Israel, that it was by the name of Jesus Christ the Nazarene, the one you crucified, whom God raised from the dead, by this name and by no other that this man is able to stand up perfectly healthy, here in your presence today. This is the stone rejected by you the builders, but which has proved to be the keystone. For of all the names in the world given to men, this is the only one by which we can be saved.'

May 5 Thursday: 3rd Week of Easter
Acts 8:26-40

… Further along the road they came to some water, and the eunuch said, 'Look, there is some water here; is there anything to stop me being baptised?' He ordered the chariot to stop, then Philip and the eunuch both went down to the water and Philip baptised him. But after they had come up out of the water again Philip was taken away by the Spirit of the Lord, and the eunuch never saw him again but went on his way rejoicing. Philip found that he had reached Azotus and continued his journey proclaiming the Good News in every town as far as Caesarea.

May 6 Friday: 3rd Week of Easter
Acts 9:1-20

… A disciple called Ananias who lived in Damascus had a vision in which he heard the Lord say to him, 'Ananias!' When he replied, 'Here I am, Lord,' the Lord said, 'You must go to Straight Street and ask at the house of Judas for someone called Saul, who comes from Tarsus. At this moment he is praying, having had a vision of a man called Ananias coming in and laying hands on him to give him back his sight.'

When he heard that, Ananias said, 'Lord, several people have told me about this man and all the harm he has been doing to your saints in Jerusalem. He has only come here because he holds a warrant from the chief priests to arrest everybody who invokes your name.' The Lord replied, 'You must go all the same, because this man is my chosen instrument to bring my name before pagans and pagan kings and before the people of Israel; I myself will show him how much he himself must suffer for my name.' Then Ananias went. He entered the house, and at once laid his hands on Saul and said, 'Brother Saul, I have been sent by the Lord Jesus who appeared to you on your way here so that you may recover your sight and be filled with the Holy Spirit.' Immediately it was as though scales fell away from Saul's eyes and he could see again. So he was baptised there and then, and after taking some food he regained his strength.

After he had spent only a few days with the disciples in Damascus, he began preaching in the synagogues, 'Jesus is the Son of God.'

May 7 Saturday: 3rd Week of Easter
Acts 9:31-42

… At Jaffa there was a woman disciple called Tabitha, or Dorcas in Greek, who never tired of doing good or giving in charity. But the time came when she got ill and died, and they washed her and laid her out in a room upstairs. Lydda is not far from Jaffa, so when the disciples heard that Peter was there, they sent two men with an urgent message for him, 'Come and visit us as soon as possible.'

Peter went back with them straightaway, and on his arrival they took him to the upstairs room, where all the widows stood round him in tears, showing him tunics and other clothes Dorcas had made when she was with them. Peter sent them all out of the room and knelt down and prayed. Then he turned to the dead woman and said, 'Tabitha, stand up.' She opened her eyes, looked at Peter and sat up. Peter helped her to her feet, then he called in the saints and widows and showed them she was alive. The whole of Jaffa heard about it and many believed in the Lord.

May 9 Monday: 4th Week of Easter
Acts 11:1-18

… 'Just at that moment, three men stopped outside the house where we were staying; they had been sent from Caesarea to fetch me, and the Spirit told me to have no hesitation about going back with them. The six brothers here came with me as well, and we entered the man's house. He told us he had seen an angel standing in his house who said, "Send to Jaffa and fetch Simon known as Peter; he has a message for you that will save you and your entire household."

'I had scarcely begun to speak when the Holy Spirit came down on them in the same way as it came on us at the beginning, and I remembered that the Lord had said, "John baptised with water, but you will be baptised with the Holy Spirit." I realised then that

God was giving them the identical thing he gave to us when we believed in the Lord Jesus Christ; and who was I to stand in God's way?'

This account satisfied them, and they gave glory to God. 'God' they said 'can evidently grant even the pagans the repentance that leads to life.'

May 16 Monday: 5th Week of Easter
Acts 14:5-18
… When the crowd saw what Paul had done they shouted in the language of Lycaonia, 'These people are gods who have come down to us disguised as men.' They addressed Barnabas as Zeus, and since Paul was the principal speaker they called him Hermes. The priests of Zeus-outside-the-Gate, proposing that all the people should offer sacrifice with them, brought garlanded oxen to the gates. When the apostles Barnabas and Paul heard what was happening they tore their clothes, and rushed into the crowd shouting, 'Friends, what do you think you are doing? We are only human beings like you. We have come with good news to make you turn from these empty idols to the living God who made heaven and earth and the sea and all that these hold. In the past he allowed each nation to go its own way; but even then he did not leave you without evidence of himself in the good things he does for you: he sends you rain from heaven, he makes your crops grow when they should, he gives you food and makes you happy.' Even this speech, however, was scarcely enough to stop the crowd offering them sacrifice.

May 25 Wednesday: 6th Week of Easter
Acts 17:15, 22–18:1
… 'Since we are the children of God, we have no excuse for thinking that the deity looks like anything in gold, silver or stone that has been carved and designed by a man.

'God overlooked that sort of thing when men were ignorant, but now he is telling everyone everywhere that they must repent, because he has fixed a day when the whole world will be judged, and judged in righteousness, and he has appointed a man to be the judge. And God has publicly proved this by raising this man from the dead.'

At this mention of rising from the dead, some of them burst out laughing; others said, 'We would like to hear you talk about this again.' After that Paul left them, but there were some who attached themselves to him and became believers, among them Dionysius the Areopagite and a woman called Damaris, and others besides. After this Paul left Athens and went to Corinth.

June 1 Wednesday: 7th Week of Easter
Acts 20:28-38
… 'I have never asked anyone for money or clothes; you know for yourselves that the work I did earned enough to meet my needs and those of my companions. I did this to show you that is how we must exert ourselves to support the weak, remembering the words of the Lord Jesus, who himself said, "There is more happiness in giving than in receiving."'

When he had finished speaking he knelt down with them all and prayed. By now they were all in tears; they put their arms round Paul's neck and kissed him; what saddened them most was his saying they would never see his face again. Then they escorted him to the ship.

June 2 Thursday: 7th Week of Easter
Acts 22:30; 23:6-11

… As soon as he said this a dispute broke out between the Pharisees and Sadducees, and the assembly was split between the two parties. For the Sadducees say there is neither resurrection, nor angel, nor spirit, while the Pharisees accept all three. The shouting grew louder, and some of the scribes from the Pharisees' party stood up and protested strongly, 'We find nothing wrong with this man. Suppose a spirit has spoken to him, or an angel?' Feeling was running high, and the tribune, afraid that they would tear Paul to pieces, ordered his troops to go down and haul him out and bring him into the fortress.

Next night, the Lord appeared to him and said, 'Courage! You have borne witness for me in Jerusalem, now you must do the same in Rome.'

June 8 Wednesday: 10th Week in Ordinary Time
1 Kings 18:20-39

… 'Call louder,' he said 'for he is a god: he is preoccupied or he is busy, or he has gone on a journey; perhaps he is asleep and will wake up.' So they shouted louder and gashed themselves, as their custom was, with swords and spears until the blood flowed down them. Midday passed, and they ranted on until the time the offering is presented; but there was no voice, no answer, no attention given to them.

Then Elijah said to all the people, 'Come closer to me,' and all the people came closer to him. He repaired the altar of the Lord which had been broken down. Elijah took twelve stones, corresponding to the number of the tribes of the sons of Jacob, to whom the word of the Lord had come, 'Israel shall be your name,' and built an altar in the name of the Lord. Round the altar he dug a trench of a size to hold two measures of seed. He then arranged the wood, dismembered the bull, and laid it on the wood. Then he said, 'Fill four jars with water and pour it on the holocaust and on the wood'; this they did. He said, 'Do it a second time'; they did it a second time. He said, 'Do it a third time'; they did it a third time. The water flowed round the altar and the trench itself was full of water. At the time when the offering is presented, Elijah the prophet stepped forward, 'Lord, God of Abraham, Isaac and Israel,' he said 'let them know today that you are God in Israel, and that I am your servant, that I have done all these things at your command. Answer me, Lord, answer me, so that this people may know that you, Lord, are God and are winning back their hearts.'

Then the fire of the Lord fell and consumed the holocaust and wood and licked up the water in the trench. When all the people saw this they fell on their faces. 'The Lord is God,' they cried 'the Lord is God.'

June 13 Monday: 11th Week in Ordinary Time
1 Kings 21:1-16

… So she wrote letters in Ahab's name and sealed them with his seal, sending them to the elders and nobles who lived where Naboth lived. In the letters she wrote, 'Proclaim a fast, and put Naboth in the forefront of the people. Confront him with a couple of scoundrels who will accuse him like this, "You have cursed God and the king." Then take him outside and stone him to death.'

The men of Naboth's town, the elders and nobles who lived in his town, did what Jezebel ordered, what was written in the letters she had sent them. They proclaimed a fast and put Naboth in the forefront of the people. Then the two scoundrels came and stood in front of him and made their accusation, 'Naboth has cursed God and the king.' They led him outside the town and stoned him to death. They then sent word to Jezebel, 'Naboth has been stoned to death.' When Jezebel heard that Naboth had been stoned to death, she said to Ahab, 'Get up! Take possession of the vineyard which Naboth of Jezreel would not give you for money, for Naboth is no longer alive, he is dead.' When Ahab heard that Naboth was dead, he got up to go down to the vineyard of Naboth of Jezreel and take possession of it.

June 14 Tuesday: 11th Week in Ordinary Time
1 Kings 21:17-29

... And indeed there never was anyone like Ahab for double dealing and for doing what is displeasing to the Lord, urged on by Jezebel his wife. He behaved in the most abominable way, adhering to idols, just as the Amorites used to do whom the Lord had dispossessed for the sons of Israel.

When Ahab heard these words, he tore his garments and put sackcloth next his skin and fasted; he slept in the sackcloth; he walked with slow steps. Then the word of the Lord came to Elijah the Tishbite, 'Have you seen how Ahab has humbled himself before me? Since he has humbled himself before me, I will not bring the disaster in his days; I will bring the disaster down on his House in the days of his son.'

June 15 Wednesday: 11th Week in Ordinary Time
2 Kings 2:1, 6-14

... Fifty of the brotherhood of prophets followed them, halting some distance away as the two of them stood beside the Jordan. Elijah took his cloak, rolled it up and struck the water; and the water divided to left and right, and the two of them crossed over dry-shod. When they had crossed, Elijah said to Elisha, 'Make your request. What can I do for you before I am taken from you?' Elisha answered, 'Let me inherit a double share of your spirit.' 'Your request is a difficult one' Elijah said. 'If you see me while I am being taken from you, it shall be as you ask; if not, it will not be so.' Now as they walked on, talking as they went, a chariot of fire appeared and horses of fire, coming between the two of them; and Elijah went up to heaven in the whirlwind. Elisha saw it, and shouted, 'My father! My father! Chariot of Israel and its chargers!' Then he lost sight of him, and taking hold of his clothes he tore them in half. He picked up the cloak of Elijah which had fallen, and went back and stood on the bank of the Jordan.

He took the cloak of Elijah and struck the water. 'Where is the Lord, the God of Elijah?' he cried. He struck the water, and it divided to right and left, and Elisha crossed over.

June 17 Friday: 11th Week in Ordinary Time
2 Kings 11:1-4, 9-18, 20

... Athaliah, on hearing the shouts of the people, made for the Temple of the Lord where the people were. When she saw the king standing there beside the pillar, as the custom was, with the captains and trumpeters at the king's side, and all the country people rejoicing and sounding trumpets, Athaliah tore her garments and shouted, 'Treason, treason!' Then Jehoiada the priest gave the order to the army officers: 'Take her outside the precincts and put to death anyone who follows her.' 'For,' the priest had reasoned, 'she must not be put to death in the Temple of the Lord.' They seized her, and when she had reached the palace through the Entry of the Horses, she was put to death there.

Jehoiada made a covenant between the Lord and king and people, by which the latter undertook to be the people of the Lord; and also between king and people. All the country people then went to the temple of Baal and demolished it; they smashed his altars and his images and killed Mattan, priest of Baal, in front of the altars.

The priest posted sentries to guard the Temple of the Lord. All the country people were delighted, and the city made no move. And they put Athaliah to death in the royal palace.

June 18 Saturday: 11th Week in Ordinary Time
2 Chronicles 24:17-25

... King Joash, forgetful of the kindness that Jehoiada, the father of Zechariah, had shown him, killed Jehoiada's son who cried out as he died, 'The Lord sees and he will avenge!'

When a year had gone by, the Aramaean army made war on Joash. They reached Judah and Jerusalem, and executed all the officials among the people, sending back to the king at Damascus all that they had plundered from them. Though the Aramaean army had by no means come in force, the Lord delivered into its power an army of great size for having deserted him, the God of their ancestors. The Aramaeans treated Joash as he had deserved, and when they retired they left him a very sick man; and his officers, plotting against him to avenge the death of the son of Jehoiada the priest, murdered him in his bed. So he died, and they buried him in the Citadel of David, though not in the tombs of the kings.

June 21 Tuesday: 12th Week in Ordinary Time
2 Kings 19:9-11, 14-21, 31-36

... Then Isaiah son of Amoz sent to Hezekiah. 'The Lord, the God of Israel' he said, 'says this, "I have heard the prayer you have addressed to me about Sennacherib king of Assyria." Here is the oracle that the Lord has pronounced against him: "She despises you, she scorns you, the virgin, daughter of Zion; she tosses her head behind you, the daughter of Jerusalem. A remnant shall go out from Jerusalem, and survivors from Mount Zion. The jealous love of the Lord of Hosts shall accomplish this."

'This, then, is what the Lord says about the king of Assyria: "He will not enter this city, he will let fly no arrow against it, confront it with no shield, throw up no earthwork against it. By the road that he came on he will return; he shall not enter this city. It is the Lord who speaks. I will protect this city and save it for my own sake and for the sake of my servant David."'

That same night the angel of the Lord went out and struck down a hundred and eighty-five thousand men in the Assyrian camp. Sennacherib struck camp and left; he returned home and stayed in Nineveh.

June 29 Wednesday: Sts Peter and Paul
Acts 12:1-11

King Herod started persecuting certain members of the Church. He beheaded James the brother of John, and when he saw that this pleased the Jews he decided to arrest Peter as well. This was during the days of Unleavened Bread, and he put Peter in prison, assigning four squads of four soldiers each to guard him in turns. Herod meant to try Peter in public after the end of Passover week. All the time Peter was under guard the Church prayed to God for him unremittingly.

On the night before Herod was to try him, Peter was sleeping between two soldiers, fastened with double chains, while guards kept watch at the main entrance to the prison. Then suddenly the angel of the Lord stood there, and the cell was filled with light. He tapped Peter on the side and woke him. 'Get up!' he said 'Hurry!' – and the chains fell from his hands. The angel then said, 'Put on your belt and sandals.' After he had done this, the angel next said, 'Wrap your cloak round you and follow me.' Peter followed him, but had no idea that what the angel did was all happening in reality; he thought he was seeing a vision. They passed through two guard posts one after the other, and reached the iron gate leading to the city. This opened of its own accord; they went through it and had walked the whole length of the street when suddenly the angel left him. It was only then that Peter came to himself. 'Now I know it is all true,' he said. 'The Lord really did send his angel and has saved me from Herod and from all that the Jewish people were so certain would happen to me.'

July 8 Friday: 14th Week in Ordinary Time
Hosea 14:2-10

... He shall bloom like the lily, and thrust out roots like the poplar, his shoots will spread far; he will have the beauty of the olive and the fragrance of Lebanon. They will come back to live in my shade; they will grow corn that flourishes, they will cultivate vines as renowned as the wine of Helbon. What has Ephraim to do with idols any more when it is I who hear his prayer and care for him? I am like a cypress ever green, all your fruitfulness comes from me. Let the wise man understand these words. Let the intelligent man grasp their meaning. For the ways of the Lord are straight, and virtuous men walk in them, but sinners stumble.

July 9 Saturday: Our Lady of Aberdeen
Isaiah 6:1-8

... The foundations of the threshold shook with the voice of the one who cried out, and the Temple was filled with smoke. I said: 'What a wretched state I am in! I am lost, for I am a man of unclean lips and I live among a people of unclean lips, and my eyes have looked at the King, the Lord of hosts.'

Then one of the seraphs flew to me, holding in his hand a live coal which he had taken from the altar with a pair of tongs. With this he touched my mouth and said: 'See now, this has touched your lips, your sin is taken away, your iniquity is purged.'

Then I heard the voice of the Lord saying: 'Whom shall I send? Who will be our messenger?' I answered, 'Here I am, send me.'

August 1 Monday: 18th Week in Ordinary Time
Jeremiah 28:1-17

... 'The Lord, the God of Israel, says this, "I have broken the yoke of the king of Babylon. In two years' time I will bring back all the vessels of the Temple of the Lord which Nebuchadnezzar king of Babylon carried off from this place and took to Babylon. And I will also bring back Jeconiah son of Jehoiakim, king of Judah, and all the exiles of Judah who have gone to Babylon – it is the Lord who speaks. Yes, I am going to break the yoke of the king of Babylon."'

The prophet Jeremiah then replied to the prophet Hananiah in front of the priests and all the people there in the Temple of the Lord. 'I hope so' the prophet Jeremiah said. 'May the Lord do so. May he fulfil the words that you have prophesied and bring the vessels of the Temple of the Lord and all the exiles back to this place from Babylon. Listen carefully, however, to this word I am now going to say for you and all the people to hear: From remote times, the prophets who preceded you and me prophesied war, famine and plague for many countries and for great kingdoms; but the prophet who prophesies peace can only be recognised as one truly sent by the Lord when his word comes true.'

The prophet Hananiah then took the yoke off the neck of the prophet Jeremiah and broke it. In front of all the people Hananiah then said, 'The Lord says this, "This is how, two years hence, I will break the yoke of Nebuchadnezzar king of Babylon and take it off the necks of all the nations."' At this, the prophet Jeremiah went away.

After the prophet Hananiah had broken the yoke which he had taken off the neck of the prophet Jeremiah the word of the Lord was addressed to Jeremiah, 'Go to Hananiah and tell him this, "The Lord says this: You can break wooden yokes? Right, I will make them iron yokes instead! For the Lord of hosts, the God of Israel, says this: An iron yoke is what I now lay on the necks of all these nations to subject them to Nebuchadnezzar king of Babylon. (They will be subject to him; I have even given him the wild animals.)"'

The prophet Jeremiah said to the prophet Hananiah, 'Listen carefully, Hananiah: the Lord has not sent you; and thanks to you this people are now relying on what is false. Hence – the Lord says this, "I am going to throw you off the face of the earth: you are going to die this year (since you have preached apostasy from the Lord)."'

The prophet Hananiah died the same year, in the seventh month.

August 2 Tuesday: 18th Week in Ordinary Time
Jeremiah 30:1-2, 12-15, 18-22

... Yes, the Lord says this: Your wound is incurable, your injury past healing. There is no one to care for your sore, no medicine to make you well again. All your lovers have forgotten you, they look for you no more. Yes, I have struck you as an enemy strikes, with harsh punishment (so great is your guilt, so many your sins). Why bother to complain about your wound? Your pain is incurable. So great is your guilt, so many your sins, that I have done all this to you.

The Lord says this: Now I will restore the tents of Jacob, and take pity on his dwellings: the city shall be rebuilt on its ruins, the citadel restored on its site. From them will come thanksgiving and shouts of joy. I will make them increase, and not diminish them, make them honoured, and not disdained. Their sons shall be as once they were, their community fixed firm in my presence, and I will punish all their oppressors. The prince will be one of their own, their ruler come from their own people. I will let him come freely into my presence and he can come close to me; who else, indeed, would risk his life by coming to me? – it is the Lord who speaks. And you shall be my people and I will be your God.

August 6 Saturday: Transfiguration of the Lord
Daniel 7:9-10, 13-14

As I watched: Thrones were set in place and one of great age took his seat. His robe was white as snow, the hair of his head as pure as wool. His throne was a blaze of flames, its wheels were a burning fire. A stream of fire poured out, issuing from his presence. A thousand thousand waited on him, ten thousand times ten thousand stood before him. A court was held and the books were opened. I gazed into the visions of the night. And I saw, coming on the clouds of heaven, one like a son of man. He came to the one of great age and was led into his presence. On him was conferred sovereignty, glory and kingship and men of all peoples, nations and languages became his servants. His sovereignty is an eternal sovereignty which shall never pass away, nor will his empire ever be destroyed.

August 11 Thursday: 19th Week in Ordinary Time

Ezekiel 12:1-12

The word of the Lord was addressed to me as follows, 'Son of man, you are living with that set of rebels who have eyes and never see, ears and never hear, for they are a set of rebels. You, son of man, pack an exile's bundle and emigrate by daylight when they can see you, emigrate from where you are to somewhere else while they watch. Perhaps they will admit then that they are a set of rebels. You will pack your baggage like an exile's bundle, by daylight, for them to see, and leave like an exile in the evening, making sure that they are looking. As they watch, make a hole in the wall, and go out through it. As they watch, you will shoulder your pack and go out into the dark; you will cover your face so that you cannot see the country, since I have made you a symbol for the House of Israel.'

I did as I had been told. I packed my baggage like an exile's bundle, by daylight; and in the evening I made a hole through the wall with my hand. I went out into the dark and shouldered my pack as they watched.

The next morning the word of the Lord was addressed to me as follows, 'Son of man, did not the House of Israel, did not that set of rebels, ask you what you were doing? Say, "The Lord says this: This oracle is directed against Jerusalem and the whole House of Israel wherever they are living." Say, "I am a symbol for you; the thing I have done will be done to them; they will go into exile, into banishment." Their ruler will shoulder his pack in the dark and go out through the wall; a hole will be made to let him out; he will cover his face rather than see the country.'

August 15 Monday: The Assumption of the Blessed Virgin Mary

Apocalypse 11:19; 12:1-6, 10

The sanctuary of God in heaven opened, and the ark of the covenant could be seen inside it. Now a great sign appeared in heaven: a woman, adorned with the sun, standing on the moon, and with the twelve stars on her head for a crown. She was pregnant, and in labour, crying aloud in the pangs of childbirth. Then a second sign appeared in the sky, a huge red dragon which had seven heads and ten horns, and each of the seven heads crowned with a coronet. Its tail dragged a third of the stars from the sky and dropped them to the earth, and the dragon stopped in front of the woman as she was having the child, so that he could eat it as soon as it was born from its mother. The woman brought a male child into the world, the son who was to rule all the nations with an iron sceptre, and the child was taken straight up to God and to his throne, while the woman escaped into the desert, where God had made a place of safety ready. Then I heard a voice shout from heaven, 'Victory and power and empire for ever have been won by our God, and all authority for his Christ.'

1 Corinthians 15:20-26

Christ has been raised from the dead, the first-fruits of all who have fallen asleep. Death came through one man and in the same way the resurrection of the dead has come through one man. Just as all men die in Adam, so all men will be brought to life in Christ; but all of them in their proper order; Christ as the first-fruits and then, after the coming of Christ, those who belong to him. After that will come the end, when he hands over the kingdom to God the Father, having done away with every sovereignty, authority and power. For he must be king until he has put all his enemies under his feet and the last of the enemies to be destroyed is death, for everything is to be put under his feet.

August 17 Wednesday: 20th Week in Ordinary Time
Ezekiel 34:1-11

The word of the Lord was addressed to me as follows: 'Son of man, prophesy against the shepherds of Israel; prophesy and say to them, "Shepherds, the Lord says this: Trouble for the shepherds of Israel who feed themselves! Shepherds ought to feed their flock, yet you have fed on milk, you have dressed yourselves in wool, you have sacrificed the fattest sheep, but failed to feed the flock. You have failed to make weak sheep strong, or to care for the sick ones, or bandage the wounded ones. You have failed to bring back strays or look for the lost. On the contrary, you have ruled them cruelly and violently. For lack of a shepherd they have scattered, to become the prey of any wild animal; they have scattered far. My flock is straying this way and that, on mountains and on high hills; my flock has been scattered all over the country; no one bothers about them and no one looks for them.

'"Well then, shepherds, hear the word of the Lord. As I live, I swear it – it is the Lord who speaks – since my flock has been looted and for lack of a shepherd is now the prey of any wild animal, since my shepherds have stopped bothering about my flock, since my shepherds feed themselves rather than my flock, in view of all this, shepherds, hear the word of the Lord. The Lord says this: I am going to call the shepherds to account. I am going to take my flock back from them and I shall not allow them to feed my flock. In this way the shepherds will stop feeding themselves. I shall rescue my sheep from their mouths; they will not prey on them any more."'

'For the Lord says this: "I am going to look after my flock myself and keep all of it in view."'

August 18 Thursday: 20th Week in Ordinary Time
Ezekiel 36:23-28

... I shall pour clean water over you and you will be cleansed; I shall cleanse you of all your defilement and all your idols. I shall give you a new heart, and put a new spirit in you; I shall remove the heart of stone from your bodies and give you a heart of flesh instead. I shall put my spirit in you, and make you keep my laws and sincerely respect my observances. You will live in the land which I gave your ancestors. You shall be my people and I will be your God.

August 19 Friday: 20th Week in Ordinary Time
Ezekiel 37:1-14

... They keep saying, "Our bones are dried up, our hope has gone; we are as good as dead." So prophesy. Say to them, "The Lord says this: I am now going to open your graves; I mean to raise you from your graves, my people, and lead you back to the soil of Israel. And you will know that I am the Lord, when I open your graves and raise you from your graves, my people. And I shall put my spirit in you, and you will live, and I shall resettle you on your own soil; and you will know that I, the Lord, have said and done this – it is the Lord who speaks."'

August 26 Friday: 21st Week in Ordinary Time
1 Corinthians 1:17-25

... Do you see now how God has shown up the foolishness of human wisdom? If it was God's wisdom that human wisdom should not know God, it was because God wanted to save those who have faith through the foolishness of the message that we preach. And so, while the Jews demand miracles and the Greeks look for wisdom, here are we preaching a crucified Christ; to the Jews an obstacle that they cannot get over, to the pagans madness, but to those who have been called, whether they are Jews or Greeks, a Christ who is the power and the wisdom of God. For God's foolishness is wiser than human wisdom, and God's weakness is stronger than human strength.

August 27 Saturday: 21st Week in Ordinary Time
1 Corinthians 1:26-31

Take yourselves, brothers, at the time when you were called: how many of you were wise in the ordinary sense of the word, how many were influential people, or came from noble families? No, it was to shame the wise that God chose what is foolish by human reckoning, and to shame what is strong that he chose what is weak by human reckoning; those whom the world thinks common and contemptible are the ones that God has chosen – those who are nothing at all to show up those who are everything. The human race has nothing to boast about to God, but you, God has made members of Christ Jesus and by God's doing he has become our wisdom, and our virtue, and our holiness, and our freedom. As scripture says: if anyone wants to boast, let him boast about the Lord.

September 6 Tuesday: 23rd Week in Ordinary Time
1 Corinthians 6:1-11

... You know perfectly well that people who do wrong will not inherit the kingdom of God: people of immoral lives, idolaters, adulterers, catamites, sodomites, thieves, usurers, drunkards, slanderers and swindlers will never inherit the kingdom of God. These are the sort of people some of you were once, but now you have been washed clean, and sanctified, and justified through the name of the Lord Jesus Christ and through the Spirit of our God.

September 12 Monday: 24th Week in Ordinary Time
1 Corinthians 11:17-26, 33

... Surely you have homes for eating and drinking in? Surely you have enough respect for the community of God not to make poor people embarrassed? What am I to say to you? Congratulate you? I cannot congratulate you on this. For this is what I received from the Lord, and in turn passed on to you: that on the same night that he was betrayed, the Lord Jesus took some bread, and thanked God for it and broke it, and he said, 'This is my body, which is for you; do this as a memorial of me.' In the same way he took the cup after supper, and said, 'This cup is the new covenant in my blood. Whenever you drink it, do this as a memorial of me.' Until the Lord comes, therefore, every time you eat this bread and drink this cup, you are proclaiming his death. So to sum up, my dear brothers when you meet for the Meal, wait for one another.

September 17 Saturday: 24th Week in Ordinary Time
1 Corinthians 15:35-37, 42-49

Someone may ask, 'How are dead people raised, and what sort of body do they have when they come back?' They are stupid questions. Whatever you sow in the ground has to die before it is given new life and the thing that you sow is not what is going to come; you sow a bare grain, say of wheat or something like that. It is the same with the resurrection of the dead: the thing that is sown is perishable but what is raised is imperishable; the thing that is sown is contemptible but what is raised is glorious; the thing that is sowed is weak but what is raised is powerful; when it is sown it embodies the soul, when it is raised it embodies the spirit.

If the soul has its own embodiment, so does the spirit have its own embodiment. The first man, Adam, as scripture says, became a living soul; but the last Adam has become a life-giving spirit. That is, first the one with the soul, not the spirit, and after that, the one with the spirit. The first man, being from the earth, is earthly by nature; the second man is from heaven. As this earthly man was, so are we on earth; and as the heavenly man is, so are we in heaven. And we, who have been modelled on the earthly man, will be modelled on the heavenly man.

September 26 Monday: 26th Week in Ordinary Time
Job 1:6-22

... 'The fire of God' he said 'has fallen from the heavens and burnt up all your sheep, and your shepherds too: I alone escaped to tell you.' He had not finished speaking when another messenger arrived. 'The Chaldaeans,' he said 'three bands of them, have raided your camels and made off with them. Your servants they put to the sword: I alone escaped to tell you.' He had not finished speaking when another messenger arrived. 'Your sons and daughters' he said 'were at their meals and drinking wine at their eldest brother's house, when suddenly from the wilderness a gale sprang up, and it battered all four corners of the house which fell in on the young people. They are dead: I alone escaped to tell you.'

Job rose and tore his gown and shaved his head. Then falling to the ground he worshipped and said: 'Naked I came from my mother's womb, naked I shall return. The Lord gave, the Lord has taken back. Blessed be the name of the Lord!'

In all this misfortune Job committed no sin nor offered any insult to God.

October 1 Saturday: 26th Week in Ordinary Time
Job 42:1-3, 5-6, 12-17

... The Lord blessed Job's new fortune even more than his first one. He came to own fourteen thousand sheep, six thousand camels, a thousand yoke of oxen and a thousand she-donkeys. He had seven sons and three daughters; his first daughter he called 'Turtledove', the second 'Cassia' and the third 'Mascara'. Throughout the land there were no women as beautiful as the daughters of Job. And their father gave them inheritance rights like their brothers.

After his trials, Job lived on until he was a hundred and forty years old, and saw his children and his children's children up to the fourth generation. Then Job died, an old man and full of days.

October 3 Monday: 27th Week in Ordinary Time
Galatians 1:6-12

I am astonished at the promptness with which you have turned away from the one who called you and have decided to follow a different version of the Good News. Not that there can be more than one Good News; it is merely that some troublemakers among you want to change the Good News of Christ; and let me warn you that if anyone preaches a version of the Good News different from the one we have already preached to you, whether it be ourselves or an angel from heaven, he is to be condemned. I am only repeating what we told you before: if anyone preaches a version of the Good News different from the one you have already heard, he is to be condemned. So now whom am I trying to please – man, or God? Would you say it is men's approval I am looking for? If I still wanted that, I should not be what I am – a servant of Christ.

The fact is, brothers, and I want you to realise this, the Good News I preached is not a human message that I was given by men, it is something I learnt only through a revelation of Jesus Christ.

October 5 Wednesday: 27th Week in Ordinary Time
Galatians 2:1-2, 7-14
... When Cephas came to Antioch, however, I opposed him to his face, since he was manifestly in the wrong. His custom had been to eat with the pagans, but after certain friends of James arrived he stopped doing this and kept away from them altogether for fear of the group that insisted on circumcision. The other Jews joined him in this pretence, and even Barnabas felt himself obliged to copy their behaviour. When I saw they were not respecting the true meaning of the Good News, I said to Cephas in front of everyone, 'In spite of being a Jew, you live like the pagans and not like the Jews, so you have no right to make the pagans copy Jewish ways.'

October 7 Friday: 27th Week in Ordinary Time
Galatians 3:7-14
... On the other hand, those who rely on the keeping of the Law are under a curse, since scripture says: Cursed be everyone who does not persevere in observing everything prescribed in the book of the Law. The Law will not justify anyone in the sight of God, because we are told: the righteous man finds life through faith. The Law is not even based on faith, since we are told: The man who practises these precepts finds life through practising them. Christ redeemed us from the curse of the Law by being cursed for our sake, since scripture says: Cursed be everyone who is hanged on a tree. This was done so that in Christ Jesus the blessing of Abraham might include the pagans, and so that through faith we might receive the promised Spirit.

October 13 Thursday: 28th Week in Ordinary Time
Ephesians 1:1-10
... Such is the richness of the grace which he has showered on us in all wisdom and insight. He has let us know the mystery of his purpose, the hidden plan he so kindly made in Christ from the beginning to act upon when the times had run their course to the end: that he would bring everything together under Christ, as head, everything in the heavens and everything on earth.

October 17 Monday: 29th Week in Ordinary Time
Ephesians 2:1-10
... This was to show for all ages to come, through his goodness towards us in Christ Jesus, how infinitely rich he is in grace. Because it is by grace that you have been saved, through faith; not by anything of your own, but by a gift from God; not by anything that you have done, so that nobody can claim the credit. We are God's work of art, created in Christ Jesus to live the good life as from the beginning he had meant us to live it.

October 19 Wednesday: 29th Week in Ordinary Time
Ephesians 3:2-12
... This mystery that has now been revealed through the Spirit to his holy apostles and prophets was unknown to any men in past generations; it means that pagans now share the same inheritance, that they are parts of the same body, and that the same promise has been made to them, in Christ Jesus, through the gospel. I have been made the servant of that gospel by a gift of grace from God who gave it to me by his own power. I, who am less than the least of all the saints, have been entrusted with this special grace, not only of proclaiming to the pagans the infinite treasure of Christ but also of explaining how the mystery is to be dispensed. Through all the ages, this has been kept hidden in God, the

creator of everything. Why? So that the Sovereignties and Powers should learn only now, through the Church, how comprehensive God's wisdom really is, exactly according to the plan which he had had from all eternity in Christ Jesus our Lord. This is why we are bold enough to approach God in complete confidence, through our faith in him.

October 22 Saturday: 29th Week in Ordinary Time
Ephesians 4:7-16

... And to some, his gift was that they should be apostles; to some, prophets; to some, evangelists; to some, pastors and teachers; so that the saints together make a unity in the work of service, building up the body of Christ. In this way we are all to come to unity in our faith and in our knowledge of the Son of God, until we become the perfect Man, fully mature with the fullness of Christ himself.

Then we shall not be children any longer, or tossed one way and another and carried along by every wind of doctrine, at the mercy of all the tricks men play and their cleverness in practising deceit. If we live by the truth and in love, we shall grow in all ways into Christ, who is the head by whom the whole body is fitted and joined together, every joint adding its own strength, for each separate part to work according to its function. So the body grows until it has built itself up, in love.

October 24 Monday: 30th Week in Ordinary Time
Ephesians 4:32–5:8

... There must be no coarseness, or salacious talk and jokes – all this is wrong for you: raise your voices in thanksgiving instead. For you can be quite certain that nobody who actually indulges in fornication or impurity or promiscuity – which is worshipping a false god – can inherit anything of the kingdom of God. Do not let anyone deceive you with empty arguments: it is for this loose living that God's anger comes down on those who rebel against him. Make sure that you are not included with them. You were darkness once, but now you are light in the Lord; be like children of light.

October 26 Wednesday: 30th Week in Ordinary Time
Ephesians 6:1-9

... Slaves, be obedient to the men who are called your masters in this world, with deep respect and sincere loyalty, as you are obedient to Christ: not only when you are under their eye, as if you had only to please men, but because you are slaves of Christ and wholeheartedly do the will of God. Work hard and willingly, but do it for the sake of the Lord and not for the sake of men. You can be sure that everyone, whether a slave or a free man, will be properly rewarded by the Lord for whatever work he has done well. And those of you who are employers, treat your slaves in the same spirit; do without threats, remembering that they and you have the same Master in heaven and he is not impressed by one person more than by another.

October 27 Thursday: 30th Week in Ordinary Time
Ephesians 6:10-20

... So stand your ground, with truth buckled round your waist, and integrity for a breastplate, wearing for shoes on your feet the eagerness to spread the gospel of peace and always carrying the shield of faith so that you can use it to put out the burning arrows of the evil one. And then you must accept salvation from God to be your helmet and receive the word of God from the Spirit to use as a sword.

Pray all the time, asking for what you need, praying in the Spirit on every possible occasion. Never get tired of staying awake to pray for all the saints; and pray for me to be given an opportunity to open my mouth and speak without fear and give out the mystery of the gospel of which I am an ambassador in chains; pray that in proclaiming it I may speak as boldly as I ought to.

November 1 Tuesday: All Saints Day
Apocalypse 7:2-4, 9-14

... After that I saw a huge number, impossible to count, of people from every nation, race, tribe and language; they were standing in front of the throne and in front of the Lamb, dressed in white robes and holding palms in their hands. They shouted aloud, 'Victory to our God, who sits on the throne, and to the Lamb!' And all the angels who were standing in a circle round the throne, surrounding the elders and the four animals, prostrated themselves before the throne, and touched the ground with their foreheads, worshipping God with these words: 'Amen. Praise and glory and wisdom and thanksgiving and honour and power and strength to our God for ever and ever. Amen.'

One of the elders then spoke, and asked me, 'Do you know who these people are, dressed in white robes, and where they have come from?' I answered him, 'You can tell me, my Lord.' Then he said, 'These are the people who have been through the great persecution, and they have washed their robes white again in the blood of the Lamb.'

November 2 Wednesday: The Commemoration of All the Faithful Departed
Isaiah 25:6-9

On this mountain, the Lord of hosts will prepare for all peoples a banquet of rich food. On this mountain he will remove the mourning veil covering all peoples, and the shroud enwrapping all nations, he will destroy Death for ever. The Lord will wipe away the tears from every cheek; he will take away his people's shame everywhere on earth, for the Lord has said so. That day, it will be said: See, this is our God in whom we hoped for salvation; the Lord is the one in whom we hoped. We exult and we rejoice that he has saved us.

November 5 Saturday: 31st Week in Ordinary Time
Philippians 4:10-19

... In the early days of the Good News, as you people of Philippi well know, when I left Macedonia, no other church helped me with gifts of money. You were the only ones; and twice since my stay in Thessalonika you have sent me what I needed. It is not your gift that I value; what is valuable to me is the interest that is mounting up in your account. Now for the time being I have everything that I need and more: I am fully provided now that I have received from Epaphroditus the offering that you sent, a sweet fragrance – the sacrifice that God accepts and finds pleasing. In return my God will fulfil all your needs, in Christ Jesus, as lavishly as only God can.

November 8 Tuesday: 32nd Week in Ordinary Time
Titus 2:1-8, 11-14

... You see, God's grace has been revealed, and it has made salvation possible for the whole human race and taught us that what we have to do is to give up everything that does not lead to God, and all our worldly ambitions; we must be self-restrained and live good and religious lives here in this present world, while we are waiting in hope for the blessing which will come with the Appearing of the glory of our great God and saviour Christ Jesus. He sacrificed himself for us in order to set us free from all wickedness and to purify a people so that it could be his very own and would have no ambition except to do good.

November 9 Wednesday: The Dedication of the Lateran Basilica
Ezekiel 47:1-2, 8-9, 12

… He took me out by the north gate and led me right round outside as far as the outer east gate where the water flowed out on the right-hand side. The man went to the east holding his measuring line and measured off a thousand cubits; he made me wade across the stream; the water reached my ankles. He measured off another thousand and made me wade across the stream again; the water reached my knees. He measured off another thousand and made me wade across again; the water reached my waist. He measured off another thousand; it was now a river which I could not cross; the stream had swollen and was now deep water, a river impossible to cross. He then said, 'Do you see, son of man?' He took me further, then brought me back to the bank of the river. When I got back, there were many trees on each bank of the river. He said, 'This water flows east down to the Arabah and to the sea; and flowing into the sea it makes its waters wholesome. Wherever the river flows, all living creatures teeming in it will live. Fish will be very plentiful, for wherever the water goes it brings health, and life teems wherever the river flows. Along the river, on either bank, will grow every kind of fruit tree with leaves that never wither and fruit that never fails, they will bear new fruit every month, because this water comes from the sanctuary. And their fruit will be good to eat and the leaves medicinal.'

November 10 Thursday: 32nd Week in Ordinary Time
Philemon 7-20

... I know you have been deprived of Onesimus for a time, but it was only so that you could have him back for ever, not as a slave any more, but something much better than a slave, a dear brother; especially dear to me, but how much more to you, as a blood-brother as well as a brother in the Lord. So if all that we have in common means anything to you, welcome him as you would me; but if he has wronged you in any way or owes you anything, then let me pay for it. I am writing this in my own handwriting: I, Paul, shall pay it back – I will not add any mention of your own debt to me, which is yourself. Well then, brother, I am counting on you, in the Lord; put new heart into me, in Christ.

November 15 Tuesday: 33rd Week in Ordinary Time
Apocalypse 3:1-6, 14-22

… Those who prove victorious will be dressed, like these, in white robes; I shall not blot their names out of the book of life, but acknowledge their names in the presence of my Father and his angels. If anyone has ears to hear, let him listen to what the Spirit is saying to the churches."

'Write to the angel of the church in Laodicea and say, "Here is the message of the Amen, the faithful, the true witness, the ultimate source of God's creation: I know all about you: how you are neither cold nor hot. I wish you were one or the other, but since you are neither, but only lukewarm, I will spit you out of my mouth. You say to yourself, "I am rich, I have made a fortune, and have everything I want," never realising that you are wretchedly and pitiably poor, and blind and naked too. I warn you, buy from me the gold that has been tested in the fire to make you really rich, and white robes to clothe you and cover your shameful nakedness, and eye ointment to put on your eyes so that you are able to see. I am the one who reproves and disciplines all those he loves: so repent in real earnest. Look, I am standing at the door, knocking. If one of you hears me calling and opens the door, I will come in to share his meal, side by side with him. Those who prove victorious I will allow to share my throne, just as I was victorious myself and took my place with my Father on his throne. If anyone has ears to hear, let him listen to what the Spirit is saying to the churches."'

November 16 Wednesday: 33rd Week in Ordinary Time
Apocalypse 4:1-11

In my vision, I, John, saw a door open in heaven and heard the same voice speaking to me, the voice like a trumpet, saying, 'Come up here: I will show you what is to come in the future.' With that, the Spirit possessed me and I saw a throne standing in heaven, and the One who was sitting on the throne, and the Person sitting there looked like a diamond and a ruby. There was a rainbow encircling the throne, and this looked like an emerald. Round the throne in a circle were twenty-four thrones, and on them I saw twenty-four elders sitting, dressed in white robes with golden crowns on their heads. Flashes of lightning were coming from the throne, and the sound of peals of thunder, and in front of the throne there were seven flaming lamps burning, the seven Spirits of God. Between the throne and myself was a sea that seemed to be made of glass, like crystal. In the centre, grouped round the throne itself, were four animals with many eyes, in front and behind. The first animal was like a lion, the second like a bull, the third animal had a human face, and the fourth animal was like a flying eagle. Each of the four animals had six wings and had eyes all the way round as well as inside; and day and night they never stopped singing: 'Holy, Holy, Holy is the Lord God, the Almighty; he was, he is and he is to come.' Every time the animals glorified and honoured and gave thanks to the One sitting on the throne, who lives for ever and ever, the twenty-four elders prostrated themselves before him to worship the One who lives for ever and ever, and threw down their crowns in front of the throne, saying, 'You are our Lord and our God, you are worthy of glory and honour and power, because you made all the universe and it was only by your will that everything was made and exists.'

November 19 Saturday: 33rd Week in Ordinary Time
Apocalypse 11:4-12

... When they have completed their witnessing, the beast that comes out of the Abyss is going to make war on them and overcome them and kill them. Their corpses will lie in the main street of the Great City known by the symbolic names Sodom and Egypt, in which their Lord was crucified. Men out of every people, race, language and nation will stare at their corpses, for three-and-a-half days, not letting them be buried, and the people of the world will be glad about it and celebrate the event by giving presents to each other, because these two prophets have been a plague to the people of the world.'

After the three-and-a-half days, God breathed life into their corpses and they stood up, and everybody who saw it happen was terrified; then they heard a loud voice from heaven say to them, 'Come up here', and while their enemies were watching, they went up to heaven in a cloud.

November 24 Thursday: 34th Week in Ordinary Time
Apocalypse 18:1-2, 21-23; 19:1-3, 9

... After this I seemed to hear the great sound of a huge crowd in heaven, singing, 'Alleluia! Victory and glory and power to our God! He judges fairly, he punishes justly, and he has condemned the famous prostitute who corrupted the earth with her fornication; he has avenged his servants that she killed.' They sang again, 'Alleluia! The smoke of her will go up for ever and ever.' The angel said, 'Write this: Happy are those who are invited to the wedding feast of the Lamb.'

November 25 Friday: 34th Week in Ordinary Time
Apocalypse 20:1-4, 11—21:2

... The sea gave up all the dead who were in it; Death and Hades were emptied of the dead that were in them; and every one was judged according to the way in which he had lived. Then Death and Hades were thrown into the burning lake. This burning lake is the second death; and anybody whose name could not be found written in the book of life was thrown into the burning lake. Then I saw a new heaven and a new earth; the first heaven and the first earth had disappeared now, and there was no longer any sea. I saw the holy city, and the new Jerusalem, coming down from God out of heaven, as beautiful as a bride all dressed for her husband.

December 5 Monday: 2nd Week of Advent
Isaiah 35:1-10

... Strengthen all weary hands, steady all trembling knees and say to all faint hearts, 'Courage! Do not be afraid. 'Look, your God is coming, vengeance is coming, the retribution of God; he is coming to save you.'

Then the eyes of the blind shall be opened, the ears of the deaf unsealed, then the lame shall leap like a deer and the tongues of the dumb sing for joy; for water gushes in the desert, streams in the wasteland, the scorched earth becomes a lake, the parched land springs of water. The lairs where the jackals used to live become thickets of reed and papyrus. And through it will run a highway undefiled which shall be called the Sacred Way; the unclean may not travel by it, nor fools stray along it.

No lion will be there nor any fierce beast roam about it, but the redeemed will walk there, for those the Lord has ransomed shall return. They will come to Zion shouting for joy, everlasting joy on their faces; joy and gladness will go with them and sorrow and lament be ended.

December 8 Thursday: The Immaculate Conception of the Blessed Virgin Mary
Genesis 3:9-15, 20

After Adam had eaten of the tree, the Lord God called to him. 'Where are you?' he asked. 'I heard the sound of you in the garden,' he replied. 'I was afraid because I was naked, so I hid.' 'Who told you that you were naked?' he asked. 'Have you been eating of the tree I forbade you to eat?' The man replied, 'It was the woman you put with me; she gave me the fruit, and I ate it.' Then the Lord God asked the woman, 'What is this you have done?' The woman replied, 'The serpent tempted me and I ate.'

Then the Lord God said to the serpent, 'Because you have done this, Be accursed beyond all cattle, all wild beasts. You shall crawl on your belly and eat dust every day of your life. I will make you enemies of each other: you and the woman, your offspring and her offspring. It will crush your head and you will strike its heel.' The man named his wife 'Eve' because she was the mother of all those who live.

December 15 Thursday: 3rd Week of Advent
Isaiah 54:1-10

... For now your creator will be your husband, his name, the Lord of hosts; your redeemer will be the Holy One of Israel, he is called the God of the whole earth. Yes, like a forsaken wife, distressed in spirit, the Lord calls you back. Does a man cast off the wife of his youth? says your God. I did forsake you for a brief moment, but with great love will I take you back. In excess of anger, for a moment I hid my face from you. But with everlasting love I have taken pity on you, says the Lord, your redeemer. I am now as I was in the days of

Noah when I swore that Noah's waters should never flood the world again. So now I swear concerning my anger with you and the threats I made against you; for the mountains may depart, the hills be shaken, but my love for you will never leave you and my covenant of peace with you will never be shaken, says the Lord who takes pity on you.

December 17 Saturday: 3rd Week of Advent
Genesis 49:2, 8-10
Jacob called his sons and said, 'Gather round, sons of Jacob, and listen, listen to Israel your father. Judah, your brothers shall praise you: you grip your enemies by the neck, your father's sons shall do you homage, Judah is a lion cub, you climb back, my son, from your kill; like a lion he crouches and lies down, or a lioness: who dare rouse him? The sceptre shall not pass from Judah, nor the mace from between his feet, until he come to whom it belongs, to whom the peoples shall render obedience.'

December 19 Monday: 4th Week of Advent
Judges 13:2-7, 24-25
There was a man of Zorah of the tribe of Dan, called Manoah. His wife was barren, she had borne no children. The angel of the Lord appeared to this woman and said to her, 'You are barren and have had no child. But from now on take great care. Take no wine or strong drink, and eat nothing unclean. For you will conceive and bear a son. No razor is to touch his head, for the boy shall be God's nazirite from his mother's womb. It is he who will begin to rescue Israel from the power of the Philistines.' Then the woman went and told her husband, 'A man of God has just come to me; his presence was like the presence of the angel of God, he was so majestic. I did not ask him where he came from, and he did not reveal his name to me. But he said to me, "You will conceive and bear a son. From now on, take no wine or strong drink, and eat nothing unclean. For the boy shall be God's nazirite from his mother's womb to his dying day."' The woman gave birth to a son and called him Samson. The child grew, and the Lord blessed him; and the spirit of the Lord began to move him.

December 24 Saturday: 4th Week of Advent
2 Samuel 7:1-5, 8-12, 14, 16
... "I took you from the pasture, from following the sheep, to be leader of my people Israel; I have been with you on all your expeditions; I have cut off all your enemies before you. I will give you fame as great as the fame of the greatest on earth. I will provide a place for my people Israel; I will plant them there and they shall dwell in that place and never be disturbed again; nor shall the wicked continue to oppress them as they did, in the days when I appointed judges over my people Israel; I will give them rest from all their enemies. The Lord will make you great; the Lord will make you a House. And when your days are ended and you are laid to rest with your ancestors, I will preserve the offspring of your body after you and make his sovereignty secure. I will be a father to him and he a son to me. Your House and your sovereignty will always stand secure before me and your throne be established for ever."'

December 29 Thursday: 5th Day within the Octave of Christmas
1 John 2:3-11
... We can be sure that we are in God only when the one who claims to be living in him is living the same kind of life as Christ lived. My dear people, this is not a new commandment that I am writing to tell you, but an old commandment that you were given from the beginning, the original commandment which was the message brought to you. Yet

in another way, what I am writing to you, and what is being carried out in your lives as it was in his, is a new commandment; because the night is over and the real light is already shining. Anyone who claims to be in the light but hates his brother is still in the dark. But anyone who loves his brother is living in the light and need not be afraid of stumbling; unlike the man who hates his brother and is in the darkness, not knowing where he is going, because it is too dark to see.

December 31 Saturday: 7th Day within the Octave of Christmas
1 John 2:18-21

Children, these are the last days; you were told that an Antichrist must come, and now several antichrists have already appeared; we know from this that these are the last days. Those rivals of Christ came out of our own number, but they had never really belonged; if they had belonged, they would have stayed with us; but they left us, to prove that not one of them ever belonged to us. But you have been anointed by the Holy One, and have all received the knowledge. It is not because you do not know the truth that I am writing to you but rather because you know it already and know that no lie can come from the truth.

THE CHAPLET OF THE DIVINE MERCY

Credit: Photo by Renata Sedmakova / Shutterstock.com

OPENING PRAYER

First, make the Sign of the Cross. Touch the forehead, then the chest, then the left shoulder, then the right shoulder, while saying:

In the Name of the Father, and of the Son, and of the Holy Spirit. Amen.

Recite this opening prayer once:

You expired, O Jesus, but the Source of Life gushed forth for souls and the Ocean of Mercy opened up for the whole world. O Fount of Life, unfathomable Divine Mercy, envelop the whole world and empty Yourself out upon us.

Recite the following prayer three times:

O Blood and Water, which gushed forth from the Heart of Jesus as a fount of mercy for us, I trust in You.

Then recite one Our Father, one Hail Mary, and the Apostles' Creed:

Our Father, who art in Heaven, hallowed be thy name. Thy kingdom come, thy will be done, on earth as it is in Heaven. Give us this day our daily bread. And forgive us our trespasses, as we forgive those who trespass against us. And lead us not into temptation, but deliver us from evil. Amen.

Hail Mary, full of grace, the Lord is with thee. Blessed art thou among women, and blessed is the fruit of thy womb Jesus. Holy Mary, Mother of God, pray for us sinners, now and at the hour of our death. Amen.

Apostles Creed: I believe in God, the Father almighty, Creator of heaven and earth.

I believe in Jesus Christ, his only Son, our Lord, who was conceived by the power of the Holy Spirit, born of the Virgin Mary, suffered under Pontius Pilate, was crucified, died, and was buried. He descended to the dead. On the third day, he rose again. He ascended into Heaven and is seated at the right hand of the Father. He will come again to judge the living and the dead.

I believe in the Holy Spirit, the holy catholic Church, the communion of saints, the forgiveness of sins, the resurrection of the body, and the life everlasting. Amen.

THE DECADES OF THE CHAPLET

After the Opening Prayers, the next prayers are said in sets of ten, called 'decades.' A set of five decades is called a 'chaplet.' The prayers are said using ordinary Rosary beads.

On the single large bead (before each set of ten smaller beads) recite:

Eternal Father, I offer You the Body and Blood, Soul and Divinity of Your dearly beloved Son, our Lord Jesus Christ, in atonement for our sins and those of the whole world.

Then, on each of the ten smaller beads, recite:

For the sake of His sorrowful Passion,
have mercy on us and on the whole world.

(Alternate version of this prayer: For the sake of Jesus Christ's sorrowful Passion and death on the Cross, have mercy on us and on the whole world.)

After each set of ten prayers, many persons add:

O Blood and Water, which gushed forth from the Heart of Jesus as a fount of mercy for us, I trust in You.

Repeat the above set of prayers, called a decade, five times to complete one Divine Mercy Chaplet.

CLOSING PRAYERS

Recite the following prayer three times:

Holy God, Holy Mighty One, Holy Immortal One, have mercy on us and on the whole world.

Then recite this closing prayer:

Eternal God, Your Mercy is endless, and Your treasury of compassion is inexhaustible. Look with kindness upon us and increase Your Mercy within us, so that, in difficult moments, we may not despair, nor become despondent, but may, with great confidence, submit ourselves to Your Holy Will, which is Love and Mercy itself. Amen.

Finally, make the Sign of the Cross again:

In the Name of the Father, and of the Son, and of the Holy Spirit. Amen.

INTENTIONS FOR EACH DAY OF THE NOVENA

FIRST DAY

Today bring to Me ALL MANKIND, ESPECIALLY ALL SINNERS

Most Merciful Jesus, whose very nature it is to have compassion on us and to forgive us, do not look upon our sins but upon our trust which we place in Your infinite goodness. Receive us all into the abode of Your Most Compassionate Heart, and never let us escape from it. We beg this of You by Your love which unites You to the Father and the Holy Spirit.

Eternal Father, turn Your merciful gaze upon all mankind and especially upon poor sinners, all enfolded in the Most Compassionate Heart of Jesus. For the sake of His sorrowful Passion show us Your mercy, that we may praise the omnipotence of Your mercy for ever and ever. Amen.

SECOND DAY

Today bring to Me THE SOULS OF PRIESTS AND RELIGIOUS

Most Merciful Jesus, from whom comes all that is good, increase Your grace in men and women consecrated to Your service, that they may perform worthy works of mercy; and that all who see them may glorify the Father of Mercy who is in heaven.

Eternal Father, turn Your merciful gaze upon the company of chosen ones in Your vineyard–upon the souls of priests and religious; and endow them with the strength of Your blessing. For the love of the Heart of Your Son in which they are enfolded, impart to them Your power and light, that they may be able to guide others in the way of salvation and with one voice sing praise to Your boundless mercy for ages without end. Amen.

THIRD DAY

Today bring to Me ALL DEVOUT AND FAITHFUL SOULS

Most Merciful Jesus, from the treasury of Your mercy You impart Your graces in great abundance to each and all. Receive us into the abode of Your Most Compassionate Heart and never let us escape from it. We beg this of You by that most wondrous love for the heavenly Father with which Your Heart burns so fiercely.

Eternal Father, turn Your merciful gaze upon faithful souls, as upon the inheritance of Your Son. For the sake of His sorrowful Passion, grant them Your blessing and surround them with Your constant protection. Thus may they never fail in love or lose the treasure of the holy faith, but rather, with all the hosts of Angels and Saints, may they glorify your boundless mercy for endless ages. Amen.

FOURTH DAY

Today bring to Me THOSE WHO DO NOT BELIEVE IN GOD AND THOSE WHO DO NOT YET KNOW ME

Most compassionate Jesus, You are the Light of the whole world. Receive into the abode of Your Most Compassionate Heart the souls of those who do not believe in God and of those who as yet do not know You. Let the rays of Your grace enlighten them that they, too, together with us, may extol Your wonderful mercy; and do not let them escape from the abode which is Your Most Compassionate Heart.

Eternal Father, turn Your merciful gaze upon the souls of those who do not believe in You, and of those who as yet do not know You, but who are enclosed in the Most Compassionate Heart of Jesus. Draw them to the light of the Gospel. These souls do not know what great happiness it is to love You. Grant that they, too, may extol the generosity of Your mercy for endless ages. Amen.

FIFTH DAY

Today bring to Me THE SOULS OF THOSE WHO HAVE SEPARATED THEMSELVES FROM MY CHURCH

Most Merciful Jesus, Goodness Itself, You do not refuse light to those who seek it of You. Receive into the abode of Your Most Compassionate Heart the souls of those who have separated themselves from Your Church. Draw them by Your light into the unity of the Church, and do not let them escape from the abode of Your Most Compassionate Heart; but bring it about that they, too, come to glorify the generosity of Your mercy.

Eternal Father, turn Your merciful gaze upon the souls of those who have separated themselves from Your Son's Church, who have squandered Your blessings and misused Your graces by obstinately persisting in their errors. Do not look upon their errors, but upon the love of Your own Son and upon His bitter Passion, which He underwent for their sake, since they, too, are enclosed in His Most Compassionate Heart. Bring it about that they also may glorify Your great mercy for endless ages. Amen.

SIXTH DAY

Today bring to Me THE MEEK AND HUMBLE SOULS AND THE SOULS OF LITTLE CHILDREN

Most Merciful Jesus, You yourself have said, 'Learn from Me for I am meek and humble of heart.' Receive into the abode of Your Most Compassionate Heart all meek and humble souls and the souls of little children. These souls send all heaven into ecstasy and they are the heavenly Father's favorites. They are a sweet-smelling bouquet before the throne of God; God himself takes delight in their fragrance. These souls have a permanent abode in Your Most Compassionate Heart, O Jesus, and they unceasingly sing out a hymn of love and mercy.

Eternal Father, turn Your merciful gaze upon meek souls, upon humble souls, and upon little children who are enfolded in the abode which is the Most Compassionate Heart of Jesus. These souls bear the closest resemblance to Your Son. Their fragrance rises from the earth and reaches Your very throne. Father of mercy and of all goodness, I beg You by the love You bear these souls and by the delight You take in them: Bless the whole world, that all souls together may sing out the praises of Your mercy for endless ages. Amen.

SEVENTH DAY

Today bring to Me THE SOULS WHO ESPECIALLY VENERATE AND GLORIFY MY MERCY

Most Merciful Jesus, whose Heart is Love Itself, receive into the abode of Your Most Compassionate Heart the souls of those who particularly extol and venerate the greatness of Your mercy. These souls are mighty with the very power of God Himself. In the midst of all afflictions and adversities they go forward, confident of Your mercy; and united to You, O Jesus, they carry all mankind on their shoulders. These souls will not be judged severely, but Your mercy will embrace them as they depart from this life.

Eternal Father, turn Your merciful gaze upon the souls who glorify and venerate Your greatest attribute, that of Your fathomless mercy, and who are enclosed in the Most Compassionate Heart of Jesus. These souls are a living Gospel; their hands are full of deeds of mercy, and their hearts, overflowing with joy, sing a canticle of mercy to You, O Most High! I beg You O God: Show them Your mercy according to the hope and trust they have placed in You. Let there be accomplished in them the promise of Jesus, who said to them that during their life, but especially at the hour of death, the souls who will venerate this fathomless mercy of His, He, Himself, will defend as His glory. Amen.

EIGHTH DAY

Today bring to Me THE SOULS WHO ARE DETAINED IN PURGATORY

Most Merciful Jesus, You Yourself have said that You desire mercy; so I bring into the abode of Your Most Compassionate Heart the souls in Purgatory, souls who are very dear to You, and yet, who must make retribution to Your justice. May the streams of Blood and Water which gushed forth from Your Heart put out the flames of Purgatory, that there, too, the power of Your mercy may be celebrated.

Eternal Father, turn Your merciful gaze upon the souls suffering in Purgatory, who are enfolded in the Most Compassionate Heart of Jesus. I beg You, by the sorrowful Passion of Jesus Your Son, and by all the bitterness with which His most sacred Soul was flooded: Manifest Your mercy to the souls who are under Your just scrutiny. Look upon them in no other way but only through the Wounds of Jesus, Your dearly beloved Son; for we firmly believe that there is no limit to Your goodness and compassion. Amen.

NINTH DAY

Today bring to Me SOULS WHO HAVE BECOME LUKEWARM

Most compassionate Jesus, You are Compassion Itself. I bring lukewarm souls into the abode of Your Most Compassionate Heart. In this fire of Your pure love let these tepid souls, who like corpses, filled You with such deep loathing, be once again set aflame. O Most Compassionate Jesus, exercise the omnipotence of Your mercy and draw them into the very ardor of Your love, and bestow upon them the gift of holy love, for nothing is beyond Your power.

Eternal Father, turn Your merciful gaze upon lukewarm souls who are nonetheless enfolded in the Most Compassionate Heart of Jesus. Father of Mercy, I beg You by the bitter Passion of Your Son and by His three-hour agony on the Cross: Let them, too, glorify the abyss of Your mercy. Amen.

PRAYER BEFORE HOLY COMMUNION

Almighty and everlasting God,
behold I come to the Sacrament of
of your only-Begotten Son, our Lord Jesus Christ,
as one infirm to the physician of life,
as one unclean to the fountain of mercy,
as one blind to the light of everlasting brightness,
as one poor and needy to the Lord of heaven and earth.
I ask, therefore, for the abundance of your infinite generosity,
that you may graciously cure my sickness,
wash away my defilement, enlighten my blindness,
enrich my poverty, clothe my nakedness,
that I may receive the bread of Angels,
the King of kings, the Lord of lords,
with such reverence and humility, contrition and devotion,
purity and faith, and purpose and intention
as may be conducive to my soul's salvation.
Grant I pray, that I may receive
not only the Sacrament of our Lord's Body and Blood,
but also the grace and power of the Sacrament.
O most gracious God, grant me so to receive
the Body of your only-begotten Son, our Lord Jesus Christ,

which He took from the Virgin Mary,
that I may be worthy to be incorporated into his Mystical Body,
and to be numbered amongst his members.
O most loving Father,
Grant that I may at last gaze forever
upon the unveiled face of your beloved Son,
whom I, a wayfarer, propose to receive now veiled under these species
who lives and reigns with you forever and ever. Amen.

EUCHARISTIC CELEBRATION

THE INTRODUCTORY RITES

The Entrance Procession and Song

Celebrant: In the name of the Father, and of the Son, and of the Holy Spirit.

All: Amen.

Greeting

C: The grace of our Lord Jesus Christ, and the love of God, and the communion of the Holy Spirit be with you all.

All: And with your spirit.

PENITENTIAL RITE

C: Brethren (brothers and sisters), let us acknowledge our sins, and so prepare ourselves to celebrate the sacred mysteries. *(a brief silence)*

All: I confess to almighty God and to you, my brothers and sisters, that I have greatly sinned, in my thoughts and in my words, in what I have done and in what I have failed to do, (and, striking their breast, they say:) through my fault, through my fault, through my most grievous fault; therefore I ask blessed Mary ever-Virgin, all the Angels and Saints, and you, my brothers and sisters, to pray for me to the Lord our God.

C: May almighty God have mercy on us, forgive us our sins, and bring us to everlasting life.

All: Amen.

C: Lord, have mercy. **All:** Lord, have mercy.

C: Christ, have mercy. **All:** Christ, have mercy.

C: Lord, have mercy. **All:** Lord, have mercy.

THE HYMN "GLORIA" *(When prescribed)*

Glory to God in the highest,
and on earth peace to people of good will.
We praise you, we bless you, we adore you,
we glorify you, we give you thanks
for your great glory,
Lord God, heavenly King,
O God, almighty Father.
Lord Jesus Christ, Only Begotten Son,
Lord God, Lamb of God, Son of the Father,
you take away the sins of the world, have mercy on us;
you take away the sins of the world, receive our prayer;
you are seated at the right hand of the Father,
have mercy on us.
For you alone are the Holy One,
you alone are the Lord,
you alone are the Most High, Jesus Christ,
with the Holy Spirit, in the glory of God the Father. Amen.

OPENING PRAYER

THE LITURGY OF THE WORD

First Reading

The Responsorial Psalm

The Second Reading (when prescribed).

The Acclamation before the Gospel

The Gospel

The homily

The Profession of Faith (when prescribed)

THE APOSTLES' CREED

I believe in God, the Father almighty, Creator of heaven and earth, and in Jesus Christ, his only Son, our Lord, *(At the words that follow, up to and including the Virgin Mary, all bow.)* who was conceived by the Holy Spirit, born of the Virgin Mary, suffered under Pontius Pilate, was crucified, died and was buried; he descended into hell; on the third day he rose again from the dead; he ascended into heaven, and is seated at the right hand of God the Father almighty; from there he will come to judge the living and the dead. I believe in the Holy Spirit, the holy catholic Church, the communion of saints, the forgiveness of sins, the resurrection of the body, and life everlasting. Amen.

THE PRAYER OF THE FAITHFUL *(Universal Prayer)*

THE LITURGY OF THE EUCHARIST

THE PREPARATION OF THE GIFTS

The offertory procession and song

Presenting the bread:

C: Blessed are you, Lord, God of all creation, for through your goodness we have received the bread we offer you: fruit of the earth and work of human hands, it will become for us the bread of life.

All: Blessed be God for ever.

Presenting the chalice:

C: Blessed are you, Lord, God of all creation, for through your goodness we have received the wine we offer you: fruit of the vine and work of human hands, it will become our spiritual drink.

All: Blessed be God for ever.

C: Pray, brethren (brothers and sisters), that my sacrifice and yours may be acceptable to God, the almighty Father.

All: May the Lord accept the sacrifice at your hands/ for the praise and glory of his name,/ for our good and the good of all his holy Church.

THE PRAYER OVER THE OFFERINGS

THE EUCHARISTIC PRAYER

EUCHARISTIC PRAYER - II

C: It is truly right and just, our duty and our salvation, always and everywhere to give you thanks, Father most holy, through your beloved Son, Jesus Christ, your Word through whom you made all things, whom you sent as our Saviour and Redeemer, incarnate by the Holy Spirit and born of the Virgin. Fulfilling your will and gaining for you a holy people, he stretched out his hands as he endured his Passion, so as to break the bonds of death and manifest the Resurrection.

And so, with the Angels and all the Saints we declare your glory, as with one voice we acclaim:

All: Holy, Holy, Holy...

C: You are indeed Holy, O Lord, the fount of all holiness.

CC: Make holy, therefore, these gifts, we pray,
by sending down your Spirit upon them
like the dewfall,
so that they may become for us
the Body and ✠ Blood
of our Lord Jesus Christ.
At the time he was betrayed

and entered willingly into his Passion,
he took bread and, giving thanks, broke it,
and gave it to his disciples, saying:

**TAKE THIS, ALL OF YOU, AND EAT OF IT,
FOR THIS IS MY BODY,
WHICH WILL BE GIVEN UP FOR YOU.**

In a similar way, when supper was ended,
he took the chalice
and, once more giving thanks,
he gave it to his disciples, saying:
TAKE THIS, ALL OF YOU,

**AND DRINK FROM IT,
FOR THIS IS THE CHALICE OF MY BLOOD,
THE BLOOD OF THE NEW
AND ETERNAL COVENANT,
WHICH WILL BE POURED OUT FOR YOU
AND FOR MANY
FOR THE FORGIVENESS OF SINS.
DO THIS IN MEMORY OF ME.**

C: The mystery of faith.

All: We proclaim your Death, O Lord,
and profess your Resurrection
until you come again.

CC: Therefore, as we celebrate
the memorial of his Death and Resurrection,
we offer you, Lord,
the Bread of life and the Chalice of salvation,
giving thanks that you have held us worthy
to be in your presence and minister to you.
Humbly we pray
that, partaking of the Body and Blood of Christ,
we may be gathered into one by the Holy Spirit.

C1: Remember, Lord, your Church,
spread throughout the world,
and bring her to the fullness of charity,
together with N. our Pope and N. our Bishop
and all the clergy.

In Masses for the Dead, the following may be added:

Remember your servant N.,
whom you have called (today)
from this world to yourself.
Grant that he (she) who was united
with your Son in a death like his,

may also be one with him
in his Resurrection.

C2: Remember also our brothers and sisters
who have fallen asleep
in the hope of the resurrection,
and all who have died in your mercy:
welcome them into the light of your face.
Have mercy on us all, we pray,
that with the Blessed Virgin Mary,
Mother of God, with blessed Joseph,
her spouse, with the blessed Apostles,
and all the Saints
who have pleased you throughout the ages,
we may merit to be coheirs to eternal life,
and may praise and glorify you
through your Son, Jesus Christ.

CC: Through him, and with him, and in him,
O God, almighty Father,
in the unity of the Holy Spirit,
all glory and honour is yours,
for ever and ever.

All: Amen.

THE LORD'S PRAYER

C: At the Saviour's command and formed by divine teaching, we dare to say:

All: Our Father, who art in heaven, / hallowed be thy name; / thy Kingdom come, / thy will be done on earth as it is in heaven. / Give us this day our daily bread, / and forgive us our trespasses, / as we forgive those who trespass against us; / and lead us not into temptation,/ but deliver us from evil.

C: Deliver us, Lord, we pray, from every evil, graciously grant peace in our days, that, by the help of your mercy, we may be always free from sin and safe from all distress, as we await the blessed hope and the coming of our Saviour, Jesus Christ.

All: For the kingdom, / the power and the glory are yours / now and for ever.

THE RITE OF PEACE

C: Lord Jesus Christ, who said to your Apostles: Peace I leave you, my peace I give you, look not on our sins, but on the faith of your Church, and graciously grant her peace and unity in accordance with your will. Who live and reign for ever and ever.

All: Amen.

C: The peace of the Lord be with you always.

All: And with your spirit.

Then the deacon (or the priest) adds:

Let us offer each other the sign of peace.

THE BREAKING OF THE BREAD

Meanwhile the following is sung or said:

Lamb of God, you take away the sins of the world,
have mercy on us.
Lamb of God, you take away the sins of the world,
have mercy on us.
Lamb of God, you take away the sins of the world,
grant us peace.

COMMUNION

The Priest, with hands joined, says one of the following prayers in a low voice:

May the receiving of your Body and Blood, Lord Jesus Christ, not bring me to judgement and condemnation, but through your loving mercy be for me protection in mind and body and a healing remedy.

The Priest genuflects, takes the host and, holding it slightly raised above the paten or above the chalice, says:

C: Behold the Lamb of God,
behold him who takes away
the sins of the world.
Blessed are those called to the supper
of the Lamb.

All: Lord, I am not worthy
that you should enter under my roof,
but only say the word
and my soul shall be healed.

THE PRAYER AFTER COMMUNION

THE DISMISSAL

C: The Lord be with you.

All: And with your spirit.

C: May almighty God bless you, the Father, and the Son, ✠ and the Holy Spirit.

All: Amen.

C: Go forth, the Mass is ended.

All: Thanks be to God.

VARIOUS PRAYERS

THANKSGIVING AFTER MASS

I adore You present in my heart,
O Incarnate Word,
only Son and splendour of the Father,
born of Mary.
I thank You, sole Master and Truth by essence,
for Your immense goodness in coming to me,
an ignorant person and a sinner.
With Mary I offer You to the Father:
through You, with You, in You,
may there be eternal praise,
thanksgiving and supplication
for peace among people.
Enlighten my mind;
render me a docile disciple of the Church;
grant that I may live by faith;
give me an understanding of the Scriptures.
Make me Your ardent apostle.
Let the light of Your Gospel, O Divine Master,
shine on the farthest bounds of the world.

ANIMA CHRISTI

Soul of Christ, sanctify me.
Body of Christ, save me.
Blood of Christ, inebriate me.
Water from the side of Christ, wash me.
Passion of Christ, strengthen me.
O good Jesus, hear me.
Within Your wounds, hide me.
Suffer me not to be separated from You.
From the evil enemy defend me.
And bid me come unto You –
That with Your saints I may praise You
Forever and ever.
Amen.

PRAYER FOR PRIESTS

O Jesus, eternal Priest,
keep those Your servants
within the shelter of Your Sacred Heart
where no one may harm them.
Keep unstained their anointed hands
which daily touch Your Sacred Body.
Keep unsullied their lips
purpled with Your Precious Blood.
Keep pure and unworldly their hearts
sealed with the sublime marks of Your glorious Priesthood.
Let Your holy love surround them
and shield them from the world's contagion.
Bless their labours with abundant fruit and
may the souls to whom they minister here below,
be their joy and consolation
and in heaven their beautiful and everlasting crown. Amen.
Jesus, Saviour of the world,
make Your priests and their helpers holy.
Mary, Queen of priests, pray for priests.

PRAYER FOR CONSECRATED PEOPLE

God, Father and Source of all that is good,
in every age and place,
You called forth women and men to consecrate
their lives to You.
Cognizant of the privilege of this call
and its accompanying graces,
we praise and thank You
for the consecrated lives of priests, sisters and brothers
throughout the world
and in particular those living and
serving within our own Diocese.
Your call to holiness extends to
every man, woman and child.
May the goodness and holiness of those for whom we pray
serve as beacons lighting the path for all
who seek a closer walk with You.
We ask this of You, through Jesus, Your Son,
and in the power of the Holy Spirit,
One God dwelling in everlasting glory.
Amen.

PRAYER FOR THE LAITY

Heavenly Father,
you have called us all to holiness,
by sharing in Your divine life.
Fill us with a sense of true dignity
as Your daughters and sons in the world
and Your ambassadors of justice, love and peace.
May we be witnesses to Your love in our families,
places of work, institutions of learning and recreation.
Give us the desire to be worthy of this great calling
and the courage to live up to it.
We ask this through Christ, Our Lord.
Amen.

PRAYER TO THE HOLY SPIRIT

Come, Holy Spirit,
Replace the tension within us with a holy relaxation.
Replace the turbulence within us
with a quiet confidence.
Replace the fear within us with a strong faith.
Replace the bitterness within us
with the sweetness of grace.
Replace the darkness within us with a gentle light.
Replace the coldness within us with a living warmth.
Replace the night within us with Your light
Replace the winter within us with Your spring.
Straighten our crookedness, fill our emptiness.
Blunt the edge of our pride,
sharpen the edge of our humility.
Light the fires of our love,
quench the flames of our lust.
Let us see ourselves as You see us,
that we may see You as You have promised
and be fortunate according to Your word:
"Blessed are the pure of heart, for they shall see God."

PRAYER FOR DIVINE GUIDANCE

Grant me, I beseech You, almighty
and most merciful God, fervently to desire,
wisely to search out, and perfectly to fulfil
all that is well pleasing unto You.
Order my worldly condition to the glory of Your name;

grant me the knowledge, desire and ability
to do that which You require of me,
so that I may walk with You unto my perfect end.
Give me, O Lord, a steadfast heart
which no unworthy affection may debase;
give me an enduring heart
which no tribulation can wear out;
give me an upright heart
which no unworthy purpose may tempt aside.
Bestow upon me, O Lord my God,
understanding to know You, diligence to seek You,
wisdom to find You,
and a faithfulness that may finally posses You.

PRAYER FOR DELIVERANCE

In the name of God, the Father Almighty,
Creator of heaven and earth,
in the name of Jesus Christ, His only-begotten Son
and our Lord and Saviour,
in the name of the Holy Spirit who dwells in our hearts,
through the intercession of Mary,
the Immaculate Virgin Mother of God,
and of St Michael the Archangel
and of all the Angels and Saints,
I take authority, and bind all demonic powers
and forces that have come against me.
I resist the devil, all his pressures, his attacks,
his deceptions, every instrument or agent
he would seek to use against me.
I challenge every spirit of darkness and of oppression,
and command him to depart right now away from me,
and go to the feet of Jesus,
to be bound, and not to return.
Lord Jesus, cover me with Your precious blood
and let me experience the fullness of redemption.
Amen.

A POWERFUL HEALING PRAYER

Heavenly Father,
I call on You right now in a special way.
It is through Your Power that I was created.
Every breath I take, every morning I wake up,

and every moment of every hour,
I live under Your power.
Father, I ask You now to touch me
with that same power,
for, as You created me from nothing,
You can certainly recreate me.
Fill me with the healing power of Your Spirit.
Cast out anything that should not be in me.
Mend what is broken
and root out any unproductive cells.
Open the blocked arteries or veins
and rebuild all damaged areas.
Remove all inflammation and heal any infection.
Let the warmth of Your healing love
pass through my body
to make new the unhealthy areas,
so that my body will function
the way You created it to function.
Father, restore me to full health in mind and body,
so that I may serve You the rest of my life.
Amen.

SERENITY PRAYER

God grant me the serenity
to accept the things I cannot change;
courage to change the things I can;
and wisdom to know the difference.
Living one day at a time;
enjoying one moment at a time;
accepting hardships as the pathway to peace;
taking, as He did, this sinful world
as it is, not as I would have it;
trusting that He will make all things right
if I surrender to His Will;
that I may be reasonably happy in this life
and supremely happy with Him
forever in the next.
Amen.